*THE HMAS VOYAGER TRAGEDY*

# WHERE
# FATE
# CALLS

Dedicated to those whose lives were changed
by the loss of
Her Majesty's Australian Ship
*Voyager*

THE HMAS VOYAGER TRAGEDY

# WHERE FATE CALLS

## TOM FRAME

FOREWORD BY ADMIRAL MICHAEL W. HUDSON

Hodder & Stoughton
SYDNEY AUCKLAND LONDON TORONTO

First published in 1992
by Hodder & Stoughton (Australia) Pty Limited,
ACN 000884855
10–16 South Street, Rydalmere, NSW 2116.

National Library of Australia Cataloguing-in-Publication entry:

Frame, T. R. (Thomas R.), 1962—
    Where fate calls: the HMAS Voyager tragedy.

    ISBN 0 340 54968 8.

    1. Voyager (Destroyer: 1952–1964). 2. Destroyers (Warships) —
Australia — History. 3. Marine accidents — Australian Capital Territory
— Jervis Bay. 4. Collisions at sea. I. Title.

359.32540994

Typeset by Character & Caps, North Sydney.
Printed in Australia by Globe Press, Melbourne.

# Contents

## List of Figures
*(pages 357–84)*

# Foreword

by
## Admiral Michael Hudson, AC, RANEM
### Chief of Naval Staff
#### 1985–1991

When *Melbourne* and *Voyager* collided at 2056 on 10 February 1964 I was the Assistant Fleet Operations Officer, a relatively junior officer on the staff of the Fleet Commander, having qualified as a navigation 'N' specialist in 1957, obtaining my advanced navigation, or 'Dagger' qualification in 1963. My first job as a specialist 'N' had been as Second Navigating Officer of HMS *Ark Royal*, a Royal Navy fleet carrier twice the size of *Melbourne*. Later, in 1962, I was the Navigating Officer of *Voyager*. My commanding officer at the time was a very experienced destroyer man, the then Captain David Wells, who constantly drummed into us the need for vigilance when in company with a carrier, particularly if your ship was acting as rescue destroyer.

At about 2230 on that eventful evening I received a phone call at home from the Duty Fleet Staff Officer advising me that there had been an incident in the Jervis Bay area in which *Melbourne* and *Voyager* had touched. There was no urgency to the call, nor any other details, and I was left with the impression that a few guard rails may have been bent. I was told that my immediate superior, the Fleet Operations Officer, had been advised in accordance with standing procedures and I turned in feeling confident that if this had been anything but a minor mishap I would be called again. It is perhaps a measure of the confusion that reigned that night that no such call came and the first I knew of the disaster that had occurred was when I read about it in the morning's newspaper.

I was horrified at its magnitude. A ship in which I had served had been lost; the RAN's flagship was severely disabled. But far worse than anything else, eighty-two men had lost their lives — with all the grief and tragedy that that would bring to families, friends and colleagues. Many I knew personally and had been shipmates.

Like others that day, I asked myself how could this calamity have occurred? My previous service in *Ark Royal* and *Voyager* had given me enough experience to know that carrier operations were the most demanding of all and that dangerous close-quarter situations could happen very quickly if bridge teams were not constantly alert to the

ix

movements of other ships. It was not enough to assume that the right action would occur as the result of a signal. Ships changing station, particularly at night, must be watched all the way. Unfortunately key personnel in *Voyager*, including the captain, had been lost and then, as now, no reconstruction could show conclusively what had occurred on the bridge of *Voyager* during her last critical minutes nor why she had been allowed to reach a stage of *extremis*.

I can recall that at the time I was critical of both ships, a view coloured by my relative lack of experience. Since then I have had the privilege of commanding four of Her Majesty's Australian Ships, including *Vendetta* (a sister ship to *Voyager*) and *Melbourne*. I was also on board *Melbourne* as the Fleet Operations Officer in 1968 when the USS *Frank E. Evans* collided with her in the South China Sea and I had the unpleasant duty of being the naval adviser to the prosecutor for Captain J. P. Stevenson's court martial. I have served as the Fleet Commander. What that experience has taught me is that 'there but for the grace of God' go a lot of us. The sea, at the best of times, is a harsh taskmaster and becomes doubly so when one imposes the challenge of naval warfare and the complexity of operating in a multi-ship environment.

All of this has made me very cautious about apportioning blame, particularly when one was not present and when reconstruction depends to a large degree on supposition. However, I cannot ignore that in this case mistakes must have been made. A collision did occur — and that brings me to this book.

One may ask: what purpose can be served by publishing a book about an incident of naval history which some may prefer to forget? For those who lost loved ones and for those who suffered personally it will raise sad and bitter memories. Others will perceive that they have been dealt with unfairly and will treat it with hostility; and there will be those who for their various reasons seek to denigrate a fighting service, which in my view is second to none. There will, however, be many others who, whilst knowing that *Melbourne* and *Voyager* collided almost thirty years ago, will not be aware of the totality of events surrounding not only the collision itself but also the background to two Royal Commissions and how they unfolded. Nor will they be aware of the heroism of people such as Chief Petty Officer Jonathan Rogers, Midshipman Kerry Marien and Electrical Mechanic William Condon, all of whom lost their lives while striving to rescue their shipmates.

There is a new generation now at sea and whilst the Royal Australian Navy may not have an aircraft carrier there is still much to be learnt from a professional study of what occurred in 1964. There are lessons too for politicians and public servants; and I would hazard that there are lessons even for those who practise the law.

When Lieutenant Tom Frame approached me in 1988 for approval to undertake his doctorate in history into the *Melbourne-Voyager* disaster he was my Research Officer, a position I had established shortly after I became Chief of Naval Staff. The posting had a dual purpose. One was to assist me, but the other was to give selected young officers early opportunity to participate in naval administration at the higher levels and to further their own experience by the study of naval history and the analysis of today's events. Through publication of many articles, documentaries and other books, Tom has more than amply demonstrated a competence well beyond his years.

In his summing up, Lieutenant Frame has been harsh in some of his judgements of people and events, and the Navy itself does not emerge unscathed. I by no means agree with all his conclusions but he has exercised his right as an individual to express his views and it is at least partly for the protection of that right that those in the Australian Defence Force serve. There is no doubt in my mind that following World War II there was a diminution in the effectiveness of the Navy and this should come as no surprise to anyone, considering the major reduction of ships and personnel after 1946. It started to pick up again in the mid 1950s and the transition lasted through to the mid-1960s. Since then the RAN has grown in maturity and whilst no organisation will ever be perfect I believe the lessons of the past have been well learnt and the criticisms of isolation from the Australian community, complacency and lack of professionalism are no longer valid.

Australians today can be very proud of their Navy, as I was proud to serve. I congratulate Tom Frame on a job well done.

M. W. H.

# Acknowledgements

A book covering a subject such as this could not have been completed without the generous help of very many people who generously gave of their time, hospitality, encouragement, knowledge and wisdom.

I am grateful to all those who consented to be interviewed. The long list included in the bibliography contains the names of some very distinguished Australians I had the honour to meet. I am especially thankful to the *Voyager* survivors who were prepared to assist with my research despite the trauma the mere mention of *Voyager* causes them. Alex Hagerty, John Wilson, Bernard Verwayen, Michael Patterson, John Milliner, Bruce Cameron, Andy Matthews and Gary Evans were particularly helpful. Captain James Kelly and Commander Alex Bate, the officers on *Melbourne*'s bridge at the time of the collision, were always ready to assist and advise. The effect of the collision on their naval careers and personal lives was substantial.

I must also acknowledge the great support and encouragement I received from the families of the late Captains Robertson and Stevens. Captain Brian Robertson and Malcolm Robertson granted me access to their father's private papers while Mrs Beatrice Legoe and Sandy Stevens permitted me to use documents and photographs they had retained. Peter Cabban was always helpful and co-operative. He neither thrust his opinions upon me nor insisted that I accept his views. *Voyager* changed his life as well.

Rear Admirals Bill Graham and John Stevens, Commodores Ian Burnside and Ian Broben, and Commanders Graham Wright, Angus Cameron and Nigel Perry went out of their way to assist and to encourage. Lieutenants Mark Harling and Ben Hall again helped as they do with all my projects.

I am grateful to the Navy for granting me study leave to complete the doctoral thesis on which this book is based. My university supervisor, Dr Roger Thompson, and head of department, Professor Peter Dennis, were a ready resource of good advice and wise counsel. I am thankful to the Australian War Memorial which provided me with a research grant. The staff in the Memorial's Historical Research

Section, under the leadership of Peter Stanley, were always helpful and I am appreciative of their goodwill.

I owe particular thanks to Admiral Michael Hudson, Chief of Naval Staff from 1985 to 1991, for granting me access to the Navy's records and for his guidance throughout this project. In the two years that I worked as his research officer I gained a close understanding of the naval-political interface, and a perception of the many demands and expectations placed on the professional head of the Navy.

Commodore Alan Thompson was the greatest source of encouragement throughout this project. He took a personal interest in my work and always gave very sound advice on approaching his colleagues in the legal profession for help. As a naval lawyer, he pointed my research efforts in that area in the right direction and the book would be poorer without his constant assistance. For legal advice I also thank Commander Peter Hohnen RANR and Graham Hryce.

Robert Hyslop ISO, the recognised authority on Australian naval administration, was the chief sounding board for my ideas and theories. The benefit of Robert's deep knowledge and personal involvement in naval administration for nearly forty years gave me many valuable insights into how the naval and civil staffs coped with the loss of *Voyager* and the many real difficulties and constraints they faced.

Complementing all of this assistance is the wonderful support I have received from wife Helen. She has had to endure much while I have researched and written this book. Her constant interest in all that I do is more than I could have reasonably expected.

I must stress that the views expressed in this book are mine, and mine alone. This is not in any sense an official or endorsed history produced for or by the Royal Australian Navy. I have not sought, nor does this book have, any official sanction for, or concurrence with, the opinions it contains. I take full responsibility for everything that appears in this book.

Quotations and other material from the Royal Commissions' transcripts and reports are copyright Commonwealth of Australia and are reproduced by permission. Selected figures are from the *Admiralty Manuals of Seamanship*. I am grateful to the Royal Australian Navy and the Australian War Memorial for the use of their photographs.

Tom Frame
Department of History
Australian Defence Academy
Canberra ACT

November 1991

# Dramatis Personae

**HMAS** *Melbourne*
Captain R. J. (John) **Robertson**
  Commanding Officer, January–April 1964
Captain H. D. (David) **Stevenson**
  Commanding Officer, April 1964–1965
Commander H. E. **Bailey**
  Executive Officer
Commander H. J. (Harry) **Bodman**
  Engineer Officer
Surgeon Commander B. T. (Brian) **Treloar**
  Fleet Medical Officer
Acting Commander J. M. (James) **Kelly**
  Fleet Navigating Officer
Lieutenant Commander G. (George) **Halley**
  Damage Control Officer
Sub-Lieutenant J. A. (Alex) **Bate**
  Watchkeeping Officer

Chief Communications Yeoman R. W. (Robert) **Barker**
  Bridge Communications Supervisor
Leading Tactical Operator R. (Robert) **Everett**
  Bridge Communications Staff

**HMAS** *Voyager*
*1963*
Captain D. H. (Duncan) **Stevens**
  Commanding Officer
Commander E. W. (Edward) **Tapp**
  Electrical Officer
Acting Commander W. H. (Bill) **Money**
  Engineer Officer
Lieutenant Commander I. I. (Ian) **Blaikie**
  Supply Officer

Lieutenant Commander P. T. (Peter ) **Cabban**
  Executive Officer
Lieutenant R. N. (Richard) **Carpendale**
  Torpedo & Anti-submarine Officer
Lieutenant S. B. (Scott) **Griffith**
  Navigating Officer
Lieutenant D. J. (David) **Martin**
  Gunnery Officer
Lieutenant T. (Terence) **Redman**
  Gunner
Surgeon Lieutenant M. C. (Michael) **Tiller**
  Medical Officer
Lieutenant C. J. (Christopher) **Tuke**, RN
  Captain's secretary

Leading Sick-Berth Attendant J. R. (John) **Wilson**
  Medical staff

*1964*
Captain D. H. (Duncan) **Stevens**
  Commanding Officer
Lieutenant Commander I. A. G. (Ian) **MacGregor**
  Executive Officer
Lieutenant H. D. (Harry) **Cook**
  Navigating Officer
Lieutenant J. L. (James) **Dowling**
  Gunnery Officer
Lieutenant D. H. M. (David) **Price**
  Torpedo & Anti-submarine, and Watchkeeping Officer

Chief Petty Officer Coxswain J. (Jonathan) **Rogers**
  Head of the Ship's Company
Communications Yeoman K. B. (Kevin) **Cullen**
  Bridge Communications Supervisor

Leading Seaman M. J. (Michael) **Patterson**
  Survivor from Operations Room
Tactical Operator R. J. (Robert) **Burdett**
  Survivor from bridge area
Tactical Operator G. W. (Gary) **Evans**
  Survivor from bridge
Ordinary Seaman W. A. E. (Alex) **Degenhardt**
  Survivor from wheelhouse
Ordinary Seaman B. W. (Brian) **Sumpter**
  Port Lookout

Ordinary Steward B. J. (Barry) **Hyland**
  Officer steward

## Australian Commonwealth Naval Board
*1963*
Senator the Hon. J. G. (John) **Gorton**
  Minister for the Navy and President
Vice-Admiral Sir Hastings **Harrington**
  Chief of Naval Staff and First Naval Member
Mr T. J. (Tom) **Hawkins**
  Secretary, Department of the Navy
Rear-Admiral V. A. (Victor) **Smith**
  Second Naval Member (Personnel)
Rear-Admiral F. L. (Frank) **George**
  Third Naval Member (Technical services)
Captain A. G. (Alan) **McFarlane**
  Fourth Naval Member (Supply)

*1964*
Hon. F. C. (Fred) **Chaney**
  Minister for the Navy and President
Vice-Admiral Sir Hastings **Harrington**
  Chief of Naval Staff and First Naval Member
Rear-Admiral V. A. (Victor) **Smith**
  Second Naval Member
Rear-Admiral F. L. (Frank) **George**
  Third Naval Member
Rear-Admiral A. W. R. (Alan) **McNicoll**
  Fourth Naval Member
  (relieved in June 1964 by Rear-Admiral R. I. (Richard) **Peek**)
Rear-Admiral T. K. (Tom) **Morrison**
  Deputy Chief of Naval Staff (non-Board Member)

*1967*
Hon. D. L. (Don) **Chipp**
  Minister for the Navy and President
Vice-Admiral Sir Alan **McNicoll**
  Chief of Naval Staff and First Naval Member
S. (Sam) **Landau**
  Secretary, Department of the Navy
Rear-Admiral J. M. (Jack) **Mesley**
  Second Naval Member
Rear-Admiral F. W. (Fred) **Purves**
  Third Naval Member

Rear-Admiral W. D. H. (Bill) **Graham**
Fourth Naval Member

**FOCAF**
*1963*
Rear-Admiral A. W. R. (Alan) **McNicoll**
*1964*
Rear-Admiral O. H. (Humphrey) **Becher**

**FOICEA**
*1964*
Rear-Admiral G. G. O. (Galfrey) **Gatacre**
(relieved in June by Rear-Admiral A. W. R. **McNicoll**)

**1964 *Voyager* Royal Commission**
Hon. Sir John **Spicer**
Royal Commissioner
J. W. (Jack) **Smyth**, QC
Leading Counsel Assisting the Royal Commission
I. F. (Ian) **Sheppard**
Junior Counsel Assisting the Royal Commission
Captain R. I. (Richard) **Peek**
Naval Adviser and expert witness
Lieutenant Commander J. B. (John) **Snow**
Naval security adviser
Captain N. (Norman) **Bolton**
Nautical adviser, Department of Transport and Shipping
R. J. (Robert) **Herd**
Naval architect, Department of Transport and Shipping
N. A. (Norman) **Jenkyn**, QC
Leading Counsel for the Navy
H. J. H. (Humfry) **Henchman**
Junior Counsel for the Navy
L. W. (Laurence) **Street**, QC
Leading Counsel for the Stevens family
J. B. (John) **Sinclair**
Junior Counsel for the Stevens family
F. M. (Fred) **Osborne**
Instructing Solicitor for the Stevens family
C. L. D. (Leycester) **Meares**, QC
Leading Counsel for the interests of Lieutenant Price

W. H. (Sandy) **Gregory**
Junior Counsel for the interests of Lieutenant Price
D. S. (David) **Hicks**, QC
Leading Counsel for Captain Robertson
E. P. T. (Peter) **Raine**
Junior Counsel for Captain Robertson
Rear-Admiral H. B. (Harold) **Farncomb**
Instructing Solicitor for Captain Robertson

**1967 *Voyager* Royal Commission**
Hon. Justice Sir Stanley **Burbury**
Royal Commissioner and Chairman
Hon. Justice G. A. G. (George) **Lucas**
Royal Commissioner
Hon. Justice K. W. (Kenneth) **Asprey**
Royal Commissioner

F. T. P. (Francis) **Burt**, QC
Leading Counsel Assisting the Royal Commission
P. (Philip) **Jeffrey**
Junior Counsel Assisting the Royal Commission
P. (Peter) **Murphy**, QC
Leading Counsel for the Navy
H. J. H. (Humfry) **Henchman**
Junior Counsel for the Navy
W. P. (Bill) **Ash**, QC
Leading Counsel for the Stevens family
J. B. (John) **Sinclair**
Junior Counsel for the Stevens family
J. T. (Jack) **Hiatt**, QC
Leading Counsel for Lieutenant Commander Cabban
C. A. (Chester) **Porter**
Junior Counsel for Lieutenant Commander Cabban
R. G. (Ray) **Reynolds**, QC
Leading Counsel for Captain Robertson, June–September
G. J. (Gordon) **Samuels**, QC
Leading Counsel for Captain Robertson, September–December
E. P. T. (Peter) **Raine**
Junior Counsel for Captain Robertson
B. S. J. (Barry) **O'Keefe**, QC
Counsel for Surgeon Lieutenant Tiller

**Federal Parliament**
*1964*
Right Honourable Sir Robert **Menzies**
  Prime Minister
Right Honourable Sir Garfield **Barwick**
  Minister for External Affairs
Hon. P. M. C. (Paul) **Hasluck**
  Minister for Defence
Hon. B. M. (Billy) **Snedden**
  Attorney-General
Senator Sir Shane **Paltridge**
  Minister for Defence
Hon. Dr A. J. (Jim) **Forbes**
  Minister for the Army and the Navy

J. D. (John) **Jess**
  Liberal Party Member for La Trobe

Hon. A. A. (Arthur) **Calwell**
  Leader of the Opposition
E. G. (Gough) **Whitlam**
  Deputy Leader of the Opposition
C. R. (Clyde) **Cameron**
  Labor Member for Hindmarsh
S. J. (Sam) **Benson**
  Labor Member for Batman

*1967*
Right Honourable H. (Harold) **Holt**
  Prime Minister
Hon. N. H. (Nigel) **Bowen**
  Attorney-General

D. J. (Jim) **Killen**
  Liberal Member for Moreton
Rev. Dr M. G. (Malcolm) **Mackay**
  Liberal Member for Evans
E. H. (Ted) **St John**
  Liberal Member for Warringah
H. B. (Harry) **Turner**
  Liberal Member for Bradfield

## Others

Professor C. R. B. **Blackburn**
  Expert medical witness, 1964 Commission
Dr J. H. W. (John) **Birrell**
  Expert medical witness, 1967 Commission
Sir John **Bunting**
  Secretary, Department of Prime Minister and Cabinet
Vice-Admiral Sir Henry **Burrell**
  Chief of Naval Staff, 1955–58
Captain D. A. H. ('Nobby') **Clarke**
  Commanding Officer of HMAS *Anzac*, 1963–64
Vice-Admiral Sir John **Collins**
  Chief of Naval Staff, 1948–55
Surgeon Rear-Admiral R. M. (Michael) **Coplans**
  Medical Director General
Lieutenant Commander T. A. (Thomas) **Dadswell**
  Naval pilot
Captain A. T. (Ed) **Dollard**
  Naval Attache in Tokyo, 1963
Vice-Admiral Sir Roy **Dowling**
  Chief of Naval Staff, 1958–61
Captain W. J. (Bill) **Dovers**
  Commanding Officer of HMAS *Sydney*, 1963
Commander P. H. (Peter) **Doyle**
  Fleet Operations Officer, 1964
Captain I. (Ian) **Easton**
  Commanding Officer of HMAS *Watson*, 1964
A. (Tony) **Eggleton**
  Co-ordinator of Navy Public Relations, 1964
  Press Secretary to the Prime Minister, after 1965
Dr K. J. (Kerry) **Goulston**
  Gastroenterologist and expert medical witness, 1967
Vice-Admiral H. (Harold) **Hickling**
  Retired Royal Navy Flag Officer and author
Commander R. E. (Ted) **Lesh**
  Director of Communications, 1964
Commander B. L. (Bruce) **Loxton**
  Commanding Officer of HMAS *Parramatta*, 1963
Sir William **Morrow**
  Gastroenterologist and expert medical witness, 1967
Captain E. J. (John) **Peel**
  Australian Naval Attache in Washington, 1964
T. S. (Stuart) **Philpott**
  Deputy Secretary, Department of the Navy

Dr V. D. (Vern) **Pleuckhahn**
  Pathologist and expert medical witness, 1967
Commodore J. M. (James) **Ramsey**
  Australian Naval Representative United Kingdom, 1964
Dr J. G. (James) **Rankin**
  Expert medical witness, 1967
His Honour Judge T. G. (Trevor) **Rapke**
  Naval Judge Advocate General
R. (Ray) **Richards**
  Employee of A. H. & A. W. Reed, publishers
Captain (later Commodore) D. H. D. (Dacre) **Smyth**
  Commanding Officer of HMAS *Creswell*
  Australian Naval Representative United Kingdom, 1967
Sir Jack **Stevens**
  Father of Captain Stevens
Mrs B. L. (Beatrice) **Stevens**
  Wife of Captain Stevens
Captain J. P. (Philip) **Stevenson**
  Commanding Officer of HMAS *Sydney*, 1964
  Commanding Officer of HMAS *Melbourne*, 1969
Commander (later Captain) A. A. (Alan) **Willis**
  Commanding Officer of HMAS *Voyager*, 1962
  Commanding Officer of HMAS *Vendetta*, 1964
Captain G. J. (James) **Willis**
  Commanding Officer of HMAS *Vampire*, 1963
Commander L. F. (Larry) **Winch**
  Chief Naval Judge Advocate

# List of Abbreviations and Acronyms

AA        Anti-aircraft
AAP       Australian Associated Press
ABC       Australian Broadcasting Commission
ABR       Australian Book of Reference
ACNB      Australian Commonwealth Naval Board
ACT       Australian Capital Territory
ADC       Aide-de-camp
AG        Attorney General['s Department]
AIF       Australian Imperial Force
ANMI      Allied Naval Manoeuvring Instructions
ANO       Australian Naval Order
ANRUK     Australian Naval Representative United Kingdom
ANSB      Allied Naval Signalling Book
A/S       Anti-submarine
ATP       Allied Tactical Publication
AUP       Australian United Press
BR        [Admiralty] Book of Reference
CAG       Carrier Air Group
CAS       Chief of Air Staff
CGS       Chief of General Staff
CINCFEF   Commander-in-Chief Far East Fleet
CNJA      Chief Naval Judge Advocate
CNO       Chief of Naval Operations (US)
CNO       Commonwealth Naval Order
CNPR      Coordinator of Navy Public Relations
CNS       Chief of Naval Staff
COSC      Chiefs of Staff Committee
CPD       Commonwealth Parliamentary Debates
CSIRO     Commonwealth Scientific and Industrial Research
          Organisation
DCNS      Deputy Chief of Naval Staff
DCS       Deputy Crown Solicitor
DD        Destroyer

| | |
|---|---|
| DDG | Guided Missile Destroyer |
| DFRB | Defence Force Retirement Benefits [Act] |
| DNC | Director of Naval Construction (Admiralty) |
| DNI | Director of Naval Intelligence |
| DSC | Distinguished Service Cross |
| DSO | Distinguished Service Order |
| DSTR | Director of Staff and Training Requirements |
| DTG | Date Time Group |
| FF | Frigate |
| FFG | Guided Missile Frigate |
| FND | Flinders Naval Depot |
| FOCAF | Flag Officer Commanding Australian Fleet |
| FOCE | Flag Officer Commanding Establishments |
| FOICEA | Flag Officer in Charge East Australian Area |
| FPLP | Federal Parliamentary Labor Party |
| HMAS | Her Majesty's Australian Ship |
| HMCS | Her Majesty's Canadian Ship |
| HMNZS | Her Majesty's New Zealand Ship |
| HMS | Her Majesty's Ship |
| HMS/M | Her Majesty's Submarine |
| IDC | Imperial Defence College |
| JAG | Judge Advocate General |
| MP | Member of Parliament |
| MV | Merchant Vessel |
| NAS | Naval Air Station |
| NATO | North Atlantic Treaty Organisation |
| NB | Naval Board |
| NGS | Naval Gunfire Support |
| NOICJB | Naval Officer in Charge Jervis Bay |
| NOL | Navy Office Letter |
| NSW | New South Wales |
| OIC | Officer in Charge |
| OOW | Officer of the Watch |
| OTC | Officer in Tactical Command |
| QC | Queens Counsel |
| QR & AI | Queens Regulations and Admiralty Instructions |
| RAAF | Royal Australian Air Force |
| RAN | Royal Australian Navy |
| RANC | Royal Australian Naval College |
| RANR | Royal Australian Naval Reserve |
| RANTAU | Royal Australian Navy Trials and Assessment Unit |
| RANVR | Royal Australian Naval Volunteer Reserve |
| RCN | Royal Canadian Navy |
| RN | Royal Navy |
| RNZN | Royal New Zealand Navy |

| | |
|---|---|
| ROP | Report of Proceedings |
| Rtd | Retired |
| SAR | Search and Rescue |
| SEATO | South East Asian Treaty Organisation |
| SecNav | Secretary of the Department of the Navy |
| TAS | Torpedo and anti-submarine |
| USN | United States Navy |
| USS | United States Ship |
| VCNS | Vice Chief of Naval Staff |
| WRANS | Women's Royal Australian Naval Service |
| | |
| 1NM | First Naval Member |
| 2NM | Second Naval Member |
| 3NM | Third Naval Member |
| 4NM | Fourth Naval Member |
| 1SL | First Sea Lord |
| 2SL | Second Sea Lord |

# Introduction

'Where Fate Calls' was the motto of Her Majesty's Australian Ship *Voyager*. It was very much the ancient sailors' creed and could have been carried by any warship. Guided by traditions but subject to age-old suspicions, sailors acknowledge a certain inevitability about their calling. Luck seems to be so much a part of seafaring, and destiny the dominant factor for those who sail the seas in men o' war. Perhaps more than anywhere else in human endeavour, providence plays a leading role.

Much has been written of what makes a navy, but most writers agree that a navy must be firmly disciplined and maintain a number of balances if it is to survive not just the rigours of war but the demands and the frustrations of peacetime. When discipline is lacking, or a navy concentrates on one area of its administration to the neglect of another, sooner or later the consequences are apparent. Mutinies, collisions and groundings are signs that larger problems exist. Sometimes the shortcomings are known and ignored by those with power to correct them. At other times they are met with shock and disbelief that things had been allowed to get so out of hand. Without vigilance and proper attention to the plethora of factors that ensures a navy continues to function as it should, by its very nature the failure will be manifest in short order.

The Royal Australian Navy (RAN) was established in 1911 with the traditions and the structures that had made the British Royal Navy one of the greatest naval forces ever known. There was a strong and pervasive sense of inheritance.

Although Australia looked to Britain, maintaining a navy relied upon the observance of some universal principles. Foremost was the importance of maintaining a balance in all things. There should not be too much hardship or firm discipline. Relations between officers and sailors had to remain within limits. The human factor was most prominent. Sailors who were not adequately cared for rebelled. Officers who paid scant regard to their duties and responsibilities became a hindrance to the effective running of the fleet. Poor morale or a lack of discipline reduced operational effectiveness and efficiency. Poorly trained officers and sailors were a liability to their ships and a danger to themselves.

By the end of World War I the RAN had experienced a mutiny (the RAN Bridging Train mutinied in 1916 when they were not paid) and a collision at sea (the RAN Flagship, the battlecruiser HMAS *Australia* collided with HMS *New Zealand* just before the Battle of Jutland in 1916 and was unable to participate). Both were only minor incidents, but they were useful in giving the RAN some good experience in learning how to handle situations when things go wrong. Both instances required sound leadership and flexible administration.

Both World War II and the Korean War added to the Navy's depth of experience at a time when Australian officers were preparing to take over command of the RAN from the British officers who had led it through its formative years. It ensured a vigilant observance of the principles that make for an effective fighting unit.

The conclusion in 1955 of the United Nations (UN) Armistice Patrols off the Korean Peninsula, in which RAN ships took part, marked the end of a very long period in which the RAN maintained high levels of operational readiness. But by this stage, the Navy was in an advanced state of matériel decline. The ships of the fleet were ageing while the Navy's finances slowly declined. Strategic guidance accorded a marginal role to the Navy in the defence of Australia. From 1958, the RAN suffered a series of major accidents with each accident more serious than the one before. There was increasing loss of life. There had been accidents before but never so many in close succession. The message these accidents seemed to proclaim was that professional naval standards were declining. This message was reinforced in the minds of many outside the Service when, on 10 February 1964, during naval exercises off the south coast of New South Wales, the destroyer HMAS *Voyager* crossed the bows of the aircraft carrier HMAS *Melbourne* and was sliced in two. Within a matter of minutes, 82 men perished. The disaster would prove to be a watershed in the operational and administrative history of the RAN and a controversy of national proportions in Australian general history.

This book describes and explains the tragic collision and the long-running legal and political controversy that followed. It is the first comprehensive account of the whole affair. Given the extent and duration of the *Voyager* controversy, it is surprising that more has not been written. The two books by Vice-Admiral Harold Hickling, *One Minute of Time* and *Postscript to Voyager*, written very soon after the two *Voyager* Royal Commissions, are primarily polemic works and were not ever intended to be serious works of history. Given the paucity of primary sources available to Hickling in 1965 and 1968, and the haste with which both books were written, they could not have been otherwise.

In the years since the publication of Hickling's second book in 1969, there have been several small additions to what is publicly known about the *Voyager* tragedy, but these are oblique references in works of Australian political science. General works dealing with the history of the Navy all draw upon Hickling's two books for their facts and their interpretation.

There has been only one attempt within the Press to have the *Voyager* case re-opened. In 1974 Evan Whitton wrote two stories for the *National Times*. The first (4 February) was entitled '*Voyager*: Operation Cover-Up', and it caused a sensation. Whitton had approached the Whitlam Government to have certain Government files on *Voyager* made available to the public. The Government refused. The documents sought by Whitton in that article have been used and are cited in this book.

The story of the *Voyager* tragedy transcends the finer points of navigation and shiphandling. It involves the interaction of several interest groups: the Navy, the Federal Parliament, the media, and the legal and medical professions, and involves the interplay of politics, bureaucratic inertia, institutional conservatism and the emergence of spirited public advocacy.

Another important area to be examined in the context of the loss of *Voyager* is the limitations of Royal Commissions as means of inquiry into events of misadventure and their use as a tool of the executive government.

This book will look at the Navy's changing attitude to parliamentary and public accountability; its attitude to other areas of the executive government; the Naval Command's understanding of its responsibility for matters of administration and operations; and most notably, the end of the Navy's 'closed shop' mentality.

At the heart of the disaster and what has made it such a tragedy, however, is the expression and conflict of strong personalities and complex human reactions.

The foremost objective in this volume has been to set down an accurate account; to lay bare the facts from which observations, interpretations and judgements can be made. Establishing the facts proved to be the most difficult task.

The approach I adopted while researching this book was that of an open-minded inquisitor. This was inevitable, given that *Voyager* was the subject of two Royal Commissions and substantial litigation outside of those inquiries. In utilising considerable oral sources, interviews I conducted resembled interrogations of those who were involved as I sought from them only what could be proved, and once proved, made public. Surprisingly, very few of the one-hundred or so people I interviewed withheld information or tried to mislead me. Only occasionally did those I interviewed insist that their views were either offered in confidence or were not to be directly attributed to them. Many of the facts I was able to independently verify were first brought to my attention in such interviews.

As a serving officer of the Royal Australian Navy, the decision to write this book was extremely difficult. Many friends and senior officers whose judgement I respected advised me to write about any other subject but the loss of HMAS *Voyager*. It took me six months to consider fully the consequences of what I was undertaking and finally to make up my mind to proceed. Perhaps *Voyager*'s rather ironic motto, 'Where Fate Calls', had something to do with it. Whatever the reason, I remain convinced that the only way the story of *Voyager* could be accurately and truthfully told was by someone 'inside' the Navy. Although I have great empathy with the officers and sailors involved, and feel a conscious loyalty to the RAN, the overriding duty of the historian to be objective has taken precedence. This has meant I have had to make many judgements in this book about individuals and their actions, and about the service that has meant so much to me. I have been conscious of the possibility of being distracted and influenced by the feelings of these individuals and the reaction of the Navy. However, I have been guided by the wisdom of Polybius:

> For as a living creature is rendered wholly useless if deprived of its eyes, so if you take truth from History what is left is but an idle unprofitable tale. Therefore, one must not shrink either from blaming one's friends or praising one's enemies; nor be afraid of finding fault with and commending the same persons at different times. For it is impossible that men engaged in public affairs should always be right, and unlikely that they should always be wrong. Holding ourselves, therefore, entirely aloof from the actors, we must as historians make statements and pronounce judgement in accordance with the actions themselves.

A number of the judgements offered in this book will not be very palatable, especially to those who assisted me with this book. I can only say that I have been led by the evidence that has been available to me in coming to the views and conclusions that seem most reasonable.

Many lessons were learned from the loss of *Voyager* and they ought not be forgotten nor disregarded, because they have continuing importance. It is not beyond the realms of possibility that another Australian naval ship might be lost or seriously damaged in the future as a result of either negligence or human error. It could be a collision with another ship, a grounding that leaves the vessel a total loss, or a failure to contain damage inflicted by an enemy in war. One would hope that the lessons learned from 1964 would ensure that such a tragedy would be handled far better than was the loss of *Voyager*.

While naval ships take to the sea, the possibility of collisions will continue in even the largest and most professional navies. That they occur at all, is the greatest tragedy.

# 1

# A Navy in the Making

W HEN THE Royal Australian Navy (RAN) celebrated its Golden Anniversary in 1961, it had been 300 years since the fighting fleets of Britain had been formally designated the 'Royal Navy'. Although the RAN had been created by royal decree in 1911, its customs, traditions and ethos were those of the parent navy from which it had been grafted. In the RAN's formative years, replicating the most powerful navy in the world made good sense. In British eyes, Australian success would be determined by the faithfulness of the copy.

This sentiment was expressed by Sir Joseph Cook, the then Minister for the Navy on 20 December 1918:

> The Royal Australian Navy has been working in and with the Royal Navy. During the war it has therefore been relatively easy to work to a single standard. It is fundamental to the idea of Empire naval defence that there should be a complete standardisation of personnel and ships and equipment and that this should be to the level of the best. Only the best is good enough for any Navy in the British Empire.[1]

After exercising control over the RAN ships during World War I, the Admiralty continued to exercise considerable influence over naval affairs in Australia throughout the inter-war years. Promoting a common approach was nowhere more stringently practised than in the crucial area of junior officers' training. It was believed that if those who led the RAN were trained to fit a Royal Navy mould, the RAN would be in sound hands and a strong bond of friendship and goodwill would exist between the two navies.

The RAN College at Jervis Bay was an institution unparalleled in Australia.[2] Boys from 13 years of age were selected on the basis of aptitude for service as naval officers, without reference to their family background, and were trained to have a rigid English public school outlook. They were indoctrinated into the ways of the Service and imbued with the hope of one day becoming an admiral. Separated from family and isolated from society, with the Jervis Bay site selected for that specific reason, the Navy was to be everything to these boys. Their first loyalty was to the Navy.

1

There was little difference in outlook between an Australian and a British naval officer during the RAN's first thirty years. Australian officers spent long periods of time in Royal Navy ships or under Royal Navy or captains. The two services and their officer groups were virtually interchangeable.

The need for continuing close alignment was reaffirmed in 1936. In a memorandum to the Minister for Defence, the Secretary of the Naval Board stated that the RAN had achieved its operational efficiency through a close relationship with the Royal Navy, particularly in the areas of training, naval matériel (construction, acquisition and supply), and intelligence. In considering personnel, the memorandum said the Admiralty had made an undertaking

> to consider Australian naval officers for appointment in due course on their merit, to the highest commands in the Empire Navy. This undertaking is made practicable only because the training of RAN officers is identical with that in the Royal Navy and it is essential, in order that this opportunity shall remain open to Australian officers, that full co-operation between the two Navies is maintained and that qualifications for promotion, including seniority, should continue, as at present, to be the same in each Service.

For its part, the Admiralty encouraged the Dominions to feel dependent on its wisdom and expertise as a means of strengthening its centralising policy and ensuring the Admiralty had as much control over the Dominion navies in peacetime as it would wish to have in wartime. Hyslop concludes, in his pioneering study of Australian naval administration, that:

> The Admiralty influence was further strengthened by the existence in Australia of a Navy Office moulded on Admiralty traditions and methods, and by its own undoubted effectiveness as an administrative and political organisation.[3]

Behind the ships and their officers and sailors serving at sea, was Navy Office, first located in Melbourne and relocated to Canberra in 1959. It was from Navy Office that the RAN was controlled and administered — by the Australian Commonwealth Naval Board (ACNB). The Naval Board, as it was known, was created on 12 January 1905 and charged with 'the administration of all matters relating to the Naval Forces'.[4] Coincident with the establishment of the RAN in 1911, the Board's membership was reconstituted to include the Defence Minister (who acted as president), three naval members, a finance member and a civil member. The Board consisted of two parallel administrations with a naval officer heading the uniformed side and a senior public servant heading the civilian side.

Navy Office staff did not exert operational command over the RAN. This responsibility was vested in the Flag Officer Commanding Her Majesty's Australian Fleet (FOCAF); usually a rear-admiral. An important distinction was maintained between the control of the Navy as a whole and command of the ships forming the Australian Fleet.

Between 1911 and 1973, the Naval Board exercised control over the policies under which the RAN operated. The professional head of the RAN, modelled after the First Sea Lord of the Admiralty, had the dual title of the First Naval Member (1NM) of the Naval Board and the Chief of Naval Staff (CNS), and was appointed by the Commonwealth Government. As a vice-admiral, CNS ranked above the FOCAF and the Flag Officer in Charge, East Australia Area (FOICEA). The senior official of the civilian element at Navy Office was the Secretary of the Department of the Navy, who also headed the public service staff. When the Navy did not warrant a separate government department, he was known as the Naval Secretary. He was usually secretary of the Naval Board as well, and managed the conduct of its business.

With time, the Board gradually extended its control over naval administration, with enhanced authority and a host of delegated powers. With the Naval Board meeting at Navy Office in Melbourne until 1959, and the political head of the Navy — either the Defence Minister or the Navy Minister — located in Canberra, the Board exercised great control over the administration and control of the RAN. If there is a persistent theme in Australian naval administration, it is the effort of successive Naval Boards to make the RAN as independent as possible from other areas of government activity. This meant the Navy enjoyed, or suffered, a minimum of external bureaucratic involvement.

Over its first fifty years, the Royal Navy officers who controlled the RAN brought with them British ideas and practices. When Australians took over they continued the process of borrowing from the Royal Navy, particularly in the areas of legislation and fleet operations. By 1961, the RAN's administration was a complex mixture of often conflicting regulations and instructions. The Board routinely exercised functions for which it had no Australian statutory authority and tended to ignore external restrictions on its activities. The Navy's degree of independence from government and from Australian society, was considered a strength rather than a weakness.

The officers who made up the Naval Board were in no great hurry to cut the RAN's ties with the Royal Navy and the Admiralty. As RAN officers had been controlling their own Service for only a short period, there was a view that Australians ought first to prove they were able to operate the RAN as the Royal Navy had done, before embarking on an independent programme. The decade following the departure of the last British admiral in 1953 was a prolonged test for the RAN. It needed to prove its professionalism so as to earn the respect of both the Royal Navy and the United States Navy, with which it had increasing contact.[5]

The RAN's relationship with the Royal Navy had created an attitude that served to blind most naval officers to the reality that Parliament shared responsibility for naval affairs with the Naval Board and that both were, therefore, accountable to the Australian people. The Naval Board was often seen by outsiders as arrogant and unwilling to acknowledge external accountability.

The RAN was still heavily dependent upon the Royal Navy for assistance in training, operational assessment, weapons trials, intelligence, and personnel management procedures. There was also continuing reliance on the loan of Royal Navy personnel. Gaining greater independence would be slow and incremental. The purchase of non-British equipment, such as Dutch radars for RAN frigates and the acquisition of American destroyers, were first and faltering steps.

The RAN remained, as far as officers were concerned, a very British institution. The world in which Australian naval officers moved was separated from the body politic, and from Australian society. This attitude was reinforced through the relatively large number of Royal Navy officers on exchange with the RAN. The world of the sailor was vastly different. Their training and employment was largely restricted to Australia and Australian ships. Officers and sailors moved in two different worlds with divergent attitudes and values, and there were bound to be tensions. In the main, Australian naval officers were left to operate the RAN as they saw fit.

Despite its pretensions and public affectations, the RAN was, like the Royal Navy from which it sprang, essentially a middle-class institution with an ethos that reflected the attitudes and values of that social group. The prime virtues of the middle-class are thrift, self-reliance and hard work. Its equivocal qualities include:

> a loyalty to the Establishment and to the status quo; a genuine dislike of creating a fuss; and instinctive reserve and highly developed sense of privacy which by transference leads to deep antipathy to poking one's nose into other people's business.[6]

This middle-class ethos partly accounted for the steady decline of the RAN in the first decade in which Australian officers exercised control over it. Other than the first RAN CNS, Vice-Admiral Sir John Collins, the RAN officers who made up the Naval Board might have been good ships' captains, but they were generally unimpressive admirals. The Naval Board tended to concentrate on minor issues that should have been dealt with by subordinates. This was partly a consequence of a long succession of Navy Ministers abrogating their responsibility as president by not attending Board meetings. The state of the Navy was greeted with stoicism by the admirals, reflecting the Navy's desire to remain 'The Silent Service'. The Naval Board did not want to make a fuss and continued to believe it could operate the RAN with ever-diminishing budget outlays. So while professional standards were being maintained in individual ships, the Fleet was gradually ageing and becoming obsolete. There seemed to be little the naval officers on the

Board could do to arrest the decline. They were isolated from political power and influence. The RAN was rapidly losing capabilities and becoming irrelevant to Government thinking on Australian defence and security.

There was a feeling within the Navy that it had become marginalised. The period after 1956 was a strategic and operational hiatus for the RAN. Australian naval involvement in Korea had ended with the demise of the United Nations Armistice patrols in 1955. Australia then made a commitment of two ships to the British Commonwealth Far East Strategic Reserve based in Singapore. These six-month deployments were busy but not overly demanding. The ships that remained in Australia were constrained by limited supplies of fuel and ammunition.

From a wartime peak of 337 ships in commission and 39,650 serving personnel, the RAN in 1958 consisted of 41 ships and just over 10,000 personnel. The two carriers *Sydney* and *Melbourne*, and the Fleet Air Arm were an enormous drain that left few resources for other fleet requirements. Although a reduction in the size of the Navy after World War II had been expected, the Navy had not envisaged the decline continuing for so long. Ageing World War II ships were not being replaced and there were few new acquisitions. The only genuine construction programme during the postwar period was for three *Daring* Class destroyers which were built largely as escorts for the Navy's carriers.[7] The first ship in the class to be laid down was HMAS *Voyager*. In 1957, the carrier HMAS *Sydney* ceased operational flying and a proposal to disband the Fleet Air Arm and decommission the second carrier, HMAS *Melbourne*, was being considered.

By 1959, the RAN was on the verge of being reduced to a coastguard. Of the three Services, the Navy was considered of inferior status to the other two and was portrayed, predominantly by senior RAAF officers, as inappropriate to Australia's strategic circumstances and irrelevant to modern war fighting tactics and operations. Although the Naval Board believed it had marshalled some very cogent arguments to support the retention of *Sydney* and *Melbourne*, Cabinet remained unconvinced.

The Navy's future appeared bleak, and the admirals of the late 1950s possessed few political skills. As Robert Hyslop, who was in the Navy Department for more than thirty years, remarks:

> Before 1959 Vice-Admiral Sir William Creswell was the only senior officer to exhibit the characteristics of the famous political admirals of the Royal Navy in the nineteenth century, and Vice-Admiral Sir John Collins was the only senior officer serving in the RAN who was at ease in his relationships with political persons. Indeed, the Australian antipathy to politics and politicians was strong among naval officers. My own observation is that they had difficulty in understanding politics and they doubted whether politics was either valuable or essential.[8]

A possible reason for what Hyslop describes is found in Nicholas

Rodger's criticisms of officer development in the Royal Navy, which are equally applicable to the RAN.

> The Navy trained its officers but failed to educate them. Thus it has a poor record of persuading influential and clever men who want to learn but who will not be preached at . . . The training which produces fine junior officers is not necessarily all that is needed to mould a commander-in-chief or a first sea lord . . . In the past, the Service has suffered repeatedly from leaders whose qualities as junior officers and technical experts had promoted them to a level where they needed instead, and lacked, the capacity to bring a trained mind to bear on novel problems.[9]

The major problem for the members of the Naval Board seemed to be understanding that they were required to act politically as part of their service. They tended to fall back on the 'simple sailor' excuse when problems became too complex for the Board to handle. The senior officers during 1955–62, when Vice-Admirals Dowling and Burrell were CNS, seemed not to appreciate that politics was involved whenever there was a conflict able to be resolved through discussion and compromise. But at the same time that the Naval Board wanted to be free of politics, it sought to influence the ways things were done and to change the thrust of public policies. Thus, as Hyslop concludes, 'They pitched headlong into politics but they did not know it'.[10] Consequently, the Naval Board's performance had never been polished, consistent or concerted. What the RAN most needed in 1958 was a tough and determined minister to arrest its declining fortunes.

The arrival of Senator John Gorton as Navy Minister in late 1958 was to provide the boost the Navy desperately needed. He took the initiative and formed a close working relationship with the Board, becoming its most forceful advocate. He attended every Board meeting and took seriously his responsibilities as president. In the year after he became minister, Navy Office also moved to Canberra and this changed the attitude of naval administrators and the tenor of naval administration considerably.

Elected to the Senate in 1951 after service during World War II as an RAAF fighter pilot, Gorton felt he had been overlooked for a ministerial post in the mid-1950s when Senators Paltridge and Henty were promoted over him. By the time he was appointed Navy Minister, Gorton was full of energy and enthusiasm. One of Gorton's biographers, Alan Trengrove, wrote:

> The Navy Department had never encountered anyone like him, but this didn't bother Gorton. He had no inhibitions about going down the line for information, occasionally disconcerting his more senior advisers by the obvious possession of information which they did not know he had. He had moreover a thorough grasp of financial problems — for which naval officers do not have much training — and he spent long hours on the [budget] estimates, keeping his own counsel, and making them very much his own.[11]

Supported by an efficient and well-oiled civilian administrative machine in the Department, within two years Gorton was able to turn the Navy's fortunes around and arrest the decline.

During the Gorton years, which lasted to the end of 1963, the Navy acquired four Type 12 frigates which were built in Australia, purchased six minesweepers from the Royal Navy, ordered two *Charles F. Adams* Class Guided Missile Destroyers (DDGs) to be built in the United States, plus four *Oberon* Class submarines, and took delivery of a squadron of Westland *Wessex* helicopters. The Fleet Tanker HMAS *Supply* returned after service with the Royal Fleet Auxiliary, and Cabinet authorisation was obtained for the construction of a new survey ship, HMAS *Moresby*, and an escort maintenance ship, HMAS *Stalwart*. The *Adams* Class DDGs were the RAN's first attempt to operate American equipment, while the *Oberon* submarine returned to the RAN a capability it had not had since the Great Depression when the two *O* Class submarines *Otway* and *Oxley* were returned to Britain.

During Gorton's time the fixed-wing component of the Fleet Air Arm also had a reprieve and the carrier *Sydney* was saved from the scrapyards with her conversion to a troopship, a role she would perform throughout the Vietnam conflict. The possibility of a second carrier in addition to *Melbourne* was also kept alive in the Gorton years. All of this was achieved against a general feeling that the Defence Minister, Athol Townley, was most favourably disposed towards the RAAF, and despite the indifference of Prime Minister Menzies to the Services.[12]

Such was his immediate success as Navy Minister that Gorton acquired additional responsibilities. In March 1960 he was appointed Minister Assisting the Minister for External Affairs (Sir Garfield Barwick) and, in February 1962, Minister in Charge of the Common- wealth Scientific and Industrial Research Organisation (CSIRO). The political correspondent for the *Age* wrote on 28 January 1963 that Gorton 'has emerged as one of the most capable and personable junior Ministers, with a healthy mixture of imagination and toughmindedness'.

By the end of 1963, when he relinquished the portfolio to become Minister for Works and Minister in Charge of Education and Science, Senator Gorton had achieved outstanding success in arguing the Navy's case within Cabinet. The RAN was in a state of transition. Most of the remaining World War II vintage fleet was to be paid off, either for scrap or into reserve.

With the prospect of a new fleet and the possibility of war with Indonesia before the end of 1964, the Navy possessed a new optimism, confidence and sense of purpose. With the start of that year, operational readiness would be the principal concern of the Naval Board.

# 2

# Preparing for War

ALTHOUGH THE peacetime roles and activities of the RAN were considered important, preparing for war remained the Service's foremost concern. Early in 1964, fears of a major conflict with Indonesia had escalated considerably. As the RAN consisted predominantly of an aircraft carrier and her consorts, it was likely that both *Melbourne* and a *Daring* Class destroyer would be deployed to any conflict in the region.

The pride of the Navy was undoubtedly the flagship of the Fleet, the aircraft carrier HMAS *Melbourne* (Figure 1). As a capital ship, she was a mark of the RAN's professionalism and standing among the world's navies. The carrier was also central to Australia's war-fighting plans and capability. She would provide air cover for the Fleet and be the command and control centre for any conflict at sea.

*Melbourne* started her life as HMS *Majestic*, the lead ship in a new class of aircraft carriers built in Britain at the end of World War II. The keel was laid down on 15 April 1943 at the Vickers-Armstrong yard at Barrow-in-Furness and she was launched on 28 February 1945. Construction was halted with the end of the war. *Majestic* remained untouched until 1949, when building was resumed for the RAN. She was then renamed *Melbourne*. The second Australian warship to bear the name, her motto was '*Vires Acquirit Eundo*' ( 'She gathers strength as she goes'). After building was completed she underwent the usual trials and exercises before commissioning on 28 October 1955. Her complement was 67 officers and 887 men, excluding the Carrier Air Group.

The flagship's commanding officer in 1964 was Captain (Ronald) John Robertson, DSC, RAN. Born on 8 August 1916 at Queenscliff in Victoria, his father, Donald John Robertson, was a captain in the 1st AIF during World War I. His grandfather, Colonel Jack Ernest Robertson, was then commanding officer of the Queenscliff military establishment. After the war, Donald Robertson returned to civilian life but was drowned in Port Phillip Bay in 1920. John and his younger brother then lived with their maternal grandparents at seaside Queenscliff, where he developed a love for the sea and ships. His mother worked as a school teacher.

Having decided to join the Navy at the age of 10, he went from Geelong Grammar School to the Naval College in 1930. He was thought to be a promising young officer and graduated second in his class of twelve cadet-midshipmen in 1933. A tall and slender youth, he had gained sporting colours in rugby, hockey, rowing and athletics and was winner of the Governor-General's cup for sporting excellence. His first ship was the heavy cruiser *Australia*, which shortly after he joined took the Duke of Gloucester back to England, via the West Indies. Her junior officers were then disembarked to continue their training with the Royal Navy. Most of Robertson's class did not return to Australia until mid-1937. Deciding to specialise as a communicator, Lieutenant Robertson returned to Britain in October 1938 to undertake his specialist course. The possible outbreak of war led to the course being shortened and Robertson was posted on exchange with the Royal Navy to the Reserve Fleet destroyer HMS *Malcolm*.[1]

He was mentioned in despatches three times during the war. The first was during 1940, when *Malcolm* was involved in the Allied evacuation of Dunkirk. On the second occasion he was praised for his skill during the evacuation of the Hook of Holland as Signal Officer to Captain D.16 (16th Destroyer Flotilla).

> His organisation of the Signal Department stood up to a very severe test and his initiative and coolness under enemy bombing were exceptional. Captain (D) reports that he was of invaluable assistance to him in every way and that he owes much to his exceptional all-round ability.[2]

After serving in the European theatre until late 1942, Lieutenant Robertson returned to Australia to join the staff of the Director of Signal Communications in Navy Office. After a brief period of exchange with the Royal Navy in 1944, when he served with the Allied Naval Commander of the Expeditionary Force, Admiral Sir Bertram Ramsay, Robertson was appointed as Flag Lieutenant and Communications Officer to Commodore Harold Farncomb, the Commodore Commanding the Australian Squadron. It was in this period, early 1945, that he was mentioned in despatches a third time when serving in the heavy cruiser, HMAS *Shropshire*. He was praised for his 'gallantry, skill and devotion ... in the successful assault operations in Lingayen Gulf, Luzon Island'. Robertson also won the Distinguished Service Cross (DSC) while in HMS *Malcolm*.

After the war, his career was divided between seagoing service in HMA Ships *Hobart, Bataan* and *Arunta*, and shore appointments. As one of the RAN's communications experts, he was placed in charge of the RAN Signal School at Flinders Naval Depot in 1947.

In 1956, Robertson was appointed to his first command, the RAN training ship and converted sloop, HMAS *Swan*. His navigator was Lieutenant Jim Kelly, who had won the DSC in Korea following the famous escape of HMAS *Murchison* down the Han River under devastating fire from advancing Chinese Communist forces. After serving as Chief Staff Officer to FOICEA, Robertson took command of the new destroyer *Vendetta*, with the rank of captain, in 1958. Following a successful period in command of *Vendetta*, Robertson was posted to Navy Office as Director of Naval Plans and then selected for the Imperial Defence College (IDC) course in London. This course was more or less a prerequisite for promotion to flag rank.

On returning to Australia in 1962, Robertson served in Navy Office as Director of Naval Reserves before taking command of HMAS *Melbourne* in January 1964. Previously, he had been the Executive Officer of the carrier HMAS *Sydney* for sixteen months in the period when she was still engaged in fixed-wing flying operations. It had been three years since he had last been at sea.

On assuming command of *Melbourne*, a most prestigious appointment, Robertson had every reason to feel confident of promotion to rear-admiral on completion of his twelve or eighteen months in the ship. His six predecessors in command of *Melbourne* had all been promoted to rear-admiral. Of those predecessors, two went on to become CNS and were later knighted.

Robertson was considered somewhat dour, serious, and at times difficult, by his contemporaries, but he was a dependable officer and an upright man. He kept largely to himself. He was married to Bettina and they had four children.

Vital to the deployment of *Melbourne* were the escorts which would protect her during a conflict. The workhorses of the Australian Fleet were the three *Daring* Class destroyers — *Voyager*, *Vendetta* and *Vampire*. They performed an enormous range of operational tasks and spent prolonged periods away from Australia as part of the nation's contribution to the Commonwealth Far East Strategic Reserve based in Singapore.

*Voyager*'s name had not been a happy one for the RAN. The first *Voyager*, a V Class destroyer of World War I vintage loaned to the RAN by the Royal Navy prior to World War II, achieved a place in history by sinking the first Italian submarine of the war only three days after Italy's entry into the war on the side of the Axis Powers. On returning to Australia from the Mediterranean in late 1941, *Voyager* was refitted and subsequently deployed to Portuguese East Timor where she was to assist in the evacuation of Portuguese nationals and the resupply of Australian commandos who were waging a guerrilla war against the Japanese. On approaching Betano Bay on 23 September 1942, *Voyager* ran aground on a reef 500 yards from the shore after some poor shiphandling. Changing tides and determined efforts to refloat the ship led to her propellers becoming deeply embedded in the sandy bottom of the bay. The following day the Japanese became aware that *Voyager* was stuck fast. To prevent her from falling into enemy hands, the ship was abandoned and demolition charges placed in the engine-room were detonated. The ship's back was broken and the first *Voyager* suffered an inglorious end at the hands of the RAN. This would have been a bad omen to the superstitious.

The first ship of the *Daring* Class to be laid down was the second *Voyager*, in 1949. She was built at Cockatoo Island Dockyard in Sydney and launched on 1 May 1952 by Mrs Menzies, the wife of the then Prime Minister (Figure 2). After a long period of trials and evaluations, as usually occurs with the first ship in a new class, *Voyager* was commissioned on 12 February 1957 under the command of Captain John Crabb. The commissioning service was conducted by an Anglican naval chaplain, the Reverend Fred Kyte.

A souvenir booklet was distributed to those attending the commissioning.

> This class of ship is a departure from the conventional destroyer both in general design, armament, and number of personnel carried. She has the striking power of a light cruiser . . . coupled with the latest anti-submarine weapon and detection devices. Furthermore, her manoeuvrability is superior to that of even the most modern conventional destroyer, owing to the fitting of twin rudders.

*Voyager*'s construction also embodied new technology and techniques.

> *Voyager* has the first all-welded hull to be built in Australia. During construction, entire sections of the ship were built upside down in the shipyard, the whole then being assembled into one unit on the stocks. Apart from ease of construction, the all-welded hull has two advantages — firstly it is lighter than the conventionally riveted hull, with a consequent improvement in the 'power–weight ratio', and secondly, if the ship is damaged, such damage is more localised than in a riveted ship, where rivets may well be sprung far from the seat of damage.

The ships were not without their flaws. In addition to some shortcomings in the design of the wheelhouse, problems were created by the design and layout of the bridge. A naval architect who served in a *Daring* as an RAN Reserve officer for several weeks in 1962, observed

> [I] became concerned over problems inherent in the very poor layout of the bridge and its equipment disposition. In essence it was a dangerous and non-functional layout, creating unnecessary difficulties in moving from place to place and danger in so doing. I listed ten related problems contributing to the difficulties in operating such a ship, particularly in action conditions.[3]

Problems caused by the many different levels of the bridge deck were confirmed by several officers with long experience serving in *Daring* Class destroyers before they were modified to a single level bridge between 1969 and 1973.

After commissioning in Sydney, *Voyager*'s operational service consisted almost entirely of long deployments to the Strategic Reserve.

After six years in service, *Voyager* had earned a reputation as a sometimes unreliable but nonetheless hard-working ship, having steamed 218,300 miles since commissioning. The uncharacteristically large number of defects for a ship of her age meant that *Voyager* was sometimes known as an unhappy ship. The latest of the mishaps she suffered was in late 1962 when parts of the aluminium superstructure parted from the steel hull during a heavy storm off Sydney. The need for repairs prevented *Voyager* from participating in the Empire Games to be held in Perth. A naturally disappointed ship's company was the result.

On 31 January 1963, *Voyager* sailed from Sydney for her sixth deployment to the Strategic Reserve. The ship would be away from her home port for six months. She had a new commanding officer, Captain Duncan Stevens, who had taken over from Commander Alan Willis on 2 January 1963. On her return to Sydney on 3 August 1963, *Voyager* proceeded to Williamstown to commence a long refit, which was to last until the first week of January 1964. The condition of *Voyager* when she began this refit was described as only 'fair' by the Fleet Commander in a report covering his inspection of the ship in July 1963.[4] He also noted some serious flaws in her gunnery system.[5]

The refit was a demoralising time for those who remained on board. *Voyager* was manned by a ship's company that had settled in Sydney and most expected the refit to be conducted at Cockatoo Island Dockyard, given that it had a better reputation for this type of work. Morale dropped considerably, with the men separated from their families and facing the prospect of returning to the Far East for another long deployment in early 1964.

Of all the problems requiring attention, the most pressing was *Voyager*'s gunnery system. Lieutenant Peter Sinclair was sent to meet *Voyager* on her arrival in Darwin from the Far East in July 1963, and to sail with her to Sydney. As gunnery specialist with the RAN Trials and Assessment Unit (RANTAU) his task was to determine why *Voyager*'s gunnery had been so poor during her deployment to the Strategic Reserve. That this was a special task prompted by the 1963 deployment and the opportunity for rectification was offered during the forthcoming refit period. Between Darwin and Sydney, Sinclair conducted a series of pre-refit trials and prepared an exhaustive defect list before the ship entered dock at Williamstown.[6]

*Voyager*'s refit was of shorter duration than that usually allocated a ship of her class at that point in the maintenance cycle. There were two reasons for this. The first related to cost, and the second to the need to have *Voyager* ready for service in the Strategic Reserve early in the new year. At a meeting of the Naval Board on 22 November 1963, a new refit policy was introduced in an effort to divert funds from refit and maintenance to capital works and acquisition. In future, captains of ships would be advised of the total amount allocated to the refit and the cost of individual equipment items. The aim was to give officers in command some discretion in using their refit funds to ensure the final cost did not exceed the allocation. If need be, they were empowered to omit certain items from the refit on a selective basis while 'carrying out the maximum possible self-maintenance'.[7]

By November 1963, *Voyager* was in an awful state. The ship was dirty and disorganised. The ship's company were given sub-standard accommodation in *Quickmatch* which was also alongside at Williamstown. Several officers and sailors serving in *Voyager* at the time remarked that they had never seen an RAN ship in such a condition. In the December 1963 Report of Proceedings to the Fleet Commander, Stevens stated

> The refit is progressing satisfactorily, and the general appearance of the ship is noticeably improved both internally and externally since ship's staff undertook all cleaning duties . . . The health, morale and conduct of the ship's company are remarkably good when the length of the refit and the conditions under which they work are considered.[8]

There is evidence that captains were under some pressure to contain the cost of their ship's maintenance within the barely adequate allocations they had received.[9] Lieutenant Charles Thomason, an officer serving at HMAS *Cerberus* while *Voyager* was in refit, later alleged that when *Voyager* sailed,

> batteries for the automatic emergency lighting were not available because someone had either forgotten to order them or else it may have been part of a cost saving exercise to meet measly budget restrictions. There was not enough money in the refit allocation to buy the batteries outside the normal dockyard or naval store channels. The entire outfit of 20-man inflatable life rafts were landed for survey when *Voyager* went into refit. These were sub-contracted to an outside firm so they were put beyond the grasp of immediate naval control and decision-making process. So that when *Voyager* had to complete her refit and sail, the reasonable thing to do would be to sail with a complete outfit of life rafts surveyed or not. However, since the life rafts were in the sub-contractors hands, all that could be done was to exhort that firm to complete the surveys and for the life rafts to be sent up to Sydney to be collected by *Voyager* before she departed for the Far East.[10]

Although substance for these claims, which are apparently based on first-hand knowledge from 1963, cannot be found in official records, it is quite possible that a shortage of funds prevented some of *Voyager*'s lifesaving equipment from being surveyed as required. If Thomason's claims are accepted, and such patently inadvisable cost-cutting did take place, one suspects that there may have been other areas neglected in *Voyager*'s refit. However, there is no evidence to suggest that *Voyager* did not have a complete outfit of life rafts when she sailed from Sydney, or that the state of these life rafts had a bearing on any subsequent event.[11]

By way of contrast, *Melbourne*'s refit in the latter part of 1963 commanded a much higher priority. The carrier's refit involved some minor conversion and Garden Island dockyard took on an additional 100 men to complete the work.[12]

The man responsible for *Voyager*'s readiness for sea service was her commanding officer. Captain Duncan Herbert Stevens, RAN, was a man of vastly different temperament and professional background to Robertson. The son of Major-General Sir Jack Stevens, a well-known wartime citizen-soldier, Duncan was the lowest achiever in the Naval College term of 1935, although he did gain colours for cricket, rugby and hockey. He was thought to be a reliable junior officer during World War II but was not rated as an outstanding prospect for early promotion.

Stevens had had command of four minor vessels and one major vessel before *Voyager* and these had produced only one noteworthy incident. When in command of the Boom Defence Vessel HMAS *Koala* in 1949, an officer of the watch with little knowledge of navigation, as it later appeared, drove the ship ashore. In the court martial that followed, the then Lieutenant Stevens was charged with hazarding and stranding his ship. He was found guilty of the charge of hazarding his command and was reprimanded — the lightest penalty a court martial can award. The Fleet Commander commented in his confidential report on Stevens that

> It is regrettable that *Koala* was stranded on passage to Sydney, but it is considered that although Stevens, who had not spared himself for the previous week, erred in his desire to make the quickest possible passage, and overestimated the efficiency of one of his officers, he is now a wiser and sounder seaman as a result of the experience.

In 1958–59, he served as Executive Officer of HMAS *Melbourne* and had first-hand knowledge of that ship and carrier operations.

Very few Australian officers had worked with Stevens in the three years prior to his taking command of *Voyager*. In early 1960 he was posted to the Royal Navy Staff College under training and spent the next two years on exchange at the Admiralty in London, with the rank of commander. At the end of 1963 he was promoted to captain and given command of *Voyager*. Nothing untoward had arisen concerning *Voyager* during Captain Stevens's first year in command, and the Fleet Commander at that time, Rear-Admiral Alan McNicoll, commented in his official report that he 'has conducted himself to my entire satisfaction'. He was thought to be a highly experienced destroyer captain and thoroughly familiar with manoeuvring around aircraft carriers.

A man of medium height and build, Stevens was gregarious, with a passion for sport and outdoor activity. He was known to have a quick and at times explosive temper but he did not hold grudges against those with whom he served. Stevens enjoyed being in the Navy. He was well liked by his contemporaries and respected by several admirals with whom he had personal friendships.

As commanding officers, Robertson and Stevens had enormous and absolute responsibilities. The Navy promoted Shakespeare's aphorism that 'In persons grafted with a serious trust, negligence is a crime'. The warships they commanded were extremely complex organisations that required sound cooperation and stringently observed principles of organisation. The officer appointed second-in-command was given the title 'Executive Officer'. In larger ships, such as aircraft carriers and cruisers, he was also known as the 'Commander', as this was his rank. In smaller ships where the Executive Officer was of lieutenant commander rank or below, the title 'First Lieutenant' was also used. He was always an officer of the seaman specialisation. The Executive Officer had specific responsibility for ship's husbandry, seamanship evolutions and discipline. He was president of the officer's mess, or wardroom as it was known, of which the captain was not a member. He would also act as Commanding Officer from time to time as preparation for his own command.

There were several departments within the ship's organisation. The Executive Officer was head of the seaman department. The Supply Officer was head of the stores, pay and secretariat department. The Engineering Officer and the Electrical Officer each headed their own departments. If a doctor was carried, the Medical Officer was overseer of another department, albeit small. Each officer was answerable to the Commanding Officer for his department.

The ship's company, which consisted of the senior sailors and junior sailors, was headed by the senior coxswain and organised along departmental lines. Men from all departments were divided into watches which provided for the continuous performance of duties at sea. Groups of men who lived and worked together were arranged in divisions. Each division had a divisional senior sailor and a divisional officer who had primary responsibility for the personal record-keeping, morale, discipline, welfare and training of the sailors in that division. A sailor with a personal problem, a request, or a complaint had to have the matter channelled through the divisional system, although a sailor could request an interview with the captain on any issue. All this organisation was aimed at ensuring an efficient ship which enjoyed good morale.

Warships were small, complex communities of men drawn from many backgrounds, with a wide range of professional skills. Over a period of several months, usually the duration of a work-up (a period of adjustment, cleaning-up and training for a ship after commissioning or a major overhaul) following a maintenance period, the officers and ship's company of a warship became a close-knit team able to maintain their ship at peak operational efficiency. The commencement of a work-up was usually a hectic time. Ships underwent extensive trials and tests, during which time the bridge staff and command teams became acquainted with each other and the particular command style of the captain. Those who had not been to sea for some time usually found that the learning curve was initially steep.

The start of 1964 had seen *Melbourne* and *Voyager* in similar situations. Both ships had been in refit for extended periods and were preparing for work-up exercises which would see them ready for service in South-East Asian waters. *Melbourne* was due to sail for the Philippines in April for an important South-East Asian Treaty Organisation (SEATO) exercise, while *Voyager* would have a repeat of 1963 and relieve *Vendetta* in the Strategic Reserve. Both ships had a large number of new faces. Of the officers in *Melbourne*, 39 per cent had been in the ship for less than three months, 15 per cent for three to six months, 12.5 per cent for six to twelve months and 33 per cent for a period in excess of twelve months. In *Melbourne*, there was a new captain, Robertson, a new navigator, Jim Kelly, a number of new watchkeeping officers including a young sub-lieutenant, Alex Bate, while the Fleet Commander, usually embarked in *Melbourne*, Rear-Admiral Humphrey Becher, had recently taken up his appointment. Becher was a specialist gunnery officer and a distinguished destroyer captain who had won the DSO and the DSC and Bar for his service during World War II and the Korean War. He had been the second captain of *Melbourne* in 1957–58.

In *Voyager*, there was a new executive officer, Lieutenant Commander Ian MacGregor, a new navigator, Lieutenant Harry Cook, and new watchkeeping officers including a Royal Navy exchange officer, Lieutenant David Price.

Both *Melbourne* and *Voyager* had the added challenge of making sailors out of the raw recruits who had graduated from the Recruit Training School at *Cerberus* in October 1963. These recruits had been sent to both ships in large numbers to replace trained men in the schemes of complement: *Melbourne* was given 184 ordinary seamen and *Voyager* 72. They all required close supervision and most were at sea for the first time. This meant that both ships were trying to fulfil a training as well as an operational function. The proportion of experienced men to sailors under training was of greater concern in *Voyager*, with her smaller complement. Chief Coxswain Jonathan Rogers, the most senior sailor on board, felt disquiet about the number of recruits and raised the matter with several officers.[13]

At the start of the new year in January, *Melbourne* had undertaken some basic sea trials, while *Voyager* sailed unaccompanied from Williamstown on 25 January 1964 for Sydney and followed this with two weeks alongside at Garden Island. On 6 February they sailed from Sydney independently for post-refit work-up exercises. *Voyager*'s gunnery was still the subject of special attention. When the RANTAU team under Sinclair departed *Voyager* for *Vendetta* in early February, two civilian technical officers from Williamstown Dockyard, Stan Parker and Eric Bird, were asked to remain on board to complete the fine-tuning of the gunnery system.[14]

*Melbourne* and *Voyager* had operated together on (Friday) 7 February but had not engaged in close quarters manoeuvring or stationing. Both ships anchored that night in Jervis Bay. At 0030 on 8 February, *Voyager* was sent to sea to recover a battle-practice target which was drifting in Shoalhaven Bight. *Voyager* remained at sea throughout the night and the following day in an effort to take the target in tow. She was later joined by *Melbourne*, which provided a team of divers to assist. *Voyager* returned to Jervis Bay and anchored at 0730 on Sunday, 9 February. At 1200 the same day, *Melbourne* also returned to Jervis Bay, having waited for the arrival of HMAS *Kimbla*, which took the target in tow. The officers of *Voyager* had been invited to lunch in the flagship and arrived shortly after *Melbourne* settled at anchor. Over lunch, *Voyager*'s navigator, Lieutenant Cook, mentioned to one of his Naval College term-mates, Lieutenant Paul Berger, that Stevens had been 'riding' him very heavily and that he was not looking forward to the coming week.

While at anchor, a series of sporting events and competitions between the two ships' companies was arranged at the RAN College, HMAS *Creswell*. Both captains went ashore after lunch that afternoon to watch the sport. The commanding officer of the Naval College was Captain Dacre Smyth, who had very recently assumed command. Smyth invited both captains to his house for drinks but only Stevens accepted. Stevens had two brandies then reverted to milk, saying that he had to take it easy as he was going to sea the next morning, with a busy week ahead.

On the morning of 10 February, both ships prepared to get under way for the very full programme of exercises. Throughout the day *Voyager* circled *Melbourne* and conducted a series of trials and exercises designed to refresh everyone in both ships with seagoing routines and to provide the opportunity for some of the problems associated with the ships' time in dockyard hands to be located and corrected. *Melbourne* practised anti-aircraft (AA) tracking, conducted radio sea trials and exercised emergency stations. *Voyager* participated in the same AA exercise in addition to an anti-submarine (A/S) exercise with HMS/M *Tabard* and a shore bombardment.

After the evening meal, the ships prepared for a series of night-flying exercises. This was the first time either ship had been engaged in close quarters manoeuvring for nearly six months. In *Melbourne*, the captain and navigator were on the bridge with the officer of the watch (OOW), Sub-Lieutenant Alex Bate. Earlier in the day, the senior watchkeeper, who was also the diving officer, had been flown to *Kimbla* which had fouled the target towing line in her propellers. The senior watchkeeper was listed on the watchbill for 'the first' — the watch between 1950 and 2350 — but Bate was to stand the watch in his absence.

Despite his rank, Bate was not an inexperienced watchkeeper. He had earlier spent fourteen months in the minesweeper HMAS *Gull*, joining the ship with her five sisters in the United Kingdom for their delivery voyage to Australia with HMAS *Supply*, which was then reverting to RAN service. During the minesweeper's work-up at Rosythe, Bate was the 'Special Sea Dutymen' (the ship's 'first eleven') OOW. He had stood day and night watches in *Gull* for the three months that the ship was on passage to Australia. Although he had been in *Melbourne* for nearly one year, and kept night watches on the bridge as Assistant OOW, this was his first watch as OOW at night.

In *Voyager*, the captain was on the bridge after his evening meal. The OOW was Lieutenant David Price. He had not served in Australia nor in an RAN ship before. In the limited time he had spent in Australia, he seemed reserved to those who met him and did not give the appearance of being overconfident.

After joining the Royal Navy in 1952, Price was appointed midshipman in 1955, acting sub-lieutenant in 1956, lieutenant in August 1958 and gained his watchkeeping certificate the following year. As a trained watchkeeping officer, Price served in the small pre-World War II minesweeper *Plover* during 1958–59 and spent the next two years in the *Ton* Class coastal minesweeper *Fiskerton*.

He was posted to *Bellerophon* (the Portsmouth Reserve Fleet) in 1962 and then to the training establishment HMS *Vernon*, where he undertook his torpedo and anti-submarine specialist course.[15] Price did not have extensive bridge experience and had not been to sea for more than two years when *Voyager* went to sea in early 1964.

His reports suggest he was an unremarkable officer.[16] While under training in HMS *Bermuda*, his captain said his performance was 'to my satisfaction. He has made reasonable progress in this ship and should develop into a sound officer'. In his first report from *Plover*, dated 31 July 1958, the captain stated: 'He needs to develop his powers of anticipation, but this is my only criticism of his work.' The captain of *Fiskerton* said in his report on Price dated 31 May 1961 that his performance was 'to my satisfaction. He is a keen and conscientious officer who always has the best interests of the ship at heart. But he must make efforts to be more tactful in his dealings with seniors and juniors'.

As OOW Price was responsible for '(i) the safety of the ship in all its aspects, particularly her safety from collision and grounding, subject to any orders which he may receive from the commanding officer, (ii) so far as it is within his control, the safety of all persons on board'. This responsibility remained with the OOW until he handed over his watch to another qualified officer, or he was relieved by the captain. In

*Daring* Class destroyers, OOWs were usually officers in the rank of lieutenant and aged between 23 and 31. The OOW was the captain's representative on the bridge, and every officer on board, regardless of rank, was subject to him. Although it was a duty with many concerns, the OOW 'is to take care that he is never prevented, through over-attention to detail, from discharging his primary responsibility for the safety of the ship'. To assist and understudy Price on *Voyager*'s bridge, as part of his training, was Acting Sub-Lieutenant J. S. Davies.

Also on the bridge was the navigator and the Executive Officer. The latter, MacGregor, was already on friendly terms with the captain, who was grateful for a second-in-command with whom he felt confident. His predecessor, Lieutenant Commander Peter Cabban, had left *Voyager* and resigned from the Navy on 8 January 1964. Cabban and Stevens had not enjoyed a good working relationship. Stevens and MacGregor had served together before and liked each other's company.

As the sun began to set, Captain Stevens was the only 'old hand' on the bridge of either ship. The others — Robertson, Kelly, Bate, Cook, MacGregor and Price — were all in new positions and becoming familiar with their surroundings.

The simultaneous appointment of Robertson and Kelly had been noted at Fleet Headquarters with a little concern. However, both men had been undergoing courses in 1963 that precluded any alternative posting arrangement. It was considered acceptable because Kelly had been a qualified navigator since 1954 and had served in *Melbourne* from 1961 to 1963, and Robertson himself had spent sixteen months in a carrier.

Rear-Admiral Becher's Fleet Operations Officer, Commander Peter Doyle, was also new, having taken up his posting in January 1964. In addition, there was also a new Navy Minister, Fred Chaney (Gorton's long reign having ended on 18 December 1963 with a Federal election), and a new Secretary of the Department of the Navy (Sam Landau).

None of this has been outlined to suggest that anyone on either ship or ashore was incompetent or ill-prepared for the duties and responsibilities assigned to them. But this was a time when many individuals were finding their way and settling into new positions and responsibilities.

There was added interest in these particular night-flying exercises as it was the first occasion on which the carrier's flight deck was floodlit (Figure 3). A check had been made by Commanders Kelly and Bailey while the ship was at anchor in Jervis Bay the previous weekend to ensure none of this red lighting was visible on the starboard side of the carrier.[17] It consisted of one light near the base of the bridge island, and an experimental directional red floodlight set up on the gun direction platform giving a downward beam from near the top of the island. This light was being trained onto the angled flight deck until the senior

Gannet aircraft pilot, Lieutenant Commander Toz Dadswell, who had been making 'touch and go' runs across the carrier's deck, informed Flying Control in *Melbourne* by radio that the glare from the light was blinding him during his approach.[18] The light was then trained onto the forward lift.

Night flying was always difficult, both for aviators and flight-deck crews. As a routine exercise it was only undertaken by a worked-up Carrier Air Group (CAG) and ship. On this occasion, the aircraft had come from the RAN Air Station at HMAS *Albatross* and would return there following the exercise. Although not all *Melbourne*'s personnel were required, since the fixed-wing aircraft were not being handled on deck, there was still a great deal of activity, and the flight deck and bridge were tense places to be.

The exercises planned for that evening were by no means difficult but there was a feeling of apprehension on the bridges of both ships.

# 3

# *Where Fate Calls*

AT 1800 ON 10 FEBRUARY 1964, *Voyager* closed *Melbourne* for the first time that day, for the transfer of mail by heaving line. The evolution completed and the sun beginning to set, *Voyager* was ordered away from the carrier and stationed five miles ahead while they both waited for darkness to fall.

Both ships prepared for a busy few hours of night-flying exercises. *Melbourne* would be working with Squadrons 816 and 805 from the CAG, which was then at the Naval Air Station (NAS) at Nowra. The aircraft had been detached from the carrier for the duration of *Melbourne*'s refit and were returning for the first time in many months. They were due to return to the carrier permanently two or three days later, after practising deck landings and take-offs. Three Gannet aircraft were expected between 2000 and 2030 and two Sea Venoms between 2030 and 2100.

At 1830, the ships were 20 miles to the south-east of Jervis Bay in deep water. There was a low easterly swell, smooth seas and light variable winds. As the anemometer, the instrument used to check wind speed, fluctuated between 17 and 19 knots — less than *Melbourne*'s speed through the water — Robertson suspected that it was faulty and ordered a hand-held anemometer be used on the flight deck. There was no moon, the night was clear, and visibility was estimated at 20 miles.

*Melbourne* and *Voyager* were 'darkened' for the exercise, with only operational lighting visible to the other ship. This consisted of the green starboard and red port sidelights, a white stern or overtaking light, masthead lights and, in the case of *Melbourne*, the experimental flight-deck floodlighting which was meant to have been visible only on the port side to avoid being mistaken for the port sidelight (Figure 4). *Voyager*'s lights were burning at full brilliance (Figure 5). The two sidelights in the carrier were dimmed so that their visibility range was about one nautical mile with the unassisted eye, that is, without binoculars. Neither *Voyager* nor the aircraft operating in the vicinity had complained that *Melbourne*'s lights were too dim.

For nearly one hour after 1845, *Voyager* remained in her station, five miles ahead of the carrier, while the two ships conducted radar calibration trials. Sunset was at 1945. *Voyager* was then ordered to rejoin *Melbourne* in preparation for night-flying exercises. The destroyer altered course to the south and took up a position ahead of the carrier when Captain Robertson, as Officer in Tactical Command (OTC), signalled *Voyager* that the flying course — the course on which the carrier would proceed while operating with aircraft — was 180 degrees at a speed of 20 knots. On execution of the flying course signal, *Voyager* was to take 'Planeguard Station No. 1' — a position 20 degrees on the port quarter of the carrier at a distance of between 1,000 and 1,500 yards (Figure 6).

*Voyager*'s function as planeguard was to recover any aircraft that happened to ditch into the sea (Figure 7). With *Melbourne* steaming to the north and the flying course being to the south, *Voyager* would be roughly in the correct position when the ships turned together to 180 degrees on the execution of the signal. There was one basic principle governing this sort of exercise: the planeguard keeps well out of the way of the carrier while it operates aircraft.

At 1950 the ships turned together to the flying course and *Voyager* assumed her station. As the winds were light and variable, Robertson would need to alter course and speed so as to get the maximum amount of headwind down the flight deck of the carrier. He was able to do this by signalling small variations. At 1957 he ordered the course changed to 175 degrees, and eight minutes later increased the speed to 22 knots. The Sea Venoms from the CAG arrived on time at 2030 from NAS Nowra to conduct 'touch and go' exercises from the carrier's deck, at which time Robertson again altered the flying course, this time to 190 degrees. *Voyager* maintained her correct station throughout these simple manoeuvres.

With insufficient wind available for the exercise on a southerly course, the two aircraft were directed to return to the Nowra while *Melbourne* sent a signal to *Voyager* at 2040 advising: 'flight operations will be delayed for about ten minutes'. At 2041, Robertson ordered a 'turn together to 020 degrees, ships turning to starboard' which placed *Voyager* ahead of the carrier (Figure 8). After steadying on the new course of 020 degrees, Robertson decided at 2047 to compare the wind across the deck on a course of 060 degrees. On a course of 060 degrees, *Voyager* should then have been 30 degrees on *Melbourne*'s port bow (Figure 9).

During the few minutes that the ships held this course and the wind speed was compared, *Voyager* was noticed by Robertson to be 'ahead' of station, being to starboard of her correct position, at a range of 1,500 yards from the carrier. This was not excessive, given the turns that had been carried out. By this time darkness had fallen and all that could be seen with confidence from the carrier were the destroyer's navigation lights. At 2052, after finding that the wind was better on the previous course, Robertson ordered a turn from 060 degrees back to 020 degrees with ships 'turning together to port'. This was done by voice VHF communications. Neither morse code nor encryption had been used for relaying any signal. Before *Melbourne* steadied on the new course and while the turn back to 020 degrees was in progress, Robertson informed *Voyager* of his intentions for flying: 'Flying course 020 speed 22 knots'. This was acknowledged by the destroyer (Figure 10).

On receipt of the signal, *Voyager* was to resume Planeguard Station No. 1, that is, 20 degrees on the port quarter of *Melbourne* at a distance of 1,000 to 1,500 yards. The destroyer would then proceed with the carrier on the flying course of 020 degrees. The manoeuvre for *Voyager* to take her new station was a familiar one. *Melbourne* would have expected *Voyager* to turn in a large circle away from the carrier, with *Melbourne* passing ahead while the destroyer completed her turn and assumed a station astern. As *Voyager* would be on the starboard bow of the carrier when the alteration of course to 020 degrees was completed, Robertson expected *Voyager* to alter course to starboard, taking the destroyer away from the carrier, before assuming station. This was also the shortest route (Figure 11).

*Voyager* initially turned to starboard under 15 degrees of wheel. Both Robertson and Kelly had expected *Voyager* to alter to starboard and confirmed their observations with each other. This was at approximately 2053. For the next twenty seconds *Voyager* appeared to maintain a heading of around 065 degrees at 1,300 yards from the carrier. She then altered course to port with 10 degrees of wheel which led Robertson — who observed all of *Voyager*'s movements from the starboard bridge-wing without binoculars — and the carrier's bridge staff, to assume *Voyager* was doing a manoeuvre that was later referred to as a 'fishtail'.

This manoeuvre would allow *Voyager* to reduce speed while waiting for the carrier to overtake. As *Voyager* was beyond 1,000 yards from the carrier, broad on the starboard bow, and had appeared to return to the new course of 020 degrees, there was no danger and Robertson had little reason to be concerned. However, he did not take a bearing or a radar range of *Voyager*. Nor did he consult Kelly about his interpretation of the destroyer's subsequent movements. It is at this point, 2054, that the situation began to change (Figure 12).

When *Melbourne* had gained her new course of 020 degrees, *Voyager* was continuing with her turn to port and was then 1,100 yards from the carrier. For over one minute, Robertson constantly watched *Voyager* and maintained the belief that she was conducting a 'fishtail'. This presented no danger, as he expected the destroyer to alter course at any time in that period.

While their ship altered course to port towards the carrier, the captain and the navigator of *Voyager* were no longer looking at *Melbourne*. They were conferring with Communications Yeoman Kevin Cullen at the chart table which was on a platform forward and below the bridge covered in a canvas flap to shield the bridge from the lighted chart table (Figure 13). It is most probable that they were discussing the interpretation of signals sent from *Melbourne* using ATP 1A Volume 1 — *Allied Naval Manoeuvring Instructions* (ANMI) or ATP 1A Volume 2 — *Allied Naval Signal Book* (ANSB). The OOW, Lieutenant Price was, however, responsible for keeping a close watch on *Melbourne*.

At 2055, *Voyager* was still altering course to port broad on the starboard bow from *Melbourne* at a range of only 1,000 yards. A dangerous situation had developed. The next 15 seconds were crucial as the ships continued to close. If the bridge staff in the destroyer were to avoid a collision, action had to be taken in that short period. *Voyager* persisted with her turn and now began to close the carrier rapidly. As neither ship had taken avoiding action, the two ships were now 800 yards from each other and a collision was inevitable; they were technically *in extremis*.[1]

Thirty seconds after 2055, with *Voyager* still turning to port, immediate concern developed among *Melbourne*'s bridge staff as Kelly exclaimed 'Christ! What is *Voyager* doing!' He moved to the compass and took a bearing of the destroyer to assess her movement relative to the carrier (Figure 14). *Voyager* maintained her turn and Kelly ordered 'half astern both engines'. This order to the engine-room was increased by Robertson who ordered 'full astern both engines' several seconds later, after coming onto the bridge from the bridge-wing (Figure 15).

The possibility that *Voyager* was not aware of her position relative to *Melbourne* did not occur to Robertson. Thus, no sound signals or messages were sent to warn *Voyager* that she was standing into danger. The carrier had little chance of altering either her course or speed in the distance available. *Melbourne* would take at least six minutes to decrease her speed adequately. When *Voyager* was just 80 yards away, *Melbourne* had lost perhaps a single knot of speed. Tactical Operator Everett on the carrier's bridge voiced what was in the mind of everyone: 'We are going to hit her'.

On the port bridge-wing of the destroyer, the side of the ship nearest to *Melbourne*, the lookout was Ordinary Seaman Brian Sumpter. This was his first time at sea. He did not have any experience on which to make a judgement, but it was apparent even to him that there was something very wrong. He shouted 'Bridge!' and turned around to see Price looking through binoculars. He then dropped the binoculars and stared at the approaching carrier, as if mesmerised. The shout from the lookout brought Captain Stevens back onto the bridge from the chart table. It took Stevens a few moments to regain some night vision and establish the position of his ship relative to the carrier (Figure 16). At approximately thirty seconds after 2055 he ordered 'Full ahead both engines. Hard a-starboard'. He then turned and said, 'Quartermaster, this is an emergency. Pipe Collision Stations'.[2] Price, who had the bridge microphone in his hand, echoed his captain's orders to the wheelhouse on the deck below in an attempt to either pass ahead of *Melbourne* or to turn inside her. It was all far too late (Figure 17). When the order was given in *Voyager*, the ships were 370 yards bridge to bridge but only 250 yards bow to bow. A collision was imminent and the only question was where *Melbourne* would hit *Voyager* (Figure 18).

Below decks in *Voyager* life was going on as usual. Watchkeepers slept before going on duty, others read, played cards or bingo, wrote letters or ironed their uniforms for the next day. Ordinary Seaman John Jersovs, aged 19, was standing his watch amidships on the port side of *Voyager*.

> I saw *Melbourne* exercising a way off. I had a look out to sea and then a wave hit me a split second before the collision. I saw no lights from the carrier, heard no warning as it hit about 20 feet forward of where I stood. The deck bent up in front of me, the bridge seemed to collapse, rigging, pipes, the funnel and all sorts of gear seemed to be falling around me.

The huge bulk of the carrier loomed overhead in the dark and then crashed through the destroyer. The point of impact in *Voyager* was the after end of the bridge and the operations room, which was one deck below. On *Voyager*'s bridge, Stevens, Price, Cook, MacGregor, Cullen and Davies were killed instantly. Lieutenant Commander Thomas Dadswell, flying overhead in a Gannet aircraft, saw a fireball and said to his observer, '*Melbourne*'s collected *Voyager*' (Figure 19).

Leading Radio Electrical Mechanic John Milliner was in the forward half of *Voyager* at the time of the collision.

> I was in the cafe playing Tombola [bingo] at the time of the collision — the coxswain 'Buck' Rogers was calling the numbers — there was a garbled pipe seconds before the impact — no. one in the cafeteria understood it but I never knew why. When someone queried the pipe, I answered jokingly 'We're sinking' and the next second we were.
>
> The ship rolled violently to starboard and instead of coming back, as it always had, she kept going. After I had disentangled myself from bodies and flying furniture, I found myself standing on lagged air-conditioning trunking which runs along the deck-head as the bow section had almost completely turned over.
>
> I was totally disoriented. It was pitch black and the strange thing is that I cannot recall any noises. It was as though I was alone in absolute silence. The thoughts that ran through my mind at that moment, apart from praying, were 'I wonder what it is like to die' and very clearly thinking 'my son and unborn baby will have no father'.
>
> I was a smoker at the time and reached into my shorts for my lighter. Without thinking of the consequences, I flicked it and saw that it gave just enough light to see some sailors opening a hatch which turned out to be in Number 1 Seamen Mess just forward of the cafe. I made my way towards the hatch and was so

25

disoriented that I was not sure where it was leading. While waiting my turn as a queue had formed, some were screaming in panic and the others stood back and let them through.

When it came to my turn. I poked my head through the opened hatch and experienced the most wonderful sensations — the clean smell of the ocean and the sky above. I was ecstatic to be out of that dark tomb and slid thankfully down the hull into the water. I swam away but when I turned round to look back, the bow, which was protruding out of the water, starting rolling towards me as it filled with water. I swam away from it in a panic and when exhausted, I looked again and saw the bow sink beneath the waves. This was the most horrific sight that I have ever witnessed. I could almost touch it. I thought it was the whole ship, not realising that we had been cut in half.[3]

Following the collision, *Melbourne* slowed and stopped dead in the water as the two sections of the severed destroyer slid down the carrier's sides. The bow section, which had completely rolled over, scraping *Melbourne*'s port side during the collision, had floated on its starboard side for five minutes. Destabilised by the weight of two 4.5-inch gun turrets, the bow section then rolled over completely, and floated keel up for a further five minutes before it sank. The after section defiantly remained afloat. Had *Voyager* continued turning to port and rammed *Melbourne*'s side, the point of impact would have been 20 feet forward of the carrier's bridge island.

Rescue operations began immediately. For the next four hours the men of *Melbourne*, and some of the survivors from *Voyager*, worked to recover those in the water. Of the 314 personnel on board, 232 officers and men were recovered from the water and the after section of the ship. The bow section had contained 225 of the ship's company. The survivors were battered and bleeding with a vast array of injuries. Many were wearing pyjamas stained black from the fuel oil from *Voyager*'s ruptured tanks. Nearly all were sick from swallowing sea water. Eighty-two had been killed: 14 officers, 67 sailors and one civilian dockyard employee.

At 2100, Robertson sent an emergency signal from *Melbourne* to the local administrative authority, Flag Officer in Charge East Australian Area (FOICEA), Rear-Admiral Galfrey Gatacre. Information copies of the signal were also sent to the Naval Board in Canberra, FOCAF, the Naval Officer in Charge Jervis Bay Area (NOICJB) at HMAS *Creswell* and NAS Nowra. It read: 'Have been in collision with *Voyager* in position 120 Point Perpendicular 19'.[4] The collision had occurred in a position 19 nautical miles off Point Perpendicular, the northern head of Jervis Bay, at a bearing of 120 degrees. The first signal was unclassified. At 2114, the Damage Control Officer in *Melbourne*, Lieutenant Commander George Halley, informed Robertson that the carrier had suffered major damage but was in no danger of sinking.[5]

Fourteen minutes later, Robertson sent his second signal to the same addressees, although this time it was classified 'Emergency' and

'Confidential': *'Voyager* has lost her bows but is still floating. Am rescuing survivors. Sea calm'.[6] It is more than likely that the staff at Fleet Headquarters in Sydney did not understand the extent of the disaster from Robertson's first two communications. The third signal, sent at 2140, nearly three-quarters of an hour after the collision read:

> *Voyager* has settled by the bows. Waterline at forward end of torpedo tubes. She still has lights onboard. Further information will be signalled when available.[7]

It appears as though Robertson thought *Voyager* had lost only part of her bows forward of the two 4.5-inch gun turrets in the collision, and not the forward half of the vessel. It was not until the next day (11 February) that Robertson was aware of the extent of the damage *Melbourne* had inflicted on *Voyager*.

The first signal from shore was sent at 2158, informing *Melbourne* that

1. *Snipe* and *Teal* proceeding maximum speed to render assistance
2. *Hawk, Ibis* and *Curlew* being despatched by NOICJB
3. SAR and helicopter despatched by NAS Nowra
4. *Stuart* being sailed as early as practicable.[8]

An examination of subsequent events confirms that the Fleet Commander's staff were not fully aware of what had happened to *Voyager*. At 2210, the Fleet Operations Officer, Commander Peter Doyle, contacted the Duty Engineer Officer, Lieutenant Peter Hugonnet, in HMAS *Sydney* which was then refitting in Captain Cook Graving Dock at Garden Island, and instructed him to prepare *Sydney* for immediate undocking by the morning as *Voyager* would be arriving for urgent repairs. Four minutes later, HMAS *Kimbla* was instructed to 'Proceed at best available speed to position 120 Point Perpendicular Light 19 miles and prepare to tow *Voyager*'.[9]

Realising that he had yet to make a report on damage to *Melbourne*,[10] Robertson sent a signal to the Naval Board with an information copy to the Fleet Commander headed 'Damage to *Melbourne*':

> Number One and Two trimming tanks flooded to five deck. 4A ship's company heads damaged and holed forward port and starboard. Cable locker may be holed. Ship watertight aft of 16 bulkhead. No personnel casualties.[11]

The magnitude of what had happened was becoming more apparent with news of the damage sustained by the carrier. At 2300, *Melbourne* was informed that Admiral Becher, who was in Canberra, had departed for the Naval Air Station and expected to arrive there at 0430. A helicopter would fly the Fleet Commander out to the carrier.[12]

At the RAN College at Jervis Bay, news was being received that there had been some sort of accident in the adjacent exercise area. There were five members of the 1960 Term in *Voyager*. Four members of this College Term had been drowned in the HMAS *Sydney* whaler tragedy in late 1963. Acting Sub-Lieutenant Davies had also joined the College on the same day as the 1960 Term but as a Matriculation Entry Cadet. Those sent to *Voyager* were selected by alphabet: Midshipmen Lindsey, Marien, Maunder, Morgan and Perry. *Voyager* was their first ship after completing the training cruise. Only Midshipman Kingsley Perry survived.

As survivors from the collision were being rescued from the water, first-year cadets at the College were being put through their initiation ceremonies. In the midst of the frivolity alarms sounded and the rescue craft left the boat harbour. The initiation ceremonies added to the unreality of the night as survivors from *Voyager* were landed at the College and the gravity of the disaster gradually became known.

At around 2300, Halley and *Melbourne*'s Engineer Officer, Commander Harry Bodman, went to the stern section of *Voyager* by boat in an effort to determine if what remained of the destroyer could be salvaged. *Voyager* was lolling dangerously and a decision was made not to board her.[13]

Just before midnight, Robertson again reported on the state of *Voyager*:

> *Voyager* is floating stern in the air waterline at the after end of the torpedo tubes. Forward bulkhead of B boiler room has held. B boiler room has some water in it and is probably flooding further. Forward portion of ship has probably sunk.[14]

Shortly afterwards, at 0018, he was forced to send another signal. It was short and horrific: '*Voyager* has sunk'.[15]

At Garden Island, Hugonnet, who had been busily preparing *Sydney* for undocking, was told there was no longer the need for such urgency; *Voyager* was not coming back. The awful finality of the disaster began to hit the Navy.

The news was gradually conveyed to the Australian people. Rumours that all was not well with the Navy started to circulate around 2200. The head of the Canberra bureau of Australian United Press (AUP), John Farquharson, was the first to hear that a tragedy of some kind had occurred at sea.[16] He was asked by the Sydney Office of AUP to contact the Navy to check whether there had been a collision. Apparently, the press police roundsman had been ringing around his regular contacts and had got a crossed line with Garden Island. After hearing something about ships colliding, he thought it was worth looking into further. He rang the home number of the Co-ordinator of Navy Public Relations (CNPR), Tony Eggleton (later to become Federal Director of the Liberal Party), to be told by his wife Mary that Eggleton was at Navy Office. This was a good indication that something newsworthy had happened. Earlier in the evening Eggleton had been informed by the Duty Officer at Garden Island — in language that reflected the lack of clarity in Robertson's signals — that '*Voyager*'s bow had been detached from her stern'.[17]

It was evident to Eggleton that something serious had happened. He was met at Navy Office by the Deputy Secretary of the Department of the Navy, Stuart Philpott, and told that he was not needed, and that if he were, he would be called.[18] Eggleton insisted that he should stay to render whatever assistance he could, only to be warned not to say anything to the press until the CNS, Vice-Admiral Sir Hastings Harrington, had decided what information would be released.

At 2330, Eggleton issued a press statement in an effort to give the media some information. It was unavoidably brief.

> *Melbourne* and *Voyager* have been in collision twenty miles off Jervis Bay. *Voyager* is badly damaged. *Melbourne* has sustained some damage to her bows. Further details are awaited.[19]

This statement was issued without the authority of the Naval Board, although it was subsequently approved. Farquharson informed the Sydney bureau of AUP but was unable to pass the news any further because the AUP teleprinter operator had gone home.[20] He then contacted John Bennetts, political correspondent with the *Age*; Gordon Burgoyne of the ABC; and John Webb of the *Daily Telegraph*. They were given up-to-date information by Eggleton, who exceeded the limits set earlier in the night of what could be released. As their correspondents were aware of the story before midnight, the only newspapers to have coverage of the tragedy the next day were the *Age* and the *Canberra Times*.

Several hours after the collision, international news services reported the tragedy across the world. The main story and photograph on the front page of the *Scotsman* was the loss of *Voyager*.[21]

Eggleton also contacted the commanding officer of the Naval Air Station and advised him that a large group from the media would shortly descend on the Naval Air Station and HMAS *Creswell*, and that he should allow them entry into the establishment and provide them with access to facilities. With typical naval officer's caution, the Captain asked whether this was an instruction from the Naval Board. In taking what was a large professional risk, Eggleton said that it was and should be treated as such.[22]

At midnight Robertson decided to send the Naval Board a brief outline of the events leading to the collision. This was the first occasion on which he would convey his version of the disaster (Figure 20).

1. *Melbourne* had been flying course 190 speed 22, *Voyager* plane guard station 1. Flying suspended due to lack of winds and ships turned together to starboard to 020 to search for wind. Further turn made together to 060 then back to 020. At this time *Voyager* bearing 040 degrees 1500 yards. Flying course was then altered by signal to 020. *Voyager* turned about 30 degrees to starboard and appeared to slow down then to port across *Melbourne* bows. At time of collision she was at approximately right angles to *Melbourne* who hit her abreast the

> after end of the bridge. *Voyager* did not appear to be doing more than about 15 knots. *Melbourne* had ordered full astern.
>
> 2. *Voyager* then passed stern first slowly down starboard side of *Melbourne* and came to rest just abaft the stern.[23]

With *Voyager* sunk and the survivors recovered, there was little point in the carrier remaining in the area. Her bow was badly damaged and she needed to return to Sydney for docking. At 0100, Robertson signalled Fleet Headquarters that *Melbourne* was 30 miles off Jervis Bay. She was making 6.5 knots through the water with revolutions set for 8 knots. An estimated southerly set of 3 knots would slow *Melbourne*'s progress even further. Her arrival in Sydney was provisionally set for Wednesday morning; one and a half days after the collision.[24]

The Fleet Commander, Becher, arrived on board by helicopter at 0300. He met with Robertson, inspected the damage to the carrier and spoke to survivors from *Voyager*. Just six hours had passed since the collision. Becher wrote a personal letter to Harrington, and sent a signal marked 'Exclusive Confidential'. The signal read:

> For CNS: I hope to despatch to you personally by air through Nowra a copy of Robertson's report to me. You might find this useful in preparing any preliminary statement by the Minister. Without prejudice, I believe Robertson's Report gives the true picture. Enclosed also in the envelope will be several copies of photos of *Melbourne*'s bow damage. I hope to get this before noon. Weather fine and *Melbourne* progressing nicely but I have instructed Robertson to play it cool.[25]

Becher's private letter to Harrington was more revealing and provides an accurate insight into how the Navy's senior officers viewed the disaster:

> As soon as possible I will convene a Board of Inquiry and I am thinking of asking FOICEA if he will lend me [Captain] Mesley — an ex-carrier captain — to preside. I will also try to get at least one recent destroyer captain on it.
>
> *Melbourne* is a mess up forward as you can see from the photos. We are making 8 knots through the water and making good about 4.5. Everything holding very firm and of course the collision bulkhead (No. 13 I think) is completely intact. *We will attempt nothing more.*
>
> This is not the happiest day in my life and my heart is sad for a lot of wives and families.
>
> My love to Janet and sorry my visit had to end so abruptly. Got to Nowra at about 0230 safely. The press will be in on me when I arrive in Sydney. I will clear a proposed press statement with ACNB before I arrive. [Becher's emphasis][26]

Hope had all but faded of finding anyone alive by sunrise the next morning. At 0650 *Stuart* had found no further survivors or bodies.[27] She reported to FOICEA again at 0950:

> Three air searches by average sortie of four Gannets and four Wessex of area within 15 mile of *Melbourne*'s dan[buoy] have shown great deal of debris within 1 mile of dan. No bodies or survivors.
>
> Ships have searched through area round dan and back to geographical position of wreck about 15 miles to north but with no results.

Consider probability area has received high coverage and possibility of recovery of survivors now slight.

Intend ships once again search area but now accepted reduced rate of search by recovering as much debris as possible.[28]

By 1440, *Stuart* had reported that *Melbourne*'s dinghy and whaler were being towed back to Jervis Bay and that most of the debris had been recovered.[29] At 1800 that day, *Stuart* ended her search and, with last light, RAAF *Neptune* aircraft ceased their searches as well.[30] Instructions were sought for the offloading of debris and flotsam from *Voyager*.[31] FOICEA informed *Stuart* that it was to be retained on board and landed at Garden Island on the ship's return to Sydney.[32] A final sweep through the area was conducted during daylight on Wednesday by naval aircraft with all the minesweepers, except *Gull*, which was en route to the collision scene.[33] On Thursday and Friday a Gannet aircraft transited through the area to check that no bodies had risen to the surface.[34] An oil slick remained until the following weekend as a reminder of *Voyager*'s watery grave. Four weeks later, part of *Voyager*'s main notice board was found off the New South Wales coastal town of Kiama.[35]

The Navy made a thorough search of all Fleet baggage stowages for the belongings of *Voyager* victims and reviewed all its promotional films to ensure none featured personnel lost in the destroyer.[36] The Naval Board announced the day following the collision that 'as a mark of respect for those who lost their lives in HMAS *Voyager*, colours are to be half-masted from 1200 to sunset'.[37]

At 1430 on the day after the collision, the Minister for the Navy, Dr Jim Forbes, and the Minister-Designate, Fred Chaney, departed Canberra with Harrington, accompanied by Eggleton, in a *Dakota* aircraft bound for Nowra.[38] They then embarked in a Navy helicopter for passage to *Melbourne*, which was making its way slowly up the New South Wales coast.

By this time, Robertson had already completed his first formal report to the Naval Board on the circumstances leading to the collision. This was dictated in the early hours of the morning after the collision and passed to Becher, who provided copies to the Ministers and Harrington. It was a brief document limited to outlining the ships' movements and the associated signals.[39] After speaking with Harrington and more than 160 survivors who had been systematically questioned by interview teams made up of *Melbourne*'s officers, Robertson altered his first report with a two-page clarification. The second paragraph read:

Although I was not aware of it at the time, *Voyager* was cut in two by *Melbourne*'s stem. The stern half behaved as stated, the bow half passed down the port side of *Melbourne*, turned over on its side and came to rest off the port quarter.[40]

When both reports[41] were despatched the following day, Becher wrote on a covering letter that they were 'forwarded for the consideration of the Naval Board without comment at this stage in view of the procedure for an enquiry into this matter announced by the Prime Minister'.[42]

The Australian people and the international community were shocked by the enormity of the disaster. The Lord Mayor of Sydney, Alderman Jensen, started a '*Voyager* Dependents' Relief Fund', while donations for survivors and their families were received by the Navy.[43] After only four days, the Lord Mayor's appeal had collected £8,250.[44]

Only hours after the collision, sympathy messages had begun to arrive from all over the world. The first to arrive at 0700 was from the Admiralty in London.[45] Others soon followed from the New Zealand Naval Board, and the navies of India, Ceylon, South Africa, Japan, Malaysia, France, Italy, Pakistan, Denmark, Holland, Chile, Portugal and West Germany. Telegrams, letters and notes arrived from municipal councils, ex-service associations and community groups, including the Calcutta Cricket Club which had challenged *Voyager* to a match during her visit to India in March 1961. The Queen Mother also sent a telegram saying her 'thoughts and sympathy are very much with the relatives of those who have lost their lives'.[46]

Those who seemed to be the most understanding of the tragedy and expressed the greatest sympathy were fellow naval officers, particularly Americans. The United States Navy's most senior officer, the Chief of Naval Operations, wrote:

> All of us who serve and love the sea live with the knowledge that a tragedy like *Voyager*'s may strike at any time. As you will remember, we mourned the loss of the men of *Thresher* last year, and the sympathy of our Australian friends then was received with warm gratitude. As we have stood together in the bad moments, so, I confidently hope, we will always stand together in the good.

Perhaps the most moving tribute came from second year pupils at Niri Primary School in Japan. Their teacher, Kenzaburo Nishiyama, wrote to the Australian Ambassador in Tokyo, Sir Lawrence McIntyre:

> When the second year children of the Niri Primary School of Imari City went to Karatsu on a School Excursion in May last year, they were lucky enough to visit *Voyager* which was in Karatsu at the time. It was great fun for the children and they have very pleasant memories of time they spent on board the huge ship.
>
> The boys and girls were extremely surprised when they heard the bad news. They felt sorry about the men who were lost in the sea. They sincerely hope that the injured crew will soon be well. They express their deep sympathy with the bereaved families and also with the people of Australia on the loss of the ship and so many men.

Each child wrote a letter of sympathy in Japanese and these were forwarded to Canberra.

The Royal Navy expressed its genuine solidarity with the RAN. The First Sea Lord wrote personally to Harrington:

We were appalled to hear last night about the tragic loss of the *Voyager*, and even more to hear today how many of her ship's company went down with her.

I did not know Stevens myself; but I do know what a splendid officer he was and that he made his mark during his time in the Admiralty and was greatly liked and respected by everyone.

We work so closely with your Navy that I can truly say that we feel your loss almost as if it was our own.

Those missing from *Voyager* were to be presumed dead on 17 February, one week after the collision. Their dependents would receive their full pay and allowances until that date.[47] The funerals of the three whose bodies were recovered were held on 14 February. A private funeral was held for *Voyager*'s commanding officer at the Northside Crematorium in Sydney. Those naval officers invited to attend were asked by the Stevens family to wear plain clothes.[48] The widow of Able Seaman R. W. Parker requested that her husband's body be buried at sea.[49] The wife of the single civilian lost in the ship, Stan Parker, a dockyard technician, asked if she could visit the place where *Voyager* had gone down and lay a wreath. The Navy met both requests.

A full naval funeral was held for the navigator, Harry Cook, who was buried at Rookwood cemetery after a service at HMAS *Watson*.[50] His parents seemed to be practically the only ones with a consoling word for the Navy by the end of that dreadful week. They wrote in a letter to Becher:

This has been a grievous blow to us, making the first gap in a united family. At the same time, we feel proud that our son has given all for his country: from the time he entered [the RAN College] he was a dedicated man, and never once did he utter a single regret for the career he had adopted. So far as we are concerned, his passing was tantamount to falling in battle, and while it has left us sad and lonely we have no feeling of recrimination whatsoever.[51]

A national day of mourning for those lost was scheduled for 21 February, with major memorial services held throughout Australia. The Federal Government and Opposition were represented at each major service. Bishop Muldoon, Auxiliary Bishop to Cardinal Gilroy, addressed the Memorial Service held in St Mary's Cathedral in Sydney and tried, as the Cook family had tried, to accept the loss of 82 men as the nation might accept losses in war and revere the qualities of those who had given their lives for a cause.

The truth is this: eighty-two men have died, and in dying they have placed each and every one of us in their debt. They have placed us in their debt simply because they have died in the service and defence of our country as truly as though an enemy had been invading our shores. They were inspired by patriotism, by love of country, as truly as were the men and women of our nation who laid down their lives in time of war.[52]

The main service was held in St Andrew's Presbyterian Church in Canberra and was conducted by the Right Reverend H. Harrison, an

RAN Reserve Chaplain and Moderator-General of the Presbyterian Church of Australia, and the Right Reverend Kenneth Clements, the Anglican Bishop of Canberra and Goulburn. Three-quarters of those who died were either Anglican or Presbyterian. It was a familiar and reassuring naval service with the hymns 'O God Our Help in Ages Past', 'Eternal Father Strong to Save', and 'Abide With Me'. The naval Psalm, 'They that go down to the sea in ships', was said. A commemoration was read by the Reverend Norman Symes, a wartime RAN Reserve Chaplain, with the address given by the Venerable John Were, Archdeacon to the Navy and Senior Naval Chaplain. A memorial service was also conducted at St Martin-in-the-Fields in London for those families in Britain who had lost relatives in *Voyager*. Her Majesty the Queen was represented by the First and Principal Naval Aide-de-Camp, Admiral Sir Wilfrid Woods.[53]

The memorial services' efforts to ennoble the deaths were felt by many to be hollow and forced. Far from being a sacrifice for the country's defence, 82 men had died in a horrible accident resulting from human error or negligence.

There was little to be salvaged by the Navy from the funerals. Many Australians were outraged by the loss of the ship and wanted answers. Perhaps it was this feeling that was best summed up by Bishop Muldoon.

> My dear friends: thanks be to God that we are still a people that values one human life more than a battleship, for that is a true scale of values.

The drive to assert that scale of values was about to start.

# 4

# *Lost Faith and Confidence*

COLLISIONS AT SEA are not uncommon. Whereas warships, with their highly trained crews, superior navigational aids and additional watchkeepers, are often better prepared than merchantmen to avoid collisions, two fundamental aspects of naval life keep the likelihood of accidents involving warships relatively high.

First, naval ships are required to be ready to fight or to meet a range of emergencies at short notice. To be so prepared, they carry their own fuel and ammunition at all times, which significantly increases the risk of accident in simply being at sea. Second, to be efficient in war, navies need to practise in peacetime under simulated conditions of combat. As many manoeuvres have to be performed at great speed, at close quarters with other vessels, and at night, there remains a high level of risk.[1]

Collisions have occurred in even the most professional navies, including the Royal Navy. Of the thirty warships lost worldwide through collision during World War II, six were British.[2] This would have created a public scandal, had wartime restrictions not kept the public ignorant of the number and magnitude of the tragedies.

The year 1960 was a particularly bad one for the Royal Navy. There were 25 groundings, 17 collisions between ships underway and 68 berthing accidents. Ninety-one of these accidents involved ships of minesweeper size and above. In fact, one out of every three ships in commission was involved in an accident. This prompted the release of a confidential Admiralty Fleet Order on the subject.[3] It began:

> Their Lordships are concerned at the heavy toll of collisions, groundings and berthing accidents, which continues at an alarmingly high rate year by year. Not only does this seriously affect the operational availability of our ships, but also results in a heavy drain on Navy [financial] votes.[4]

It is interesting that the Admiralty seemed more concerned about the costs of these accidents than with declining professional standards or negligence. In his study of collisions at sea, Peter Padfield offers something of a concession when he says

> it is worth noting here that the Royal Navy's collision record for normal passages — steaming from A to B, is remarkably clear. HM Ships do not as a rule hit each

other or hit merchant ships in the course of their voyaging.[5]

He suggests that the reason for the number of collisions at sea being so high, even after the installation of radar in most larger ocean-going vessels after World War II, was in part a product of the inadequacy of the existing regulations for their prevention. The international rules for preventing collisions were drastically overhauled in the decade after Padfield's book was released, which indicates there was some truth in this statement.

The RAN's safety record had probably been better than that of its main operating partners in terms of collisions since 1945. None of the six recorded collisions required major repair work. It was a series of other accidents, not specifically related to navigation, that had brought the RAN to the close attention of the Australian Parliament and people by 1964, raising concerns about its professional standards.

The first substantial postwar accident was an explosion in the troopship HMAS *Tarakan* alongside at Garden Island in 1950. Nine sailors were killed as a result of the explosion and fire that followed, and *Tarakan* was beyond economical repair. For the next eight years there were few serious accidents and the RAN could boast a better than average safety record. In July 1958, however, the first in a series of accidents brought unwanted attention to the Navy. The newly completed *Daring* Class destroyer HMAS *Vendetta*, under the power of her own engines for the first time, rammed the dock caisson at Williamstown Naval Dockyard and nearly flooded the dry dock. In *Quickmatch*, which was undergoing a refit in the dry dock at the time, 'abandon ship' was ordered as water rushed through the fracture caused by *Vendetta*'s bow. A major disaster that could have involved the loss of both ships was narrowly averted. *Vendetta*'s captain referred to the accident later as

> a straight case of human error. My order 'half astern both engines' was not carried out. Instead, *Vendetta* moved forward at half ahead both engines. I repeated my original order four times. Still she continued forward. There was nothing I could do to stop *Vendetta* impaling her bow in the gate of the dry dock.[6]

The commanding officer and the navigator of *Vendetta* incurred the displeasure of the Naval Board and the chief coxswain was admonished. The able seaman who manned the engine-room telegraphs in the wheelhouse was found guilty of negligence in the performance of his duties. Dealing with the matter by disciplining a sailor caused some minor controversy in Parliament when an Opposition member accused the Navy of punishing a scapegoat.[7] The commanding officer of *Vendetta* was Captain John Robertson.

Two years later, in 1960, the two RAN *Battle* Class destroyers, *Tobruk* and *Anzac*, were involved in a gunnery exercise off Jervis Bay. During the course of the exercise *Tobruk* was holed by a shell from *Anzac*. So bad was the damage caused by a single sand-filled practice round that *Tobruk* returned to Sydney, beyond economical repair. In the inquiry that followed, a malfunction in *Anzac*'s gun direction equipment, a type not previously encountered, led to a 6 degree 'throw-off' of the shell being nullified. Two officers incurred the displeasure of the Naval Board for negligence.

In the following month, the ammunition carrier HMAS *Woomera*, blew up and sank, with the loss of two lives. Although the cause could not be proved, it was generally believed that the fire which led to the vessel exploding was caused by the ignition of a flare within a silk parachute held onboard. The flare had ignited when a sailor allegedly attempted to remove the silk from a parachute pack. The court martial which followed acquitted the captain and first lieutenant of all charges laid against them. However, the Naval Board decided to review the court martial proceedings and found that the captain should incur the displeasure of the Naval Board for his deficient leadership in failing to control his officers and sailors after they had abandoned the ship. The *Woomera*'s commanding officer resigned from the Navy over his treatment following the court martial.

In October 1963 five junior officers from the training ship, the converted aircraft carrier HMAS *Sydney* (III) under the command of Captain Bill Dovers, were drowned. A group of junior officers had been ordered, as a training evolution, to sail three of the ship's whalers around Hayman and Hooke Islands. This was a twelve hour trip, during which the whalers would be out of sight for most of the time, and the weather was known to be extremely variable. The commanding officer of HMAS *Anzac*, which was in company with *Sydney*, warned Captain Dovers of the dangers and offered to take his ship to the north of Hayman Island so as to be nearby in case of an accident. Dovers declined the offer.

The first two whalers were despatched without incident. By the time the third whaler had departed for the trip at 0500, with four midshipmen and one Naval Reserve sub-lieutenant on board, the wind had stiffened and the seas had become rough. While out of sight, the whaler must have capsized. This would have been at around 0900 or 1000. All five men were drowned. A search party from *Sydney* was not sent until 1900 that day.

Under the direction of the Minister, Senator Gorton, a Naval Board of Inquiry convened and was open to the public and the press. However, given that it was held in HMAS *Sydney* while she was at anchor in Cid Harbour, adjacent to Hayman Island, it would have been difficult for even the most intrepid reporter to cover the proceedings. In addition, the Board of Inquiry's report to the convening authority was not released.

As a result of the findings, the commanding officer, the executive officer and the training officer of *Sydney* were brought to trial by court martial. The president of the court martial convened to try Captain Dovers, which was held in public, was Captain John Robertson. The other four members of the panel included Captain Duncan Stevens.

After all the evidence was heard, the executive officer and training officer were acquitted. Captain Dovers was found guilty of one of the two charges brought against him. On reviewing the case, the Naval Board, with the assistance of Judge Trevor Rapke of the Victorian County Court, a former member of the RANVR, quashed the verdict, but Rapke advised that Dovers could be retried on a new charge. The decision to overturn the verdict was based on a legal technicality relating to the wording of the charge. In his letter to all the members of the Court explaining why the finding had been quashed, the Second Naval Member, Rear-Admiral Victor Smith, stated that the prosecution failed to show that

> (a) the duty defined in the charge was in fact imposed on the accused, and
> (b) that the accused culpably omitted to perform such duty.[8]

Admiral Smith said that by quoting Admiralty Book of Reference (BR) 11 — *Admiralty Memorandum on Naval Court Martial Procedure*[9] — which had been used as the basis for establishing a neglect of duty, the judge advocate had misdirected the court. Smith stated, 'The notes on that page are misleading and confusing, if not wrong in law'.[10]

A member of the court martial, Captain Ian Easton RN, protested the quashing in a letter to his administrative authority, FOICEA.[11] Further, he claimed that if BR 11 was invalid as the basis for proving incumbent responsibility, then there were no grounds for charging any officer with dereliction of duty and that the system of naval justice needed revision.

> It is submitted that as long as no action is taken to amend, cancel or endorse [the notes in BR 11] it will be virtually impossible for a conviction of neglect of duty to be upheld.[12]

Dovers had been nominated for the IDC course and was due to sail for England on the Monday following the court martial, which was held on a Friday. After the finding of guilty was delivered, he was told he could go. When the Board later decided to quash the verdict, Dovers was at sea. This made it very difficult to retry him. The Naval Board then showed no further interest in the matter.

Newspaper editorials and letters to the editor expressed intense public dissatisfaction with the way the Naval Board had handled the tragedy. The RAN's reputation for justice had tumbled and the nation's respect and trust in the Navy's leadership was undermined.[13]

The following year did not start well for the Navy. In January 1964, the RAN Fleet Tanker, HMAS *Supply*, was alongside at Garden Island. During the night, the engine-room was flooded and the ship sank.

Fortunately, such was the draught of the ship and the shallowness of the water that the upper decks were not awash. The real dangers lay in the ship rolling over and in raising the RAN's heaviest ship from a position alongside a wharf. The finding of the subsequent inquiry was that the engineering officer in *Supply* had committed an error of judgement but not neglect of duty. Disciplinary action was considered, but neither recommended nor taken.

By February 1964, the RAN was the subject of Parliamentary and press interest. Whereas politicians and the press had once been content to allow the RAN to sit in judgement of itself, an affirmation of its integrity and the store of public goodwill built up over many years, the whaler tragedy had ended any possibility of such inquiries being tolerated in the future. However, the Naval Board seemed unaware of the pressure being applied to the Government to initiate a thorough review of naval administration. The Labor Opposition, for its part, attributed the accidents to long-term Government neglect of the Navy.

It was in this context that the Australian public was informed of the loss of *Voyager*.

# 5

# *The Calm Before the Storm*

T HE NAVY was unprepared to handle the collision of *Melbourne* and *Voyager*, or its aftermath. As a first measure, locating and informing key individuals proved difficult.

At Navy Office the duty staff officer had received the first signal regarding the collision at 2114, just over a quarter of an hour after it had occurred.[1] He then contacted Naval Board members and the directors of relevant Navy Office functional areas. At the same time, the duty supervisor in the Main Signal Office informed the civilian head of 'N' Branch, who telephoned the Deputy Secretary of the Department and Eggleton, the CNPR.

Becher was not in his flagship. As the Fleet Staff had not embarked in *Melbourne*, and the planned exercises were straightforward and involved only two ships, there was nothing that demanded his presence on board. At the time of the collision he was attending a dinner with Harrington in Canberra. Both admirals were informed almost immediately of the collision by the duty staff officer. It was Harrington's responsibility to ensure that the Navy Minister was informed.

At that moment there were effectively two Navy Ministers. After the 1963 election, Prime Minister Menzies had expanded the size of the Cabinet to twenty-seven portfolios, but an amendment to the *Ministers of State Act* was required to accommodate the enlarged number. Until this was done, Dr Jim Forbes, who was Minister for the Army, was also appointed Minister for the Navy. Although Forbes was signing documents as Navy Minister, he allowed Fred Chaney, the Minister-Designate, to make the decisions that would affect the Navy's handling of the disaster in the longer term.

Both Chaney and Forbes had seen active military service in World War II. Chaney, as an RAAF pilot, had won the Air Force Cross. Forbes, a graduate of the Royal Military College, Duntroon, had been an infantry officer, and had been decorated with the Military Cross. After the war Chaney had been a school teacher before being elected as Federal Member for Perth in 1955. He had made a name for himself in 1962–63 as Government Whip when the Coalition had a majority of only one on the floor of the Parliament.

The Navy was Chaney's first ministry. He did not believe the Navy Minister should have been president of the Naval Board. Unlike Gorton, who attended nearly every meeting of the Board and took an interest in all aspects of naval activity, Chaney deliberately kept some distance from the Board to ensure he was not caught up in matters that were not properly within his domain as the political head of the Navy.[2]

On 10 February Chaney and his Departmental Secretary, Sam Landau, were both in Sydney for a tour of naval establishments. However, they had changed hotels and not left word as to where they could be contacted. The Deputy Departmental Secretary, Stuart Philpott, immediately took charge at Navy Office when news of the accident was received. He telephoned Forbes, who was attending an official dinner in Melbourne, and informed him of the collision. Forbes asked if the Prime Minister had been informed and Philpott indicated that he would make certain this was done.[3] By 2215, Gatacre had located Chaney and Landau and had informed Chaney that a collision had occurred and that *Voyager* had been damaged.

Just before 2300, Gatacre telephoned again to advise that the collision had been worse than was first understood. Chaney replied that the Prime Minister needed to know and that, as Minister, it was his responsibility to tell him. Chaney immediately contacted the Secretary of the Department of Prime Minister and Cabinet, Sir John Bunting, knowing that Bunting knew the Prime Minister's private telephone number at The Lodge. Bunting said he would inform the Prime Minister, and did so immediately.[4] Bunting told me that, thereafter, Menzies had received briefs directly from Harrington. (The contents of those briefings cannot be verified, although Harrington's widow recalled that the flurry of activity caused by the collision ceased at around midnight.[5] By that stage, Harrington would not have known that *Voyager* had been cut in half and was going to sink.) Chaney then contacted Forbes to assure him that Menzies had been informed.

A legend later developed that Menzies was not told at all of the collision. This seems to have originated with the press. In a leading story on Captain Robertson, published on 26 August 1964, the *Daily Mirror* stated, 'it is reliably reported, [that Sir Robert Menzies] first heard of the tragedy in a radio news broadcast'.[6] This story was cited by Hickling in his book *One Minute of Time* and had become well-established 'fact' by the time Sir James Killen came to write his autobiography in 1985. Killen recounts the legend as a plausible explanation for Menzies's decision to hold a Royal Commission.

... the Prime Minister was not told of the collision and first heard of the news in an ABC broadcast ... Menzies was rightly indignant. It is at times a neat point when a Minister should be told by his advisers as to a particular happening. And that is the case with advice being passed on to a Prime Minister. Clearly in the case of the *Voyager* tragedy the Prime Minister should have been told immediately.[7]

The question of when the Stevens family was informed of the tragedy was also to be a matter of major contention. It was later alleged[8] (on the basis of hearsay) that Stevens's father had contacted Menzies around 0530 and had attempted to influence him on the way the disaster would be investigated. This is a serious charge against the propriety of both Sir Jack Stevens and Menzies, and one that deserves to be examined.

Captain Stevens's wife, Beatrice, had been contacted by Captain David Stevenson (commanding officer of HMAS *Sydney*) at around 2300 and informed that *Voyager* had been sunk but that her husband was safe and embarked in *Melbourne*. Stevenson did not contact Sir Jack Stevens with the news until around 0645. At approximately 0700, Sir Jack telephoned Rear-Admiral Harold Farncomb, a retired naval officer then working as a solicitor. Sir Jack said that *Voyager* had been in a collision and that his son would need legal representation. Farncomb suggested that he contact another solicitor, Fred Osborne, who agreed to represent Stevens and indicated that he would arrange for suitable barristers to be retained when briefs could be prepared. Shortly after making the call to Osborne, Sir Jack was informed that his son was dead.

> I then had to break the news to my wife who, like myself, was completely shattered. Our whole life had centred around our only son. All my planning in recent years had been to make life easier for him than it had been for me. The bottom seemed to fall out of life for both of us.[9]

He contacted Osborne again and said there was no longer any urgency. At around 0830, Mrs Valerie Becher and Captain Stevenson arrived at the Stevens's home in Elizabeth Bay to convey the news to Mrs Stevens that her husband had been confirmed dead and that Sir Jack had also been informed.

There is no evidence that Sir Jack spoke with the Prime Minister before Menzies announced the form of inquiry he would establish. At any rate, it would have been impossible for Sir Jack to have reached Menzies by telephone at that hour of the day. Certainly Menzies would not have telephoned Sir Jack, as Menzies would not have known that *Voyager* had been sunk or that Captain Stevens had been killed.

Navy Office and Fleet Headquarters did not know of the recovery of Stevens's body until at least 0230.[10] Prior to that time, Stevens had been listed as missing. Indeed, the first survivor lists were those used by the naval chaplains, who came on duty after 0200.

With the Prime Minister and the Navy Minister informed of what was then known, Harrington rang Admiral Smith between 2330 and 2359. Smith says he advised Harrington to call the Naval Board together immediately to discuss a strategy for handling the disaster. Harrington said it could wait until the next morning, and Smith later regretted not having pressed the matter more firmly.

Sir Garfield Barwick told me that early the next morning, Menzies was distressed to learn that the collision had been far worse than he had been led to believe.[11] In a discussion with Barwick, Menzies outlined the sequence of the previous night's events, said he was annoyed at the Navy's failure to keep him properly informed and expressed a fear that it might close ranks and attempt a cover-up. To avoid the latter, Menzies wanted to have naval officers involved in, and made responsible for, the inquiry process. He discussed possible courses of action with Barwick, including placing a judge at the head of a Naval court of inquiry. Although Barwick was Minister for External Affairs, he also retained considerable influence within the Attorney-General's (AG) Department which was headed by Billy Snedden. Menzies also spoke to several other callers that morning about what he might do.[12]

The Naval Board, apparently unchastened by its public mauling over the handling of the whaler tragedy and unaware that there was little public trust in naval inquiry procedures, thought it would be investigating the matter. Becher's private letter to Harrington, which has been cited, revealed his belief that the inquiry would be left to him to arrange and that a Naval board of inquiry would be the most effective means of investigation. Another admiral suggested that the Navy should court martial the senior survivor from *Voyager* to ascertain the facts of her loss. This was the method employed during World War II when ships were lost in action and did not necessarily imply any guilt on the part of the individual being court martialled. It was simply the most convenient means of inquiry.

To agree on a course of action, a meeting of the Naval Board was convened at around 0830 the morning after the collision. Both Chaney and Landau had returned to Canberra by motor vehicle during the night. Harrington presided over the meeting, although Chaney was in attendance. The minutes of the meeting record that:

> The First Naval Member outlined the circumstances as far as they were known ... The regulations provided that a Board of Inquiry be held in such circumstances. It was a matter for consideration whether the press should be admitted to the Inquiry and, in this regard, it was noted that they were permitted to attend the 'whaler tragedy' inquiry ...
>
> The Secretary pointed out that the loss of the ship could be considered a national calamity and, in the circumstances, the exclusion of the press from the Board of Inquiry would not be realistic. He considered, in addition, that in view of the nature of the mishap, consideration might also need to be given to the appointment by the Government of some outside authority to conduct the investigation, such as a judge, assisted by naval officers as expert professional advisers.[13]

Forbes, the Navy Minister, arrived at Navy Office just as Harrington was informing the meeting that a Naval board of inquiry would be convened. Forbes was astounded by what he heard and told Harrington that the method of investigation would not be determined by the Naval Board, given the magnitude of the tragedy. At about 1030 a message was received at Navy Office that Menzies wanted to see Forbes and Harrington immediately.

Menzies, with Barwick in attendance, gave Harrington an opportunity to express his views on what action should be taken to investigate the collision. Harrington put the view strongly that a Naval board of inquiry was the normal practice in these situations and was the most appropriate action. Menzies said he had decided to modify the 'normal' practice by appointing a judge to head a Naval court of inquiry, and to be responsible for its conduct and report. Chaney said later that Harrington understood and accepted the need for an externally supervised inquiry.[14]

Despite his anger about not being adequately briefed on the gravity of the collision, this was not a malicious action on Menzies's part. He was too good a politician and too resolute a leader to be distracted by emotional considerations.[15] The idea for such a departure from normal procedure followed an explosion in the Heavy Landing Ship, HMAS *Tarakan*, in January 1950. At that time he had recently become Prime Minister and Josiah Francis was Minister for the Navy. Menzies wanted a Naval court presided over by a federal judge to investigate the disaster — which had left nine dead.[16] However, there was no statutory means in existence enabling such a court to be convened. The Prime Minister therefore ordered the preparation of the necessary regulations to allow such a court to be available when required.[17]

A first draft of the regulations was received by the Navy from the Parliamentary Draftsman on 15 February 1950.[18] A revised draft tightening security was prepared in response to suggestions by the Secretary of the Navy Department, Tom Hawkins, which were passed to the Draftsman between 20 and 22 February 1950.

The Service members of the Naval Board were not convinced that the regulations were either necessary or desirable. The Second Naval Member of the Board, whose responsibilities related principally to personnel matters, argued that the regulations were a vote of no confidence in the Navy Minister and the Naval Board:

> No court of inquiry such as is now proposed, has been found necessary in the Royal Navy, where they have had practically a decade of experience to each year of the RAN's existence. Surely it is unusual to introduce a new law without some indication of the necessity for it or inadequacy of the existing regulations.[19]

He then outlined his views on the many serious disadvantages of such a court, making the somewhat high-handed remark that

> Whatever may be said to the contrary by some disgruntled member or written in the press by some irresponsible journalist, Naval personnel prefer that their actions in relation to Naval service be judged within the Service itself.[20]

After concluding that these regulations would detract from the disciplinary authority of the Naval Board, the Second Naval Member strongly urged that the proposal be rejected. Vice-Admiral Sir John Collins, as CNS, concurred with these views. But the Minister could not dismiss the matter that easily. The Garden Island Vigilance Committee and the Secretary of the New South Wales Labor Council were adamant that such a court be set up. They had hoped the court would also have the power to award compensation in favour of its findings.

A redrafted regulation was sent to the Naval Board on 28 February 1950 by the Solicitor-General, Kenneth Bailey. The Attorney-General had examined the Navy's proposed changes and did not object to them. Yet, the matter was brought to an abrupt end on 15 March 1950 when Hawkins wrote, not to the Solicitor-General but to the Parliamentary Draftsman, informing him that 'the Minister for the Navy has decided not to proceed with the Regulations'.[21] It appears as though Menzies's requirement was forgotten, even by Menzies himself, because there is no evidence that any inquiry was made as to its promulgation until February 1964.

On the night *Voyager* was lost, Menzies recalled the *Tarakan* explosion and was under the impression that the regulation he directed be prepared in 1950 had indeed been promulgated.[22] This impression was the basis of a statement he issued the following morning at 1000:

> My colleague, the Minister for the Navy, is making a statement about the sinking of the *Voyager* and the great loss of life which has occurred.
>
> It is a shocking disaster unparalleled in the peacetime history of Australia. The Government and the Naval Board extend their very deep sympathy to the bereaved families who have sustained so sudden and so tragic a loss.
>
> I want to announce at once that there will be a prompt and thorough investigation into this tragedy. I have decided that the normal machinery for Naval investigations is inadequate for the present purposes. There will therefore be a full public investigation conducted by a judge. I cannot, of course, yet say who the judge will be. I will also discuss with my colleagues whether he should be assisted by Naval experts acting as assessors. But the main thing I want to make clear at this early stage is that the investigation is to be prompt, thorough, public and conducted by a judge.[23]

It was left to Dr Forbes to issue a statement on the circumstances of the collision as they were then known.[24] This was at a press conference held at 1230.

Menzies had decided upon a form of 'Naval court' and instructed the Navy Department, following his public statement, to make the necessary arrangements. Midway through that afternoon when the relevant files in Navy Office were consulted, there was a realisation that the court Menzies had in mind was not provided for by any existing legislation or regulation. Menzies was then advised by the Naval Board that its predecessors had not carried out his instructions.

Robertson later commented:

> Rumour has it that the Prime Minister's first idea was to have two naval assessors,
> presided over by a judge. However, he found that this was not possible without
> a special act of Parliament. Parliament was not sitting at the time and therefore
> he was forced to have the Royal Commission.[25]

The Naval Board was obviously unable to comply with Menzies's
instructions. The passing of a regulation to establish a naval court did
not require the involvement of Parliament, but it was affected by many
other difficulties and constraints. Foremost were the shortage of
draftsmen in the Attorney-General's Department and the well-known
slowness of the Navy Department in drafting any regulations. The
suggestion that the Navy, the area from which the draft regulations
would need to come, could have had something prepared in forty-eight
hours would have been considered, as civil servant Neil Preston
suggests, something of a joke.[26]

The Prime Minister realised immediately the expectation his public
statement had created. To have the naval court of inquiry regulations
promulgated would have taken much longer than he was prepared to
wait. He could not convene a marine court of inquiry under the
Commonwealth *Navigation Act* as this Act specifically excluded naval
ships. Even the *Royal Commissions Act* presented a problem in that it
would need to be altered to allow for the assessors Menzies had
mentioned in his statement. Such an amendment would have required
the recall of Parliament.

The whole incident had become an administrative mess. Ultimately,
the Prime Minister had to settle for a Royal Commission, which was
announced to the press two days later, on 13 February.[27] As the *Royal
Commissions Act* (1902–33) did not allow for assessors, and Menzies had
no intention of adding to its provisions, the role of naval experts could
only be advisory.

Menzies was stuck with a Royal Commission, something he had
wanted to avoid in spite of later telling Parliament, 'I decided instantly
that it ought to be a Royal Commission' and it was to be perhaps the
only unintentional Royal Commission in Australian history. Menzies
issued a statement on 13 February:

> We have decided that the investigation of the *Voyager* tragedy should be
> conducted by a Judicial Commissioner appointed under the *Royal Commissions Act*.
>     The Commissioner will be the Hon. Sir John Spicer, the Chief Judge of the
> Industrial Court. There is no provision under the *Royal Commissions Act* for the
> appointment of assessors. The Commissioner will be assisted by Counsel who
> will, of course, be assisted in their turn by technical experts. The function of
> counsel will be to help in the most thorough-going examination of all relevant
> circumstances.
>     My colleague, the Minister for the Navy, is discussing with the Naval Board
> the appointment of counsel to represent the Board. Should any other applications
> be made for representation, the Commissioner will decide them.[28]

The Royal Commission was directed to inquire into and report upon the cause or causes of the collision; the circumstances and factors leading up to the collision and, where relevant, the suitability and preparedness of the ships, their equipment and ships' companies for the exercise; and finally, the facts and circumstances relating to the rescue and treatment of survivors.[29] From the wording of the Commission's terms of reference and the expressions used, it was obvious the Navy had not been consulted. The terms had been framed by Menzies and Barwick.

Although he had appeared as counsel before Royal Commissions, and had been involved in setting them up as Attorney-General, Barwick was not a great supporter of this form of inquiry. He is attributed with the remark that 'the only resemblance between a Royal Commission and a Court of Justice is the furniture in the courtroom'. However, there were advantages in holding a Royal Commission, and in some circumstances they offered the Government the only appropriate course of action. The *Royal Commissions Act* provided

> that a royal commissioner may summon any persons to attend, give evidence and produce relevant books, documents and writings. A royal commissioner has power to take evidence on oath. The penalty for failure to attend or produce documents is a fine of £500. A royal commissioner may take evidence in private or direct that evidence be not published. The Act provides that statements made by witnesses before a royal commission shall not be admissible as evidence in criminal or civil proceedings.

In sum, it has considerably greater power than a Naval board of inquiry. As one of the Navy's parliamentary supporters, Gorton said he expected Menzies to hold a Royal Commission and that the Naval Board would have understood the inevitability of this action, given the magnitude of the disaster. 'Whatever the Navy had found through its investigation would have been labelled as a whitewash by the media and the public'.[30]

The Navy and the nation were stuck with the loss of *Voyager* being investigated by a Royal Commission. Most agreed that it was not the best means. In an article in the *Australian* Brian Johns reported that the decision was 'regarded even by Government members as hasty'.[31]

The Federal Opposition praised the Government for deciding to hold a Royal Commission. Opposition Leader, Arthur Calwell, said it was imperative that the disaster be publicly investigated and that the terms of inquiry should be as wide as possible.

The press coverage of the collision and its investigation was to play a major role in determining the course of the controversy. The Navy started at a disadvantage. A certain amount of ill-will was created between the press and the Navy during the night of the collision. The Naval Board was not forthcoming with details about the accident and the press immediately sensed a cover-up. Robertson later asserted that the delay in informing the press 'was instrumental in putting the press against the Navy. Once again, it is not possible to blame anyone else but the Naval Board themselves'.[32] It was ironical that Robertson should make this criticism, given that the delay was mainly due to the lack of clarity in his signals reporting the collision. Robertson's signals had created the impression at Fleet Headquarters that *Voyager* had merely lost her bows; something that would not normally have led to great loss of life.

The Naval Board later conceded:

> Insofar as public relations were concerned, we got off to a bad start and never really recovered from it. We subsequently learned that our failure to issue the initial statement promptly was a contributory factor in this matter, but there were good reasons, which we still consider valid, for the attitude we took at the time.[33]

The Melbourne *Herald* of 12 February 1964, which went to print before Menzies's announcement, captured the public feeling in its editorial:

> Some measure of risk may be unavoidable in service at sea. But the principle of matching safety precautions to the risk, as far as is humanly possible, should be a part of every peacetime exercise. People will want the fullest assurances on this point.

The *Age* of 14 February greeted the announcement of a Royal Commission with approval:

> Yesterday's prompt announcement by the Prime Minister that a judge will conduct a full public investigation into the sinking of the *Voyager* was necessary. The nature and magnitude of the disaster puts it beyond the scope of the normal naval court martial in which a service in effect looks at itself and decides how far any shortcomings are exposed or concealed. It is important in a tragedy of this scale that a far reaching public inquiry be held so that no doubt is left in the public mind about what happened and why.

The Sydney tabloid *Daily Mirror*, on 11 February 1964, took a different line on the matter of risk and revealed a total ignorance of the way ships were conned. This ignorance obscured much of the subsequent reporting.

> Both the *Voyager* and *Melbourne*, with which she collided, were fitted with radar and were, in fact, steered by radar. What freak of human frailty made this latest scientific aid fail to give ample warning of an impending collision? . . . We expect losses of ships and men in times of war. They should never occur in peace.

The *Mirror* also was the only newspaper to link *Voyager* with previous naval accidents and was the least restrained in its criticism of the Navy:

> This time we don't want the Navy sitting in judgement of itself as with the very recent Hayman Island [whaler] disaster. There was a strange, almost cold air of complacency about that inquiry and the subsequent court martial, when it was found that nobody was to blame for the loss of five midshipmen.
>
> The brutal fact is that public confidence in the RAN, for all its splendid traditions, has been severely shaken . . . In the meantime the Australian public is asking: what is wrong with our Navy?[34]

As for the form of inquiry, only the *Sun*, on 14 February in its editorial, commented on this aspect:

> Now we have a civilian judge who ... can call whom he pleases and, because no one is on trial, he is not bound by rules of evidence. He can listen to evidence, technically hearsay, to which there would be instant and sustained objection in a court, and he can decide its worth after hearing it. A royal commission is a form of inquiry the public understands.

There were many officers and sailors who felt that the Navy's honour had been slighted and its admirals denigrated by the announcement of a Royal Commission. If the Navy could not be trusted by the Parliament and Australian people to investigate a matter within its responsibility then ... what? The awful consequence of this lament — one that few were prepared to contemplate — was that the admirals should have resigned *en masse*.

But not everyone connected with the Navy had faith in its procedures. Robertson later said:

> If my guess is true that the admirals of the RAN considered the collision would not have occurred if they had been in my shoes, then I personally would not have had much confidence in a Naval Board of Inquiry in this case. The disease 'hindsight', combined with the pressure that there undoubtedly was to find a scapegoat, may well have proved too much for a Naval Board of Inquiry, meeting as it would have done at a time when emotions were running high.[35]

Sir Jack Stevens family shared a similar view:

> No other form of inquiry would have satisfied the public, although it was bitterly opposed by the Navy which would have preferred to see a normal Board of Inquiry. Had this latter body conducted the inquiry, Duncan's reputation would have been blasted for all time. This I knew from my conversation with senior naval officers. The dead have no friends, the living must be protected.[36]

A retired commander spoke for many in the Navy and the naval ex-service community in a letter to the *Sydney Morning Herald* of 15 February:

> Naval incidents should clearly be dealt with by Naval authorities and in this case the magnitude of the disaster in terms of loss of life or loss of ship should not be confused with the business of a straightforward inquiry into a collision at sea. The tactical error which produced the collision remains the same error, whether *Melbourne* scraped paint from *Voyager*'s stern with no loss of life or sank her with all hands.
>
> With hysterical precision, the Government swept aside all the long standing and well tried naval procedures, implying immediately that its Naval Board of Admirals and its Flag Officer commanding the Fleet were incompetent to investigate the matter. There was no pause in which to gauge public opinion, only an immediate decision indicating complete distrust in the integrity of the officer corps of the Royal Australian Navy.

A similar sentiment appeared in HMAS *Yarra*'s Report of Proceedings for the month of February 1964, when *Yarra* was stationed in Singapore:

> The circumstances of [*Voyager*'s] loss were debated at length but the matter which caused at least as much comment by other Commonwealth naval officers was the taking of the inevitable inquiry from the Naval Authority and placing it in the hands of the Civil Authority by the institution of a Royal Commission.

The 'other Commonwealth naval officers' were no doubt Royal Navy officers, who would have used that oft-quoted remark that 'this would never have happened in the Royal Navy. The Board of Admiralty would have resigned'.[37]

But the resignation of the Naval Board over the establishment of a *Voyager* Royal Commission would have achieved very little. It would certainly not have led the Government to abandon the Royal Commission, while the public would have interpreted a mass resignation as the flight of guilty men who had failed in their responsibilities.

Yet the problem of excluding the Navy and its expertise from the investigation was something that had been of concern to Menzies. He believed that the Navy was ideally placed to help the Commission make sense of the evidence and arguments presented to it, while he wanted to make the Navy feel it had a role and a voice in how the inquiry was conducted. Although the *Royal Commissions Act* did not allow for Naval assessors, a letter was sent from the Deputy Crown Solicitor's office to the Fleet Commander on 18 February stating:

> It would be of great assistance and benefit to Counsel assisting the Royal Commission if a naval officer with appropriate experience could be made available to confer with and advise Counsel on matters relevant to the Royal Commission of Inquiry.
>
> The officer selected would need to have experience relevant to be in command of vessels such as HMAS *Melbourne* and HMAS *Voyager*. If no one officer has the relevant experience, it would be of assistance if two officers could be made available.
>
> I should mention that Counsel assisting the Royal Commissioner are anxious to have this assistance at the earliest available moment.[38]

The Naval Board willingly and promptly acceded to this request, the nominees being confirmed in a later letter from the Secretary of the Navy Department:

> Although these officers have, in fact, already reported to you this letter serves to confirm that Captain R.I. Peek, the captain of HMAS *Melbourne* until 5 January 1964 and Captain J. P. Stevenson, until 14 February 1964 captain of HMAS *Vendetta*, a sister ship of HMAS *Voyager*, have been made available to advise Counsel assisting the Royal Commission.
>
> Similarly, Captain J. S. Mesley, one time captain of HMAS *Melbourne* and Commander J. L. W. Merson, until 7 January 1964 in command of the Type 12 frigate HMAS *Yarra* and who thus possesses recent experience in Fleet Operations, have been made available to advise Counsel representing the Navy.[39]

The appointment of Peek was convenient for the Navy. He was to be promoted to rear-admiral in July and could be spared for the intervening period. He would play a major role in the Commission's proceedings. He had made his feelings clear about the collision in a private note to Robertson.

> A note of sympathy — a hellish time for us all and particularly for you.
> I am sure that there was nothing you could have done to avoid *Voyager* when she came across your bows and I wish that the press and public could somehow be made aware of the inevitable hazards of exercising and the complete reliance one has to place on the other ship doing the right thing.[40]

Peek's experience at sea was more broad and impressive than that of Robertson. He was appointed to his first command, HMAS *Shoalhaven* and the First Frigate Squadron, in 1951. He later commanded the destroyers *Bataan* and *Tobruk*. After completing the IDC course in 1961, he was given command of *Sydney*. After several months, and having spent very little time at sea, Peek was posted to *Melbourne* in command where he remained for eighteen months.

In addition to Peek, Captain A. Pearson, a master mariner, was seconded from the Commonwealth Department of Transport and Shipping to advise on navigation, while another departmental officer, Robert Herd, a naval architect, was provided to give expert opinion on the ships' construction and manoeuvring data.

It emerges from the dates and times shown on signals that Captain J. Philip Stevenson was the Navy's initial selection as assessor but was later listed after Peek on the basis of the specific request for an officer who had been in command of *Melbourne* or of *Voyager*. Stevenson had commanded neither ship. His role at the inquiry was to be a minor one.

It is important to note that the Naval Board took the opportunity presented by the request from counsel assisting to appoint its own 'assessors'-cum-advisers in Mesley and Merson. Evidently, the Navy believed that the more its people were involved, either formally or informally, the more its voice would be heard and its interests served. It was also made very clear by the Naval Board to its Department that every effort would be expended in making available to the Commission all the relevant information. Nothing was to be withheld.[41]

Later, on 9 March, Lieutenant Commander John Snow, the Fleet Communications Officer, was also made available to assist the Royal Commission as an expert witness, although his primary function was to advise the Commission on matters of security where they related to evidence and argument, and to speak on the Naval Board's behalf in requesting that parts of the Commission be held in camera.[42] Although there was the occasional lament from counsel appearing before the Commission, Snow recalled that there was never any suggestion that the requirement to protect classified information was used or manipulated by the Navy to serve its own interests.[43]

The RAN set about preparing itself for the Commission while the two Ministers for the Navy, Forbes and Chaney, attempted to shield it from its critics and avoid an expansion of the Commission's terms of inquiry into an examination of its operating techniques and procedures, training methods and systems of control and communication. The Federal Opposition and some sections of the press were still contending that there was something basically wrong with the Navy for it to be so accident prone. In a letter sent to Prime Minister Menzies on 21 February, Dr Forbes suggested that it was unwise to extend the Commission's terms on the grounds that it might inadvertently lead to criticism of the U.S. Navy and the Royal Navy, who used the same techniques and procedures as the RAN. He went on to say

> ... it can be expected that some attempt might well be made to link the *Voyager* tragedy and other major accidents in which RAN ships have been involved in recent years. This could have serious effects of a damaging nature on the morale of the Service, and to the Government. Mr Chaney and I do not think therefore that the Government should concede that there is anything inherently wrong with the Navy, its officers, crews or equipment.

Whatever may have been the concerns prompting public debate on widening the terms of reference, it was for the Royal Commissioner, Sir John Spicer, to determine whether there was anything wrong with the naval administration.

As a senator, the Honourable Sir John Spicer had been Attorney-General under Menzies from 1949 to 1956. He was a workmanlike politician but is not remembered for being a forceful Attorney-General. He left politics and was appointed Chief Justice of the new Industrial Court in 1956, where he was considered a good leader. He was familiar with public administration and had recently presided over two separate inquiries into aircraft crashes and three marine courts of inquiry.

Despite later criticism of the appointment of a former Cabinet Minister as Royal Commissioner, Spicer was virtually the automatic selection.[44] The Industrial Court conducted marine courts of inquiry (the *Commonwealth Navigation Act* being part of its jurisdiction), and was known to be under-utilised at the time of the collision. Within the legal profession, however, there was some ambivalence towards his appointment. A number of the judges and barristers who spoke with me said they did not regard Industrial Court judges as 'proper' judges, in that they did not discharge traditional judicial functions. They were thought to have little experience or expertise in handling contradictory evidence or determining the reliability and credit of witnesses. Hence, Spicer may not have been the best choice to head such an inquiry.

The Commissioner sat alone when the inquiry first convened on 25 February 1964, in Sydney. There were five counsel at the Bar table, each with his junior counsel. Opposite each pair of barristers was a clerk or an assistant. There were seldom less than twenty people spread around the Bar table, all jockeying for the most room and the greatest privacy. Behind counsel were the designated 'naval assessors' and an assortment of other naval officers called by counsel (particularly that for the Navy) from time to time for advice and information. Between the Bar table and Sir John Spicer were four Commission officials and two shorthand court recorders. Inside the court were a Commonwealth police officer and an usher. Perhaps symbolising his precarious position, Captain Robertson was given a place at the Bar table, initially alone.

The public benches were straight-backed wooden forms arranged in two rows, accommodating around thirty people. The press contingent consisted of four to six reporters who occupied a press box alongside the Bar table, facing counsel. The number of people present during the Commission's sittings was over seventy. It was cramped and uncomfortable for all involved and the situation could only get worse as an enormous number of papers, charts, diagrams and maps would be tendered as evidence and distributed to counsel. The courtroom doors remained open and people were free to come and go as they pleased.

The crucial role of counsel assisting the Commissioner was played by Jack Smyth QC, with Ian Sheppard as his junior.

Smyth was suggested by Barwick. He was a leading member of the Sydney Bar, with a reputation for devastating cross-examination. His job was to represent the public interest: test the evidence presented, challenge every argument, and explore every possible cause for the disaster.

Sheppard had been admitted to the Bar in 1952 and, like Smyth, was a member of Wentworth Chambers in Sydney. Sheppard had had some experience with civil shipping cases, having appeared in the Admiralty Division of the New South Wales Supreme Court on several occasions. Both Smyth and Sheppard were instructed by the Crown Solicitor on behalf of the Commonwealth.

Counsel for the Navy was Norman Jenkyn QC, with Humfry Henchman as his junior. Jenkyn was known to have an attraction to Government briefs and had appeared for the Navy on previous occasions. The Naval Board had actually wanted Laurence Street QC, and had made a request for his services through the Crown Solicitor only to find he had already been engaged by Mrs Stevens. Henchman had been involved in maritime cases before and was known to have a good grasp of technical matters.

Street had just returned from appearing before the Privy Council. A former Naval Reserve officer, he had had considerable experience appearing in the Admiralty Division of the NSW Supreme Court and possessed great knowledge in shipping cases. This was his first brief as a QC. He appeared with his junior, John Sinclair, who was a graduate of the RAN College, having joined the Navy in 1940. Sinclair served throughout the war before resigning in 1950 to begin a career in the law. He personally knew many of those involved in the tragedy.

The instructing solicitor for the Stevens family was Commander the

Hon. Fred Osborne, who had held three portfolios in the Menzies Government from 1956 until 1961, when he lost his seat of Evans in the 1961 general election. He was to play a major role in the inquiry. Osborne had extensive naval experience, having been commissioned into the RANVR in 1938. Osborne won the DSC and Bar during his distinguished wartime service in command of the Royal Navy ships *Gentian, Vanquisher* and *Peacock*. After leaving Parliament in 1961 he practised as a solicitor but remained active in the Liberal Party. Osborne was later President of the NSW Division of the Party between 1967 and 1970.[45]

Commander Alec Black, a Naval College term-mate of Stevens, offered to assist the Stevens family interests as a communications specialist. Sir Jack Stevens later wrote that his advice and guidance, and access to inside information, had helped the family's interests substantially. Sir Jack would himself play a major part.

Originally a post office clerk and a cook during World War I, Sir Jack Stevens commanded the Sixth Division, 2nd AIF, from 1943 to 1945. After the war he was successively general manager of the Overseas Telecommunications Commission, Secretary of the Department of National Development, Secretary of the Department of Supply and chairman of the Atomic Energy Commission. He was knighted in 1955 and left the public sector the following year to become a director of several companies, including Mount Isa Mines, Vickers Australia, Commonwealth Industrial Gases, the National Bank and Custom Credit. In effect, he acted for his late son.

A Royal Navy officer on exchange who was commanding HMAS *Watson*, Captain Ian Easton RN, also asked the Commissioner if he could appear in a limited way for Lieutenant David Price RN, *Voyager*'s OOW. Spicer said that he would reserve his decision, but that Easton could appear for Price in the immediate term, should it prove necessary. After the first day's sitting, a letter was also forwarded to the Attorney-General asking that the Commonwealth accept the cost of counsel for Price's widow (as it had done for Stevens's widow). This request was granted and Easton made himself available to assist Price's interests.

Appearing for Price were Leycester Meares QC, with Sandy Gregory as his junior.[46] Meares had been a Lieutenant Colonel in the 2nd AIF, while Gregory had had naval experience. He had served in the Royal Naval Volunteer Reserve from 1940 to 1946 and had been awarded the DSC for his service as a junior engineering officer in a Royal Navy battleship during the war. After the war he was a Surveyor to Lloyd's Register of Shipping (London and Sydney) before being admitted to the Bar in 1957. Gregory saw their role as preventing counsel from pushing blame, as distinct from responsibility, onto Price as a subordinate officer who could not defend himself.[47]

Robertson decided against engaging counsel and made no request for any costs to be borne by the Commonwealth. He told Henchman, and later Ray Reynolds QC, that, given the circumstances of the collision and the correctness of his own actions, he had absolutely no need for representation. Robertson told Reynolds he fully expected the Commission to blame *Voyager* and exonerate *Melbourne* and thought that engaging counsel on his behalf would only serve to convolute the inquiry. Robertson thought the Commission would be like the many naval boards of inquiry in which he had played a part over more than thirty years.

When Street had suggested to Robertson before the Commission began that he should have counsel and that they would need to meet to plan tactics, Robertson said he would speak for himself and would not agree on any tactics. How he was intending to lead evidence which only he could properly put before the Commission is unclear. He may have expected Jenkyn to ask the right leading questions. His private papers reveal that he had no understanding of Royal Commission proceedings and had given virtually no thought as to how he would defend his interests from the array of counsel who could have led adverse evidence.

The Royal Commission was able to draw upon a large pool of nautical expertise, which included Peek, Mesley, Stevenson, Merson, Pearson, Herd, Snow, Winch, Black, Easton, Farncomb and Robertson. One could add to this the naval service of Street, Osborne, Gregory and Sinclair.

After a number of formalities, Smyth asked that proceedings be suspended for a period to allow the large amount of preparatory work to be completed. At that time, a number of interviews and statements from those involved had still not been taken. Every officer and sailor in both ships was interviewed; this meant 232 interviews and statements from the *Voyager* survivors and over 900 from the men in *Melbourne*. After only 20 minutes of sitting, Spicer granted this request and the Australian public were kept waiting for another three weeks.

It seems surprising that separate counsel was not arranged for either Kelly or Bate. Given the readiness of the Attorney-General to have the Commonwealth accept the costs of counsel for Stevens and Price, both of whom were dead, there was little reason to believe that the same provision would not have been granted Kelly and Bate. Robertson had, of course, refused counsel on the grounds that it was not needed. This probably led Kelly and Bate to the same conclusion, although there was an absolute dearth of legal advice available within the RAN to any officer or sailor at that time.

The Navy brief was likely to be unworkable. There were clearly too many competing and conflicting interests. Hints to this effect were made to Jenkyn, but he resisted every effort to 'split' the prestigious brief. Street's comments when he first approached the Commission should have suggested something to Jenkyn:

> If this had been a Marine Inquiry after a collision between merchant ships the owners would have borne the costs of representation including those of the ships' officers. In the event of the interests of any officer being divergent from those of the owner the Merchant Service Guild would provide representation for him.[48]

During an interview, Street suggested to me that Navy counsel should have been briefed on only two of the three inquiry terms of reference, namely, that the ships and officers were adequate and equipped for the task and that the rescue of the survivors was handled properly. Counsel could then have been specifically arranged for Robertson on the first term of reference, dealing with the cause of the collision.[49]

Jenkyn, however, was of the opinion that having separate counsel for Robertson, Kelly and Bate could have created an impression that the Navy was divided and unsure of what it believed, with the Naval Board being of one opinion, the senior seagoing officers (represented by Robertson) being of another, the middle ranking officers (Kelly) holding another view, while the junior officers (Bate) possibly seeing things differently again. While Robertson had refused counsel, and Kelly and Bate had not pushed for representation, Jenkyn was happy for them to remain unrepresented at the Bar table. At any rate — or so Henchman told Bate — the Navy brief would cover Bate's interests and those of Kelly. The only advice the young sub-lieutenant was given prior to the Royal Commission was simply 'to tell the truth' as he saw it.[50]

Much had happened in the three weeks following the Commission's first brief hearing. In addition to the interviews with survivors from *Voyager* and the ship's company of *Melbourne*, statements were taken from the pilots involved in the search operations, signal office watchkeepers and medical staff. Any individual with any involvement in the collision or the rescue of survivors was interviewed. Requests from counsel were made for every conceivable naval book of reference and regulation that might shed some light on the reasons for the disaster. Copies of every signal sent on the night of the collision were requested, security clearances were arranged and completed by the Australian Security and Intelligence Organisation (ASIO), and endless meetings were held between counsel and those whose interests they represented. Not trusting the Navy from the outset, Smyth requested the original signals and the communicators' log books.[51]

The Navy was also chastised for its anxiety, before the Commission began, over the security of classified material. Having made repeated representations on the matter, Bunting wrote to Landau on 12 March:

> [T]he Prime Minister has announced that the inquiry will be a thorough judicial investigation and that the investigation will be prompt, thorough and public. The

Commissioner appointed is an Executive Councillor and a former Minister of the Crown. Nothing the Prime Minister has said suggests that there should be made public any information which is of a genuinely classified nature and which deserves to remain so.[52]

Anticipating requests for performance reports on the officers concerned, the Navy was determined — with good reason — to limit the information made available to counsel and, by implication, the information that would become public knowledge.[53] Two forms for performance assessments were in use. The first was Form AS 206. It was a confidential report in which officers were scored out of 9 for their performance in the areas of assessment. The report also contained a narrative which was meant to reflect the score. The second was Form AS 450, also known as a 'flimsy', because of the thinness of the paper. A 'flimsy' summarised, in a few sentences, the general assessment made on Form AS 206. One was meant to reflect the other. The officer being reported on was given a copy of the 450 but not the 206. The system's greatest strength, which had evolved over a number of years, was the freedom it allowed an officer submitting the report to express views and opinions. But that strength relied upon complete confidentiality. The AS 206 was not produced at civil criminal proceedings, nor at courts martial.

The Navy doggedly insisted that the information contained in these reports should not be made public. It feared that once absolute confidentiality had been breached, a precedent might be set, or reporting officers might feel disinclined to be as frank as they had been in the past. For the moment, none of the counsel pressed for disclosure and accepted the comments contained in the 450.

The amount of information requested by counsel was excessive but it was the inevitable consequence of the Commission's terms of reference, which were far too broad. Soon there was masses of information that needed sorting and explaining to counsel by the naval professionals.

By the time the Royal Commission reconvened on 17 March, more than five weeks had passed since the collision. Behind the scenes it appeared as though the reason for the collision could lie in any or all of five areas. First, that signals sent between the ships were either mistakenly sent, received or misinterpreted. Second, that *Voyager* had mistaken her position relative to *Melbourne*. Third, that *Voyager* correctly assessed her position relative to the carrier but miscalculated the area in which she had to manoeuvre. Fourth, that the state of training and readiness in either or both ships was poor, and fifth, that there was an equipment failure in either or both ships that went undetected. Over the following months, counsel assisting and appearing before the Commissioner would propose a range of theories that put the cause in one or all of these areas.

# 6

# *The 1964 Royal Commission*

DESPITE THE BREADTH of its terms of reference, the Royal Commission was principally concerned with the final movements of both *Voyager* and *Melbourne* prior to the collision. Notwithstanding some political pressure, it was not authorised to probe the existence of any underlying flaws in naval training or administration. Establishing what had occurred in *Melbourne* was to be a relatively straightforward matter as no one in that ship was killed. The greatest difficulty lay in explaining *Voyager*'s actions, as all but one junior member of the bridge staff had been killed. Having found the cause or causes of the collision, the Royal Commissioner was to apportion blame and responsibility. This would be a part of his findings. There was, of course, an enormous difference between blame and responsibility. A fundamental distinction also exists between negligence and errors of judgement. Naval regulations made the captain absolutely accountable and, therefore, totally responsible for his ship. In most naval inquiries, the apportionment of responsibility tended to dominate the distribution of blame.

The proceedings of the Commission were organised by Smyth in consultation with Spicer. The hearings would be arranged around the terms of reference and to some extent by the availability of naval witnesses. As counsel assisting the Commissioner, Smyth would open the proceedings and foreshadow the evidence and argument he would present. This would be followed by the examination of witnesses called by Smyth, and then witnesses called by the other parties represented at the Commission. Each would give their evidence before being cross-examined and re-examined by other counsel. After receiving all the evidence and hearing all the witnesses, counsel would make their final submissions. These were crucial, as they summarised the case for their clients and sought from the Commissioner a finding most favourable to their interests. The Commissioner would then retire to consider the evidence and all the arguments put to him before coming to conclusions on which he could make findings, as required by the terms of reference.

The opening address by counsel assisting was vital. It would effectively set the tone and mould the character of the entire inquiry. It would interpret the terms of reference and suggest the major issues and questions on which the Commissioner would have to make a judgement. The Naval Board could not have expected what followed.[1] After explaining the terms of reference, Smyth outlined arrangements for the questioning of witnesses, and the evidence he would present. He claimed this evidence showed the Navy's provision of safety and lifesaving equipment was woefully deficient, and procedures for its use were totally inadequate. This amounted to a far-reaching attack on the administration of the Navy and went well beyond the immediate circumstances of the collision. Smyth then alluded to variations in evidence and alleged there were serious flaws in the manner in which the RAN conducted its operations.[2] The Naval Board were immediately placed in a defensive position, and Smyth had to face the prospect that he would not enjoy the wholehearted and enthusiastic assistance of the Navy.

This also placed Captain Peek in a difficult position. He had been provided to Smyth as an assessor, but it became obvious by the end of the first session of hearings that Smyth and Peek held very different opinions about the Commission. Meares, Gregory, Street,[3] and Sir Garfield Barwick told me they believed Smyth was informed by his 'naval assessors', which probably meant Peek, that the inquiry would be a straightforward affair: *Voyager* was clearly responsible for the collision in failing to keep out of *Melbourne*'s way. This led Smyth to think the Navy wanted see the blame dumped conveniently on the dead. Rather than guiding Smyth towards the view he should take, the advice made Smyth determined to prove his assessors were wrong.[4]

Smyth made little use of Peek throughout the Commission, and Peek apparently did not seek to press his views. Notwithstanding the disagreement between the two, Peek was also in an invidious position. In the middle of the year Peek would be promoted to rear-admiral and become a member of the Naval Board. Thus, his views would have been naturally coloured by his feelings of loyalty to the Naval Board. This is not to say that he was prevented from disagreeing with the Board in any advice he offered to Smyth. However, one can imagine he would have been reluctant to offer such advice if there was even the slightest possibility that he would have been called by Smyth as an expert witness to state his opinion publicly.

From the beginning of Smyth's address, it would have been apparent to Jenkyn, as counsel for the Navy, that his task was not so much to assist the Commission to ascertain the causes of the collision, as to defend naval procedures. As these procedures were determined and promulgated by the Naval Board, the interests foremost in Jenkyn's brief were those of the Naval Board. As he received his instructions specifically from the Naval Board through the Deputy Crown Solicitor, he was already placed in the precarious position of siding with the Naval Board in any dispute or disagreement it might have with any of the other naval personnel covered by the single Navy brief.

The second day of the inquiry was taken up with the evidence of Rear-Admiral Humphrey Becher. He was an important witness. In addition to being the first to be called, he was the Fleet Commander and possessed a solid reputation as an experienced destroyer and carrier captain. Although the Commission was in its early stages, Becher's answers to Smyth's questions suggested that at least one admiral had already formed a firm view about what had happened and who was to blame. Smyth may have placed the Navy in a defensive position but it was Becher who took things further and forced Robertson into a similar situation.

Becher gave his assessment of the circumstances leading to the collision and what he would have done had he been captain of both ships. His strongest statement was that *Voyager*'s movements did not constitute 'a tidy manoeuvre' and, had he been in the position of Officer in Tactical Command (OTC), would have concerned him much earlier than they seemed to have concerned Robertson.[5] The most valuable point he made was to stress that 'every moment at sea could have an element of risk if the incorrect thing is done'.[6] Becher's comments were newsworthy in the extreme.

The Royal Commission attracted prominence daily in every Australian mass-circulation newspaper. From the outset, the editors seem to have abandoned any thought of analysis. Opinion was suspended until the Commissioner's report was released.

As expected, the tabloids led with dramatic headlines and the most 'startling' revelation from the hearings. Unlike the broadsheets, the tabloids often supplied their readers with charts and graphics to aid explanation.

The reporting was generally fair and reasonable, considering the subject matter and its complexity and unfamiliarity to the lay audience. And although the coverage tended to focus on peripheral issues which contained some human interest angle, the Naval Board had little reason for complaint.

The Board was correct in its assessment of the impact of newspaper reporting on general perceptions of the Navy and its leadership under the existing Naval Board. Given the extent to which the *Voyager* story saturated the newspapers and dominated editorials before the Commission's hearings began, the press played a major role in shaping the views of ordinary Australians and in sustaining *Voyager* as a matter of national importance. The 'Silent Service', as the Navy prided itself on being known, became a victim of one of its traditions. In the absence of a strong and pervasive reputation, the press filled a void which the

Naval Board was unable to counter. Having become a matter of national importance, there was every chance that *Voyager* would become a national controversy. Thus, when naval officers and sailors gave their evidence, they were on a national stage. Some felt the pressure of the Commission's high profile more than others, as their performance as witnesses showed.

The first half of the third day of hearings was again taken up with Becher in the witness box. To add to the controversy of the second day, Becher admitted that Robertson had called on him the previous evening. Admiral Becher said that Robertson 'warned me of what he was likely to ask'.[7] Smyth was incredulous that such senior naval officers would have thought nothing of discussing evidence before its presentation at the Commission.

> Smyth: Did it occur to you that it might be undesirable, or might even be misconstrued, if, after you had given evidence in the box, an interested party should have a discussion with you in relation to that evidence?
>
> Becher: I am afraid it did not, for which I might be remiss, but I am afraid it did not.[8]

Smyth appeared to take the view that the Navy was, even at this early stage, attempting to manage the information presented to the Commission. Robertson began to experience the consequences of his decision to represent himself.

To make things even more difficult for *Melbourne*'s captain, Becher led Spicer to believe that Robertson should have taken some action to avoid the disaster. In answer to what he would do if a ship under his control was executing a manoeuvre in an unseamanlike way, Becher unhesitatingly replied: 'I would immediately challenge him and his movements'. He further agreed that if there was even the slightest risk from another ship, it would be his duty to intervene. The Admiral said that, in the case of the events leading to this collision, that moment would have been when *Voyager* altered course to port. Smyth pressed Becher on when the moment for intervention would have been in his mind. Becher replied, 'When his turn to port was recognised as such'. This would have been at 2054, two minutes before the collision. This intervention would include, Becher agreed, in answer to a question from Smyth, reaching for the radio-telephone and saying 'What on earth are you doing'?[9]

Coming from a naval officer in his position and with his reputation, Becher's evidence naturally had a tremendous influence on both Spicer and Smyth.[10] Becher's evidence effectively suggested that Robertson should have become concerned by *Voyager*'s movements much earlier and that he should have taken action earlier to avoid a dangerous situation developing.

Robertson failed to launch a counter-attack on Becher, although he had ample grounds for doing so. *Voyager* was well ahead of the carrier and over two-thirds of a mile away at the moment Becher claimed he should have intervened. Robertson could also have referred Becher to an incident several days before the collision, when *Voyager* was taking station on *Melbourne* for an entry into Jervis Bay. On that occasion, *Voyager* made a mess of manoeuvring into her station and had to reverse her turn, a severe action in the circumstances, in order to avoid *Melbourne*. Becher was on *Melbourne*'s bridge at that time and his only comment had been, 'He has discovered his mistake. There is no need to tell him'.[11]

Robertson's reticence in questioning Becher was explained by a natural reluctance to embarrass or criticise his senior officer, particularly in public. His counsel, if he had had one, would not have felt so constrained. Having heard Becher's evidence, and noting that Robertson's reconstructions of the collision had changed several times over the preceding five weeks, Smyth appears to have come to the view that Robertson had tried from the moment of the collision to provide an account which best served his own interests. This became a basic premise when Smyth came to question witnesses who had been on the carrier's bridge during and after the collision.

Smyth asked the first member of *Melbourne*'s bridge staff to enter the witness box, Leading Tactical Operator Everett, whether Robertson had told his officers 'what he thought had happened' on the morning after the collision, and if anyone had disagreed. Although Everett said he had disagreed and outlined his version of what had happened, he was adamant that Robertson had shown no interest in bullying anyone to accept his version of events.[12]

The first material setback for Robertson was the evidence given by Chief Communications Yeoman Barker, who was questioned on the signals sent to *Voyager*. Barker was emphatic that all were sent correctly and that after *Voyager* altered back to port at 2053, someone on the carrier's bridge asked whether the destroyer had sought permission to cross *Melbourne*'s bows. After ascertaining that the answer was no, he looked towards *Voyager* and saw that Kelly had noticed that her port-side light was visible. At that moment, Barker said he heard someone on the carrier's bridge say that *Voyager*'s range was 3.5 cables (1 cable = 200 yards). Kelly then ordered the engines half astern and *Voyager* appeared out of the dark. Barker said that if *Voyager* had been alerted at that moment, she could have 'got clear by clapping on speed, and going across the *Melbourne*'s bow'. The implication was that Kelly should have given a warning to *Voyager* rather than worrying about *Melbourne*'s engines. Barker had been the Chief Yeoman in *Voyager* the previous year, and this gave his view added credence.[13]

When asked by Smyth why he made no effort to warn *Voyager* if he believed a collision was imminent, Barker said it was not within his authority to 'get on the radio-telephone to give her a warning', as Smyth suggested.[14] Yet he later conceded that this action would have averted the collision. As Robertson had the authority to issue such a warning, and the need for it was obvious to Barker, this amounted to a criticism of Robertson by one of his own bridge staff. Jenkyn then pointed out that Barker was an expert on communications and was not an authority on seamanship.[15] However, the point had been made by someone with reasonable knowledge who deserved credibility.

Barker was to prove a valuable witness for the interested *Voyager* parties as well. In cross-examination by Street, Barker appeared to have less confidence in his own area of expertise than in areas where he was not an authority. Street took Barker through *Melbourne*'s log and pointed out that three messages sent in the hour prior to the collision had not been recorded as being acknowledged by *Voyager*.[16] Although Barker said he was certain they had been acknowledged, he had not said this in a statement he gave the Crown Solicitor after the collision. Street then showed Barker the signal sent from *Melbourne* to *Voyager* ordering a change of course to 190 degrees, which was transmitted without a time at the end of it. He asked whether this 'would give you any uncertainty if you were receiving it?' Barker replied: 'I would know something had been missed. You always put the time at the end of a message.'[17] However, the signal had not been queried by *Voyager*. It was, in fact, sent and acted on by *Voyager* at 2041.

> Street: Does not that suggest some looseness in the signalling practice being followed by *Melbourne*'s bridge on that night?
>
> Barker: It is a simple procedure thing. But as you say it has not been followed.

Barker's answer led Street to believe that the most likely cause of the collision was an error in signalling, although not necessarily in *Melbourne*. He was to maintain this view throughout the Commission.

In later cross-examination it emerged that if an incorrect signal was involved, it was almost certainly to have been incorrectly conveyed or misinterpreted by *Voyager* rather than to have been an error originating from the carrier. There were two reasons for this. First, Robertson was aware of the signal he had sent and *Melbourne* complied with it. Second, the voice of the tactical operator was audible throughout the carrier's bridge and Barker testified that he heard Everett send the correct signal.[18] In testimony received later, Commander George Jude commented that Everett did speak rather loudly because he was conscious of Everett's voice after he came on watch at 1950.[19] Robertson said that he personally instructed Everett to speak loudly and to face the captain's position when he was sending signals so he could be heard. If the signal had been incorrectly transmitted, Robertson, Kelly, Bate and Barker would have heard the error and cancelled the incorrect signal.

Both Street and Meares pressed Barker on his recollection of a discussion — referred to by Street and Meares as a conference — held on *Melbourne*'s bridge the morning after the collision. Although Barker could recall disagreeing with Robertson on the angle at which *Voyager* crossed *Melbourne*'s bows, he had no recollection of anything Robertson had said. Meares was particularly harsh: 'May I suggest to you that this conference was a sort of round-table conference in which you were all trying to resolve any doubts about it or uncertainties in your minds?' Barker was agitated and this showed in his reply: 'That is not true. Nobody was ever asked to resolve any uncertainties.'[20] It appeared to others at the Bar table as though the naval witnesses were influenced by Robertson's presence and that they were giving answers that assisted Robertson's case. There was nothing really sinister about this. Robertson was respected and well-liked by his officers and sailors. Naval witnesses, like Barker, appeared to feel they had to be loyal to him, even as witnesses.

By the end of the first week of sitting, the Navy and Robertson had not fared too well. The second week commenced in much the same way. *Melbourne*'s OOW, Sub-Lieutenant Alex Bate, took the stand and was forced to agree with Smyth's contention that he 'could not be described as a very experienced First OOW'.[21] Bate explained that prior to the collision he was on the port side of the carrier's bridge looking for merchant ships.[22] Thirty seconds before the collision he heard Kelly say 'What the hell is *Voyager* doing?' and turned to see the blurred superstructure of *Voyager* at a range of 700 yards. Unsure of what was happening, he rushed to the bridge radar with Kelly and saw that *Voyager* was 600 yards away.[23]

Smyth returned to what would become a persistent theme and suggested to Bate that since he believed a dangerous situation had developed, it would have been prudent to have sounded the bridge siren — located 8 feet from the radar. Failing that, he should have directed the tactical operator standing near the radio-telephone to have alerted *Voyager*. Bate said he was at that time giving engine orders, although he conceded that *Voyager* had a much greater capacity for manoeuvre than *Melbourne* and, therefore, a better chance of avoiding a collision.[24]

To make matters worse for Robertson, Street showed Bate Robertson's report of the collision which stated that *Voyager* had initially turned to starboard, but was then seen, including by the OOW, to turn to port. Bate said he heard Robertson say *Voyager* had altered to port, but had only taken a quick glance.

> Street:   ... you put your signature to this form verifying something as correct when you had not the faintest idea what was in the document you were verifying?
>
> Bate:   You have just proved this, yes.[25]

On being challenged by Street as to why he signed a document that he could not totally substantiate from his own observations, Bate stated that he had been instructed to do so by Robertson's secretary in *Melbourne*. Worse still, he had signed the collision forms before they were completed by Robertson.[26] After this admission, Bate said he was not now prepared to authenticate what Robertson had put forward. The credibility of Robertson and the Navy's procedures continued to decline.

The seventh day ended with more humiliation for Robertson. After indicating that he wanted to cross-examine Bate, Robertson was told he would have to wait until the next morning. Smyth then asked Spicer to direct that Bate not be approached or interviewed overnight. Before Spicer could answer, Robertson said: 'I have been caught out once'. Spicer glared at Robertson and said, 'He should certainly not to be interviewed, directly or indirectly, by you or anybody on your behalf'. Robertson could only reply, 'I understand that'.[27]

Robertson's situation had become untenable. He was not performing well at the Bar table and his position had deteriorated every day. He had come to feel acutely that he was on trial, with Smyth acting as the prosecutor. He appeared powerless in defending his own position and reputation, and ineffectual in dealing with the submissions of other counsel. There was little alternative but for Robertson to take the advice he had been given from the start of the Commission and seek representation.

This decision was a painful one, especially since he had earlier been offered counsel and had refused. Street had personally implored him to engage counsel after the disastrous seventh day of the hearing. Jenkyn spoke with him as well and pointed out that the Naval Board could not be expected to side exactly with his version of events or agree with their significance. Finally, the problem of the scope of the Navy brief was acknowledged. This was affirmation that the principal problem with Jenkyn's brief was that it was too large and cumbersome and unable to carry all the interests and points of view being expressed by Naval personnel. Jenkyn strongly advised Robertson to arrange representation but permanent damage had already been done to his standing at the inquiry.[28]

The next morning (Day 8) Robertson spoke with Smyth, who agreed to ask Spicer for a one-week adjournment while he organised counsel to assist him. In putting Robertson's request, Smyth remarked that 'We think it highly desirable that he should be given that opportunity'.[29] After sitting for only 5 minutes that morning, Spicer again agreed to adjourn the Commission. A great deal of time would not be lost. Included in the week was the Easter break.

In seeking a commitment initially from the Navy to pay for his legal expenses, Robertson completely misread and misunderstood his position and the Navy's inability to help him. Robertson saw Becher first and asked whether he should send a signal to the Naval Board requesting that his legal fees be paid. Becher informed Robertson that this was not a matter for the Navy to decide, and advised him — given the urgency of the situation — to send a telegram to the Prime Minister setting out his request.

Robertson was evidently unhappy with Becher's response. He asked to speak with Landau who informed Robertson that Becher's advice was correct. Landau had already made verbal representations on Robertson's behalf and informed the Prime Minister's and Attorney-General's Department that the matter would need attention before 1 April when the Commission resumed. Robertson then sent a telegram to Menzies, although he did not specify what counsel he needed.[30]

The next day (26 March) Robertson was informed by the Deputy Crown Solicitor, at the direction of the Attorney-General, Billy Snedden, that the Commonwealth would not pay for senior counsel. However, in a letter to Robertson dated the same day, Snedden said only that 'It is not possible for me, at this stage, to completely define the extent of financial assistance which the Commonwealth will provide.'[31]

Rear-Admiral Harold Farncomb, representing Alfred Rofe and Sons, (Robertson's solicitors) sent a telegram to the Prime Minister asking for his intervention. This was followed by a letter to Snedden outlining Robertson's need for senior counsel.[32] In reply to Farncomb, Snedden stated that 'Captain Robertson's position is not, in my opinion, the same as that of the relatives of Captain Stevens and Lieutenant Price,[33] and implied that Jenkyn's presence at the Commission would also serve to protect Robertson's interests.[34] One assumes that Jenkyn would protect the Stevens family's interests as well. Any other interests Robertson had, Snedden stated, would be outside the Commission's terms of reference. In his reply of 15 April, Farncomb attempted to strengthen the arguments he had earlier put to Snedden, but there was really nothing new for Snedden to consider.[35]

Robertson submitted an official letter to the Navy outlining the circumstances of his case on 16 April.[36] He concluded it by stating that, 'I make the above submission in order that the Naval Board may be aware of the circumstances surrounding my decision to obtain legal representation and so that they might be in a position to take any action that they consider appropriate in the circumstances'.[37]

There is no evidence to suggest the nature of the action Robertson hoped or expected the Naval Board would take. It appears, however, that individual members of the Naval Board did try to exert personal influence on the Attorney-General's Department. On 8 May, Rear-Admiral McNicoll wrote to Robertson 'I'm so glad that justice finally prevailed over your legal expenses. It was an interesting operation and I'll tell you about it some time.'[38]

Nevertheless, for the next month, Robertson's case was argued within the Attorney-General's Department, with a resolution in Robertson's favour not being made until the first week in May. During Question Time in Parliament on 6 May, in answer to a question from Liberal backbencher John Jess, Snedden said, 'I have reconsidered this matter in the light of representations made by the honourable member'.[39] The reason for Snedden taking such an unsympathetic and patently unpopular view of Robertson's case has not been adequately explained. In his letter to Farncomb reconsidering his earlier decision,[40] there is no indication as to why he changed his mind.

Robertson seems not to have properly understood his status at the Commission. He later wrote, 'for myself and for the Navy it was indeed an unprecedented action to take, for as a serving officer I was forbidden by regulation to deal with politicians, or even with my parliamentary representative. There are naval procedures for things you want to air, or grievances you wish to raise. You are required to go to your immediate superior officer and so through the chain of command'.

Of course, had the Navy taken up Robertson's request and failed to achieve the desired commitment from the Commonwealth, there would have been the suspicion that the Navy had sabotaged Robertson's efforts in securing a fair hearing. At any rate, the issue of his legal fees was not a matter for the Navy to decide. Only Cabinet had the power to grant his request and it made sense that it should be treated at the highest possible level, hence sending the telegram to Menzies. Robertson's statement that he was forbidden to deal with politicians, including his local parliamentary member, should have carried with it the qualification that this restriction related only to naval matters. It is of relevance that in his private and confidential memoirs, Sir Jack Stevens states that

> I was approached during the Spicer Commission by a senior naval officer to desist in our 'attacks' on Captain Robertson. (This followed cross-examination of Robertson and Bate by Street.) The senior naval officer came to my house in Vaucluse. I do not know who, if anyone, authorised his visit which he asked me not to disclose. I told him it was and never had been our policy to attack Robertson unless he or his officers made statements in evidence reflecting upon my son.[41]

While Robertson was fighting the battle over his legal expenses, the Naval Board had to face the problem of whether Robertson should remain in his posting. It was apparent that he was now fully involved with the Commission and unable to give his command the close attention it required. Remaining in *Melbourne* had already affected his preparedness for the hearings. However, if he were to be removed there would be adverse comment from many quarters, including from within the Navy.

In the weeks after the collision, Robertson had written to the next of kin of every officer and sailor lost in *Voyager*, and worked on his full official report on the disaster. Robertson's time was also taken up with repairs being effected to *Melbourne* at Cockatoo Island Dockyard and the constant demands of running the small city that the carrier was. It was obvious that he would be needed to appear before the Royal Commission and it was likely his evidence would take a considerable period of time to present. On 28 February, Captain Peek had informed the Naval Board, from his discussions with Smyth, that the Commission was not likely to complete its sittings until June or July.[42] There was also no indication of when Robertson would be called.

The matter of the timing of Robertson's appearance before the Commission was put before the Minister, Chaney, on 28 February. On 3 March Chaney wrote to the Minister for Defence, Paul Hasluck:

> It is becoming apparent that some difficulty may be experienced by reason of the fact that the Royal Commission will not complete sitting until after [*Melbourne* is planned to sail from Sydney for the SEATO exercise], probably the end of June or July, 1964. Concern is therefore expressed that a large body of officers and men may be detained until the inquiry is completed and this may prevent the *Melbourne* from sailing.
>
> I think it is right to assume that it is highly desirable from a national point of view that *Melbourne*, with the Fleet Commander on board, should take part in the SEATO exercise and I am therefore putting this matter before you so that you may consider what steps can be taken to see that the witnesses from *Melbourne* meet all the requirements of the Commission of Inquiry before the salient date.[43]

Hasluck spoke with the Prime Minister the same day.

> Both the Prime Minister and I think that it would be quite proper to ask the Royal Commissioner to call all of these witnesses at an early stage of the Inquiry so that they will be released from further attendance and will become available for the manning of *Melbourne* and other ships of the Royal Australian Navy. The Prime Minister suggests that the most convenient procedure for Counsel representing the Navy before the Commissioner is to make the request direct to the Commissioner at the earliest possible hearing. We feel sure that if the request and the supporting argument are put fairly and clearly to the Commissioner he will respond to them.[44]

Smyth's instructing solicitor, F. J. Mahoney, indicated on 16 March that Smyth proposed to call Becher first, followed by two officers from HMAS *Albatross* and forty-four witnesses from *Melbourne*. When this was done, witnesses from *Voyager* would be called. He also advised the Navy that the Commissioner was aware of the need to release *Melbourne*'s personnel as early as possible to allow the ship to sail with minimum disruption.

As *Melbourne* was undergoing repairs prior to sailing for South-East Asia, and given that the deployment was to be a lengthy one, there seemed to be no alternative but to post Robertson ashore for the duration of the Commission, and the time taken to publish its report.[45] A replacement would need to be found for him in *Melbourne*. It appears some thought was given to this matter very soon after the collision.

When some idea of how long Robertson would be required by the Commission was obtained, a decision was made to post him from *Melbourne*. That he was being 'temporarily relieved of his command' was publicly announced at 1000 on 26 March and Becher informed the ship's company at 0900 of what was to happen.[46] Captain David Stevenson (no relation to Captain J. Philip Stevenson), was appointed to *Melbourne* in temporary command on 2 April from HMAS *Sydney* where he had been captain since November 1963. Captain J. P. Stevenson was appointed in temporary command of HMAS *Sydney* on 6 April.

The Naval Board's decision to replace Robertson was prompted by more than just a concern for his involvement in the Commission. Throughout 1964 there was a fear that Australia might become involved in combat operations either in Indonesia or in South Vietnam.

When the Royal Commission resumed on 1 April, Sub-Lieutenant Bate was again in the witness box and David Hicks QC (representing Robertson) was given leave to appear with his junior, Peter Raine.[47] Sitting alongside the Bar table with Robertson was Farncomb. The Minister for the Navy, Fred Chaney, also attended the Commission for the first time, sitting in the public gallery.

During the morning's proceedings, both Bate[48] and Kelly were questioned on the disappearance of a page from the OOW's notebook from *Melbourne*, which had come into Smyth's hands in the period of the adjournment. This was the high point in Smyth's aggressive attacks on the naval witnesses. A page had been removed from the notebook and a small part left at the seam of the book. Bate was forced to agree with Smyth that the 'torn page' which followed showed an alteration of course at 1957 on the night of the collision, and that it could have been significant. The pages following the torn page were in Bate's handwriting. When asked about its removal, Bate said he did not know why it had been removed, or who had torn it out.[49] The book was examined by handwriting experts and Smyth continued to question Bate about it. The tabloids were given another sensational headline — 'Page Torn from Ship's Notebook'. The matter of the torn page would emerge again later in the Commission.

Bate agreed that an entry for a 'fix' (of the ship's navigational position) at 2100 had been crossed out in the notebook, but explained that it had been the time when he intended to take a new fix and this was a reminder. As the collision occurred at 2056, the fix was never taken.[50] Hicks then questioned Bate in an effort to show that Robertson had not put any pressure on Bate to sign the six copies of Form AS 232 — Report of Collision or Grounding — that Robertson was required to submit to the Fleet Commander. Bate said there was no pressure but that he had done what his captain had directed him to do. The point was lost by Hicks.

It was apparent that Bate's role was minor and that Kelly and Robertson acted in some respects as though they were alone on the bridge in the moments before the collision. As with Bate, Kelly had no idea of what to expect at the collision. He described himself as being 'naive and like a babe in the woods'.[51] Kelly agreed with Smyth's comment that although he was occupied with finding the wind, he should have watched *Voyager*, or at least ensured that Bate was observing her movements.[52] Kelly said he did not try to communicate with *Voyager* or to warn her of any impending danger.[53] Kelly was, however, vulnerable. Three incorrect bearings of *Melbourne*'s position had been given after the collision and these attracted the attention of Smyth. The first was simple enough: Kelly had given *Melbourne*'s position as a range and bearing of Point Perpendicular lighthouse from the carrier, whereas the bearing should have been the reciprocal — what *Melbourne* bore from the lighthouse. The bearing had actually been taken by the OOW or the Assistant OOW.[54] When the position was reported at the Naval Air Station, there was no confusion as they understood how the bearing had been reported and knew where *Melbourne* was. Certainly, she was not 20 miles inland.

Kelly then had to defend the variation in his view to that put by Robertson that *Voyager* had passed across *Melbourne*'s bows at something more than 290 degrees or at right angles.[55] He also conceded that *Voyager* had not been told of *Melbourne*'s altered turning circles as a result of her recent refit. Although the alteration was very minor, producing a larger turning circle (in other words, a slower turn), and would have had no real effect on the relative movement of the two ships prior to the collision, it helped Smyth to discredit Kelly and suggest that *Melbourne* may not have reached the 020 course until much closer to the collision.

Kelly's examination produced a new twist. Smyth began to imply that naval witnesses were misleading the Commission. This prompted Jenkyn to ask Kelly whether he had been 'influenced from any quarter to tell any account of this incident other than the version as you saw it and believed it?' and 'Have you felt any sense of pressure of any kind from Captain Robertson or anyone else ... to say anything other than what you personally believe?' Kelly replied no to both questions.[56]

Smyth then developed a line of questioning that evidently impressed Spicer. In his various reconstructions and draft reports of the collision, Smyth had Kelly concede that if *Voyager* had altered course to starboard even as late as 40 seconds prior to the collision, she could have avoided hitting *Melbourne*.[57] Smyth then pointed out on one particular drawing prepared by Kelly, as part of an earlier draft of Robertson's report, that the time could even have been 30 seconds. In acknowledging this, Smyth asked Kelly why this had not been included in paragraph 31 of Robertson's final report of the collision:

Kelly:    I do not remember any discussion about it.

Smyth:    Do you remember hearing from anybody that it might be suggested that had *Melbourne* given *Voyager* a warning this collision might never have happened? You knew that was going to be suggested before the inquiry began, did you not?

Kelly:    Yes.

Smyth:    Was that the reason ... why it was cut out, this paragraph 31?

Kelly:    Not that I know of.

Smyth:    If paragraph 31 be correct, then it is clear that had *Voyager* been given a warning 55 seconds, 50 seconds before the collision, she could have avoided comfortably? That is clear, is it not?

Kelly:    Yes.

Spicer:   Did Captain Robertson tell you he was cutting out that paragraph?

Kelly:    I don't remember. The captain used to produce many drafts and I probably did not see every ...[58]

He was interrupted by Smyth before he could finish.

There was nothing sinister in the changes made to Robertson's numerous reports to the Naval Board during their various iterations. His first report was despatched with great haste a few hours after the collision. A one page clarification was sent the same day. A report on the period between the collision and the carrier's arrival in Sydney on 12 February was sent on 19 February. Although it mentioned the events leading to the collision, it concentrated on the rescue operation. A very comprehensive document, it contained reports from those in charge of the carrier's rescue boats, the aircraft circling overhead at the time of the collision, the Search and Rescue (SAR) craft, HMAS *Stuart*, and three of the five minesweepers employed in the rescue.

Robertson's major report was submitted with Form AS 232 on 5 March.[59] Although Robertson had advised on 19 February that it would be completed by 23 February, it appears from Robertson's private papers to have been redrafted four or five times. Despite Smyth's criticisms, Robertson was remarkably frank about his thinking in the few minutes prior to the collision. Although Robertson sought to make the best use of all the information then available to him, and showed little interest in deception, the tone of the report was more guarded than those of the previous three weeks. He also wisely declined to offer in his final report a theory to account for *Voyager*'s final movements.

All the available evidence suggests that Robertson acted on his own and without any direction or advice from the Naval Board. However, he voluntarily subjected his reconstructions to no fewer than three experienced RAN navigation specialists. The comments they offered do show some minor differences of opinion on the relative motions of both ships, as determined by variations in the theoretical amount of speed both ships may have lost during their final turns and the reliability of published turning data.

Smyth persisted with this line of questioning and referred to the first draft of Robertson's report. When describing *Voyager*'s turn to port as the first part of a 'fishtail', Robertson had crossed out the word 'unseamanlike' and replaced it with 'not the best practice but possible if tightly controlled'.[60]

Smyth: So it is the element of danger that would make it unseamanlike?

Kelly: In these circumstances, yes.

Smyth: Well, if you see a vessel conducting itself in unseamanlike manner ... would you not then regard it as your duty to take some step to communicate with that vessel either by siren or radio-telephone?

Kelly: Yes.

Smyth: And had that paragraph [29] been right as originally drawn, would you agree that *Voyager* should have been communicated with at one and a half minutes before the collision?

Kelly: Yes.[61]

*Melbourne*'s 2nd OOW, Sub-Lieutenant F. M. Jefferies, probably lowered Spicer's view of the competence of *Melbourne*'s bridge staff even further when he admitted that he had not recorded *Melbourne*'s increase of speed from 20 to 22 knots at 2015. After being shown the OOW notebook, he also conceded that his previous statement that he had not written anything in the OOW's notebook on the night of the collision was untrue.[62] He was also unable to explain why a page had been torn from the notebook.[63] He knew this was not permitted.[64]

After dealing with *Melbourne*'s personnel first, to enable them to rejoin their ship, Smyth called the first of the *Voyager* witnesses. He also pointed out that the evidence of these witnesses would be relevant to the Commission's third term of reference relating to the treatment and rescue of survivors.

The major difficulty in the way of arriving at a satisfactory explanation of the collision was the absence of personnel who were responsible for *Voyager*'s movements in the three minutes prior to the collision. All four officers and the communications yeoman on the bridge at the time were killed. The only survivors from the bridge were Tactical Operator Gary Evans (the signalman at the communications desk) and Ordinary Seaman Brian Sumpter (the port lookout). The only man to survive from the wheelhouse was the port engine telegraph operator, Ordinary Seaman Alex Degenhardt, while Leading Seaman Michael Patterson, a radar plotter, survived from the operations room.

The first to be called was 19-year-old Sumpter, who had spent only one day at sea in HMAS *Derwent* prior to going to sea in *Voyager* for trials. Sumpter had gone on duty as port lookout only a matter of minutes before the collision. After *Melbourne* continued to close the destroyer, Sumpter called out to the bridge. There was no answer but he turned and saw Price looking at *Melbourne* through his binoculars. Sumpter looked around to face the carrier again before hearing Price order the engines astern.[65]

There was great import in Sumpter's evidence. It appeared that *Melbourne* was at Red 75 at the time he turned towards Price. It was then between 1 minute 40 seconds to 1 minute before the collision.[66] On closer questioning he said that Price later looked through his binoculars.[67] As Robertson remarked in his notes for Hicks's use, 'He would not have used glasses if he suddenly saw *Melbourne* in an unexpected position. Given that the final orders to avoid the collision were given at around 30 seconds before impact, it is possible that *Voyager*'s bridge might have taken as much as 1 minute to assess the situation, only acting when a collision was imminent.'

The evidence of Sumpter effectively ruled out the possibility of port wheel having been inadvertently left on. The bearing change was appreciable and therefore observable.

Robertson commented privately to his counsel,

> If *Voyager* got into this position through an error of leaving the 10 degrees of port wheel on, surely, when the OOW suddenly discovered that *Melbourne* was on his port bow instead of astern, he would immediately have gone hard astarboard rather than pick up his binoculars and look at *Melbourne*.[68]

But too much was made of Sumpter's evidence that none of *Voyager*'s bridge staff came near the port bridge-wing compass repeat to take a bearing of *Melbourne*.[69] It was one thing to say that no one took a bearing, but quite another to state that no one moved to a position where they could have observed *Melbourne*. As the bridge of *Voyager* was compact, Price could have moved away from the pelorus towards the port side of the bridge, observed *Melbourne*'s sidelights and noted her position, and then returned to the pelorus, all in the space of several seconds. If Sumpter had been looking towards *Melbourne*, this could have happened without his knowledge.[70]

However, Robertson believed Sumpter's evidence that he saw the OOW (Price) using binoculars was

> *the most important piece of evidence we have heard yet.* Whatever the relative bearing of *Melbourne* was when Price looked at her through binoculars one would infer that at least he thought he knew what he was doing. This fact combined with the rumour that Stevens may well have left the handling of his ship to Price would indicate that Price was confused about some fact rather than that *Voyager* was doing something which no one on the bridge knew she was doing. This, of course, means that my original theory that whatever was happening *Voyager* was not looking at *Melbourne*, is completely wrong. [Robertson's emphasis][71]

This was a highly significant concession that Robertson never made in public and which he never made again, even in his private papers.

While keeping his watch on the bridge of *Voyager*, Tactical Operator Gary Evans sat in front of the captain's chair and could remember Stevens being seated with the Communications Yeoman, Kevin Cullen, at Stevens's right hand.[72] On the night of the collision he had been using a telephone style handset to receive and80acknowledge VHF voice signals from *Melbourne*. Evans stated that when the turning signal was received he reported it to Price, apparently within the hearing of Stevens and Cullen. However, he did not report any of the signals received that night directly to Stevens and could not be certain that Stevens had actually heard any of them.[73] It is possible, with the background noise associated with steaming at more than 20 knots, that neither Price nor Cullen actually heard the signal over the tactical primary loudspeaker which projected distorted sound. The signal was acknowledged by Price. Evans stated that *Voyager* steadied on 020 degrees before receiving and acting on the flying course signal.[74]

Evans was in a key position as the tactical operator on duty on the bridge. He may have been the only member of the bridge staff to have actually heard *Melbourne*'s turning course and flying course signals. Evans said he believed the cause of the collision was that *Melbourne* gave a final order to turn to port and failed to turn herself, or was slow to turn. It was a curious explanation for someone who had been on *Voyager*'s bridge and who had personally received all *Melbourne*'s signals.[75] In fairness to Evans, it should be stated that in giving his evidence he did not want to be held to the accuracy of any of the courses he recalled prior to the collision.[76]

The next witness threw some doubt on the credibility and reliability of Evans. Tactical Operator Robert Burdett spent two hours in the water after the collision and had some difficulty remembering the events before impact. Although in error, he said he could recall a turn from 190 to 060 degrees because Cullen had reprimanded Evans for not passing the order to Price quickly enough.[77] However, he said there was no discussion on *Voyager*'s bridge about *Melbourne*'s movements, nor was there anything unusual. Burdett also thought that the bridge loudspeakers were performing poorly.[78] Much was made of this by Street. During cross-examination, Burdett agreed with Street's statement that 'it was difficult to hear what was being said over the speaker' because of the distortion.[79] The distortion was the product of two things. The first was a technical fault in the loudspeaker. This had apparently been reported by Burdett to the ship's electrical maintenance staff, but not repaired. The other reason was that

> the captain's chair was up and aft a bit and you could not see the [loud]speaker from the captain's chair. I think it was blocked out a bit by the signalman's booth ... There was another speaker on the other side of the signalman's booth right next to the captain's chair but it was removed during refit. That was the one that was used for tactical primary [communications] before the refit.[80]

The only seaman officer to have survived the collision, Lieutenant John Conder RN, when asked by Street whether it was easy to hear signals coming through the loudspeaker when *Voyager* was steaming at 20 knots, replied:

It depends on the volume of the loudspeaker. Generally speaking I would say it would be fairly difficult to listen to it at something like 20 knots.

Street:   If he was standing at the pelorus he would not hear the tactical primary?

Conder:   I do not think it would be easy for him to hear it.[81]

There were similar concerns raised about the material state of *Voyager* from the evidence given by the survivors of the destroyer's operations room. The most important evidence was offered by Patterson, whose evidence was taken in camera and the transcript subsequently released. Patterson was thought by some at the Bar table to be an unreliable witness from the outset. After being rescued by one of *Melbourne*'s boats, Patterson spent the next two days in the carrier, where he claimed he saw a plot of the ship's final movements in *Melbourne*'s operations room. There was some suspicion about why Patterson went to the operations room. It appears that after commencing a plot of the exercise at 2005 in *Voyager*, he stopped plotting positions about four minutes before the collision because, he claimed, the ship was heeling from the turn and he was physically holding on to keep his balance.[82]

While the final turn to port was in progress, MacGregor (*Voyager*'s First Lieutenant) asked Patterson if he had either *Melbourne* or the Royal Navy submarine *Tabard* on his radar screen. Patterson stated he looked at the radar screen but could see neither of them because the carrier was in *Voyager*'s radar blind arcs.[83] Patterson claimed he heard nothing about *Voyager*'s changes of course because the intercom between the operation room and the bridge was not working.[84] He further claimed that it had not been working since he joined the ship and that he had not observed *Melbourne* on radar since his watch began over an hour before.

One very useful piece of evidence that Patterson did offer, if only inadvertently, was that he distinctly remembered *Voyager* heeling during her final turn to port. Patterson said that all the pens, pencils and parallel rulers rolled off the plotting table onto the operations room deck.[85]

This heeling was subsequently confirmed by Able Seaman Howis, who stated that a can of beer on a table in front of him slid out of his reach,[86] while Able Seaman Bannister recalled that the dice he and three others were using with a board game, rolled under the bunk they were sitting on when the ship turned.[87] There could be no doubt that the bridge staff would have felt the ship heel as it maintained port wheel. This effectively discounted the possibility that the final turn was effected without the bridge staff being aware of it. In other words, port wheel had not been unintentionally left on.

After giving his evidence on the twenty-first day of hearings, Patterson read a newspaper report covering Evans's evidence. Patterson had expected Evans to give certain evidence, but when this did not emerge, Patterson gave a supplementary statement to the Deputy Crown Solicitor.

In essence, Patterson stated that he heard a voice calling out from the darkness after the collision, '*Melbourne* told us to turn to 270 but she didn't'. He heard these words called out on several occasions in an hysterical voice. When Patterson was recalled to the inquiry and asked by Smyth why he had not mentioned it in his evidence, Patterson replied:

> I did not attach great importance to the matter at the time. When I came into court I had completely forgotten about it.[88]
>
> Smyth:    Were you able to identify who it was?
>
> Patterson:    No, I could not put a name to the voice at the time.[89]

There was, however, little doubt that Patterson believed the voice was that of Evans and that he had expected Evans to have remembered what he had said in the water and included it in his evidence. Both Evans and Burdett were recalled.[90]

Evans, choosing his words carefully, said that he did not hear the voice mentioned by Patterson. When asked by Smyth, 'Do you say it did not happen?,' he replied, 'I will not say that'. He conceded that when in the water he might have been calling out in the same way that the voice heard by Patterson had been calling out.[91] When asked about the voice, Burdett said that he was unable to help as he had heard nothing at all. It is worth mentioning that Evans and Burdett were close friends, although another of the tactical operators serving in *Voyager* at the time, Robert Jocumsen, said that after the collision he sensed that Burdett bore some resentment towards Evans.[92] After both Evans and Burdett had been examined, Smyth sought to question Patterson further. He was prevented from doing so by Jenkyn who wanted to delay his cross-examination until the matters raised by Patterson could be given further consideration. Four days later Patterson was recalled.

In his later evidence, which was taken in camera, Patterson said that after he had given his statement to the Deputy Crown Solicitor, he had a conversation with both Burdett and another tactical operator from *Voyager*, Owen Sparks. The date was 27 April 1964. Patterson recalled that

> Sparks said that he saw Evans in Balmoral [Naval] Hospital and Evans had told him that *Melbourne* had told *Voyager* to turn. Evans also told Tactical Operator Burdett something similar outside this court.[93]

Although Patterson could not recall if either Sparks or Burdett had mentioned courses, he was under the clear impression that it was a course to the west and was definitely not the turning course of 020 degrees signalled by *Melbourne* at 2052. Patterson spoke with Evans about these matters on two occasions. He states that on neither occasion did Evans make any comment.[94]

Jenkyn attacked Patterson's recollection on the grounds that he could not remember a course. It was obvious that the Navy's counsel did not consider that Patterson's evidence brought great credit to the RAN, as it inferred that both Evans and Burdett had not helped the inquiry to the full extent that they were able. He also thought that Patterson may have been attempting to find a cause for the collision which shifted blame on to *Melbourne*.[95] With Patterson resolutely standing by his evidence, Jenkyn took another approach in attempting to discredit him. Jenkyn asked Patterson about his injuries and his psychological state since the collision.[96] This was grossly unfair to Patterson, who had suffered personal discomfort in offering his latest evidence.[97]

The attack on Patterson's credibility continued. Two days later, three witnesses claimed that Patterson was intoxicated on the night of the collision. It was alleged by Able Seaman A. C. O'Connor, who had been on duty at *Melbourne*'s plotting table during the collision, that Patterson had said he 'was a bit wonky because he had had four cans of beer the night of the accident'.[98] It was claimed that Patterson made a similar statement to Leading Seaman R. J. Wallent, who had also been on duty in *Melbourne*'s operations room. The day after the collision, Wallent alleged that Patterson attempted to see *Melbourne*'s plot of the collision. When he was informed by Petty Officer B. T. E. Spalding that the plot was no longer in the operations room, Spalding offered to sketch it for Patterson. Spalding said in evidence:

> Then I said to him 'How come you did not hold us on the radar?' and he said 'I don't know; I was a bit confused. I had had four cans of beer before I went on watch and I only had an ordinary seaman on duty with me, and I wasn't sure what was going on.'

Having heard this evidence repeated over commercial radio, Patterson asked for an opportunity to reply. When asked about the allegations that he had consumed four cans of beer, he said he had in fact had only three-quarters of a can and had never said otherwise. Patterson angrily denied having said to another sailor 'they are not going to blame me for the loss of eighty-two men'. He admitted that he was 'panicky' after the collision, but not hysterical. Had Patterson engaged his own counsel, he could have pointed out that the performance of O'Connor, Wallent and Spalding in maintaining an accurate plot in *Melbourne* had been called into question at the inquiry, and that all three stood to gain from denigrating Patterson. Despite the evidence of these three, their immediate supervisor, Sub-Lieutenant David Isles (an ex-sailor), stated there was nothing that suggested to him either on the night of the collision, or later, that Patterson was in any way affected by alcohol.[99] In fact, Isles spoke with Patterson during the first ten minutes of the voice exercise which was in progress when the collision occurred.

Robertson later wrote of Patterson:

> We, at the Bar Table, were surprised that the judge was impressed by Patterson. We did not think he was a good witness. There were rumours at the time that he was very disturbed emotionally.... The inference we drew was that he (Patterson) was well aware that his plot in the *Voyager* was not up to date at the time of the collision and he was worried lest the judge would put blame on him for this as being a contributory cause of the collision. These facts were obvious to naval officers, but not, of course, to Spicer.[100]

It is fair to ask how Robertson could have possibly known these things about Patterson's private life.

But despite the attacks on Patterson's credibility Spicer seemed persuaded by the truthfulness of Patterson's recollection that he did hear a voice calling out from the water.

Burdett and Sparks were recalled to the Commission to answer questions in relation to Patterson's evidence. However, for reasons that were not fully explained at the inquiry, neither was put back into the witness box. The only other survivor to corroborate Patterson's 'voice in the water', was Able Seaman Andrew Matthews, who said he heard a voice call out, '*Melbourne* didn't turn, *Melbourne* didn't turn'. Matthews was not far from Patterson and obviously heard the same voice, while another witness, whom Patterson could not identify, stated one week after the collision, when the survivors met at *Watson* after returning from leave, that the voice was that of Evans.[101] Yet another survivor recalled Patterson commenting on the voice when the survivors returned to *Watson* after their leave.[102]

Patterson's evidence about *Voyager*'s radar blind arc was also thoroughly tested. Radar Plotter Low, who had earlier been in charge of the operations room, as no officer was present, said that of the two available radars, one was 'not really good'. The other set was working normally. Low was relieved by Patterson and made him aware that the only contact was *Melbourne*, which was in close visual range.

Acting Petty Officer Brennan confirmed Low's comments on *Voyager*'s radars. He said that although there had been some trouble earlier in the day with the radar blind arcs being larger than normal, they were functioning normally at the time of the collision.[103] Leading Radio Electrical Mechanic Gracie also testified that the radar troubles were minor and that the radar on the bridge was functioning properly on the night of the collision.[104]

The evidence of Ordinary Seaman Alex Degenhardt, the only survivor from the wheelhouse, could have changed the Commission's view of *Voyager*'s final movements. In a statement given to one of *Melbourne*'s officers the morning after the collision, Degenhardt confirmed that the orders relayed to the wheelhouse from the bridge had been starboard 15, followed by port 10, and then the final orders given immediately before the collision. However, two weeks later he made another statement which included an order of midships from the bridge, followed by a course to steer. He could not recall the course but thought it might have been 032.[105]

Degenhardt was cross-examined extensively on this by all counsel except Gregory, who reserved his right to do so later. It emerged that when Degenhardt returned from survivors' leave he had been summoned by Captain Ian Easton, the commanding officer of *Watson*, and questioned on his recollections.[106] It will be recalled that Easton had sought leave to represent Price until counsel was arranged. This evidence contradicted that given by other witnesses, but it did leave open for Spicer the possibility that *Voyager* was on a steady course prior to the collision.

Robertson could not accept that *Voyager* was on a steady course, and later remarked that Degenhardt was 'an odd sort of witness'.[107] In Robertson's view 'the original statement of Degenhardt was correct and his subsequent evidence about going midships and steadying was pure imagination as a result of him thinking to himself about what must have happened'.[108]

The witness whose testimony could have altered the entire course of the Commission was Ordinary Steward Barry Hyland. He stated that at 1930, less than ninety minutes before the collision, he had served Stevens a triple brandy, that is, three tots of brandy in a single glass.[109]

The RAN had inherited the practice of a daily alcohol issue from the Royal Navy. But whereas the RN has traditionally issued rum, the RAN abolished the rum issue during the Great Depression. An issue of beer was started in 1954.[110] Although not forbidden by naval regulations, captains and watchkeepers in ships at sea did not drink. This was an unwritten law with a tradition of being universally observed. Other officers, such as the engineer and the supply officer, were permitted to drink and usually did so with the evening meal. Sailors were granted a daily beer issue, although not on the first night at sea. This issue consisted of one 26-ounce can per day per man. Drunkenness was also defined as an offence under section 28 (i) of the *Naval Discipline Act*:

> A person is drunk within the meaning of this section, if owing to the influence of alcohol or any drug, whether alone or in combination with any other circumstances, he is unfit to be entrusted with his duty or with any duty which he might be called upon to perform, or behaves in a disorderly manner or in a manner likely to bring discredit on Her Majesty's Service.

It was a definition that counsel stated was more stringent than that which the civil courts apply.

The Naval Board, which was privately astonished by this revelation, expected Smyth to seize on this evidence as a means of further discrediting the Navy. Smyth had previously elicited evidence that some watchkeeping personnel in *Voyager* had consumed alcohol, but no one had expected to hear that either Stevens or Cook had had anything to drink. Professor C. R. B. Blackburn of the University of Sydney was earlier asked by Smyth to advise on the effect this blood alcohol level would have had on Stevens's performance. As Blackburn concluded that it would not have impaired his performance in any way, Smyth informed the Commission that alcohol was not a factor, and that was the end of the matter.[111]

Other counsel seemed content not to probe this matter further, although Street had Blackburn agree that the uncertainties in the actual level of blood alcohol resulting from the handling of the corpse and the method of acquiring the blood sample, would have tended to raise the blood alcohol content to a level higher than was present at the time of death.[112] Robertson, who knew little about Stevens but who stood to gain from making the most of his fellow captain's actions in drinking at sea, refused to have Hyland questioned by Hicks. He felt it was both unnecessary and in bad taste.[113] Robertson was aware of the opportunity he had let pass.

To make matters worse for the Navy, and to further complicate the Commission's proceedings, Gatacre wrote to Landau on 1 April setting out his explanation of the collision.[114] It was his belief that on receipt of the flying course signal, *Voyager* had to wait for another signal informing her that flying was resumed before taking up her planeguard station. 'Therefore,' declared Gatacre, '*Voyager* should not have started to move to her new station on receipt only of the 2054 signal giving a new flying course.' Having realised the need for another signal after starting the turn to port from 060 to 020 degrees, Gatacre speculated that either Price or the helmsman had left port wheel on, that this was undetected by anyone and led to *Voyager* assuming a collision course. There could be no doubting Gatacre's confidence about his version of events. He concluded his letter to Landau by informing him

> Such then is the explanation which in my long bridge experience and specialist knowledge in navigation I find entirely reasonable and so likely as to be almost certain.[115]

He also advised Landau that he had been asked by Street to attend his chambers for an interview. Gatacre said he felt bound to give his explanation of the collision to Street. In any event, as he was to retire on 10 June 1964 he had nothing to lose.

The Naval Board was incensed, and a meeting was hastily convened between the Director of Naval Communications and Jenkyn. Gatacre had taken it upon himself to present views that were not shared by his fellow admirals. What was worse, the obvious differences in opinion between the Board and Gatacre would only serve to reduce the Commission's confidence in the capacity of the Navy to offer expert opinion. The Board was evidently of the view that experts were meant to be of like mind.

Street was not interested in Gatacre's views, as they did not seem to assist the interests of his client, but they were taken up by Smyth who saw an opportunity to exploit this division of opinion. After speaking with Vice-Admiral Tom Hayward, USN, who had recently flown his flag in the nuclear-powered carrier USS *Enterprise*, and who agreed with Gatacre about the need for an additional signal, Gatacre wrote to the Australian Naval Attache in Washington, Captain John Peel, asking him to confirm his view with senior American officers. Peel's response, dated 8 May 1964, was a perplexing one:

> I had never heard any different interpretation than that agreed by you and Admiral Hayward — it all seemed clear enough to me and I have never heard it done any other way but that which you outlined.
>
> I managed to catch VCNO (Air), Admiral Thach, this morning and he completely agrees ... My other contacts at captain level found it difficult to believe that there should be any difference to the opinion expressed by you. As this seems such a universal attitude I don't consider it necessary to make further personal inquiry.

This was exactly the opposite view of that held by the Naval Board. It also said very little for the unanimity that the Board claimed existed within the Allied navies over the interpretation of tactical signalling.

Gatacre appears to have had a private agenda in seeking to involve himself in the Commission. He later showed little mercy to anyone involved in the tragedy. In his autobiography, Gatacre was critical of Becher for not being on board at the time of the collision and was unsparing of Robertson for not giving any instruction to *Voyager* when her movements became unclear.[116] It was his opinion that had neither erred in judgement, a collision would not have occurred. As for *Voyager*'s movements, he was still insistent that the destroyer needed a supplementary signal and that this requirement was discovered in *Voyager* after she had altered to starboard to take up her station astern.

In this later account,[117] Gatacre suggested that Stevens countermanded *Voyager*'s initial turn to starboard, a movement probably ordered by Price, and ordered the ship back to course 020. Price then ordered 'Port 10', followed by 'Steer 020'. Gatacre believed that the helmsman may have either repeated 020 and mistakenly steered the ship around to 200, or that he in fact repeated back 200 and that this was not corrected. For this to have happened, Price would have either not bothered to listen to the helmsman repeating the order or failed to notice the ship had proceeded beyond 020. The ship continued to turn to port until only 30 to 40 seconds before the collision, when Price realised what had happened. Gatacre explained Stevens's actions by saying that he ordered a return to 020 because he was either puzzled by the flying course signal or wanted to consider his options in taking up planeguard station. Thus, Gatacre believed, he was acting with caution, because he knew that he would remain out of *Melbourne*'s way until he was ready to take up station. This would account for Stevens stepping down to the chart table and would have been a reasonable action to take. There was, unfortunately for Gatacre, no evidence to support any part of his theory and this made it subject to a plethora of objections.

He was unable to explain why it would take so long for the captain, the communications yeoman and the navigator to sort out any confusion in signals received, or why, for two to three minutes Price would take no notice of the carrier. Gatacre's aim was to find an excuse for Stevens's conduct, however specious that excuse may have been. Gatacre claimed his was an acceptable theory which might console the Stevens family.[118]

There were two problems with the view Gatacre put before the Commission. First, the Naval Board did not state that an additional signal was incorrect, but that it was superfluous.[119] Second, the signal group used by *Melbourne* had been in common use since 1961. Although Gatacre told Landau on 1 April that 'I remind myself, however, that I have had greater sea experience and vastly more bridge experience than the captain of HMAS *Melbourne*,'[120] he had not been to sea since 1959. His contention that *Melbourne* had sent the wrong signals was totally incorrect. Further, the signals used specifically required *Voyager* to move on receipt of the flying course signal.[121] Becher was able to confirm, prior to Gatacre giving evidence, that the view held in the Fleet was that of the Naval Board and not that of Gatacre.[122] However, a contrary and dissenting view put by a senior RAN officer assisted Smyth's objective of showing flaws in the Naval Board's administration and the fallibility of naval tactical signalling and manoeuvring.

For the second half of April and the early part of May, the Commission heard detailed accounts of the escape of survivors from the sinking destroyer and their difficulties with emergency and lifesaving equipment. To familiarise himself with the equipment, Spicer was given a comprehensive demonstration of all items at Garden Island and inspected the rescue craft used on the night of the collision. It emerged that there were indeed serious flaws in the preparedness of *Voyager* for an emergency. Several escape hatches could not be opened, some emergency lighting had not functioned, while most of the lifejackets were stowed together in an inaccessible location. The Commission heard evidence from survivors that they did not know how to operate lifesaving equipment and that some could not swim. Although the sensational evidence foreshadowed by Smyth dealing with these aspects of the collision did not materialise, the Commission was presented with a number of accounts which clearly implied that men had lost their lives because of these shortcomings.

The star witness at the Commission was undoubtedly Robertson. After briefing his counsel and preparing his arguments, *Melbourne*'s captain finally entered the witness box on 12 May. Although there was subsequent public criticism of his being called last, as would have happened in a Naval board of inquiry, Robertson was not unhappy. He later wrote that he considered 'Smyth's procedure of leaving me till last was the fairest in the long run'.[123]

Robertson was in the witness box for six days. His demeanour was that of a man who believed he had nothing to fear nor hide. He said he had confidence in both Kelly and Bate and believed, despite having been in command for only five weeks, he had a good ship's company.[124] He described the events leading to the final turning and flying course signals. Robertson said that after the turning course signal was made, *Voyager* moved immediately to port and seemed to settle on 020 degrees. When the order was given, *Voyager* was very fine on *Melbourne*'s bow and probably moved quickly beyond 020 degrees to regain her station. At around the time the flying course signal was sent, Robinson thought *Voyager* turned to starboard but he was not absolutely sure.[125] His uncertainty would subsequently prove to be significant. In notes prepared later he said that after the turn to 020 degrees, *Voyager* was out of station:

> *Voyager*'s correct station at this time was 030 degrees at a range of between 1,000 and 1,500 yards. This means that *Melbourne* should have bore 210 degrees from *Voyager*. My guess is that at about this time, the OOW in *Voyager* took a bearing of *Melbourne* and found that it was 220 degrees. The OOW must have decided to go to starboard to get back into station. Note that this move is in the wrong direction.
>
> *Voyager*'s alteration to starboard at this time happened very soon after my signal was passed. It is possible that her alteration was a reaction to that signal. On the other hand it could well have been a movement ordered as the signal was coming through as I suggested above. At the time I though it was a prompt reaction to my signal.[126]

It was this prompt and decisive reaction that made him think she was responding to that signal.[127]

After watching *Voyager* move to starboard, Robertson went onto the starboard bridge-wing of the carrier and saw her steady before altering to port. He said he continued to watch *Voyager* from this position until he gave the order to reverse the carrier's engines.[128]

His interpretation of *Voyager*'s final movements was crucial. He said that after she appeared to be on a parallel course, the destroyer was 'sitting there, to my recollection, for some appreciable length of time — again I cannot estimate — it might be twenty seconds, it might be thirty, it might be only ten. I just watched her sitting there'.[129] It was during this period, when *Voyager* held her position relative to the carrier, that Robertson formed the view that the destroyer was carrying out a fishtail (Figure 21).[130] He then noticed that her turn to port brought her on to a collision course with *Melbourne* and moved quickly from the bridge-wing into the bridge and caught the end of Kelly's order to bring the engines half astern.[131] After ordering full astern, Robertson said he considered altering *Melbourne*'s course but realised that it would have had no effect. For the next thirty seconds, he watched the collision develop and felt powerless to do anything about it.[132]

Robertson believed there were two possible explanations for *Voyager*'s final movements. The final turn to port was either the result of port wheel left on mistakenly,[133] or came about because *Voyager* believed she was on *Melbourne*'s port bow, lost the tactical picture, became confused and persisted in this confusion until collision was imminent.[134] By this stage in the Commission he was inclined to disregard the first explanation.

Thus, Robertson was left with the contention that '*Voyager* was on a deliberate turn to port on the mistaken assumption that she was on *Melbourne*'s port bow' (Figure 22).[135] He preferred this view because of his belief that *Voyager* had altered to starboard after the flying course signal had been sent:

> If *Voyager*'s movement to starboard was a reaction by the OOW to my signal for her to resume her [flying] station, then the movement to port must have been a captain's contradiction of this reaction and a decision that it was clear to go to port. Note that it is not possible to take a bearing from the centre line pelorus of a ship in this position relative to *Voyager*. I conclude therefore that *Voyager* did not take an accurate bearing of *Melbourne* during this period, and guess that she relied on the visual appearance of *Melbourne* which showed that *Voyager* was near enough to right ahead [of the carrier] which made it safe to turn either way to her new station. Note that if *Voyager* had been in this position, it would have been quicker and therefore more seamanlike to go to port.[136]

Thus, Stevens was personally to blame because he countermanded Price's initial order — which was correct. While keeping his public criticism veiled, Robertson was critical of Stevens in private correspondence to his counsel. He noted the 'stories that one has heard recently about Captain Stevens leaving a lot of the handling of his ship to his officers' and was critical of Stevens for being over the chart table during a manoeuvre, and for earlier sitting in his chair on the bridge. 'If I had been on the bridge of *Voyager* as the captain, with *Voyager* in station somewhere ahead of *Melbourne*, I would certainly not be in my chair. On these occasions one is very much on one's toes. And so far as I am concerned, I would definitely be in a position where *Melbourne* can be continuously observed until we get into a comfortable station.'[137]

There were two central elements in Smyth's hostile cross-examination of Robertson. Citing Becher as an authority, Smyth attempted to obtain certain concessions from Robertson about what he could have done. He also made much of the fact that Robertson had recently taken command of *Melbourne*, suggesting that Robertson was inexperienced. The second prong of his attack was on Robertson's reactions when he realised a dangerous situation had developed. Once again, Smyth returned to his, by now, familiar comment that Robertson should have used the radio-telephone to give positive direction to *Voyager*.

Robertson did an exemplary job in defending his actions on the night of the collision, and during the weeks that followed (Figure 23). Rather than attempting to construct a version of the collision which best suited his interests, Robertson, by his research and painstaking efforts at gathering manoeuvring data, emerged as a helpful witness who wanted to assist the inquiry with finding the causes for the Commission. Where there had been disagreements with his version of events, or with the measurements he had used for his reconstruction, Robertson was open about their existence. By the time his reconstruction of the collision, dated 6 May 1964, was tabled at the Commission (Figure 24), many hundreds of hours had been devoted to interpreting and arranging the navigational data. There was no reason, other than a conclusion that Robertson was dishonest, for the Commissioner not to accept his reconstruction. Indeed, even after the evidence of naval architect Herd was received and the variations between his calculations and those of Robertson were found to be insignificant,[138] Smyth was unable to point to any error or deficiency that warranted the reconstruction's rejection either in part or in total.

With so many competing and conflicting arguments and views being presented, the Commission made its progress very slowly. To better their understanding of the circumstances in which the collision occurred, the Commissioner and counsel spent a night at sea in *Melbourne* on 19 May, following the completion of her repairs at Cockatoo Island.[139]

As *Melbourne* had started exercising at sea, the party was flown out to the ship from Mascot airport in two Navy helicopters to watch 'touch and go' exercises, with HMAS *Vendetta* acting as planeguard. *Vendetta* conducted one change of station from the starboard bow of the carrier to *Melbourne*'s port bow but there was no re-enactment of *Voyager*'s fatal last manoeuvre and neither was the party given an opportunity to see *Melbourne* from the bridge of a destroyer. Although Hicks QC attended, Robertson chose not to be present.

Some time during May, Menzies had become concerned about the direction and progress of the Royal Commission and, in particular, the role of Smyth. Such was Menzies's distress that he consulted Barwick, who was by then Chief Justice of the High Court, with the intention of having quite specific instructions given to Smyth about the way in which the Commission would be handled until its conclusion. Barwick pointed out to Menzies that although Smyth was being briefed by the Crown Solicitor's office and was having his fees paid by the

Government, he was not required to act on their instructions. Barwick also told Menzies it would have been improper for new instructions to have been issued at this point in the Commission.

The contents of this conversation was relayed by Barwick to Hicks, who later mentioned it to Robertson. When Hicks was told is not clear.[140] However, Hicks added that 'In any event, the head of the Judiciary does not and cannot tell the Government what it should do'.[141]

When the Commission's proceedings opened on 28 May, Spicer said he hoped the hearing of evidence would be completed by the end of the following day, with the Commission resuming on 9 June, when Smyth would deliver his final address. Spicer's expectation was not realised and the Commission sat for the last time on Saturday, 30 May. The final major witness was Captain Peek. He gave short, precise answers and limited his comments to only those matters raised in questions. He might even have been described as a reluctant witness.

If it could be said that the Naval Board had a view of why the collision occurred, Peek would have been in the position to have made it known. Yet he was reluctant to commit himself to any firm views. Jenkyn asked him if he thought Street's suggestion that *Voyager* had misinterpreted *Melbourne*'s flying course signal as being a variation on 020, such as 200 or 220, was possible. Peek's answer was evasive but nonetheless revealing:

> No, I do not. On the assumption that the captain of *Voyager* was a competent captain, and this is I think borne out by his record, I cannot believe he would not watch *Melbourne* constantly during the turn together.[142]

Peek was prepared to discard the theory of a misinterpreted signal solely on the basis that Stevens would not have failed to look at the carrier, notwithstanding the fact that a turn to the west would have put *Voyager* astern of the carrier.[143]

As 'naval assessor' to Smyth, and Robertson's predecessor in command of *Melbourne*, the view put by Peek naturally carried great weight at the Commission. He proposed three 'most likely' theories (Figure 25).[144] In the first, he suggested that Stevens countermanded the turn to starboard with a direct order of 'Port 10'. When the captain gave such an order it meant he had taken over the 'con' of the ship. Price then assumed that the captain had the ship, although he did not confirm this with Stevens by asking 'Captain, sir, do you have the ship?', and allowed the ship to manoeuvre as his captain had ordered. For his part, Stevens believed Price still had the con and went off to examine the tactical signalling manual at the chart table.

In the second of his theories, Peek suggested that after ordering 'Port 10', Price ordered 'Wheel amidships' prior to the ship's head actually bearing 020. Not having given the helmsman a course to steer, the ship continued to swing towards the carrier and a collision occurred through the inattentiveness of Price.

The third, the one he seemed to favour, was based on a mistaken signal. Given that a turn together from 020 degrees to 220 degrees would have put *Voyager* near her planeguard station, Peek thought that if *Voyager* had received both the turning course and the flying course as 220 degrees, she could have continued under the equivalent tactical rudder and ended astern of *Melbourne* with only a slight station adjustment required. Peek contended that a better method may have been to reduce speed and increase rudder. But if only the flying course were taken as 220 degrees, and *Voyager* thought she needed to wait for another executive signal, Peek said '*Voyager* would have to lose 30 degrees of bearing ... she would have to drop 30 degrees off *Melbourne*'s bow to be in station on a flying course of 220 degrees'. This meant that the turn to starboard may have been intended as a movement to lose bearing, something which did achieve a bearing loss of 25 degrees. At this point, the third theory returns to the previous two which suggest that port wheel was mistakenly left on.

None of Peek's theories was advanced with much conviction.

An alleged weakness in the theory that had *Voyager* moving to a mistaken course somewhere between 220 degrees and 270 degrees is that the destroyer's final movements would still have led to *Voyager* being some distance out of station on completion of the mistaken change of course. But if one considers *Voyager*'s previous efforts at stationing, which were no more than adequate for a ship on her first night of manoeuvres with a new bridge team, discounting the theory on these grounds is giving *Voyager*'s bridge staff more credit than they deserved, while the radar blind arc prevented her from precisely assessing her range from the carrier. The fact that this was the first night fleetwork exercise after a lengthy refit should have been given more weight in assessing the ability of *Voyager*'s bridge to sharpen their perceptive skills in exercising what is often called the 'seaman's eye'. But this was not something on which Captain Peek offered a comment.

The final question put to Peek by Meares was a loaded one, designed to obscure responsibility for the collision.

> Meares: May I put this to you now: that if it were your unfortunate task, having listened to the evidence, to reach any conclusion as to what happened in relation to *Voyager*, you would find yourself in the position, would you not, of saying: 'I simply cannot say?'
>
> Peek: Should I be put in that unfortunate position I would say that the matter was inexplicable.[145]

This was an admission of significance. Peek was here effectively agreeing that a Naval board of inquiry would be just as unlikely to find the cause of the collision. Of course, Peek could have said that the Commission had not heard the right evidence, or enough of it, but he did not. For those who were later to claim that a naval inquiry would have found the answer, Peek had already destroyed their case. All that now remained was for counsel to put their final submissions to the Commissioner.

# 7

# *The Appeal of Inexplicability*

T HE COMMISSION had so far heard 44 days of evidence and argument. There was some inconsistency and contradiction in what had been heard, and some of the matters on which Spicer would be expected to make a finding lacked a firm evidentiary foundation. For instance, could Spicer be certain about what Stevens actually did in the few minutes before the collision. But did it matter? Was it enough for Spicer simply to establish that Stevens was responsible, as commanding officer of *Voyager*? Was there enough evidence for Spicer to accept Robertson's reconstruction of the collision and its implicit consequences for his findings? The task of making plain the issues requiring a judgement was vested in Smyth, as counsel assisting. Smyth's only concern in the case was to serve the public interest, that is, to establish the facts relating to the collision and its causes, regardless of their consequences for the Navy or the Government.

Smyth began his summing up on 9 June 1964. He would speak for three days in an address that would take up 260 pages of transcript.[1] He dealt with the first and second terms of reference, which he considered under three headings. The first was the experience of each individual concerned with the navigation of the two ships; the second, the experience of each bridge in working as a team; and third, the experience of the two ships, as then manned, in manoeuvring together. He opened with Robertson.

Robertson was described by Smyth as a very competent captain of destroyers and small craft. But he had never commanded a carrier, had not been to sea for the previous three years, had not previously worked with anyone on *Melbourne*'s bridge other than Kelly, and even that had been nearly eight years earlier. Smyth pointed out that Robertson had never been OTC of a carrier and a destroyer manoeuvring together.

Kelly had not served at sea since early 1963 and this was his first experience as navigator in a carrier. Bate, by his own admission, was a relatively inexperienced OOW, while Jefferies, the 2nd OOW, had no prior experience in carriers. Everett, the tactical operators' supervisor, had previously served in *Melbourne* but had not, until five days before the collision, been stationed on the bridge. The carrier's starboard lookout, Ordinary Seaman Russell, had only six minutes' experience as a lookout. Smyth said that a more experienced lookout would have alerted the OOW. He then pointed out that it was only by chance that Kelly had noticed *Voyager*'s movements and taken positive action. The only person on the bridge of *Melbourne* that Smyth spoke of positively, in terms of experience, was Barker, who had served in *Voyager* until 9 August 1963, when he was posted to the carrier. But this was practically the first time Barker had taken charge of *Melbourne*'s bridge communications during tactical manoeuvring.

Smyth then examined the experience levels on *Voyager*'s bridge. He started with the only member of the bridge staff in whose experience he seemed to have had confidence. Smyth remarked that Stevens was a very competent destroyer captain and had considerable experience in operating with carriers in planeguard stations and in related manoeuvres. MacGregor was described as an experienced and competent seagoing officer, who served throughout 1963 in *Melbourne* as Fleet Gunnery Officer. Price's experience was limited to smaller vessels and he did not appear to have any prior experience in carrying out manoeuvres with carriers. He had not been to sea for over two years. Smyth concluded that inexperience did feature in the collision.

Referring to the second element of the inquiry — the experience of each bridge in working as a team — Smyth said it was limited to the previous five days. As to the third element — the experience of manoeuvring together prior to the exercise in which the collision occurred — Smyth said this was confined to manoeuvres which had taken place from 6 February 1964, and there had been virtually no practice of them prior to the collision. Smyth suggested that these manoeuvres, particularly those involving aircraft, which tended to distract bridge staffs, should have been conducted at a later stage in the work-up programme.

As for *Voyager*'s final movements, Smyth argued that *Melbourne* was unlikely to have been on course 020 degrees for much more than 90 seconds prior to the collision and that *Voyager*'s final turn to port was a result of the turning signal (to 020 degrees) rather than the flying course signal. Once she had altered to port, Smyth stated that *Voyager* held a steady course somewhere between 270 and 290 degrees. As the time-keeping in *Melbourne* was shown to have varied, Smyth contended that the reconstructions presented to the Commission by Robertson were not reliable.

Smyth submitted to the Commissioner that on the evidence, a finding was warranted that there was some misunderstanding between *Voyager* and *Melbourne* as to the course to which *Voyager* was ordered to turn. If there was such a finding, Smyth argued, then it also established the initiating cause of the collision. Smyth hinted at a possible reason for the misunderstanding. The naval system of acknowledging signals by use of the word 'Roger' rendered the occurrence of mistakes likely. He suggested that it should be revised by having each message repeated as received back to the originator. Smyth was here echoing the case earlier alluded to by Street. It appeared to him also that the failure of anyone on *Voyager*'s bridge to realise they were standing into danger was a crucial factor. He could not believe that no one on *Voyager*'s bridge was looking where the ship was heading.

Whatever the initiating cause, Smyth did not dispute what was known from the outset. Although *Voyager* may have mistaken or misinterpreted signals sent to her by *Melbourne*, she was clearly at fault in failing to maintain a proper lookout and failing to keep out of *Melbourne*'s way.

According to the rules of manoeuvring at sea, *Melbourne* did all that was required of her. But in terms of actually avoiding a dangerous navigational situation and ultimately the collision, Smyth was critical of Robertson who, he thought, should have intervened at a point when the collision could have been averted. Smyth asserted that Robertson's failure to intervene in time was a contributing cause of the collision. Concerning Bate, Smyth said he failed to keep a proper lookout and neglected to ensure that others were keeping a proper lookout. Bate's evidence that he saw Robertson go out onto the bridge-wing of *Melbourne*, but that he did not see him after that, supported Smyth's contention that Bate could not be sure that an officer was observing *Voyager*. Smyth said that if Bate had kept a proper lookout, a collision might have been avoided. Kelly was also implicated in Bate's alleged failure to carry out his duty properly as OOW.

Given his earlier attitude, Smyth was relatively charitable to the Navy in his remarks on the rescue of survivors and the state of *Voyager*'s equipment. He pointed out that of twenty-three escape hatches in *Voyager*, eleven were without wheel spanners, while one had been closed with the aid of a length of pipe to give added leverage to the wheel spanner. Some of the destroyer's emergency lighting failed to operate after the collision and the life jackets were not stowed in easily accessible locations throughout the ship. In concluding his submission on this term of reference, despite the shortcomings Smyth was satisfied that procedures and equipment met reasonable expectations. It was a better result than the Naval Board had expected.

Jenkyn was the next to deliver his final address, and he too spoke for three days.[2] Before he began, an urgent message was sent to the Naval Board from FOICEA staff stating that

> Smyth's submission indicated a deep-rooted criticism against *Melbourne* ... Navy's counsel desire a direction from the Board on the attitude they are to take on various points put forward by Mr Smyth.[3]

Jenkyn opened his address by confronting some of the general allegations that had been put to naval witnesses and by clarifying the nature of his brief — something he failed to do at the start of the Commission. Jenkyn stressed that the Department of the Navy did not want to conceal anything that would throw light on the causes of the collision.

> As Counsel for the Navy, I have no special brief for either *Melbourne* or *Voyager*, but I have a very real interest in seeing as far as possible that the real facts are ascertained irrespective of whether they justified proper criticism of those in command of either vessel.
>
> In particular, I am concerned that principles on which responsibility rested were correctly placed and that responsibility for the collision should not be placed upon the shoulders of any officer, or officers unless that responsibility was on the evidence, and on the evidence alone, clearly established in accordance with those principles.[4]

Jenkyn also emphasised that the Navy's operating procedures, particularly those relating to signalling, had been 'tempered by time and tested in the furnace of war. We feel that any criticism of those practices and standards should be advanced with much caution.'[5] Jenkyn lamented Smyth's attribution of sinister motives to some areas of evidence that could be simply explained. He mentioned the 'missing page' from the OOW's notebook, the critical appraisal of log entries, the lengthy cross-examination on erasures, and alterations and additions to reports. 'The net result has been, however, that a number of *Melbourne*'s officers have been placed under a cloud of suspicion ... a cloud under which they still remain ... because my friend [Smyth] has neglected to publicly withdraw what was implicit in his cross-examination of these witnesses.'[6]

Jenkyn commenced his version of the events leading to the collision by disputing Smyth's view that *Melbourne* was on a steady course of 020 for only ninety seconds before the collision. He said the evidence showed it was on such a course at least two and a half to three minutes before the collision. Upon receipt of the new flying signal, *Voyager* should have taken up her planeguard station 200 degrees relative to the flying course, that was 20 degrees on *Melbourne*'s port quarter on a true bearing of 220 degrees. Her actual movement, in turning initially to starboard, was upon receipt of the flying course signal. He rejected Smyth's assertion that the signal had been misinterpreted, because it could not be proved with evidence, although he could not prove that *Voyager* had indeed received or interpreted the signal correctly. To say that she turned upon receipt of the signal did not prove that it had been correctly relayed by Evans, Cullen or Price.

Jenkyn contended that a submission that *Voyager*'s final movements could be taken to be the result of mistaking a signal to turn to 020 degrees for a signal to turn to 220 degrees, not only failed to get support from a single knowledgeable witness, but was positively rejected by the experts who had been called, including Gatacre and Peek. The submission was not convincing because it necessitated a similar mistake in the flying course signal. If the turning signal, understood to be 220 degrees, was shortly afterwards followed by a flying course signal of 202 degrees, it would unquestionably call for an immediate verification. The possibility that the signal was incorrectly heard over the tactical voice net was discounted by Everett and Barker in *Melbourne*, and by Evans in *Voyager*. But as Evans was more likely to have made the error, it could be alleged that his view might have been coloured by self-interest.

Yet Jenkyn did not rule out the possibility of a mistake:

> We say it is possible that a mistake could have been made in *Voyager* as to the flying course signal, but no finding could be made to that effect. It is pure conjecture. There could not be a finding that Tactical Operator Evans made any such mistake without a grave injustice being done to him ... Evans was a very competent tactical operator and gave his evidence in a very commendable way. He must have created a very favourable impression in Your Honour's mind. It is very unlikely that Lieutenant Price, Communications Yeoman Cullen and Captain Stevens would have misinterpreted any signal properly given by Evans.[7]

After arguing that the Navy's signalling procedures and personnel were beyond criticism, Jenkyn did not see that his concession, virtually in the next sentence, that

> It is possible that upon receipt of the flying course signal, doubt was expressed by someone on the bridge of *Voyager* as to whether it was necessary to await a further signal,[8]

constituted a lack of confidence in both. First, because they could have produced doubt, the procedures were clearly not beyond improvement. Second, if the bridge staff of *Voyager* were beyond criticism, why did Jenkyn even admit the possibility that they may not have been familiar with signals that he had previously described as straightforward?

Jenkyn's address, surprisingly, raised more questions than it answered. It appeared as though he wanted the Commission to avoid coming to any definite findings. In considering *Voyager*'s failure to maintain a proper lookout, Jenkyn said

> It would seem that while a finding that there was an absence of a lookout in *Voyager* was inevitable, there was a far greater difficulty in determining what the circumstances were on board *Voyager* which caused or resulted in the failure of observation. This seems to be a real matter the Commission must look for.[9]

Jenkyn also agreed that *Voyager* did not appear to realise she was getting into a difficult position until collision was virtually inevitable. The absence of survivors from *Voyager* to testify what was in the minds of her bridge staff, Jenkyn submitted, meant the Commission would be unable to reach a finding on some aspects. For this reason, Jenkyn warned that it would be quite unfair to say with regard to *Melbourne* that you should tend to throw responsibility on that ship [*Melbourne*] because the people of *Voyager* are dead. It is wrong to say that therefore there should be a shrinking away from finding one way, but an ease in finding another way.[10]

It appeared as though he also wanted to persuade the Commission against making any finding of blame. He told Spicer that

to make positive findings of fact by way of speculation as to the reason for *Voyager*'s turn on to a collision course with *Melbourne*, and to conjecture from that speculative reason what officer or officers in *Voyager* were responsible for the cause of the course which was then pursued would, we believe be a most unjust way on which to base any possible condemnation. It would be more likely to lead to a miscarriage of justice than to the elucidation of the truth.[11]

This led Jenkyn to Robertson's role. Given that the Naval Board and Robertson did not necessarily share a common cause, that Robertson now had his own representation in Hicks and Raine, and that the Board stood to gain by diverting criticism for the collision onto Robertson, counsel for the Navy was remarkably generous to Robertson in his final submission.

Arguing against Smyth's submission that Robertson's failure to intervene was a cause of the collision, Jenkyn asserted that it was contrary to the law relating to contributory negligence.

The destroyer was playing a subsidiary role in the exercise ... the carrier had the right of way so that it could attend to its flying exercise without interruption.

It would be an understatement in these circumstances to say that Captain Robertson would have complete faith in Captain Stevens' ability to so control and manoeuvre his own destroyer ... that the possibility of a collision was unthinkable.[12]

Thus, when *Voyager* turned to starboard and then altered back to port, and it took her some time to steady on 020, this could have been interpreted by Robertson as *Voyager* being unsure as to whether she was required to move to planeguard station with this signal, or on receipt of an additional signal. This was a tacit admission of Gatacre's already discredited view. 'Nor could Captain Robertson for a moment have reasonably contemplated that the turn away to starboard after his flying course signal had been given was simply a preliminary move to a mistakenly contemplated turn of 220.'[13]

Jenkyn agreed that it was only about 45 seconds before the collision that Robertson became aware that *Voyager* was so near to the carrier and on a closing course, and he defended Robertson's lack of reaction.

Captain Robertson is being placed, at this stage, through no fault of his, in a position where the 'incredible' was about to take place, an 'incredible' that need not have taken place if 45 seconds before the collision, the *Voyager* up to that stage had turned away.[14]

Spicer interrupted and returned to the crucial argument put by Smyth that Robertson should have given *Voyager* some warning.

Spicer:    The 'incredible' need not have taken place if at the 45 seconds *Melbourne* had given five short blasts.

Jenkyn:    To have given five short blasts would have taken 15 seconds.

Spicer:    Well, pick up the telephone.

Jenkyn:    It has to be given, and while this is going on — is this in conjunction with the order 'engines full astern' or before 'engines full astern'?

Spicer:    I would have thought you could do both. He has an OOW there.

Jenkyn:    Is that not rather applying a standard of perfection to a person who is being put into a situation of almost mortal agony at that particular stage by an incredible happening? A criticism is being made of him that in the moment of agony he took a course which under all the laws, including the law as laid down in the House of Lords in the *Otranto* case, was said to be the action best calculated in these circumstances to assist, by a stand-on vessel, and that is to give engines full astern and that is precisely what he did do.[15]

Jenkyn went on to emphasise that whatever action *Melbourne* would have taken at that point would not have averted the collision because it was clear *Voyager* was unaware of her own position relative to *Melbourne* and would have needed to ascertain this before taking any remedial action. Jenkyn vigorously defended Robertson in arguing that his action was in no way a contributing factor because it could not be proved that he failed to do any part of his duty. Jenkyn cited *Halsbury's Laws of England* to highlight the correctness of Robertson's conduct.

> It must always be a matter of some difficulty for the officer in charge (OIC) of a stand-on vessel to determine when the time had arrived for him to take action and some latitude has to be allowed for him . . . it is quite impossible to determine mathematically the point at which the stand-on vessel must act . . . If the OIC is found to have been watching the other vessel and doing his best to make up his mind when to act, he ought not to be held to blame for waiting a moment too long before acting or acting too soon . . . The liability of the stand-on vessel is to be judged on the supposition that she is only aiding action by the other vessel and she is not to be held to blame because of the other vessel's inactivity.[16]

As for Bate and Kelly, the other two officers from *Melbourne*, remembering that they were now special responsibilities of his as Robertson had arranged separate counsel, Jenkyn stressed that they had done what was required of them, and expert opinion confirmed that this was so.

During the critical few minutes after 2052, Bate was conning the ship around from 060 to 020 degrees and had taken a bearing and range of *Voyager* to ascertain her position. Jenkyn also protested the assertion given prominence in the newspapers that Bate was to blame for the collision. The crux of Smyth's criticism of Kelly, that he was under an obligation to keep a lookout himself as Bate was inexperienced, was denied by Jenkyn, who contended that Kelly had reason to be confident in Bate's ability. He said that Bate had kept many day watches in *Melbourne* and had been given his watchkeeping certificate by Captain

Peek some months earlier. As Kelly had a number of other duties to perform, Jenkyn said it bordered on the absurd to suggest he should have been keeping a constant watch on the OOW.

In closing his address, Jenkyn returned to the theme with which he had begun:

> The reasons that prompted *Voyager*'s actions were unknown and are incapable on the evidence of being established by proper legal inference.
> The solution still remains as it was when this Commission started . . . in the realm of conjecture, and the collision is inexplicable.[17]

It was appropriate that Street, representing the interests of the Stevens family, should follow Jenkyn. This would give Street the opportunity to answer Jenkyn's criticisms of his (Street's) version of events.[18]

Throughout the Commission, Street had succeeded in deflecting Smyth and Spicer towards *Melbourne* and the actions of her officers. He had attacked the Navy counsel for siding with Robertson and isolating *Voyager*. The failure of Hicks to attack the Naval Board gave the added appearance of a common cause between Robertson and the Naval Board. As Robertson still considered he had a future in the Navy, he was naturally reluctant to criticise those who would determine his next promotion. The great strength of Street's argument was the evidence that there had been no difference of opinion within *Voyager*'s bridge staff as to their actions prior to the collision, and this suggested they knew, or thought they knew, where the destroyer was in relation to *Melbourne*. Street emphasised that 'somewhere in the passing of a word of mouth signal it is apparent, in our submission, that there had been a distortion . . . [and] we believe the basic cause of this collision was an inherent weakness in the signalling system'.[19]

To avoid drawing objections from Jenkyn, Street said he made no imputation against any tactical operator, but he suggested that the responsibility of passing verbal messages was too heavy to be placed on a man of junior rank. In asserting that there could be no criticism of Stevens's actions before the collision, Street was also attacking the line of argument that Stevens had become disoriented, which was not surprising. In addition to pointing out that for this to be true it would also need to apply to Price, Cook, MacGregor and Cullen, who were also on the bridge, Street was right to question the ease with which Stevens could have become disoriented. There were only two ships involved in the exercise. The previous manoeuvres had been straightforward and the ships had changed course in a substantial way only once.

There was one more compelling factor that Street should have mentioned. At every point in her final manoeuvre, *Voyager* was able to see *Melbourne*'s starboard sidelight. It was the only green light and witnesses had claimed it was visible from *Voyager* even at a range of

2,000 yards. Thus, *Voyager* was constantly in a position to see she was on *Melbourne*'s starboard side.

Street advanced a theory that conflicted with Robertson's evidence. Street argued that the short turn to starboard was a station-keeping manoeuvre carried out at 2051 or 2052, while *Melbourne* was still steering 060 degrees, but that it was only detected after *Melbourne* had turned to the new course of 020 degrees. As the turning course signal was sent at 2052, *Voyager* was returning a heading of 060 degrees, accounting for the visibility of the starboard sidelight, and reversed wheel to port in response to that signal. Street postulated that *Voyager* misinterpreted that signal as ordering a course to the west — possibly 270 degrees — and believed *Melbourne* to be turning. The flying course was sent at 2053 and was again mistaken to be a westerly course. For the next three minutes, *Voyager* failed to appreciate that *Melbourne* had not turned, and the collision resulted.

Although Street argued in his submission that 'the basic cause of the collision was the inherent weakness of the signalling system',[20] in a letter to me, Street said:

> The difficulty, of course, lies in the human problem that those who mistakenly transpose figures are not even themselves aware of their mistake and thus there was no positive evidence to support my theory.[21]

(As the signalling system did not permit the repeating back of messages, *Melbourne* had no way of knowing, other than for the signal to be actually queried, that it was correctly received and relayed within *Voyager*. The signalman was the only link between two ships moving at high speed.)

Evans having said he received the turning course signal as 020 degrees, Street asked the all-important question: did he actually say 020 when relaying it to Stevens and Price? Again, to avoid a challenge from Jenkyn, Street said he did not question the truthfulness of Evans, although he had mixed up call signs during cross-examination, but asked whether Evans could possibly know that he had said the wrong course. Street asked Spicer to find that the course *Voyager* was steering was 270 degrees and that *Voyager* would only have steered such a course if directed.

Favouring the evidence that *Voyager* was on a steady course prior to the collision, Street argued that this course must have been between 270 and 290 degrees. This revealed a weakness in Street's argument. It would have been more convincing if the course was a variation of the numerals two and zero, such as 200, 202 or 220.[22] Unchallenged on this weakness in his version of the collision, Street stated that none of the preceding counsel 'has thought it permissible from all the evidence to seek to ascribe any specific aspect of fault against *Voyager* or her captain'.[23] This was too much to claim, but it stood, because Jenkyn had concentrated on rebutting any suggestion that the Navy's signalling methods were flawed.

Street's theory had a number of weaknesses. It is unlikely that Price would have waited almost ten minutes to put *Voyager* in her correct station after her alteration to 020 degrees. At any rate, Evans stated that Stevens realised *Voyager* was out of station by 2048 and that prompt action followed. This movement to regain station would also have needed to be slight, despite *Voyager* being some 25 degrees ahead of her station, for it to have eluded detection by *Melbourne*. In sum, it is most unlikely that *Voyager* was not in her correct station by 2052 when the turning course signal was sent. Street's theory must also reject Robertson's evidence that he saw the destroyer alter to starboard immediately after the flying course signal was sent.[24] The effect of Street's theory was to reduce to a minimum the involvement of Stevens and any failure of judgement he showed in *Voyager*'s last few moments.

This view reflected that of Sir Jack Stevens, who had made his own independent detailed analysis of the collision. He thought that the final signal was 'distorted' to '270 or something like that' in being passed within *Voyager*. When the final signal confirming 020 degrees as the course for flying operations was received, Stevens detected

> a difference in what he believed had been the immediately prior signal and this one, went to the chart table to compare the two signals under the only light available, stepped back to the bridge and gave his final order in an attempt to avoid the collision. Captain Peek's evidence that no competent captain would take his eyes off the other ship in such a manoeuvre is far too dogmatic in the circumstances as I interpret them.[25]

Meares was the next to present his final submission and continued to support Street and their common cause.[26] In his submission he said that there was no evidence that *Voyager*'s officers had been distracted, and the failure to see *Melbourne* was therefore the fault of every person on the destroyer's bridge. Meares strengthened Street's argument by agreeing that *Voyager*'s final turn was the result of a corrupted signal. It was argued that Evans passed the signal having transposed the first two words in it. If he transposed the first two words, that is, Foxtrot Corpen 020 was reported as Corpen Foxtrot 020, Meares suggested, he would have given a turning signal. There was also the possibility that he jumbled the numerals and gave a course around 200 degrees, although Meares was unable to counter the evidence, as it was then accepted, that *Voyager* had been on a steady course to the west, or north of west. These courses would have included the numeral 7, 8 or 9. However, Meares's theory impressed Spicer, who subsequently praised its cogency.

As expected, Meares echoed the contention offered by Street that no adverse finding could be brought against Stevens. This being the case, Meares submitted that no blame could be found on the part of Price or anyone else on *Voyager*'s bridge. Gregory told me that the best they could hope for was a finding that the collision was inexplicable.[27]

The end of Meares's address brought Hicks to his feet and a change of pace for the Commission.[28] Hicks began his address with a long preamble in which he described the position of Robertson before the Commission. He said Robertson was a witness like any other who had been called to ascertain the facts relating to the collision. Hicks attacked Smyth bitterly for the evidence he put before the Commission and the way in which he had led it as counsel assisting. This made it appear as though there was a case being put against Robertson, in the first instance, and the bridge staff of *Melbourne*, in the second. Hicks stated that Robertson had been put in a defensive position from the day the inquiry started, and this led Hicks to attack the conduct of the Royal Commission itself:

> We would say that we trust this is not a situation where you will get a trial by Royal Commission, because that is opposed to every basic tenet of justice and would be unfair and would involve a miscarriage of justice.[29]

Robertson's case had much in common with that presented by the Navy, with Hicks agreeing with Jenkyn's conclusion that *Voyager* was at fault in failing to keep out of the carrier's way, but that the reasons for this and the causes of the collision were inexplicable. However, realising that the case put by Street and Meares for *Voyager* left too much 'in the air' and allowed too much space for a criticism of Robertson, Hicks attacked Meares's submission that the signal was corrupted on two grounds. First, that it could not have happened, and second, that it was opposed to all the evidence. Spicer dealt with the first objection: 'I do not know. I think Mr Meares did not make a bad fist of it. You cannot dismiss it out of hand, I do not think.' As for the second, it was not demonstrably opposed to the evidence. It was more a matter of it being very possible, but without evidential support. Certainly it was wrong for Hicks to say it was opposed or in conflict with the evidence. But Hicks then effectively played into Meares's hands by seeking to show that *Voyager* was on a continuous turn to port, which would have given her a heading similar to that required in Meares's theory. This was part of his argument for the timing of Robertson's reaction to *Voyager*'s final turn.

Hicks warned the Commission not to make the mistake of viewing the situation before the collision with the benefit of hindsight, and to use an accepted legal standard in determining when Robertson should have acted. This brought something near an apology from Spicer:

> This troubles me more than anything else and all I am saying is that, does not a point of time come, and maybe it is too late, when he says this turn to port is more than an ordinary alteration of course, it is going on too long? I know it is all in a small space of time. It does come, but the whole point is: when should it have come?[30]

It was becoming obvious that Spicer would need to be convinced that this moment of time was very close to when Robertson actually reacted. Hicks attempted to persuade Spicer:

> Captain Robertson decided to take action at a point which cannot be precisely fixed, but which was probably about half to three-quarters of a minute before the collision ... That is when he went into the pelorus platform to give the order 'full astern'.[31]

Spicer was still not convinced:

> I think we can take that as being a bit after the time when he first had doubts. I am only wondering, when he first had the doubts, whether he should have done something by way of warning.[32]

Hicks's reply had little chance of convincing a sceptical Commissioner:

> Captain Robertson has told the Commission that he cannot tell at what time he had doubts, but it could not have been a long period of time.[33]

Realising that the various theories being proposed did not strengthen his position, Hicks kept his arguments to matters that could be established. He submitted that *Voyager* was on a continuous turn and that the final manoeuvre was initiated by the flying course signal, alternatively that the starboard turn was contemporaneous with the flying course signal or so close to it as to give that appearance to Robertson. Hicks's strongest argument was that even if Robertson had warned *Voyager* or taken evasive action before he did, that would still not have avoided a collision. Therefore, Robertson was distanced from any blame. He rejected the imputation of Smyth's remarks that the duties of the OTC imposed some absolute responsibility on Robertson. There was no regulation to support this view. Stevens at all times remained totally responsible for his ship and its safe navigation.

While Robertson felt betrayed by Becher, he openly expressed the loyalty he felt he owed to Bate, whom he sought to protect. In private notes prepared for Hicks, Robertson stated:

> I would like to make it quite clear that I personally would completely exonerate Bate from any implication at all in the causes of the collision. By regulation he has the safety of the ship on his shoulders. However, I was there, I was watching, and I was in command. I should like to make it abundantly clear in the [final] address that I do not blame Bate in any way.[34]

In the final instance, Robertson's case revolved around the question posed by his solicitor, Rear-Admiral Harold Farncomb. What would a reasonably competent man do, knowing there is a reasonably competent man in the other ship, experienced in destroyers and in working with carriers? There were two ways of handling this question. The first was to portray and explain Robertson's behaviour in terms used in the question, that is, Robertson acted as a 'reasonably competent man'. The second was to challenge its fundamental assumption, that is, that the other man was not reasonably competent. Robertson and Hicks decided on the former method, rather than attack the competence of *Voyager*'s bridge staff. In the context of a Royal Commission, with two of *Voyager*'s officers represented by very able senior counsel, this was probably the wisest course of action and the one most likely to appeal to Spicer. As Robertson's was the only side likely to probe the ability of *Voyager*'s officers in any depth, the officers and men of the destroyer were spared the investigation that *Melbourne*'s officers endured.

Having a right of reply, Smyth defended his submissions throughout the Commission.[35] He started by claiming an injustice had been done to Evans, whom he described as a 'very fine young man'. He said there was no evidence to support the view put by Street and Meares that Evans had erred, while Evans himself had never ceased to claim that he had interpreted the signal correctly. But, once again, this was not the argument that had been put. It was suggested that Evans may have *relayed* the order incorrectly. There was never a suggestion that he interpreted it incorrectly. Nor did Smyth take totally into account the changes in Evans's statement or Patterson's additional evidence.

Smyth restated his view that *Voyager* had been turning in accordance with the turning signal rather than a flying course signal, and said he thought there had been some misunderstanding on *Voyager*'s bridge as to what the destroyer had to do. This was, in effect, little different from what Street and Meares had argued, albeit on a different premise.

Smyth's most strident criticism was left to last. He referred the Commission to *Regulations and Instructions for the RAN*, paragraph 2704, where the responsibilities of Flag or Senior Officers towards their fleet, squadrons or ships under their command are laid down. Under these circumstances, Smyth submitted that Robertson should have taken positive control of *Voyager* when he saw her make a turn to starboard (assuming this followed the turning signal and preceded the flying signal). In Smyth's opinion, the time to intervene would have been long before the collision became inevitable. By his calculation it was at two and a half minutes before the collision.

Spicer seemed persuaded by Smyth's submissions, although he was attracted by the argument put by Street and Meares. He later said:

> If the view is accepted that messages were transmitted from *Melbourne* ... and were received in *Voyager*, then obviously if the messages had been obeyed there would have been no collision. So something must have happened in *Voyager*, some mistake has taken place which was the initial cause of the collision. What it was, we do not know.[36]

With this sombre reflection, the inquiry ended its public sittings at 1445 on 25 June after the recording of 4,380 pages of transcript, and the Commissioner retired to prepare his report. The Commission had cost taxpayers in excess of £150,000. Spicer was now on his own. What he thought of Robertson's actions loomed as the most potentially contentious aspect of his report.

It would be far from true to suggest that all naval officers believed Robertson was completely blameless. A signal issued to the British Far East Fleet by its commander-in-chief, on receiving news of the collision, implied a judgement on Robertson:

> Commanding officers are reminded of the following points:
>
> 1. It is exceptionally difficult for an escort to judge inclination and varying rate of turn of a carrier.
> 2. The large number of red lights in a carrier are confusing.
> 3. The safest method is to keep planeguard astern when executing the signal to proceed to planeguard station at a safe and appropriate moment during a turn into the wind.[37]

The very selective content of this communication suggested some of the areas in which one very senior Royal Navy officer believed Captain Robertson may have been unwise. Paragraph three implied that Robertson would have been better served by turning the ships in succession rather than together at 2041. Had he executed the turn in this way, *Voyager* would never have been ahead of the carrier. This was a signal that did not receive wide circulation.

A retired RAN admiral, in a letter to me, commented on this very matter:

> The Commission failed to pursue why *Melbourne*, in the initiation of wind-chasing, did not adopt the simpler, prudent, seamanlike option of tucking *Voyager* in astern and altering course by corpen. Such action would have obviated any chance of collision, notwithstanding possible errors in transmission or receipt of course heading.[38]

In an earlier interview, the same admiral had argued that Robertson should have sounded a warning and taken more bearings of *Voyager* than he did.[39]

The view that Robertson should have stationed *Voyager* in 'Formation 1' — directly astern of *Melbourne* — was advocated by Admiral Sir Victor Smith, a one-time captain of *Melbourne*, who said this would have relieved Robertson of any concern about the destroyer's whereabouts while he was searching for the wind.[40]

Another retired admiral, who had commanded *Melbourne* during his career, said:

> It could also be postulated that the first mistake might have been the signalling of a new flying course of 020 degrees whilst both ships were still completing a turn together to a new course. If (and here is the wisdom of hindsight) both ships had been allowed to settle on the new course of 020 degrees, *Voyager* may have been less disoriented during the assumption of her planeguard station, if that is in fact what happened.[41]

In notes later issued by the RAN Navigation School at HMAS *Watson*, there were several points of guidance which supported these views:

(a) Do not execute the next manoeuvre before all ships have completed the current one.

(b) Do not alter course or speed whilst a manoeuvre is being executed.

(c) Keep an eye on the navigational safety of all ships.

(d) Watch the positions of all ships relative to their correct stations and delay executing the next signal if necessary.

The challenge for Spicer was to arrive at a finding which accounted for the collision. This would not be easy. Other than Smyth, who sought to blame Robertson and the cumulative effect of deficient naval procedures, every interested party represented at the Commission had argued that the collision was inexplicable. If the causes of the collision could not be found, it was impossible to apportion blame. It remained for Spicer to decide whether he had been presented with enough evidence, given that the officers on *Voyager*'s bridge had all been lost, to form conclusions on which to base findings. Spicer would have been aware that a finding of inexplicability would not be popular with the public.

# 8

# The Spicer Report

T HE COMMISSIONER completed his report on 13 August 1964 and presented it to the Governor-General.[1] It was made public on 26 August when tabled by Menzies in Federal Parliament. It produced a range of public reactions. The tabloid *Daily Mirror* instructed its readers to expect 'the most important document in the history of Australia's armed forces ... The report is expected to produce the most searching examination ever conducted of an Australian fighting service, in which efficiency, organisation and procedure will be highlighted.'[2]

Something much less than that was actually received. Press analysis of the Spicer Report was superficial, with most space devoted to extracts from it. The headlines were consistent. The *Sun* led with 'Judge Puts Blame on *Voyager*'; the *Australian* with '*Voyager* to Blame'. Having decided that the Commissioner failed to provide some answers, the editorial writer at the *Daily Mirror* suggested:

> it could well be time that we brought in some top naval troubleshooter from elsewhere ... Traditionally, we would expect any imported expert to come from the Royal Navy, but there is no special reason why this should be so. In fact, it is more probable today that we could find the right man in the United States Navy, the world's biggest, whose attempts to eliminate human error go as far as running 'dry' [alcohol prohibited] ships.[3]

The *Age* brought down its verdict on the report on 1 September, after its correspondents in the parliamentary press gallery had had time to assess the reaction of government ministers. It revealed that

> Ministers are frankly disappointed in the report ... No one questions Sir John's finding that a turn by *Voyager* beyond the course set by *Melbourne* was the primary cause of the collision. But Sir John also noted, as possible contributory causes, what to ministers seem to be serious departures from the standards of efficiency expected of the Navy.
>
> What worries ministers is that Sir John suggested neither reasons nor remedies for these apparent shortcomings ... Ministers feel Sir John's report has raised too many doubts about naval efficiency for the Government to take no action, but they are uncertain about the action to be taken.[4]

The *Age* followed this report with an editorial statement that

'Reaction to the royal commission report on the *Voyager* has, on the whole, been highly critical ... Most people expected the inquiry to provide a clear-cut explanation of why it happened and who was responsible.' The editorial concluded with the hope that the deficiencies of the report might be remedied when it was the subject of parliamentary debate to 'ensure that no allegations go unchallenged, that no suspicions are allowed to linger, and that confidence in the Navy is restored'.

The *Daily Mirror*'s political correspondent, Ray Kerrison, reported that one angry MP said, 'By the tone of this report you would think the sinking of *Voyager* was a naval victory. Members from both sides of the House privately expressed feelings ranging from quiet concern to outright dismay.'[5] Both Sir John Bunting and Menzies's daughter have confirmed that the Prime Minister was disappointed with the Spicer Report. I also spoke with other government ministers of that period who were of the same general opinion.

Most analysts agreed that the RAN had emerged relatively unscathed. The *Age* reported that

> At navy headquarters the general reaction to the Royal Commissioner's report was a feeling of relief. Sir John Spicer had not been nearly so critical as some people had feared.[6]

In comparison with other Royal Commission reports of the period, the Spicer Report was of average length. The Royal Commissioner obviously tried to keep his report as brief as possible, while using very straightforward language. However, the narrative was disjointed and often confusing. The report alternated without warning between Spicer's own view and that of counsel, and he consistently neglected to cite the evidence and the argument on which his conclusions and findings were based.

There was not a single political commentator nor a politician who was prepared to say it was a good report. It was apparent that Spicer had not grasped the significance of much of the evidence, as the report is characterised by speculation and tentative assertion.

The structure of the document was roughly along the lines of the terms of reference. Spicer opened his report by describing the two ships, the officers responsible for their safe operation, the collision and the damage to both vessels. There followed a narrative of the signals and movements prior to the collision and Spicer's conclusion that some confusion may have been created by the existence of several conflicting interpretations on *Voyager*'s bridge of signals sent by *Melbourne*. He wrote: 'The operative effect of the last flying course signal is not wholly free from doubt ... The evidence does not disclose which view was held by Captain Stevens or other officers in *Voyager*.'[7]

Spicer then offered his first controversial finding, which was that

*Voyager* was on a steady course of around 270 degrees prior to the collision. After pointing out the degree of uncertainty created by varying recorded times for *Melbourne*'s signals, Spicer 'inclines to the view' rather than reaches a 'firm conclusion' that *Voyager*'s final movements were induced by the turning course signal, which he agrees was sent at 2052. What effect the flying course signal, which he says was sent at 2054 or 2055, had on *Voyager*'s bridge staff Spicer neglects to say. His explanation for the short starboard turn was lame. It was the result of some initial misunderstanding of the turning course signal. As a purported finding of fact, this was highly dubious.

The Royal Commissioner then returns to his finding that *Voyager* was on a steady course, and attempts to provide justification. The only firm evidence he cites is that of Dadswell. 'I attach considerable importance to this evidence of an independent observer as indicating the nature of the tracks of the two vessels immediately before the collision.'[8] This implied that he was unable to accept Robertson's evidence, primarily because he was an interested party in the Commission. He also found that *Melbourne* steadied on 020 degrees at 2055, just as the flying course was being signalled, rather than at 2053 (or slightly before), as Robertson contended.

Yet his explanations for these findings were far from convincing. Dadswell was presumably concentrating on flying above the ships at nearly 200 knots, in darkness, and was not prepared to say he was absolutely certain that *Voyager* was on a straight course for at least a minute, as Spicer concluded.[9] Degenhardt could not remember the course the helmsman was supposedly given to steer after the starboard and port alterations of course. As for the voice in the water shouting the course '270 degrees', it did not necessarily mean the ship had reached that course by the time of the collision.

In sum, the evidence simply did not support Spicer's conclusions. If *Voyager* steadied on 270 degrees at 21 knots for more than one minute prior to the collision, working back she would have had to bear about 060 degrees and be 1,700 yards from *Melbourne* at 2053 (Figure 26). The collision would then have occurred at 2057. However, as it was generally agreed (including by Spicer) that the collision occurred at 2056, by 2057 *Melbourne* would have gained more than 700 yards and *Voyager* would have passed astern. In other words, *Voyager* was either making good a speed of 27 knots during a turn (this would have required her to have engine revolutions ordered for 29 or 30 knots) or Spicer's finding was a physical impossibility. It also plainly contradicted another of his findings: that *Melbourne* had settled on course 020 degrees for more than one minute, despite a firm body of evidence that it had been more like three minutes.

There was another major shortcoming in the report. Spicer acknowledged that there was some variation in the times that signals were logged by *Melbourne*. The only time recorded in *Melbourne*'s log for the flying course signal was 2054. By this time *Voyager* was well on her port turn and the signal, if sent at this time, did not alter her actions. The time logged for the turning course was 2052 in the ship's log and 2053 in the tactical operator's log. Working back from the time of collision as his datum, Robertson's various reconstructions led him to record it as four and a quarter minutes before the collision. Robertson made less of the actual times and more of the sequence of events and the evidence for the order in which they occurred. This made good sense, given the difficulties presented by the inaccurate timekeeping.

Without justifying his methodology, Spicer chose 2042 — the alteration from 190 to 060 degrees — as his datum and worked forward.[10] The problem with this method of reconstruction was that Spicer was forced to accept some of the obviously inaccurate times recorded in the logs (evidenced by the physical improbability of several manoeuvres being conducted in the time his scheme required them to be completed) and this left his reconstruction with very little time in which to have *Melbourne* settle on 020 degrees and for *Voyager* to settle on or about 270 degrees. Events were therefore crammed into the period 2054 to 2056. In effect, Spicer was inclined to accept evidence relating to *Voyager*'s movement over that confirming *Melbourne*'s movement. Thus, *Melbourne*'s was determined, and made subject to, that of *Voyager*.

If the evidence of Robertson or naval architect Robert Herd is accepted, *Melbourne* was on a steady course for some three minutes prior to the collision.[11] The carrier's theoretical and actual turning data permits such a conclusion. Before steadying on 020 degrees, Robertson's bearing of *Voyager* was 040 degrees. While the ship was still turning, the flying course was sent. *Voyager* was then at a range of 1,200 yards. The alteration of courses to starboard (to 060 degrees) and then to port (back to 020 degrees) took 40 seconds. Under port wheel, the destroyer's advance (at 18 to 19 knots) was 600 yards. By the roughest measure, it can be seen that if *Melbourne* remained steady on 020 degrees at 21 knots (she was more than likely steaming at 19 or 20 knots), it would take at least two minutes for the collision to occur. Thus, unless one is prepared to conclude that Robertson and Kelly knowingly misled the inquiry, the flying course must have been sent slightly more than three minutes prior to the collision.

Criticisms of Spicer's reconstruction can be taken even further. If 2042 is the accepted datum, the duration of turns and time spent on steady courses can be used to verify its accuracy as a starting point. If the turn from 190 degrees to 020 degrees takes five minutes thirty seconds (a conservative estimate based on a tactical diameter of 2,400 yards under 10 degrees of rudder) and that course is held for one minute, a period generally agreed by Spicer, the alteration to 060 degrees was ordered at 2048 and 30 seconds. The turn to 060 degrees took one minute and was then held for four minutes, again an accepted duration, the return to 020 degrees must have been ordered at 2053 and 30 seconds. If the turn from 060 degrees to 020 degrees took another minute, the flying course would have been sent very near to 2055. *Melbourne* is then on a steady course of 020 for one minute and the collision occurs at 2056. This was definitely not a view put by any counsel at the inquiry.

If, however, the very strong evidence is accepted that *Melbourne* was on a steady course for three minutes, the collision would need to have occurred at 2058. To make the sequence of known events fit within parameters he had set himself, Spicer selectively discarded the evidence that *Melbourne* was on a steady course for three minutes. If he accepted that the turning course was sent at 2052, and this he appears to have done, he should have argued *Melbourne* took three minutes to achieve an alteration of course from 060 to 020 degrees — a mere 40 degrees. The technical data does not support this view. It would be nearing exaggeration to say the carrier would take much more than sixty seconds to achieve this alteration. One could also add that *Melbourne*'s trim (the fore and aft inclination of the ship) was at that time favouring a slightly tighter turning regime.

If one also accepted Spicer's conclusion that *Voyager*'s final movement was in response to the turning signal, and that the flying signal was sent at 2055, it produces the unlikely situation that *Voyager* was already well advanced on her port turn and had turned beyond the signalled course of 020 degrees. Unless there was a mistaken signal, there is no reason to believe she would not have settled on 020 degrees. A contrary conclusion also conflicts with evidence that *Voyager* steadied briefly on 020 degrees. It is equally difficult to conclude that *Voyager* would have taken three minutes to achieve a turn of 40 degrees. One minute or less would have been needed to complete the alteration of course. Spicer effectively became entangled in his own conclusions, which became more awkward and less convincing as they were advanced to cover a longer period and additional manoeuvres. Whatever way the finding is analysed, it conflicts with much of the evidence presented to the Commission, especially that given by Robertson and Kelly.

The cause of the collision, Spicer concluded, was the failure of *Voyager*'s bridge to maintain an effective lookout. This was obvious from the first day. However, he was not prepared to be specific in allocating individual blame. Having ascertained that the destroyer was at fault, Spicer sought to establish whether *Melbourne* may have contributed to the cause of the collision. This covered over eight pages of the report and included a portion of transcript, an extract from *Regulations and Instructions for the RAN*, the citation of findings by Lord Buckmaster in *SS Kitano Maru* vs *SS Otranto*, and a quotation from *Halsbury's Laws of England*. The latter two related to interpretation of the international rules for the prevention of collision at sea. They were largely irrelevant, given the circumstances of the collision, but they allowed Spicer to quote from some legal authorities in support of his wholly uncomplicated judgements. Then followed the most controversial part of his report.

Whereas Spicer passed no remark about the conduct of *Voyager*'s officers, he made direct comment on the actions of the three officers on *Melbourne*'s bridge. He dealt with Robertson first. After indicating that he could not criticise Robertson for the timing of ordering the carrier's engines astern, the Commissioner stated:

> In my opinion it should have been indicated by three short blasts but the failure to give that signal did not, in my opinion, contribute to the disaster save to the extent that even the first blast at an appropriate stage may have served as a warning and been sufficient to alert *Voyager* to a danger of which those in control of her may not have been aware.[12]

Spicer then considered whether Robertson should have queried *Voyager*'s movements when she altered course back to port (Figure 27).

> The moment *Voyager* turned to port forward of the beam her action should, as it seems to me, have created some doubt at least in Captain Robertson's mind as to what her intentions were, and the moment the movement to port passed beyond such as would have brought her back on course, it seems to me that Captain Robertson should have made some enquiry or passed some signal, whether by whistle or otherwise, to *Voyager*. Whether action of this kind would have avoided the collision I am unable to say, but I feel that the chances of a collision occurring might have been lessened if some such action as I have indicated had been taken by Captain Robertson.
>
> I cannot but feel that some such action would have been taken by a more experienced officer in tactical command and it may be that his inexperience, coupled with his knowledge of the experience and capacity of Captain Stevens, led to some hesitation in interfering on this particular occasion.[13]

He dealt next with Kelly. Noting that Bate possessed only limited experience, the criticism was short and to the point: 'I think in all the circumstances Commander Kelly should himself have paid more regard to *Voyager*'s movements than he did.'[14]

As for Bate himself,

> In these circumstances I think he failed to exercise sufficient care as officer of the watch to protect his own vessel from collision. He did not himself maintain sufficient watch over *Voyager* at a time when he was unaware whether any other watch was being maintained on the bridge.[15]

He was also critical of Bate for not giving some warning to *Voyager*.

The failure to make any signal to *Voyager* was at the focus of the Commissioner's criticisms:

> I am unable to comprehend why no warning was given to *Voyager*. Ready means of communication were available and some warning, even at a late stage, would seem to have been a wise course of action.[16]

The comment that VHF radio should have been used to warn of a collision was often heard in marine inquiries during this period. The loss of the luxury liner *Andrea Doria* after a collision with *Stockholm* in 1956 highlighted the contribution VHF communications could have made to collision avoidance. This prompted international efforts to make it mandatory for all vessels over 300 tons to be fitted with VHF radios and for them to be used in aiding safe navigation. Given that there were some cases where misuse of VHF communication had actually contributed to a collision, the benefits of this navigational 'aid' were probably overstated in the early 1960s. Although Spicer did not suggest anything unreasonable, most navigators, if placed in the position of Robertson or Kelly, would have thought about their own ship first. Whether or not issuing warnings or commands to *Voyager* over VHF radio would have prompted the best avoiding action by the destroyer is speculatory.

How harsh were Spicer's remarks on the performance of *Melbourne*'s officers, especially Robertson? Did they constitute a comment or a criticism? If it was the latter, did it amount to saying that Robertson had been negligent and, therefore, at fault? If Robertson were at fault, it would involve both causative potency and blameworthiness.[17] This constituted, in the words of Lord Maugham,

> a failure to exercise that degree of the skill and care which are ordinarily to be found in a competent seaman ... It is negligent not to take all reasonable steps to avoid danger in navigation, and the nature of those steps must of course depend on the surrounding circumstances, and they may call for the utmost possible precautions.[18]

The substance of Spicer's remarks, which were unconditional and admitting of no mitigating circumstances, constituted a criticism of Robertson so severe that it implied he was at fault and, therefore, partly to blame for the collision. Adopting Maugham's description of negligence by a mariner, Spicer had concluded that Robertson did not take all reasonable steps to avoid danger, and had been negligent.

Perhaps Spicer did not realise the manner in which his assessment of Robertson's performance would be received by Robertson, or any naval officer. Conversely, Robertson would not have been aware that in the vast majority of collisions at sea involving merchant ships, very few resulted in court actions where one ship was completely freed from blame. While it is one thing to apportion blame for the specific purpose of deciding damages in a civil action, it is very difficult for any party involved in a collision to be completely absolved from some contributory role. There is great wisdom in the old nautical adage that 'A superior seaman uses his superior judgement to keep out of situations requiring his superior skills'.

The section dealing with contributing causes was a rambling and unrelated group of paragraphs that did not lead to any clear conclusion.

Spicer was in no doubt that both ships were fully prepared for sea service of the type in which they were engaged before the collision. Despite the expectations of the press, not one contributory cause was identified.

The latter part of the report covered the rescue and treatment of survivors. Spicer was satisfied that the Navy responded effectively and efficiently to *Melbourne*'s signals and he could not criticise Robertson's decision not to send a distress signal to all ships. As for the recovery of survivors, the Commissioner praised the evacuation which showed 'a considerable absence of panic among men'. As for the sinister absence of wheel spanners, Spicer concluded: 'There does not appear to have been any loss of life due to the absence of wheel spanners.'[19]

Although Spicer was critical of the Navy's provisional swimming test and the fact that some men could hardly be called swimmers, he concluded that 'it seems unlikely that very many men were lost once they had escaped from the ship'.[20] He was also satisfied that sufficient survival and life-preserving equipment was available, and was full of praise for the handling of survivors and their subsequent treatment.

The report ended with six appendixes. The first was a list of the names of those lost in the collision. The next five were reconstructions; the first, by Robertson, was submitted with his initial report to the Naval Board. The second was a rough drawing by Dadswell. The third and fourth were those made by Robertson on 5 March and 6 May respectively. The final reconstruction was produced at the Commission after the evidence of Herd had been considered. As stated earlier, Spicer did not offer a reconstruction of his own based on his findings. (Had he done so it would have looked significantly different to that proposed by Robertson.) This was a major shortcoming of the report.

Many of Spicer's findings and conclusions should have come as no surprise to the Naval Board. On 16 July 1964, Rear-Admiral Peek submitted a number of questions to Harrington about the Navy's possible responses to the Commission's findings. The Naval Board was already bracing itself for a finding critical of the three *Melbourne* officers 'for a lack of judgement or slow reaction time'. In answer to a question about what the Navy would do if there were no court martial, the Deputy CNS, Rear-Admiral Tom Morrison, stated that if the Board agreed with the Commission's findings it would either admonish or reprimand any officers concerned. If it disagreed, no action would be taken.

On 29 July, Smith raised with Harrington the 'possible advantages of a Board of Inquiry into the *Voyager* loss'. This notion was apparently still in the minds of Board members and, from Smith's comments, it was effectively the preferred option.[21]

Towards the end of June 1964, anticipating the release of the Spicer Report, Harrington asked for expert legal advice on the way ahead. The

Board received confidential information from its Chief Naval Judge Advocate (CNJA), Commander Larry Winch, on 31 July. He warned the Board that Spicer would complete his report on 21 August 1964 but that the Navy had virtually no chance of having Spicer privately reconsider his findings or recommendation before the Report was publicly released. The Department of Civil Aviation had approached Spicer after he concluded his report into the crash of a Viscount airliner to reconsider some of his recommendations because they were difficult to apply. Spicer had bluntly refused.[22]

At the same time, Winch also gave the Naval Board some advice, as specifically requested by Harrington, on how to handle the release of the Report.[23] Taking his lead from Smyth's final address, Winch thought the Report might be critical of Robertson, Kelly and Bate and find that they were negligent in failing to perform their duties properly. If this were the finding, the Board had two choices: first, determine whether the evidence adduced at the Commission produced a *prima facie* case against them; or second, ignore the Commission and set up a Naval board of inquiry under *Regulations and Instructions for the RAN* (Article 2301), with the possibility of a subsequent court martial. Winch strongly recommended against the second course because

> the transcript of the Royal Commission contains a full account of all witnesses who could throw any light on the tragedy. The evidence adduced at the Royal Commission can be used as the basis for an application for trial by court martial but the evidence cannot be used at such a trial in support of the charge. Such a charge must be supported by evidence given afresh and under oath by witnesses called for the purpose.[24]

A problem could arise, however, if one of the officers criticised by Spicer wanted to be court martialled to 'clear the air'. Other than during war service, the *Naval Discipline Act* did not give any officer the right to claim trial by court martial. However, a convening authority could grant a request for court martial if satisfied that (a) the charges to be laid were correct and sufficient; (b) that they were properly framed and carefully drawn up; and (c) that the evidence, if contradicted or unexplained, would probably suffice to ensure a conviction. If these three conditions were not fulfilled, the court martial would be, as Winch concluded, 'a mockery and give the appearance of a whitewashing which, it is submitted, is just what the Naval Board wish to avoid'.[25]

Winch's report is of value in assessing one of the more considered opinions that the Board received into the most likely causes of the collision. Winch was obviously convinced from the evidence, despite the argument put by Street and Smyth, that *Voyager*'s turn to starboard was the result of the flying course signal rather than the turning signal, and there was likely to have been less confusion over the turning course signal as it was made by the 'immediate execute' method.[26] The danger point, in Winch's mind, was 50 seconds prior to the collision, shortly after which Robertson reacted. As to the Board's attitude towards the three *Melbourne* officers, Winch recommended that the Navy adopt the final submissions of its counsel as its official view of the collision.[27] As Jenkyn had argued strongly that no blame was attributable to any of them, and that each was carrying out his duties adequately, such should be the opinion of the Board. Winch concluded that there was no *prima facie* case of negligence against Kelly or Bate. He made a separate conclusion concerning Robertson:

> If anything can be said against Captain Robertson, it can only be that it took him 2 to 5 seconds to react when the situation suddenly became, in his opinion, dangerous. Although it may be said that there is some opinion evidence that he reacted too late, this is in the main, hindsight, and does not constitute a *prima facie* case of negligence.
>
> Any court who could convict Captain Robertson of negligence would, I submit, have their tongues well and truly in their cheeks.[28]

The Board had been very well advised. At its meeting on 7 August 1964, the Board decided that Winch's report 'should be used as an *aide-memoire* when the findings of the Royal Commission are made available'.[29]

Cabinet asked the Naval Board through the Navy Minister on 26 August to prepare its response to the Commissioner's Report, particularly those passages dealing with the conduct of the three officers from *Melbourne*.[30] The Naval Board had already started to consider its response in detail. What seems amazing now is that no attempt was made by the Board to have an appreciation of the collision prepared by the Naval Staff. It was common practice following a collision, grounding or accident for a group of officers (usually navigation specialists) at Navy Office to prepare a summary of the event and identify the lessons learned. Because no such appreciation had been prepared, when the time came for the Board to respond to the Commissioner's report, it was not adequately prepared to refute his version of events with its own version. Such a version could have been painstakingly prepared and reworked over the five months after the collision. It could have been supervised by Peek or Mesley who heard much, if not all, of the evidence. Whatever the reason for this failure to prepare an appreciation, the Navy was not in a position in August 1964 to provide an expert theory or explanation of what had happened.

The Board accepted that there were inconsistencies in *Melbourne*'s clocks and that timekeeping practices needed to be standardised throughout the Fleet.[31] Regarding the flying course signal, the Board said that its view was the only permissible view and was critical of Gatacre and others 'without recent sea experience' for their differing views.[32] As for what induced *Voyager*'s final movements, the Board was astonishingly silent and relied upon a citation of Jenkyn's final address at the Commission. This suggested that the Board believed *Voyager*'s final movements were in response to the flying course signal, solely on the grounds that the turn to starboard took place after this signal was sent. At least the Naval Board had confidence in Robertson's recollection. However, the point was made in passing only. The Board offered no all-embracing theory for the collision and appeared determined not to comment on any specific cause or causes. However, it conceded that there were some ambiguities in some tactical signalling procedures and these would be resolved after consultation with the RAN's operating partners.[33]

The Board then turned to the primary cause of collision as concluded by Spicer, and agreed with the Commissioner's finding that it was not possible to identify those who had actually made an error. This was of lesser importance, as responsibility always rested with the captain.[34] Harrington was most annoyed that Stevens had not been watching *Melbourne* and asked in a penscript note tucked into his personal copy of the Spicer Report 'What could the matter of grave importance [which had him at the chart table] be?' As for the suggestion that Stevens was unsure as to the action he should take, the Naval Board did not agree that this uncertainty should have distracted a captain to the extent that he would neglect the safety of his ship. Further still, if Stevens had been confused by the signal,

> he should have asked for repetition or verification and maintained a safe course and speed while this was being obtained and the differences of opinion resolved.[35]

> It is not considered that a difference of opinion constitutes a matter of such importance as to justify the captain neglecting his primary responsibility for the safety of the ship.[36]

What the Naval Board thought of Robertson's actions became a highly controversial matter. The Board had two views: one which was expressed privately by Board members and one which Cabinet was offered. The view expressed to Cabinet reflected Service solidarity.

The Board in all its submissions agreed that *Voyager* was to blame and that ultimate responsibility rested with Captain Stevens. It defied every attempt to place any responsibility for the collision with Robertson. The attitude adopted by the Board towards Robertson's role was a practical one, in which he was clearly given every support:

> In the case of Captain Robertson, the Naval Board agrees with the Commissioner, in considering whether he should have taken steps to alert *Voyager*, that it is impossible to say whether action by him 'by whistle or otherwise' would have avoided the collision. The Naval Board also agrees that the putting astern of *Melbourne*'s engines should have been indicated by three short blasts but the failure to give that signal did not contribute to the disaster.

In reaching a judgement in such a matter one has to endeavour to put oneself in the place of the responsible officer who, faced with an almost incredible situation has to make up his mind from moment to moment as to what is happening and as to what he should do.[37]

The Naval Board believed that Robertson could have given positive direction to *Voyager* to take station when her actions appeared indecisive but conceded that

the movement to port beyond such as would have brought *Voyager* back on course would not have been apparent to Captain Robertson for an appreciable time.[38]

The Board did not believe, even privately, that Robertson's failure to make a signal to *Voyager* contributed to the collision. Nor was it negligent conduct. As for Spicer's statement that Robertson should have queried *Voyager*'s movements when she started back to port, the Board said it was difficult to give an opinion because inconsistencies in the times being kept made any reconstruction of the final movements unreliable. On other occasions and in other places, Board members were not so restrained in their comments on Robertson.

What the Board never mentioned in Robertson's defence was the doubts it now had about the navigational lighting in RAN ships. In the DCNS Newsletter, issued twice yearly and classified 'secret', there was the admission in May 1965 that

the navigational lighting fitted in HMA Ships may be ambiguous and inadequate for ship safety when ships are manoeuvring at close range ahead of the beam of a consort, both for normal navigational purposes and for night flying.[39]

The newsletter seemed to accept that *Melbourne* would have had great difficulty in assessing the full extent of *Voyager*'s relative movement. Two and a half minutes before impact *Voyager* bore 054 degrees from *Melbourne*. One minute prior to the collision her bearing was 057 degrees, and yet her heading had changed considerably.

The chief deficiency and the main problem were the absence of a second steaming light and the proximity of the sidelights to the main steaming light and/or masthead obstruction light. In *Voyager*'s case, a 50 degree alteration to port with range closing from more than 1,500 yards to less than 1,000 yards would not have been readily apparent. This movement, which equated with the period when *Voyager* went from being in a safe position to a dangerous one, was estimated at 33 seconds. The newsletter's conclusion was something of an understatement: 'It is therefore apparent that the lack of visible aids in determining an escort's movements can delay avoiding action.'[40]

Two clear observations had been made. The first was that, ahead of the beam, an escort's bow and steaming light could not adequately indicate that a turn towards the carrier was in progress until the turn had progressed much more than 50 degrees. The second was that relying on a supposed knowledge of the intentions of the other ship was dangerous. Ships were therefore advised by the Fleet Commander to be diligent in positively ensuring that other ships in company had turned when ordered in the direction previously signalled, because the means of detection were not straightforward.

Harrington was alone in believing that there was not a problem with navigational lighting:

> My experience is that any captain who relies on any one navigation system, be it lights, the plot, signalled information or his own eyes, is unwise and fiddling about with the navigation lights, which are, at best, occasional aids only in fleetwork, will not create a situation any better than it is at present ... To my knowledge the question of navigational lighting was considered in detail in the early 1950s by HMS *Dryad* and the present arrangements worked out.[41]

Other members of the Naval Board were so concerned about lighting arrangements that clarification was sought from both the U.S. and Britain on the reasoning behind current arrangements. While waiting for a reply, a second steaming light would be fitted to RAN *Daring* Class destroyers as an added safety precaution.

The point to be stressed here is that shortcomings in equipment and procedures demonstrated by the collision and the Commission were acknowledged but were never cited in defence of Robertson. McNicoll, who had been a member of the Naval Board during the first half of 1964, later claimed it was Harrington's personal conviction that Robertson had been 'overconfident and slow to react' during *Voyager*'s final turn toward *Melbourne*. Further, this same deficiency in Robertson's ability was also evident when *Vendetta* struck the dock wall at Williamstown in 1958. Although McNicoll overstated the case against Robertson, whom he gradually came to dislike personally, there is some support for the belief that Robertson lacked a 'seaman's eye' — the ability to assess distance at sea — in comments written by Harrington in his personal copy of the Spicer Report:

> Kelly, who had been watching the anemometer, saw the danger at a glance and ordered half astern *before* Robertson, who had been intently watching the whole tragedy occur from its very inception.[42] [Harrington's emphasis]

As for Kelly and Bate, the Board in its submission to Cabinet agreed with Winch and was completely satisfied that both officers had performed their duties properly; the conduct of neither contributed materially to the collision, nor was there any negligence on their part.

On the basis of all the opinion it had received, Cabinet was informed that 'the Naval Board considered that there was no justification for disciplinary action against any of the three officers concerned'.[43]

Winch's statement that the Board was unable to initiate action against any of the three, had it even wished to do so, was supported by the Attorney-General's Department, which had been asked to examine the matter. Citing a provision in the *Royal Commissions Act* that served to protect witnesses by precluding the use of their evidence in any civil or criminal proceedings in any Commonwealth or State court, there was no other evidence to support a charge. At any rate, the only charge the Naval Board believed it could bring against Robertson was failing to 'blow three short blasts when his engines were put astern'. This, it concluded, would 'achieve a result which would be in the nature of an anti-climax'.[44] The truth was that it had no interest in bringing any charges.

The statement of jurisdiction cited from the Act also included, by implication, naval courts martial. The only evidence on which a charge could be brought against the three officers had already been given at the Commission and could not be used, or even used if adduced by any other means or in any other form before any other inquiry. And as Robertson's submission of Form AS232 — Report of Collision or Grounding — was not admissible in trials convened under Section 19 of the *Naval Discipline Act*, there was no scope for bringing any charges of negligence.

The Board believed there were veiled criticisms of its policies in the Spicer Report, particularly the Commissioner's comments on Robertson's alleged lack of experience.[45] Resentment was felt most by Harrington because as CNS he personally determined the allocation of commands, which included that of Robertson to *Melbourne*. The Board provided a wealth of data to show that Robertson's appointment was in keeping with naval practice elsewhere in the world. He had been Executive Officer of the carrier HMAS *Sydney* for sixteen months earlier in his career and had had two previous sea commands. The Board defended Robertson's having had three years ashore prior to commanding *Melbourne* on the grounds that officers needed to gain a broad range of experiences, including that as staff officers, and that the skills acquired by Robertson during his thirty-five years of naval service would not have been substantially diminished during that period. It also pointed out that Robertson had spent two years as Captain 'D' 9th Destroyer Squadron when in command of *Vendetta*, which placed him in permanent tactical command of a group of destroyers.[46]

Not content to leave the matter there, the Board cited the back-grounds and experience levels of captains then serving in command of aircraft carriers in the Royal Navy and the U.S. Navy. In the Royal Navy, each captain cited was commanding his first carrier, while most had had only one previous command. The average time spent ashore before assuming command had been three and a half years while the average seniority was six years and eight months. Robertson, on the other hand, had served for seven and a half years in the rank of captain.[47] The American situation was very similar. The average time spent ashore was three years and four months.[48]

Spicer's lack of familiarity with seagoing had led him to make far too much of the differences between commanding a carrier and a destroyer, and this was rightly seized on by the Naval Board.

As for the operational state of *Voyager*, the Board made the surprising concession that: 'There can be no doubt that something was very wrong on the bridge of *Voyager* on the night of 10 February'.[49] It went on to concede that evidence concerning wheel spanners and defective radars indicated 'that *Voyager* had not reached an acceptable standard of efficiency'[50] and undertook to revise procedures for thoroughly inspecting ships on completion of refits and prior to work-ups.

After detailing its response to Spicer's comments, conclusions and findings, the Naval Board was determined to highlight that the RAN had made great progress in the few years prior to the tragedy and that these achievements should not be lost in the rush to criticise the Service. The Board ended on a note of foreboding:

> So far as discipline and morale are concerned, the Board believes that this is currently at a high level. It is believed, however, that morale will inevitably suffer if such attacks as have been made during the past few months that are shown to be unjustified continue unanswered.
>
> If Cabinet, after consideration of this report, feels that appropriate action is being taken to remedy such deficiencies as have been revealed, and that the Navy as a whole continues to serve the nation effectively as an instrument of Government policy, it is believed that the early public expression of this viewpoint by the Government will be the best means of meeting the situation. In this way, personnel will be made aware of their Government's support, and it is considered that this would be the most effective way of preventing a decline in morale and restoring public confidence in the Navy.[51]

The Report prompted a rethinking of several operational practices. Although the Navy had publicly defended the tactical signalling system in use, the Commission did reveal some inadequacies and inconsistencies and this led the RAN to recommend a series of changes in the signalling manual to its NATO operating partners.[52]

The Commission had demonstrated that although instructions for stationing planeguard destroyers were adequate, instructions for the conduct of ships while in this station were not. Of particular concern was action to be taken by a planeguard destroyer when flying operations were not actually in progress, and upon receiving a new flying signal. Although the Naval Board said there was no doubt that the planeguard destroyer should take up her station on receipt of the new flying course and without further direction, and there probably was not any doubt, it still proposed that the manual be amended to read:

> A rescue destroyer, having taken station, is to maintain that station relative to the carrier air operating course and is to manoeuvre to maintain station without further orders on each occasion that the air operating course is altered by signal whether flying operations are actually in progress or not.

As to whether 'turns together' were more dangerous than 'turns in succession', the Naval Board stated that it depended on the circumstances and left the decision to the discretion of the OTC. This seemed to be an exoneration of Robertson. However, the Board went on to say:

> If a carrier is looking for the wind it could be quicker and simpler to use turns in succession with the rescue destroyer following round astern of the carrier.[53]

This was another subtle criticism of Robertson's actions in ordering an alteration together at 2042. Perhaps showing his frustration at the alleged dangers of either manoeuvre, Harrington wrote on his copy of the document, 'It would, of course, be safer to stay in harbour'.[54]

The method of signalling the carrier's minor adjustments of course and speed was revised. It was recommended that 'minor adjustments' should be defined as being not more than 10 degrees of course and 2 knots of speed, that these should be sent as action, not information, signals to rescue destroyers, with rescue destroyers directed to manoeuvre to maintain true bearings from the carrier. Recommendations for the simplification and clarification of possible interpretations of signals referring to the progress of flying operations were also made.

For all the criticism naval people had heaped on the legal profession via the Commission, the lawyers had been able to highlight at least a dozen areas of inadequacy in existing instructions for fleet operations. The location and operation of bridge and operations rooms loudspeakers was reviewed in this context, together with the placement and briefing of bridge lookouts.

There were a host of other changes prompted by the loss of *Voyager*, particularly in the use of lifesaving and safety equipment. Naval training was reviewed to ensure a greater familiarity with the operation of life rafts and helicopter winching, and a higher standard of proficiency in swimming. A new mechanism was devised which did not require the use of wheel spanners to open scuttles. A new policy was introduced for life jacket stowages, and the operation of life rafts would be demonstrated as part of every ship's work-up.

Instructions regarding the issue of alcohol were repromulgated by FOCAF and FOICEA to prohibit a 'beer issue' when ships are engaged in planeguard duties or while flying operations are in progress or imminent. The Naval Board also pointed out that 'Officers have the privilege of buying alcoholic liquor for drinking in their mess at lunchtime and in the evening. An officer is required to be temperate at all times in his drinking. It is most unusual for any watchkeeping officer to drink any alcohol whenever his ship is at sea.'[55]

The matter of navigational lighting mentioned previously is significant in assessing the extent to which the RAN was prepared to undertake a self-assessment in the wake of the collision. While Harrington appears to have believed there was little of a general nature to be learned from the collision, and actually resisted some of the changes proposed on the grounds that past procedures and practices had stood the test of time, the Naval Board generally accepted proposals for change when the need for them was demonstrated.

In answer to its press critics, the Naval Board could assert that there was no excessive traditionalism or professional arrogance to inhibit the Board's reception of suggestions for doing things differently, or better than they had been done before. Although some senior officers attempted to portray this change as being coincidental with the collision and its aftermath, the Naval Board strove to show the Parliament and the press that it was anything but a hidebound organisation incapable of self-initiated reform. Whether or not the Board was sufficiently persuasive in this regard was yet to be seen.

# 9

# *The Dust Begins to Settle*

CABINET DISCUSSED both the Commissioner's Report and the Naval Board's response on 4 and 10 September 1964.[1] The first meeting outlined the theme of the Government's response to the Spicer Report:

> [T]he central subject should be the nationally important matter of the efficiency of the Navy. The atmosphere to be established and maintained is that the Navy's real efficiency is to be rated as very high, that the *Voyager* incident has been, and is, most seriously regarded, and that the Government and the Navy will together build upon lessons derived from the experience for the future greater safety and efficiency of the Navy.[2]

Cabinet decided that the question of courts martial of the three *Melbourne* officers had been disposed of by legal advice received by the Naval Board. At its 10 September meeting, Cabinet decided that

> it would be an unhelpful precedent to table the report of the Naval Board and that the Government will therefore decline to table it.[3]

Menzies had earlier told Parliament:

> I did not say that we would present the Report of the Naval Board. The Naval Board through the Minister for the Navy advises the Government. All sorts of advice is received in this way from our expert advisers.[4]

Cabinet decided that reports of previous naval accidents would not be tabled either.

Two actions resulted from these Cabinet deliberations. First, it was decided that a Naval Accidents Investigating Committee would be established similar to that operating within the RAAF, and second, that a Cabinet Committee would be formed

> in order to examine methods of training and organisation of the Navy with a view to recommending any improvements that appear to be necessary.[5]

The loss of *Voyager* was debated in Parliament, with the opening address presented by the Prime Minister. Menzies covered the matters raised by Spicer, and his principal findings, including his criticism of the three *Melbourne* officers. He defended his decision not to make the Board's response public by saying that the Board's

---

relationship to the Government is one of great confidence and indeed secrecy. When the Government after receiving advice announces a decision or makes a statement of fact or policy, it takes the responsibility for what it does.[6]

Menzies remarked that publishing the Board's confidential report would have created a harmful precedent. He announced that no action would or could be taken against the officers because of the legal advice he had received.[7]

The Navy emerged very well from the Prime Minister's address. He made the point that the Naval Board would have most wanted him to make, and that was that

life at sea has its hazards, and that this is plainly true in the case of the Navy, which must prepare itself to fight by day or by night in all sorts of circumstances and weather and whose preparations can be effective only by practising by day or by night every sort of manoeuvre which may be needed in war.[8]

His verdict on the way ahead was positive and constructive. There was nothing fundamentally wrong with the RAN:

We believe that under these circumstances the Navy can go on with its vital service to the nation in co-operation with the Government and with the moral backing of the Australian people. I repeat that we have a fine Navy, with a gallant and devoted company of officers and men. It is the task of all of us in authority to remove any discoverable impediments to its full effectiveness.[9]

The member for the Melbourne bayside seat of Batman, Sam Benson, seemed to be the logical choice to lead the debate for the Opposition, despite the fact that he was a backbencher and the Spicer Report had been personally tabled by the Prime Minister.

Benson was a merchant marine captain who had served with the RAN during World War II. His only post-war contact with the RAN was in July 1952 when he was involved in Naval National Service training for thirteen days. He retired from the RANVR in 1954. Benson's experience was limited and not recent. However, this did not stop him surging into the debate with allegations that had been dealt with and dismissed long before the Spicer Report was given to the Parliament.

When he opened the debate for the Opposition, Benson argued that Admiral Becher should have been in *Melbourne* while the ship was working-up and hinted that the

Admiral's presence could have prevented this accident, because his greater experience and authority surely would have prevailed. For instance, when no wind was apparent he, undoubtedly, would have called off the operation.[10]

He went on to make much of Robertson's lack of experience and stated that Bate was too young and inexperienced to be the carrier's OOW.[11] He went as far as saying that Bridge Watchkeeping Certificates were 'not worth the paper they are written on' and that the stationing of planeguard destroyers 1,000 yards astern of the carrier was nonsensical.[12]

He had no experience on which to base his remarks and no familiarity with naval exercises involving carriers or modern destroyers, and was unable to state matters of detail correctly. For instance, *Melbourne's* displacement was 19,000 tons and not 29,000 tons, as Benson had stated. As might be expected, given his background, he pointed out that the scandalous standards of professionalism which allegedly afflicted the RAN 'do not obtain in the Merchant Navy'.[13] He also called for naval captains to sit for pilotage exemptions as their ships usually 'blundered into Australian ports'.

Although it was not widely known at the time of the debate, on 15 February 1963, *Melbourne* was transiting through Port Phillip Bay, with HMAS *Quickmatch* stationed one mile astern. Both ships were steaming at 7 knots. Benson, as the pilot of the liner *Australia*, overtook *Quickmatch* at 14 knots, cut in between the two warships and passed across *Melbourne's* bows without permission. The carrier's commanding officer, Captain Richard Peek, complained about Benson's handling of the ship he was piloting, and the complaint was passed by the Naval Board to the Victorian Marine Board.

In reply, Benson said that *Melbourne* had reduced speed without warning him, yet he was aware that it was incumbent upon ships in overtaking positions to keep well clear of vessels being overtaken, which always retain the right of way. In an attempt to embarrass the RAN, Benson cited this incident in Parliament as an example of the RAN's alleged incompetence, but neglected to mention that he was an interested party. It made the front page of the *Australian* on 18 September 1964 and was described as a 'near collision'.

Benson concluded his speech by stating that the Navy was fundamentally deficient:

> It is obvious that the Navy is not aware of its shortcomings. Therefore, the Government must set in motion the necessary machinery to reorganise the Navy. The Navy appears to be too aloof and unrealistic in these things. It is remote, it is out of station and for its own good must be quickly brought into line.[14]

It was unfortunate that Benson's speech should have attracted favourable comment in all the major metropolitan newspapers. Respected political correspondent Alan Reid remarked that Benson 'contributed a thoughtful, balanced speech which simultaneously revealed his commonsense and deep feeling for the Navy'.[15] In the *Daily Mirror*, political correspondent Ray Kerrison described Benson as the Opposition's 'incredible trump card':

> As Mr Benson, calmly, incisively played the role for the first time of a devil's advocate, Mr Chaney sat at the table receiving notes scribbled furiously by naval departmental experts. Facing Mr Benson, Mr Chaney must have felt like a man looking down the barrel of a gun — that had been loaded and cocked. A layman

in naval affairs, he was facing criticism of a man who had learned his drill in the battering waves of wartime Atlantic convoys.[16]

The Opposition frontbench was not so pleased with Benson's speech. Benson failed to demonstrate, as his Parliamentary colleagues had hoped, that the circumstances of the collision reflected any deep-seated problems in naval administration. Clyde Cameron believed the Opposition's position had been compromised in the debate 'by the apologetic contribution of our leading spokesman, Captain Sam Benson'.[17]

It was a pity that so few people in either the Parliament or the press knew enough about the Navy or the tactical manoeuvring of ships at sea to dismiss the superficial and inaccurate views put by Benson as the Parliament's 'authority' on naval matters.

Chaney responded to Benson's address and so emphatic were his rejections of Opposition jibes about the Navy that he was taunted by Cameron, Dr Jim Cairns and Fred Daly for 'getting so excited'.[18] He covered the points raised by Benson, criticised the staleness of his experience and reiterated a number of the points made by Menzies.

The next Opposition speaker, Kim Beazley, made a positive and constructive address which focused on the inability of the matters raised in the Royal Commission to be referred to court martial. He pointed out the justifiability of public disquiet over the collision and attacked those parts of Menzies's address which covered the state of naval preparedness.[19] William McMahon, a former Navy Minister, replied to Beazley's address by returning the discussion to navigational matters and the facts of the disaster as revealed by the Commissioner's report. He did not deal with Beazley's general comments but attacked Benson for overstating his ability to make conclusions about matters that others, including a Royal Commission and the Naval Board, had not been so certain.[20]

Cairns criticised the Government for suggesting the cause of the accident could not be known. Obviously knowing nothing about the navigational issues, he restated the view put by Benson and was critical of the Navy for having programmed an exercise that he believed both ships were ill-prepared to undertake.

Newspaper reporting of the debate was less than convinced by Menzies's reasoning that the Naval Board's report ought not to be released. The *Age* remarked in its editorial, 'Surely he could have revealed more of the Board's general assessment of naval standards'.[21] The *Daily Mirror* said 'the Government must not be allowed to bury the *Voyager* debate in a secret file. The public wants to know'.[22] The Melbourne *Herald* was unimpressed by the Prime Minister's proposals for the future:

It is not enough to announce that the Minister for the Navy and the Naval Board will set their own committee system to look into service administration and investigate future accidents. Only an obviously impartial and independent review of service procedures can now restore full confidence'.[23]

The *Australian* was sharply critical of Chaney.[24] Political correspondent Brian Johns wrote:

It will put his career back ten years — and if he can recover at all, it will take him the life of three parliaments . . . Among Opposition members there was anger and ready anticipation of political retribution for the flustered jibes which occupied so much of Mr Chaney's speech. They see Mr Chaney as the man to be rattled over the *Voyager* issue and they intend to concentrate their attack on the inexperienced minister.

Alan Reid commented in the *Bulletin* of 26 September that 'Navy Minister Chaney did his political reputation considerable harm in replying to Benson. Where Benson had been calm, he was emotional'.[25] The *Sydney Morning Herald*, which was partial to the Federal Government, moved to defend Chaney by quoting a 'highly placed naval officer' who said the Navy would remember Chaney for having defended them 'when the fashion was to put the boot in. He identified himself with us, although he was not the minister at the time of the collision'.[26]

The Navy could be thankful that the *Australian* was still not persuaded that there was something fundamentally wrong with the Navy:

The Government, it seems, does not realise what the public is really seeking from the *Voyager* case. The need is for an assurance, in practical terms, that in the RAN tradition does not crush initiative; that evolutionary change is not considered radicalism; and that original thinking and practical decision-making are not the close preserve of the top echelon.

In short, that the Royal Australian Navy is not a hidebound anachronism in a world of highly progressive defence thinking.

When the debate reopened on 24 September, Calwell moved a censure motion against the Government 'for the succession of naval disasters for which it is primarily responsible'.[27] This was a tactic designed to prompt debate. Question Time, usually scheduled for 10.30 a.m., was cancelled and the censure motion was to be debated until a vote would be taken at 4.00 p.m.

The Leader of the Opposition returned to his theme that

the *Voyager* case is the latest and most convincing proof that all is not well, and has not been well for some considerable time now, in the Royal Australian Navy.[28]

He went on to argue that the frequency of naval accidents 'is sufficient to draw the conclusion that a pattern of inefficiency exists'.[29] Calwell's speech covered most of the ground of the first debate as part of a general attack on the state of the RAN.

In replying to the motion, Menzies attempted a defence of the Naval Board and its actions:

125

> We at no time asked the Naval Board to investigate the events of that night ...
> I venture to suggest that it would have been an impertinence on the part of any
> higher naval authority to say: 'Well, we will now have a little private inquiry of
> our own, and if we disagree with the Royal Commissioner, that is all right we
> will act on our own view'. This would have been criticised from one end of the
> country to the other; yet some people have talked as though this is what the Naval
> Board should have done.[30]

So much for the notion of the Board holding a parallel inquiry. It would
obviously have had no political support. Menzies argued that the Naval
Board acknowledged there were defects in the way things were done
because it had accepted the need for change as a result of this and other
accidents. Having made that point, Menzies said the appointment of a
Cabinet committee to review the Naval system of administration was
designed to identify any 'improvement to be made'.[31] Despite the
rhetoric and the political necessity of such action, Menzies was
conceding that there might have been something wrong with the Navy
and that it could take outsiders to pinpoint what it was.

Speaking in favour of the censure motion, Gough Whitlam said that
while there was nothing wrong with asking outsiders to review
Australian naval practices, it was an insult to the Minister for the Navy
to have a ministerial committee appointed to assist him. Whitlam also
came to the defence of Smyth, who had been attacked in the Senate
debate the previous evening:

> It is true that Mr Smyth's conduct at the Royal Commission did shake the Naval
> Board up. Let us recall that until this year the Navy, alone among the Services,
> did not have a Judge Advocate General. All the inquiries which the Prime
> Minister mentioned, except the court martial of Captain Dovers, were in private.
> Thus, frankly, it did the Navy good for a competent public inquiry to be held.[32]

The remainder of Whitlam's speech reviewed the criticisms first
uttered by Benson, and he suggested that the Naval Board ought to have
a Naval Reserve officer as one of its members, as was the case with the
Military Board. He even suggested the appointment of a civilian
mariner. By this stage the debate about *Voyager* had become bogged
down and was making little progress.

The involvement of John Jess, Federal Liberal backbencher, in the
debate altered its tone completely. He said the censure motion had 'some
right on both sides of the chamber' and that had the motion been
'against the Government because of the conduct of the Royal
Commission and the events flowing from it, I would, without hesitation,
have voted with them [the Opposition]'.[33] Jess was openly critical of the
Government's handling of the tragedy. He said the Royal Commission
had been abused and not conducted correctly, and that it should not
have been set up in the first place.

> I think there should have been a naval inquiry and I think that when its findings
> were complete they should have gone to a court martial which should have been
> held in public.[34]

He went on to criticise the appointment of judges from the Parliament, and their appointment to head inquiries in which the Government had an interest. This was the only time Spicer had been criticised during the Parliamentary debate. Turning next to Smyth, Jess said that he (Jess) 'personally resented the way the inquiry was conducted and the way in which the evidence was led by him' (Smyth).[35]

As for the three officers criticised by the Commissioner, Jess took the submission of Jenkyn to be the view of the Naval Board: they were not guilty of any negligence. He finished by stating that

> if this Parliament does have any control over these matters, if it is to accept its responsibility, it should have another look at this matter.[36]

What Jess actually wanted the Parliament or the Government to do was not entirely clear. Was he advocating a parliamentary inquiry, a Naval board of inquiry, or a court martial?

Of the speakers that followed, Cairns made the point that in the previous ten years, there had been ten different Ministers for the Navy and that one had served for over five years. Therefore, the others had served for an average of six months each. He criticised the Government's handling of the portfolio in this respect and there was little that could be said in its defence.

After three and a half hours of debate, with the Minister for the Navy the final speaker, the motion was defeated along party lines. This was far from being the end of *Voyager* as a political problem for the Government. The editorials next day predictably criticised the Government for failing to order, in the *Australian*'s words, 'a thorough overhaul of Navy leadership and procedures'.[37] It was also critical of Chaney for being 'singularly sensitive to criticism of his portfolio and pronouncedly hostile to critics. Certainly he is not the man to prescribe the ills of the Navy'.[38] The most vigorous defence of the Navy had to wait until the matter was debated in the Senate on 23 September 1964.

The debate was opened by Senator McKenna, Opposition Leader in the Senate. He clearly was not familiar with naval matters, as his turns of phrase and expressions showed. In describing the background to the collision, McKenna said the three officers on *Melbourne* were 'relatively inexperienced in the duties they were to perform' while those in *Voyager* were 'fully experienced but they, too, were not accustomed to working together'.[39] After describing the conditions at the time of the collision he concluded, 'I say with great deliberation that the fact that there was a collision at all under those conditions is, on the face of it, the result of plain gross negligence. There are no other terms in which to describe it'.[40]

Senator McKenna turned next to blame and believed that Spicer had been rather diffident in its apportionment. McKenna implied that others beside those in *Voyager* were to blame and repeated the criticism of

Robertson for not sounding a warning to *Voyager*. His comments are almost comical. 'I have heard the noise that these large vessels make when they give these blasts and they are rather world shattering events. They pervade the whole atmosphere and they could have been an element of warning.'[41] He was goaded by Senator Cormack, who attempted to correct McKenna by pointing out that, 'One short blast means "I am turning to port".'[42] Unfortunately, the senator was not entirely correct, as one short blast meant an alteration to starboard. The remainder of McKenna's speech was a poor paraphrase of the Spicer Report. He cited the changes to be made to naval administration as a result of the collision, and then proceeded to blame Gorton as the former Minister for the Navy:

> If the Government will, as the Prime Minister said, accept its proper responsibility it will dismiss from office all members of the Naval Board at the time of the disaster and also, I submit, the former Minister for the Navy, Senator Gorton.[43]

The end of this speech brought Gorton his first opportunity to speak. Throughout the year Gorton's name had not been linked with *Voyager* although he was, in effect, the minister responsible for the tragedy — if it reflected any long-standing deficiencies — as it had occurred just six weeks after he left the portfolio he had held for over five years. In a sympathetic biography of Gorton by Alan Trengrove, the suggestion is made that *Voyager* may have permanently damaged Gorton's political standing:

> Had Gorton still been Minister for the Navy, his subsequent career could have been greatly affected because, though it might have been difficult to attach any responsibility for the catastrophe to him, the mere association of his name with it probably would have deprived him of any remote chance of one day being prime minister.[44]

Other writers were more direct. In Whittington's *The Twelfth Man?* an analysis of Australian prime ministers, he expresses his surprise that Gorton was not held more accountable for the loss of *Voyager*. He further suggests that Gorton should have offered to resign over the affair:

> If there had been inefficiency and maladministration, if Navy morale was low, if the wrong men were being appointed to senior positions, if the men at the top were of poor or mediocre calibre, the Minister must have known and should have known, and in any case was bound to accept responsibility. In other days, or perhaps in other countries, a Minister would have felt obliged to resign on principle. Certainly a Minister's resignation might have stopped the rot in Navy morale that began with the demotion of officers of lesser rank who had been involved.[45]

In addition to the last statement, which was in any event totally inaccurate, the principle of a minister accepting responsibility and resigning was also being questioned in Australia and abroad at this time. The traditional idea was that a minister was responsible for all the actions of his department. But in the 1960s this was being questioned in Britain and, therefore, in Australia. Where previously the minister would have resigned in the face of a disaster such as *Voyager*, by 1964 this was not nearly so clear-cut. Resignation was not urged by anyone simply on the basis of the disaster itself. In the case of *Voyager* it would not have been clear which minister should have resigned. Should it have been Gorton, Forbes or Chaney?

Certainly Whitington's statement that 'there can be little doubt [Gorton] knew of and approved of and even influenced the promotion and appointment of many of the Navy's senior officers and administrators', was far-fetched.[46] Gorton recognised the limits of his involvement in departmental affairs and realised the impropriety of interfering with the promotion and posting of naval personnel.

That Gorton did feel in some way responsible was demonstrated in his speech. He began by telling the Senate,

> I believe that in these circumstances all honest criticism of the events of that night, or of the other matters which have been raised against the Navy, should be regarded as constructive criticism.[47]

After remarking that the opinion of a Royal Commissioner was one among many, he gave a spirited defence of Kelly and Bate and said 'I am certain that the entire volume of naval professional opinion virtually unanimously would reject the view that either Sub-Lieutenant Bate or Commander Kelly had in fact been guilty of any negligence in the performance of their duties'.[48] Gorton then proceeded to answer the criticisms made by Benson, and cited, for good measure, the incident of Benson being reported to the Victorian Marine Board. 'I think it should be realised,' Gorton commented, 'in this instance Mr Benson is acting as an advocate in his own case and is not completely detached and completely impartial when making his allegation against the Navy'.[49]

In turning to the Spicer Report, Gorton accepted the spirit of the Commissioner's criticisms about the rescue and the provision of life-saving and emergency apparatus. However, he was concerned about impressions created during the Commission which continued to affect public confidence in the Navy. Without hesitation, Gorton attributed most of the controversy to the 'completely untrue statements of Mr Smyth'.[50]

Senator Murphy: Are you attacking Mr Smyth?

Senator Gorton: You must draw your conclusions as to what I am attacking. I am not seeking to attack any individual. I am seeking to attack a series of events which unfairly and unjustly reflected on the Naval Service without having any proper basis for such reflection.

It was giving the press headlines that served as the basis of Gorton's attack:

> No Service has been so damaged by a partial presentation of the facts, in some cases by completely unsubstantiated presentations of the facts, as was the naval service, which was improperly damaged by Mr Smyth QC, during the course of the Commission's inquiry . . . that is the only thing in this whole affair for which I accept blame.[61]

Gorton concluded his speech by rejecting the suggestion that there was something fundamentally wrong with the Navy and argued that there was much in the RAN for which the nation ought to be proud.

The final speaker, Senator McClelland, suggested that if Smyth had acted improperly, it was the duty of Counsel for the Navy to have brought it to the attention of the Commissioner. He also pointed out that Gorton had defended Kelly and Bate but had 'deliberately excluded any reference to Captain Robertson. Do I understand from that that the Minister was thereby saying that he felt that the Captain was negligent in the incidents that occurred that night?'[52] The debate was adjourned before Gorton was given an opportunity to respond.

Liberal Party Federal parliamentarian, Peter Howson, wrote in his diary:

> Another melancholy debate. We haven't come out of this too well. It has had the effect of uniting the ALP and giving them an issue to fight on. By far the best speech on our side was made by John Gorton in the Senate last night. I feel the PM has taken it all rather too lightly.[53]

A leading article published in the *Australian*, by its parliamentary correspondent, Dominic Nagle, was headed 'Gag Put on *Voyager* — Government is mauled: scores a hollow victory'. He claimed that 'The Government won a technical victory as expected. But not since the debates of early 1962 has the Government taken such a mauling on such an important subject.'[54] Alan Reid, writing in the *Bulletin*, expressed a similar view, but with a little more realism. 'The Government took a bad beating . . . It had to be beaten, even if only because no semantics could possibly transform a collision at sea . . . into a triumph of Australian arms'.[55]

The press had had its say. Members of the public had theirs in the letters to the editor columns in the major newspapers. The persistence of disquiet was obvious.

Meanwhile, Smyth referred Gorton's speech to the New South Wales Bar Council, which agreed to hold a special meeting the same day to consider the senator's remarks. The President of the Bar Association, Mr John (later the Right Honourable Sir John) Kerr, publicly supported Smyth and criticised Gorton. Smyth declined to comment until the Bar Council had made its ruling. Two days later, Smyth obtained permission from the Bar Council to issue a statement in reply to Gorton's speech.

He stated that he had not 'made unsubstantiated statements at the Commission' and that Gorton's allegations were 'without foundation'.[56] On 29 September, the Attorney-General, Billy Snedden, defended Smyth in Parliament and said he had acted 'according to his professional duties'. When pressed on whether the view put by Gorton was the Government's view, Menzies avoided the question by commenting that Gorton had the right to 'express any view on a matter which concerns proceedings which related to events while he was Minister for the Navy'.

The RAN had not emerged well from the second debate in the Lower House. The performance of those who had sought to defend it had been variable. The Navy was the subject of numerous editorials and more adverse publicity than it could have hoped to counter.

The main counter to public criticism was to demonstrate that it was 'business as usual' for the RAN. It was opportune for the Naval Board that Menzies announced a record programme of military expansion on 10 November 1964. The RAN was the principal beneficiary. This announcement diverted attention from public criticism of the Navy and pointed to a positive future for the Service.

A change of leadership would accompany this new programme. The Government announced that Air Chief Marshall Sir Frederick Scherger had been granted an extension to his term as Chairman of the Chiefs of Staff Committee, while Harrington would be relieved as CNS the following February by McNicoll.

The *Australian* interpreted this as a move designed to block Admiral Harrington from succeeding Scherger.[57] There is no evidence, however, that Harrington either wanted the job or was prepared to curry Government favour as a means of boosting his chances for selection. In fact, Harrington did not even enjoy his time as CNS.[58]

The public were obviously concerned about safety within the Navy, as *Voyager* had an adverse affect on recruiting. The DCNS Newsletter for November 1964 described the Navy's recruiting performance for that year:

> As forecast in the last newsletter, recruiting has proved extremely difficult. After an initial increase in applications following the *Voyager* disaster, the number of applications fell appreciably during the period of the Royal Commission, and until after the findings were published. The continued adverse and often ill-informed press comment is believed to have contributed to the fall ...[59]

The relationship between the Navy and the press had traditionally been benign, but the whaler tragedy and the loss of *Voyager* changed the attitude of the press completely. The Navy was now marked for close and critical attention.

Times had changed and the Naval Board needed to change with them. To enhance the Navy's now tarnished public image, the Naval Board agreed to a number of public relations initiatives.[60] In terms of organisation, the CNPR became Director of Public Relations and had his authority extended to cover Navy public relations staff in subordinate area commands. Press Liaison Officers were to be appointed within each command, while full-time public relations staff was increased.

In response to Parliamentary concerns, the Ministerial Committee for Review of Naval Organisation, Procedures and Methods foreshadowed by Menzies was appointed and met for the first time on 8 October 1964. It requested from the Naval Board an enormous amount of material on the history of the RAN's organisation, administrative procedures and personnel management and training. The Naval Board minutes contain no hint of hesitation in providing the Committee with this information, which was bound to keep it occupied, if not distracted, for many months.[61]

The Naval Board also considered the creation of a Standing Naval Committee of Investigation, as directed by the Prime Minister on 15 September. The lack of enthusiasm for the initiative within the Naval Board was obvious. At its meeting on 25 September, the Board noted that

> the types of cases the Committee would investigate would have to be clearly defined and that an assessment would need to be made of the extent of the work involved in order to determine whether personnel selected for the Committee could undertake the task in addition to their present duties.[62]

The Second Naval Member was asked to prepare a paper on the subject.

On 6 October, having considered a minute on the subject from Admiral Smith, the Board was concerned about the status and future of boards of inquiry, which they obviously wanted to continue. Whereas Smith had proposed a Naval Committee of Investigation, which appeared to subsume some of the functions of boards of inquiry, the Naval Board considered that

> the requirement was rather for a Committee more analogous to the Standing Committee which investigates air accidents in the Air Force and that it should function separately from Boards of Inquiry.[63]

It is difficult to perceive that there was much of a difference in practice between the two.

Having noted a minute from Landau that the Navy had to provide some evidence of progress in this area, should it be publicly asked, the Board decided to appoint an officer as Director of Accidents Investigation, responsible to the Deputy CNS. His title was soon altered to Co-ordinator of Naval Safety — a suggestion made by the Ministerial Committee reviewing naval affairs. The appointment of the first officer to the position was announced on 20 December 1964. This statement also mentioned that the Ministerial Committee 'had held a series of meetings and were giving consideration to a range of matters affecting naval administration'.[64] Such a bland statement was unlikely to induce much optimism about what the Committee might achieve. When Calwell asked Chaney about the Committee in Parliament on 1 April 1965, he could only say

> The Committee has held a series of meetings since its inception. It has under continuing consideration a wide range of matters affecting naval administration.[65]

In other words, it had yet to achieve anything. On 16 May 1967, Harold Holt asked the Navy Minister about the Committee and its progress. In reply, the Minister enclosed copies of the statements setting up the Committee and the position of Co-ordinator of Naval Safety, and a copy of his predecessor's reply to Calwell.[66] The Committee had been a failure but, at least from the Navy's perspective, Parliament's concerns about the Navy had been eased.

By the end of 1964, the Naval Board hoped to put *Voyager* into the past. The Royal Commission report had been debated in Parliament — the unavoidable fallout had further hurt the Navy — and a series of actions to be undertaken by the Navy had been outlined. Morale had taken a heavy blow but the Naval Board staunchly believed there was nothing wrong with the Navy or its administration. With Australia seeking to play a role in ending Indonesia's confrontation with Malaysia, RAN ships would be permanently deployed to South-East Asian waters. It was also likely that Australia would become involved in the Vietnam conflict and the Naval Board could see that this would mean some involvement for the Navy.

Yet, *Voyager* would have a lasting effect. Command at sea and perceptions of loyalty had been irrevocably changed. Rear-Admiral Andrew Robertson, who was a commander at the time of the collision, told me that '*Voyager* was a watershed for the RAN. The old navy with its absolute supremacy over its own affairs had died. A huge gulf had opened between those serving at sea and the Naval Board, with the confidence and respect of the navy to its leadership never really restored'.[67]

It seems morale was most affected at the lieutenant to commander levels, where there was a perceived crisis of loyalty caused by the alleged absence of loyalty shown by Becher to Robertson. Every officer of these ranks during those years who was interviewed by me strongly shared this view. Certainly it was an opinion that Chaney had encountered during his trips to sea with the Navy in 1965 and 1966.

The *Sun-Herald* described the Navy's plight aptly in its editorial of 30 August 1964:

> Blame for the sinking of *Voyager* has been apportioned, six months after the disaster. It will take much longer than that for the public's confidence in the Navy to be restored.

# 10

# *The Demise of Robertson*

AFTER THE COMMISSIONER adjourned on 25 June 1964 to write his report, Robertson was given a temporary billet and directed to undertake a study of naval training procedures. Notwithstanding the Commission's findings, Robertson fully expected to be restored to his command some time during September when *Melbourne* returned to Sydney from her deployment to South-East Asia. Many others shared his view. On 8 July Robertson received a note from Norman Jenkyn QC accepting a dinner invitation to the flagship. This invitation was evidently made by Robertson towards the end of the Commission's sitting.[1] Shortly after, Robertson received a note from one of his Naval College term-mates, Captain John Peel, who wrote: 'I am looking forward to your immediate appointment back to *Melbourne*'.[2] It was apparent that some of those serving in the carrier also expected him to return. Surgeon Commander Brian Treloar, the Fleet Medical Officer embarked in *Melbourne*, wrote to Robertson on 11 July 1964 remarking 'We are all thinking of you during this waiting period and are sincerely hoping that commonsense will prevail over sensationalism. We are all looking forward to your speedy return to the team.'[3]

Robertson's supporters, both inside and outside the Navy, hoped for a favourable result, but none was overconfident. A letter from another of Robertson's term-mates summed up the general attitude. 'I feel for you at this time and hope that you emerge unscathed, as I think you should, and that Mr Smyth is made to look the goat that I think he is'.[4]

The first formal mention of Robertson's fate was in a minute dated 16 July 1964 from Rear-Admiral Peek to Harrington. Peek posed three questions which were answered in the handwriting of the Deputy CNS, Rear-Admiral Tom Morrison:

Does Robertson go back to sea?    Yes.

Is this a Board decision?    Board.
[This answer conformed to the previous pattern which asked whether action was to be taken by the Board, the seagoing admirals or by CNS]

If he does not go back to sea will it have an adverse effect on the Navy generally?
It may have an adverse effect on *Melbourne*'s ship's company.

This is a crucial indicator of the thinking among the Navy's most senior officers. It is particularly noteworthy that at least one admiral, Tom Morrison, assumed Robertson would be returning to *Melbourne*.

John Jess had heard a rumour on 30 June 1964 that Robertson might not be returning to the carrier in command but be posted as commanding officer of the naval training establishment, HMAS *Watson*, in Sydney. The rumour had probably come from Captain David Stevenson who must have spoken to Jess when the Naval Board informed him privately that he would be remaining permanently in command of the flagship.

Armed with this information, Jess made inquiries with Chaney's office and advised the Navy Minister that Robertson would not accept the appointment because it had been previously filled by junior captains, or even an acting captain, and would be considered by Robertson as an effective demotion. Although there is no indication from Robertson's private papers as to when he first heard about this, there is no doubt that Jess, being a close friend and a relative by marriage, would have ensured Robertson knew speedily that such a rumour existed.

Robertson's next posting was formally confirmed in a letter from Harrington dated 23 August 1964 which he received on 27 August, one day after the Spicer Report was tabled in Parliament.

> I write to inform you of your next appointment which is to be *Watson* on the return of the present captain to the United Kingdom.
>
> The appointment will appear on the next list so as to be public before *Melbourne*'s return on 1 September.
>
> I am aware that this appointment will not be very pleasing to you and I can only say how sorry I am that your *Melbourne* appointment was not entirely fortunate.[5]

There was nothing unusual about Robertson being informed of his new job in this way. The posting of all naval officers in 1964 was a strictly veiled affair. The Director of Officers' Appointments did not ask officers for their posting preferences or seek to ascertain or accommodate their personal wishes. A billet and a commencement date were determined within Navy Office and the nominated officer was duly informed. Officers of captain's rank, especially those selected for seagoing command, were normally advised in a letter from CNS (who handled the posting of all captains) of their new appointment with as much warning as was administratively possible to allow the necessary domestic arrangements to be made.

Although it was an accepted procedure of some antiquity, the closed method of appointing officers was a shortcoming in the management of their careers. It has since given way to a degree of negotiation between those making the appointments and the officers concerned. Certainly, a senior officer like Harrington would have recoiled from the suggestion that Robertson ought to have had explained the reasons for his posting to *Watson*. In Harrington's view, Robertson was a serviceman and would dutifully go wherever he was sent — without discussion or argument.

It seems being posted to *Watson*, of all the appointments he could have been given, was the source of Robertson's greatest dissatisfaction. But this was not the only suggestion made for his future within the Naval Board. Admiral Smith, as Second Naval Member with overall responsibility for officers' appointments, proposed promoting Robertson to commodore and posting him to London as Australian Naval Representative United Kingdom (ANRUK).[6] Although this might have been construed outside the Navy as a form of protest by the Naval Board over Spicer's criticism of Robertson, Harrington did not oppose it on these grounds. Despite his apparent dislike of Robertson, Harrington felt genuine compassion for him.[7] He believed that rather than having Robertson sent away, he should remain in Australia and be appointed to a less demanding posting which would give him ample time to recover from the ordeal of the collision and the Commission, and take whatever action he wanted with respect to its findings.

The reputation of *Watson* in those days was that it was virtually a part-time command. Commander Ken Gray served as executive officer of the establishment in 1960 with Captain George Oldham in command. Believing there was insufficient work for both a captain and a commander, Oldham would spend only one or two days each week at the establishment.[8] For the remainder of the time he stayed at home. Surprisingly, Oldham was promoted to rear-admiral at the end of his time at *Watson*. Privately, Harrington hoped that Robertson would submit a redress of grievance to the Naval Board, which would give the Navy a chance to conduct either some form of internal inquiry or major review of its own. This was something Harrington verged on initiating several times after 3 September — the date of Robertson's posting to *Watson*.

The Naval Board had tried to do what it thought was best for Robertson, given that Board members never seriously considered he would resign. There was every chance that Robertson could still have been promoted to Flag rank had he remained in the service. Captain Dovers had certainly not been barred from promotion over the HMAS *Sydney* whaler tragedy. Indeed, the Deputy Departmental Secretary, Stuart Philpott, who was also a personal friend of Robertson, wrote several months later that 'I would have expected you to be promoted to rear-admiral in February 1965, but as you know such promotions are not arranged by the civil staff'. He also added that Robertson would have been in line for possible promotion to vice-admiral and appointment as CNS in 1971.[9] He would have contested this appointment with Rear-Admiral Richard Peek, who ultimately became CNS.

Robertson received the letter from Harrington advising him of his new posting along with dozens of other letters, telegrams and cards congratulating him on the findings of the Spicer Report. The writers of nearly every letter Robertson received believed he had been cleared of any blame. There is no doubt that this correspondence sat uneasily, because he did not reply to any of it. At about the same time, the Naval Board had also finally decided on the disciplinary action it would take against him and the general attitude it would adopt towards Spicer's criticisms. This was partly covered in the previous chapter. After reviewing the grounds on which Spicer based his remarks, the Board concluded that

> the only charge which could be laid against Captain Robertson would stem from his failure to blow three short blasts when his engines were put astern . . . In these circumstances, the Naval Board does not consider that Captain Robertson's omission amounts to negligent conduct, and is of the opinion that trial by court martial on this charge would not result in a conviction.[10]

The 'angle' to take on Spicer's criticisms of Robertson proved a vexing question for the newspapers. Both the *Sun* and the *Australian* featured front-page pictures of a smiling Captain Robertson, quoted as saying he was 'relieved' to read the findings and 'glad it is all over'.[11] A 'human interest' article by Ron Saw in the *Daily Mirror* was headed 'Skipper came through with flying colours'[12] while its editorial stated

> The finding of the Royal Commission . . . does nothing to remove the very deep public unease about this peacetime tragedy . . . It blames the dead for the collision and expresses some curiously mild criticism of the *Melbourne*'s personnel.

Evidently, not everyone was on Robertson's side.

Robertson had already decided the course of action he would take if not reappointed in command of *Melbourne*. He replied to Harrington's letter advising of his next posting several hours after it was received:

> Thank you for your letter which reached me here this morning. It was kind of you to let me know in advance.
>
> I fully understand the reasons which have prompted you to make this decision and I do not quarrel with it. I only wish I were capable of explaining to you the damage you are doing to the RAN in general.
>
> You must, of course, realise that as a matter of principle, I shall have to resign my commission. How and when I shall do this I have not yet decided.
>
> In the meantime it would be helpful if some thought could be given to my pension entitlements in view of the special circumstances of the case.

Robertson's posting was not promulgated on the next list of appointments, as previously promised by Harrington, and did not appear until 4 September. This fuelled press speculation. By that time Becher was back in Australia and the admirals had had a chance to meet. They decided it was not possible to send Robertson back to *Melbourne*.[13]

The ship was fully operational under Captain David Stevenson and there was a strong feeling that Australia would soon be involved in a war with Indonesia which would involve the use of substantial naval power. To have sent the inevitably tentative Robertson back in command would have disrupted the carrier's command team and adversely affected her operational efficiency at a time when this could not be contemplated. This was even conceded by Robertson's most staunch advocate, Admiral Hickling:

> Melbourne had returned to Australian waters on 1 September. Under the command of Captain David Stevenson she had gained for herself an enviable reputation as a smart and efficient ship in the Far East, where she had been taking part in SEATO exercises. It is bad for a ship's company to be constantly changing captains, for between the ship's company and the captain there is a very special relationship, a mutual confidence, a respect and comradeship fostered by continuity.[14]

During the previous month Indonesian infiltration began across the Straits of Malacca into Malaysia and tension increased. Britain felt that Indonesian claims over archipelagic waters, including the strategically vital Sunda and Lombok Straits, needed a direct challenge, and formed a formidable naval fleet to prove its right of innocent passage through these waters under international law. The RAN was receiving intelligence and detailed reports from the Royal Navy which assessed that war was probable.

The RAN was preparing to despatch Melbourne to increase Australia's regional profile and add appreciably to the fleet's combined naval air assets. Although the right of passage was demonstrated and firing by either side was averted, Indonesian infiltration across the Straits of Malacca continued.

By the end of 1964, the 'Confrontation' with Malaysia having been formally declared by Sukarno, RAN ships including Melbourne were taking an active role in protecting Malaysia through naval displays of strength and resolve, and anti-infiltration patrols. Melbourne was the foremost symbol of Australia's support for Malaysia. She had to be fully worked-up and ready for diverse operational contingencies.

The extent to which the Naval Board believed that war was likely was completely disregarded by Robertson and the press. The Board was obviously not in a position, owing to the security implications, to make public this assessment of regional affairs although it was principally for this reason that Robertson could not return to Melbourne. The Board acted on what it perceived were the best interests of the Navy and the nation. It was a justifiable decision and one which showed great courage and firmness of purpose.

After receiving official notice of his posting on 8 September, Robertson submitted his formal letter of resignation on 10 September.

> I have the honour to acknowledge receipt of my appointment to HMAS Watson

in command to date 9 November 1964, and to submit, with the greatest respect, that this appointment in effect, dismisses me from my previous command, namely HMAS *Melbourne*, with all the consequences that will necessarily follow.

This, Sir, as you will realise places me in an intolerable position. No charges have been preferred against me nor have I been requested or instructed to explain any circumstances which might possibly be thought to warrant my removal from the command of one of Her Majesty's Australian Vessels.

In the circumstances, therefore, I request that I may be permitted to resign my Commission as an officer in Her Majesty's Fleet. I enclose my commission with this submission.[15]

McNicoll, as FOICEA (Robertson's administrative authority) and the admiral closest personally to him, asked to see Robertson on 13 September. McNicoll tried to persuade Robertson at least to delay his resignation until he had taken up his appointment at *Watson*. McNicoll believed he was acting with too much haste and feared he might come to regret making this decision under enormous personal strain and anguish, remembering that the posting was meant to have some therapeutic value. Robertson, however, was resolute.

Although he hoped the parliamentary debate on 15 September may have forced a political solution in his favour, Robertson was not optimistic. He was greatly angered by two matters raised during the debate. The first concerned Menzies's statement that he could not be court martialled, something Robertson never accepted.

Robertson believed he was a victim of political expediency. He later wrote in a note to his counsel:

In my opinion, the whole tenor of the Prime Minister's statement creates a slur against Kelly, Bate and myself ... It is true to say that evidence as given before a Royal Commission is not admissible as such at the subsequent court martial proceedings. There is no objection, however, to the court martial calling the same witnesses as were called at the Royal Commission and asking them the same questions and getting from them the same answers. This is quite normal procedure. They cannot, of course, drag out of us the reasons we gave for the actions we took, but the fact that we took that action can be established by the evidence of others. Therefore, for the Prime Minister to hide behind what he calls legal opinion is merely avoiding the issue. He should have come out and said that there was no charge to be laid against any of us and therefore there was to be no court martial or he could have said that there were charges to be laid and that a court martial would proceed.[16]

Commander Larry Winch, the member of the Naval Staff who had advised the Board that disciplinary action was not possible, later wrote to Robertson: 'I thought you were sold down the river unscrupulously ... Your resignation is the Navy's loss, but if from your example a little rubs off onto us, it will make for a better Service.'[17]

The decision not to table the Board's response was the second source of Robertson's anger:

I wonder whether the Naval Board report said that there were no charges to be laid or whether it said that the charges were there but could not be sustained due to the inadmissibility of the evidence?

I wonder if the Board changed its opinion about the cause of the collision after seeing the Spicer report? Were there pressures brought to bear on the Board, and if so who was behind them? What really did go on behind the scenes in Canberra after the Royal Commission report was presented?[18]

The answer to the last question was very easy: nothing. There were no pressures brought to bear on the Board and it did not change its view of the collision as a consequence of Spicer's report. Without any concrete evidence, Robertson fell back on a 'conspiracy theory'.

After the debate in Parliament on 15 September, the Government realised the extent of support for Robertson and the existence of public concern that he would be denied a pension if he resigned. Brian Johns, writing in the *Australian* on 22 September, reported that Senator Shane Paltridge, the Defence Minister and Government Leader in the Upper House, had hardened in his attitude towards Robertson because of the publicity he had been receiving since the Commission had concluded. Paltridge, who was known to be one of Menzies's closest confidantes, was determined that there would be no bargaining with Robertson.[19]

On 17 September, the Naval Board met specifically to consider his position. It decided that Robertson's resignation would be accepted and that he be called to Navy Office the following day to ascertain whether he wanted any special representations to be made on his behalf for the granting of a pension, and whether he was willing to contribute an additional lump sum for a pension to be granted. Harrington drafted a letter to Robertson after the Board's meeting, but it was never sent. It read:

The Board appreciates your position. It reserves the right to appoint officers as it sees fit.

The Board does not wish to dispense with your services. Nevertheless, having regard to all the circumstances it has decided to forward your application [to resign] for consideration by the Governor General.[20]

Chaney asked Robertson to see him in Canberra on 18 September. The Minister informed Robertson that notwithstanding his own wishes, he was not entitled to a pension under the *Defence Force Retirement Benefits Act* (DFRB Act). At the same meeting it was agreed that his resignation would take effect on 28 September 1964.

The decision having been made, Harrington showed some charity.

It is my opinion, however, that although he has no entitlement to anything other than a return of his contributions without interest, every endeavour should be made to obtain a pension for him as an act of grace.[21]

The next day Admiral Smith, the Second Naval Member, recommended to Harrington that in order to satisfy the conditions of the DFRB Act and grant Robertson a pension, he should be 'retired in the interests of the Service'.[22] The reasons are illuminating. Smith suggested that Harrington should tell the DFRB Board that Robertson would not be returning to *Melbourne* because his return would have disrupted the ship's operational effectiveness. This much was true.

> Furthermore, it is not intended that Captain Robertson should return to command *Melbourne* at any future date as such action would deprive other aspiring captains of lesser seniority of this command.[23]

It was further stated, although inaccurately, that Robertson could not fulfil the requirement for promotion to Flag rank in that he would not have commanded a carrier for a period of at least twelve months. Thus, he could not be considered for promotion and accordingly had a limited future in the RAN.

Smith's comments on promotion to flag rank did not reflect the current policy or practice but it appeared to establish a case for granting Robertson a pension. That one member of the Naval Board was prepared to devise this 'story' showed the extent to which the Board was sympathetic to his position and eager to help.

Landau tried vigorously to persuade Chaney to put to the DFRB Board Smith's view that Robertson be retired in the interest of the Navy. As the matter involved some ministerial discretion, Chaney agonised over the matter for several days.[24]

A man of undisputed conscience, Chaney was aware that the case his department had proposed on Robertson's behalf was not entirely truthful. As a politician, he also realised that to make a submission on these grounds after Robertson had resigned would have strengthened the case of those who portrayed Robertson as a scapegoat dismissed from his ship by a critical Naval Board that did not have the courage to explain its reasons publicly. Chaney informed Landau that no case would be put to the DFRB Board on the grounds proposed. Robertson would not get the pension of £1,771 he would have received had he been, as the Act required, 'retired to meet the needs of the Service'.

Robertson's resignation was further discussed by Cabinet on 22 September 1964, when a special act of grace payment was considered. Cabinet resolved that 'no payment should be made other than those for which the law provides'.[25] To have the matter dealt with before the resumption of parliamentary debate on the Spicer Report on 23 September, Menzies called a special meeting of the Executive Council on 22 September for the specific purpose of accepting Robertson's resignation later that day. His resignation accepted, Robertson was then appointed to the Emergency Reserve List. His commission was returned to him on the recommendation of the Naval Board. When Robertson's resignation appeared in the *Commonwealth Gazette* some time later, it also revealed that Robertson had been appointed an honorary aide-de-camp to the Queen on 8 September 1964 but that the appointment had expired when his resignation became effective on 28 September.[26]

As Cabinet was meeting, the Navy began preparing for the onslaught of criticism it would receive when the resignation took effect. Smith advised Landau that if Robertson had been unhappy with the way he was treated, he was obliged to submit a complaint or a redress of grievance through his administrative authority to the Naval Board.[27] However, the damage had been well and truly done. Robertson's name and face were on the front page of every metropolitan newspaper. He had become a celebrity and had achieved the status which was the mandatory precondition for fervent public advocacy — he was seen as an innocent victim of a faceless and cowering bureaucracy.

The *Daily Mirror* headed its editorial on 18 September: 'What a Raw Deal!'

> Captain Robertson is the Naval Board and the Navy Department's scapegoat. His axing, thinly disguised as a shore posting, is a disgraceful underhanded move by the Government. The case of Captain Robertson is of grave concern to the public.

The *Sunday Mirror*'s article on 20 September was entitled, 'The Ordeal of Captain Scapegoat'.

Robertson's resignation, rumoured then confirmed, continued to dominate the newspapers and the parliamentary debate then in progress. For over two weeks the press followed the tortuous progress of his resignation. Believing his career had ended before it had even started, Bate submitted his resignation but the Naval Board refused to accept it. Kelly and Bate also wanted courts martial as a means of answering Spicer's criticisms of their conduct. As with Robertson, their desire to be court martialled fell on deaf ears. Neither was ever informed of the Naval Board's attitude towards Spicer's criticisms or its assessment of their performance on the night of the collision.

Kelly and Bate continued to serve — Kelly as Fleet Navigating Officer until the end of 1965, and Bate as a watchkeeping officer on *Vampire*. Kelly later commanded a destroyer and retired as a captain in 1979. Bate was promoted to commander some years later and commanded a frigate. He transferred to the RAN Emergency Reserve with that rank in 1987. In many ways, Kelly and Bate were the forgotten men of the *Voyager* affair despite the legacy of trauma and anxiety which was left by the collision.

In the wake of the parliamentary debate, Robertson had replaced the ill-fated *Voyager* as the focus of public attention. In what was a helpful corrective, the *Age* editorial of 23 September suggested that Parliament and the nation should not be distracted by the controversy over Robertson:

> There is no doubt the Navy has been shaken up. But while Captain Robertson remains the centre of controversy it is important that Parliament should not be

distracted from the basic need to ensure that the Navy is ready, experienced and well led at all times. There must be no more unexplained disasters.

This also fell on deaf ears. Riding on a wave of public support, Robertson was receiving hundreds of letters, all of which were highly sympathetic to him and virulently critical of the Naval Board. One letter, from a fellow RAN captain, described the mood within the RAN well at that level. Captain Anthony Synnot, who was then serving on secondment as the Malaysian CNS, wrote:

> It is very difficult from this distance to follow what is happening; however it was clear from the outset that the blame did not lie with the *Melbourne*. The unwarranted anguish, strain and mental torture that the Commission and the Press must have put you to was quite unjustified. It is most distressing to me and to all others of us up here. It could have happened to any of us.[28]

But what would resigning achieve? Robertson's personal correspondence clearly shows his decision to resign was purely and simply a matter of principle. He regarded Spicer's criticisms as a serious censure which he sought to have lifted by an additional inquiry, or negated by his return to *Melbourne* in command. There was nothing personally vindictive about his decision. Nor was it conceived as a protest. Although Robertson vowed to 'clear his name', he seems to have given little thought about how, as a civilian, he might achieve the justice he sought. There was a hint of concern over this in a letter he received from Naval College term-mate, James Ramsey:

> I can only hope that with the Board and the Government against you, you can get some satisfaction out of your next move. I am entirely with you on principle, but I hope you have some back-up at home because a lone battle against the 'authorities' is hardly likely to succeed.[29]

His resignation having taken effect at midnight on 28 September 1964, Robertson was free to comment publicly on the whole affair for the first time. Early on 29 September, he gave a press conference on the lawn of his Neutral Bay home. The next day, a reporter with the *Daily Mirror* wrote:

> For the Press, it was the biggest day since the Beatles. Precisely 40 of us — reporters, photographers, radiomen, TV interviewers and their crews — gathered in the morning sun ... At 0855, he [Robertson] glanced at his watch and marched to his position in front of the cameras and microphones. In his best bridge voice, loud and clear, he announced, 'I will now read my statement. You may then ask any questions.'[30]

The press conference lasted for two hours and marked the start of his campaign against the Naval Board, which he held primarily responsible for what had happened to him.[31] He criticised the Board for the way in which it had handled the affair, emphasising the particular roles played by Harrington and Becher. He also mentioned Gatacre for his destructive remarks at the Commission. Robertson lamented not having been asked for his version of events by the Naval Board, but said he did not consider that he was, or was ever meant to be, a scapegoat. What seemed to disappoint him most was that he had not been given an opportunity to discuss his next posting with the Naval Board. However, he remained firmly convinced that he should have been sent back to *Melbourne* at some stage in the future.

Robertson was perfectly correct when he pointed out that the distance between the Naval Board and naval personnel was too great. The lofty podium on which the Board believed it sat precluded it from explaining, let alone justifying, its actions to anyone. Robertson could not understand his treatment, and drew the worst inference from every event. Smith wrote to Harrington and Landau after Robertson's press conference disputing most of the allegations of unjust treatment made by Robertson. He said there had been no need for a ministerial statement on his appointment to *Watson*; Robertson had no right to expect a personal copy of the Spicer Report; and he should not have made public Harrington's letter to him advising him of his next posting without Harrington's approval. In addition, Smith disputed Robertson's claim that morale had suffered and denied that he had been 'dismissed his ship'.[32]

The Naval Board was adamant that if Robertson had wanted to convey any information or make any representation, he should have submitted a request to do so. As it had received Robertson's interim and final reports on the collision, it was of the view that Robertson had conveyed all he wished to convey to the Board.[33] Indeed, Hickling said Robertson's 'was a model report, concise and to the point, nothing was left out, no superfluous word intruded'.[34]

However, given the isolation that Robertson felt and the silence of the Board, it is not hard to see why Robertson saw things as he did. He sincerely believed his 'honour' and good name had been slighted, something that featured in a personal letter he wrote to Archdeacon John Were on 9 October:

> It's a sad and sorry affair in lots of ways but on the other hand although I had naturally have rather stayed on there was no doubt in my mind that I had no alternative in the circumstances.
>
> One can only make decisions which one hopes are right as one passes through life and hope that the future will take care of itself — not entirely, of course, but another way.
>
> There is no hope for the future if one is to live it in a state of shame for not having done what had to be done. All rather involved but I feel sure that you understand.[35]

After his press conference, Robertson gave personal interviews with several radio and television news programmes and his name became a household word. He was approached by Station HSV7 in *Melbourne* to appear on 'Meet the Press' and was even invited to stand for the

Australian Republican Party as a candidate for the next Senate elections. Hugh Curnow, an editor at the *Bulletin*, strongly encouraged Robertson to write his memoirs and advised a strategy for their newspaper serialisation.[36] Robertson told several reporters that he intended to write a book on collisions at sea, but this never eventuated.

While the tabloid newspapers had become advocates for Robertson's cause, the editorial writers for the three major metropolitan newspapers were much less supportive. The *Age* said:

> It is difficult to see what other course the Naval Board could have taken but that of giving him a new appointment of captain's rank. One wonders what the critics in full cry would have said had Robertson been returned to command HMAS *Melbourne*. Would there have been a new chorus berating the Naval Board and the Government for complacency and disregard of the Commission's criticisms? The personal drama of Captain Robertson should now be closed. The broader and more important aspect of the disaster remains.[37]

The *Australian* even had some sympathy for the Naval Board:

> [T]here is no reason to believe that the Naval Board made Captain Robertson's appointment with the sole purpose of victimising him; nor can it be expected that the Board will make the other factors public; nor would it restore public confidence in the Navy, if having made the decision, the Board reversed it in the face of an ultimatum.[38]

The *Sydney Morning Herald* was the only newspaper to adopt a hostile attitude to Robertson:

> A naval officer of his long experience could not have reasonably expected, in all circumstances, that he would be reappointed to command HMAS *Melbourne*. Nor was there any reason why the Naval Board should, as some of its critics suggest, have 'given him a hearing' . . . That he chose not to serve in the same rank in another capacity is his own affair.[39]

It is impossible to know what the Naval Board imagined Robertson would do after he had left the RAN. In resigning, he had shown himself, as far as the Board was concerned, unpredictable and irrational. Any sympathy Board members may have felt ended when he published five major feature articles in the *Australian*. Although it was not made known at the time, Robertson was assisted by two journalists, one from the *Australian* and one from the *Daily Mirror*.

Robertson could easily have been vengeful in these articles. However, he was fair in most of his comments and repeated many of the sentiments he had expressed on various earlier occasions.[40]

The first article covered the circumstances of the controversy and established the grounds for his criticism of Harrington, Gatacre and Becher, particularly the latter for his remark to Robertson during the night of the collision that 'There was nothing you could do'. Robertson made far too much of this. There is a big difference between a sentiment expressed in the emotion of a tragedy to calm a shocked person and the matter dispassionately considered. The former is a comforting sentiment; the latter a considered opinion. (With hindsight, Becher should have perhaps said nothing when he arrived on board the carrier after the collision. But this would have been heartless.) Robertson's bitterness and resentment was made clear in his closing statement:

> If the five seagoing admirals of the Australian Fleet had been on the bridge of the *Melbourne* on the night of the collision and if each of them had had the opportunity to intervene when he considered it necessary, then the collision would have occurred in the same way.[41]

In notes prepared for his counsel under the heading 'Sudden situation', it is apparent that Robertson failed to understand one important rationale for the criticism levelled at him:

> It has been suggested (e.g., Senator Gorton in Parliament) that because Kelly ordered 'Half astern' before I gave 'Full astern', his reaction was quicker than mine, thus showing that I had been standing there open-mouthed and doing nothing. I would suggest, however, that a more objective and unbiased appreciation will show that these two orders, given almost contemporaneously by two different observers, points very clearly to the sudden arrival of the dangerous situation.[42]

Robertson clearly missed the point. Kelly gave his order instantly on seeing *Voyager* moving towards the carrier whereas Robertson had been watching the whole situation develop from the bridge-wing. Other than Kelly having coincidentally noticed *Voyager* at the very moment that a collision became imminent, the Fleet Navigator's reaction, which occurred perhaps five seconds before that of his captain, reflects adversely on Robertson. In other words, it was immediately apparent to Kelly that *Voyager* was where she should not have been. As achieving this position must have taken some time, it should have become apparent to Robertson before Kelly. This created the inference that Robertson could have been slow to react to a dangerous situation. Alternatively, one could conclude that Kelly had excellent powers of anticipation.

In the second *Australian* article, Robertson provided his explanation of the collision and opened his criticism of Spicer, whom he said 'did not have the deep naval knowledge necessary to extract this story from the evidence before him'. The article featured a diagram and commentary, and was presented in such a way that readers with superficial knowledge or limited understanding of fleet manoeuvres would have accepted his reconstruction and understood his theory about why the collision had occurred.

Having put his case and stressed that he was not in any way to blame, the third article was headed 'Why I Resigned from the Navy'. Robertson claimed his career to date should have afforded him better treatment than that which he received in 1964. He even went as far as commenting upon the dock wall collision at Williamstown in 1958, in contending that the 'vanity of experience' principle had been invoked against him even then. It suggested something like a conspiracy and could have been left unsaid. He was on more appealing grounds when he spoke of loyalty and devotion to service. This included a shot at the Naval Board: 'I believe the Naval Board has sold its birthright. I do not know whether the Board will be able to buy it back. I hope it can.' He predicted the Navy would suffer a severe loss of confidence in its leadership. It was a familiar theme in Australian literature and had a parallel in the Anzacs at Gallipoli — good men, poorly led.

The fourth article contained the least substance. Robertson claimed the Naval Board had two voices: one it used in public, the other it reserved for its political masters. It covered the conduct of the Royal Commission and then drifted into a series of ponderables that created suspicion but little compulsion for official action.

The fifth and final article was Robertson's parting broadside at the Naval Board. Although the article was headed 'What's Wrong With the Navy', it was another catalogue of criticism of the Naval Board. According to Robertson, 'the failure in leadership from the top is basically what's wrong with the Navy.' He asked whether 'the organisation and pattern of administration as a whole is capable of providing the leadership required'. This was a tantalising question, given that Robertson had been, to a very large degree, a product of that organisation and administration. Unfortunately, he gave no answer. After writing about the Navy's need for more forceful leadership, new management techniques and better public relations, he criticised the attitudes of both naval and civil staff in Navy Office in Canberra:

> These two groups of short-sighted men are the cause of much unnecessary friction, jealousy and inefficiency ... The fact that too many men in the higher executive positions allow petty jealousies to interfere with their work permeates through both the naval and civil sides. In my opinion it can only be eradicated through corrective example set at the top.

He was especially critical of parochialism within the Navy, something he argued also emanated from the Naval Board. His solution was simplistic.

> I would suggest the employment of a firm of management consultants to go into Navy Office in Canberra. Such firms are specialists in this field, and although not capable of making any miraculous overnight improvement are able to provide the extra thinking capacity at executive level which is so urgently required if these faults I have mentioned are to be put right.

As for the Navy's future, Robertson had an abiding faith in the quality of naval officers and appears to have felt the Navy's leadership was the product of a bad lot rising to the top at the worst time. In citing the Navy's need for a Nelson — that supreme naval father and a vital part of the rallying mythology — Robertson concluded his article on a positive note:

> It gets back to having the right men in the right place at the right time — men

who not only select the right ideas and make the right decisions but who are
prepared to fight to get these ideas translated into action.

The articles had a great impact on the *Australian*'s readership, which
was swelled by their publication. There were many letters to the editor
supporting Robertson and condemning the Naval Board. Despite
Robertson's restraint, the articles were highly controversial and were
widely discussed in naval and government circles. Never before had the
RAN been so openly or harshly criticised. That these criticisms came
from a recently serving senior officer and that he had widespread public
sympathy over his treatment throughout the Royal Commission, made
them all the more convincing to those who read them.

The Naval Board hoped this would-be 'martyr' would soon be
forgotten. There was never any mention of Robertson's resignation in
*Navy News* and no further mention of *Voyager*. John Robertson had not
done what was 'in the best interests of the Service'. He was an outcast.
The Board hoped that he would gradually drift into obscurity and that,
along with *Voyager*, he too would soon be forgotten.

# 11

# A Soliloquy of Shame

ON THE FIRST anniversary of the loss of *Voyager*, naval memorial services were held around the nation. The Naval Board, not unexpectedly, wanted the official commemorations to be low-key.[1] Two chaplains from NAS Nowra, the Reverend Walter Wheeldon and Father Franks Lyons, conducted a memorial service from a Navy Wessex helicopter over the site of the ship's loss and cast a wreath into the sea. In *Melbourne*, Archdeacon John Were conducted a service at which 500 were present. These commemorations were to be the last on the direction of the Naval Board, which decided that *Voyager* would not be specially remembered each year, but numbered among those RAN ships lost at sea.[2]

Apart from the president, members of the Naval Board were confident about handling the legacy of the disaster both inside and outside the Service. When public interest faded, the matter would be over. Chaney believed the Board was too hasty in its efforts to drop the subject of the Royal Commission. He thought the main problem was 'that naval officers had no idea of how low their public image had fallen and the low public esteem in which the Navy was held'.[3] One key indicator was recruiting. The hoped-for improvement in November 1964 had not been achieved by May 1965. As a consequence, the Board authorised the production of new recruiting material, including films and handouts, and sought to bring naval recruiting and public relations functions much closer together.

A change of personalities would clear the air and refresh higher naval administration. Rear-Admiral Alan McNicoll was named as Harrington's successor as CNS. It was fully expected that he would be favoured over Becher, whose performance during the *Voyager* Commission had won him few accolades.

As a middle ranking officer, McNicoll distinguished himself during World War II with the dangerous work of disarming eight torpedoes in a captured Italian submarine. He was awarded the George Medal. After the war he was consistently promoted ahead of his peers until, in 1957, he attained Flag rank on being posted as Head of the Australian

Joint Defence Staff in London. By the time he was promoted vice admiral and appointed CNS, he was self-assured and seemed pompous and domineering. McNicoll successfully avoided the taint of association with *Voyager* and wanted to leave the distasteful matter far behind. In a year he would be knighted as well. Certainly, he showed no interest in reversing any apparent or real injustices associated with the Spicer Royal Commission.

Yet, having reached the top of his chosen profession, McNicoll's ambition was far from satisfied and he sought further preferment. The position of Chairman of the Chiefs of Staff Committee (COSC) attracted McNicoll and he let it be known within Parliament House that he was interested in the job. However, McNicoll knew that the next incumbent, according to the unofficial but strictly observed order of rotation, was to be an army officer. It would be fair to say that McNicoll had a personal agenda which had the potential to conflict with what was best for the RAN. If nothing else, avoiding any controversy would have earned him ample credit with the Government.

Robertson's often dogmatic personality did not allow him to forget the injustice he believed he had suffered at the hands of Sir John Spicer. Robertson was an individual with a point to prove. From 1 October 1964, he had been employed by the *Australian* as a special defence correspondent. This employment was helpful to his cause, although he always considered it to be of a short-term nature. While working as a journalist, Robertson made no further specific comment on *Voyager*.

There was little newspaper coverage of *Voyager* in early 1965. The press believed it was finished and politically dead, although the *Sydney Morning Herald* gave it a temporary reprieve in its editorial of 26 March 1965:

> After the hammering that he and his government took in parliament during the debate on the Opposition Censure Motion last September, the Prime Minister cannot be unaware of the extent of public uneasiness aroused by the evidence given to the Royal Commission, and by the attitude taken by some senior naval officers before it. Nothing has transpired since to allay that disquiet, or even to suggest that any steps have been taken to allay it.

Despite the absence of public interest, private efforts aimed at helping Robertson continued unabated. One form of pressure constantly exerted was protest letters written to a number of senior Government ministers. Within the Parliament, Jess continued to press Robertson's right to a pension or a payment in lieu. If there was to be a political resolution, Jess was now Robertson's only hope.

John Jess was a physically imposing man with an aggressive and forthright personality. Both Jess and Robertson were aware that direct political action rather than public advocacy offered Robertson his best chance of settling his grievances.

Robertson had known Jess for some time. Robertson's wife, Bettina, was related to Jess by marriage, and a friendship existed between the two men well before the events of 1964. From the time Robertson's intention to resign was known, Jess attempted to persuade Menzies that some compensatory payment should be made to Robertson. He had his first interview with Menzies on the subject in September 1964 after the Commission's report was debated in Parliament. Shortly afterwards, Robertson spoke with retired Lieutenant Commander Peter Cabban, *Voyager*'s executive officer until four weeks before the collision, who had recounted his experiences with Captain Stevens. Cabban claimed that Stevens frequently drank alcohol to excess while *Voyager* was in harbour, but was emphatic that he never drank at sea.

Robertson conveyed the substance of this discussion to Jess, who was convinced that it was relevant to the cause of the disaster. Menzies did not consider that the evidence, as it then existed, was sufficiently compelling and was not moved to reopen the inquiry. It seemed the only way of achieving 'justice' for Robertson was to establish some new ground. Cabban's allegations appeared to offer the greatest hope.

In New Zealand, Vice-Admiral Harold Hickling, a Royal Navy officer who had retired some fifteen years earlier, had followed the events of the *Voyager* Royal Commission with more than a passing interest. Hickling obtained a copy of the Spicer Report and read Robertson's articles in the *Australian*. Having written two books on his own naval career and possessing a conviction that Robertson had suffered unfairly, Hickling decided to write an account of the collision in the hope of correcting the injustice he believed Robertson had suffered. Hickling wrote to Robertson on 18 November 1964 outlining his project and asking for assistance.[4] Robertson had little to lose and agreed to help Hickling in return for a fishing trip in New Zealand. Robertson travelled across the Tasman on 8 January 1965 and the two started working on a book that would be published at the end of that year. It would be called *One Minute of Time*.

What 'justice' for Robertson meant in practical terms was not made clear. Did Robertson want to be reinstated to command of *Melbourne*, granted a pension, or have the findings of Spicer overturned? Not even Hickling seemed to know what Robertson wanted.

Hickling was something of a 'terrier': small, aggressive, energetic and given to sniping. Although aged over 70, he was the driving force behind Robertson's campaign. Robertson's wife firmly believed that her husband owed an enormous debt to Hickling and his energetic advocacy.[5]

Hickling felt that his own naval career amply qualified him to write a book about the collision and the Commission, even though he had never served or lived in Australia, nor had he worked closely with the RAN.[6]

Hickling also brought to his book a deep resentment of any civilian involvement in naval affairs. Although he gained the rank of vice-admiral, he was never given any part in administering the Royal Navy nor had he any experience of working in a political environment. It may be, therefore, that he was less than the amply qualified and unbiased observer he claimed to be.

In the course of collecting material for Hickling's book, Robertson explained to Hickling that he had spoken to Cabban and that he might be able to provide some background information on Captain Stevens. What sort of information Robertson was referring to, or why it was relevant to the collision, was not made clear. On returning to Australia, Robertson invited Cabban and his wife to dinner at his home and suggested to Cabban that his knowledge would be of value to Hickling in preparing a character profile of Stevens. He then offered to lend Cabban his tape recorder for the purpose of making a confidential statement for Hickling.

That same night, 29 January 1965, and without any notes or references, Cabban dictated a statement lasting forty-five minutes. Robertson had the statement transcribed and Cabban signed it. The statement was then sent to Hickling.[7] (The full text of the Cabban Statement is provided in Appendix I.)

A copy of the Cabban Statement, as it became known, was retained by Hickling's publishers in New Zealand, A.W. & A.H. Reed. It met with the response Cabban was anticipating. Ray Richards, a senior staff member at Reed, wrote to Robertson:

> It is a shattering document and raises a hundred questions that should have been raised by the Naval Board and the Commission. And there must be another dozen officers who could give damning testimony along the same lines. Without the extent of alcoholism or heavy and prolonged drinking there would surely have been no collision — there can be no possible escape from that conclusion.[8]

There was little doubt that both Robertson and Hickling were persuaded by Cabban's evidence and, one assumes, its relevance to the causes of the collision. In a letter to Robertson, Hickling's companion stated that

> As the picture of D.S. [Duncan Stevens] emerges, one begins to feel that the collision was inevitable — if not then, some other time or place. At least that is how it strikes me.[9]

If the contents of this letter had been made public, it would have become a crucial document. How the Cabban Statement struck a disinterested observer related directly to popular perceptions of Stevens and the public's desire for another inquiry.

The problem faced by Hickling, Robertson and the publishers was whether or not to mention Cabban by name. Realising the import of Cabban's statement and the inference made in the book that vital evidence had been withheld, a decision was finally made against mentioning Cabban by name or identifying him as an ex-naval officer.[10] Robertson was still not comfortable about using Stevens's drinking habits as a lever for gaining a new inquiry, as his comments on one of Hickling's early draft chapters reveals:

> My initial reactions regarding the triple brandy are that references to it in the text of the story may well give the wrong impression. It certainly hits you in the face when you read it — but perhaps I am too sensitive. I wonder whether a completely separate chapter pointing to the gaps in the evidence on this subject and inferring that there was some kind of collusion to suppress the rest may not be a better way. After all, no one knows, nor will they ever find out, whether or not the drink question had any bearing on the collision. But we do know that much of the evidence on this subject was suppressed and also that some at least of the character evidence given for Stevens was incomplete to put it mildly.[11]

Despite his reticence about using this evidence, Robertson's personal view of Stevens had obviously undergone a transformation since the Spicer Commission. Hickling adopted an ambivalent view. He had written to Robertson on 13 May 1965 remarking,

> The drinking question is fading more and more into the background and I am beginning to feel you were right in not letting Hicks use Cabban's evidence.[12]

Robertson also sought comments on the collision and the Commission from other naval officers. One of the respondents, Captain George Fowle, told Hickling: 'To cast reflections on a man who cannot speak for himself is unpleasant, but at one stage certainly, Captain Stevens was an alcoholic, something of course which cannot well be proved unless evidence can be given.'[13] Cabban was obviously going to be that evidence.

To assist Hickling's research, Robertson wrote to the Department of the Navy on 24 March 1965 seeking copies of his letters and reports concerning the collision, and asking that 'permission could be given for these reports to be freely used as the basis for published material'.[14] In a reply from the Director of Naval Intelligence (DNI), Robertson was reminded of the relevant section of the *Crimes Act* which made it an offence to disclose information in reports that had not been made public.[15] Further, the DNI pointed out that permission would only be given if the reports were to be used 'as the basis for producing your own story'. There is little doubt that the Navy knew Robertson already had copies of the documents he was seeking in his letter.

Landau wrote to Robertson on 8 April enclosing the papers Robertson had requested, with some editing for security purposes having been completed by Naval Intelligence.[16] However, Landau reiterated the condition that they were supplied on 'the clear understanding that they should not be published. There is no objection to any information they contain being used as a basis or background for articles prepared for publication.' Robertson took this to infer that 'my request to use these reports has been refused'.[17] Two weeks later Landau confirmed that Robertson was not 'authorised to publish the reports, or extracts from them, as such'.[18]

As these were official reports, they were the property of the Navy and could not be quoted without its permission. Yet, the essence of the documents could be relayed in print. Why the Navy took this action is unclear. Most of the information had been tabled at the Royal Commission. Although the position of the Navy as stated by Landau was technically correct, it appeared to be an obstruction to further discussion of the collision.

On 3 May 1965, having already supplied the documents to Hickling, Robertson again wrote to Landau pointing out his previous letter 'does not answer my question ... The purpose of my letters has been to seek permission for them to be released for publication.'[19] Landau stated in reply that permission for them to be published was not granted, and as far as he was concerned, the matter was closed.[20] Robertson thought about writing again. He drafted a letter lamenting the Navy's obstinacy and the need for him to explain in print that he had been refused permission to publish his reports. He decided to let the matter rest and advised Hickling to use the reports but without indicating that they were direct quotations.

The exchanges between Robertson and the Naval Board generated a great amount of ill-will and created suspicion on both sides. The Naval Board was still unsure about what Robertson intended to do. Robertson believed the behaviour of the Naval Board confirmed his view that it was not interested in finding out why the collision had occurred.

While Hickling was working on his book, Robertson showed the Cabban Statement to Jess who confirmed that Robertson had doubts about the 'fairness' of using the statement for his own ends:

> It took me many days of argument and persuasion to get Robertson to agree that Cabban's evidence might be relevant. Involved in this was his deep concern that the Navy would be harmed, and this he would not be party to. Cabban considered that his experiences in *Voyager* with her captain should be examined and considered, but also stressed this should be in confidence. He stated his willingness to be examined and to give his information to the Prime Minister or anyone nominated by him. Both were adamant at all times that publicity should be avoided both in fairness to the Stevens family and the Navy. After my first interview with Sir Robert Menzies I advised them that the Prime Minister was unwilling to see Cabban or investigate the matter further. Eventually they consented to let me have what is now known as the Cabban Statement, provided that it be shown only to the Prime Minister and Cabinet.

With a signed copy of the Cabban Statement in his possession, Jess sought another interview with the Prime Minister in mid-1965, and on this occasion he was more sympathetic. Menzies remarked that even if only half of the statement were factual, he would find it difficult to believe a man such as Stevens could be given command of a warship.

Time passed and Jess heard nothing from Menzies. Fearing the Prime Minister was going to ignore the allegations, Jess indicated that he would bring the matter up in the party room. A week later he saw Menzies for a third time. By this stage a copy of the Statement had finally been passed to the Department of the Navy which had made its own inquiries, albeit very superficially. Without being aware of anything that had gone on before, something which angered Chaney, the Navy Minister asked a series of questions:

> How can it have any effect on the Commission's findings? What is gained by using it in any forum? If there is substance in the statement it raises the question: how does such a person retain command?[21]

Chaney also recalled, in an interview with me, Harrington's remark during the Spicer Commission that if the consumption of brandy were made an issue, that is, Hyland's evidence, 'the Navy would close ranks'.[22] He was concerned also that the Statement had been kept from him for over six months and his departmental officers could not provide an adequate explanation for withholding it from him. It was now more than twelve months since Spicer submitted his report and nearly a year since Jess first saw Menzies. Chaney's response is significant in that it reveals the Navy's initial approach to the statement.

In a minute dated 23 August 1965, Landau stated that Smyth had been contacted and confirmed that, in his opinion and in the statements of other *Voyager* officers, Stevens's drinking was of no relevance. Smyth and Sheppard formed the 'impression that Cabban seemed to bear an underlying grudge against the Navy and Captain Stevens'.[23] The Navy had also asserted that Stevens was a competent destroyer captain and that it had no reason to doubt that he was anything less than that on the night of the collision. The minute mentioned McNicoll, Rear-Admiral Morrison and Captain James Willis as officers who could testify to Stevens's capabilities and character. The final paragraph revealed the Navy's hand:

> It has not been possible to make a close factual check of the various statements made in Cabban's document, as this would involve extensive consultation with numerous officers and reference to records. *This would be undesirable.* Admiral McNicoll is the only officer who has been consulted. As Flag Officer Commanding the Fleet at the time, he says there was no report of the collision between *Voyager* and *Vampire*, nor of the near collision between *Voyager* and *Ark Royal*.[24] [emphasis added]

This was a remarkable confession. None of the factual details of the Statement had actually been checked. Other than McNicoll, no one had been consulted and the relevant records remained unexamined. How then could the Naval Board say that Cabban's allegations were either untrue or irrelevant to the causes of the collision? McNicoll did not even want to be pressed on Stevens's professional ability. He said he was 'an officer of average intelligence, completely engrossed in the Service, but not more than an able, experienced, run-of-the-mill destroyer captain. I could not in any way describe him as outstanding.'[25]

Most noteworthy is the illogical assertion in the last sentence of the minute that because there was no report of the collision between *Voyager* and *Vampire*, it did not happen. Consequently, it was unlikely that anything contained in the Statement had actually happened. Chaney forwarded Landau's minute to Menzies the following day.

The Prime Minister offered to have the matter investigated further but was not convinced that anything useful would come from reopening the case. Shortly afterwards, during a Cabinet meeting, Menzies spoke with Gorton, the former Navy Minister, about the allegations and remarked that he was considering a new inquiry. Gorton informed Menzies that if another inquiry were held, as minister responsible for the Navy during the year to which the allegations related, he would be forced to resign.[26] The fact that this discussion took place was not revealed to Jess and has not been previously disclosed publicly. However, it is possible that McNicoll was told of the discussion by Gorton. To have a promising minister like Gorton resign was politically unacceptable to Menzies, who again took no further action. The Prime Minister was able to deflect further pressure from Jess until the time of his retirement in January 1966. When Harold Holt succeeded Menzies, he was to find *Voyager* hidden away in a bottom drawer of the prime ministerial desk. It was something he would have wished Menzies had either dealt with or taken with him.

By the end of 1965, then, *Voyager* was still a politically dead issue. Something was needed to return the disaster and the fate of Robertson to public prominence. The release of Hickling's book met this need. *One Minute of Time* was launched with a flurry of publicity. Hickling gave a news conference and both he and Robertson agreed to be interviewed. It seemed *Voyager* might have another life.

The release of the book came just as the Navy's general press coverage had started to improve. The 13 November 1965 edition of the *Bulletin* carried a very positive lead story about the rejuvenation of the Navy. The article, by respected defence writer Tom Millar, was headed 'The Navy after Years of Neglect: Will the New Policy Last?' Millar made only passing mention of *Voyager* when he said, 'Twelve months ago the Navy and the nation were still recovering from the shock of the *Voyager* disaster and the apparent (largely unproven) implications of inefficiency in the Service'.

Hickling made no secret of the fact that *One Minute of Time* was written to assist Robertson. It was effectively the collision and its aftermath as seen by *Melbourne*'s captain. Based on source material that was arranged to show Robertson in the most favourable light, the narrative was disjointed, over-simplified and replete with special pleading. The story jumped from the frequent intrusion of episodes from Hickling's own career to the events of 1964.

Hickling's view of the collision was little different from Robertson's. Indeed, it is likely that Hickling's view was an amalgam of his own suppositions and the version put by Robertson in the *Australian*. Yet, Hickling made much of the independence of his authorship of the book. This was fiction. The book was extensively redrafted by Robertson, who provided most of the factual material and commentary, and Ray Richards, an editor employed by the publishers. They attempted to blend Robertson's analysis and pleading with Hickling's reminiscences. In his last letter to Hickling before *One Minute of Time* was published, Richards said:

> There's no question that this would be a pale imitation of the real book if John [Robertson] had not been intimately involved. The consequence of this is that we have deleted the reference to his not having contributed directly to the book. On the other hand, we do not say that he has done so.[27]

Earlier, Hickling had written to Robertson:

> Do you mind if I write Chapter 13 — your solution — as if it was my brain wave and not yours. It will help to anticipate any criticism that we have been in collusion — which indeed we have not been.[28]

Robertson tried to control the content of the book but affirmed on a number of occasions that Hickling was free to write whatever he wished. The things that most irritated Robertson were the drawing of inappropriate and inaccurate parallels, overdone humour and constant attempts at levity, misplaced sarcasm, persistent derision of lawyers, and imagined conversations and dialogue. He also objected to Hickling's solution to the problem of what the Naval Board should have done with Robertson after the Royal Commission. Hickling suggested that Robertson should have been made a commodore and sent to the United States to stand by the first *Charles F. Adams* Class destroyer being built for the RAN in Michigan. Robertson pointed out that

> There was not time to send me off on such a job as you suggest. I had to finish my sea time and be available for promotion at the very latest by the end of 1965, otherwise I would have been passed over for promotion by officers junior to me. The *Perth*, the first of the guided missile destroyers, is still not commissioned at the time of writing this.[29]

Hickling ignored Robertson's comments. His version created the impression that this course of action was what Robertson had wanted. It led the Board to think that Robertson had lost his sense of perspective as these destroyers were to be commanded by mid-seniority captains and certainly not commodores. The Board would also have been surprised that such a posting would have been acceptable to Robertson.

Hickling sought advice which was later ignored. Several paragraphs were, however, deleted from the book on the insistence and advice of Robertson and Hicks QC, the latter giving some wide-ranging comments on the book including an opinion on any defamatory content.[30] The deleted sections, representing more contentious views, included Hickling's introduction of Sir Jack Stevens as a man who 'exercised considerable influence in Governmental circles and was friendly with the high-ups in Canberra, including the Prime Minister. He was also ambitious with a strong personality and accustomed to getting his own way.'[31] Hickling also inferred in earlier drafts that both Spicer and Smyth were susceptible to improper direction by Menzies.

While Robertson had given enormous assistance to Hickling, several serving naval officers had also helped Robertson. Foremost was Captain Bill Graham, Captain of the Port in Sydney. Graham was a long-time personal friend who, Robertson said, 'acted as an extracurricular solicitor for me during the Royal Commission and is thoroughly familiar with all the happenings'. Robertson had also received assistance with minor details from a rather reticent Captain David Stevenson, Robertson's replacement in *Melbourne*. Robertson told Hickling that Stevenson 'was apologetic about having had to refuse his assistance with the book. He explained that, in his position, he did not feel that he could make any general contribution, but he is quite prepared to answer or deal with any specific questions'.[32] Some of the documents found in Robertson's private papers also indicate that substantial amounts of confidential material were being covertly passed to him from inside Navy Office.

*One Minute of Time* was generously reviewed in all the metropolitan newspapers. In the *Age*, former CNS, Vice-Admiral Sir John Collins, praised Hickling's effort, although one suspects his review was flavoured by his agreement with the author's views.[33] Collins referred to the Commission's hearings as 'inept meetings' and accepted most of Hickling's criticisms of the Government and the Royal Commission.

The review in the English *Naval Review* also concentrated on the form of the inquiry.[34] Citing a recent article in the *Times* on Royal Commissions, the reviewer lamented that Australia had learned nothing from Britain on the failings of this form of inquiry. The writer asserted that the main drawback was the duration of the inquiry, which was prolonged by irrelevancies. Given this attitude, what might be said of Cabban's allegations? This favourable review ended as Hickling would have hoped:

> The whole affair, which in effect constituted a substitution of appropriate legal jurisdiction by the legislature, came in for much criticism in the Australian [Parliament], in the Australian press and in that of New Zealand and the United States, and appears a sorry instance of how naval matters should *not* be investigated or discipline preserved.[35]

What this writer failed to understand was that the conduct of the inquiry, rather than its form, was the subject of criticism.

Reviews of the book by non-defence writers, such as John Yeomans of the *Herald*, were impressed by Hickling's credentials as a 'decoration-encrusted' retired admiral and a veteran of a collision involving naval ships.[36] Yeomans accepted all of Hickling's arguments and assertions without question but neglected to ask Hickling what he thought his account might achieve. In the *Sydney Morning Herald* John Gunn, an ex-RAN officer, praised Hickling's style, repeated his theory, without comment, of why the collision occurred and shared the author's lament at Robertson's resignation.

Neither review took up Hickling's allegation that vital witnesses were not called, nor did they propose a course of action that might result in 'justice' for Robertson. What reviewers and other commentators did not notice was Hickling's insinuation at several press meetings that Stevens was unfit to command *Voyager* at the time of the collision. Hickling told the *Age* that Stevens

> must have been in great pain with stomach ulcers just before the collision. This was why he drank a triple brandy when he never usually drank at sea. Something must have been worrying him for him to break a lifelong habit. He may have been tired — and when we get tired we get a sort of premature satisfaction.[37]

In referring to the triple brandy, Hickling remarked in his book:

> This is to me a distasteful subject, as it must be to most people and to senior naval officers jealous of the reputation of their service in particular. But if a true and factual story is to be told we had better face up to it ...
>
> It would have been entirely reasonable if the Commission had considered the service careers of the officers on the bridge of *Voyager*, both officially through their records and by cross-examination of the officers who had served with them, especially at sea in the months preceding the tragedy ... Anything that could have contributed to an understanding of the temperaments and abilities of the *Voyager* officers and could be reasonably elicited, bearing in mind they could not speak for themselves, would surely have been helpful to the Commissioner, and to a broader appreciation of factors contributing to the collision.[38]

In spite of the book's many serious shortcomings, the interest in *Voyager* was so great that the first edition of 18,000 copies was sold within two weeks of release. But the question remained: what would it achieve? Tom Millar commented in the *Bulletin* that

> Lessons were, of course, learned from this tragedy and have been since applied throughout the Navy. Legal provisions have changed to allow for different judicial procedures in an inquiry into a disaster of this kind.
>
> Had the loss of *Voyager* not followed a number of accidents, there may not have been the public outcry, the political activity on both sides, and the Royal Commission. Yet all of these were, in a sense, signs of immaturity, an unawareness of the problems and risks involved in maintaining a fighting service, and an unreadiness to back up the officers who carry such great responsibilities in the defence of us all.[39]

The release of Hickling's book prompted a fresh series of letters to editors of the major Australian newspapers and another round of correspondence to leading Government members, but the Government continued to state that there were insufficient grounds for another inquiry, which it contended would achieve very little anyway.

Hickling's book served more as an interesting account of a dramatic event than as a compelling case for action on Robertson's behalf. It lacked a specific lament: if Robertson had been unjustly treated, how was this to be reversed?

The key to a new inquiry remained Hickling's remark that several witnesses with the capacity to comment on the collision and its causes were told they would be called but did not appear. Whitlam questioned Chaney about this on 9 December 1965:

> Will the Minister state the names and qualifications of those witnesses, the nature of the evidence they would have been able to give, and the reason for not calling them?[40]

Chaney replied that he had read the book and remembered the passages to which Whitlam had made reference. However, 'I am not in a position to say who were the witnesses referred to by Admiral Hickling'. There was really only one witness in question — Cabban. On being questioned as to their identity again by Whitlam, Chaney changed tack:

> I am assured by counsel that everybody who was interviewed and told they would appear before the Royal Commission did so. Therefore I believe that what is stated in this book does not exactly accord with the facts.[41]

Whitlam persisted: 'Does the Minister know their names?' Chaney stonewalled and answered 'No'.

Although the Labor Opposition had joined Jess in voicing disquiet about the Royal Commission, there was some unexpected support for the Stevens family on the Opposition backbenches. Sam Benson wrote to Sir Jack Stevens: 'I am disgusted with Vice-Admiral Hickling's effort which is uncalled for and which has only caused more anguish to persons whose feelings should be spared in this matter. I am writing this letter to you ... because happenings on the night when *Voyager* was sunk were not your son's responsibility'.[42] This was certainly a novel view, as even counsel for the Stevens family at the Royal Commission had admitted that Stevens was responsible for the loss of *Voyager*.

Jess had used the debate on the DFRB Act during the previous month (October 1965) to highlight Robertson's case, although Jess made several statements for which no evidence has come to light. He said that Robertson had been told, 'If you allow yourself to be dismissed for the good of the Service, and we think this may be possible, you will be entitled to your full pension'.[43] It is possible that Rear-Admiral Smith foreshadowed this proposal to Robertson although, as has been shown, it was never endorsed by the Naval Board. Sam Benson also joined the debate by calling on the Government to look at his case again in the hope of having Robertson reinstated to the Navy or granted a pension.

Jess arranged an interview with Holt soon after Menzies retired in January 1966 and presented him with a copy of the Cabban Statement. Jess stated that Cabban and Robertson did not want it to become public knowledge. When Holt asked Jess what he expected him to do about it, Jess replied, 'That, Sir, is hardly for me to say'. This created a ridiculous situation. It was obvious that the Statement would have to be made public if the inquiry were to be reopened. There was no possible way for its contents to remain secret when they would serve as evidence in gaining justice for Robertson.

The attitude being displayed by Jess, Robertson and Cabban was founded more on hope than sound judgement. Sooner or later, the existence of the Statement would be leaked to the press. If the Statement were to be used as the basis of any new finding, whether or not it altered Robertson's situation, there was no avoiding the necessity for it to be made public. What Jess, Robertson and Cabban tried to avoid was the charge that they were denigrating the character of a dead man. Whatever their intentions, it would be a charge not readily dismissed.

As the Statement could not be made public at that time, Holt seems to have done little other than hope that even Jess would lose interest in the matter. There was practically no chance of this happening. Throughout most of 1966, Jess gathered supporters within the parliamentary Liberal Party but failed to have the matter reopened. In August 1966 he stepped up his campaign.

However, he and his group, numbering not more than eight, underestimated the difficulty they would face in getting answers out of the Navy and the extent to which it would oppose all efforts to reopen the case. After he had failed to see Holt throughout July 1966, Jess wrote to him on 11 August 1966:

> I enclose a copy of a precis of Cabban's evidence, which was given to Mr Smyth, in which in paragraph 3, page 9, you will see that the QC stated that he would be an important witness and would be heard much of during the inquiry. However, in fact, during the conduct of the inquiry at no time was Cabban, or the other officers who gave similar evidence, even called.[44]

This letter had been prompted by a note Jess had received from Cabban who was becoming concerned about what had happened to his statement and Jess's inability to have any parliamentary action taken on it. This correspondence from Cabban[45] is important in revealing his attitudes and motivations.

In almost melodramatic prose, Cabban states that the 'opportunity to act honourably has been spurned by the Government' which connived 'to procure a false report' from Sir John Spicer. Cabban is critical of the Naval Board for allowing a Royal Commission and for accepting the Commission's report. His real motivation for writing emerges towards the close of the letter when Cabban refers to the involvement of alcohol and 'the fact that the ship was in collision only five weeks following my relief as Executive Officer, and the total removal of the restrictions placed by me on drinking at sea by officers. This indicates a blind fear of any encroachment on privilege regardless of life or cost.' Thus, the picture emerges of a man who believed he had saved *Voyager* from a tragedy by his vigilance in enforcing drinking restrictions, with the inference that alcohol was a primary cause of the collision. By his own words, Cabban has cast himself as a central figure. He concluded:

> Please write me of your intentions in this matter as I am reluctant to submit to the pressures which are on me to publicise the facts in my own possession if I can be assured that positive action is possible without a repugnant ventilation of dirty linen. I believe the time is suitable for much credit and honour to be obtained by the Government by an honest and open reappraisal of the situation.

The copy of this letter supplied later to the Navy has a single line comment penned to it by the Minister (Chaney): 'What does he want?' It was a fair question. At the same time, the Government received a minute from within the Attorney-General's Department stating that counsel at the Royal Commission were told by Cabban that he 'would not, in the witness box, repeat those allegations which tended to discredit Captain Stevens' and this had recently been confirmed.[46]

Jess informed Holt in a letter dated 11 August 1966 that *Voyager* was of 'considerable importance to the Government and the Liberal Party' and said that Cabban was considering going public himself.[47] This was misrepresenting Cabban's written remarks, but it helped to force Holt's hand. Jess said that a number of questions needed to be answered. They included the effect of Captain Stevens's drinking on the safe navigation of *Voyager*, whether the Naval Board knew that Stevens had a reputation for drinking and if the fact that the Royal Commissioner and the instructing solicitor for the Stevens family (Osborne), both former Federal ministers, had any influence on the non-disclosure of information about Stevens's drinking.

The Naval Board was becoming tired of Jess's insistence on a new inquiry, and surprised that Jess was now suggesting the Royal Commission had been a whitewash and that Spicer had been party to it. The Board believed that the statement was 'discredited by the inconsistencies within it and points which have been disputed'. At the heart of the matter was an uncertainty about what Robertson and Jess wanted:

> It is difficult to see what the enclosed correspondence now seeks to achieve. The inference seems to be that by disregarding Cabban's evidence an injustice was allowed to be perpetrated against Captain Robertson. But this completely ignores the fact that the Royal Commissioner placed the primary cause for the collision with *Voyager*.[48]

Cabban himself said that Stevens never drank at sea, so what was the import of his allegations inasmuch as they explained the causes of the collision? On 23 August, McNicoll wrote to Chaney suggesting ways of dealing with the Statement.[49] McNicoll said that while the Statement could be checked with Stevens's officers at that time, it had been shown to Captain James Willis whom McNicoll described as a

> most responsible and reliable witness on the events of the final six months' operations preceding Captain Stevens' death . . . Captain Willis found the Cabban document difficult in that few of the charges were in any way specific. The contradictions were obvious, and many of the events which were presented in a sinister light, had completely natural explanations . . . Among the inconsistencies noted by Captain Willis is the fact that Captain Stevens invariably wrote to his wife before turning in, a practice which is clearly incompatible with a brandy induced stupor. Again, the fact that in his forties he opened the bowling for his ship's cricket team, the Fleet Champions — also accords strangely with the allegations of drinking brandy by the bottle.[50]

It is surprising that McNicoll took such a hostile line. His response was clearly mixed with personal emotion as he committed many of the errors, such as extravagant prose, for which he was critical of Cabban. And to suggest the Statement could be dismissed solely on the opinion of Willis was stating something about Willis's memory that both McNicoll and Willis would come to regret. McNicoll also had other concerns in mind which had drifted to prominence in his thinking.

Chaney relayed the contents of McNicoll's minute to Holt the next day, 24 August 1966,[51] and again things came to a halt. Jess agreed not to persist with the matter in the lead-up to the 11 December 1966 Federal election. The Navy was very careful to have only one set of papers relating to the Statement and to limit to the absolute minimum the number of people with knowledge of the Statement's existence.[52] The Navy's greatest fear was of a leak to the press.

Holt announced his new Ministry on 13 December 1966. There were three new ministers — Bert Kelly, Don Chipp and Nigel Bowen QC. Chaney was dropped from the Ministry. Howson says

> The Prime Minister explained that Chaney's demotion was due to the over-representation of Western Australia compared with South Australia and implied no reflection on his capabilities . . . Holt was not a vengeful man and had retained Chaney when he inherited the Ministry. But if someone had to go, then Chaney was the defensible choice.[53]

Twelve months after Hickling's book had brought *Voyager* back to public prominence, Robertson and Jess were no closer to 'justice' for Robertson or another inquiry. While Jess's parliamentary colleagues hoped he would tire of the matter after successive rebuffs, he ended 1966 more determined than ever to get what had so far eluded him.

## 12

# A Victory for Public Advocacy?

IN THE NEW YEAR of 1967, Jess continued to lobby for another *Voyager* inquiry. After receiving pledges from his parliamentary colleagues that the Cabban allegations would be considered in detail, he withdrew the matter from party room discussion on three separate occasions. These efforts were noted by the Melbourne *Herald* on 9 February, and the paper continued to follow the *Voyager* story closely. Jess had a meeting with the new Minister for the Navy, Don Chipp, who was of vastly different background and temperament to his predecessor.

In 1967, the Navy was still the most junior portfolio. The new Minister, the youthful Chipp, had been elected to the Federal Parliament as member for the safe Victorian Liberal seat of Higinbotham (later renamed Hotham) in a by-election in 1960 with a majority he increased in the general election of 1961. Chipp had served during World War II in the RAAF and rose to prominence in 1956 as Chief Executive Officer of the Olympic Civic Committee which was established to make arrangements for the Melbourne Olympic Games. The Navy was not Chipp's only responsibility. He was also Minister in Charge of Tourist Activity and was preoccupied in the early months of 1967 with the creation of a tourist commission.

Although as a backbencher he was known for occasional outspoken criticisms of his parliamentary colleagues, Chipp accepted without alteration the policy the Naval Board had devised for Chaney on the handling of the Cabban Statement. The new Minister called for the Navy's files on the matter and 'tended to agree with the view which the Department and the Admirals were putting to me — that Cabban's allegations were basically untrue and largely a figment of his imagination'. Despite this setback to his cause, Jess found he had a forceful ally in the newly elected member for the safe New South Wales Liberal seat of Warringah, Ted St John QC, who took an immediate interest in the case.[1]

In early March, *Voyager* began a new life in Parliament after a question from Harry Turner, a lawyer by profession, about Captain

Robertson. In a speech in reply to the Governor-General's address, Sam Benson agreed that Captain Robertson

> received a pretty raw deal and that the Government should have seen fit to give him his full DFRB Fund pension. But there are, of course, two sides to any question. There are few survivors from the *Voyager*, most of the very gallant men of her crew lost their lives. What is going to be gained from resurrecting this affair? ... I think it was wrong of [Hickling] to bring out some of the matters he brought out in his book ... I will end this part of my speech by saying that he had more accidents than most.[2]

Benson seems to have forgotten, in arguing the point, that eighty-two men were lost but 232 survived, while Hickling had been involved in only one accident during his naval career. Several days later Sir Jack Stevens wrote to Benson, 'We are most grateful for your continued interest in the *Voyager* tragedy and we earnestly hope that the matter will not be resurrected'.[3]

On 9 March, Jess and Mackay met with Holt to discuss reopening the case. Jess wrote to Holt again on 23 March to ensure the Prime Minister realised that the matter would soon come to a head:

> In view of the fact that you will be going overseas ... I would be grateful if you could let us know your decision, as soon as you return, in order that I may not miss the opportunity to exercise my rights in raising this matter at a full Party meeting.[4]

Another delegation of Government backbenchers also met with Holt on the subject. It consisted of Sir Wilfred Kent Hughes, Bill Wentworth and Edmund Fox. Hughes wrote to Holt on 20 March 1967 and suggested that, as the nation was at war with North Vietnam, Robertson ought to be recalled and that

> the RAN prohibit the consumption of alcohol when ships were at sea. There are several other matters which the Navy should enquire into 'in camera' such as routine reports on officers' capabilities and conduct. The previous decisions cannot be allowed to remain unchallenged.[5]

The point should perhaps be made here that of the eighty-nine members of the House of Representatives in 1966 who were not Ministers, Opposition Executive or Speaker, fifty-five had served in the armed forces.[6] They should have more readily understood the separation between ranks and had more empathy for Service problems. Debate on defence matters should have proceeded on a firmer footing than at any other time in Australian parliamentary history.

On 10 April 1967, Chipp, who was becoming concerned about Jess's determination to see *Voyager* reopened, went to see his close friend Peter Howson, Minister for Air. Howson's attitude to Jess's efforts is probably typical of those Government members who opposed those efforts:

> Unfortunately if he [Jess] pursues this course he will bring the Navy into a great deal of disrepute and also the government as a whole, as he will intend to suggest

there was a miscarriage of justice. Don [Chipp] and I talked it over together,
feeling that at present it is wise to let him bring the matter into the party room
but after that to try to reason with him to prevent him from taking it into
Parliament, especially as the information he has is completely unsound and can
be easily demonstrated so.[7]

Finding that the Prime Minister had only just read his letter of
23 March 1967 on the eve of the 12 April party meeting which listed
*Voyager* as an agenda item, Jess again agreed to have the matter removed
from the agenda. Holt told Jess that he had not received his letter until
mid-April. Given that he had exerted enormous efforts to have the letter
in the Prime Minister's hands before his departure overseas, Jess was
angered by Holt's poor excuses and continued vacillation.[8] Holt
informed Jess on 21 April that he had left his office before the letter
arrived and that it was placed below the papers on Cabinet business
Holt attended to on his return from overseas.[9]

William McMahon, a former Navy Minister Coalition parliamentary
tactician, spoke to Jess on 11 April and relayed the contents of the
discussion to Holt. Jess told McMahon he wanted parts of the Royal
Commission reopened as its proceedings had not been just and fair to
all concerned; that he wanted Stevens's alleged drunkenness examined;
and that the 'wrong' decision made by the Commissioner on the
conduct of Robertson, Kelly and Bate needed to 'be corrected'.[10]

Jess told Chipp around the same time that if these three conditions
were not met, he would raise the matter in the party room.
Furthermore, if the Party did not then support him, he would consider
three possible courses of action: resigning from the Liberal Party;
resigning his seat in Parliament; or raising the matter on the floor of
the Parliament. Chipp was still firmly opposed to the case being
reopened or an ex gratia payment being made to Robertson. Chipp had
little sympathy for Robertson and said that his counsel had the right
to call whatever witnesses he wished at the Commission. He felt
Robertson should have called and questioned Cabban, if his evidence
was sufficiently compelling.

Support for Jess was growing slowly and now included Fox, Turner,
Kent Hughes and Senator Reg Wright who questioned the adequacy
and efficiency of the Commission itself. There were two courses open
to Holt: either to refuse to reopen the case, or to have the matter
reopened by Cabinet on a submission from the Defence Department.
McMahon advised Holt against giving Robertson any payment.

The Prime Minister decided to have the matter put to Cabinet for its
consideration, and a joint submission dated 27 April 1967 was prepared
by Allen Fairhall, Minister for Defence, and Chipp. The submission
assumed that Jess's concerns related solely and specifically to
Robertson. In other words, Jess was concerned about the Cabban
allegations only inasmuch as they served to assist Robertson's case.

The difficulty was that no one seemed to know what Jess, Robertson or Cabban wanted out of another inquiry. Jess believed that Cabban should have been interviewed by Chipp or another Cabinet member.[11] Chipp told Jess he had been strongly advised by the Naval Board against speaking directly with Robertson or Cabban.[12] Cabban was evidently something of an enigma.

The executive summary attached to the joint Defence–Navy submission stated that there was no miscarriage of justice to Robertson at the 1964 Commission and that no 'real case existed for an ex gratia payment' to be made to him.[13] The decision to offer some payment

> would be counter-productive. It would mean that Cabinet's original decision had been wrong, and that the Government had delayed nearly three years in correcting an injustice. It is extremely doubtful, moreover, whether this would satisfy those who, on the basis of Cabban's statement, are querying the propriety of the Royal Commission hearings and findings. The more likely result would be to strengthen their doubts'.[14]

As for the new allegations, the Cabban Statement was

> imprecise and contains numerous contradictions. It makes allegations which are damaging not so much through the specific nature of the charges, but by implication, and many of the events which are presented in a sinister light have completely natural explanations.[15]

The submission concluded

> For our part, we believe there is sufficient evidence available, as indicated in this paper, to discredit the statement, and that those who wish to pursue this matter should be given the opportunity to do so at an early date, within the Party Room. We hold this view despite the risk that versions may leak out publicly, to the embarrassment of the Government, to the detriment of the Navy and, more particularly, to the further distress of Captain Stevens' family, and to all the relatives of the other 81 dead. In our opinion avoidance of the subject is no longer desirable, and the sooner it is aired and put into proper perspective, the better.[16]

On 2 May, Holt informed Jess that Cabinet had considered the submission prepared by Fairhall and Chipp and would not reopen the case or grant any compensation to Robertson. Cabinet had agreed that 'no new material or factor which has come to light since then would, either on the score of justice or of equity, warrant a reconsideration of that decision'.[17] Jess's options had now been reduced to one: he had to take the matter to the Party Room and from there to Parliament.

While the submission was being prepared, Chipp had decided to gather some comments on the Cabban Statement from those Naval officers in a position to either corroborate or refute it. He did this only after seeking permission from McMahon, as the Liberal Deputy Leader, who said that the statements ought to be witnessed rather than sworn.[18] Thus, it would be easier for witnesses to subsequently reconsider their evidence if they were not committed to sworn statements. Over the next two weeks, these comments were obtained with the presumable expectation that they would assist the Navy's cause.

Meanwhile, the dispute between Jess and his supporters and the Naval Board had become bogged down on the characters of Stevens and Cabban — the Navy painting Stevens as a competent naval officer who deserved respect, at the same time dismissing Cabban as an unbalanced and scheming malcontent. Having tied the Navy's fortunes to the reputation of Duncan Stevens, McNicoll compiled a series of extracts from the final four confidential reports which covered Stevens's time at the Admiralty and in command of *Voyager*.[19] These were freely circulated to parliamentarians and later the press.

Admiralty report dated 18 September 1961:

> The more I see of this officer the more I am impressed by him and the more I like him. He is bluff and cheerful but by no means a 'blow hard'. He gets on well with everyone and earns their respect for his professional knowledge and vigour. His common sense is refreshing.

Admiralty report dated 14 January 1963:

> A vigorous and forceful officer who deserves the goodwill which exists between him and all his contacts.

British Far East Fleet report dated 15 August 1963:

> A popular and pleasant officer, who has a ready smile and is fine company. He has worked hard and well with the Far East Fleet to good effect. Very enthusiastic and rarely disheartened. There is sound material here but I cannot rate Stevens's chance of reaching Flag Rank higher than good.

Flag Officer Commanding Australian Fleet dated 6 January 1964:

> A very keen officer of average intelligence who is devoted to the Service. He has a volatile nature, considerable dash and much enthusiasm. He does not strike me as having great abilities, and has probably reached his ceiling, though he will always give his best to the Service in any capacity.

This report was drafted by McNicoll when FOCAF. He further remarked in this minute that

> It is of some interest that Stevens's promotion to Captain was clinched by a very favourable report on his performance while on exchange in the Admiralty. It therefore seems clear that any personal and professional deficiencies were not apparent to his Royal Navy superiors.

It is perhaps surprising that McNicoll would cite these reports when he privately had little confidence in them. On 29 August 1964, in a private letter to Landau, he wrote:

> Form AS 206 is a nonsense and should be abolished in favour of a modern method. Any system which gives as many marks for 'social qualities' as it does for 'leadership' is patently absurd. Captain promotions should be done by *all* admirals, and before confirmation all selected should undergo a rigorous medical examination, with a substantial psychological content.[20]

McNicoll had a personal interest in the case as well. If it were proved that Stevens had been either unfit to command or acting improperly while commanding *Voyager* and that McNicoll knew or ought to have known as Fleet Commander, he would be liable for censure. Although he claimed later that he had seen little of Stevens during 1963 and did not have the opportunity of noticing anything untoward, a comparison of the monthly reports of proceedings of *Melbourne* (with McNicoll embarked) and *Voyager* reveals that the two ships spent a considerable period in company.

These were also among the opportunities that Captain Peek had to witness *Voyager*'s performance and for Cabban to have made a report on Stevens's state of health.

While seeking permission to use the statements Chipp had collected in response to the Cabban Statement, the matter was referred to a parliamentary Liberal Party meeting on 3 May 1967. It was a very tense meeting that brought to the surface the depth of feeling surrounding *Voyager*. When the vote was taken on a motion calling for a reopening of the case, it was more than ten to one against.

Rumours of backbench pressure for another *Voyager* inquiry reached the newspapers on 4 May, although there was no indication of the nature of the evidence Jess claimed the 1964 Commission had not considered. The *Australian*, on 5 May 1967, led the way in supporting Jess in its editorial headed '*Voyager*: the truth must out':

> If there is an untold story about the sinking of the *Voyager* it should be told immediately. The claim by Mr John Jess MP that essential evidence was not placed before the Royal Commission which investigated the disaster, demands, at the very least, a public statement by the Prime Minister; and if the evidence is as serious as reports hint, he should reopen the inquiry.
>
> Mr Holt is wrong to think that by refusing either course he can shut off all public uneasiness about the collision off Jervis Bay. The claims have been given too much publicity for this tactic to succeed . . .
>
> There is also the reputation and morale of the Navy as a whole to be considered. If any allegations are being made against it, the service will be harmed less if they are not secreted behind party doors. Mr Holt would do much better to clear up the whole business once and for all, in the open.

Jess also appeared on ABC television and said he planned to make his allegations public during the following week from the floor of the Parliament, and was prepared to risk his political future in doing so.

Despite some popular perceptions to the contrary, Sir Jack Stevens was powerless to do anything. He had offered to former Navy Minister, Fred Chaney, some of the sympathy letters he had received showing the high standing in which his son was apparently held. There was no response to this offer and Sir Jack was not approached by any minister for assistance. Having noted Benson's previous attitude towards the matter, Sir Jack sought his assistance on 7 May 1967:

> I am not concerned in any way with the efforts of Jess to gain some recompense

for Robertson for his early retirement from the Navy. I am, however, deeply concerned that, in making this attempt, Jess may — under parliamentary privilege — seek to blacken my son's character and efficiency and thus cause further agony of mind, not only to the members of his family but also to the relatives of those other men who also lost their lives in the disaster ...

I do not wish to see the verdict of the [1964] Royal Commission challenged. Indeed it would be a mistake to do this in the context of the debate which may take place this week. We have learned to live with this verdict and would prefer to have no reference made to it.

If you feel so disposed, and if the opportunity is given you, may I ask that in respect of this issue of character and fitness, you will help me and my family.[21]

It was not until 8 May that references to Cabban first appeared in the newspapers. Alan Ramsey, writing for the *Australian*, referred to an ex-officer who wanted to tell his story which contained 'some grave allegations against a key figure in the tragedy; allegations which, if true, shed new light on how Australia's worst peacetime naval disaster came to happen'.[22] Ramsey quoted Jess as saying he (Jess) wanted another inquiry to ensure that 'this thing could never happen again'.[23] The inevitable letters to the editor on this subject followed. All supported Jess's call for another inquiry, and all based their demand on seeking justice for Robertson. This was a remarkable show of support given that Jess had not disclosed whether this new evidence might have helped Robertson's case.

Howson later asked Jess not to feel so strongly about the matter that he should have cause to resign from Parliament.

Late to join the cause was Dr Malcolm Mackay, a Liberal backbencher from New South Wales. Mackay had served in the RANVR during and following the war and had a number of contacts within the Service. His background as a senior ordained minister in the Presbyterian Church and a member of the board of Longreach Oil led Whitlam to refer to him as 'Your Oiliness'. Mackay wrote to Holt on 4 May apologising for his outburst in the Party Room which was critical of the Prime Minister and Chipp, and supportive of Jess.[24] From his own inquiries concerning Stevens, he told Holt, 'I have little doubt he was a man with grave problems relating to alcohol,' and went on to state:

I would immensely deplore any raising of this matter in public or in the House, and will urge John Jess not to do so. But this does not mean that I do not equally strongly urge you to consider that leading figures in the Navy are covering up, from no doubt good as well as personal motives, the fact that this man was appointed to command one of HMA Ships when he was known to have a problem with drinking to excess. Young men died for that dereliction of duty, if this was, as I am firmly led to believe, reasonably common knowledge in the Navy.[25]

Mackay concluded by stating that a new inquiry should be 'secret and *not* through Service channels to serving officers alone' (Mackay's emphasis). After the same Party Room discussion, St John accepted an offer Chipp made to allow members of the Government to examine the documents relating to *Voyager* which he held in his possession.[26]

St John was to have an enormous impact on the future direction of the *Voyager* affair. He was a controversial figure even before his election and was to have a political career that was without precedent or parallel in Federal Parliament. St John did not join the Liberal Party until 1964 but rapidly rose to a position on the State Executive. He was an acting judge of the New South Wales Supreme Court and had since 1961 been President of the Australian Section of the International Commission of Jurists. The latter sought to promote and protect human rights and included many distinguished judges and barristers among its executive, including Professor Zelman Cowen, Gough Whitlam and Sir Kenneth Bailey.

As a jurist and a campaigner for the victimised, St John wore his principles openly as he passionately pursued a range of convictions. There was little surprise when he became interested in the *Voyager* case. Moreover, he approached it as an advocate rather than as a politician aspiring to a ministerial portfolio.

St John was among the six Government members who were permitted to view the papers held by Chipp. One member leaked some of the allegations to the press. Although Chipp suspected St John may have done the leaking, he had no proof. In his autobiography, Chipp commented that he was having 'some residual worries about this sordid business' but there is no record of this apparent weakening resolve.[27]

After looking at these papers, Chipp suggested that St John contact Smyth and Sheppard to ask for their opinions. Both barristers refused to discuss the matter with St John, who was already known to them at the NSW Bar. This served only to make St John more suspicious. St John then interviewed Robertson and asked him for his opinion of Cabban's Statement. Robertson was now becoming less concerned about Stevens's reputation. He said he had 'no doubt that Cabban's Statement represents substantially the truth of the matter'. Mackay and St John then arranged to see Cabban and were thoroughly convinced that he was telling the truth.[28] They also came to suspect that all that was known by Spicer or Smyth had not been recorded. They questioned the expert opinion of Professor Blackburn at the first inquiry on the effects of alcohol on the mind and body as well, and insinuated that Blackburn had been chosen because he was well disposed to the Stevens family's interests. St John and Mackay were less concerned with any alleged injustice done to Robertson, feeling it was 'of minor importance compared with the broader issues which we have mentioned'.

Mackay then wrote to the Prime Minister expressing his disquiet and mentioning that Cabban had supplied them with the names of several people who were no longer in the Navy (and, therefore, whom they seemed to presume were beyond being influenced) who could substantiate the statement.[29] Chipp hurriedly asked for their names.

St John informed him that they would only be given to a Select Parliamentary Committee and regretted that he could 'give no further assistance for the moment'.[30]

The press was now involved in the emerging controversy. Rumours of the Cabban allegations were floating around Parliament House but would not be confirmed by anyone, even Jess. It took a Melbourne-based tabloid press journalist, in Canberra on other business, Richard L'Estrange of the *Truth*, to break the story. He pieced it together from two members of the parliamentary press gallery, the secretary to a senator, and a Liberal parliamentarian who was neither Jess, Mackay nor St John. The story appeared on 9 May 1967 with the heading '*Voyager* scandal — this is what it's all about. DRUNKEN DUNCAN. Captain with triple brandy'. The news caused a national sensation. The story published by *Truth* focused on an incident mentioned in the Cabban Statement.

Holt was under siege. Whitlam had by now learned that the Liberal Party was tearing itself apart from within over *Voyager*. On 9 May during Parliamentary Question Time, Whitlam asked Holt the question he had put to Chaney nearly eighteen months before: the names of the two witnesses allegedly not called at the 1964 Commission. Holt evaded the question, telling Whitlam that it was a matter for the relevant Minister, in this case Chipp.

An answer to the question was sought from the Navy by the Prime Minister's Department. Attached to the letter from Sir John Bunting to Landau was a separate slip of paper which read:

> Mr Yeend, PM's Department, advised he is quite happy for this to be left unanswered and when the present debate on *Voyager* is over he will prepare a reply.[31]

The Government was persisting with its efforts to avoid a parliamentary confrontation. By this stage Jess had decided that enough was enough and gave notice on 10 May that during General Business when Parliament next sat he would move that a select committee be appointed to investigate whether any evidence relevant to the collision was not heard at the 1964 Commission and whether a

> further Commission should be issued to three judges or some other tribunal to consider the findings, report and recommendations which ought to have been made in the light of such further evidence.[32]

On the same day Holt announced that the motion would be debated on 16 May 1967. His decision to do so surprised some political commentators who believed he could have further delayed the matter in the hope that backbench resolve would weaken. He was quoted by the *Australian* on 12 May as saying, 'I am not shutting out the possibility of a select committee if there is a residual belief in Parliament that there should be one after this debate. We are not trying to cover anything up.

We want to see the right thing done'. This was extraordinary in itself. Motions of this sort would not normally be dealt with for a period of months after notice was given.

> The Cabinet decided that it should forthwith act itself to initiate a Ministerial Statement and debate on the matter in the House in the following week, and should announce to the House on the morrow its intention in this regard.
>
> The Cabinet agreed that the Attorney General should draft and present the Ministerial Statement, taking up the central issue of Cabban's evidence but without unnecessary reproduction of its detail. In this connection, it felt that there might be merit in indicating that the whole of Cabban's evidence would be shown to the Leader of the Opposition.[33]

Holt's aim was clearly to retain the initiative. The crucial factor continued to be the Senate, where the Government did not have the numbers, and Liberal Senator Reg Wright had threatened to introduce a similar motion to the one that Jess would propose in the Lower House. After the 1965 Senate Election, the Government had 30 Senators, Labor 27, the Democratic Labor Party two, with one independent. The Parliamentary players went away to prepare their arguments.

The press was divided. The *Sydney Morning Herald* on 12 May questioned the cost and the value of another inquiry, but according to the *Age*, it was 'the Government's responsibility ... to satisfy the public [that] it is pursuing, rather than obscuring, justice and truth'.

The Naval Board continued to denigrate Cabban rather than conducting its own investigation of the allegations. In a memorandum to the Navy Minister dated 15 May, which seems to have been prompted by Mackay's letter of 8 May, McNicoll said that whereas Mackay had described Cabban's 'high moral character, idealism and principalled awkwardness',[34] McNicoll believed 'they add up to what might be less charitably described as a self-righteous egomania'.[35] He went on to say that Cabban resented Stevens and had nothing but contempt and antipathy for him. This, he argued, coloured his judgement and his Statement. Later, he alleged that Cabban had attempted to perpetrate deliberate falsehoods and that these could be refuted by other observers, 'men of far steadier character than Cabban himself'. However, McNicoll conceded that

> the fact Stevens had a brandy at all at that time is astonishing ... One feels that there must have been some special reason which caused Stevens to do so at that time ... I think it is more likely that Stevens' ulcer was paining him acutely and that he adopted his usual remedy in order to help him get through the exercise. If he had been an alcoholic he would have had a bottle concealed in his cabin and would not have called for a drink openly from the steward. It seems to me far more likely, too, that what distracted his attention in the few minutes before the collision was not alcohol but pain.[36]

On 15 May 1967 the Naval Board prepared a long letter for the Prime

Minister dealing with the letter Holt had received from Mackay and St John dated 8 May, and building on the attack launched by McNicoll, whose memorandum on the 'Character of Cabban' was enclosed.[37] In what was another scathing attack on Cabban and the two parliamentarians, the Naval Board suggested that Cabban was obviously lying, given that it had collected numerous refutations of the Statement. Also attached was a minute outlining the history of Stevens's health prepared by Surgeon Rear-Admiral Michael Coplans, the Naval Medical Director-General.[38] Coplans said there was nothing wrong with Stevens at the time of the collision as there was no record that he was suffering pain from his duodenal ulcer at any time in 1963. Coplans also felt, having seen a copy of the Melbourne *Truth* on 13 May, that he should make his own personal statement on Captain Stevens's character. It concluded:

> I do not believe that Captain Stevens, with his history of dyspepsia and peptic ulceration, would knowingly suffer the pain, and the risk of possible complications, of aggravation by over indulgence in alcohol.[39]

When Parliament met on 16 May, *Voyager* was the major item for debate and Jess put his motion calling for the appointment of a select committee to inquire into the tragedy. At the same time, Senator Reg Wright introduced a similar motion into the Senate. This motion was more threatening to the Government with its slender majority and it feared that Wright's motion might have been passed.

Rather than debating the motion put by Jess, the debate was on a ministerial statement from the first speaker, the Attorney-General, Nigel Bowen QC. He largely repeated the essence of the Navy's opposition to reopening the case. At the conclusion of his speech, Bowen tabled the selection of statements gathered by the Navy. They were published as a Parliamentary Paper[40] and contained a copy of the record of interview with Cabban by Police Sergeant Turner, a copy of the Cabban Statement and sixteen virtual refutations of what Cabban had stated. These refutations were from several officers, including Captain (G. J.) Willis, Rear-Admiral Peek, Captain Loxton and Lieutenant Commander Griffith. They were remarkably similar in tone.

A letter had been sent to these selected officers on 19 April 1967.[41] At the time, James Willis was in Britain, although he had already commented upon the Statement. Peek was then commanding the Fleet, Griffith was First Lieutenant of HMAS *Parramatta*, and Loxton was commanding HMAS *Yarra*. Willis, Peek, Griffith and Loxton all variously denied having any recollection of the incidents described in Cabban's Statement; stated that what Cabban had described was highly improbable if not impossible; or imputed a different significance to that attributed to certain events by Cabban. Loxton stated that Cabban was lying. Cabban alleged Loxton told him that

174

Stevens had consumed a bottle of brandy on his return with Loxton to Williamstown Naval Dockyard from Sydney, following the court martial of Captain Dovers. In reply Loxton said:

> The statements of Lt Cdr Cabban are generally inaccurate. In particular, it is not true that, on the occasion he refers to, Captain Stevens drank a bottle of brandy, nor was he in any way affected adversely by alcohol. Further, I have never told Lt Cdr Cabban otherwise.

Comments were also sought from Captain Alan Willis, younger brother of James Willis, and Surgeon Lieutenant Michael Tiller, the latter having resigned from the Navy to study at the Royal College of Surgeons in Britain.

When these statements were tabled by Bowen, and later published, excluded were those from Alan Willis and Tiller. Willis corroborated the Statement where it related to the period he commanded *Voyager*, and the observance of bar hours. And although he agreed with Cabban's Statement that Willis thought Griffith was a poor ship-handler, it was with qualification. Willis's statement consisted of matters of mundane detail rather than opinion or interpretation. Alan Willis did not know his statement had not been included but believed that it added little to corroborate the Cabban Statement. Even in the matter of bar hours, Willis believed that Cabban overstated his role, in that bar hours were properly laid down in each ship's Captain's Standing Orders and that Cabban, as president of the wardroom mess, had far less prerogative in the matter than he suggested in his Statement.[42]

Alan Willis signed his statement on 24 April 1967 and had it witnessed and despatched on the same day.[43] Landau may have felt some justification for excluding this statement among those passed to the Attorney-General as it did not relate in any way to the matters that were of public concern. But a different set of circumstances related to the procurement of a statement from Tiller.

Given that Landau knew that *Voyager*'s former medical officer was in London, it is surprising that he waited two days after despatching letters to those within Australia before writing to ANRUK, Commodore Dacre Smyth. This letter, dated 21 April, requested Tiller's comments and suggested to Smyth, because of the urgency, that they be cabled to Australia.[44] Smyth sent Tiller's statement back to Australia by airmail express and it arrived before the end of the month, probably 29 April.

On 4 May, Chipp asked his Department whether he could, if the need arose, use the statements that had been gathered, in Parliament. He was advised that those from the serving officers could be used but that the permission of Tiller, who was now a civilian, would need to be sought.[45]

This is surprising because the word 'confidential' was never used in the 21 April 1967 letter. The clear inference was that the Naval Board, rather than Tiller, now wanted his comments kept confidential.

In fact, there was no commitment given by the Navy to Tiller that his comments would be kept secret. Nonetheless, in the hope of delaying the inclusion of Tiller's damaging statement in the papers the Navy Minister wanted to cite in Parliament, Chipp asked Landau to contact Tiller by telephone and discuss the possibility that his statement be made public. Contact was finally made at 7.45 p.m. on 9 May. Tiller said that he had not been given any background information about the extracts which 'seemed to come from nowhere' and that he had not been given much time to consider his words, which Commodore Smyth had asked him to keep brief. When informed that his comments would be made public and that they might be cited in an inquiry, Landau records that Tiller said

> he had been thinking about the extracts and wasn't completely happy about his comments on them in their present form because of the haste in which they had been made, and the insistence on brevity. He wouldn't like them used in public. He said that if this matter were going to be brought out in public he thought it would be reasonable for him to spend a little more time and thought before replying. In these circumstances he wanted them destroyed.[46]

A second letter was then sent to Commodore Smyth asking for a fresh set of comments from Tiller. Landau was evidently in no rush to have Tiller's remarks, as he sent his letter to Smyth airmail when it could have been sent as a confidential signal.[47]

Chipp, Landau and McNicoll were later to claim that Tiller's original statement was garbled and incomprehensible, largely because of its brevity. Chipp stated:

> The doctor named Tiller had sent a hastily written reply, couched in 'Signalese' which could not be properly understood ... I wanted permission of the signatories to produce the documents publicly. All agreed except Tiller, who ... said he would like to give the matter more thought and send a considered reply, and that he wanted the existing reply destroyed.[48]

This appears to have been done, as there is no trace of Tiller's original statement.[49] However, Chipp's statement does not give an accurate version of what happened in Navy Office.

Tiller's experience of naval life was limited. He joined the RAN as an undergraduate to complete his medical training. The son of an Anglican clergyman, he had sought Navy support in covering his university expenses. He spent three years attached to the junior recruit training establishment near Fremantle, HMAS *Leeuwin*, before driving across the Nullarbor to join his first ship, *Voyager*. After spending most of 1963 in *Voyager*, he transferred to the frigate HMAS *Gascoyne* and was serving in that ship at the time of the collision. When his period of obligatory naval service was over, Tiller resigned from the Navy.[50]

Why a medical officer who served for only a short time in the RAN and who was never familiar with 'signalese' would choose to express himself in this way more than two years after he left the Navy is baffling. There is no evidence that Tiller ever used 'signalese' in naval correspondence. There is also some doubt about the brevity of the first reply. On the letter from Smyth to Landau dated 27 April, covering Tiller's first comments, Smyth added the following penscript to the foot of the letter.

> I am *not* encrypting Lieutenant Tiller's comments because it will be no quicker than this Air Mail *and* it is a long job for two of my busy staff officers.[51] [Smyth's emphasis]

This suggests, and it has been subsequently confirmed, that rather than being brief, Tiller's comments were long and involved. Tiller said in a letter to the author that

> the statement that my 'signal' was incomprehensible raises a number of other queries, which I am sure are associated with people protecting their tails.[52]

In a statement about this matter given later in 1967, Tiller said that after signing his first statement

> I received a telephone call which I think was from Mr Landau in Canberra. He asked if I would like to withdraw my comments. I agreed and he asked further if I would mind if my comments were destroyed. I also agreed to this as I felt that I did not wish to be involved in this matter in any way. I got the feeling at the time that Mr Landau was keen for me to consent to destruction of my answers. It was quite a long conversation.[53]

He also later commented that during night exercises,

> I formed the habit of sleeping on a stretcher on deck. This was because I heard of a couple of near collisions which took place and I wanted to be in a position to get off the ship quickly if that was necessary. The Captain often shouted at other officers and I felt the ship was perhaps not run as smoothly as it might be.[54]

Given these sentiments, it was little wonder that the Naval Board were concerned about Tiller's evidence.

The inescapable conclusion to be drawn is that Chipp did not want to have Tiller's comments tabled in Parliament and that certain members of the Naval Board were prepared to prevent some vital evidence from being publicly disclosed. Landau obviously used every means available to delay receiving the statement and prompted Tiller to water down his remarks with the spectre of them being made public. There is little doubt that McNicoll was not aware of Landau's actions, and may even have been party to them. On 19 May, Commodore Smyth informed Landau that Tiller had read the Cabban Statement:

> He took away with him the extracts from it, but his present intention is to choose not to make any comment on the allegations contained therein.

The Naval Board had succeeded in preventing Tiller from making a public statement. If the Naval Board had nothing to fear and nothing to hide, it was a strange way to behave.

A similar set of circumstances applied to the statement given by Lieutenant Commander Griffith, who gave his first response to the Cabban Statement in the presence of Landau while in Navy Office, probably around 20 April. However, after thinking about what he had written he returned the next day to alter his statement. He stated in response to one extract from the Cabban Statement:

> I cannot recall at any time being unable to see the captain if I so wished or needed. I do not recall any instances of the captain arriving on board heavily under the influence of alcohol.
>
> In regard to the passage from Sydney to Melbourne, Captain Stevens was on the bridge when the ship left harbour and on entering Port Phillip Bay. The occasions when the captain would have been otherwise required on the bridge were seldom if at all.[55]

This statement was in contrast to the one he gave to the Solicitor General, Anthony Mason,[55a] on 15 May 1967. Griffith in this interview stated:

> My understanding is that Captain Stevens had the reputation of being a heavy rather than a moderate drinker. I know of no occasion on which I have seen him intoxicated ... I have, however, seen him early in the mornings when his facial appearance was consistent with heavy drinking the night before, but this was only a general impression and should not be treated as anything else ... I illustrate this by the trip from Sydney to Melbourne [Williamstown Dockyard for refit]. The morning the ship left Sydney, Captain Stevens gave the appearance of having had a heavy night, but nevertheless, he was on the bridge, he was quite sober and carried out his duties in a competent manner.[56]

What he neglected to add was that Stevens then handed over command to Cabban, who was himself suffering from influenza, and retired to his cabin for the remainder of the passage.

Griffith told me that he felt very unsettled about responding to Cabban's statement. When he first commented on the document at Navy Office, he gained the impression that Landau hoped the allegations were not true, but Griffith was adamant that the Secretary made no attempt at influencing him. As far as Griffith could tell, *Voyager* had become a 'face-saving' exercise for the Naval Board. On a personal level, he failed to see what good could have come from reopening the case.[57]

The extent to which Griffith was prepared to be critical or open in his description of Stevens's conduct in the 15 May statement, compared with the earlier one that he made at Navy Office, said a great deal about how the Naval Board regarded this continuing intrusion into its affairs and the extent to which it desperately hoped that the Cabban Statement was demonstrably false. Griffith's earlier statement was included in the papers presented to Parliament; his later statement was not. However, the Navy was able to include a letter dated 16 May from retired

Commodore John Plunkett-Cole who said the name 'Drunken Duncan' was a rhyming nickname, like 'Sexy Rexie' or 'Dirty Bertie', and that nothing should be inferred from it.[58]

Surprisingly, a statement was not sought from *Voyager*'s Gunnery Officer, Lieutenant Commander David Martin (later Governor of NSW), although he was mentioned in the Cabban Statement. After the Spicer Report was released, Martin had been uneasy. He believed that the Commission had badly erred in assuming that Stevens was fit to command *Voyager*. Such was his concern that he sought the advice of at least two senior officers, to whom he expressed his feelings. One of these officers listened with interest but advised him to leave the matter alone as no good could come from any attempt to reopen the case.

The Naval Board's determination to resist another inquiry was understandable. The Cabban Statement contained many damning allegations about personal and professional standards of conduct within the RAN, although it was unsworn and substantially untested. There was little doubt that if the Statement was to be publicly dissected, it would be a grubby affair, and the Navy would be dragged through the mire of an inquiry which would examine the consumption of alcohol within the RAN and the extent to which drinking and excessive behaviour were the norm. The day-to-day running of the Navy would be opened to challenge and possible ridicule by people the Naval Board did not believe would understand the practicalities of seagoing service.

There was also the possibility of the Navy having to turn against Robertson. He remained a very popular figure within the Navy and was still viewed as a scapegoat and a martyr by sections of the press and the public. This had the potential to alienate the Naval Board even further from the officers and sailors of the Navy. Added to this was the strong possibility that the inquiry would find nothing that warranted overturning the conclusions of Sir John Spicer. The Navy doubted an inquiry would find anything new relating to the causes of the collision and thus, the entire exercise would have been pointless.

Rather than ending public disquiet, the Naval Board's method of procuring these 'anti-Cabban' statements served to create further suspicion. Even the Board's affectation of honesty and openness had now been abandoned. St John offered this stinging criticism:

> The printed document *Loss of HMAS* Voyager denigrating the Cabban Statement, is, in my view, a dreadful blunder in the light of what we now know and what was already known to these Ministers when the papers went to press. The authority issuing it denied there was any substance at all in the Cabban Statement. It is a carefully edited and selected document which does the Government little credit.

This criticism was most fairly directed at the Board, and its leading officials, McNicoll and Landau, who had considerable influence and power over Chipp.

While the best course of action to have taken in the long run was to investigate the allegations thoroughly and accept whatever was revealed, there was an abject refusal within the Naval Board to believe that anything in the Statement was true. This refusal resulted not in a genuine effort to obtain contrary evidence but in a determination to prevent anything further being known. However, when the matter spilled onto the floor of Parliament, the Naval Board would be required to defend not only Captain Stevens but also its actions in trying to avoid another inquiry. The Parliamentary debate was, therefore, a test for the Board as well as Captain Stevens. Notably, Bowen had not sought to defend the Naval Board or its actions prior to the debate in his statement to Parliament.

Although the Attorney-General referred to extracts from the Cabban Statement, Cabinet had earlier decided that the Statement itself would not be tabled.[59] The next to speak in the debate was Jess. After reminding Bowen that he had not been a Member of Parliament during the debate of the Spicer Report, Jess spoke for well over an hour about the 1964 Commission and its failings, the injustice done to Captain Robertson, the essence of Cabban's statement, and the Navy's efforts in refuting it. It was a vociferous attack on the Government and his own Party:

> Today I stand in this House confronting my own Government . . . I am still loyal to the Liberal Party. I support it and I support the Government. The Prime Minister said last week that members of this House and of his party had the right to bring before the House matters which they felt should be raised, and I am exercising that right today. On a question of principle I had to make a decision as to the action I should take. Having had my submissions rejected by the Government, and having put them before my party, I feel it is now my duty to bring the matter to the final arbitrator, which must be this Parliament, the members of which sit here representing the people of Australia and not particular political parties. This should not be a party issue. This is an issue of justice.[60]

The speech was far too long, made so by an unnecessarily lengthy critique of Bowen's address. It also suffered from repeated pleadings in defence of his own stand on the issue, coupled with constant affirmations of his loyalty to the Liberal Party.

Chipp was made furious by Jess's remarks. The man who had defeated him for preselection for the safe Liberal seat of La Trobe had made a damning indictment of his department. He was the next to take the floor:

> The allegations that we have just heard from the honourable member for La Trobe are very serious. In fact, this House has rarely heard more serious allegations about a man. Furthermore they have been made about a man who is now dead — indeed, about a man who died in the service of his country.[61]

Chipp argued that the Cabban Statement was unreliable and grossly inaccurate. He outlined the way statements refuting the allegations had been collected and stressed their import. Chipp's closing plea was to 'ask honourable members to judge where the weight of evidence is and to come to a fair and logical conclusion.'[62]

Chipp's approach to the whole controversy was straightforward:

> Once I had formed my own conclusions about the Cabban allegations, it was my duty to defend with vigour and conviction the charges made about Stevens, the Navy generally and its officers and men, because under the Australian-British system of government, public servants and people serving in the armed forces are unable to defend themselves publicly.[63]

The Minister for the Navy ruined any prospect for compromise or negotiation in emphasising that there were no shades of virtue in the dispute, and hence no need for an inquiry. He gave no ground and was given none in return.

St John, the next to speak, was still very much an unknown quantity. This was his maiden speech, and maiden speeches were, by convention, non-controversial and never interrupted. But ministers had every right to fear the worst given St John's opening:

> I rise to make my maiden speech conscious of my loyalty to the party of which I am proud to be a member and of my duty to the electors of Warringah who have done me the honour to elect me to represent them in this House, but conscious above all of my sovereign obligation to speak the truth as I see it in the interests of the people of this, my country.[64]

After explaining his interest in the case and stating that he was 'not concerned with any possible injustice to Captain Robertson', St John proceeded to outline how and why the truth about *Voyager* might have been either lost or obscured. In spite of the efforts of Bowen and Chipp to discredit Cabban, who sat in the public gallery throughout the debate, St John argued that he believed Cabban to be a truthful and honest man:

> I believe this man is telling the truth. I would not care if the Minister for the Navy, with all due respect to him, brought along a stack of statements from serving officers saying that they could not remember or could not corroborate.[65]

Chipp had to be restrained in his seat by Snedden, such was his anger at St John's remark. After having his speech interrupted by the dinner adjournment, St John launched a savage attack on the Navy's argument that much of Cabban's statement was irrelevant to the causes of the collision. St John said that if it was true that Stevens was perpetually drunk or recuperating from drinking, and he firmly believed it was, how could it possibly be irrelevant?

> Is not this one of the facts and circumstances leading up to the *Voyager* disaster? Or have I lost the meaning of the word 'irrelevant'? Are we playing a battle of semantics? What is the meaning of the word 'irrelevant'?[66]

Holt could contain himself no longer and broke convention by interjecting, 'What is the meaning of the word "evidence"?'

St John cut Holt in two with his reply:

> I did not expect to be interrupted by the Prime Minister. We all have been invited
> to debate what comes to us second hand. The Prime Minister's interruption
> demonstrates better than anything else that this kind of matter can be sifted only
> by a proper judicial committee.[67]

The big winner was St John. Everyone was aware that Holt had been
embarrassed, including the press, who were showing great delight in
the proceedings. Bowen, who was sitting next to Holt, placed his hand
on Holt's arm to calm the outraged Prime Minister.[68]

However, St John overstepped the line and lost much of the support
he had accumulated when he said of Captain Stevens that, if the
allegations were true, 'This man is a chronic drunkard.'[69] This was a
serious misquotation of Attorney-General Bowen's masterful understatement that Cabban alleged Stevens 'frequently drank to excess'.[70]

St John then went on to suggest that the collision was a case of
drink-driving. As for corroborating the Statement, St John said he had
a long list of people who could be called and that he was not convinced
by the Minister for the Navy reading out statements he had gathered.
St John was interrupted for a second time, on this occasion by Chipp.
After forty-five minutes of anguish for the Government, St John
resumed his seat.

The speech received universal media acclamation. The *Adelaide News*
said 'Few could remember a more courageous and impressive maiden
speech ... the most forceful case for a new inquiry'.[71] Max Walsh of the
*Australian Financial Review* noted that one of St John's forebears appeared
for John Hampton in the 'Ship Money Case', one of the most famous
in British constitutional history:

> By any yardstick it has been an astonishing parliamentary debut. In thirty
> minutes of devastating forensic display, the Napoleonic-statured Sydney QC
> showed himself to be one of Parliament's most accomplished and persuasive
> debaters and at the same time perhaps irremediably blighted his political career.
> The motives which dictated this course of action are obviously confused and
> obscure but from his own words we can gather that a major contributing cause
> was the prideful consciousness of the family tradition.[72]

John Stubbs said in the *Australian* that

> Because Mr St John had, with his stature and ability, made dissent on the
> Government backbenches a respectable thing for the first time in many years,
> the debate and its result were — regardless of where the truth lies — a triumph
> for Parliament.[73]

There have been few occasions when pure oratory had led an
Australian Prime Minister to change his mind — and this was one of
them. Bowen regarded St John's speech as the turning point when the
press abandoned their reticence about supporting Jess's campaign and
the Prime Minister's resolve began to give way.

Harry Turner, the Member for Bradfield, probably the safest Liberal seat in the Federal Parliament, followed St John and explained his interest in the case and his conviction that it should be reopened. He made two points that those speaking before him had not made. Should those who refuted the statement be believed over Cabban simply because they were more senior? And was a different standard of proof being applied to Cabban? Chipp interrupted and criticised Turner for 'rubbishing a dead man'. Turner was unrepentant in his reply:

> Well, I have rubbished a dead man, for a start. This is regrettable — it is most regrettable — but I am concerned about eighty-two people who are dead and others who may be dead hereafter. I am not going to remain silent and not speak about facts, however painful they might be, if the cost of not speaking about those facts is that this thing could happen again.[74]

The next speaker was Jim Killen (later to be Minister for the Navy). After asking the Stevens family, who were in the public gallery, to show some charity towards the Parliament in spite of the debate, Killen argued on the strength of Professor Blackburn's statement that the amount of alcohol consumed by Stevens on the night of the collision would have had no effect on his judgement or mental capacity. Killen also defended Sir John Spicer and asked those who had been in the Parliament with him to 'acknowledge the utter integrity of the man and the sheer probity of his conduct'.[75]

Other than Jess's insistence that Robertson had been the victim of injustice, there had been little mention of him at all in the intervening debate, although Turner talked about the personal tragedy the collision had become for *Melbourne*'s captain. The final speaker in the debate during that first evening was Leslie Irwin, who attempted to amend the motion put by Jess to include the reinstatement of Robertson to naval service or the provision of an ex gratia payment. The amendment was not seconded. In fact, it would not have received support because both St John and Mackay had indicated to Holt that this was neither sought nor wanted by those who had joined with Jess.

The debate had been a disaster for the Government. At the Cabinet meeting held before the next day's sitting of Parliament a wait-and-see attitude was adopted.

Chaney, the former Minister for the Navy, was the first to speak the next day. He expressed amazement that St John would believe the allegations, and remarked that naval officers could be trusted when they gave their word. (Everyone except, one presumes, Cabban.) Chaney argued that reopening the case would affect the morale of the Navy and, by implication, the nation's security. He conceded that morale had fallen during the first Commission but that the Navy had arisen again to full stature and had performed admirably during the 'Confrontation' and in waters off Vietnam.[76]

The Government was to receive some support from Sam Benson,

now Independent Member for Batman. He started his speech by tabling a copy of Captain Stevens's final 'flimsy' which read: 'He has conducted himself to my entire satisfaction. A keen and enthusiastic captain of HMAS *Voyager*'. The Navy had not made available McNicoll's fuller commentary on Stevens's performance. Benson claimed once again to be an expert, but his speech showed him to be far from that.

Benson stated that although he was a supporter of Robertson, he had to challenge the allegations being brought by Cabban. The charges 'were untrue because the things that are alleged just could not happen'.[77] Benson said that a hopeless alcoholic, if that is what Stevens was, could not remain undetected for so long. He said that it was 'impossible' to bring liquor on board a ship without it being recorded and that Stevens would have hidden his drinking if it were as bad as Cabban alleged. He moved that the motion be amended to note that the Parliament 'places on record the confidence which it has in the Chief of Naval Staff...'[78] This was a complete reversal of his attitude of three years earlier.

The only useful thing to have come out of Benson's speech was his announcing that he had been informed by Surgeon Commander Roger McNeill the previous evening that Stevens had consuslted him privately about his ulcer condition. McNeill told Benson that the ulcer had been causing Stevens a great deal of pain and that this would explain much of his behaviour. It was convenient timing on McNeill's behalf, but produced little reaction during the debate.

The only member from the Opposition benches to make an impact on the debate was Clyde Cameron, who followed the matter very closely. He had interviewed Cabban as well and 'gained the impression that he was perhaps slightly pro-Liberal; or maybe apolitical. At any rate, he gave no clear indication to me that he was either for or against the Labor Party'.[79]

Cameron discussed the Naval Board's knowledge of Stevens's condition and their responsibility to be certain an officer was fit for command. He also picked up some of the inconsistencies contained in the refutations of Cabban's Statement. For instance, he pointed out that while the navigator of *Voyager* could recall his ship hitting *Vampire* during Stevens's first and only attempt at bringing the ship alongside, Captain James Willis, who had previously been held up as a reliable witness said 'I have no recollection of the alleged collision'. He did not say the incident did not happen, but that he could not remember it. Cameron voiced his opinion that the Government could not resist the demand for an inquiry 'without laying itself open to the charge that it fears the result'.[80] Cameron then went on to ridicule Benson, citing his statement in Parliament in 1964 that 'There must be an overhaul of the top echelon [of the Navy], because its members, and its members alone are responsible'.[81]

After citing Benson's criticism of the Navy for its handling of the HMAS *Sydney* whaler tragedy, Cameron showed that Benson had been generally critical of the RAN:

> He had not finished with the Navy, by a long way. He was still after its blood and he still means what he then said. He does not retract one word. He believes every word, and so do I and most other people. The honourable member for Batman is an expert, an ex-naval officer, and who would know better the shortcomings of the Navy? Who in this Parliament would be a more authoritative person to speak on the subject of the Navy?[82]

Cameron had neutralised Benson and his speech. He closed by calling upon the Government to hold another inquiry.[83]

William McMahon was next to speak and asked the Parliament how it was hoped a new inquiry could improve upon Sir John Spicer's finding that *Voyager* was culpable. He then proceeded to attack St John for his remark that Stevens was a 'chronic drunkard' and for challenging the honesty and integrity of Professor Blackburn. McMahon ended the debate by informing Parliament that

> The Government has not closed its options. The Prime Minister after considering all the points that have been raised will take the matter back to the party room and then decide exactly what is to be done.[84]

The Parliament adjourned for dinner while the Government went off to lick its wounds. Cabban states that political journalist Alan Reid approached him, Jess and others during the adjournment and informed them that Sir Frank Packer, owner of Australian Consolidated Press, had told Holt that, given the progress of the debate, the newspapers could forestall the matter no longer and that the Government had to have another inquiry. Cabinet met briefly before the evening sitting and decided a new inquiry was now unavoidable. Although a Select Committee[85] of Parliament had been mentioned, the feeling in Cabinet was that

> the only form of inquiry open in the circumstances was a judicial committee, the terms of reference of which would need to be tightly but clearly drawn to identify the basic points at issue. The Cabinet agreed that the course which the Government would follow would be announced to the House following discussion at the Party Meeting the following morning.[86]

After dinner, Holt addressed the Parliament with what he termed a 'ground clearing' operation, opening and covering the principal matters in dispute. He said that his predecessor had earnestly sought an explanation for the *Voyager* disaster and that he would not be party to any attempt to obscure the truth. He went on to say that Spicer was a man above reproach in his conduct and should not have been criticised as he had been. Holt then went on to read from Stevens's 'flimsies' which had, by now, been made available to the Government and mustered all the evidence he could gather to assert Stevens's good character.

Holt stalled any attempt to bring the debate to its conclusion with a vote on the motion. He said it was 'for the House to judge what course we should adopt'.[87] As to the avenues of inquiry, he mentioned a select committee but spoke strongly against it. 'There is the possibility of another judicial inquiry',[88] he said, although he again queried what the inquiry would prove. After another day of self-destruction, the Liberal Party would again consider the matter in the Party Room.

The Government had suffered by its own hands and Holt was unwilling to let the debate continue any longer. There was little hope of restraining the 'rebel' backbenchers while the newspapers and the public were hankering for another inquiry. The long haul for Jess was over on 18 May 1967. In a statement made to the Parliament, Holt said that a select committee to investigate *Voyager* was not appropriate. He said that although the matter had been thoroughly debated in Parliament and that most would say there was little left to discuss, there was an element of disquiet. Then came the moment the Navy had been dreading for over two years:

> So the Government has concluded that there should be a further inquiry and that it should be a judicial inquiry conducted probably by three judges.[89]

The Prime Minister said that although the precise terms of reference had yet to be finalised, they were substantially those proposed by Jess. They were announced in Parliament the next day and Holt confirmed that

> The inquiry will necessarily take the form of a Royal Commission, because it is under the legislation concerning Royal Commissions that we can set up the inquiry. To do it any other way would require legislation.[90]

Holt made this decision without consulting his Attorney-General — who would have advised against it — and against a body of opinion in Cabinet which continued to oppose a new inquiry. Bowen felt that Holt overreacted to the political pressure being exerted and agreed that any indication from Packer that his newspapers would no longer support the Government's opposition to another inquiry would have played a major role in Holt's thinking.[91]

It made sense not to convene a Select Committee as Jess and his supporters had proposed.[92] The likely candidates for appointment to the committee were those who had already trenchantly put their views. To have excluded Jess, Turner, St John and Mackay, as Bowen would have needed to do in the interests of fairness, would have in itself created a controversy.

The Salmon Royal Commission into Tribunals of Inquiry in Britain, which had not long before delivered its report, concluded that the record of Select Committees of Parliament to investigate allegations of public misconduct was 'to say the least, unfortunate'.[93] The Commissioner, Lord Justice Salmon, went further in an address to the Hebrew

University in Jerusalem, saying that these committees were indeed 'wholly unsatisfactory' on the basis that they have no 'claim to impartiality'.[94] This is not to say that they should never be used as an alternative to Royal Commissions, but for a matter such as *Voyager*, a Select Committee inquiry would have been most inappropriate.

Whatever the form of the inquiry, Jess had achieved his objective. It was now to be seen whether it was justified.

# 13

# *An Inquiry Into an Inquiry*

THE DECISION to hold another inquiry was very much against the sentiments of Cabinet, which still could not see the value of doing so. This was partly reflected in the three terms of reference which were framed to exploit the weaknesses apparent in the case put by Jess and St John. The Commissioners were to investigate:

1. Whether any of the allegations made by Lieutenant Commander P.T. Cabban in the document attached to the Letters Patent regarding the drinking habits and seamanship of Captain D.H. Stevens were true and being true established that Captain Stevens was unfit to retain command of HMAS *Voyager*.

2. If it is found in answer to Question 1 that Captain Stevens was unfit to retain command of HMAS *Voyager*
    (a) Did the Naval Board know or ought they to have known of such unfitness to retain command and were they at fault in failing to relieve him of command?
    (b) Should the findings made in the report of the Royal Commission relating to the loss of HMAS *Voyager* be varied, and if so, in what respects?

3. Whether the allegations in the document disclosed evidence which was available to counsel assisting the Royal Commission and was improperly withheld from the Commission.

Neither Jess nor St John was completely happy with the terms of reference. As St John commented:

> The terms of reference displayed a fair deal of ingenuity. The questions were arranged like so many Chinese boxes, in a form which we feared might stifle full inquiry. There followed some correspondence and a press release in which we tried to have the terms widened but the Government stood firm.[1]

This sort of criticism was not unexpected. Cynics have often argued that governments have the power to manage the outcome of inquiries through the appointment of commissioners and setting the terms of reference. In this case, rhetoric was not overcome by truth. Whitlam tried to have the terms augmented, and in effect widened, from the floor of the Parliament and in a letter to Holt. The matter was considered by Cabinet's Defence and Foreign Affairs Committee on 25 May 1967. The Committee did not believe there was justification in amending the terms of reference and felt that the Royal Commission had the ability to alter its terms, if it felt it necessary to do so, in the course of its inquiry.[2]

The selection of Commissioners was vital to the character of the inquiry. The Attorney-General had in mind Sir Norman O'Bryan, a retired Victorian Supreme Court judge, as chairman, with Justice Kenneth Asprey of the New South Wales Supreme Court and Justice George Lucas of the Queensland Supreme Court as Commissioners. For reasons that could not be verified, O'Bryan did not take up the appointment, which ultimately went to Sir Stanley Burbury, the Chief Justice of Tasmania, who also served as chairman.[3] The choice of commissioners from three different States and the distribution of Government briefs to barristers around Australia was a deliberate move on the part of Bowen. He believed it was fair for the Government work to be shared by the respective State Bars. It also avoided a concentration of opinion from one Bar, as had occurred in the first inquiry, which was dominated by the New South Wales Bar.[4]

The practice of appointing multiple commissioners was well established for matters which were of a political or controversial nature, such as the Petrov case in the 1950s. *Voyager* warranted three commissioners on two grounds. First, there was no doubt the matters referred to the commissioners were highly controversial. Second, in some respects the Commission was to serve, as Whitlam remarked at the time, as a 'Court of Appeal' on the Spicer Report. Multiple commissioners avoided the unwanted situation when, if one judge overturned the ruling of another, it was not a case of one view against another equally valid view.

There was universal support for the new inquiry from the newspapers. The *Australian*, in its editorial of 19 May 1967, applauded the Prime Minister's decision to hold another *Voyager* inquiry:

> If it is true, as Government spokesmen claimed on Tuesday, that there is no possibility of anything emerging from the new inquiry to change the official finding on what caused the disastrous collision between *Melbourne* and *Voyager* on February 10, 1964. That is not the point of the present discussion. The Royal Australian Navy's system of command appointments and officer assessment is the paramount issue in the charges made against the late Captain Stevens.

This editorial had not paid enough attention to the Parliamentary debate or the controversy surrounding the Cabban Statement. The debate was not about the RAN's officer career management — if this had been the prime issue there would not have been the agitation for a Royal Commission. Cabban's allegations were significant only inasmuch as they related to the collision. While the Cabban Statement may have caused some public disquiet about officer career management as it existed in 1963, it was the tantalising claim that Cabban's evidence contained the 'real' explanation for the collision that made Jess's campaign newsworthy and controversial.

The decision to have a new inquiry was made at great political cost to Holt's leadership, as Alan Ramsey noted in the *Australian*:

> Over the past two weeks the Prime Minister and his Cabinet colleagues have suffered a series of humiliating reverses. These reverses not only bring into question the ability of Mr Holt to succeed as chief architect in the administration of national affairs; they also, for the first time since he took office, acutely expose the vacuum created in the Government ranks by the retirement of Sir Robert Menzies.[5]

Another political correspondent suggested that Chipp had emerged poorest from the debate:

> The *Voyager* case has profoundly affected a number of political careers and reputations, and the greatest sufferer this week was the Minister for the Navy, Mr Chipp.
> Mr Chipp was, of course, obliged to defend the Navy and its reputation, but he should have kept calm about it ... Mr Chipp also introduced the nickname 'Drunken Duncan' into the debate for the first and only time, thus conferring parliamentary privilege on its use. With friends like that, the Navy does not need enemies.[6]

In his autobiography, Chipp says 'I reluctantly supported the idea' of another inquiry. However, I found nothing in any official file nor did anything emerge from interviews I conducted with those involved, to suggest he did anything to bring about the inquiry. Given the virulence with which he opposed it during the parliamentary debate, the most he did was to accept the inevitable.

There is little doubt that had Gorton been Prime Minister rather than Holt, as Alan Reid contended, 'there would have been no inquiry'.[7] Gorton was totally against another inquiry and resented the attacks being made on the Navy for events that had occurred while he had been Minister. Gorton recently confirmed that he would have resisted an inquiry whatever its political cost.[8]

The Opposition seemed content with the outcome. Only the member for Oxley, Bill Hayden, felt the need to comment: 'It will not be another whitewash, will it?'[9]

As expected, the Naval Board did not meet the decision to hold another Commission with any enthusiasm. At that time a number of its ships were engaged in operational service in the Vietnam conflict. The RAN was at war and men would soon be lost in action. While the Royal Commission would be looking at the health and drinking habits of Captain Stevens, the Naval Board would be striving to avoid weakening the resolve of those serving their country off the coast of South Vietnam.

Robertson had assumed a very low profile in all of this, although he was delighted to have finally gained an opportunity to challenge the findings of Spicer. However, he was greatly angered by a report appearing in the *Australian* on 19 May which stated that

> Government sources said that some weeks ago Mr Holt indicated the Government might take up the matter if it knew what Captain Robertson was prepared to accept. It is understood that he had made it known he would have to be taken back into the Navy, with the inclusion of his three years seniority and back pay that he had lost by his resignation. He is also understood to have asked to have restored all pension rights that he would have been entitled to had he not resigned. The terms were considered out of the question, and the matter was dropped.

Robertson was incensed and denied there had been any such approach. A clipping of this article in Robertson's private papers has 'Not True!' scrawled across it twice in Robertson's handwriting, while the offending sentences have been underlined so many times the page is torn.

The Stevens family were naturally distressed by the prospect of another inquiry from which they stood to gain nothing. They were, and remain, genuinely shocked by Cabban's allegations, which they considered were totally inconsistent with their own knowledge of Duncan gained over many years of close contact. The decision having been made to hold another inquiry, public statements were issued by Captain Stevens's widow and father. Mrs Stevens said:

> I have been sickened and upset during the past few days by allegations made about my husband Duncan. He lost his life in *Voyager*. He has never therefore been able to speak for himself . . . My faith in my husband is unshaken. I welcome the P.M.'s decision to have a judicial inquiry which will restore his name. I only hope the legal procedures will be quick.[10]

Sir Jack took a different and perhaps safer line, and said his son 'was not a paragon of all virtues but he was a decent Australian, a dedicated naval officer, a good all-round athlete and a wonderful son'.[11]

There was some consolation for the Stevens family from the many letters of support and encouragement they received. There were more than forty unsolicited letters from the public and several from serving officers and naval families.

In defence of Captain Stevens, his family could cite the many letters they received when *Voyager* was lost, including three from officers who had served with him throughout the Far East cruise in 1963. They were from Lieutenants Griffith, Martin and Redman. It is worth quoting extracts from all three as they show the depth of feeling each had for their former captain and how they were likely to feel about giving evidence that might have been adverse to him. First, the letter from Griffith:

> I personally feel the loss of a good friend for whom I have a very high regard. Duncan was a fine man indeed. We shall all miss him dearly.[12]

The letter from Martin provided the Stevens family with their understanding of the 1963 deployment:

> My year with Duncan in that fine ship, was I think, the best and happiest time

I have had in the Service. He was always cheerful and outstandingly helpful, and much of the advice he gave me I will always rely upon. Please remember what a happy ship he had, and how much his sailors liked him.[13]

The third letter, from Redman, was significant in that he was a very experienced officer who had risen through the ranks and who had had his fair share of commanding officers:

Captain Stevens was more than just my captain, he was also my friend, and I shall always remember his many kindnesses.[14]

There had also been letters from two serving flag officers, Rear-Admirals Morrison and Smith. Morrison said he was 'extremely pleased and very lucky to have him as my Commander while I was in the *Melbourne*'.[15] Smith remarked that he had 'always especially admired his integrity, cheerfulness, willingness to help others and his enthusiasm. As you know we were together in the Frigate Squadron and there I was able to appreciate fully his many fine qualities.'[16]

Gaining sympathy was one thing; rebutting Cabban's allegations was quite another. Mrs Stevens wrote to her husband's friends and acquaintances seeking additional assistance. A letter dated 23 May to a family friend, R. Boyd McMurrick, who spent time with Stevens in Hong Kong in 1963, was typical of this early period (later letters were far more circumspect):

Duncan enjoyed his grog — got high and merry at times — like all normal people do, but I could never accuse him of being a chronic alcoholic or drunkard and incapable of being captain of his ship. His ulcer I know was affecting him a great deal in 1963 [although] he never mentioned it much in his letters.

... We expect the judicial inquiry to be set for sometime in August so naturally want any information as soon as possible.[17]

McMurrick's reply, too, was typical although, not unexpectedly, it was not tabled at the Royal Commission:

At no time could Duncan be accused of being a chronic alcoholic. He liked his grog and enjoyed many a good dinner party in my home where we wined and dined well ... To my knowledge Duncan liked his grog no more than a normal naval officer or a normal man. We all get high and merry at times but surely this doesn't mean we are all alcoholics.[18]

In notes for counsel prepared by Mrs Stevens dated 2 June 1967, there is a record of telephone conversations with both Griffith and Captain Loxton who indicated their non-corroboration of the Cabban Statement. Griffith also told Mrs Stevens he had been 'contacted by Mr St John before the parliamentary debate and asked if he would corroborate. He immediately informed the Naval Board of St John's approach'.[19] There were other offers of help. They included ones from Ian Blaikey, *Voyager*'s supply officer in 1963, who had left the Navy and was working in the news section of ABC Radio in Melbourne, and Commander John Goble who 'offered to help regarding the character and nature of Cabban as an aviator. Says he grounded Cabban and was in *Supply* in 1963 in Hong Kong and could have given Cabban advice at the time he sought it from Peek.[20]

A body of opinion giving a very different picture of Stevens to that painted by Cabban was gradually growing. Mrs Stevens received supportive letters from WRANS and sailors who had worked at the family residence at *Cerberus* while Stevens was Training Commander. There were also many letters from neighbours of the Stevens, all denying that they had ever seen him drunk. Sydney broadcaster Ron Casey, a swimming coach in 1964, said he saw Stevens regularly in the early morning with his son at swimming training and noticed nothing to suggest he had been drinking.

The Navy's attitude to assisting the Stevens family was revealed in a letter from the now retired Rear-Admiral Becher:

> For a couple of months, since Don Chipp asked me to see him, I have known what was going on. I assured Chipp then, that I was absolutely certain that the allegations were completely and utterly false. I hope now, I will have the opportunity to swear the same in front of three learned judges.
>
> Alan McNicoll, whom I saw on Wednesday, asked me when I told him I was sending you a note, to assure you that, on all Duncan's file, there is not even a suggestion that he drank too much. Duncan and I became very close when he was my second-in-command in *Melbourne* ... I am now very glad that I wrote then, in his confidential report that 'this officer is of sober habits' ...
>
> Duncan's name will be completely cleared and he will be confirmed as a loyal, enthusiastic, fine man with whom so many in the Navy were pleased and proud to serve.

Although there was contact between naval personnel and the Stevens family after the second inquiry was announced, it could not be properly termed collusion. On 23 June 1967, Commodore Dacre Smyth wrote from London to Mrs Stevens:

> Jim Willis and I have often talked together in my office and he just can't wait to get at Cabban. But even if Cabban does get his just deserts, nothing can make up to you the nightmare of this ghastly campaign.[21]

On the same day Smyth wrote to Osborne:

> I had not seen Duncan for over three years, so I do not feel that I can usefully comment on the Cabban statement. Many men better qualified than I will no doubt point out its inconsistencies and inaccuracies, which seem almost to indicate a paranoid tendency in its author ...
>
> [Duncan] was often individualistic, and was certainly not a dull conformist to the traditional naval officer mould. He may well have sometimes been brusque and loathe to suffer inefficiency, but I cannot believe that he was a martinet, or an oppressive officer, or a drunkard.[22]

One of the principal witnesses, Captain James Willis, mentioned in his letter to Mrs Stevens that

> I understand my comments were tabled during the debate in Parliament, and that there was some suggestion that they were made under pressure from some

sinister 'they' — nothing could be further from the truth, of course.[23]

In a letter dated 10 July, Willis, who was out of Australia for part of 1966 and 1967 attending the Imperial Defence College course in London, stated he had still not been contacted by the Naval Board. 'Have heard nothing from any of the powers that be about the inquiry, but imagine that something will be forthcoming soon as the opening is only about one week away'.[24]

It was curious that Willis had yet to be contacted. On 26 June 1967 the Deputy Crown Solicitor wrote to eight officers serving overseas asking if they could corroborate Cabban's allegations. The letter was drafted by Peter Murphy QC as counsel for the Navy and closed with the intentionally leading comment, 'I might add that I have not been able to obtain corroboration of these allegations from other witnesses already in Australia'. Whitlam later raised an objection to the wording of these letters in a question to the Attorney-General in Parliament.[25]

The task before the Commissioners was a difficult one in many respects, not least the close interest of politicians. Although they had followed similar career paths into and through the law, the three Commissioners were very different men. Sir Stanley Burbury, as Chief Justice of Tasmania, was the necessary choice of chairman. Although Tasmania was not known in legal circles for having produced many outstanding lawyers, such were the limited legal actions the island managed to produce, Burbury was nonetheless considered to be a very good Chief Justice and above what might have been expected of that State. He had earlier been involved in a Royal Commission into the Tasmanian fruit industry and was 'not all that busy' when he was approached to preside over the Commission. Burbury was advised that the Commission was likely to last for only four or five weeks. He had not previously met the Commonwealth Attorney-General or the other two Commissioners. Burbury stated that he had no difficulty with any of the terms of reference but felt it was a curious thing to have them based on 'a scrappy statement that was only ever meant for private use and which was unsworn'.[26] He was a thoughtful man and known to be conservative in most things, including the law.

Justice Kenneth Asprey, a judge of the New South Wales Supreme Court since 1962, had had a busy and varied practice at the Bar and was known to be a very forceful advocate, a common attribute among barristers at the New South Wales Bar.[27] A quick mind coupled with a well-developed self-view and an aggressive streak made him at times impatient and severe with those appearing before him. He did a lot of his thinking and reasoning aloud and occasionally closed his mind about matters towards which he should have kept it open.

Justice George Lucas possessed a character that was halfway between the usually mild Burbury and the occasionally abrasive

Above: Looking astern of HMAS *Voyager* during pre-commissioning trials.

Left: Looking towards the bow. (RAN)

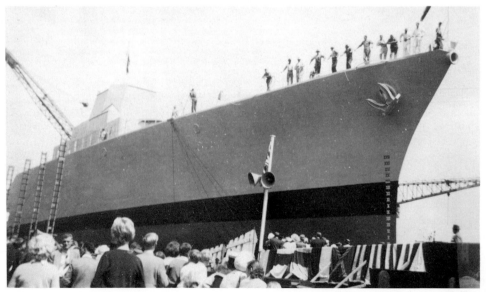

Top: HMAS *Voyager* at sea (probably 1963).

Left: The launching of *Voyager* at Cockatoo Island, 1 May 1952.

Right: The commissioning of *Voyager* in 1957. (RAN)

Above: Admiral Sir David Luce arriving on board HMAS *Voyager* in 1963. On Captain D. H. Stevens's right is Lieutenant D. J. Martin. (RAN)

Below: *Voyager* at sea. (RAN)

Opposite, above: Looking down at *Voyager*'s bridge. (RAN)

Opposite, below: Captain Stevens seated on the chair in which he died while commanding *Voyager*. (RAN)

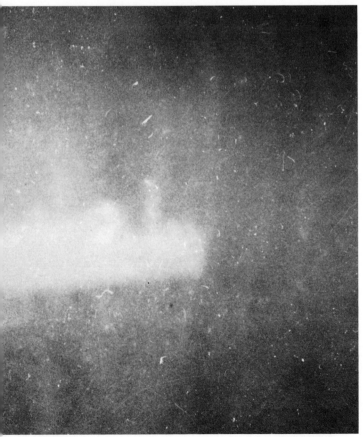

Above: The stern section of HMAS *Voyager* floating after the collision. This photograph was taken from HMAS *Melbourne*'s flight deck. (RAN)

Left: *Voyager* sinks. (RAN)

Above: Survivors from HMAS *Voyager* being picked up by rescue craft from HMAS *Melbourne*. (RAN)

Below: Survivors from *Voyager* recovering in *Melbourne*. (Naval Historical Collection, Australian War Memorial)

Right: Injured survivor from *Voyager* is helped off *Melbourne* after she docked in Sydney. (RAN)

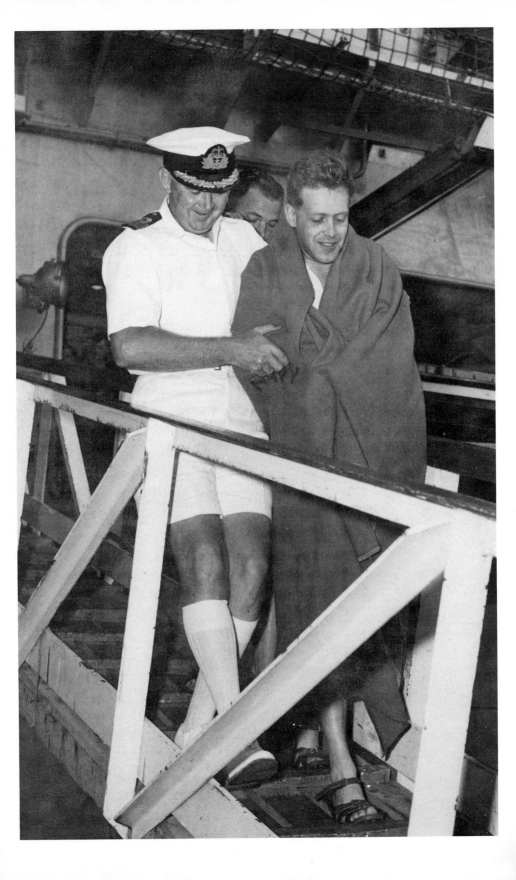

Three views of HMAS *Melbourne*'s damaged bow. (RAN)

Above: HMAS *Voyager* at sea. (RAN)

Right: Survivors from *Voyager* after being picked up by HMAS *Melbourne*'s whaler. (Naval Historical Collection, Australian War Memorial)

## CANBERRA EDITION

# THE AUSTRALIAN

NUMBER SIXTY-EIGHT

TELEPHONE 4 4221

THURSDAY OCTOBER 1 1964

PRICE FOURPENCE

EXCLUSIVE

# CAPTAIN ROBERTSON'S STORY

INSIDE

Above: The Australian Commonwealth Naval Board in 1964. From left: Rear-Admiral F. L. George, Rear-Admiral V. A. Smith, Vice-Admiral Sir Hastings Harrington (Chief of Naval Staff 1962–65), Mr S. Landau. (RAN)

Below: The Australian Commonwealth Naval Board with the Commonwealth Administrator in 1967. From left: Rear-Admiral V. A. Smith, Mr S. Landau, Vice-Admiral Sir Alan McNicoll (Chief of Naval Staff 1965–68), Lieutenant-General Sir Edric Bastyan, Rear-Admiral J. S. Mesley, Rear-Admiral F. N. Purves, Rear-Admiral W. D. H. Graham. (RAN)

HMAS *Melbourne* meets her end in 1985. (RAN)

Asprey. Lucas was much respected in the Queensland Supreme Court. He was also the only Commissioner to have undertaken military service in World War II.[28] Not much was known of him outside his home State but he was to make a very balanced contribution to the Commission's proceedings.

The all-important position of counsel assisting the commissioners had gone to Francis Burt QC, a Perth barrister and son of a former Chief Justice of Western Australia. Burt had a good reputation as a lawyer and was much admired by the Commissioners. An imposing man with enormous powers of persuasion, he argued from the outset that the Commission should be conducted entirely in open session. This view was shared by Burbury who was reluctant to exclude any evidence, given the circumstances of the first inquiry.

Burt's junior was Philip Jeffrey. The other government brief was taken by Peter Murphy QC, a Melbourne barrister, who had long experience at inquiries of this nature. He was assisted by Humfry Henchman who had been Jenkyn's junior at the 1964 Commission.

Briefs for parties claiming an interest in the proceedings were a mixture of faces from the 1964 Commission and newcomers. Appearing for the Stevens family were Bill Ash QC and John Sinclair, with Fred Osborne as the instructing solicitor. Osborne would have preferred Street QC to have taken the brief but he had been elevated to the New South Wales Supreme Court bench. He then unsuccessfully tried to engage Ray Reynolds QC (who had accepted a brief from Robertson), and then Gordon Samuels QC. The Stevens family brief ultimately went to Ash. In his favour, Ash had the assistance of Sinclair's naval experience, his personal knowledge of Cabban since 1942, and his involvement in the previous Commission.

David Hicks QC, counsel for Robertson in 1964, was now on the New South Wales District Court bench. Despite it not being clear at this stage what Robertson hoped the new Commission would achieve, he was represented by Ray Reynolds QC, with Peter Raine acting as his junior.

Appearing for Cabban were Jack Hiatt QC and Chester Porter. Porter, who had been suggested by St John to Cabban, recommended Hiatt as leading counsel.[29] Sandy Gregory would act for the interests of the Price family at Commonwealth expense but these were thought to be less involved in the new Commission.

The sensation of the *Voyager* tragedy going around again was made even more obvious by the use of the same courtroom as in 1964. It was an inquiry that made history. Never before had a matter been the subject of two Royal Commissions. The Commission formally opened on 13 July 1967.

# 14

# The Indictment of Stevens

THE COMMISSION'S formal opening on 13 June 1967 lasted just thirty-three minutes and covered a range of preliminaries, including an application from Burt to the Commission that the Cabban Statement be suppressed until evidence was finally given. Of most significance was Burt's explanation of the terms of reference and the matters on which the Commission would need to hear argument and make findings. He emphasised that

> this Commission is not what has so often been referred to as the second *Voyager* inquiry. To call it that would really be to miss the central point of the present inquiry.[1]

Burt stressed that the Commission did not call for the rehearing of any evidence that related to the events immediately preceding the collision. In an attempt to prevent the Commission becoming a bottomless pit, he also tried to limit the scope of the inquiry to those matters which related specifically to Stevens's unfitness to command and the extent to which, if at all, Spicer's finding ought to be altered on that basis. This having been said, the Commission adjourned until 18 July 1967 to allow counsel to gather evidence and prepare submissions.

After Burt's clear statement that the Commission ought not to hear navigational evidence, it must have been obvious to Robertson that he would have to use Cabban and his allegations about Stevens if he were to gain anything from the Commission. When the Commission resumed on 18 July, Burt continued to outline the scope of the inquiry:

> ... we are not really concerned with the happenings of the night of the collision, or not specifically concerned; perhaps it lies on the periphery of this inquiry, but that is the highest status one can give it.[2]

He later suggested that even if Stevens had had a violent heart attack on the bridge of *Voyager*,

> it would not seem to me to throw any light upon or indeed be relevant to the behaviour of the officers on the bridge of *Melbourne*.[3]

The one situation he was prepared to accept was that Stevens was proved incompetent, which was vastly different from being unwell, although he saw no grounds at that stage of the Commission for such a view. He also tried to prevent any ground covered by Spicer from being re-examined at the Commission by declining to tender the whole transcript of the 1964 Commission as an exhibit. He further stated that less than one per cent of the 1964 Commission was at any rate relevant to the current inquiry and that very limited extracts would be tendered.

Burt then outlined the circumstances behind Cabban's involvement, from his interview with Police Sergeant Turner soon after the collision to interviews with Sinclair and Smyth to the construction of the Cabban Statement. Burt was at pains to reduce the significance of the document in terms of the Commission's subsequent proceedings:

> The origins of the document, it seems to us, is to a very high degree reflected in its structure. It is not a pleading. Nor is it an indictment. It is really a conversation piece. It is made, so to speak, off the cuff by a man who had no idea that it would ever see the light of day.[4]

Burt attempted to use the Statement as an indication of signs that the Commission needed to consider as a means of drawing other related evidence, rather than conducting a detailed exegesis of the Statement itself. He also hinted at the line of argument he was later to adopt: that Stevens was physically unwell more than he was affected by excessive consumption of alcohol. Burt then had his junior, Philip Jeffrey, read the entire Statement. Finally, the whole of the controversial document entered the public arena.

After noting those incidents in the Statement which could be dated and proved, and following a rearranging of the Statement into a proper chronological sequence, Burt asked the Commissioners to bear in mind two things. First, that although Stevens was dead and unable to defend himself, if the facts sustained any conclusion about his conduct then it ought to be fearlessly made. Second, given the nature of the inquiry, notions such as onus of proof and beyond reasonable doubt were unrealistic. He cited a judgement by the then Justice Dixon who said that 'it is enough that the affirmation of an allegation is made out to the reasonable satisfaction of the tribunal'.[5]

As for Stevens's drinking habits, Burt was at pains to point out that the Commission's interest in them was only so far as they related to his fitness to command a warship. And the nature of the consumption was of interest only in the manner that it affected Stevens. Burt criticised St John's description of Stevens as a 'chronic alcoholic' and went as far as saying that the evidence showed that this was not true.

As to whether the Naval Board ought to have known about Stevens's condition, Burt left the matter entirely open, although he suggested that many situations could develop which would prevent the Naval Board from knowing things it ought to know in spite of established procedures to ensure it is kept informed. As Burt had suggested from the outset that Stevens was more likely to have been unwell than an alcoholic, his remark that

> procedures both general and medical devised by the Naval Board for the recording of information appear to me, untutored in these matters, to be in all respects adequate if not excellent,[6]

was of great comfort to the Naval Board.

The third term of reference, which asked whether any information was 'improperly withheld' from the 1964 Commission, was one Burt appeared to dismiss from the outset. It was perhaps the most political of the terms of reference and he argued that the conduct of Smyth and Sheppard was entirely within the professional conduct expected of a barrister.

Having outlined the principal matters he believed would most exercise the judicial minds of the Commissioners, Burt outlined the way in which he intended to organise the Commission's proceedings, as was his duty as counsel assisting. Starting with Cabban, who would be called to give evidence and to be examined on his Statement, witnesses would be called to give evidence on the origins of the Statement, the reasons for Cabban not being called at the 1964 Commission and the handling of the Statement since its coming into existence. This would serve to answer the third term of reference and get it out of the way immediately.

After receiving Cabban's evidence the Commission would look at Stevens's health, to be followed by matters relating to alcohol and blood alcohol levels. Only after this had been done would Burt call any witness to corroborate or dispute the truthfulness of the Cabban Statement. It was at this point that Burt first expressed some concern about the Navy's ability to assist the Commission. Two copies of *Voyager*'s Report of Proceedings for 1963 had apparently been mislaid within Navy Office. As this period was of particular concern in terms of the Commission's inquiries, it was inevitable that the worst suspicions were created. Four other copies, two received by the RAN and two by the Royal Navy, had either been destroyed or were no longer held.[7]

Cabban was, as expected, the first witness to take the stand on the third day of sitting. After displaying some nervousness, he appeared to relax and sat while giving his evidence. Burt systematically took him though his naval career and the circumstances relating to his appointment to *Voyager*. The character of the accuser appeared as relevant as that of the accused.

Peter Thomas Cabban was born on 12 March 1928 in Newcastle. He joined the RAN College in 1942 and made steady progress during his training. Promoted acting sub-lieutenant in 1947, Cabban was an officer of average ability and promotion prospects. Awarded his bridge watchkeeping certificate in 1949, he commenced training as a pilot in February the following year. Over the next six years, Cabban served as a naval aviator in various postings. In June 1955 he trained to become a maintenance test pilot and served until November 1956 in that capacity at HMAS *Albatross*. After the crash of a Gannet training aircraft in which he was the pilot, Cabban was permanently grounded as 'temperamentally unsuited to operational flying'.

In an effort to shape a new career for him in general service, Cabban was posted to HMAS *Warramunga* in January 1957 as a watchkeeping officer. He spent one year in the ship before being sent to the Jervis Bay Naval Airfield as officer-in-charge. With the completion of the mandatory period of service in the rank of lieutenant, he was promoted to lieutenant commander. After failing in successive attempts to have his grounding as a pilot overturned, he submitted his resignation from the RAN. It was not accepted and Cabban was sent to the training establishment HMAS *Cerberus* as the Ships' Company Divisional Officer. This was not a sought-after appointment for an officer with hopes of high naval rank. In January 1959, he was selected to undertake a course in Work Study in Britain when the Naval Board decided it would form a team to commence this activity within the RAN. After serving in the newly established Fleet Work Study Team for two years, he was appointed Executive Officer of HMAS *Tobruk*. When a decision was made that the destroyer would not recommission from reserve, Cabban was appointed Executive Officer of HMAS *Sydney*, which was then undergoing conversion to become a troopship. After a year which *Sydney* mostly spent alongside at Garden Island, he was posted in September 1962 as Executive Officer of *Voyager*.[8]

Cabban and Stevens were professionally and personally incompatible and an unlikely command team. They were temperamentally ill-suited to have even served closely with one other. Stevens respected Cabban but did not like him; Cabban liked Stevens but did not respect him. Mrs Stevens stated that her husband had instant concerns about Cabban and recalled them in a private statement she prepared for the Stevens family's counsel on 20 June 1967. Neither this statement, nor any of the comments it contained, was ever used or cited at the Commission. It was a revealing document. This statement spoke of 'Cabban's ineffectiveness, lack of leadership and inadequate support for his captain'. Mrs Stevens also said her husband was 'not happy to rely on Cabban for any assistance'. An undated first draft of this statement went even further:

> Duncan intimated on and off that Cabban took [being second-in-command] a little too literally and freely — I recall him saying Cabban caused him more concern over his attitude to working the upper deck — his ideas were not Duncan's, he was a 'crank' on 'method' which had not proved successful as regards the general look and maintenance of the upper deck ... He and Cabban

were not compatible on or off duty — he was mildly critical of Cabban's lack of a sense of humour, of social demeanour as president of the wardroom. Personally, they had little in common.[9]

Later she mentions that her husband believed Cabban had tried to 'run the ship's company and wardroom with an autocratic mananagement routine which no one appreciated'. There is little doubt that neither Captain nor Mrs Stevens understood the character of Cabban very well.

Peter Cabban was an extraordinary man and the type of person few people would ever encounter in their lives. He was complex and contradictory; he could be both candid in self-deprecation and consciously conceited. Most peculiar was his ability to recall specific details of even minor events. In matters that had no connection with *Voyager*, he was able to recollect with incredible accuracy names, dates, places and conversations which were independently confirmed. He was an honest and truthful man.

Throughout his naval career spanning two decades, Cabban appeared to be a difficult and obstinate individual. He abounded in self-confidence and ambition, and, by his own admission, showed little restraint in disagreeing with his seniors. Cabban was foremost an individualist with a strong and resilient character. He possessed a firmly entrenched set of personal and professional principles by which he often judged others. Although an officer with well-developed self-discipline, his temperament occasionally led him to break the code of conduct he had set himself.

Cabban was never a strong 'team player'. He usually took his own counsel and was normally unmoved by the views of those he considered inferior to him. Consequently, he was an independent thinker, inclined to do things his own way with the expectation that others should accept both his right and his wisdom in doing so.

Cabban saw much of what happened in life as either black or white. Yet, he was not a moralist. His judgements on others, including those he passed on Duncan Stevens, were those of a man with a firm sense of duty and a well-defined appreciation of responsibility. Whereas he believed his duty was to implement and see observed all of the Navy's rules and regulations, his rigid personality and dour demeanour led him to be authoritarian, inflexible and even petty at times.

Cabban told me that he considered himself a coward on two grounds for having resigned from the Navy. The first was that he had fled from his fear of what he thought Stevens might have done to him because they had not enjoyed a harmonious relationship in *Voyager*. The second was a conviction that he formed in mid-1963 that *Voyager* would be lost if Stevens remained in command. After the collision, Cabban felt responsible for what had happened and believed that he should have done more to have prevented the circumstances which led to the collision. In speaking with me on numerous occasions, Cabban stressed the shock he experienced when he heard that *Voyager* had been lost and the continuing feelings of guilt he carried with him in the period after the first Commission. Cabban conceded that between 1964 and 1967 he acted more out of emotion, as a consequence of his desperate psychological state, than out of logic and sound reasoning. Cabban was driven by his feelings of guilt and believed the Commission would meet intimate personal needs, foremost being the need for affirmation that the collision was not his responsibility.

Cabban considered that his psychological state allowed him to be drawn into a second *Voyager* inquiry. He considered neither the full consequences of his involvement nor the personal cost. In spite of having been out of the Navy for twelve months when he made his Statement, Cabban felt as though he was within the Navy system and found it difficult to resist the imposing Robertson, who acted towards him as a captain would treat a lieutenant commander, although both were by then civilians. Cabban, foolishly or otherwise, accepted Robertson's instructions as orders which he ought not to question. Although he gave the outward appearance of a stable character and a balanced personality, Cabban remained deeply disturbed by some of his experiences in *Voyager* during 1963 and the collision in 1964. There was passing mention of Cabban's psychological state at the Commission. However, Cabban's feelings and the actual state of his mind, which were so important to interpreting his actions between the collision and the second Commission, were not revealed by the adversary style of the Royal Commission process.

It was remarkable that Burt was able to take Cabban through his entire statement with only two objections from counsel, both relating to the admissibility of hearsay evidence. On both occasions the Commissioners declined to make a ruling on hearsay evidence other than to ask that it be avoided until its significance with respect to possible findings was established. This was no doubt going to be a problem for the Commission as large parts of Cabban's allegations were based entirely on hearsay. However, Burt tried to ignore the Cabban Statement as much as he could in an effort to distract attention from it. From the outset it was apparent that Cabban wanted to moderate his views and opinions and it was this more considered evidence that Burt, realising the flaws in the Statement, hoped to use as the basis for subsequent argument. It was a hope he entertained for the two days he retained Cabban in the witness box.[10]

On the fourth day of hearings, Cabban was led through the events which culminated in his not being called at the 1964 Commission. His conduct had been curious to say the least. After being interviewed by Sergeant Turner, Cabban was asked to see Smyth. He told Smyth that he had heard rumours about Stevens being drunk at the time of the collision, rumours he had heard from *Voyager* survivors at HMAS *Penguin*, but that he could vouch for Stevens's strong discipline in never drinking at sea. Although Smyth was given a description of Stevens's alcohol-induced incapacity at other times, he would have found Cabban's probably excessive insistence that Stevens never drank at sea a little strange.

Apparently fearing for Stevens's reputation, Cabban sought legal advice before approaching the Stevens family with his evidence. He subsequently consulted Osborne, who took him to see Sinclair. Street did not want to speak with him. Cabban said his intention was to exclude evidence relating to alcohol being brought up at the Commission. Strangely, after he heard Hyland's evidence that Stevens had consumed a triple brandy he rang Robertson and offered him his 'knowledge of Captain Stevens as far as alcohol was concerned'. Robertson declined the offer. In early April 1964, Cabban was informed by Smyth that he was not required to give evidence and seems to have let the matter lie at that point. He told Burt he was 'pleased' not to have to give evidence. Burt then took Cabban through the sequence of events that led to the Cabban Statement being made.

Before the luncheon adjournment, Burt advised the Commissioners of the order of cross-examination. Hiatt was to follow Burt, then Murphy, and possibly Reynolds. This would allow the evidence against Captain Stevens to have been given before Ash commenced his cross-examination. Hiatt would follow Ash to cover any matters raised by Ash, with Burt retaining the final right of cross-examination. The position of Reynolds revealed the difficulty Robertson would face throughout the Commission. Reynolds, on being asked by Burbury what purpose he would have in cross-examining Cabban, would not commit himself nor directly answer Burbury's question. In fact, he revealed nothing of the approach he would take and reserved his decision on whether he would cross-examine Cabban. As it happened, neither Murphy, Hiatt nor Reynolds wanted to cross-examine Cabban on what he had told Burt. After two days of Cabban giving evidence, Ash began his cross-examination with the purpose of destroying the truthfulness and reliability of Cabban as a witness.

Ash attempted to attack Cabban on a number of fronts including his inexperience in operational warships, having been an aviator and work study specialist for a number of years; the sheer unlikelihood of the alleged events having taken place without Stevens's conduct being widely known (this was based on Ash's contention that destroyer captains have little or no privacy); gaps or failures in Cabban's recollection; exaggerations or inaccuracies in his evidence; and the impossibility of Cabban being able to vouch for Stevens's movements. The attack was sustained and relentless. However, Ash was unable to find a motive for Cabban's allegations. At the end of two hours' questioning, Cabban's Statement was still largely intact. An interesting fact that did emerge was the limited contact that Stevens had with Captain James Willis in 1963. This was in conflict with the expectations of counsel and the Commissioners that had been created by the suggestion in the Naval Board's previous statement that Willis would be able to refute the majority of the Cabban Statement.

The following day (Day 5) Cabban was still in the witness box. Ash tried to suggest to him that Stevens had plenty of work to do and that as he did all that was required of him there was little opportunity for him to be as incapacitated as frequently as Cabban claimed. He went on to criticise Cabban's overly rigorous attitude towards alcohol consumption by officers and to use Cabban's uncertainty about events to minimise Stevens's consumption to what could be positively ascertained. Ash attempted to chip away at the period covered by Cabban's allegations although he was unable to show any instance where Cabban was either grossly inaccurate or deliberately misleading.

The turning point came in the late morning of the fifth day, when Ash started to question Cabban on *Voyager*'s visit to Japan. In his statement, Cabban described the period 'as more than trying, it was quite desperate'.[11] When asked if he was exaggerating in describing the situation as desperate, Cabban denied the suggestion and pointed out that it was not the events which were desperate but his 'state of mind'. He said, 'I thought I was in a situation rather similar to that in *The Caine Mutiny*'.[12,13] This comment reflected Cabban's occasional tendency to be melodramatic. In wanting to avoid being in the same position as Lieutenant Maryk, the Executive Officer of the fictitious USS *Caine* in the novel by Herman Wouk (he had landed himself in trouble by keeping a log of the captain's actions), Cabban said he had avoided any reference to Stevens in either his letters or the audio tapes which he sent to his wife. Ash saw great opportunity in letting Cabban describe his mental desperation.

> I had no certain pattern or guide as to where I should turn or what I should do under these circumstances. I did not know if a continuation of this situation would adversely affect the safety of the ship. I felt that if I were to report my feelings in this way and I were wrong, I would be committing both the captain unfairly and myself to an extent that was not going to help. If I did not report it and anything happened, I did not know where I would stand then. I felt that the situation was close to being out of hand but I just could not see how I would explain what I saw so intimately to senior authorities.[14]

This explained much of Cabban's behaviour to that time. He had portrayed a dramatic ordeal with himself as the central character with the story unravelling around him. Ash realised that his best chance of discrediting Cabban was to concentrate on exaggerations in the Statement and to the extreme nature of some, if not all, of Cabban's personal judgements. He was relentless in pointing out the inconsistency in Cabban's attitude that the situation had indeed become desperate, although large passages of time and action did not conform to the pattern he required to form and maintain this attitude. The conclusion that Ash drew from Cabban's memory was one of great selectivity and he put this suggestion to Cabban:

> You seem to have been on the spot when this man had a few drinks but you never seem to have been on the spot when he was doing his job in harbour.[15]

Then Ash produced a photograph album presented to Captain Stevens by the Mayor of Karatsu, which was the port of call before Tokyo where Cabban had stated his position had become desperate. Using the album, Ash was able to draw Cabban into making a series of judgements about Stevens's behaviour and to give the impression that he was a man who sat in constant judgement of his captain, applying standards that were overly rigorous and unrealistic, if not varied in application. Ash was also able to have Cabban agree that Stevens performed well throughout the visit to Karatsu. But when asked whether the visit fell out of the pattern he observed to that time, Cabban foundered. He said 'I do not disagree, but I cannot agree'.[16] This placed upon Cabban the need to put an alternative explanation. He was unable to do this because he could not recall his views of the captain's behaviour, his own state of mind, or whether he was more or less anxious about this visit than any other. Ash had won the forenoon sitting and Cabban looked less secure and less confident.

Ash was determined to shatter Cabban's logic in stating that his position had become desperate during the Tokyo visit. He suggested to Cabban that he was being unreasonable in taking Stevens to the steam baths on two occasions and then allowing him to drink afterwards; on the second occasion both he and Cabban consumed five brandies. Covering the events of the following day, Ash submitted that Stevens had made no attempt to hide the fact that he was unwell and Cabban was forced to agree. Shortly afterwards, *Voyager* departed Tokyo and Cabban claimed Stevens had given him 'complete' command for the ensuing five days. After this, Cabban no longer felt that the situation was 'desperate', because Stevens did not drink for two months. Ash was unimpressed with the intensity of Cabban's descriptions. Ash avoided covering any specific detail about the visit, and simply outlined the events as they occurred.

From his build-up it was clear that Ash had evidence relating to the period following *Voyager*'s departure from Tokyo when Cabban claimed he had complete command for five days. He pressed Cabban on whether the period was exactly five days, what he meant by complete, and left him no grounds on which to alter what he had said. That something major was to follow was obvious.

Having committed Cabban to a statement in which he had complete confidence and staked his credibility as a witness of the truth, Ash tendered *Voyager*'s punishment log for the period of June 1963 showing that Stevens had awarded punishments in the period Cabban claimed he did not leave his cabin. Ash was confident that this was the issue on which he would destroy Cabban's credibility, which was still largely intact. On the face of it there seemed little Cabban could do to refute the evidence. Cabban could not remember who awarded the punishments recorded in the log. He could not remember Stevens having awarded them although Cabban would have been the prosecutor if Stevens had. If Cabban had awarded them, he would have needed the captain's approval to do so as they exceeded those a first lieutenant was able to award, although he could not remember Stevens giving him this authority. Cabban was adamant that an officer awarding the punishment must sign the log to that effect. He was just as insistent in saying that Stevens had not awarded them in the five days after *Voyager* departed Tokyo.

Cabban suggested that the punishments were awarded after the five days that he had had command, and that Stevens had antedated them, or an error was made when the record of the offences in the working or 'rough' punishment log were translated into the official punishment log, and that this oversight was undetected by either Chief Coxswain Rogers, or Stevens, or even himself. Cabban seemed to favour the first probability: that Stevens deliberately antedated the punishment return and that Rogers was party to a deception designed to ensure Stevens had some record to show that he was in command throughout the five-day period. This was consistent with Stevens's instruction to Cabban that nothing was to leave the ship suggesting he was not in command. Cabban then asked to speak with his counsel, a request refused by Burbury. By the end of the fifth day and the first week, Cabban's reliability had been challenged.

The sixth day was to see a major new turn in the cross-examination of Cabban. The evidence began with Hiatt asking Burbury if he might be allowed to lead Cabban in giving evidence which related substantially to the matter of the punishment returns. Burbury agreed, after gaining Ash's concurrence. In two extraordinary passages of transcript covering cross-examination by Cabban's own counsel, Hiatt, and then Ash, Cabban stated that seeing the punishment returns at the previous day's hearings had penetrated his state of hysterical amnesia. He was able to recall the whole incident. Cabban said at the time the punishment returns were tendered, he had been unable to speak, was emotionally affected and wanted to speak with his counsel — which the Commissioners had refused. On termination of the day's hearing, he said that he immediately mentioned this matter to his counsel, who consulted Burt to ensure it was not later alleged that Cabban had concocted a story over the weekend.

He could now recall sitting in his cabin in Subic Bay, some time after the ship had arrived, when Stevens stormed in, said something to the effect of, 'You are not going to get me like this,' and threatened to charge Cabban with mutiny for attempting to use the punishment log to show he was not in command. Cabban contended that Rogers had spoken to him in a state of distress some time shortly afterwards and told Cabban that Stevens had instructed him to retype the punishment returns. Cabban directed Rogers to do as his captain ordered. When this incident was mentioned later by Murphy in examination of another witness, the witness suggested that Rogers may have just learned that he had a terminal medical condition and this might have accounted for his distress. However, an examination of Rogers's medical file reveals no evidence of such a condition nor even a hint that he was not in perfect health.

After further cross-examination, Cabban stated he now recalled that Stevens had informed him when he handed over command on leaving Tokyo that if he, Cabban, attempted to have another senior officer come on board during the period of transit he would have Cabban arrested and charged, Cabban presumed, with mutiny. Cabban believed that his only way of answering a mutiny charge, if it were subsequently brought, would be through the punishment log, which indicated Stevens had been ill. Cabban did not want to make anything of being in command and hoped it would not be noticed by any administrative authority examining the return.

The assertion now being made was that if Stevens did take exception to the punishment log, the threat he made to Cabban when the ship departed Tokyo would lie dormant until carried out at a time of Stevens' choosing. Further still, Cabban said Stevens gave the impression he was keeping a log on Cabban's performance and behaviour and that he might use it to have his Executive Officer either charged with mutiny or committed for retention in a psychiatric institution.

The Commissioners and Ash found it hard to believe that Stevens would even contemplate charging Cabban with attempted mutiny for sending a signal to the effect that Stevens was not in command. Captain James Willis, Cabban stated, had instructed Stevens to give command to Cabban and that neither Surgeon Lieutenant Tiller nor Cabban were required to make any report of the incident. When Ash suggested that Cabban could call Willis as a witness at any trial for attempted mutiny, Cabban said it would make no difference if he had already been committed to the Psychiatric Unit at Concord Repatriation General Hospital in Sydney as a psychiatric case. He appears to have believed that a naval medical officer could have signed a deposition declaring that treatment was necessary, while the mutiny charge would have substantiated the committal.

Ash doubted that Cabban really believed that this was possible and suggested that his fears of mutiny were a later construction on the events. Cabban's understanding of mutiny was superficial and related more to insubordination than mutinous conduct.[17] He also believed that Stevens may have feared the extent to which he took matters into his own hands as Executive Officer as constituting some diminution of Stevens's command. The way Cabban explained his fears and the threats he alleged Stevens had made against him was far from convincing. He was not able to show a clear pattern in his own behaviour or in that of Stevens which suggested a mutiny charge was ever seriously considered or based on demonstrable fact.

Ash continued to chip away at Cabban's credibility towards the end of the sixth day. Cabban was unable to be specific when questioned about an incident in which *Voyager* had the carrier HMS *Hermes* in tow. Cabban alleged the tow line parted because Stevens had applied full power in *Voyager* in a fit of pique after his ship came too close to *Hermes* in her approach. Ash was able to show that Cabban had mistaken the ship involved, pointed out that he had not been on the bridge to observe Stevens's actions, and had Cabban concede that it was not really indicative of Stevens's seamanship ability but of his temperament.

Ash was right in pressing Cabban on his reasons for providing this information to Admiral Hickling, information which was largely irrelevant to Hickling's book and in which many of the facts and inferences were either incorrect or inaccurate. The effect of this cross-examination, based to some degree on the Cabban Statement, was to prove amply that the Statement was indeed no more than a conversation piece and was not even reliable. This was what Burt had realised from the outset in suggesting the Statement should be used only as a point of departure. However, Ash could have made much more of the Statement inasmuch as it was the basis of the terms of reference. Ash's failure to do this was fortunate for Cabban. To further compound his mishandling of the brief, Ash unwittingly added to the case against Stevens by probing other incidents Cabban had not mentioned in his statement. Whereas Ash sought to cast doubt on Cabban's power of recollection, his approach in fact added to the number of allegations that he, as counsel, would subsequently need to defend.

Ash turned next to two alleged dangerous situations that developed with HMS *Caesar*. After Ash had asked Cabban about the details of the incidents, Cabban had suggested that the involvement of Lieutenant Harry Cook, *Voyager*'s navigator in 1964, as the navigator of *Caesar* on those occasions might have had something to do with the loss of *Voyager*. Burbury ruled that Ash was straying into matters of navigation which were not included in the terms of reference (this was the first time the terms of reference had been mentioned since Burt's opening address). He said the Commission was not 'to inquire into any of what I might call the navigational aspects of the collision'.[18] Burbury ruled that what Cabban thought about Cook or his conduct on the night of the collision was not relevant, even though Ash argued that Cabban's purpose in mentioning it was to imply that Stevens should not have trusted Cook and that this constituted a failure on his part as *Voyager*'s captain.

Cabban's evidence relating to Stevens's temperament particularly strained his credibility. The incidents that he cited to show that Stevens had an unpredictable temperament were unconvincing. Rather than showing that Stevens was prone to rash outbursts, it hinted at a degree of over-sensitivity on the part of Cabban. Even Cabban's objection to the use of bad language by Stevens from time to time was rejected by the Commissioners who regarded it as part of the 'hurly burly' of life at sea.

The cross-examination then turned to the period after the ship had departed Tokyo and Stevens had gone for two months without a drink. On the ship's arrival in Sydney, Cabban stated that Stevens immediately started drinking. The following week Cabban submitted his resignation, which he simply left on the desk in Stevens's cabin. At that stage, however, Cabban and Stevens were apparently on very favourable terms. Cabban said 'I felt the battle was over and that he was alright and that everything was going to be fine'.[19] Cabban was also insistent that Stevens said he would recommend Cabban for promotion and felt he was bound to be on the next promotion list. The sixth day of hearings ended with Ash covering the period *Voyager* spent in Sydney prior to departing for a refit at Williamstown.

The following day, Ash took Cabban through a series of activities that involved Stevens in the week Cabban had stated his captain arrived at work every day affected by alcohol and immediately retired to his cabin after informing Cabban that he had 'command' for the day. Cabban alleged that Stevens would be attended by his steward at around 1600 when he would start drinking again. The thrust of Ash's reply to this was that Stevens attended a range of meetings and official functions and that this was clearly inconsistent with Cabban's Statement. When Cabban was asked to reconcile his Statement with the evidence presented, he could only say

> that was the general impression that lasted in my memory at that time. I think I could give a more accurate statement now day by day of what happened. Mr Ash has revived my memory quite well.[20]

The subsequent line of cross-examination aimed to show that in addition to being factually incorrect, the picture of Stevens painted by Cabban was obviously misleading to anyone who had read the Statement. The letter from Hickling's companion to Robertson in February 1965, which was quoted earlier but not produced at the inquiry, was firm evidence that this was very much the case. It was becoming clear that Ash wanted to show that the motivation for the Commission being established was to ease public outrage at the Cabban allegations, and that, having shown the Statement created a false impression, the matters under review needed no further examination. In other words, Ash sought a way to have the Commissioners discharge their duties without conducting an exhaustive inquiry. By easing public concerns and demonstrating them to be quite unfounded, the Commission could be wound-up and the matter closed. This was a useful tactic for Ash to employ, given the pivotal role public concern had played in the creation of the Commission. He was also critical of Cabban for retreating from his Statement but leaving its inference.

On reconsidering the matter and conceding that it was not true for the first three days of the week in question (5 to 7 August 1963), Cabban stated positively that on completion of the luncheon following the presentation of the Pakistan Shield (7 August), Stevens had told him he was retiring to his cabin. Cabban further recalled that Stevens looked tired and unwell but could only point to the Thursday of that week when Stevens appeared to be adversely affected by alcohol. When asked by Ash to comment on that part of his statement covering the week in Sydney, Cabban conceded 'I would say that it is inaccurate' and that it was only meant to 'create in Admiral Hickling's mind the impression I had in mind when I dictated it'.[21] It is at this point that Cabban started to sound apologetic about his Statement by adding that it was not meant for 'the average reader' but only for Hickling. He proceeded to imply, albeit in a veiled way, that he would not have commented as he did had he known his Statement was to become a public document. This suggestion would have brought him little sympathy from the Commissioners, who already felt an inclination towards protecting Stevens's reputation.

As the morning proceeded, Cabban struggled to preserve the integrity of his Statement. On several occasions he suggested in reply to cross-examination that other witnesses would be better able to speak on the matters he had referred to in his Statement. Burbury retorted, 'Never mind about that. You answer the questions from your own knowledge.'[22] Strengthened by Cabban's concession about the week spent alongside in Sydney harbour, Ash was partially successful in challenging the general accuracy of Cabban's statement that during the 1963 Far East cruise Stevens

> drank for very long periods in harbour until he became violently ill and then would spend days in bed being treated by the doctor and his steward until he was again fit to start drinking.[23]

Ash then turned to *Voyager*'s passage from Sydney to Williamstown as a means of demonstrating that Cabban's description and evaluation of Stevens's conduct, both on this occasion and elsewhere, consistently varied with more straightforward and perfectly acceptable explanations.

On departing Sydney on the morning of Saturday 10 August 1963, Cabban said that Stevens had arrived on board smelling of alcohol and that passing through the heads at Port Jackson, Stevens informed Cabban he could take charge of the ship for the passage to Williamstown. But whereas Cabban said Stevens was physically incapable of exercising command because of alcohol, Ash said it was not an unreasonable thing for Stevens to have allowed Cabban to 'command' the ship. As the passage was straightforward and Cabban was soon going to leave the Navy, it could be seen as an entirely reasonable, if not generous, thing to do. Cabban believed it was, in his experience, a highly unusual thing for a captain to do, despite having limited experience on which to comment. Although Ash could have made much more of Cabban's limited experience, pointing out that prior to serving in *Voyager* Cabban had not been to sea in an operational combatant for any length of time since 1957, he again failed to do so. The inference of Cabban's Statement, that Stevens was unable to command for that period, remained, although there was no mention of alcohol or vomiting during the passage. Once the ship arrived in Williamstown and was placed in the hands of dockyard staff, leave and training requirements meant that Cabban and Stevens did not see each other for some eight weeks.

Attention then turned to the alleged second prolonged drinking bout following the Far East cruise, which Cabban said started after Stevens had returned from the court martial of Captain Dovers in Sydney. According to Cabban, after returning to Williamstown on (Monday) 2 December 1963 and apparently after drinking a considerable quantity of brandy, Stevens vomited the following day and informed that he would have command for the next seven days. In his Statement, Cabban said

> This was a fairly accurate assessment as he was in fact inside his cabin for the next seven days although he was able to start drinking brandy again on about the fourth day taking it very gently.[24]

Thus, the period in which Cabban had command extended from 3 to 10 December. However, Ash produced punishment returns showing that Stevens had dealt with defaulters on 6 December. Although not disputing that Stevens had held the defaulters parade, Cabban said he believed the punishment return had been altered or amended and conceded nothing of its import. Cabban seemed to imply again in relation to punishment returns that the records had been adjusted by several naval officers to assist counsel for the Stevens's interests.

Notwithstanding this disputed evidence, Ash pointed out that

Stevens spent the weekend with friends ashore and, without conflicting with Cabban's evidence, could have dressed and conducted the defaulters parade before returning to his cabin. For the second time that day, Cabban had to concede that his Statement may have given the wrong impression and that it was also incorrect in that the period of his 'command' was more likely to have been three days rather than seven.

Having shown the Cabban Statement to be inaccurate in places, Ash began the eighth day by turning on its author in attempting to suggest that Cabban was critical of Stevens as a consequence of his work study training and experience, and as an officer who sat in apparent judgement of his superior. Drawing on the fact that Stevens had an ulcer, and that this condition was seriously exacerbated by worry and stress, Ash argued that Stevens was increasingly affected by Cabban's demeanour and critical attitude. Ash also suggested to Cabban that he was, in effect, keeping a mental file on his captain's behaviour.

After being questioned further by the Commissioners on the origins of his Statement and whether Cabban believed it would be used for a purpose other than as background for Hickling's book, Ash ended his cross-examination.

The Naval Board had already made clear its attitude towards Cabban and his allegations. From the outset, it was apparent that Murphy's aim, as counsel for the Navy, was to discredit Cabban and thereby destroy the impact of his Statement. Although the Board was not yet prepared to concede a common cause between itself and the Stevens family's interests, Osborne stated later that he tried to convince Chipp that they had a common cause and ought to work together during the Commission. Osborne recalled that the Navy Minister was evasive and non-committal.[25] Murphy confirmed in a discussion with me that the Naval Board believed Cabban was a 'crank' who would be easily discredited.[26] When added to the fact that most of those who served in *Voyager* liked Stevens and disliked Cabban, there would be no shortage of willing witnesses to support the Naval Board's view. Murphy also told the author that the Naval Board believed that Robertson, as OTC, was responsible for both ships, and that he had a history of being slow to act in dangerous navigational situations.

Murphy began his cross-examination by establishing that Cabban believed Robertson had suffered an injustice and that this injustice was partly the product of the 1964 Commission's failure to hear Cabban's evidence. Cabban agreed that he saw his contribution as helping to reverse the injustice suffered by Robertson, although he was not specific as to how it would be achieved. Murphy then turned to Cabban's career in the Fleet Air Arm to argue that Cabban held a grudge against the Navy and that this was the real motivation behind his actions.

Throughout the Commission, Cabban had attempted to portray

himself as a highly competent and professional naval officer in all respects. Murphy showed from his career in the Fleet Air Arm that he was, at the very least, on occasion less than an adequate naval aviator. In April 1953, Cabban was suspended from flying by the captain of HMAS *Sydney* after six aircraft accidents. He was described as accident prone. Between February and September 1955, Cabban was involved in another four accidents. He was then sent to Britain to train as a maintenance test pilot before returning to NAS Nowra in mid-1956. There were another four accidents involving Cabban during the period September to November 1956, culminating in an accident in which the aircraft he was piloting was written-off. As Burt had mentioned earlier (Day 2), a Board of Inquiry was held into the last accident which resulted in Cabban being permanently suspended from flying on the grounds that he was 'temperamentally unsuitable'.

There was little doubt that Cabban was unhappy about the treatment he had received by the Board of Inquiry. In a letter to his wife he described it as 'the worst treatment I have ever seen handed out to anybody in the Navy. It was criminal.'[27]

Murphy took Cabban through the remainder of his naval career, showing that during these years Cabban had proved to be a difficult officer who was frequently involved in disputes with other officers. Murphy was able to show that Cabban was taken to commenting on the performance of his seniors and was rigidly insistent about rules and regulations being obeyed. As a lieutenant commander, Cabban still seemed to rely on procedures and regulations for his survival and promotion prospects, and was not content to rest on his performance and assessment by others. Cabban also seemed not to care about his contemporaries' views of his ability. It was as if their judgement was either poor or that they should be discounted on the grounds that they stood to gain by their judgements.

There was much to be made, as Ash had shown, of the Cabban Statement being misleading, as its author himself was now prepared to concede that it could be misleading. The matter of whether the confidential reports on Stevens and Cabban could be tendered in evidence was again considered, with Murphy being instructed to discuss the matter with Burt, as the Naval Board had insisted on their remaining secret.

The start of the ninth day brought an agreement between Burt and Murphy that the confidential reports on Cabban would be provided to the Commissioners but not published. Murphy then returned to his cross-examination of Cabban and the Subic Bay 'mutiny' incident. Although he agreed that this was a traumatic event, Cabban could not explain some of the remarks he made to his wife in a tape one week later. There were similar apparent back-downs over the defaulters parade conducted in the five days Cabban was alleged to have been in command. Cabban had said that on the passage between Tokyo and Subic Bay, *Voyager* was running before a typhoon. Murphy countered by tabling *Vampire's* deck log from the same period showing that the winds were recorded as being Force 1 and 2 on the Beaufort Scale, and not Force 9 or 10, which constitute a typhoon.[28] Murphy ended his cross-examination by asking Cabban whether his statement could be misconstrued. Cabban agreed that it could, but only to the extent that he had conceded in his evidence.

The right to cross-examine then passed to Reynolds QC, counsel for Captain Robertson, who simply said, 'I have no questions'.[29] Cabban was then re-examined by his own counsel, Hiatt QC, whose questions allowed Cabban to express in more detail the reasoning that led him to draw particular conclusions about Stevens and his behaviour. The passage of evidence that was most significant dealt with Cabban's decision to lift his requirement that his Statement remain confidential. When asked by Justice Asprey whether it was Robertson or Jess who sought Cabban's permission to have the Statement shown to the Prime Minister and Cabinet, Cabban said he could not recall. His next admission, which related to what he thought disclosing the Statement would achieve, exposed his greatest vulnerability:

> I just understood that if the Prime Minister were to read this document — and perhaps the cabinet — they would feel that perhaps there was some other inference that could be placed on the conditions described on the night, and perhaps in so doing they might decide that the circumstances which prompted this might perhaps be reviewed to see that the security of the Navy was established.[30]

When asked whether he thought his statement could assist Captain Robertson after the Spicer Commission, he lamely replied: 'I was prepared to accept the word of people more experienced than I in these areas.'[31] This was not nearly good enough, given the controversy he had generated by offering to help Robertson and Hickling. Cabban should have realised the force of his allegations, the harm they would cause to the Navy and the hurt they would inflict on the Stevens family. He should also have satisfied himself that the allegations contained in his Statement were at least relevant to the causes of the collision before allowing them to be used for political purposes in achieving a second inquiry.

It is evident that Cabban even at this early stage sought to free himself from responsibility for the second Commission. His explanation of how he might help Robertson overcome the injustice Cabban felt had been meted out to Robertson — which related mostly to his posting to HMAS *Watson* rather than to the Spicer Report — was tentative in the extreme. It was heavily qualified with the words 'might', 'perhaps' and 'inference'. The absence of any real conception of how his Statement might have been used to cast more light on the causes of the collision, highlighted either the naivety or the conceit which led him to offer his Statement in the first instance.

In re-examination by Burt, Cabban went further and said that if Robertson had known more about Stevens's competence as a destroyer Captain, he would have had

> every reason to think that the destroyer [was] doing something he did not recognise. But [as *Voyager*] had been commanded in the Far East for 12 months by the same man, [she] must be under good control. But he just did not understand what was going to happen next. He certainly did not expect what did, or have any reason to.[32]

Thus, Cabban appears to have assumed that Stevens was under the influence of alcohol at the time of the collision and this effectively made him unfit to command, with such unfitness manifesting itself in the manoeuvre which led to the collision.

At this point in the Commission, Burt began to show some suspicions about the documentary evidence that had been tabled and used to support Stevens. In fulfilling his role as counsel assisting, he had neither attacked nor supported Cabban, although he was obviously persuaded by some of the explanations Cabban had offered for his behaviour and thoughts. Burt appears to have understood Cabban's personality and character traits. His empathy went further than the even-handedness required of him as counsel assisting, partly because he was able to separate the significance of the Cabban Statement and the matter of Stevens's fitness to command, from the circumstances and causes of the collision.

Burt had shown no interest in arguing at this point that the two were related. His approach was technically correct and avoided any pre-emptive conclusions. In fact, Burt seems to have understood the terms of reference better than Burbury and Asprey, who sought repeatedly to establish a link between the Cabban Statement and the collision. By the end of the ninth day of hearings, Cabban's position had improved, if only because his counsel were able to perceive that Burt was not hostile to Cabban or his evidence. After eight days in the witness box, Cabban was permitted to withdraw.

Cabban's evidence had been used as a basis for the Commission's inquiries. By this stage there were also clear indications of how each of the parties saw and understood their briefs. Of the Commissioners, Burbury had exerted some restraint but had allowed examination and cross-examination to proceed freely. He had questioned the relevance of evidence and argument sparingly, and avoided committing himself to any firm views relating to evidence or findings. Asprey obviously saw himself as next in line after Burbury. He frequently broke into cross-examination and had shown a readiness to engage in argument with counsel. Although not a bully, Asprey seemed to have some fixed ideas and, of the three Commissioners, appeared to be the least impressed by Cabban. Lucas, on the other hand, was quietly spoken and seldom interjected. He appeared to want the Commission's proceedings to continue with the minimum of restrictions or interruptions. Lucas gave the impression of being the most concerned of the Commissioners by the gravity of the Cabban Statement and seemed most positively disposed towards Cabban.

Burt evidently enjoyed the goodwill of all counsel, and this augured well for the remainder of the inquiry. However, it was becoming obvious that Ash was increasingly concerned by the lack of combativeness in Burt's examination of Cabban. It was not surprising that Ash and Murphy shared a common cause. Both were determined to dismiss Cabban and his evidence and this, of course, brought them into conflict with Hiatt. The role of Reynolds, who was appearing for Robertson, was the most curious. He had declined to question Cabban and this kept other counsel guessing as to what line Robertson would take and when. Reynolds's approach was simply to assess the disposition of the Commission and the represented parties towards each other before declaring his hand. There was no doubt that Reynolds would need to choose his time carefully. Nine days of hearings had merely highlighted the inability of counsel to establish a connection between the Cabban Statement and the collisions. This no doubt caused some anxiety for Robertson who had developed a convincing case for overturning Spicer on the grounds of navigational evidence. Burt's insistence that the Commission keep within its terms of reference provided little encouragement.

The Cabban Statement had not fared well, although Cabban's performance in defending a very difficult opening position was creditable. Ash had led Cabban to make numerous concessions. The statement was in places inaccurate, exaggerated, misleading and easily misconstrued. However, Cabban stood by the spirit of his statement and had support from Burt who did not want the Commission tied to an exegesis of the Statement, which he still regarded as a 'discussion' piece. Cabban desperately needed corroboration for his statement.

The Cabban Statement contained a great deal of hearsay and detail that Cabban could neither adequately confirm nor definitely remember. This is not to imply that Cabban lied either in his Statement or in his evidence. There had not been the suggestion that he had lied. Rather, and as Ash argued, it was that Cabban had overstated much of what he had seen or heard, and had placed unwarranted constructs on matters that yielded an innocent explanation more readily than the explanation that Cabban had offered.

The next phase of evidence related to Stevens's physical fitness and health, and covered matters that were largely independent of the Cabban Statement. The principal witness was Surgeon Commander Roger McNeill, who was then on the RAN Emergency Reserve and in private medical practice in Melbourne. Burt took McNeill through his naval career and the occasions on which he had served with Stevens. They first served together and became friends in 1954 while serving at HMAS *Tarangau* on Manus Island. During this time Stevens had complained of indigestion, which McNeill diagnosed as a pre-ulcer condition to be treated with the antacid Amphogel and a strict diet. McNeill had not reported or recorded either the diagnosis or the treatment he prescribed. It appears that Stevens was next affected by an active duodenal ulcer in 1959 while serving in HMAS *Melbourne*, and that this was known to McNeill.

When *Melbourne* and *Voyager* were together in Hong Kong, McNeill, being the Fleet Medical Officer embarked in the flagship, saw Stevens on three or four occasions which he described as 'social' but not 'professional' in the normal understanding of that term in this context. He said that Stevens complained of suffering from severe stomach pain but that he (McNeill) did not think the ulcer was again active. As he believed the problem was not serious, he prescribed an increased consumption of Amphogel. McNeill stated that he did not subsequently mention this to Tiller, *Voyager*'s medical officer, nor did he submit any official report, believing this to be a matter within his discretion. Burt did little to hide his incredulity at McNeill's actions. Burt believed that Stevens's condition was demonstrably serious and, given that the circumstances in which Stevens lived and worked were likely to worsen his condition, hinted that Stevens had attempted to conceal the extent of his condition by seeking out McNeill for treatment. McNeill's only explanation was that Stevens's condition did not appear to be that serious to him, and it is likely that he communicated this to Stevens who would have adopted the same view and underestimated his true state.

Burt then posed a hypothetical situation in which Stevens developed a serious condition because of his ulcer while the ship was engaged in dangerous operations during bad weather. McNeill said he would not have been concerned because *Voyager* carried a doctor. Burt then reminded McNeill that Stevens was category 'A', which classified him as being fit to serve in a ship without a medical officer. McNeill was forced to concede that Stevens should have been in a lower medical category. Being mindful of Stevens's medical history, the nature of his present naval service, the symptoms McNeil had observed and the circumstances of their observance, Burt said he could not understand why McNeill had not taken steps to inform the Naval Board of Stevens's condition, or to have upgraded the treatment he prescribed. Having received no convincing explanation from McNeill, Burt was entitled to conclude that Stevens had sought to conceal his condition and that McNeill was a participating party. Furthermore, McNeill failed to perform his duties by not making the necessary reports which Stevens's condition warranted.

The task of retrieving the adverse situation brought on the Stevens family's interest by McNeill fell to Ash. There was little he could do with a witness whose credibility had been substantially weakened. Ash quoted a letter from a Macquarie Street[33] medical specialist describing the general symptoms of pre-ulcer and ulcer conditions and suggested these generally conformed to those observed by McNeill in 1963. McNeill was also led to say that Stevens had displayed a responsible attitude towards his condition by giving up smoking and by observing a strict diet.[34] McNeill said Stevens usually drank brandy and that his alcohol consumption would not have affected his condition, and neither had he ever seen or known of Stevens drinking to excess.

As expected, Hiatt returned to the line of argument developed by Burt. He argued that although Stevens had spoken openly of his condition, he sought to conceal the occasions when it was causing him discomfort by consulting McNeill. This McNeill denied. Hiatt then questioned McNeill on his reasons for contacting Sam Benson MP during the parliamentary debate on the Cabban Statement and telling him that he was the 'principal medical officer in Hong Kong'. McNeill, who had only resigned from the Navy on 4 November 1966, seemed not to know why he had contacted Benson, although he considered the allegations being made about Stevens were 'untrue and unjust so I just rang up to sort of register a protest ... and to let Captain Benson know he had had a *serious* stomach condition' (emphasis added).[35] But while McNeill tried to have Hiatt believe he was referring to Stevens's condition in 1959, it became obvious that McNeill had described it in relation to his being the Fleet Medical Officer in 1963. McNeill's credibility continued to deteriorate. The condition he had described earlier as not being serious was now 'a serious stomach condition' that was of such relevance that Benson needed to be appraised of it in explaining Stevens's behaviour the year preceding the collision. The day ended with Stevens's medical condition unexpectedly providing the strongest evidence that Stevens may not have been fit to command *Voyager*.

Burt re-examined McNeill the following morning and returned to the non-disclosure of Stevens's ulcer condition. McNeill's standing at the Commission deteriorated even further. After stating the previous day that he had never conducted an annual medical examination on Stevens, Burt produced documentary evidence showing that McNeill had done so in 1954 and again in 1956. After reminding McNeill that he had earlier stated the appropriate time to record any disorder was on an officer's annual medical report, Burt asked McNeill why he had not made some reference to the ulcer condition he knew existed. He explained not mentioning Stevens's ulcer in the 1954 report because this was made soon after McNeill's arrival at *Tarangau* and before Stevens mentioned his dyspepsia. However, he could give no explanation as to why he had not mentioned the ulcer in 1956. Burt was clearly concerned by McNeill's answers, while Murphy made no attempt to defend McNeill's position or defend his actions.

McNeill was followed by another naval medical officer, Surgeon Commander Samuel Haughton. Haughton spoke of serving with Stevens at *Tarangau* in 1953 and gaining a very detailed and intimate knowledge of 'his life, his ambitions, his worries, his family troubles, his fears and so on'. Haughton then gave a very illuminating description of Stevens at that time in his life. He said that Stevens was an ambitious officer concerned about his promotion prospects: 'He gave me the impression of a man who was driving after an ambition that he did not have the capability to achieve'.[36]

During this period Stevens was usually tense, aggressive and self-critical, and inclined to be short and abrupt with others. He considered his posting to *Tarangau* to be a retrograde step in his career, that Manus Island was a backwater and that he was a failure. However, Haughton said a marked change came over Stevens when his wife and two sons finally arrived. He next saw Stevens in 1963 when he was commanding *Voyager*. He said Stevens looked very healthy and happy; that he had achieved his ultimate ambition and 'was riding the crest of a wave'.[37]

Haughton was an impressive witness. He was direct and confident in his answers. There was no doubt that he had high professional standards and understood his job as a naval medical officer very well. He was insistent on observing both naval and clinical procedures. His evidence suggested he would have taken Stevens's ulcer condition far more seriously than did McNeill, although this was only on the description of symptoms offered by counsel. Haughton was also the first witness to have provided the Commissioners with some insight into the character of Duncan Stevens.

Haughton's assessment of Stevens condition was confirmed by Dr Kerry Goulston, a consultant physician at the Royal Prince Alfred Hospital in Sydney, who had recently completed two years' research into stomach disorders. Despite the limited knowledge medical science possessed on the causes of duodenal ulcers and their effects on different people, he explained in detail the usual signs and symptoms and the generally prescribed treatment. Two points he made were of great significance in understanding how Stevens might have felt and reacted to his condition. Goulston said that ulcer patients were allowed to drink alcohol only when and if they had to, and to limit to a minimum the amount consumed. He said there was no reason to believe that drinking watered-down alcohol might have assisted in any way. It was also common for ulcer patients to feel ill one and a half to two hours after eating if the ulcer were active.

Sir William Morrow, a leading gastroenterologist, followed Goulston. He had conducted a medical examination of Stevens during September 1963 and found that he was fit and well, although diffident in describing how he felt. The Naval Medical Director-General would not have approved of this consultation as all naval personnel were strongly discouraged from seeking medical attention without a referral from the Service.[38] Morrow noted on a record that he kept of Stevens's consultation: 'Drinks too much on shore'. However, he stated that this did not mean Stevens drank to excess; it was meant to imply he drank too much given his ulcer condition. Morrow concluded that Stevens's ulcer was not active at the time of his examination but he did concede that it could have changed from being inactive to active virtually overnight. Morrow said the drinking of diluted brandy had a largely psychosomatic effect, and that among many ulcer sufferers 'there is a belief that diluted spirit, not necessarily whisky but brandy too, does give them relief of pain ... but we know it really exacerbates the ulcer in the end'.[39]

The Commissioners quite justifiably tried to limit the expert medical opinion presented. At the insistence of Asprey, the Commission was ready to accept the views of Morrow, although to a very large extent Morrow was compromised as an expert witness in that he had treated Stevens and was obviously an advocate for his own cause. Yet Asprey was insistent that only Morrow needed to be heard. It was fair to ask why Asprey had such a high view of Morrow's opinions. Asprey and Morrow were long-time personal friends and Asprey had himself been treated by Morrow for a duodenal ulcer in the late 1950s, at which time Morrow had advised him to drink diluted brandy or whisky for the temporary relief of pain. While Asprey may have felt his first-hand knowledge of Morrow's competence justified the weight he placed on his testimony, this should not have blinded him to the existence of other expert views which differed from Morrow's. It should also be mentioned that Morrow was at the time of both the collision and the second inquiry, a specialist consultant physician to the RAN. Had Morrow disclosed this to the inquiry, he could have been asked to explain why he did not make a report to the Navy on Stevens's condition after he saw him on 23 September 1963.[40]

To complete the passage of evidence relating to Stevens's health, the RAN Medical Director General, Surgeon Rear-Admiral Michael Coplans, was asked for his views of McNeill's actions with respect to naval regulations and procedures. After outlining the details of naval medical administration, Coplans stated that it was an offence for any officer or sailor to conceal or feign a medical condition. Further, that if the circumstances regarding Captain Stevens's interviews with McNeill in Hong Kong and Cabban's Statement were accepted, McNeill should have arranged an interim medical survey and if necessary recommended a downgrading of Stevens's medical category. As for his opinion on whether Stevens had concealed his condition, Coplans suggested that most people who suffered from ulcers had learnt to live with their condition, and while it was not incumbent on them to report any symptoms of an ulcer, it would be prudent to do so.

It was obvious that McNeill would stand alone for his actions. Coplans seemed quite prepared to criticise his behaviour, including his failure to consult Tiller over Stevens's condition. When asked by Hiatt what would have happened to Stevens had McNeill convened the interim medical survey and found that his ulcer was active, Coplans said Stevens would have been removed from the ship, admitted to hospital for six weeks, been medically downgraded and given a shore posting for twelve months. In other words, Stevens would see a repeat of the events of 1959 when he was landed at Hong Kong and spent six weeks under care at the Royal Naval Hospital. Although in 1959, he was serving as *Melbourne's* Executive Officer and could be relieved by another officer of that rank serving in the carrier, as an officer in command he would have had to be posted elsewhere. For an officer who was in the midst of experiencing his ultimate ambition, and who placed his hopes of future preferment on his seagoing ability, this established a clear motive for concealing the true state of his condition by desperately wanting to avoid a medical survey.

After sixteen days, the case against Stevens had been put in its entirety. It was alleged that Stevens was unfit to command on two separate grounds, although the charitable would have said the causes were related. He was unfit to command through excessive consumption of alcohol and because of a debilitating medical condition. For the next fifty days of hearings, a succession of witnesses were called to give evidence on Stevens's actions over the fourteen months from the time he assumed command of *Voyager* until the collision.

The case against Duncan Stevens related almost exclusively to his conduct since assuming command of *Voyager* in January 1963 when he was 41 years old. It was probably unfair to Stevens for the Commissioners, and those with an interest in the case, to base an appreciation of this man and his character solely on the evidence presented before the inquiry over a short span of his life. As with any individual, in understanding his or her personality, both the strengths and weaknesses, the length and breadth of view play a vital role. Had the Commissioners enjoyed the luxury of examining the whole life of Duncan Stevens, they would have discovered a very different man to the one portrayed by both his supporters and detractors.

Duncan Stevens grew up with opportunities and privileges that his father had only dreamed about, such as attending the elite Wesley College Preparatory School in Melbourne.

In January 1935 Duncan was entered into the RAN College on

Western Port Bay, some eighty kilometres south-east of Melbourne. From the outset, Duncan Stevens was not a leading performer. In his final exams before graduating from the Naval College, he obtained a lowly third class pass. The only subject in which he did better than a grade of 'fair' was in gunnery, where he was rated 'good'. His seamanship instructor wrote, rather disparagingly, on his final report that he was 'keen and tries to use what brain he has'.[41]

The same barely passable results were recorded for his midshipman's sea time in HMAS *Canberra*, and in his courses for promotion to lieutenant the following year. He recorded a mix of second and third class passes. However, Stevens achieved steady progress in his training which coincided with a range of experiences during World War II serving in four ships — the cruisers HMS *Shropshire* and *Australia*, and the destroyers *Vendetta* and *Napier*. He had seen active service in the South Atlantic, the Burma Campaign and the Borneo Campaign and was present at the signing of the Japanese surrender in Tokyo Bay on 2 September 1945. His reports were good, but not outstanding.

On 1 January 1942, Stevens had obtained his watchkeeping certificate. He was now 'qualified to take charge of a watch at sea as a lieutenant and to perform efficiently the duties of that rank'.[42] The captain of *Shropshire* said he needed to exert 'a little more energy in everything he does', while two reports from *Vendetta* mentioned an inclination for unreliability. His captain in *Napier* said he 'has a pleasant personality and good manners but could well develop initiative and powers of concentration'. Stevens's war service qualified him for the 1939–45 Star, Atlantic Star, Africa Star, Pacific Star with Burma Clasp, War Medal and Australian Service Medal. He did not gain any decorations nor was he mentioned in a dispatch.[43]

In March 1945 Stevens returned to *Shropshire*, which had been transferred to the RAN, and served out the war in that ship. He then spent short periods in the frigate *Barcoo* and the corvette *Gladstone* before being posted to the destroyer *Quiberon* as Executive Officer in 1947. It was a successful appointment, his captain noting on his departure that he was an 'efficient Executive Officer with very good professional ability, energy and initiative who must not allow his imagination to get the better of him'. What the latter comment referred to was unclear.

Duncan Stevens's career changed after 1948. He was appointed to command the small Boom Defence Ship HMAS *Kangaroo* in September 1948. This type of ship, workmanlike and lacking any pretension, seemed to best suit Stevens's abilities and temperament. It was physically very demanding and this appealed to his love of outdoor activity. He was obviously in his element, as his reports show. Life gained even more vigour when he married Beatrice Phippard on 20 May 1949 at the Dreger Harbour Naval Establishment at

Finchhaven in New Guinea.

For the first time in his career, Stevens was consistently praised for his achievements. The Naval Board commended him for his service while in command of *Kangaroo* in and around New Guinea between September and October 1948.[44] In January 1949, Stevens transferred to another Boom Defence Vessel, *Koala*, again in command. For a second time his performance came to the attention of senior officers. He was commended for 'the efficiency and high morale of his ship. These qualities were developed by his personal zeal and leadership'.[45] In January 1950 Stevens was given command of the only seagoing tug in commission, HMAS *Reserve*, and directed to tow an Admiralty floating dock from Darwin to Brisbane. It was considered a difficult and possibly dangerous undertaking. However the dock arrived safely and for the third time in three years, Stevens was praised by the Naval Board for his efforts.[46]

At the end of his time in *Reserve*, Stevens was promoted to lieutenant commander. This was an automatic promotion based on the affluxion of time. Promotion to commander and beyond was by selection. Stevens was then sent to the corvette, *Cowra*, a training vessel, in command. After what was a non-eventful fourteen months in his fourth command, Stevens was posted ashore for the first time since the start of World War II. He was sent back to New Guinea in August 1952 as Executive Officer of HMAS *Tarangau* (Manus Island) and Deputy Naval Officer-in-Charge, North-East Australian Area. Stevens was later placed temporarily in command and given the rank of acting commander. He remained there until 1955.

The years 1948 to 1955 saw a marked change in Stevens and his performance. He had gone from being considered a mediocre officer with few real prospects to an officer whose abilities and potential had been demonstrated. Although he was not an outstanding prospect for promotion to admiral, he was now considered a better than average officer. Those destined for flag rank at his age were not commanding small ships in remote waters. They were serving in combatant ships as specialised warfare officers. Stevens had not specialised and was happy to remain a 'salthorse'. He had not proved himself in any shore or staff postings but his seagoing ability would carry him for a few more years yet.

A real challenge for Stevens was to be appointed in command of the newly converted fast anti-submarine frigate, HMAS *Quickmatch*, in mid-1955. He reverted to his substantive rank of lieutenant commander on taking up the appointment. For the first time in eight years he was back in mainstream naval service commanding a major warship that had been significantly altered for specific operations and which was shortly to be recommissioned. It would be a testing time as Stevens would be under the watchful eye of the captain commanding the frigate flotilla,

Captain Victor Smith, and the Fleet Commander, Rear-Admiral Henry Burrell. Stevens was thought to be an able frigate captain and was promoted commander at the end of June 1956.

Stevens's next appointment was Executive Officer of HMAS *Cerberus*. As this coincided with the build-up to the 1956 Melbourne Olympic Games, and the Navy had offered to provide marshalling staff, Stevens would occupy a high public profile. His time at *Cerberus* was aided by the friendship he had with the commanding officer, Commodore John Plunkett-Cole, who had served with Stevens before and seemed to approve of his forceful, if not occasionally domineering, leadership style.

Having proved himself at sea in command and ashore, Stevens was posted in July 1958 as Executive Officer of the flagship, HMAS *Melbourne*. This was a sought-after posting and a continuation of the steady progression of his career. However, as mentioned earlier, in 1959 Stevens was landed in Hong Kong by direction of the Fleet Medical Officer, Surgeon Commander Brian Treloar, and admitted to the British Naval Hospital at HMS *Terror* with an active duodenal ulcer.[47] He spent a period in Hong Kong before being sent back to Australia for sick leave. It appears that the ulcer developed while he was serving in New Guinea, where he was treated by the naval medical officer at *Tarangau*. Although he understood the nature of his condition and how it could be exacerbated, it took being removed temporarily from his ship to make Stevens understand the extent of his condition.

After eighteen months in *Melbourne*, Stevens was sent to Britain to complete a staff course and was then posted to the Admiralty as Commonwealth Liaison Officer in the Directorate of Tactics and Weapons Policy. He was apprehensive about the staff course and a staff posting because administration was not one of his strong areas and he was anxious that this weakness might influence his chances of promotion to captain. Stevens believed he performed best at sea and sought a sea posting to demonstrate his abilities. His fortunes again changed in the second half of 1963.

His name was on the 30 June 1962 promotion list to captain. Shortly after, Stevens was appointed in command of HMAS *Voyager* from 2 January 1963. He was delighted to have been given *Voyager* and an opportunity to get back to sea.

Privately, there were mixed reactions from his contemporaries over his promotion. Stevens had not specialised and this, in the minds of many officers, highlighted his limitations and the likelihood that he would not proceed beyond captain. Some of his friends and term-mates, the latter always being the strongest critics, were surprised by his promotion. The first to be promoted to commander and captain in his Naval College term, the promising J. Philip Stevenson, had been promoted two years before Stevens to both ranks. Although not the last to be promoted from his group, Stevens's promotions were steady rather than rapid. Of course, the Navy operated ships that required officers with the rank of captain to command them. Given that Stevens had earned reasonable reports and had exercised command at sea effectively in the past, he was always a likely candidate for command of a *Daring* Class destroyer.

On assuming command, Stevens had some concerns about the officers serving under him. In another draft statement for the Commission, Mrs Stevens recalled — from letters she received from her husband while *Voyager* was in the Far East — that he had commented upon Cabban and two other officers, Lieutenants David Martin and Scott Griffith. Of Martin: 'I recall Duncan's comments as — a naval officer with a future once he learns to appreciate and evaluate people, including sailors. Was good in his job but needed experience in handling lower deck [sailors]'. Regarding Griffith: 'Realised adverse comments by Alan Willis and knowing his previous experience — tried his utmost to instil confidence — despite detrimental effects to himself re, nerves, ulcer. Knew Griffiths "had" it and was determined to prove it. Expressed he had succeeded'.

Stevens had even greater concerns about some of the officers he gained at the end of 1963, although he was pleased to have MacGregor. Mrs Stevens noted: 'I definitely remember his remarks when MacGregor was appointed to relieve Cabban — MacGregor understood Duncan's orders, re: upper deck and ship's company (MacGregor had experience in *Daring* Class destroyers and knew its details). Duncan felt there would be no need to keep a check on MacGregor as he had to do with Cabban.' As for two new lieutenants, Cook and Price, she recalled her husband's comments on both:

> Cook — was similar to Griffith [whom he relieved] and needed to regain confidence due to previous criticism. Duncan was well aware of Cook's previous Royal Navy experience [HMS *Caesar*].
> Price — was lacking in practical experience but otherwise very capable although no experience in destroyers. This Duncan told me and it was something that stuck in my mind because I feel sure he would not let Price have 'had' control the night of the collision. Duncan would have been very much on the alert knowing both Cook and Price were 'new' to such experiences.

On the Stevens family's copy of the Cabban Statement, Mrs Stevens had written alongside Price's name that 'Duncan commented to me he was lacking in sea experience and needed watching'.[48]

Making a judgement about Stevens's personal attributes would prove inordinately difficult for the Commissioners. The inquiry would receive at least twenty statements from people who had dealings with Stevens away from the Navy and *Voyager*. The picture they painted was of a very different man from that described by Cabban. It seems there were really two Duncan Stevenses. There was the Duncan Stevens who enjoyed his

224

family life as a husband and as a father. He had a close relationship with both his father and mother who gave him every support. There was also his love for sport, particularly his passion for cricket. This Duncan Stevens liked to have a good time in the company of other people. He was content when people he liked were around him and pleased when they were happy. There were no expectations on this Duncan Stevens, who was free to be whomever he chose to be.

The other Duncan Stevens was a creation of the naval environment and all the demands it made of those who accepted responsibility and sought promotion. It was another world that required Duncan Stevens to be other than he really was, and perhaps was ever really suited to being. It asked for more than he was prepared or even able to give. This created a tension between the two worlds in which he moved and the two different people he thought he had to be.

In *The Gunroom*, a novel by Charles Morgan, this tension is described in a chapter entitled 'Two worlds':

> Have you ever noticed how Portsmouth and other naval ports differ from the rest of the world? It has a definite atmosphere of its own, enveloping it, hiding it from outsiders. And the atmosphere they breathe changes naval officers only so long as they breathe it. Once outside it they are so much like the ordinary civilian that he fails to recognise them as visitors from another world.
>
> A man who works in an office all the morning and goes into polite society in the afternoon preserves the same nature throughout the day. He may alter his manners a bit but he doesn't change essentially. You naval people do. And why? Isn't it because in the Service circle, within the Service atmosphere, you have standards of life that are unrecognised elsewhere? The Naval officer's attitude towards the essentials of life — so long as he remains within the atmosphere — is altogether different from the attitude of other human beings.
>
> At any rate, it is not a natural condition, and is bound to produce phenomena of which those outside have no knowledge, no understanding.[49]

Although Duncan Stevens may not have been a contradictory character or in possession of a complex personality, the changing environment in which he lived and worked was both highly contradictory and complex. Understanding the many diverse forces and pressures that motivated a man like Duncan Stevens, and most naval officers, was of secondary importance to the lawyers, who concentrated more on his actions and their consequences. However, if they were to reconcile the apparent inconsistencies in his behaviour, they needed to look into these 'two worlds' and consider the tensions each created in the other. No one really bothered to look that deeply.

Over the span of his forty-one years, a clearer picture emerged of Duncan Stevens. He was a straightforward man who enjoyed life and thought it was important to have fun. On occasions throughout his life he lacked drive, commitment and perseverance. He worried about the challenges he needed to face, and was angered when things did not go his way. He was a son with feelings of insecurity; a man who lacked strength of character; and an officer whose ambition did not match his ability. This was the 'real' Duncan Stevens who commanded *Voyager* on the night she was lost.

# 15

# For What Purpose?

WHILE THE PRESS and public were generally worried that a man of Captain Stevens's alleged condition could be placed in command of a naval ship, the central proposition was that Stevens's inability to command may have attributed to the collision. Had Stevens been the captain of a ship that had survived an operational deployment, there would not have been the public clamouring or political involvement, and certainly a Royal Commission would not have been convened. Regardless of whether Cabban, Jess or St John had actually demonstrated the relevance of Stevens's drinking to the causes of the collision, the newspaper editorials assumed there had to be a connection. Consequently, if Stevens was unable to exercise command of *Voyager*, the collision might not have occurred, or would not have occurred for the reasons it did, and Robertson's responsibility would need to be revised. The logic applied assumed the situation was far more straightforward than it was. Yet, there was a strong belief that if Cabban's allegations were shown to be true, Spicer's criticisms of Robertson would invariably require revision.

The great challenge for Robertson would be to show that Cabban's allegations warranted a reconsideration of the navigational evidence presented at the first inquiry in conjunction with submissions that Robertson would put to the Commission demonstrating that Spicer's findings were wrong. If there was a case to be made that Spicer would have reached different findings had he heard Cabban's evidence in 1964, then the reasons for his evidence not being heard needed to be explained. This led the Commission to the second term of reference and prompted the involvement of Reynolds QC.

Was relevant evidence improperly withheld from the Spicer Commission? This was a question that could have been asked of most inquiries of this nature after the event. The greatest difficulty faced by a counsel assisting at a Royal Commission is to determine from an often vast amount of available evidence what is relevant and what is not. A Canadian QC, experienced in assisting commissions, has identified the essence of the problem.

The question of how much Commission Counsel should tell the Commissioner about the evidence to be given has troubled most Counsel. Some Commissioners merely want to know, in a general way, what any given witness is likely to be testifying about and how long he is apt to be. Other Commissioners, I am told, practically insist on seeing the interview notes in advance, possibly in order to assist in the preparation of their own cross-examination. It is difficult to know how to handle that situation.[1]

Hallet raises the second dilemma faced by counsel assisting: 'Should he ultimately present all the information collated or should he exercise an independent discretion and exclude all that which he regards as irrelevant or unhelpful'.[2]

Several witnesses from the 1964 Commission were called to explain why they declined to call Cabban to give evidence at that inquiry. Those called on Day 10 included John Braund from the Deputy Crown Solicitor's Office who had acted as instructing solicitor to Smyth at the 1964 Commission; Senior Constable Wright who had been present when Cabban's initial statement was taken after the collision; and Fred Osborne and John Sinclair who had acted as instructing solicitor and junior counsel respectively for the Stevens family's interests. Braund explained the manner in which statements were extracted from witnesses; Wright detailed the circumstances relating to Cabban's Statement and said he and Sergeant Turner believed Cabban had been drinking and was also emotionally affected by the collision; and Osborne and Sinclair explained that Cabban's evidence did not assist the interests of their clients, the Stevens family.

Robertson was the next witness to be called and questioned about the origins of the Cabban Statement. He recounted details that had already been well-established yet he too was unsure as to who asked Cabban for permission to have his Statement circulated more widely. Burt's junior, Philip Jeffery, asked Robertson why he thought Cabban's evidence was relevant in January 1965 when he had refused to either hear it or use it during the 1964 Commission. He replied that Cabban may have been useful to Hickling and that only after he had spoken with Cabban at length had he realised the significance of his evidence. As to its relevance to his situation, Robertson said

> I felt quite certain that if the situation revealed by the information which is outlined in Mr Cabban's document — if it were believed to be true — it would throw such a different emphasis on the whole collision that practically every paragraph of the Commission's report would need revision.[3]

In subsequent questioning, Robertson asserted that the general ambience of the Spicer Commission, which was hostile to him, would have been completely different if Cabban had been heard. Wisely, Robertson declined at this stage to comment on how Spicer's report might have been different but strongly contended that it would have been. Moreover, he stated that if Cabban were honest and his allegations were true, Stevens was a man 'whose sense of responsibility had been so eroded he was not sufficiently reliable to be left in command of a man-o'-war'.[4] Yet he declined to demonstrate how his unreliability manifested itself in the events leading to the collision. Robertson also suggested that 'this situation was known to naval authorities before the collision took place'.[5] With these words, Robertson ended any possibility of support from Navy counsel.

The Commissioners pressed Robertson on the relevance of the Cabban Statement to Spicer's criticisms of his (Robertson's) actions before the collision. Perhaps under close instruction from his counsel, Robertson avoided pointing to any specific relevance. He returned to what was little more than an inference that it would have changed the way Spicer 'looked at the evidence being presented to him'.[6] By their questions, the Commissioners did not seem convinced by Robertson's assurances. Robertson had had his chance and had not made the most of it.

Robertson knew this as well. He suggested a different approach in a note to Reynolds. Having tried to avoid criticism of the Naval Board, he suggested a two-prong attack on the Board for failing to pass to the inquiry all relevant documents, and for complicity in subterfuge with naval witnesses.

> I feel that an omission on my part was not very helpful in that when I was asked why I was encouraging Jess, I merely said, 'To put the record straight'. I reckon I could be much more definite and say that I did not consider, nor do I consider, that the true facts behind the collision and its real causes — both direct and indirect — were ever uncovered. Having been involved in the sinking of one destroyer and the loss of 82 lives, I am anxious to do all I can to ensure that no future naval officer will be put in the same position as I was for the same reasons.[7]

This change of attitude for Robertson was another step in a gradual abandonment of reticence about criticising the Board. On each occasion that Robertson's situation had become desperate over the last three years, he became willing to do whatever was necessary to pursue his interests. He had become an opportunist when his former values and principles became liabilities in achieving the vindication he sought from the second Commission.

Before the examination of Robertson continued on the eleventh day, Hiatt made a submission to the Commissioners in relation to the Subic Bay incident. He claimed that this was a critical issue and crucial to assessing Cabban's general credibility. To that end, Hiatt stated that Cabban was prepared to undergo psychiatric examination by a panel of psychiatrists nominated by Burt. The aim was to have Cabban's claim of amnesia verified. This was a highly unusual request which took Burbury by some surprise. He decided that the request would be considered by all counsel appearing at the Commission before a ruling would be made. Nothing more was made of it at the Commission.

When Robertson re-entered the witness box, the Commissioners returned to the issue of the relevance of Cabban to Spicer's findings. Robertson had obviously considered the matter overnight. However, he tried to avoid the issue by saying that he could not answer the question briefly. When pressed, he did not even mention the Cabban Statement. Instead, he questioned the competence of Spicer and the actions of Smyth, claiming that they made Spicer's task impossible. Burbury informed Robertson that he had not answered his question about the relevance of Cabban to Spicer's findings and that he could not understand why Cabban was relevant now when he had not been during the Spicer Commission. Robertson was rattled. The following passage of transcript covers the mood of the Commission well.

> Lucas:     I must confess I am very anxious, speaking for myself . . .
>
> Burbury:  We all are.
>
> Lucas:     I know my fellow Commissioners are very anxious that it should be made very clear what your point is. I must confess at the moment I am still not clear in my mind about it.[8]

The Commissioners were surprised that Robertson was unable to clearly articulate the relevance of Cabban when he had aided and abetted those who sought another inquiry based on Cabban's evidence. He should, of course, have expected questioning on this fundamental issue. It became apparent that the Commission needed to digress into Robertson's disagreements with the Spicer Report before returning to the issue of whether or not Cabban was relevant to them. Having heard a brief account of why Robertson believed Spicer was wrong, with emphasis on his finding that *Voyager* had steadied for a 'minute or so' before the collision, Asprey returned Robertson to the Cabban Statement and affirmed that they could only alter Spicer's findings on the basis of that Statement.

The main problem Robertson faced was his continuing refusal to state that Stevens was not a competent captain. There was some logic in this. If Robertson attacked Stevens, he could expect to be attacked by counsel for the Stevens family. To date, he had avoided supporting Cabban by having Reynolds ask no questions. The time was fast approaching when Robertson had to attack the credit of Stevens and prepare himself for criticism from Ash, and probably Murphy as well. At the end of his examination by Jeffrey, Robertson had only said that the Royal Commissioner had rejected his theories about why the collision occurred because Spicer assumed that Stevens was a competent captain. He had failed to demonstrate the specific relevance of the Cabban Statement, relying on a general inference that obviously did not convince the Commissioners.

Jack Smyth was then called to give evidence, principally in relation to the third term of reference although more was to be made of his evidence than whether or not he improperly withheld Cabban's evidence from the Commission. Burt sought from Smyth an assessment of Cabban and his evidence, as it appeared to him in 1964. He said he believed Cabban had a grudge against Stevens; that Stevens had hindered his promotion; that his Statement was 'highly coloured' and presented exaggerated views of Stevens's 'drinking'; and, that he was an unreliable witness. Smyth stated that he checked some of the matters mentioned by Cabban with other officers, including Griffiths, but they received no support. Smyth's final view at the time was that whether or not what Cabban said was true, it was irrelevant to the causes of the collision and was, therefore, inadmissible evidence.

Smyth spent the whole of the twelfth day of the inquiry in the witness box. The most vigorous cross-examination came from Reynolds who questioned Smyth on the formulation of his submissions to Spicer and the effect they had had on Spicer and on his final report. It was apparent that Reynolds wanted to attack Spicer's assumption that Stevens was a competent destroyer captain, to undermine the rejection of Robertson's theories by both Smyth and Spicer. Against an accomplished adversary, Reynolds made slow and arduous progress. Smyth was unwilling to concede very much about Cabban's allegations, principally because such concession represented a criticism of his own performance as counsel assisting the 1964 Commission.

> If I had been given all of this material I would have certainly probed all of it
> but whether I would have called it or not later would have been an entirely
> different matter.[9]

When asked by Reynolds whether Cabban's evidence would have altered the entire course of the 1964 Commission, Smyth replied, 'I do not think so'.[10] For Smyth, his assessment of Cabban had rendered his Statement next to worthless. In answer to a question from Reynolds in which he was asked 'Let us not mince words. Did you think he was a psychiatric case?', Smyth replied, 'To tell you the honest truth, I did. But I would prefer not to say it. I do not claim any psychiatric knowledge, but I have struck that sort of witness before. I could be quite wrong, but that is what I thought'.[11] By the end of Smyth's re-examination by Burt which dealt with statements Smyth had made between 1965 and 1967 relating to Cabban's evidence, Robertson's position had not improved. Smyth had not made any helpful concessions, neither had he agreed that Cabban's evidence could in any material way have assisted Robertson at the 1964 inquiry.

When the thirteenth day of hearings began, Burbury took the initiative with respect to Robertson's position and intervened with a series of questions for Reynolds. He took this action because the Commissioners were anxious 'to know how it is claimed that if the Cabban Statement were accepted in substance, some variations in findings adverse to Captain Robertson ought to be made'.[12] Burbury then summarised his understanding of the basic submission being put by Reynolds. The third of the three propositions he outlined contained the vital element.

> If Sir John Spicer had believed that Captain Stevens was a man of the type that Cabban paints him in the Cabban Statement, he might have been prepared to give Captain Stevens the kind of margin of error which ... he felt unable to attribute to him, and therefore led him to reject Captain Robertson's reconstruction [Reproduced as Appendix 5 in the Spicer Report].[13]

Burbury invited Reynolds 'at a convenient time this week to make ... a short opening statement of how it is claimed that the findings of Sir John Spicer, adverse to your client, should be varied'.[14]

The remainder of the day was taken up with evidence from Ian Sheppard, junior counsel assisting the 1964 Commission. Sheppard largely substantiated what his leader (Smyth) had already stated. What Sheppard did reveal was that after Robertson's first report on the collision was submitted, but before evidence was first heard at the Commission, Smyth formed the opinion that substantial criticism could be levelled at Robertson. It was on this basis that Smyth advised Robertson to engage counsel and supported his application for the Commonwealth to meet the expense. Following Sheppard was Eric Neilson, instructing solicitor to counsel for the Navy at the 1964 Commission. He outlined his initial contact with Cabban, the taking of a statement from him, and its subsequent handling.

This brought to an end another phase of the Commission and largely completed the hearing of evidence relating to the third term of reference. Although the four days on which evidence was heard on this matter showed that there was nothing sinister about Cabban not being heard at the 1964 Commission, it provided few insights into the other areas of inquiry. It did not assist Cabban or Robertson. It may have gone to the credit of the Naval Board but it certainly helped the Stevens family. With both Smyth and Sheppard answering against the relevance of Cabban to the causes of the collision, it provided further weight with two separate views that there was no connection.

While the Cabban Statement was being confirmed or denied by witnesses, there remained the issue of whether navigational evidence and argument would be heard from Robertson's counsel. As Reynolds had shown no interest to date in assisting Cabban's cause, his entire submission would rest on showing that Spicer's findings were open to challenge. At the end of the sixteenth day of the inquiry, Reynolds handed the Commissioners a statement putting the case for a variation of Spicer's findings where they related to Captain Robertson. It was not until the thirty-ninth day of the inquiry that attention was again turned to Robertson's interest in the proceedings. On this occasion it was prompted by the calling of Rear-Admiral Peek as a witness and objections from Ash to the consideration of navigational evidence.

Ash wanted the Commission to limit its inquiries to the period covered by Cabban's statement which ended on 8 January 1964. Despite pointing out that this was 'literally speaking' the extent of the Commission's charter, Burt was of the understanding that this

> did not seem to be a desirable point at which to terminate the inquiry and it would be satisfactory to carry it forward, not perhaps in great detail, but at least until the date of the collision.[15]

But Burbury added

> there must be some nexus between the drinking habits and seamanship of Captain Stevens and possible variation in the finding [of Spicer].[16]

Reynolds's strategy was to have the Commission accept his evidence and his arguments — which may have established a connection between Cabban's evidence and Spicer's findings — before making a ruling on its admissibility. Reynolds sought to avoid committing himself to a construction on Cabban's evidence or any limitation of the relevance it might have had to any of Spicer's findings. The only form of resistance Ash could offer was a threat to prolong the inquiry by seeking a reconsideration of all the evidence presented to Spicer.

Both Burt and Ash were concerned about the evidence that would be elicited from Peek, although for different reasons. Burbury realised that the examination of Peek could not proceed without a statement by Reynolds of the matters relating to navigation he wanted to cover. Reynolds advised that they were limited and would, in the case of Peek, who was an expert witness, be questions regarding the theories explaining *Voyager's* final movements. The Commissioners were clearly unsure as to whether to allow Reynolds to ask his questions in that they seemed unrelated to Cabban's evidence, but Burbury was prepared to be indulgent.

> Burbury: Do I understand that you are not pressing upon the Commission to — what I will call — open the flood gates and listen to a lot of evidence relating to the causes of the collision?
>
> Reynolds: As at present advised, apart from my own client, we would not be seeking to call evidence.[17]

It was apparent that there were still some misgivings about what Reynolds proposed.

The following morning Burbury gave him what could be fairly described as a warning.

> We wish to be certain that we fully understand in what way and for what reasons Captain Robertson claims that Sir John Spicer's findings, so far as they were critical of himself, should be varied. We will, therefore, provisionally permit cross-examination along the lines indicated by Mr Reynolds, as possibly assisting us in that regard. If it appears that matters are being opened up which have no fairly arguable relevance to term of reference 2(b), then we may have to intervene.[18]

Reynolds began his cross-examination of Peek by having him agree that the standards of performance expected of a captain in the Fleet were very high. Reynolds then described a series of hypothetical situations drawn from the Cabban Statement. He asked Peek what he would have done had he been aware of these situations as they occurred. As expected, Peek said that if the substance of the Cabban Statement were accepted he would have decided that Stevens lacked responsibility, was unfit to command on medical grounds, and would have been court martialled. Reynolds then attempted to connect the view that Peek would have formed of Stevens's ability had he been aware of Cabban's evidence, with the navigational aspects raised at the 1964 Commission. The difficulty Reynolds faced was relying on Peek to establish the connection since he was unable to do so himself. Peek was quite prepared to express his disagreement with Smyth's theory that *Voyager*'s final movement was in response to the flying course signal. He was also prepared to say that *Voyager* was manoeuvring in accordance with the flying course signal which gave Stevens the discretion to determine how he would assume the proper station. But as for demonstrating the relevance of Cabban, Peek was of no use.

It was not until ten days later (Day 50) that Reynolds made what could properly be termed an opening address which he hoped to develop on behalf of Robertson. Reynolds acknowledged at the outset that his submission depended on the Commissioners finding that Stevens was unfit to command. Reynolds also attempted to persuade the Commissioners that their decision on whether to alter Spicer's findings should not rest merely on whether Stevens was unfit to command. If additional evidence was presented it ought to be heard. Asprey suggested that what Reynolds wanted was more of a re-hearing of certain aspects of the first inquiry than an appeal from its findings. As this gave Reynolds an opportunity to be heard, he happily agreed. Robertson's case was made up of six main arguments.

First, if at the 1964 Commission the respective courses of *Melbourne* and *Voyager* prior to the collision were not in dispute by either ship, there were reasonable grounds for levelling criticisms at the officers on the carrier's bridge.

However, there was dispute about the courses. Reynolds argued that any criticism of *Melbourne*'s officers must be considered and determined in the light of what *Voyager* did prior to the collision. This was the second point.

As his third point, Reynolds conceded that if the two ships were on a steady course for one minute prior to the collision, Spicer's criticism of Robertson had to stand. But if Spicer had found that *Voyager* was on a turning course until 20 seconds before the collision, Reynolds contended that Spicer would not have made a finding critical of Robertson, Kelly or Bate.

As his fourth point, Reynolds said that Spicer's findings were predicated by the acceptance of Stevens as a highly competent destroyer captain and the rejection of Robertson as an inexperienced aircraft carrier captain. Had Spicer known of Cabban's evidence and questioned Stevens's competence, Reynolds then argued, he would not have rejected Robertson's submission that *Voyager* mistook her position relative to *Melbourne*.

In his final submission, designed to provide a fall-back position if the majority of the Cabban Statement were not accepted, *Voyager* was in any event on a turning course on her way to planeguard station.

Reynolds's submission did not satisfy the Commissioners' requirement for the relevance of Stevens's unfitness to command to be demonstrated. Asprey was the most concerned about this aspect.

> What you are putting is that the mistake [leading to the collision] is such that it can be explained only on the basis of some great error that anybody could have made — even a fit man … If your forceful arguments were given effect, they could be given effect without any references to anybody's unfitness on the night in question.[19]

There was more to the Commissioners' concerns than just semantic purity relating to their terms of reference. While they were naturally reticent about overturning Spicer too readily, the very fact of overturning Spicer would create the impression that Stevens's drinking — which had a higher importance in Reynolds's submission than his ulcer condition — had contributed to the causes of the collision. Reserving their judgement on whether to allow Reynolds to develop his submission further, Burbury again sought an indication of how many witnesses Reynolds proposed to call in arguing his case. In addition to Robertson and Cabban, and possibly one or two others, Reynolds hoped to dispose of his submission quickly. Burbury asked other counsel to consider the witnesses they would need to call in response to Reynolds's submission.

The Commissioners returned to Robertson's case two days later (Day 52). It was almost certain that Reynolds would face opposition from other counsel, particularly Ash and Murphy. Reynolds said that he would adopt the submission put by Norman Jenkyn QC — Navy counsel at the previous inquiry — that *Voyager* was altering course until just prior to the collision which he hoped would not involve placing any additional blame on the bridge of *Voyager*. Reynolds's tactic was obviously to minimise the possibility of his submission being attacked by Ash and Murphy.

Burbury was reticent about permitting Reynolds to proceed. His understanding of the terms of reference required the Commissioners to express an opinion rather than consider a redetermination of the facts. Murphy was not as obstructive as he could have been. His main contribution was in suggesting to the Commissioners that it was necessary for unfitness to command to be proved not only at some time prior to the collision, but as a continuing state, and that such unfitness was an operating factor on the night of the collision and pertinent to its causes. This was a tall order and one which the evidence had not as yet gone anywhere near showing. Ash argued that Robertson had had his chance, that his theories had been rejected, and that it was unfair to evaluate Spicer simply on the basis of his report. The proper way to vary Spicer, Ash asserted, was to rehear the witnesses Spicer had heard. As this would occupy the Commission for a considerable period, Ash submitted that it should not even be attempted.

Burt provided the most damaging objection to Reynolds's submission in pointing out that Spicer's criticism of Robertson was that he did not warn *Voyager* that she was standing into danger and that this criticism remained valid whatever *Voyager*'s movement, steady (straight) or turning, prior to the collision. Attacking Reynolds's concession that Robertson relied upon a finding that Stevens was unfit to command, Burt questioned how this finding could affect Spicer's conclusion that *Voyager* was on a steady course. In other words, Stevens being unfit did not mean *Voyager* was turning. This was the weakness in Reynolds's submission. Indeed, Sheppard later stated in a letter

> I do not see how [Cabban's evidence] would have affected Captain Robertson's culpability one way or the other. The whole question was whether he should have sounded a warning when he realised the ships were on a collision course. It is difficult to understand how Stevens' drinking habits could have had any relevance to this matter.[20]

Before the criticism of Robertson could be displaced, the steady course had to be rejected. In strictly observing the construction of the terms of reference, the Commissioners were not entitled to overturn Spicer on this matter. Robertson's position was again desperate. The Commissioners decided to defer ruling on the submissions.

The fifty-third day of hearings appeared to mark the end for any chance Robertson may have had to argue his case. Burbury announced the Commission's ruling on Reynolds's submission when it commenced hearings. His statement needs to be cited in some length.

> It is not part of the function of this Royal Commission to hear new evidence or to re-hear any of the old evidence as to the immediate circumstances of the collision or the navigational aspects of it. This Commission does not sit as a General Court of Appeal against the findings of Sir John Spicer. The Commission as we see it, must take Sir John Spicer's findings as they appear in his report, and consider only whether in the event of the Commission finding that the late Captain Stevens was unfit to retain command, that finding requires any variation in Sir John Spicer's findings, and if so in what respect.
> ... Therefore, for these reasons we will exclude all evidence as to the navigational aspects of the collision ... It follows that we reject the application by Mr Reynolds to call expert evidence from Captain Robertson as to the

navigational aspects of the collision, because although this would not be factual evidence it would nevertheless be fresh evidence as to the collision itself.[21]

Burbury also pointed out that this ruling was on the assumption that Stevens was found to be unfit, a matter on which the Commission had as yet adopted no view.

When hearings commenced the next morning (Day 54), Reynolds addressed the Commission and said that if the submission of Burt was accepted, Robertson could get nothing from the inquiry. This being the situation, Reynolds stated that there were strong grounds for having the Government widen the terms of reference to allow Robertson to put his case. This seemed to have had the desired effect as the door was left slightly open. Burbury stated that

> if ultimately you could persuade us that Sir John Spicer's line of reasoning in making the finding he did as to the course of *Voyager* was vitiated by an erroneous assumption of fact as to the late Captain Stevens' complete competency, alertness and concentration, then I would think that would mean that we would have to examine his finding in relation to Captain Robertson and the course of *Voyager* critically and consider whether we ought not to substitute some other inference for ourselves than that adopted by Sir John Spicer.[22]

But this only marginally improved Robertson's situation as it related to submissions he would find difficult to prove, and which he had so far attempted to avoid.

There appeared to be another major setback to Robertson's case. Reynolds had been appointed to the New South Wales Supreme Court Bench and Robertson would need to brief another QC in all that had happened at the Commission in time for a final submission. Reynolds recommended a friend, Gordon Samuels QC, and approached him on Robertson's behalf. This was a selection which naturally angered the Stevens family's instructing solicitor, Fred Osborne, who had earlier sought to engage Samuels to represent his clients. At that time Samuels had been busy with another case.

It would take a great deal of tactical cunning for Samuels to persuade the Commissioners to even hear the submissions on navigational aspects in which Robertson had placed so much store.

# 16

# Gordon Samuels and Pieces of String

FTER THREE MONTHS of hearings, there was still a belief in
Parliament and the press that the primary purpose of the Royal
Commission was seeking 'justice' for Robertson. Yet the
prospect of his gaining anything from the inquiry was declining.

Taking over the Robertson brief was an enormous undertaking for
Gordon Samuels. After a short recess, he was expected to be familiar
with the proceedings and report of the first Commission, the events
between the Commissions and the progress of the second Commission
which had been going for four months. He was also expected to have
the Commissioners hear Robertson's arguments on the navigational
aspects when Reynolds had previously been unsuccessful. It is also
relevant that Samuels had 'read' with Asprey while Samuels was
training as a barrister and that Asprey had a deep affection for his
former pupil.

The arrival of Samuels marked a change for the Commission.
Samuels was pleased to have the brief.

> The inquiry was, I think, one of the most exciting matters I had at the Bar,
> principally because it involved a field previously quite unfamiliar and because
> we started well behind.[1]

In early November the Royal Commission moved into another,
smaller, court as the chamber it occupied was required for a pressing
Federal case. The new courtroom was poorly ventilated, acoustics
were bad, and public seating was reduced. In an effort to improve
conditions, a fan was set up at the rear of the chamber. It achieved
little other than making it more difficult to hear the Commission's
proceedings. The press was now denied desks and had to cross the
floor of the courtroom when coming and going. Fortunately, the major
evidence had been tendered and only closing arguments and final
summations remained.

There was another change in the mood of the Commission. On
10 November 1967, Burbury announced that Lucas was unable to
continue sitting because of ill-health. This was rightly considered a

major blow to Cabban's position because Lucas appeared most positively disposed towards him and his evidence. There was nothing sinister about Lucas's inability to continue.

(A legend later developed, propagated by Cabban's supporters, that Lucas had left the Commission because he could no longer tolerate the behaviour or the attitudes of his two fellow Commissioners, and that although illness was a convenient cover, he shortly afterwards returned to the Queensland Supreme Court Bench. This allegation has been virulently rejected by all three Commissioners. Justice Lucas told me that he started having severe headaches two weeks before his eventual departure from the Commission. These headaches culminated in his collapse from an aneurysm the day before his formal departure on 10 November. He spent the next month in hospital and did not hear any cases until the new sitting period in 1968. Inquiries with the Supreme Court show that he did not fully return to work for some three months in all.)

Henchman then informed Murphy that he had been appointed a judge of the New South Wales District Court. This did little to help the position of the Naval Board.

Burbury announced on the sixty-first day that the order of the final addresses would be Burt, Hiatt, Ash, Murphy and Samuels with Burt to present the closing submission, as was his right, as counsel assisting the Commissioners. When he began the first of his two addresses on the sixty-seventh day,[2] Burt stated that his approach to the first term of reference, Stevens's fitness to command, would be to isolate the specific allegations which formed the basis for dispute and to relate these to the evidence.

Burt appears to have generally accepted Cabban's description of numerous events during the Far East cruise although he did not ascribe the significance to them that Cabban did. For instance, he was prepared to accept that Stevens was indisposed for several hours in HMS *Rothesay* which he attributed more to gastritis than excessive consumption of alcohol. As for Tokyo, Burt's submission was simply that every night over a five-night period, the evidence of Arthur Jamieson (an Australian Embassy official), Willis and Captain Dollard (Australian Naval Attaché in Tokyo) showed that 'on no night while the captain was in Tokyo did he stay the course, except for the first night'.[3] This was a very cunning way for Burt to put his submission. By emphasising what was known of Stevens's condition, Burt left it open to the Commissioners to decide how it was caused. They could choose the ulcer, drinking, or a combination of both. All the possible findings were left open.

When he continued on the next day (Day 68), Burt argued that the evidence supported the sense of the Cabban Statement although it was in places exaggerated. Citing one clear instance, Stevens was alleged to have returned on board *Voyager* heavily under the influence of alcohol every morning after the Far East cruise while the ship was in Sydney. Burt stated that evidence showed this was clearly not true and that Cabban had a tendency to exaggerate.

There were, of course, other matters in which the Commissioners had either to accept or reject the word of Cabban over another witness. By way of example, there was no corroboration for the conversation between Cabban and Willis which resulted in Cabban taking 'unofficial' command of *Voyager* for five days from Tokyo to Subic Bay.

As an allied submission, Burt said the Commissioners had to determine whether documents, such as *Vampire*'s rough-weather log and *Voyager*'s punishment returns, both of which covered the period Cabban was allegedly in command between Tokyo and Subic Bay, had later been changed. If these records had been altered, as Cabban claimed, it reflected directly on Stevens's fitness to command. In essence, the first term of reference was largely based on the Commissioners either accepting Cabban as a truthful witness or rejecting him as a malicious and vindictive liar.

Burt also pointed out that the author of the terms of reference had read more into Cabban's comments on Stevens's seamanship ability than Cabban had intended. Stevens's shiphandling ability was not in doubt.

As for the second term of reference, whether the Naval Board should have known, Burt stated that there was no evidence that any member of the Board knew of any unfitness within Stevens to command. He said that McNeill, Tiller, Leading Seaman Sick Berth Attendant Wilson and Captain Dollard should have made reports to the Naval Board, but none did so. On the matter of a variation of Spicer's findings, Burt reiterated his previous submission that Robertson's difficulty was showing that a finding adverse to Stevens on fitness to command could overturn Spicer's view that *Voyager* was on a steady course prior to the collision. Furthermore, regardless of whether *Voyager* was steady or turning, the criticism of Robertson remained valid.

The third term of reference, whether Cabban's evidence had been improperly withheld, Burt disposed of very quickly by saying that Cabban and his evidence had been available but Smyth had decided against putting him into the witness box. He said that the evidence had not been withheld and Smyth had not acted improperly.

Cabban and the Naval Board had emerged well from Burt's address; Stevens and Robertson had not.

In his final submission,[4] Hiatt launched a virulent attack against the Naval Board. He claimed the Naval Board felt it was under attack from Cabban and had acted to hinder the Commission's inquiries into Stevens's fitness to command by discouraging witnesses and branding Cabban as a malcontent. Hiatt claimed that the Board had used its control over documentary evidence to support Stevens and discredit

Cabban while pressuring naval witnesses to ensure their testimony reflected the view put by the Board. Conversely, the strongest corroboration for Cabban came from non-naval witnesses.

In effect, Hiatt believed the Naval Board had attempted a very subtle cover-up, and had succeeded to some extent, yet it had failed to show Cabban to be the man that was portrayed by McNicoll in his memorandum of 15 May 1967, entitled 'Character of Cabban'. On being asked by the Commissioners to substantiate his allegation that naval witnesses had been intimidated, Hiatt said he could not prove the point but argued that the inference had to be drawn. Given the gravity of the allegation, this was not nearly good enough for the Commissioners who directed Hiatt to consider his position overnight. The following morning he withdrew his remarks.

The Cabban Statement, Hiatt said, had been corroborated from the most unlikely of sources and did not contain exaggeration. He conceded that it had been inaccurate in several places but explained that Cabban had been giving his general impressions.[5] Given that Cabban had made his Statement and presented his evidence entirely from memory and had remained consistent throughout the eight days of his examination and cross-examination, this went substantially to his credit as a witness. As to the specific incidents mentioned in the Statement, Hiatt said they were generally corroborated. Where they were not, as in the case of the punishment returns[6] and in the details of the Tokyo visit, Hiatt alleged that there had been attempts at falsifying records in the first instance, and presentation of deliberately misleading evidence in the second. Hiatt went as far as alleging that both Dollard and Loxton had been less than completely truthful in giving their evidence.

In closing his final submission, Hiatt described his client's Statement as an honest attempt to record his experiences while in *Voyager*. He said that Cabban had resisted the efforts of others to have the Statement made public, avoided publicity and rejected any form of personal gain. He did not address his remarks specifically to any of the terms of reference, although he sought an affirmation from the Commissioners that Cabban was a truthful and reliable witness, and that his Statement was for the greatest part an accurate description of *Voyager*'s 1963 Far East cruise.

Ash began his reply[7] by exposing the flawed assumption that Cabban's allegations were relevant to the cause of the collision. He pointed out that there was serious doubt as to whether Stevens actually consumed the triple brandy on the night of the collision, and at any rate, Stevens was described as being in very good health across the three days prior to the collision. Ash attacked Robertson for using Cabban as a lever to force another inquiry, and Cabban for never attempting to restrict the use of his Statement.

The line taken by Ash was to limit his attack to the Cabban Statement for its inaccuracies, exaggerations and misleading inferences. He referred to his own cross-examination of Cabban in which he had consistently reduced the period of Stevens's incapacity stated by Cabban. Ash pointed to the evidence of Stevens being a fit and active man who loved sport and physical activity.

On the second day of his final submission, Ash argued that Cabban was an unreliable witness and that Cabban's opinions and judgements of what he heard and saw were not those experienced by others. Consequently, he asked the Commissioners to reject Cabban's submissions where they related to the truthfulness of other witnesses and the integrity of naval records. As if to suggest that his client's position was predicated by a finding that Cabban did not have command for five days out of Tokyo, Ash cited the evidence of one sailor who said he could not recall captain's defaulters having been taken by anyone other than Stevens, while others had recalled seeing Stevens some time within the five-day period claimed by Cabban. In all, it was a weak submission which relied on too few witnesses and too liberal an interpretation of Stevens not being incapacitated. The fact of his having been seen by one of the ship's officers, Lieutenant Richard Carpendale, did not prove that Stevens had been fit to command or had been acting in command.

On the third day of his final address, Ash attempted to discredit Hiatt's allegation that naval witnesses were partial to Stevens while asserting that the recollections of many witnesses had been impaired by the passing of time. Wisely, Ash did not comment on the reasons for Stevens's behaviour as a way of avoiding making any concessions relating to Stevens's ulcer or drinking habits. However, the evidence presented of Stevens's performance at the birthday mess dinner in Singapore was so overwhelming that he had to offer some defence. Ash, understating the import of the whole incident, said Stevens's behaviour was either due to illness, or a combination of illness and drink, but claimed that it did not affect morale, the efficient running of the ship or his fitness to retain command.

In his fourth and last day addressing the Commission, Ash covered the main incidents referred to by Cabban in an effort to place Stevens's command of *Voyager* into a larger context and to cast further quantitative doubt on Cabban's statements. The only concession adverse to Stevens that he finally made was the birthday mess dinner. As for Stevens's health, Ash argued that Stevens was in perfect health, and that both McNeill (at Hong Kong) and subsequently Tiller had confirmed this. Further, Ash claimed that Stevens had never sought to conceal his ulcer condition or any other ill-health. Consequently, Ash implored the Commissioners to give a negative reply to the first term of reference.

What Ash did not cover in his submission was Robertson's position.

After retracting some fairly strong criticisms he had made of Robertson on the second day of his address, Ash made no effort to attack Robertson's use of Cabban's evidence to gain another inquiry. Ash could have exploited Burt's argument that Cabban's evidence did not alter Robertson's position or the criticisms of Spicer. Whatever his reasons for not attacking Robertson, Ash weakened his own position. Anything that Robertson gained from the Commission would be at the expense of Stevens.

Murphy decided to take a different line in arguing for a finding of 'no' to the first term of reference.[8] Given the corroboration the Cabban Statement had received from a range of witnesses, he chose not to attack its truthfulness but its alleged unreliability, exaggerations and distortions. Murphy's approach was to demonstrate how damning Cabban's criticisms were when properly assessed and understood, and how much his portrayal varied from the picture that had emerged of Stevens throughout the Commission. In trying to show that Cabban and his counsel had retreated from Cabban's initial statement, Murphy hoped to reduce the value placed on the Statement as a means of discrediting its author. It was a subtle tactic that made much of the circumstances in which the Statement was originally conceived, while avoiding much of the evidence and argument that served as corroboration. Murphy had now committed himself to the 'sickness' interpretation of Stevens's actions and could make very little comment on the issue of drinking.[9]

The Naval Board, having entered the Commission arguing that there was nothing adverse in its view of Stevens's performance while commanding *Voyager*, had little choice but to persist with this view throughout. This led Murphy to frame his submission in terms of answering whether any of the allegations were true. After contending that they were not true, he conceded that Stevens had an ulcer, was periodically sick and tired, and delegated command to his executive officer when necessary. Murphy stated that there was nothing unusual in this and Stevens had acted responsibly.

The Naval Board was also committed to attacking Cabban's motives in making his Statement. Murphy argued that Cabban was motivated by the residual ill-will he felt towards the Navy for his grounding as a pilot in 1956, and his attitude towards the 1964 Commission and its alleged injustice to Captain Robertson. He described Cabban as a man who was 'willing to wound and yet afraid to strike',[10] and he remained so throughout the Commission. His allegations were those of a man who 'is careless with the truth or whose capacity to make rational judgements had been completely lost because of his prior bias or his preconceived ideas'.[11] As such, his judgement was 'warped, unbalanced and cannot be relied upon',[12] while his evidence could only be used when totally corroborated by reliable witnesses.

Murphy dealt only briefly with Hiatt's allegation that naval witnesses followed the 'Navy line' when they gave their evidence. This, and other charges that the Naval Board had attempted a cover-up, were rejected on the grounds that Hiatt had no proof that this had occurred. Murphy's task in this respect was made easier by the fact that Hiatt had alleged the cover-up and intimidation was blatant. Had he argued that it was achieved with more subtlety and ingenuity, Murphy's task would have proved much more difficult.

On the second day of his final address, Murphy turned to the submissions that had been made by Robertson's counsel. It was at this point that the Naval Board most clearly revealed its hand towards the man it had attempted to support in 1964. At first, Murphy agreed with Spicer's finding that *Voyager* had been on a steady course prior to the collision. He mentioned Spicer's reasons for coming to such a view without any reservation, and then suggested that Robertson should have been aware of a dangerous situation and as OTC should have taken appropriate action as soon as *Voyager* had passed beyond a heading of 020 degrees when forward of *Melbourne*'s beam. This was almost a complete about-turn on the view the Board had expressed throughout 1964. It certainly took Robertson by surprise. The Commissioners decided that before Murphy proceeded further on navigational aspects, Samuels would put his submission and Murphy would then respond to these arguments. Murphy told me that at no time during the Commission had he any intention of advancing any theory for the causes of the collision.[13]

The challenge to Samuels was to have the Commissioners hear the new evidence while exploring the relationship between Stevens's behaviour and the navigation case he would present if permitted. The attitude of the Commissioners appears to have altered slightly with the commencement of final submissions. Burt argued that they should not hear navigational evidence; Hiatt made no comment; Murphy said there was no justification. It was almost as if there was a fear that the Commissioners would overturn Spicer's findings if Robertson were heard. In response to Murphy's submission to limit the evidence to be covered, Justice Asprey remarked

> ... for myself I would not like to leave any stone unturned, I want to fully appreciate what is being submitted on Captain Robertson's behalf.[14]

Burbury was of a like mind. He advised Murphy that the Commission needed to hear Robertson's submissions in the event that it did find that Stevens was unfit to retain command.[15] What prompted Burbury to say this, something he could have said four months earlier, is unknown. It certainly would have saved Reynolds a great deal of argument.

This was the opportunity that Samuels needed. His opening remarks made it difficult for the Commissioners not to hear his full submission.

... we think we can establish as a fact once and for all how the collision happened ... and that we can present a most compelling inference as to why it happened.[16]

Having noted that there was some space in which he could develop an argument, Samuels did not immediately take up the matter of Stevens's health or drinking, so as to avoid the appearance to other counsel, particularly that for Stevens and the Navy, that he was hostile to them.

Samuels's long address[17] began by exploiting the obvious change in the Naval Board's attitude towards Spicer's criticism of Robertson between 1964 and 1967. Whereas Jenkyn, counsel for the Navy in 1964, rejected Smyth's system of building the times and manoeuvres from 2042, Murphy had no objection to it. Conversely, where Jenkyn was prepared to accept the evidence of Tactical Operator Evans that *Voyager* steadied on a course of 020 degrees after the turning signal, Murphy was not. Furthermore, Murphy agreed with Smyth on matters on which the Naval Board had previously disagreed.

Samuels's argument was much the same as that put by Jenkyn — that *Voyager* had been on a turning course in response to the flying course signal which allowed her to manoeuvre with discretion. Consequently, Samuels argued that Spicer was wrong in three major respects: he was wrong in finding that *Voyager* was on a steady course; wrong in finding that she was manoeuvring in response to the turning course signal; and wrong in attributing any blame to Robertson as a result.

A connection was still needed with Stevens's unfitness to command. Samuels said that Spicer believed Stevens was a competent captain who knew what he was doing on the night of the collision. By implication, Spicer asserted that a competent captain would be more likely to have put *Voyager* on a steady course. By ascribing a deliberate intention to *Voyager*'s final movements and that Stevens alone was responsible for the port turn — it being inconceivable that Price would have countermanded his own order — Spicer rejected the possibility that the destroyer had been on a continuous turn and discounted many of the errors and failures that were implicit in such a finding. Samuels argued that if Spicer had been aware of Cabban's evidence, he would have been prepared to accept a wider margin of error on the part of Stevens and, one assumes, to have admitted the possibility or even the probability that *Voyager* was turning prior to the collision.

Robertson's notes for Reynolds earlier discounted the theories based either on wheel having been left on or confusion over who had the con. Robertson was by now convinced that *Voyager*'s turn to port was intentional. The reason? Robertson concluded that Stevens was unfit to command. Yet his reasoning had more to do with incompetence than incapacity although it was unlikely he would argue either very strongly, if at all.

Further testing the waters, Samuels remarked that he was reticent about attacking Spicer's findings. Burbury responded:

> I do not see why you should. I am very used to Courts of Appeal making most trenchant criticisms of my judgements and I have never regarded myself as having a vested right in them. Please do not feel inhibited.[18]

There was now nothing restricting what Samuels could say. The door was fully open for Robertson's submissions. Although he had played a minor role in Robertson gaining another hearing, Cabban was now of importance to Samuels's submission, which still required a finding of 'yes' to the first term of reference that Stevens was unfit to command. Samuels's arguments in favour of this finding were tentative in the extreme yet he overruled Robertson who continued to resist his counsel making mention of Cabban's evidence.

At any rate, Samuels did not need to say much about this because the finding of unfitness was largely dependent on the submissions of both Burt, counsel assisting the Commission, and Hiatt, Cabban's counsel. However, he argued that Stevens did on occasion drink excessively, was unwell from time to time because of his ulcer, and that his ulcer was affected by his alcohol consumption. It was described as a 'self-fortifying, self-destructive cycle'.[19] Samuels asserted that Stevens's self-discipline had been eroded and this was on no occasion more apparent than in drinking a triple brandy on the night of the collision. The 'triple brandy' emerged as the key to showing that Stevens was unfit on the night of the collision. Samuels argued that Stevens drank the brandy because he was either an alcoholic or needed to ease ulcer pain. He suggested it was probably the latter.

By ascribing the triple brandy as a medicinal drink, Samuels hoped to reduce objections to his submission. Given that this was a medicinal brandy, Samuels contended that Stevens must have been in some physical distress and 'was not in a condition to exercise complete concentration and judgement which the duties of his command required'.[20] Consequently, Stevens was unfit to retain command of *Voyager* at the time of the collision.

This was still a very loose and subjective submission. What Samuels needed to show, but could not, was that Stevens's behaviour either followed a pattern or was so fundamentally inadequate and of an inherent and continuing kind, that it existed at the time of the collision. Robertson certainly had no doubts that this was true. In a notebook he maintained during the Commission, he wrote after Murphy's address

> Isn't it incredible that at the end of all the evidence we've heard, the Navy says — 'Yes, this man was quite fit to retain command'.[21]

Elsewhere, in notes prepared for his counsel dealing with the connection between Cabban's evidence and the collision, Robertson caustically remarked that Stevens suffered from

Impatience, impetuosity and finally, an attitude of laissez faire to his responsibilities. [There was] no need to take a bearing, no need to keep on the ball, to arrive sober, to stay sober, to thank wardroom, and finally, no inhibition about faking records to cover-up.[22]

The conclusion that Stevens was unfit was left 'hanging' while Samuels turned to the navigational aspect of his submission. He said that the prime difference between the actions required by a turning signal or a flying signal was that in the former, *Voyager* had no discretion as to the course she took whereas in the latter, *Voyager* would have full discretion. And that if this were so, Robertson was not obliged to challenge her movements which were acceptable within the bounds of her captain's prerogative. If accepted, no blame could be attributed to Robertson and the finding of Spicer should be overturned. Samuel's task was to prove that *Voyager* was not on a steady course prior to the collision but on a continuous turn. Robertson believed that the most readily demonstrated weakness in Spicer's findings was to do with times: 'His logic and approach to the problem are to say the least childish, and his arithmetic is wrong'.[23]

This was Robertson's last chance to put his case. As it was a final submission, new evidence could not be called. Samuels had to convince the Commissioners purely on the strength of his arguments based on the existing evidence, having ultimately failed to establish a direct and demonstrable causal link with Cabban's evidence.

The strategy devised by Samuels and Robertson was to give the Commissioners small pieces of paper with coloured ships drawn on them. Samuels used these to demonstrate his argument on a mooring board which featured a reconstruction of the collision and a series of overlays. He supplied each Commissioner with a set of 'models' and a mooring board. This seemed to impress both Burbury and Asprey who appeared to gather very quickly the issues in dispute and the essence of Robertson's submission. For most of the seventy-seventh day of the inquiry, Samuels took the Commissioners through the signals and manoeuvres that preceded the collision, and led them to his contention that Stevens may have 'lost the tactical picture'.

The following morning, Samuels attacked Spicer's reconstruction of the collision on the basis of the times he accepted for various events. Working back from the point of the collision, Samuels was quickly able to demonstrate that *Voyager* could not have been on a steady course for a minute before the collision. This appeared to impress Burbury who had made no attempt to limit Samuels's submission.

This [submission] seems to involve a proposition that once you discover that Sir John Spicer's line of reasoning is vitiated by a material error as to any matter, it then becomes our duty to go on and to consider almost all of his findings.[24]

This was further encouragement for Robertson. Citing evidence heard by Spicer which was inconsistent with his own findings, Samuels started to build a theory which could replace that adopted by Spicer. He questioned the basis on which Spicer had found that *Voyager* was on a steady course, casting great doubt on the evidence of Dadswell, the Gannet pilot, his recollection of what he had seen while flying overhead, and the circumstances in which he had made his reconstruction. With the aid of several pieces of string placed on the mooring boards, Samuels was able to demonstrate that by combining the accepted parameters of *Voyager*'s speed and turning data, and the known positions of the destroyer during the four minutes preceding the collision, there was practically only one valid reconstruction of the collision: *Voyager* must have been on a continuous turn before the collision and, by a process of deduction and reduction, that this turn was induced by the flying course and not the turning course. This reconstruction was the same as that dated 6 May 1964 which was presented by Robertson to the first inquiry. On the basis of this reconstruction, Robertson was able to prove that Spicer's version of the collision was manifestly wrong and had to be rejected.

Having provided a description of *Voyager*'s movements, Samuels had also to show why she had manoeuvred as she did. There was nothing surprising in the explanation offered. It was a reiteration of what Robertson had repeatedly said since soon after the collision. Samuels contended that Stevens lost the tactical picture and mistakenly believed he was on *Melbourne*'s port bow. He turned to port, thinking it was safe to do so, and the collision resulted. The primary and initiating cause of the collision was that Stevens had become confused. Samuels inferred that this confusion was related to Stevens's alleged unfitness to command. He suggested that his version involved less criticism of Stevens than that proposed by Spicer. This seemed to attract Burbury.

> What you are saying is you are not attributing such a gross margin of error to the late Captain Stevens as Sir John Spicer implicitly imputed by his finding.[25]

Consequently, when *Voyager* turned to starboard and back to port, manoeuvring in a manner which was considered unseamanlike, those on *Melbourne*'s bridge were entitled to believe that she was competently commanded and would not continue with her turn to port until the point of collision. Given the situation confronting Robertson, Samuels argued that Robertson did the only proper thing and ordered the engines full astern.

> We are not concerned with degrees of culpability. All that we have tried to do is to suggest a solution to a problem that has not yet been solved, i.e., how did the disaster happen and why did it happen? On the basis of the solution we submit also that the criticism made in the report of Captain Robertson, Kelly and Bate is totally unjustified.[26]

After a brilliant marathon address lasting five days, Samuels had highlighted the flaws in Spicer's logic and destroyed his Report.

Robertson had made the most of the opportunity presented to him, largely through the efforts of his leading counsel.

Samuels was followed on the eighty-first day by Sandy Gregory, counsel for Lieutenant Price, who also had comment to make on navigational matters. He had not said much during the Commission and offered a short final submission. Gregory did not take issue with Samuels's submission relating to *Voyager*'s final course although he did question the assumption that all the signals sent by *Melbourne* were properly received and interpreted by *Voyager*. He said there were grounds for believing there was some doubt in the minds of those on *Voyager*'s bridge as to what the flying course signal required the destroyer to do. There was also the possibility that the signal could have been corrupted in being passed from Tactical Operator Evans to Price and then to Stevens. As it appeared *Voyager* was deliberately proceeding to the west at the time of the collision, a corrupted or misunderstood signal was most likely the cause.

As for *Voyager*'s officers 'losing the tactical picture', Gregory asserted that very little was known about what had happened on the destroyer's bridge prior to the collision. He asked the Commissioners to retain all of Spicer's findings, including those which cast general rather than individual blame on *Voyager*. As he shared in many respects a common cause with the Stevens's interests, Gregory argued that Stevens was perfectly well on the night of the collision and that everything was calm on *Voyager*'s bridge. Gregory closed by stating that there was nothing before the present Commission which could apportion any more blame on Lieutenant Price than was placed in a general way by Spicer.

When Murphy, counsel for the Navy, rose to respond to Samuels's submission he was presented with a cleft stick. On the one hand he had to acknowledge the submission put by Jenkyn in 1964, but on the other he could not support Robertson. While assuring the Commission that the Naval Board was determined to assist the Commission in ascertaining the causes of the collision, his submission was destructive and largely uncooperative. Murphy argued that it was difficult to establish absolutely the facts leading to the collision. Thus, a number of theories were possible. He conceded that Robertson's latest theory was possible but it did not discount others which were equally plausible. Murphy argued that reconstructions of the collision had to be tentative by virtue of what was either not known or could not be adequately proved. Thus, Robertson's reconstructions were helpful but not conclusive. Sensing the importance of discrediting Robertson, Murphy surveyed the many explanations, opinions and theories Robertson had offered since the collision and the many real inconsistencies that existed between them. This was a good argument. Robertson had indeed changed his mind about what he thought had happened and Murphy made the most of this in asking the Commissioners to accept his latest

249

theory for what it was — a theory rather than a factual explanation.

As for the need to vary Spicer's findings, Murphy asked the Commissioners to retain them as they were not demonstrably wrong. He contended that, at any rate, a finding that Stevens was unfit would not change the facts and circumstances of *Voyager*'s final movements. The view of the Naval Board, Murphy stated, had never been that *Melbourne* was the prime cause of the collision. Murphy suggested that Robertson, as OTC, should have taken action as soon as he was in doubt as to *Voyager*'s movements. Whether or not this imposed a duty on Robertson against which he could be held responsible, and whether any failure to act was tantamount to blame for the collision, was not made clear. But Murphy agreed that Stevens had a clear and definite responsibility for the safety of his ship and that this was inescapable. As for Kelly and Bate, the Board again changed its view. Although in 1964 it had stated to Cabinet that no blame was attributable to either officer, Murphy said the Board did not agree with Spicer's criticism of Kelly but believed the criticism of Bate should stand. The extent to which the Naval Board had changed its view would not be obvious because only Murphy had seen the Board's submission to Cabinet. Robertson and Bate especially, had every right to feel betrayed.

Murphy concluded by reminding the Commissioners that Spicer had spent many months gathering evidence, hearing witnesses and considering arguments, and therefore Spicer's views and findings could not be lightly discarded. The Naval Board believed that all the theories advanced remained 'in the realm of conjecture' and that the cause of the collision was still inexplicable.

Responding to Samuels's submission on the eighty-third day, junior counsel for the Stevens family, John Sinclair, revived the theory that the 020 turning signal had been corrupted in transmission to a course of 270 degrees and that *Voyager* turned to this course without noticing that *Melbourne* had steadied on 020 degrees.

There was little chance of Sinclair's submission overwhelming that put by Samuels. Robertson had made great gains from Samuels's address. And, despite what was said about degrees of error, Robertson's gains were at the expense of Stevens. Ash seems to have been aware of this danger because he privately prepared some detailed notes for an argument which he did not present to the Commission. These notes survive in papers retained by the Stevens family. The argument Ash considered putting to the Commission consisted of a personal attack on Robertson. He asserted that no evidence had been provided which warranted Spicer's findings being overturned.

> This commission, now in 1967, has to put itself back into the mind of Mr Justice Spicer in 1964, and re-evaluate possible findings that he would make in that situation. It is submitted that this is impossible to do ... The situation, by reference to well-established principles adopted by an appellate court, would be

akin to the appellate court reassessing the demeanour and credibility of witnesses, which of course is the very thing that all the authorities preclude.[27]

Having perceived that the Commissioners saw themselves as an appellate court, Ash concentrated more on his objections to an overturned finding than in answering the allegations against his client. He realised, as most did, that the Commissioners had to overturn Spicer on the matter of *Voyager* being on a steady course if Robertson was to succeed. This realisation led him to attack the weakest part of the case against his client — the connection between Cabban's allegations and the causes of the collision.

> It was not the aim of the Parliament in setting up the Commission that 'unfitness to command' should be used to 'open the door' for Captain Robertson 'to have a second bite at the cherry' on navigational matters.[28]

This was the focus of his attack against Samuels.

Ash correctly pointed out that for Robertson's navigational evidence to be heard, Samuels needed to find a way of introducing it before the Commission. Having attempted to cite Stevens's duodenal ulcer as a reason for unfitness, Samuels was forced to retreat to a notional date of 31 December 1963, since evidence revealed the ulcer was not active in the few days before, or on the night of, the collision. While conceding five exacerbations of the ulcer during 1963 which Ash described as 'several innocent misassessments by an enthusiastic man',[29] he argued that the ulcer was inactive by the time Stevens consulted Sir William Morrow on 23 September 1963, and that evidence from the night of the collision confirmed that there was 'no sudden rush of ulcerated duodenal pain'.

> Stevens's unfitness was not a cause, or a contributing cause of the collision. Not only was it not a *causa causans*; it was not even a cause *sine qua non*, because it was not a cause at all . . . We submit in short that a finding of unfitness as at 31 December is not open at all unless it can be causally connected with the collision.[30]

Ash's planned attack on Robertson was scathing. He described Robertson as 'clearly one of those men who will entertain no criticism of himself' and suggested that Spicer's comments on Robertson were a 'very mild application of Rear-Admiral Becher's evidence'. He also rejected Samuels's description of Robertson having suffered a 'miscarriage of justice'.

> What was the injustice? His posting and his voluntary resignation? If so, it was not a matter for the Commissioners to consider.

Ash believed that each exacerbation was independent of the others and that when they subsided, Stevens was 'restored to that latent condition which was as such acceptable to the [Naval] Board'. As for his drinking, Ash stated that it was only excessive when considered in relation to his ulcer condition.

In concluding his working notes, Ash proposed a clear finding of 'no' to the first term of reference. He advocated an utter and complete vindication of Stevens on all the incidents referred to by Cabban, except for the birthday mess dinner and the 'misassessment of himself at Tokyo'. Thus, if the Commissioners were silent on any incident in their report, it could be taken as being adverse to Captain Stevens.

Why Ash proposed these arguments but did not put most of them in submissions to the Commission cannot be properly explained. His instructing solicitor, Osborne, told me[32] that he was adamant that Ash should fully oppose Robertson on navigational matters, and was angered by Ash's refusal to make strong submissions in the area. This had been the great strength of counsel appearing for the Stevens family at the 1964 Commission. The Stevens family had nothing to gain and everything to lose by opposing Robertson but Ash remained reluctant to join the battle, possibly because his understanding of navigation and fleetwork was superficial. Ash told the Commissioners on several occasions that he had not come prepared to dispute navigational matters, and may have believed that he would have only weakened his clients' position by putting submissions he imperfectly understood. Laurence Street QC, leading counsel for the Stevens family in the first Commission, told me that

> At the second Royal Commission, *Voyager*'s case was not as persuasively argued as it might have been and that it was not fully comprehended.[33]

This is understating the case against Ash. By failing to oppose Samuels he lost the tactical initiative and an opportunity to use the strengths of the arguments put by Street three years earlier.

Samuels made a short address in reply. He alleged the Naval Board had attacked the credibility of Robertson; had deliberately misinterpreted his theory and reconstructions; and had abandoned its previous position because it was favourable to Robertson. He asked the Commissioners to remove Spicer's criticism of Kelly, Bate, and Robertson.

In his final address, Burt commented upon all the submissions put by counsel. He ended on navigational aspects and maintained the view he had put at the start of the Commission: this was not a second *Voyager* inquiry or a court of appeal sitting in judgement over Sir John Spicer. Burt argued that it was not possible for any finding based on fact in 1964 to be displaced by a finding that Stevens was unfit. Yet he was still prepared to be generous to Robertson.

> I think it is apparent from what I have said ... that it is difficult to reach a conclusion on the present terms of reference [on whether Spicer's findings should be varied] but if you do reach it, it might well be something that might call for a variation of the report to be made.[34]

Burt felt that Spicer had made a finding as to the final movements of both ships and that it was impossible to displace these findings without rewriting the Spicer Report. Additionally, the terms of reference for the Commission did not allow it to do so. Burt was plainly sympathetic to Robertson's position but reiterated that the question to be answered by the Commissioners was whether the criticisms of Robertson were fair on the basis of what Spicer found rather than on the basis of Robertson's own version of the events. The door was left open for Spicer's criticism of Robertson to be removed if the Commissioners were prepared to accept Robertson's version and Samuels's defence of his conduct.

After eighty-five days, the hearings were adjourned. The Commissioners retired to write their report. Lucas had already started writing some sections of the final report and passed these to Burbury and Asprey when he took leave. The tone of the report would be determined by the Commissioners' concern that Stevens had no opportunity to answer the allegations being made against him. This would significantly temper their findings. Justice Asprey gave a good insight into his thinking about the position of Stevens, and what could and should be concluded, by quoting an extract from *Corbin On Contracts*:

> Facts are stubborn and impressive; and it is facts rather than legal doctrines that play a major role in judicial decision. Facts always precede rules; and it is only after a Court has knowledge of the facts of a case that it finds or constructs the law that it applies.[35]

Asprey went further in a letter to me:

> In other words, it is not only a waste of time but also an unreasonable course to make *conclusive* apportionment of blame or a *conclusive* denial of blame for the happening of an incident where there is an absence of the relevant facts leaving only a one-sided version of the operative cause or causes of the happening of that incident. That was the case with the *Melbourne–Voyager* affair.[36] [Asprey's emphasis]

In contrast to their role in publicising the divisions within the Government over the Cabban Statement and their clamouring for another inquiry, the press played a minor role during the Commission.

The Melbourne *Herald* provided a daily report on the previous day's hearing. The headlines were sensationalised when they could be — 'Cabban seeks mental check-up', and 'False picture of drunken captain' were representative of what was left in the air. The body of news stories consisted of extracts from or a paraphrase of the transcripts of evidence. Other than in its editorials at the beginning and end of the Commission, the newspaper offered no opinion or analysis of the Commission's hearings.

While its reporting resembled that of the tabloid *Herald*, the *Australian* occasionally lapsed into sensational headlines drawn from statements and remarks made at the Commission: 'Your captain has passed out. He will be returned when fit'; 'Drunken captain should go — Admiral Peek tells what he would do'; and 'I never saw captain incapable — Cabban'. The headlines and the reporting did not seem to favour one side or the other despite the fact that Robertson had been an employee of the *Australian* for over eight months. There was again neither interpretation nor analysis to accompany the narrative.

The coverage provided by the *Age* was the most consistent of the three newspapers in terms of headlines, and length and position of report. There was a tenor of restraint and an attempt to focus on the most significant portion of the hearings rather than the most sensational. There was no analysis.

It is difficult to assess the impact the headlines and reports might have had on the Australian public and on naval personnel. As with most Royal Commission reporting, the daily reports served mainly as reminders that a Royal Commission was in progress, and gave only a vague hint as to what had been led in evidence. Most emphasis was given to the publication of the Commission's findings. To the publicity sensitive, the headlines were likely to cause considerable angst. However, it was the handling of the final report by the press that overshadowed all that came before, as Robertson had found in 1964.

For their part, the Commissioners were aware of the press's reporting and the public attention their deliberations were receiving. However, as senior judicial officers they were familiar with this situation. They were largely unconcerned by the reporting and did not have cause to refer to it during the course of the inquiry. Yet they were mindful of the public's main interest in the case, finding an explanation for the collision, as their report would make abundantly clear.

# 17

# A Verdict on Stevens

T HE COMMISSIONERS had been given the unenviable task of determining whether Captain Stevens's general well-being during 1963 was primarily affected by an active duodenal ulcer, the effects of excessive consumption of alcohol, or both. Or were there other factors which were never disclosed and never discussed?

Whatever the finding, it would invariably have some bearing on Stevens's likely physical condition on the night of the collision and also impose a probable reason for Stevens drinking a triple brandy. If he did consume alcohol, what need did it meet? Was it because he was an alcoholic and craved a drink or because he sought relief from debilitating ulcer pain? Either of these two findings would allow Robertson to infer that Stevens was unfit to be in command of *Voyager*. But if it were shown that Stevens did not consume a triple brandy, he had suffered a grave injustice and all the suspicions about his conduct and his health immediately before the collision were groundless. The only evidence that he drank any alcohol on the night of the collision was the post-mortem conducted on his body, and the testimony of the captain's steward, Barry Hyland.

Little was made of alcohol consumption during the inquiry in 1964, as has been shown.[1] When Professor Blackburn claimed that Stevens's blood alcohol level had no bearing on his performance, Smyth did not pursue the matter further. Hyland's evidence was received without thorough cross-examination although his evidence given at the Commission conflicted with an earlier statement. He had stated shortly after the collision (6 March) that he had served the captain a brandy; in his testimony, it had become a *triple* brandy. Nothing more was made of this conflict of evidence in 1964.

The interest of the 1967 inquiry in the triple brandy was similar but not identical. The primary concern was to prove positively whether Stevens drank any alcohol. If he did, the issue now was not the extent to which a triple brandy might have impaired his performance, but Stevens's reasons for drinking any alcohol. There were two avenues of approach to these issues. The first was to re-examine Hyland on his recollections. The second was to review the circumstances, conduct and report of the post-mortem on Stevens's body. If achieving nothing else, it would cast doubt where previously there was none.

In fairness to the medical experts who were asked to comment on the post-mortem report, there were many variables influencing any comment or judgement. Stevens's body had been in the water for four hours when recovered; it was not refrigerated after being taken from the water; and the post-mortem was not conducted until sixty hours after death — in a small country town by a general practitioner with limited experience in this type of work. At this time it was not a legal requirement for post-mortems to be performed by pathologists. The details provided in the report on Stevens's body were a bare minimum of what was usually provided, while some of the clinical techniques did not conform to the normal strict standards employed in post-mortem analysis. By way of example, Surgeon Lieutenant Tiller later commented: 'It seems to me somewhat strange that they were able to produce a blood alcohol level on Duncan Stevens following the accident, but yet no comment was made in regard to his gastrointestinal tract'.[2] Of course, had such an observation been made and a comment offered, it would have shed light on whether Stevens's ulcer was inflamed to any appreciable degree at the time of the collision. There was clearly room for speculation on the available scientific evidence.

Ascertaining whether Stevens actually drank a triple brandy involved reconciling four pieces of evidence. The sample of blood taken from Stevens contained a blood alcohol level of 0.025 per cent. Three ounces of brandy were 'needed' to produce this level of blood alcohol. A man of Stevens's age and physical condition would break down alcohol at the rate of approximately 0.02 per cent per hour. Hyland said he had served Stevens a maximum of 2.475 ounces of brandy ninety minutes before the collision. Therefore, the recorded blood alcohol level was too high for the amount Stevens is alleged to have drunk. The inescapable conclusion was that at least some part of the alcohol content of the blood sample must have been derived from sources other than its consumption. This conclusion was supported by expert opinion.

Dr Vern Pleuckhahn was introduced to the Commission as an eminent pathologist and an authority on the matters presented to the inquiry. After the individuals involved in conducting the post-mortem gave their evidence, Pleuckhahn concluded that: 'It is very much more probable than not that contamination and bacterial growth in the sample of blood taken have contributed to produce the alcohol concentration of 0.025 per cent'.[3] However, he added that this could not be said as a matter of certainty. But with this much doubt established, a definite possibility existed that some or even all of the alcohol in the sample could have been due to contamination of the sample or post-mortem changes in body chemistry.

As this expert opinion did not completely exclude the possibility that Stevens did drink some quantity of alcohol, there remained the question of whether Stevens was an alcoholic or seriously alcohol dependent. This was a matter of great importance for the Commissioners who were concerned about the serious damage that had previously been done to Stevens's reputation on the basis of doubtful evidence. Pleuckhahn confirmed the conclusions offered by Professor Blackburn in his report to the first inquiry of 24 March 1964. In Pleuckhahn's opinion, the amount of alcohol consumed by Stevens was below the

> threshold value of blood alcohol concentration which can cause an impairment in skills and an increased liability to be involved in an accident.
>
> On the evidence supplied to me it is my firm opinion that Captain Duncan Stevens was not affected by alcohol at the time of his death and that the effects of alcohol on the capabilities of Captain Stevens can be excluded as a possible cause of the collision.[4]

This was not a view shared by other experts in the field. Dr James Rankin from St Vincent's Hospital in Sydney, Victorian police surgeon Dr John Birrell, and Dr Norman McCallum, Head of the Victorian Police Forensic Science Laboratory, were approached by Jess during the Commission for their opinions and expressed a willingness to offer alternative views to those put by Blackburn and Pleuckhahn. The Commissioners, principally at the insistence of Asprey, were only prepared to hear Birrell.[5]

Birrell remarked[6] that Pleuckhahn was a pathologist and had no experience in the observed effects at low alcohol levels.[7] Birrell conceded that 0.025 per cent was not significant but if considered in conjunction with undigested alcohol in the stomach, it could have been more important. He also suggested that Stevens may have partly induced a duodenal ulcer through a consistently heavy consumption of alcohol over a number of years.[8] (This suggestion is rejected by Dr Kerry Goulston, a leading Australian gastroenterologist.[9] He states that current thinking suggests ulcers may be caused by a parasite while there is a paucity of medical evidence linking high alcohol consumption with ulcers.[10])

Rankin had been prepared to put to the Commission similar views to those of Rankin. Based largely on the evidence that Stevens did drink a triple brandy, Rankin was convinced from the outset that Stevens was alcohol dependent. Whether or not the gastric ulcer problem was separate from or linked to alcohol dependence, he was unable to determine. However, Rankin stated that it was common medical knowledge that gastritis is a complication of alcohol dependence and there is also an association between gastro-duodenal ulceration and hazardous alcohol consumption.[11] Taking into account Goulston's expert knowledge, it would appear that Rankin is firmer in his conclusions than the evidence allows.

If, however, there was doubt that Stevens did not drink any alcohol on the night of the collision, it is obvious that the allegations of alcohol dependence instantly collapsed. It is for this reason that the Commissioners quite justifiably concentrated on the strength of the evidence that he did.

The scientific evidence elicited at the 1967 Commission had certainly cast significant doubt on the post-mortem report. The Commissioners could now turn to the evidence of Hyland. For the reasons stated earlier, Officer Steward Hyland was not cross-examined at length at the first Commission. Other than the cross-examination of Porter, whose purpose was ambiguous, the questioning of Hyland served to highlight the inconsistencies in two previous statements and his testimony before the second inquiry.

Hyland's evidence presented a difficulty to the Commissioners in that he could recall two occasions when he served Stevens a brandy. The first occasion (one week before the collision) was in the captain's day cabin, and the other (allegedly on the night of the collision) was in his sea cabin situated one deck higher in the ship. In spite of Hyland's insistence that his recollections of the night of the collision were clear, he knowingly contradicted his statement of 1964 while adding to his recollections with additional detail that suggested he had confused the second of the nights on which he had served the captain a brandy.[12]

The confusion and the contradiction were most easily resolved by shifting the events described by Hyland to the previous evening (Sunday) when *Voyager* was at anchor in Jervis Bay. After watching some sport at HMAS *Creswell*, Stevens went to Captain Smyth's residence where he had two brandies followed by milk before returning to his ship at around 1900. It is likely that shortly after he returned to *Voyager*, he ate his evening meal in the day cabin. Soon after this, he asked Hyland to serve him a brandy, which he drank. There is sufficient similarity between the circumstances of the two nights for them to have been confused by Hyland who admitted that he had undergone a terrible experience on the night of the collision.

Two further points ought to be made about the evidence of the triple brandy. There is a very strong tradition in the RAN that captains do not drink at sea.[13] (This is in contrast to the situation in the Royal Navy which was generally more liberal.) It is difficult to conceive of Captain Stevens breaking this rule but making no attempt to conceal the fact. Whereas he could have poured and consumed the drink in secret, he had involved a very junior sailor who was likely to convey what had happened throughout his mess deck. There is also the matter of the empty glass. Stevens appears to have left the empty brandy tumbler in full view from the door of the cabin for a period of thirty minutes or more. It is almost beyond belief that Stevens would have been so open about breaking such a strict prohibition and one which he had praised publicly to several people throughout his career.[14]

The second point to be made, and one completely ignored at the second Commission, relates to the existence of alcohol in the blood of Lieutenant Cook. As the navigating officer, Cook was bound by the same code on drinking at sea. If the blood alcohol level of 0.015 per cent recorded in his post-mortem report is ascribed to the consumption of an alcoholic drink a short period before the collision, it seems that on the very same night that Captain Stevens decided to break a life-long rule, Cook happened to do so as well. This is most unlikely.

Putting aside the possibility of sheer coincidence, Cook is unlikely to have had any alcohol to drink for fear of detection by his captain. It should be recalled that Stevens and Cook had served together for only a short period. Cook was eager to please Stevens and would hardly have risked creating a poor first impression by drinking at sea. This would have been considered most unprofessional and definitely unwise. Cook certainly did not join Stevens for a post-dinner drink. Several officers who served with Cook after 1959 and who knew him well, commented that he would have been one of the very last RAN officers to have broken this convention. Although of little evidentiary value, the fact that Cook did not have a reputation as a drinker is of significance.

In fairness to Stevens and to Cook, the taint of misconduct implicit in the allegation that they drank alcohol on the night of the collision has neither been proved nor shown to have much credibility. The evidence is very weak and open to question. On balance, it is considerably more likely that neither drank any alcohol prior to the collision. And even admitting the possibility that they did, expert opinion (even that of Birrell) suggested that the recorded levels of blood alcohol would not have impaired the performance of either officer. Smyth was correct at the first Commission in concluding that the consumption of alcohol played no part in the causes of the collision.

However, Stevens may still have suffered from a degree of alcohol dependence. In researching this book and interviewing more than thirty naval officers who either served with Stevens or who knew him sufficiently well to pass valid judgement, none was of the view that he was either a drunkard or an alcoholic or that his nickname of 'Drunken Duncan' was coined because of past drinking. Many could recount incidents when Stevens had been as drunk as those he was with. Indeed, the statement was made by more than one officer that if Stevens were to be condemned for his alcohol consumption, many others were liable for the same censure. Alcohol was integral to the culture of the Navy. It played an important role in leisure and in social activity generally. For officers, the Wardroom Bar was normally the hub of activity in ships and isolated shore establishments. Alcohol was served during lunchtime, after work, with dinner, and following most sporting or ceremonial occasions. There is no disputing that a majority of naval officers below the rank of captain or senior commander in the late 1950s and early 1960s, regularly drank large quantities of alcohol which left them in a condition that would shock many unfamiliar with naval life. In those years an officer's capacity for alcohol was yet another reflection of his standing in the eyes of his peers.[15]

Stevens's reputation was for a lower alcohol capacity than what was considered 'normal' while he seemed to have suffered from the after-effects more than most. To single out Stevens for particular criticism would be too harsh and somewhat unfair. He was just like many other naval officers of his day. He drank too much, too often. His drinking was undisciplined and unwise for a man of his standing. According to Cabban, it greatly diminished his sense of responsibility and severely affected his ability to exercise command over *Voyager* and all who sailed in her. This did not make him a drunkard or an alcoholic but it did suggest he had some problems with his drinking, problems that were either ignored or went unnoticed, the gravity of which appears to have increased during 1963.

But was he a healthy man with a healthy man's capacity and toleration for alcohol while he commanded *Voyager*? Was he a man in very poor health throughout 1963 and did his health render him unfit to command? There was great difficulty in obtaining any positive statements about Stevens's health after 1959. He was not examined by a Navy doctor between July 1960 and February 1963 although the normal procedure in the RAN was for all officers to be subjected to an annual medical examination. However, Stevens's service with the Royal Navy, where medicals were only carried out every four years, meant that he was not examined and was able to avoid an examination.

For a considerable part of 1963 Stevens was unable to perform his duties either partially or completely. The dates listed below are minimum periods of Stevens's incapacity in 1963 as generally accepted by counsel at the Commission.

| | |
|---|---|
| 31 January | Confined to his cabin for one day after *Voyager* sailed from Sydney |
| 13 February | 'Recurrence of ulcer pain' |
| 25–27 February | Confined to cabin for two days after *Voyager* left Singapore |
| 18–21 March | Ill while *Voyager* was in Singapore |
| 23–24 March | Ill while *Voyager* was in Singapore |
| 30 March–2 April | Confined to cabin for two days when *Voyager* was in Hong Kong |
| 6 April | Ill while *Voyager* was in Hong Kong |
| 16 May | Ill while *Voyager* was in Hong Kong |
| 5–10 June | Ill during visit to Tokyo |

| 10–15 June | Confined to cabin for at least two days when *Voyager* transited from Tokyo to Subic Bay and ill for a period of five days |
| 10–12 August | Confined to cabin after *Voyager* departed Sydney for Williamstown |
| 2–5 December | Confined to cabin for three days while *Voyager* was in Williamstown |

In addition to these periods of illness, the Commissioners could also draw upon a large number of other incidents, some of a general nature, which had been corroborated either in part or in full by the testimony of witnesses, and which impinged upon any assessment of Stevens's health, well-being and self-discipline. These incidents covered the interaction of alcohol and ill-health later attributed to ulcer pain. The extent of the corroboration is also outlined.

First, Stevens was confined to his cabin for twenty-four hours after *Voyager* departed Sydney (and possibly later from Darwin) for the Far East in January 1963. This was confirmed by Lieutenant Griffith,[16] Lieutenant Carpendale[17] and Officer Steward Eddy,[18] who said he had heard this from Petty Officer Steward Watson at the time.

Second, Stevens's inability to see out the mess dinner held in his honour on his birthday during *Voyager*'s first visit to Singapore. Only one witness, Lieutenant Commander Blaikey, said he noticed nothing unusual about the evening.[19] Fifteen other witnesses gave testimony adverse to Stevens. Petty Officer Steward Freeman said that Stevens had had five or six drinks after lunch on the day of the dinner.[20] Leading Steward Leatherbarrow said he saw Stevens drinking in his day cabin and that he was slouched and heavy-eyed.[21]

Lieutenant Commander Wright said Stevens 'entered the wardroom looking flushed and was unsteady on his feet'.[22] Steward Menkins remarked that he looked as though he had been drinking,[23] and Tiller said he 'looked dull and as if he was not fully aware of what was going on'.[24] Lieutenant Somerville recalled that he 'went down on his hands and knees' as a show of humour.[25] Howland, who sat next to Stevens at the dinner, said he looked as if he had been drinking. He 'spoke slowly and framed his words carefully'.[26] Sub-Lieutenant Forrest mentioned that 'during the soup course, Stevens was doubled up as if in pain'.[27] Petty Officer Watson said he 'had difficulty with the meal and left assisted'.[28] Lieutenant Holmes stated that the 'atmosphere in the wardroom was embarrassed and hushed'.[29] Martin was not in attendance but heard about the dinner five weeks later.[30]

Third, Stevens's behaviour at the reception at Hong Kong during *Voyager*'s second visit on 13 May 1963 for the resident British Army Group. Martin said that Stevens 'was slightly flushed, that he was talking slightly more loudly and slightly more than usual, and I remember feeling a twinge of embarrassment for my guests who were in the group at the same time'.[31] Martin thought this was caused by alcohol. A civilian at the same party, Piet Liebenshutz, said Stevens had difficulty framing his words and was shabby in appearance. He attributed this to drinking.[32]

Fourth, Stevens's inability to see out the lunch held on board HMS *Rothesay* on 16 May 1963. This was due to illness, not intoxication. He then slept for several hours in an officer's cabin in *Rothesay*.[33]

Fifth, Stevens's general demeanour during *Voyager*'s visit to Karatsu from 24 to 28 May 1963. Leading Seaman Britton recalled seeing Stevens at a nightclub and that he appeared flushed and unsteady.[34] An Australian liaison officer, Squadron Leader Farrelly, remarked that Stevens did not look well at any stage and did not seem 'to have much life in him'. Farrelly said that Stevens drank consistently rather than excessively.[35]

Sixth, Stevens's inability to fulfil many of the programmed events during *Voyager*'s visit to Tokyo from 5 to 10 June 1963. Martin remembered that Stevens looked unwell throughout the visit and that his ulcer was very active and caused him pain and discomfort.[36] He remarked that Stevens drank more than he should have and that he 'was disappointed in his captain'.[37] Able Seaman Mead stated that after the party held by the Australian Ambassador to Japan on 6 June, Stevens returned on board 'glassy-eyed and unsteady'.[38] Most probably that same night, Stevens had dinner with a group of Australians at the Gaslight Restaurant. An embassy official, Arthur Jamieson, said that Stevens's head was nodding, that he was slumped in his chair and that he overheard him say to Willis, 'You will look after me, won't you Jim'.[39]

At the reception held the following day in HMS *Alert*, Howland said that Stevens seemed quite normal at the outset but towards the end of the party it was obvious he had been drinking. That night he attended a buffet dinner given by the Australian naval attache in Tokyo, Captain Dollard. Farrelly said that Stevens 'looked under the weather' from the start and predicted he would have difficulty seeing the night through.[40] This was the worst he had seen Stevens. Jamieson, who was also present, commented that Stevens looked 'as if he had more to drink than other people'[41] and even Dollard thought he was 'overtaken by alcohol'.[42] When Stevens appeared unable to continue, Farrelly arranged for a car to transport him back to *Voyager*.[43]

The next day Stevens participated in a picnic organised by the Dollards. He was described by Willis as looking unwell. Dollard said Stevens was unable to attend a reception hosted by a Japanese admiral in the early evening, remaining at the Dollards' home where he vomited before returning to *Voyager*.[44] When Willis heard that Stevens was unable to attend a church parade the following morning, he saw the captain in his sea cabin looking 'washed out, tired and slightly sorry for himself'.[45] However, he made a remarkable recovery to attend a luncheon held in *Voyager* for the Australian Ambassador.[46]

Seventh, Stevens was confined to his cabin for a number of days after *Voyager* sailed for Subic Bay from Tokyo. Most witnesses agreed that Cabban had command for two to three days. Martin thought it might have been five days[47] while Howland, in his initial statement, stated it was five days. Under examination at the Commission he changed this to three or four days.[48] Chief Petty Officer Young heard rumours that it was five days.[49] Petty Officer Strachan said he had to wait for six days until Stevens had recovered to receive his rating (promotion to petty officer).[50] However, Lieutenant Commander Carpendale recalled that Stevens got up after two days. In letters to his wife — seized and examined by the Commissioners — Carpendale said that despite his ulcer Stevens 'continued to knock hell out of himself' and remarked that he had no capacity for alcohol.[51] Lieutenants Redman[52] and Holmes[53] remembered that Cabban had told them he had assumed command as the captain was ill.

Eighth, Stevens was confined to his cabin for the duration of *Voyager*'s passage from Sydney to Williamstown. Martin said that Stevens looked unwell, a state he described as the 'Tokyo look',[54] and that he did not see Stevens until the ship arrived off Port Phillip Bay. Griffith's recollection was that he looked tired and had had a 'heavy night'.[55] Lieutenant Commander Coombs recalled that on the day of *Voyager*'s departure he went to Stevens's sea cabin at about 1700 and found him under the covers of his bunk.[56]

To these specific incidents a series of witnesses made some general observations. Leading Seaman Freeman[57] and Able Seaman Irvine[58] said that on a few occasions they had served Stevens coffee laced with brandy at 0900 while *Voyager* was in harbour. Lieutenant Commander Martin,[59] Surgeon Lieutenant Tiller[60] and Officer Steward Eddy[61] recalled seeing Stevens during the day in his cabin sipping brandy while doing paperwork. Naval Shipwright Gardiner stated that up to the first visit to Hong Kong, Stevens occasionally 'looked sort of glassy eyed' in the late afternoons in his cabin.[62] Petty Officer Webber complained of having to clean vomit from the heads (toilets) near the captain's cabin,[63] and Able Seaman Murray stated he heard Stevens vomiting in these heads about twice each month.[64] Commander Money[65] and Lieutenant Tuke RN[66] both stated they had occasionally had a pre-lunch drink with Stevens when *Voyager* was not at sea. One witness, Lieutenant Keith Cleland (an RAN Reserve officer), approached the Commission offering to give evidence. He said Tuke told him that Stevens chose to travel by train from Sydney to Williamstown after Captain Dovers's court martial because he could then consume a bottle of brandy overnight.[67]

In addition to the events of 1963, there was also the incident in mid-January (possibly the 14th) 1964 when Captain D. A. H. Clarke,[68] commanding HMAS *Anzac*, stated he saw Stevens bending over a guardrail of *Voyager* obviously in great pain.[69] Ash described this as being 'in any event equivocal in its evidentiary effect'[70] and dismissed it as possibly the product of some other ailment. This was a very weak view to put but nonetheless a necessary one given that he had earlier argued that there was no pattern of ulcer pain after 31 December 1963.

The question then remained: to what extent did Stevens's ulcer condition affect his performance during 1963? The best judge of this was Stevens himself. It emerges that on several occasions during the year he was concerned his condition was so grave that it could have terminated his command. Had he not been worried by his ill-health, he would not have gone to the lengths he did to conceal his condition.

Sir Jack Stevens privately disputed the claim that Stevens actively concealed his illness:

> Many witnesses gave evidence that Duncan had mentioned his stomach to them ... These two doctors [McNeill and Tiller] may have made a faulty diagnosis but this does not constitute deliberate concealment ... The only weak link for us is his request to Leading Seaman SBA Wilson at Williamstown in December 1963 not to send for a doctor but to treat him himself.[71]

But Sir Jack misunderstands the issue. It is one thing to mention a condition and imply that it is under control, and quite another to describe the extent of its effects. If Stevens's own actions are to be used as a guide and a measure, there is little doubt that his ulcer was almost continuously active throughout 1963 and that its effects were near debilitating. Consequently, there would have been few periods in 1963 when he was fit to command *Voyager*.

At the beginning of this chapter the possibility was raised that there might have been other factors affecting the behaviour of Stevens, particularly his remarkable ability to recover rapidly from illness. A sufficient number of such incidents were mentioned at the Commission for a pattern to emerge. Several instances can be cited.

On 9 June 1967, Stevens invited Sir Laurence McIntyre, the Australian Ambassador to Japan, and Lady McIntyre to luncheon on board *Voyager*. At 1130, Cabban stated that Stevens looked very tired and was clearly unwell. Yet thirty minutes later, Stevens greeted his guests and looked in good health. Although Ash used this incident to suggest that Cabban's memory was either faulty or he had overstated Stevens's condition, Cabban stated that Stevens 'could pull himself together, though, quite well'.

Cabban said that during the week *Voyager* was alongside in Sydney before sailing for her refit in Williamstown, Stevens spent most of the working day confined to bed. However, Ash was able to show that Stevens had attended a number of pre-refit conferences.

Cabban stated that Stevens was very ill after returning from Captain

Dovers's court martial while *Voyager* was at Williamstown. Yet Stevens was able to spend the weekend with the Higgerson family, who stated at the Commission that Stevens looked perfectly well.

Stevens's remarkable ability to recover rapidly when the occasion demanded required explanation. At the Commission, none was offered nor seemed required. One explanation was offered nearly ten years later.

Don Chipp discusses the whole *Voyager* affair in his autobiography, *The Third Man*, published in 1978. It is a valuable piece of writing given Chipp's involvement as the Navy Minister during the second Royal Commission. Of greatest significance is his description of what the Commissioners allegedly uncovered during the inquiry. Most startling is the revelation that 'they', meaning the Royal Commissioners,

> also discovered another fact which never found its way into the report, and which to my mind provides the answer to a great number of puzzling features of Captain Stevens's behaviour, and more particularly, the key to the great number of contradictions given by witnesses before the Commission ...
>
> The key was given to an off-the-record session of the Commission in which a doctor offered to give evidence, provided it did not find itself on the official record. The evidence was that he was secretly prescribing amphetamines for the captain. The drug, amphetamine sulphate — now rarely prescribed — served as a relief from pain and gave the recipient a 'mild high' . . . To some people it could be quite euphoric. This explains the contradictions in the evidence of the captain being miserable, low, sick, in pain, and an hour later being bright, charming, witty and the life of the party, with no pain.[72]

Chipp states that he then (probably meaning some time in 1967 or early 1968) asked a distinguished Melbourne physician to draw a scenario of Stevens's likely health and behaviour. This appeared to explain — or at least to resemble — Stevens's behaviour. It was the first public indication that drugs had been a factor in the loss of *Voyager*. Chipp's statements seem to have been accepted without question. Then, in 1984, in an article in the *Australian* by defence commentator Peter Young marking the twentieth anniversary of the sinking, Young said: 'Much later information which did not come out even at the second Royal Commission indicated that he [Stevens] may also have been taking amphetamines'.[73]

Although he may not have fully appreciated the consequences, Chipp's statements constitute very grave allegations against the Royal Commissioners, the Department of the Navy, several of the counsel involved in the inquiry, Captain Stevens, and the unnamed doctor. In effect, Chipp alleges that the Commissioners concealed relevant evidence with the probable connivance of Burt; that they failed to cite this evidence although it related to Stevens's behaviour and possibly to the causes of the collision; and that Stevens was taking drugs that were obtained from naval sources with the assistance of a naval medical officer who had concealed this fact for three years.

It must be stressed, however, that amphetamines were not at that time prohibited drugs. Because there is no statement to the contrary from Chipp — or in the post-mortem report — there is also the inference that Stevens was taking this drug at the time of the collision.

The spectre of drugs was first raised at the 1967 Commission during the cross-examination of Lieutenant Commander Alan Kyd, a naval dentist, who took passage in *Voyager* from Singapore to Hong Kong.

> Porter: Is it correct that your first impression of the captain when he came in [to the wardroom for the mess dinner on his birthday] was that you thought he might have been taking a few drugs, a few drinks on top of a high powered drug?
>
> Kyd: That idea did occur.
>
> Porter: That was a very clear impression you had?
>
> Kyd: Yes.[74]

Ash objected to this line of questioning because it had not been put to Tiller who had by then returned to Britain and who would have been far better placed to give evidence on this matter.

There was no further mention of drugs until the forty-fourth day of the inquiry when Hiatt cross-examined Don McDonald, one of *Voyager*'s sick-berth attendants. Hiatt, Cabban's counsel, said that in view of evidence that had emerged since Kyd appeared, he felt bound to pursue a line of questioning aimed at establishing whether Stevens might have been taking any drugs.

> Just taking the evidence which has been given, we would submit it is not susceptible of a natural unassisted process of convalescence for someone to fall asleep on Saturday night quite suddenly ... be vomiting first thing in the morning, be unable to do routine duties during the Saturday morning to the extent of having to ask for relief by someone else, and then to be in a condition by quarter past twelve as described by Sir Laurence McIntyre.[75]

Burbury could see that he wanted 'to ask this witness whether, to his knowledge, the captain ever took, say, stimulating drugs?'[76] Hiatt acknowledged this was his intention. As expected, Ash objected but Burbury maintained his willingness to accept any evidence that might ultimately be relevant.

> If this is relevant to the captain's condition observed objectively from time to time, then it seems it is admissible. If the fact is that he recovered very quickly through the assistance of medicine or even some drug, that would seem to me to be relevant. So far there is not the slightest evidence about it.[77]

Hiatt then put his question to McDonald who was, incidentally, by this time a civilian.

> Hiatt: What stocks of amphetamines were kept on *Voyager* at the time of this commission?

McDonald: I cannot recall the drug.

Hiatt: Does that mean that you cannot say whether stocks were held or whether they were not, or does that mean you think they probably were not?

McDonald: I think they probably were not, but then I cannot absolutely remember all the drugs we had.[78]

Registers of drugs held on board RAN ships in this period indicate that amphetamines were held, although the records of the quantity of any drug used by ships were routinely destroyed after twelve months. By the time of the second Commission in 1967, the records relating to the drugs consumed by *Voyager* in 1963 had been destroyed. The specific form of amphetamine supplied throughout the RAN in this period was an amphetamine sulphate; the same type mentioned by Chipp. Although this does not definitely establish that the drugs taken by Stevens (assuming he did take them) were obtained from a naval source, the possibility remains open.

Finding no evidence to support the allegation that Stevens had ever taken amphetamines, the matter of drugs did not arise again and played no part in the summing up or the Commissioners' report. However, there was some investigation of this matter outside the Commission.

In a statement dated 11 August 1967, Tiller stated that on the morning the Pakistan Shield was presented to *Voyager*

Captain Stevens entered the sickbay and ordered all the sailors out. When he and I were alone, he asked me to give him a stimulant because he felt that he needed to boost himself up for the presentation of the trophy.

He looked unwell as I have described and said that he was tired. I told him that I was sorry but did not agree with giving stimulants for those reasons. He left without much comment.[79]

For some reason, Burt did not raise the matter of drugs until after the evidence of McDonald. He then telephoned Tiller in Britain and asked him several questions about Stevens and whether he took any drugs.[80] Burt also had his junior, Philip Jeffrey, ask Tiller's counsel, Barry O'Keefe QC, for some further information on matters raised in his earlier statement. O'Keefe then wrote to Tiller because he was 'anxious to find out whether or not you would want this information to be made available to those assisting the Commission.'[81] Tiller had already agreed to respond by answering written questions put to him by Jeffrey. During his telephone conversation with Burt, Tiller said he was in no doubt the stimulant Stevens wanted was amphetamine.

When I asked Burt[82] why he had not pursued the matter of amphetamines given Tiller's comments and the possibility that Stevens had taken them before and would probably have taken them later, he stated that he did not want to embark on a 'wild goose' chase in searching for evidence that would not be easy to find. At any rate, it could be said that if Stevens was unfit to command it did not need the matter of amphetamines to give it substance.

The discussion between Stevens and Tiller in the sickbay has been separately corroborated by John Wilson, the Leading Sick-Berth Attendant who was also present. He stated in a letter to me that Stevens entered *Voyager*'s sickbay between 0800 and 0900 and directed other patients to leave. As Tiller was not then in the sickbay, Stevens told Wilson he had a 'presentation to endure' and that he needed to be 'on the ball'.[83] He asked Wilson if he had any amphetamines to get him through. In reply, Wilson said that Tiller had the keys to the medical chest where such drugs were stored. Stevens left the sickbay. Shortly afterwards, Tiller arrived and Stevens returned. After a 'somewhat heated discussion', Stevens went away empty-handed.[84]

When Chipp's book was released in 1978, Wilson believed it reflected adversely on him. He feared that as the only medical staff member on board *Voyager* between August 1963 and the collision it might have been thought that he had prescribed amphetamines for Stevens. Wilson states that he contacted his local newspaper, the *Adelaide Advertiser*, where he had seen mention of Chipp's statement and claimed that to his best knowledge, Stevens was not taking amphetamines in the period he served in *Voyager*.[85] Wilson was subsequently contacted by a reporter from Australian Associated Press who was told by Wilson that 'Stevens was not on drugs'.

The suggestion that there was a secret or off-the-record session of the Commission is also trenchantly denied by the three Royal Commissioners.[86] In fact, all three were appalled by Chipp's statements, which surprisingly, they had not seen before, when shown to them by me. Burbury stated:

> I am astounded at the assertion that there was a secret session of the Commission. It is a complete fabrication without the slightest foundation. It is a grave slur on the integrity of my two brother judges and myself. Indeed, had I known of it earlier I would have contemplated asking the Attorney General to institute proceedings for contempt of the Commission.[87]

Had there been a closed session of the Commission, Burt would no doubt have been aware that it had taken place. If it had involved amphetamines he certainly would have insisted that the matter be brought before the Commission in open session. However, when I raised this with him, Burt had no recollection of any such session of the Commission and put the view strongly that it was virtually impossible for it to have taken place without his knowledge.

If the Commissioners and counsel assisting have no knowledge of any 'off-the-record' session or of the matters raised in Chipp's autobiography, then the only other possible explanation seems to be that Chipp, as Navy Minister, possessed information that was not publicly disclosed. It could then follow that when he came to write his autobiography, as a matter of conscience, he decided to reveal what he knew but sought to distance himself from the information (to avoid the possible suggestion that he improperly withheld evidence from the Royal Commission) by alluding to a meeting of which there is no record and by implicating the Royal Commissioners.

When I interviewed Chipp, he stood by his statements. When asked about his allusion to amphetamines, he commented that the (unnamed) doctor came to 'us',[88] — suggesting by this the Naval Board, its representatives or its counsel at the inquiry — and spoke about amphetamines. The choice of 'us' is significant. This is consistent with Jess's recollection that Chipp told him after the Commission concluded that Stevens was taking amphetamines and that he had known this for some time.[89]

What, then, is the evidence for Chipp's claim? What was the point of making these allegations? And how could anyone possibly have known whether Stevens had taken amphetamines on the night of the collision? In answering the first question, it could be said that an adequate explanation has never been given for Stevens's alleged rapid recovery on several occasions during 1963. The qualification, 'alleged', is warranted because there is no material evidence that it was either rapid or complete. Rather than taking drugs to assist his recovery, it is equally possible that Stevens may not have been as ill as Cabban believed or that Stevens may not have looked all that well when he was met by people outside *Voyager*. It would appear to be a question of degree in matters that are ordinarily imprecise and open to a wide divergence of opinion. It should also be pointed out that the events that Stevens attended after giving the appearance of being very sick, were not physically demanding in themselves. On the contrary, the luncheon with McIntyre and spending a weekend with the Higgersons placed no great burden on Stevens's health. At the refit conferences he would have deferred to his engineering officers.

In answering the second and third questions, the lack of detail in Chipp's remarks raises more questions than it answers. There does not seem to have been any point to his 'revelations' about amphetamines, other than to damage Stevens's reputation even further, and it would be impossible to know whether Stevens had taken any amphetamines on the day or night of the collision. There was also no comment on this matter in the post-mortem report.

On balance, Stevens should have the benefit of any doubt that he took amphetamines regularly, or at all. However, his request for a stimulant on the day of the Pakistan Shield presentation still requires explanation.

This incident is without precedent or parallel. It does not fit into any pattern and should be treated in isolation. The most likely interpretation is that on this occasion, Stevens felt particularly fatigued and unwell. He was unable to avoid attending the ceremony which was to take place at Garden Island in full view of the Fleet Commander with the press and television reporters in attendance. This no doubt made him anxious. These circumstances made this day different from most others in 1963. It would be especially demanding for Stevens who would play a leading role in extending hospitality to the Pakistani High Commissioner and other important guests over luncheon. It was probably for these special reasons that Stevens wanted something to ensure he was at his best by the middle of the day.

The issue of amphetamines is of little real consequence and serves only as yet another distraction from determining the causes of the collision. As Chipp's statements appear to be unsubstantiated, they only serve to add controversy when and where it was least needed. Surely, if Chipp had specific information about Stevens and amphetamines, he should have made a full statement to the Commission setting out when he first received information about this matter, who told him, and who else may have known. Of course, if he had this information during the inquiry and directed that it not be disclosed, such action would deserve vigorous condemnation. Chipp's statements are too damaging to be left without further clarification. Certainly Captain Stevens's reputation deserves better treatment than a devastating but anonymous narrative. The duty now rests with Chipp to clarify his statements and substantiate his allegations.

Putting aside the alleged involvement of drugs, the question remains: which was the dominant factor leading to Stevens's incapacity during 1963? Was it alcohol, an active ulcer, or the effects of alcohol on an active ulcer?

The most balanced and reasonable conclusion is that Stevens did have a duodenal ulcer which was easily exacerbated either by stress or alcohol. It seems he did not have a great capacity for alcohol and this made his 'hangovers' more debilitating than for an average person. Occasions when he was ill for several days cannot be accounted for merely by alcohol. It is usual for 'hangovers' to last around twenty-four hours. Given that Stevens never engaged in prolonged bouts of excessive drinking, it is likely that alcohol, coupled with the anxiety produced by the demands of commanding a warship in an operational zone, were directly responsible for exacerbations of his ulcer. After the ship left Tokyo and Stevens stopped drinking, he was not unwell for even a single day. He would also have been less anxious at that time because it was towards the end of *Voyager*'s deployment to the Strategic Reserve and he could look forward to returning to Sydney and a less demanding period during his ship's refit.

But was Stevens unwell, and therefore unfit to command, at the time of the collision? Other than the evidence of Captain Clarke, there is nothing to suggest that Stevens was not constantly in good health throughout January and February 1964 or that on any occasion in the new year he had too much to drink. Lieutenant Peter Sinclair, who saw Stevens at various times throughout the day in this period but who was not called as a witness, stated that at no time did Stevens smell of alcohol or give the appearance of having had anything to drink.[90]

The great weight of evidence shows that just before the collision he was probably in better health than he had been since taking command of *Voyager*. A series of witnesses who saw Stevens and spoke with him during the weekend before the collision said he looked well and was in good spirits. All the witnesses who survived the collision and who saw Stevens during the day said he looked perfectly well.

There was no evidence produced, other than inferences to be drawn from the now only *possible* consumption of the triple brandy, that Stevens was unfit to command *Voyager* on 10 February 1964 through ill-health. Of course, this is not to make a judgement on his professional ability or his competency to command a destroyer during fleetwork exercises.

All the evidence suggests that Stevens looked perfectly well on the weekend prior to the collision. Thus, if Stevens was not an alcoholic and his ulcer was not active, and he did not take any amphetamine, the collision was clearly the result of navigational factors and had nothing to do with Stevens's health or him being in any way unfit to command *Voyager*.

# 18

# The Burbury Report

THE COMMISSIONERS' REPORT was released on 25 February 1968. Its title was *Report of Royal Commissioners on the Statement of Lieutenant-Commander Cabban and Matters Incidental Thereto*, also called the Burbury Report.[1] The report proved to be as cumbersome as its full title. The confidential advice given to the Naval Board by those officers who had been involved in the inquiry to assist its counsel was that the Commission would probably find Stevens was unfit to retain command 'because of an ulcer which he aggravated by unwise drinking' but would likely find that the Board did not know of his unfitness or Cabban's allegations. As for Robertson, the Board was advised that his submission was likely to be accepted, that Spicer's finding would be overturned and that 'the criticisms which Sir John Spicer made of Captain Robertson's actions should be removed'.[2]

The release of the report coincided with a reshuffle of the Ministry by John Gorton after he had become Prime Minister following the accidental drowning of Holt on 17 December 1967. Chipp was dropped from the Ministry, principally for supporting Snedden as a candidate for prime minister on the death of Holt. (Snedden's vote could have split the pro-Gorton vote sufficiently to give Paul Hasluck the prime ministership.) Publicly, *Voyager* was blamed for the ruin of Chipp's 'first ministerial career' and Gorton was happy for his decision to be interpreted in this way.[4] The new Minister for the Navy was Bert Kelly, from South Australia.

The Burbury Report was a document of 231 closely typed pages and 38 pages of appendixes. The last of these, Appendix G, consisted of a detailed chronology consisting of *Voyager*'s movements and activities from January 1963 to the date of the collision, events in the personal life of Captain Stevens, and the major allegations made in relation to them in the Cabban Statement. The Commissioners' findings and comments with respect to Cabban's allegations were summarised below the dates relating to each allegation. They also drew conclusions and made findings about Stevens and matters which were not alleged, prompted or even mentioned by Cabban. Conversely, there were some

272

matters on which the Commissioners expressed no view. These instances, and their significance, will be discussed later.

After some preliminary discussion the Commissioners set out the origins of the Cabban Statement and what its creation and subsequent circulation was meant to achieve. Then followed the first of a series of observations describing the Commissioners' evaluation of the Cabban Statement:

> the conclusion is inescapable that it was the product of the mind of a man who had become a partisan to a cause [that of Robertson] and was influenced by his partisan attitude to paint a highly coloured picture of Captain Stevens ...
>
> The picture of Captain Stevens given by Cabban in his evidence is therefore vastly different from the picture which he gave in the tape-recording ...
>
> Cabban's sworn evidence fell far short of supporting what he dictated ...
>
> We add neither the 'Cabban Statement' nor his evidence was coloured by any dishonest motive or by any malice towards the late Captain Stevens.[5]

Of all Cabban's allegations, those of a general nature relating to Stevens's behaviour during periods when *Voyager* was in harbour, were found to be untrue. However, the Commissioners were prepared to accept his evidence on most points. They accepted that Stevens was periodically confined to his cabin through illness as Cabban had stated. They found that Cabban's allegations about the birthday mess dinner were 'substantially true'; that he was assisted on board by several sailors when returning to his ship during the first visit to Hong Kong; that he was mildly drunk during a party given in *Voyager* for the British Army Garrison in Hong Kong; that he was indisposed at the *Rothesay* luncheon; that his drinking during the Karatsu visit 'was unwise having regard to the condition of his health'; that he 'suddenly nodded off' at the dinner at the Gaslight Restaurant in Tokyo; that he again 'suddenly nodded off' at a buffet dinner held by Captain Dollard; that he was unable to attend a Japanese Admiral's dinner party and that he slept at the Dollards' home that evening before drinking a brandy and vomiting; that he was confined to his cabin through illness after the visit to Tokyo for 'a period of at least two days and possibly more'; that he was confined to his cabin during the passage from Sydney to Williamstown; and that he drank a considerable quantity of brandy when returning to Williamstown by train from Sydney and was ill for the next four days. However, Stevens 'was not a drunkard nor an alcoholic. Nor did he periodically become intoxicated when *Voyager* was in port'.[6]

The most notable absence of a definite finding concerned the alleged falsification of *Voyager*'s punishment logs, although the Commissioners were prepared to find that Cabban did not have command for five days between Tokyo and Subic Bay. Their rather tentative suggestion was a period in excess of two days which would have nevertheless prevented Stevens from taking a defaulters parade on 11 June 1963 despite his name and signature being shown as the officer who conducted the parade. Cabban's counsel argued that the two matters were directly linked.

It is significant that of the period in Tokyo, the Commissioners concluded that

> We are satisfied that during this period Captain Stevens drank far too much for a man with an ulcer condition. His drinking can only be described as unwise and undisciplined . . . We have no doubt that this relative excessive drinking seriously affected his health, caused him to be ill on Sunday 9 June and subsequently caused him to be confined to his cabin through illness for several days out of Tokyo.[7]

Yet, they still avoided commenting on the punishment log and Cabban's evidence that Stevens had threatened him with a mutiny charge despite recounting the considerable evidence that something unusual had indeed happened.

> It is not a matter on which, under our terms of reference we are required to make any finding. It is essentially a matter which goes to Cabban's credit. We do not exclude the possibility that some incident of the kind occurred, but we are unable to accept in its details Cabban's dramatised account of the incident.[8]

This was a curious conclusion to draw given that the Commissioners had heard in evidence that it was mandatory for the officer awarding the punishment to sign the log while they themselves noted that Stevens 'could not have conducted a defaulters parade on Tuesday 11 June' 1963. If the records were changed to show Stevens was in command for that period, and the Commissioners obviously admit this possibility, he must have been in a desperate frame of mind and his threat to Cabban is consistent which such a mental state. The period of five days mentioned by Cabban was also considered important by Stevens who took steps to prevent the duration of his illness being known.

It is noteworthy that the Commissioners mentioned later in their report that a defaulters parade deferred from 2 December to 5 December 1963 was explained in the punishment log as being 'delayed due to Captain absent on duty'.

> This we are bound to say shows that Captain Stevens was very anxious not to disclose the state of his health. The delay from 2 to 5 December was due to illness and not due to his being absent on duty.[9]

Why the Commissioners did not link these two incidents — which were obviously prompted by the same motive — to produce a more definite finding is difficult to understand. It shows that Stevens had learned something from the drama of the passage between Tokyo and Subic Bay, and that others were probably aware of his directions to alter the log for that period.

Before the Commissioners stated their finding on Stevens's fitness to command, they made oblique references to some of the witnesses they had heard. Griffith was 'obviously most reluctant to give evidence adverse to the late Captain Stevens', while Petty Officer Steward Freeman was 'obviously (and understandably) reluctant' as well.[10] Griffith told me that he was extremely angry with Cabban when he heard about and later read the Cabban Statement. He felt it was morally wrong of Cabban to have spoken as he did although he conceded Cabban had the right to make such a statement and admired his courage of conviction. Griffith believed the Cabban Statement was in places exaggerated although he agreed with the Commissioners' finding that Cabban had not made up any incident mentioned in his Statement. Out of loyalty to Stevens and as a product of his anger with the excesses of the Cabban Statement, Griffith stated that he felt he should neutralise the Statement, and so 'over-corrected' the picture he portrayed of Stevens in his evidence at the Commission. Regarding Stevens's shiphandling ability, Griffith thought he was not a good shiphandler and tended to rely too heavily on others.[11]

The Commissioners placed 'great reliance on Lieutenant Martin's evidence'[12] and regarded Lieutenant Holmes as 'an honest and reliable witness'.[13] Asprey told me that a number of witnesses did not tell the truth or the whole truth, and that the Commissioners considered having action taken against some of them for perjury. However, as they were mainly Navy witnesses who had sought to protect the RAN and as their evidence would not alter the findings, such action would only have served to hurt the Navy further and was not initiated. The public was aware that some of the witnesses had not been as helpful as they could.

Having made a finding on the Cabban Statement, the Commissioners also made a finding on its author.

> We regard Cabban as an unreliable witness but not as a dishonest witness. When we say he is an unreliable witness we refer rather to those parts of his evidence which involve his assessment of Captain Stevens' behaviour and condition or his judgement of a situation rather than to those parts of his evidence relating to specific incidents. In many instances indeed he emerged as an entirely reliable witness on detailed objective facts ... we do not believe that Cabban at any point of his evidence deliberately invented incidents which did not take place.[14]

Burt told me he was disappointed that the Royal Commission took a low view of Cabban's reliability as a witness given that his statement had been corroborated. He also believed it was unfair to disregard him on some matters simply because no corroboration was available.[15] Reynolds regarded the Commissioners' description of Cabban as a sublime compromise and not the way a judge would usually address the credibility of a witness.

With these preliminaries decided, the Commissioners gave their answer to the first term of reference.

> The conclusion is inescapable that (answering the question as at 31 December 1963) the late Captain Stevens was then unfit to retain command of *Voyager* because his physical condition did not conform to the very high standard of fitness required of a Captain holding that appointment ...
>
> It is not possible to say for how long after the 31 December 1963 the late Captain Stevens would have been unlikely to have remained unfit to retain command of *Voyager*.[16]

The date (31 December 1963) coincided with the end of the period covered by the Cabban Statement while the latter paragraph was an indirect means of stating that Stevens was generally unfit to retain command of *Voyager* at the time of the collision. The cause of the unfitness was

> intermittent recurrences of his duodenal ulcer trouble between January 1963 and December 1963 (to which his drinking habits contributed) ... We think this conclusion must follow even if at that particular point of time his ulcer was not clinically fully reactivated.[17]

This was a far more adverse finding than most would have expected, and went well beyond what Cabban had stated in his evidence. Neither Cabban nor his counsel had ever gone as far as alleging that Stevens was unfit to command. In finding that the reason was through sickness rather than excessive consumption of alcohol, Burt believed the Commissioners may not have realised that this was a more serious finding. Whereas if it were found that Stevens was unfit through drinking, it could be argued that when he was at sea, he was sober, and therefore fit to command when it mattered most. However, if he were unwell, he would be in this condition wherever he was. Burt considered that this was a more serious matter and a greater indictment of the Navy and its administration. Consequently, he was surprised by Murphy's submissions that this was the Navy's preferred finding.

Whether or not the Naval Board knew or ought to have known of Cabban's allegations was dealt with quickly. They concluded that McNeill *should* have made a report of Stevens's ill-health, that Tiller *ought* to have done so and that Wilson *might* have, had the circumstances been different. Whether Dollard and James Willis should have reported Stevens to the Naval Board was not answered by the Commissioners, who were content to say that neither failed in any duty imposed upon them. As none of these personnel had made any report on Stevens, and given that McNicoll was in his flagship in company with *Voyager* and nothing had come to his attention, the Commissioners concluded that the Naval Board were not aware of anything contained in the Cabban Statement.

As the position of Willis was the most precarious, he had emerged well from the inquiry. Sir James Willis told the author that he had complete confidence in *Voyager* during the 1963 deployment and would have had no hesitation in making a report on Stevens if he felt it was warranted. But his readiness to make such a report is less of an issue. There was sufficient justification in the little that Willis did know for more positive action to have been taken. Willis stated that he was aware that Stevens had stomach complaints and that this was aggravated by a little 'too much drink and a little too much activity'. He said that Stevens at times 'lacked self-control'. Yet when Cabban saw Willis in Tokyo, Willis maintains that he was surprised by the seriousness of Cabban's report. The only action Willis took was to tell Stevens that he ought not to drink as it worsened his condition. This was not nearly enough.

Stevens was evidently barely coping with the demands the deployment was making upon his health. Willis should not have been content with seeing him return to a state of health that was barely adequate. Stevens needed to be in better health than he was and probably required closer attention than he could have received from Tiller.

As for Stevens, the Commissioners concluded that he 'cannot altogether escape moral censure for failing to disclose what he must have known was a recurring condition of some seriousness'.[18]

As there was an affirmative answer to the first term of reference, the Commissioners had now to decide whether Stevens's unfitness to command justified overturning Spicer. In this the Commissioners regarded themselves 'as having the full authority of an appellate Court in reviewing the finding of facts of a trial judge sitting without a jury'.[19] This narrow conception of the Commission's status should be contrasted with the inconsistency of its general approach to the matter under review. This involved something of a reversal on its previous attitude which held that external factors, such as public interest, ought not to determine the scope or conduct of the inquiry.

> It would be a mistake to adopt a legalistic approach . . . The truth is that the limits of our duty to inquire under Question 2(b) cannot and ought not to be defined by abstract considerations . . . they are inevitably and only properly defined by our own sense of what in the public interest and in the interests of those affected by Sir John Spicer's findings, ought in justice to be done once we are satisfied that a substantial link is established between our finding of Captain Stevens' unfitness to retain command and Sir John Spicer's findings.[20]

What, then, was the substantive connection between their finding and that of Spicer? It was relayed so quickly and in such vague terms that it almost escapes detection:

> we are satisfied that Sir John Spicer's line of reasoning in relation to a number of his findings was substantially influenced if not dominated by an underlying assumption that the late Captain Stevens must necessarily have been completely

277

fit and alert and incapable of the kind of error of judgement which certain inferences which the evidence suggested were reasonably open, would impute to him.[21]

Notwithstanding the Commissioners' best efforts to couch their message in densely written prose, they had obviously accepted the sense of Samuels's submissions as a justification for re-examining the navigational aspects of the collision. What followed was a logical refutation of Spicer's findings but it was a refutation conducted in a vacuum. It did not draw upon the affirmative answer to the first term of reference and the all-important nexus between Stevens's unfitness and the causes of the collision.

The reason for this was explained by Asprey. When the Commission was convened in May 1967, before their inquiry began, the three Commissioners examined the evidence and argument presented to Spicer in 1964 and concluded that Spicer had erred. However, to avoid criticising and embarrassing Spicer, they were prepared to infer that the new evidence they heard led them to this belief. Thus, the link between the navigational aspects and Cabban was important more for appearance's sake. Their prodding of Reynolds for a link between the collision and Cabban was in the hope of finding an alternative means of overturning Spicer, and avoiding, as much as possible, having to base their findings with respect to the collision on Cabban's evidence.[22]

Adopting the principles of an appellate court, a connection between the 1967 evidence and the cause of the collision is not made because by these principles it cannot be made. The approach to Robertson's situation was on the basis of unchallenged facts and their arrangement by Spicer to produce or arrive at a finding or conclusion. Thus, if Spicer was seen to have arrived at a finding or conclusion that was internally illogical, if not impossible, then the Commissioners could replace his finding to the extent that it is illogical or 'manifestly wrong'.

However, the 1967 Commission strained the usual understanding of appellate principles and went further than an appellate court would have, for the sake of producing a finding that reflected the underlying public interest in the case, although the hub of this interest was not contained within the terms of reference.

In sum, the Commissioners must have felt the plausibility and persuasiveness of Samuels's submissions justified their overlooking the need to establish and maintain the connection between Cabban's evidence and the collision, *in the public interest*. Had they adhered strictly to the terms of reference and the logical construction that led from one to another, Robertson would not have been heard and the Commission would have produced a report of little practical value. In terms of the public interest in the case, it would have been useless.

Having found the 'door' to re-examining Spicer's findings, the Commissioners varied most of his principal findings relating to navigation and the ships' final movements. Briefly, the new findings were that

— *Voyager's* turn to starboard and her subsequent turn to port were induced by the flying course signal and not by the turning signal;

— *Voyager's* final turn to port was in the form of a continuous curve under 10 degrees of rudder until about 20 seconds before collision and not on a steady course for a 'minute or less';

— The sole cause of the collision lay with *Voyager* and the criticism of Robertson was not justified;

— Similarly no blame was attached to either Kelly or Bate;

— The action of *Voyager* in continuing her turn to port across *Melbourne's* bows was due to the mistaken belief held by officers on her bridge until 20 seconds prior to the collision that *Voyager* was on the carrier's port bow;

— *Voyager's* belief that she was on the port bow of *Melbourne* in the final stage of her port turn was induced by mistaken inclination and personal circumstances peculiar to Stevens;

— The times at which signals were sent and acknowledged could not be determined with sufficient accuracy for complete reliance. The same applied to elapsed time, courses, stations, distances and speed made good through the water;

— *Voyager's* final turn to port was not induced by either a corruption or misunderstanding of a signal from the carrier;

— Stevens was an experienced and competent destroyer captain, well versed in the manoeuvres ordered by *Melbourne* but at the time of the collision he was unfit to command *Voyager* as a result of ill health.

Although the Commissioners removed all blame from Robertson, Kelly and Bate, their justification was difficult to understand. They concluded that Spicer's findings were predicated by the view that *Voyager's* final movements were induced by the turning course signal and that this situation would have demanded a much closer watch being maintained on the destroyer. The Commissioners fail to say why this was so.

Although this was the result longed for by Robertson, its justification was unconvincing. The Commissioners having 'found' that *Voyager* was on a continuous turn, then discredited much of the evidence and argument used to establish this proposition during both commissions. The reconstructions and diagrams tendered by Robertson

> correlate facts with assumptions of fact which cannot be regarded as reliable ... they amount to little more than suppositions of little real value ... We are of the opinion accordingly, that the use of times and diagrams are an unsafe guide to explain the events of 10 February 1964 and that they should be rejected.[23]

Whatever the reasoning and justification for overturning Spicer's findings, the Commissioners did arrive at a new set of findings which were generally considered much fairer to Robertson, Kelly and Bate, and which embodied a more plausible explanation for the causes of the collision than that offered by Spicer. While not all of its assumptions, assertions and conclusions were totally convincing, there was little in them of a speculative or controversial nature.

The findings on the third term of reference, whether Cabban's evidence was improperly withheld at the first Commission, was something of an anticlimax. The Commissioners accepted the statement of all witnesses who had appeared in relation to this matter and found that

> The evidence was not in any way improperly withheld from the Royal Commission. Indeed, as it was made known to Sir John Spicer, it is not true even to say it was withheld at all from the Royal Commission.[24]

The Commissioners concluded their report with some general observations and comments on existing naval regulations and procedures relating to medical examinations of officers, duties imposed on commanding officers in foreign ports, and the availability of alcohol in RAN ships. The final acknowledgements confirmed that Mr Justice Lucas concurred with the opinions expressed in the report inasmuch as the major matters requiring a finding were concerned.

Of all the parties appearing before the Commission, Robertson achieved the most. He obtained the 'justice' he had sought after the Spicer Report. The new navigational findings justified the Commission from Robertson's perspective. Cabban had achieved all he possibly could from the Commission in surviving the personal attacks of the Naval Board. He had emerged as an honest and truthful witness whose evidence had led a second inquiry to conclude that Stevens was unfit to command and this warranted new findings on the causes of the collision. Cabban could say the Commission had been justified. However, his counsel was unhappy with Robertson's behaviour during the inquiry and his failure to say anything positive to the media about Cabban after the Burbury Report was released. St John attacked Robertson for 'washing his hands' of the suffering endured by Cabban and the Stevens family. Robertson 'had the benefits of all the fuss but pretended he was not involved'.[25] Burt said he was surprised and disappointed that Robertson had not done any more to help Cabban although he had used Cabban to have the case reopened.

Captain Stevens's image was hardly salvaged by the Commission. He had earned moral censure for concealing his medical condition; he was found to have been drunk on several occasions while on duty; he was found to be unfit to retain command at the time of the collision; and prone to lapses of judgement sufficient to have allowed a serious accident to have occurred. Sir Jack Stevens believed three aspects of the Burbury Report

> put us in a much more adverse position now than we were when the Spicer Report was published:
> (a) degree or responsibility for the collision itself;
> (b) general unfitness to command because of physical condition;
> (c) deliberate concealment of physical unfitness by Duncan [Stevens], McNeill and Tiller.[26]

There were other minor aspects of note in Sir Jack's comments, including the doubt cast on his own evidence, the suggestion that Stevens's condition may have contributed to the collision, the description of Cabban as 'loyal' by the Commissioners, and 'the complete discarding of the evidence of witnesses who favoured Duncan'.[27] (Osborne, for example, did not believe the evidence warranted a finding that Stevens was unfit to command.[28]) The positive matters Sir Jack identified were the classification of Cabban as an unreliable witness and the doubts the Commission cast upon the consumption by his son of a triple brandy.

As an aside, Sir Jack Stevens attacked the conduct of Burt QC, whom he describes as having adopted the role of 'Crown Prosecutor'.

> It was clear from his [Burt's] opening address that he accepted the Cabban allegations. When Ash demolished most of these in cross-examination, he did his best to rake up adverse witnesses to make the going hard for us.[29]

He pressed the responsibility of Burt even further.

> The Commission, in my view, showed (because of Burt) a definite bias towards witnesses who were favourably inclined towards Duncan. They accept with great alacrity witnesses like Martin who quite obviously were favourably disposed towards Cabban. Martin in 1963 was a young officer with (in Duncan's view) distinct possibilities but inexperienced and given to airing his views . . .
> The whole case was lost for us when Samuels addressed the Commission and it was obvious to anyone in the Court that it was lapping up Samuels story . . .[30]

Sir Jack was also critical of McNicoll, whose assessment of Stevens as a destroyer captain 'greatly helped to free Robertson of criticism'.[31]

Whereas by all accounts McNicoll was an unimpressive witness, the most damage to Stevens's reputation was done by Martin. Giving evidence at the Royal Commission had been a great test of character for Martin. There was a hint of this in an article published in the *Australian* in early 1988 to mark his retirement from the RAN.

> His confidence in his colleagues was troubled only twice. The first was 'in another Navy' when the men lost faith in the captain and decided to keep the ship going by working around him. The second was the *Voyager* tragedy.
> 'I was very frightened at that inquiry,' Martin admits. 'Relatively senior people had advised me not to rock the boat'.[32,33]

Martin told the author two weeks before his death in 1990 that

> I was horrified when I first saw the Cabban Statement. That was not because it
> was untrue but because I believed Cabban should not have done it. However, I
> believed that everything in the Statement could have happened, and I can
> visualise all of it taking place — but it was out of order and not sequenced.[34]

In spite of his personal feelings, it was Martin who provided the most detailed corroboration of Cabban's Statement. He told me that Stevens was liked by his officers, was very popular with the ship's company, and was also compassionate and caring. Martin described *Voyager* during 1963 as one of the most tight-knit and efficiently operated ships in which he ever served. This was because the ship was run by her officers who conducted most of the evolutions. At times lacking confidence, Martin said that Stevens sometimes refused to become involved in exercises and even delayed operations until Griffith had arrived on the bridge. In his view, the collision was caused by a lack of co-ordination on *Voyager*'s bridge. Martin asserted that, for the first time, Stevens did not have around him the officers on whom he had relied heavily in 1963, a group of officers who had been formed into a team by Commander Alan Willis in late 1962. Yet, Martin could not conceive of Stevens drinking at sea.

As for Cabban, Martin saw him as 'a tragic figure who tended to make the most and the worst of things'. In his defence, Martin remarked that Cabban suffered from a wardroom which did not support him, Commander Money being especially disloyal. Martin thought that many witnesses did not tell the truth because they wanted to do what was best for the Navy, and because they were unable to say anything adverse about Stevens at the inquiry when his widow was sitting in the public gallery.

Other than the finding that he was neither a drunkard nor an alcoholic, the Commission had been a disaster for the Stevens family and their actions in opposing it were now understandable.

The position of Lieutenant Price, *Voyager*'s OOW, remained unaltered, as expected.

The party to have emerged the most damaged from the inquiry was the Naval Board. Its concerted campaign to denigrate Cabban had failed while its hostility to Robertson had further diminished its already tarnished reputation. Its defence of Captain Stevens was unsuccessful as well. On three counts, the Naval Board had failed to convince an independent tribunal of its views and had seriously harmed its standing. It was seen to have vilified an honest and truthful man (Cabban) and abandoned an innocent man (Robertson), at the same time that it sought to protect another who had been neither truthful nor beyond reproach.

There was also the suspicion, regardless of how poorly founded it may have been, that the Naval Board and some of its representatives had withheld information from this second inquiry. What was worse,

Captain Stevens's behaviour had been less than the Naval Board would have expected from an officer of his seniority. Outsiders would have had reason to doubt the quality of the Navy when Stevens had progressed so far through the ranks. The Naval Board also found that many of its procedures and practices had been inadequate, and that it should have known more about Stevens notwithstanding the failure of certain personnel to submit the required reports.

The Naval Board could take little solace from the report. It had hurt the Navy's public image. Officers and sailors serving in the Fleet would now have better understood why the Board strived so hard to prevent another *Voyager* inquiry.

Newspaper headlines the day after the release of the report concentrated on two matters: the Commission's finding that Stevens had been unfit to command, and that Robertson had been cleared of any blame.

The *Australian* spoke for many with its editorial of 26 February 1968 headed, '*Voyager* — justice at last'. It said the Commission's report vindicated those who had sought another inquiry and decried the situation where the first Commission had been able to err so badly, as the *Australian* believed it had done. It also had a parting shot at the outgoing minister.

> The Navy, if it has not done so already, is clearly obliged to devise whatever safeguards are possible against such a situation [Stevens remaining in command]; some are suggested by the royal commissioners . . . After the ill-advised attempts to block the second *Voyager* inquiry, based apparently on inept investigation of the so-called Cabban Statement and even loss of records from within the Navy Department, Mr Chipp could not be allowed to remain Ministerial head of the Navy.

The *West Australian*, was almost alone in questioning the Commissioners' findings.

> What is difficult to accept is the commission's view that the Naval Board was not at fault in failing to relieve Captain Stevens . . . it is hard to believe that in the tight-knit society of senior naval officers no gossip or speculation had reached the Board.[35]

By this time Jess and St John had also publicly stated their expectation that Robertson would receive either a pension or some form of compensation. Alan Ramsey, writing in the *Australian*, said that 'Government sources believe there is a strong possibility that he will be offered reinstatement, although not with the four years' seniority he has lost by his resignation'.[36]

It took one of the Sunday newspapers, the *Sun-Herald*, to express some doubt about the shortcomings of royal commissions as methods of inquiry.

> The royal commission system itself must come under review. Two judicial

investigations, each exhaustive and impartial, reached widely different conclusions as to the cause of the disaster. In major respects, the findings of the second inquiry reversed those of the first.[37]

With Prime Minister Gorton's announcement that Cabinet would consider the Commission's report without delay, speculation about compensation for Robertson dominated the newspapers on 27 February 1968.

Gorton had felt some sympathy for Robertson since the 1964 Commission began and believed he had been harshly treated, particularly by Smyth. Gorton told me that although he personally doubted whether Spicer would have reached different findings had he heard Cabban's evidence, the public believed Robertson was a victim of circumstance and entitled to compensation. Gorton said that despite the Navy's opposition to a payment to Robertson, he felt on balance it was justified and would have satisfied Jess and his other parliamentary supporters.[38]

The matter of re-entry to the Navy or compensation was first considered by Cabinet on 28 and 29 February 1968:

> The Cabinet saw as a major issue of principle whether the findings of a legal tribunal should, in the matter of Service appointments, be allowed to prevail over a proper authority, in this case, the Naval Board. It was concerned that any action which the Government might now take should not set, or appear to set, a precedent in this regard . . . While wishing to make clear and sustain this position, the Cabinet felt that it must nevertheless face up to the possibility of a compensation payout and should therefore explore what basis was likely to prove a reasonable settlement.[39]

The matter was considered again on 12 March with the possibility of Robertson being reinstated to the RAN being dropped. The Cabinet still felt uneasy about the situation but knew it had to give Robertson something or Jess would again attack the Government. The resolution of this uneasiness was lame in the extreme.

> The Cabinet noted that Captain Robertson had made a voluntary decision to resign and it did not accept that the Government had been responsible for any injustice to him. However, it agreed lest it be held in the light of the findings of the Second Royal Commission that Robertson had wrongly suffered, that recompense ought to be made to him.[40]

It was now a question of whether he would receive a pension or compensation. The Treasurer, Attorney-General and Minister for the Navy recommended a lump sum payment of $60,000 with 'the basis of the calculation being not disclosed'.[41] This recommendation was accepted.

On 13 March 1968 the Prime Minister made the following statement in Parliament:

> The Government has now decided that a payment should be made to Captain Robertson and in reaching this conclusion necessarily had to take a broad view.

Whilst paying some regard to the pension which Captain Robertson might have received in certain eventualities if he had not resigned as and when he did, the Government did not regard this as the sole criterion. Other factors also had to be taken into consideration. Having considered the various ways in which this payment might be made the Government decided that a lump sum, as an act of grace, would be most appropriate and the Government has now decided to authorise payment of $60,000. In reaching this decision, the Government took the advice from the Commissioner of Taxation that he would regard payment in the form proposed as being free of income tax.[42]

Although most of the newspapers had called for at least $100,000,[43] they were not critical of the Government for offering a lesser sum, which Robertson accepted graciously.

The Navy, quite sensibly, had assumed a low profile following the release of the Burbury Report. This was the wisest course of action. However, the changeover of the Fleet command on 18 March 1968 provided an opportunity for the RAN to respond to its critics. The new FOCAF, Rear-Admiral John Crabb, said the Navy was a completely volunteer defence service and was to be admired. This was a veiled insult to the Australian Army which was being enlarged by conscripts for active service in South Vietnam. In a public address, Crabb said the Navy was

> something a lot of people can kick around. It is difficult for a Service like ours to come back and answer criticisms. This is one of those things in our exposed position we have to be big enough to take and absorb. I think the RAN has absorbed and taken enough.[44]

Admiral Peek, who was relinquishing command, said the Navy had 'suffered over the past six months from press headlines and a lot of stupid questions from legal people at the Royal Commission'.[45]

The response from the press was quick and devastating. The *Age* headed its editorial the next day 'The Untouchables'.

> Those who listened to or read the evidence at the first Royal Commission on the loss of HMAS *Voyager* must have been struck by the ill-conceived resentment of senior officers of the Navy at having their actions and methods questioned. It might have been supposed that this foolish arrogance would have been tempered by the revelations of naval inadequacies which emerged in the course of the *Voyager* inquiries.
>
> But not at all. Now we have two admirals, senior enough to know better, returning to the charge. It appears that Admiral Crabb and Admiral Peek believe that the Navy should be above criticism, and that the fault lies with 'Press headlines' and 'stupid questions' from legal people. It might be pointed out that it was not the Press or the Law which lost the *Voyager* ...
>
> The attitudes of the two admirals unhappily suggest that the higher echelons of the RAN have still to learn their lesson.[46]

The Navy would have to endure these public criticisms in silence. The Burbury Report was not debated in Parliament until 2 April 1968. The Leader of the Opposition, Gough Whitlam, opened the debate speaking against the motion that the House take note of the paper (i.e. the Report), and set about establishing the Parliament's right to debate the Report and to level criticisms at the Naval Board. This was in response to the public comments by Admirals Peek and Crabb who, Whitlam said, 'took it upon themselves to warn us off'.[47] Whitlam's speech aimed at reflecting the Commissioners' criticisms on the Government's handling of the Navy portfolio. His first point was a telling one. The finding that Stevens was physically unfit to be in command of *Voyager*, Whitlam said, 'seems to me to be an infinitely more serious finding than if the Commission had found, for instance, that drink had contributed directly to the disaster'.[48] This was an indictment of the naval system of administration.

Whitlam expressed the Commission's report as a vindication of Cabban as a means of chastising the Government for failing to act on his Statement in the first instance. But at the same time, he questioned what he saw as the determination of the Commission to denigrate Cabban, arguing that a higher level of corroboration was required for Cabban's evidence than was expected from other witnesses. It was clear that Whitlam's best option was to attack the Government for covering up matters that it had either known or should have known. In particular, he focused on the actions of Landau and said 'Honourable gentlemen will wonder how much confidence they can have in the administration of the Navy with a creature like this [Landau] in charge'.[49] It was a remark that would be thrown back at Whitlam, and repudiated by his own party, throughout the long debate.

For the remainder of his speech, Whitlam was critical of those who attacked Cabban personally as a means of discrediting his statement and the refusal of the Naval Board to have the matters raised by Cabban properly investigated. This added little to Parliament's confidence in the Commission. Whitlam's speech, which lasted fifty minutes, was described as 'devastating' and 'scathing' by the newspapers the next day.

In reply, Gorton criticised Whitlam's reference to Landau on his way to building a case which used the Commission's report to demonstrate that Cabban's major allegations had not been accepted. Gorton attempted to establish the pattern for the ensuing debate in which he hoped the Government would attack Cabban while upholding the Commission's report which was portrayed as an independent opinion above partisan criticism.

The Prime Minister's speech defended the actions of the naval officers and civil servants involved, but suggested that action might have been taken against McNeill and Tiller had they still been serving in the Navy. Despite there being a new finding for the causes of the collision, Gorton stated 'there would not have been a second Royal Commission if it had not been for what were found to be misleading accusations'.[50]

This was taken up by Lance Barnard who placed the events in their proper context.

> The debate tonight is the culmination of an extraordinary sequence of events. There is no parallel in either Australian military history or legal history for this incredible reversal of the findings of a Royal Commission by a second Royal Commission.[51]

Barnard highlighted the significance of the new findings for Robertson, Kelly and Bate but, in the absence of a declarative statement with respect to Stevens, attempted to fill some of the gaps he believed existed in the Commission's report. Rejecting the Commission's conclusion that Stevens might not have had the triple brandy, Barnard was prepared to describe the link between his drinking and the collision. Most others, including Cabban, had been unwilling to do this in the absence of substantive evidence.

> The obvious inference is that Captain Stevens had a quantity of brandy shortly before the collision because he was suffering pain from his ulcer and was distressed. This is immensely significant in the light of the Commissioners' finding that the bridge of the *Voyager* lost the tactical picture just before the collision and this could have been caused by some circumstances peculiar to Captain Stevens.[52]

The inference was still bereft of a basis in fact but it probably represented what a great many people thought.

It was appropriate for Chipp, as the former Navy Minister, to reply to the Opposition's attack on the Navy. He ended his short speech with a sombre warning to the Parliament.

> Our Navy is presently engaged in a war. Our ships' officers and men are being fired upon in anger. Our clearance divers and pilots are risking their lives daily in Vietnam. None of the Armed Services in Australian history — indeed few, if any — have ever been subjected to the microscopic examinations of two royal commissions in four years ... after the conclusion of this debate, whenever that might be, in God's name leave them alone, give them a fair go to serve Australia as they have volunteered to do.[53]

In spite of all that had been revealed, this needed to be said.

The next Opposition speaker, Bill O'Connor, returned to the shortcomings of the first Commission and went further than his party colleagues.

> I submit that to say that they were merely guilty of an error of judgement is to treat them very leniently. In my opinion, they erred seriously and were deserving of some censure.[54]

Sir William Morrow was next in line.

> Frankly, I consider that the two commissioners in the recent royal commission relied too generously on the evidence of Sir William Morrow, and their readiness to give credibility to this evidence is not shared by many doctors ... I have spoken to other doctors who have read Sir William Morrow's evidence and who laughed on reading it.[55]

Although not content with the Commission's findings, O'Connor said he wanted matters of continuing public disquiet investigated but did not want another inquiry.

This sentiment was echoed by Jess in his speech. In spite of being the prime mover for the second Commission, Jess stated that: 'No matter what the Commissioners have said in their report, I retain the right to disagree with their decisions.'[56] He then proceeded to attack the conduct of McNicoll, Landau, Spicer and Smyth. He defended Cabban, the first Government member to do so, and made some excessively fulsome remarks about truth and justice. His conclusion reiterated the purpose for which he had sought a review of the first Commission.

> The [second] Commission was never necessary. It only needed one person to hear one man and perhaps to check what he had to say and not leave the matter to two men who were concerned and who, in fact, I think even recommended compensation for the man who was victimised, Captain Robertson.[57]

The debate adjourned following Jess's speech and resumed the following afternoon with the former Navy Minister, Fred Chaney, speaking against an amendment to the motion proposed by Lance Barnard which added 'but deplores the efforts of Ministers to stifle debate on Lieutenant Commander Cabban's statement and to suppress documents substantially corroborating it'.[58]

The thrust of Chaney's address was to defend the Commissioners and Landau in particular. As the minister involved in the decision to post Robertson to HMAS *Watson*, Chaney's remarks about Robertson's decision to resign deserved attention. What he pointed out on this occasion he had not said when he was the minister. After informing the Parliament that seagoing appointments were naturally favoured over shore jobs, Chaney noted that McNicoll

> went from the post of FOCAF to what may be regarded, I suppose, as the mundane job of Fourth Naval Member of the Naval Board. There was an occasion, on the other hand, when Captain Oldham went from command of *Watson* to become Rear-Admiral Oldham in the post of FOICEA.[59]

In other words, the former minister was stating that it was quite possible for Robertson to have been promoted from this appointment.

Chaney concluded his address by departing from his party's line over the efficacy of holding a Royal Commission into these matters:

> the time has come to introduce machinery for carrying out in relation to the RAN the type of inquiry that is conducted when a marine disaster occurs involving merchant vessels. We could perhaps have a judge appointed, preferably one with some experience in these matters, assisted by assessors. The inquiry could be held in public, as my friends on the other side demand. I do believe that the one thing we should have learned from these two royal commissions is that the present system is not a fit and proper one to operate in respect of one of our own Services. Immediate consideration should be given by the Government to the suggestion I have just made.[60]

Sam Benson, who was now an Independent, proposed the replacement of Barnard's amendment to the motion with his own, which acknowledged the Parliament's confidence in the members of the Naval Board, all naval personnel and 'the way in which the Navy operates and is administered'.[61]

Opposing the arguments put by his former colleagues of the Labor Party, the unpredictable Benson denigrated Cabban as a 'strange individual' whose statement was a 'piece of exaggeration and distortion'. He then turned on Robertson, stating the first Commission 'did offer some minor criticism which was, in my opinion, fully justified by the facts and supported by well-known principles of admiralty law'. He was even prepared to say that Robertson was at fault as OTC in not taking the required evasive action, 'obstinately refused to accept' Spicer's criticism, and failed to act as a loyal serviceman when posted to *Watson*. While clearly neglecting the evidence and argument relating to navigational matters presented at the second Commission, Benson stated, 'Personally, I prefer Sir John Spicer's report'.[62]

On each occasion he entered the debate, Benson's seriously flawed knowledge of the law of the sea, of conventions applying to warships when manoeuvring in company, and of the arguments accepted and rejected by both Commissions, served only to confuse and obfuscate the debate. His suggestion that the RAN somehow believed it was exempt from the law of the sea was not supported by any evidence. It was also an odd way to end a speech proposing an amendment expressing the Parliament's confidence in the RAN.

Virtually ignoring the amendment proposed by Benson, Leslie Irwin joined Jess on the Government side in questioning the wisdom of holding Royal Commissions with respect to matters involving the Services. However, Irwin provided an unusual twist.

> There should have been an independent naval inquiry. We should have flown in an admiral from the Royal Navy and an admiral from the Royal Canadian Navy to conduct the inquiry. If this had been done we would have had first class evidence and we would not have had to go through all the ceremony and paraphernalia that is associated with a royal commission . . . It appears to me that royal commissions need to have some sort of scapegoat . . . We want to devise some better way of finding out the truth. I strongly protest against the appointment of royal commissions to inquire into matters affecting the Services. There must be something radically wrong if we cannot get a better system.[63]

The next speaker, the Liberal Member for Swan, Richard Cleaver, continued to erode the Government's solidarity and its support for the method of inquiry. He contended that

> there would be many who would hold the opinion that a complex technical matter such as this should preferably have been the subject of a Naval Board Court of Inquiry as a first step, with a royal commission appointed later to give close attention to any disturbing features of the report of that Court of Inquiry.[64]

One assumes that Cleaver understood that regulations did not exist at the time of the collision for such a court, and that he would have supported Chaney's call for a review of procedures. Cleaver was also unhappy with the Commission's report which, he argued, failed to 'give a clear measurement of what is corroborated evidence and what is not'.[65] Cleaver was right to point to the vagueness of statements which detracted from Cabban's veracity or judgement, and the convenience of this approach to the Commissioners in writing their report and arriving at their findings.

With the Opposition declining its right of reply, St John was given his chance to speak. The controversial Member for Warringah addressed his remarks to Barnard's amendment deploring the efforts of ministers to stifle debate and suppress documents relating to the Cabban Statement. It came as little surprise when he said he proposed to abstain from voting on the amendment.

St John continued his attack on Stevens's drinking habits and the way they were investigated by the Commission. He was critical of Birrell's evidence being excluded and questioned the suitability and usefulness of Morrow to comment on the case as Stevens's physician. This led St John to the matter of Stevens's fitness to command and the cause of the collision. St John saw in the Report the 'possibility, to say no more, that Captain Stevens' unfitness was indeed a cause or the cause of the mistaken belief that *Melbourne* was on the port side.'[66] (He meant *Voyager* was on *Melbourne*'s port side.)

St John was also prepared to try to prove the link but he erred in the process. While he says

> the Commissioners show a logical inconsistency, a failure to realise fully the significance of their own primary findings or to work out their full consequences in other parts of their report,[67]

his statement that

> the Commissioners have recognised that they were justified in varying the findings of Sir John Spicer only because they found that Captain Stevens was unfit,[68]

fails to consider the large amount of navigational evidence and argument that the Commissioners heard. It was the argument of Samuels that *Voyager* could not possibly have been on a straight course prior to the collision which led the Commissioners to overturn the findings of Spicer. The evidence about Stevens being unfit to command, although stated, is not closely linked to the new finding. Nevertheless, it is not true to say that this was the *only* basis on which the finding was based. This point seems to have been overlooked by every speaker during the long debate.

True to his zealous character, St John concluded with veiled criticism of the Commissioners for being 'too tolerant of human weaknesses' and for failing to

> have passed some strictures, for example, upon the many witnesses who attempted to conceal the truth about Captain Stevens, thus delaying and obstructing the course of justice, instead of finding this, and so much else so completely 'understandable'.[69]

The support of Jim Killen was not expected by those who opposed the appointment of Royal Commissions of inquiry into Service matters. As a barrister, Killen took a slightly different line.

> I have the greatest of doubts as to whether the system of Royal Commissions with judges sitting on them can be used in future in these circumstances. The Royal Commission is a very old instrument of inquiry . . . But I hope this House, whatever view any of us may take on this matter, will ponder a while and consider the wisdom of appointing judges to Royal Commissions involved in the fury and fierceness of political conflict.[70]

Killen pointed out the undesirability of a Federal court judge (Spicer) and two Supreme Court judges (Burbury and Asprey) being vigorously attacked in public by parliamentarians.

> We are exercising, as it were, some corrosive influence upon the stature and upon the integrity of their Honours. I hope that we have at last seen the end of this sort of inquiry.[71]

A straight-talking politician, Killen expressed the view that had Robertson been given a pension in 1964, the second Commission would not have eventuated. This was Killen's way of precluding any sanctimoniousness about motives based on the abiding importance of truth and justice. It was, quite clearly, an attack on Jess. Killen's speech did, however, return to the Government's argument that Cabban was discredited by the Commission while he defended the Government's hesitation in agreeing to the second Commission.

Killen's closing argument, relating to Royal Commission procedures, was an important one that had not been put before. It appeared to reveal a serious flaw in the Commission's actions in overturning Spicer's findings.

> I think it is a pity that this Commission — and here I find myself in company with some of the critics of the Commission — re-heard Captain Robertson on navigational aspects of the inquiry but did not re-hear all the others. An appellate court which decides to hear the matter *de novo* [afresh] hears all the evidence; it does not hear the evidence of one witness and then look at the transcript of the previous case for the remainder of the evidence. This would not be fair. If it happened in an ordinary civil action it would be held to be a denial of natural justice.[72]

This does not seem to have been the view of Bill Ash, QC, counsel for the Stevens family in 1967, who was counsel most likely to object, given that the finding in favour of Robertson reflected adversely on Captain Stevens and increased the relative degree of blame he was made to accept.

Speaking after Killen, the Attorney-General, Nigel Bowen QC, was constrained to defend the Commission he had instituted. He began with several points of clarification. First, the Commissioners found that Stevens's ulcer was not active on the night of the collision. Therefore, the link which others had attempted to make between his ill-health and the cause of the collision, was weakened. Second, rebutting St John's argument and supporting the Commissioners' right to overturn Spicer's findings, Bowen said that the Commissioners examined the same evidence that was before Spicer and arrived at a different conclusion. It was this that led them to exonerate Robertson.[73]

Having waited for dissension and division within the Government to manifest itself, Clyde Cameron embarked on a vicious denunciation of those he alleged had covered up the facts before the Commission.

Cameron went on to say the tests ordered on Stevens by Morrow suggested Morrow believed Stevens was 'suffering from cirrhosis of the liver' or some other disease caused by an excess of alcohol'.[74] The purpose of Cameron's speech was to suggest that if an inquiry were held to examine specifically the health of Captain Stevens, it would more than likely find more than the Commission was prepared to conclude, including that Stevens was an alcoholic.[75]

The Liberal Member for McMillan, Alex Buchanan, sought to support Benson's remarks. He defended Spicer and attacked Turner, St John and Jess. He was particularly demeaning of Robertson.

> Unfortunately, Captain Robertson has proved by other mishaps in his navigation in previous incidents that he is a slow thinker, and he did not take any action. Sir John Spicer made a faint criticism ... which was fully justified.[76]

He argued that Robertson 'in an extraordinary fit of pique, insisted on resigning' and that the award of compensation was 'disgracefully extravagant'.[77]

Gordon Bryant, in what was probably the most constructive speech of the debate, returned to the shortcomings of the Royal Commission procedure.

> How did we get a report such as the first report, which was challenged two or three years later, then re-sifted and then thrown out? Why did the Government appoint the type of people that it did to examine such a matter? I believe that the important task here tonight is to establish the principles upon which this Parliament will work in instances such as this because we are the continuing trustees of a parliamentary democracy and we are a court of last resort. Any citizen should be able to put his case before us knowing that we will raise it on his behalf.[78]

Bryant suggested that there were two main sources of Service inefficiency. The first was the innate conservatism of the military forces which was sustained by an 'old boy network' which was linked to other conservative elements within government. The second was the isolation of the Services from the community and the Service Boards from their respective Services. This was aided and abetted by the system of officer promotion that alienated senior officers from those they were promoted to lead. Bryant emphasised that the isolation of the Services from the community would be ended when the isolation of the Services from the body politic was broken down:

> there has been an increasing professionalisation of the Services in the last twenty years which has removed them from our scrutiny and from the ordinary way of life. Life is completely different in the Services. I think it is fair enough to say . . . that of the three Services the one most removed and most isolated is the Navy. Anyone who takes over the running of the Department of the Navy . . . will find that he has to shake it up and bring it back into the light of day.[79]

The next Government speaker, the barrister Tom Hughes QC, directed his remarks to the use of Royal Commissions as a tool of executive government. The thrust of Hughes's argument was that if the Parliament saw itself 'as a sort of court of appeal to review the findings of the Royal Commission . . . knowing something of the way in which judges think, that there will in future be very few Royal Commissions on which judges will consent to serve'. The solution proposed by Hughes was that Parliament should not see itself as a court of appeal and that debate should not be 'on the basis of ill-formed, half-baked ideas'.[80] This was not a very practical solution to offer men used to political debate. It also assumed that having judges serve on Royal Commissions was to be preferred.

The reference to the Commissioners being seen as referees was taken up by the final speaker, the Minister for the Navy, Bert Kelly. He said that there had been no criticism of the Commissioners when they were appointed.

> But now that the report is before us we find that a lot of people are dissatisfied with it . . . Really, I do not think this is good enough. It is no good appointing umpires and then accepting their decisions, except the ones you do not like. This is so if you have agreed to their appointment in the first place.

Just after 11 pm, debate was adjourned and the Opposition amendment was put to the House. Four Government members, Jess, St John, Turner and Cleaver, abstained from the vote which was defeated by 64 votes to 37. The amendment proposed by Benson was carried on voices. *Voyager* became a matter of parliamentary history.

The parliamentary debate did not greatly add to an understanding of what the Commissioners had found or its import. If anything, the lack of clarity in and precision of the prose in which some of the findings were expressed allowed a variety of interpretations. The content of the debate was also influenced by the composition of the groups opposing each other over the findings. The conventional parliamentary situation of the Opposition challenging the Government was mutated when the Labor Opposition was joined by a number of Government backbenchers who led an attack on the Government. There was also a side debate conducted among the lawyers in Parliament on the legislature and the role of the judiciary in inquiries ordered by the Parliament. The position of Benson only added to the confusion.

Despite the existence of numerous separate agendas, several points did emerge and they related to the conduct of naval administration. If nothing else, the debate had demonstrated that there were shortcomings in the way the RAN was operated. The part of the motion expressing the Parliament's confidence in the Navy could not obscure the continuing disquiet being felt on both sides of the House on the state of the Navy. There was still much to be done.

Whatever might have been said publicly, the second Commission did lead to substantial changes in naval administration. By 16 November 1967 the Navy had altered the procedure for the medical examination of captains, reviewed instructions for medical officers and provided new aide-mémoires, and amended the principal administrative manual, *Regulations and Instructions to the RAN*, where it dealt with reporting collisions, the submission of punishment returns and the exercise of command at sea.[81]

The new regulations stated that: 'Command is vested by CNS and can only be removed or relieved by CNS'. The occasions on which a captain would cease to command his ship included death, serious illness or injury, removal or relief by CNS, or removed by court martial. The officer succeeding to command was directed to enter the fact in the ship's log with a signature noting its assumption and subsequent relinquishment; a signal was to be sent to CNS giving all details; and, ships in company were to be informed. It was obvious the Board did not want a repeat of *Voyager*'s 1963 deployment.

The Board agreed with the Commissioners' suggestion that a closer and more rigorous medical reporting system was needed, notably that all officers with histories of peptic ulcers were required to complete a questionnaire and confirm in writing that they had revealed all relevant symptoms and that the answers given were correct to the best of their knowledge. If an officer was diagnosed as having an active peptic ulcer, he was to be posted ashore for twelve months and re-examined at the end of that period. Before such an officer was sent to sea in a command or charge position, his case was to be specifically referred and cleared by the Medical Director General.

There were other far-reaching actions. Naval manuals were to be examined and those that were unintelligible were to be rewritten so as to make them accessible to all naval personnel. The definition of command was rewritten while the handling of punishment returns and collision reports was to be reviewed and altered where necessary.

The RAN was just beginning to realise the importance of public relations and the power of the media. The appointment of a Co-ordinator of Navy Public Relations in 1964 was a start, but in 1967 there was no PR strategy and few resources were dedicated to that area. McNicoll wanted to prepare the Navy for the worst. On 30 November 1967 he wrote to the Minister:

> I suggest that we might seriously consider placing the handling of the Commissioner's report in the hands of a professional public relations firm. It affects the whole Navy and its public image, not to mention a national asset which is at present engaged in operations of war.[82]

The Minister felt that the Navy would be seen as timid if it had other people than itself handling the matter, but formal preparations needed to be made.

By the end of 1967 and after four years of being battered by *Voyager*, a Committee on Public Relations was formed and the first attempts made at defining a PR strategy. Rather than handling the matter, a professional PR consultant would be engaged to advise and assist. This committee would also help the Navy handle its response to the Report of the second Commission. The Committee told the Board after its first meeting that there was not much goodwill toward the Navy within the media, that the Commission's findings would be reported so as to emphasise the criticisms, and that good PR could only be achieved gradually.[83] In the shorter term, an officer with PR experience and a journalist would be employed to assist in the fallout from *Voyager*.[84] A signal was sent to all ships and shore establishments in early January 1968 heralding the new approach and acknowledging the need for press coverage.

> An effort is being made to increase the amount of general publicity given to the RAN and an urgent and continuing need exists for publicity photographs. A requirement also exists for photographs of HMA Ships underway and in obviously foreign ports.[85]

The Naval Board deflected criticism of itself onto a number of subordinate officers who failed to keep the appropriate authorities informed of matters they were required to by regulations. These officers were, on medical grounds, Surgeon Commander McNeill, Surgeon Lieutenant Tiller and Leading Seaman Wilson, and on disciplinary grounds Captains Dollard and Willis.[86] This was further than the Commissioners were prepared to go. The Naval Board believed that both Dollard and Willis could have been charged under Section 45 (i) of the *Naval Discipline Act* which required

> every person subject to this Act who knows or has reasonable grounds for suspecting that any other person subjected thereto is committing or has committed an offence under provision of Part 1 of this Act [which included drunkenness] to take all reasonable steps within his power to cause that person to be brought to justice.

No action or censure was ever brought against either officer.

After four years of drama and controversy, the Naval Board believed that *Voyager* was dead and buried. But all was not yet well. One could have imagined the furore that would have resulted if the public had learned that shortly after the parliamentary debate on the Burbury Report the captain of a frigate was physically removed from command. This officer was suffering from a psychological disorder which had been exacerbated by the unwise consumption of alcohol. He was deemed unfit to continue in command and was swiftly removed and later discharged from the RAN. Other than an oblique mention of the incident in one Brisbane newspaper, the matter was contained within the Navy. The need for diligent self-examination had obviously not yet passed.

*Voyager* would continue to plague the RAN. On the one hand there were the *Voyager* survivors; on the other, continuing doubts about whether the second Commission had heard all of the evidence and whether what it did hear was completely truthful. The *Australian* headed an editorial in April 1968, '*Voyager* — Still Too Many Doubts'. Of course, the causes of the collision had still not been adequately explained. While this uncertainty persisted it was unlikely that *Voyager* would ever disappear entirely from naval or national interest.

# 19

# *Inquiries and Controversy*

THE INVESTIGATION of the causes of the collision between *Melbourne* and *Voyager* was as controversial as the loss of the ship. To a large degree this was the product of decision-making on the inquiry process which was poorly handled from the outset. The decision by Prime Minister Menzies to hold a Royal Commission into the loss of *Voyager* had proved a costly one, for which the Naval Board shared part of the responsibility. Although there had been criticism of the use of a Royal Commission to inquire into the disaster, was this still the best method? Notwithstanding public fears of a whitewash, would a naval board of inquiry have been better? Or the method of investigation employed by civilian marine boards of inquiry?

Whenever there is a major disaster in Australia, including the loss of a ship at sea, there is usually a demand for a Royal Commission to inquire into the circumstances of the tragedy.

The matters that can be referred to a Royal Commission are virtually limitless. In Australia their role has been primarily for the valid purpose of gathering information. Sir Laurence Street identified the two principal types of Royal Commission in the report of the inquiry he conducted into allegations of wrongdoing on the part of New South Wales Premier Neville Wran in 1983. The first is the 'investigatory' type which includes those inquiries convened to research and provide facts for the formulation of government policy. The second is the 'inquisitorial' type which is used to investigate and report on the circumstances relating to misadventure.

Zdenkowski suggests that their performance depends on selection of criteria for assessment.

> A non-exhaustive list might include justice (compensation for victims, prosecution of wrong-doers, reversal of unjust decisions, etc); prevention (structural changes to avoid repetition of, or at least reduce the incidence of, the problem); educational impact (raised public consciousness of the problems and potential solutions); attitudinal change (changes produced by information disclosed); cost benefit (it depends on how you do your sums). Some of the factors overlap. Moreover, universal propositions are dangerous. Even if all royal

commissions do not measure up to the criteria suggested, it is likely that some will.[1]

For all that is cynically said about them, Royal Commissions have attained, as Hallet has pointed out, 'an aura of importance in the public mind because they are generally reserved for particularly important inquiries'.[2] Their primary attraction is that they can acquire information coercively if they choose. Their added appeal is that as a tool of the executive government they have the powers normally associated with the judiciary and appear to attract the same status and respect as a court of law. This is often the very intention of a government in appointing judges or very senior barristers to preside over them. However, commissions have no power in themselves to alter their terms of reference, determine government policy or bring criminal charges against any person. This is not often properly understood.

The chief objection to Royal Commissions relates to the lack of restrictions on the methods employed to gather information. Although the investigative inquiry needs to be orderly and follow a logical methodology, the case of the 'inquisitorial' constitutes a departure from the usual 'adversarial' style associated with conventional court action. Hence, it presents a number of problems relating to evidence and the rights of the individual. While a Royal Commission will usually, if conducted by lawyers, conform to the provisions of the relevant *Evidence Act* for that jurisdiction, the virtual absence of any restrictions or limits controlling the proceedings of a commission — other than the conventions and practices brought with any legal officers who happen to be involved with a commission from formal courts — means there are few constraints on the inquiry or the commissioner and few guaranteed rights or safeguards for individuals. Indeed, an interested party is questioned not in relation to a specific charge but in terms of often vague and general terms of reference. As far as its findings are concerned, a Royal Commission is not unlike judgements made in civil actions where the case must be proved on the balance of probabilities and need *not* be beyond reasonable doubt.

Thus, in the case of the first *Voyager* inquiry, Smyth was able to criticise and attack Robertson without laying any specific charge or making any particular allegation against him. In the second inquiry, hearsay evidence was admitted for the purpose of establishing certain facts about Captain Stevens's behaviour, yet this behaviour did not involve a breach of any law. There were undeniable problems associated with the Menzies decision to hold a Royal Commission. But what were the alternatives?

Jim Killen, a future Navy Minister, stated in relation to *Voyager* that

A [naval] board [of inquiry] would have conformed with naval practice and tradition. Royal Commissions are not necessarily the best equipped bodies to determine the facts. They can become unnecessarily combative forums in which advocacy can deflect and wrong conclusions are made. That certainly proved to be the case with the *Voyager* Royal Commission.

Why Menzies opted for a Royal Commission to investigate the collision has always puzzled me. The normal Naval Board of Inquiry had been proved to be a very useful means of getting at the facts, without fuss and public drama.

Chipp, another one-time Navy Minister, also had reservations about the decision to hold a Royal Commission.

Prime Minister Menzies immediately decided that because of the dimensions of the accident a Royal Commission must be held. This was against the wishes of the Naval Board. I have no doubt that, as the political head of a democracy, Menzies was correct and that his decision was inevitable. In any crisis involving the public service or the fighting services, I am persuaded that the most efficient and effective way of getting at the truth is by an expert inquiry held in camera. Allegations of corruption in the police force or the public service, or alleged scandals affecting construction of roads or buildings, can be investigated and ruthlessly pursued in secret and from within, in a fashion that cannot exist in a public hearing. Witnesses will say things in private which they will not repeat in public. This would be the method adopted in any totalitarian country, but in a democracy it has to be different because whatever the conclusions of such a secret inquiry, cries of 'whitewash' and 'cover-up' are sure to follow: justice must not only be done, but also seen to be done.[3]

The views presented by Killen and Chipp are in complete disagreement and suggest there was not a uniform view within the Liberal Party.

In 1964, there was a strong and pervasive body of opinion that the collision ought not to have been investigated by anyone other than naval officers. Naval officers believed that only they could appreciate the intricacies and subtleties of the naval art. As Hickling remarked, 'The courtroom is far too removed from the sea'. Yet the reverse did not seem to apply.

Naval officers claimed great expertise in the investigative processes of ascertaining facts, marshalling evidence and answering pertinent questions. Lawyers could not be seamen but seamen could be lawyers. This was the height of professional arrogance and the cause of so much ill-will towards the Commission, notwithstanding any objective view of its performance.

The procedure laid down by naval regulations in 1964 was for the relevant naval administrative authority to convene a board of inquiry which was a professional naval fact-finding body, not a judicial body. A board of inquiry would be followed by a court martial if a *prima facie* case of misconduct could be established against any officer or sailor as a result of the findings of the board of inquiry.[5] The decision to hold a board of inquiry remains within the discretion of the Naval Board. As Sir John Carrick pointed out, the *Naval Defence Act* did not make such action mandatory in the event of any misadventure and the Naval Board could have decided, for instance, against convening an inquiry into the loss of *Voyager*.[6] Not convening a naval board of inquiry did not constitute a breach of the Act.

There are advantages with the in-house board of inquiry approach. In the first instance, Naval boards of inquiry are readily convened with their costs borne by the Navy. They consist of experts in a field relevant to the matter under inquiry who can quickly assemble and are more than familiar with the circumstances leading to a misadventure. Thus, there should be little need for preliminary discussion about the matter under investigation. The board should quickly focus on the relevant areas with a full understanding of what may, or may not, be accepted as reasonable.

The disadvantages of this form of inquiry relate to the frailty of human nature. While a board will always have the potential to produce a flawed or inaccurate report, the officers making up a board are not specialists in detection or investigation. They have no experience in assessing the credit of witnesses. Any officer appointed to a board could harbour a grudge against those involved in the incident being investigated or stand to enhance his own promotion prospects by an adverse finding on a fellow officer. There is the additional fear that because the inquiry is not conducted in public and because those conducting the inquiry are all naval officers, there is a propensity for these inquiries to be either a 'whitewash' or an exercise in finding an expendable scapegoat. Although this fear is unwarranted, the Navy cannot avoid the general suspicion and distrust of all government in-house inquiries.

If an administrative authority determines from the findings of a board of inquiry that any individual has committed an offence under the various acts pertaining to naval service, charges are laid and the individual is brought to trial by court martial.

The procedure of trial by court martial has been developed and refined over centuries. From the earliest days of organised navies, admirals and ships captains had final authority over matters within their jurisdiction. They could punish sailors and even put them to death by hanging from the yardarm if charges brought were proved.

The creation of a distinct and comprehensive naval justice system was achieved during the days of the Commonwealth in England with the proclamation of the *Articles of War* and the first court martial in 1653. It was refined in 1661 with the introduction of the first *Naval Discipline Act* which formalised all the processes of naval justice while tailoring its practice to the practical operation of the Navy in which it would be exercised. Thus, it was necessary for all the players in a normal court to be found from among the ranks of naval officers, including those to act roughly as defence counsel, prosecution, judge and jury. In the case of the latter two, judge and jury were merged into a court-martial panel with a president who would manage the conduct of the court martial, but only share in its finding.

A court martial regarded itself as essentially a board of inquiry with few limitations on its powers or conduct. There were no formal charges, the accused answering for conduct broadly covered by the *Articles of War*, and usually no prosecutor. The president of the court martial, the Judge Advocate, was responsible for examining witnesses and taking depositions from those appearing on oath before the court martial. At the very controversial court martial held in Toulon 1744 for Mathew and Lestock which subsequently led to the death penalty, the House of Commons had insisted on sending two lawyers from the Admiralty to prosecute. However, protecting its prerogative, the court's members considered they alone were the proper persons to obtain the evidence of the witnesses and refused to allow the lawyers to be heard. This was later modified and legal officers from the Admiralty did prosecute. It was not until late in the 19th century that the accused was able to have a 'friend' to assist in his defence. However, the Navy retained the right to punish offenders on its own terms, including imprisonment in naval gaols. The aim was to keep naval justice within the Navy. The objective was assisted by civil jurisdictions which were reluctant to inquire into matters involving the Navy.

A naval court martial normally consisted of five officers who sit in judgement and pass sentence. Their verdict must be by majority opinion in the event of dissent by one or two of the members and the fact of a divided opinion is never made known. How each officer voted is kept in strictest confidence by those sitting at the court martial. In order to avoid the possibility of any pressure or influence, the most junior member returns his verdict first, followed by the next senior member with the President of the court martial, the most senior officer and an officer senior to the accused, speaking last. He has no power of veto although in a split decision he has the deciding vote.

The RAN's discipline and justice system was modelled in every detail on the Royal Navy procedures. Yet it did not enjoy the same reputation. Whereas the Royal Navy had the services of a Judge Advocate of the Fleet (who was always a QC), and an array of officers listed under the title 'Legal Advisers to the Admiralty' who examined court-martial transcripts, there was no such expert scrutiny within the RAN.

An anonymous contributor to the *Australian Law Journal* in 1950 soundly criticised the system of Australian naval justice in which judge advocates were not legally qualified and that hearsay and other irrelevant evidence was freely admitted. The point of the article was to highlight the importance of justice appearing to be done, not just being done and that lawyers were needed in the Forces:

> to the seaman — officer or man — the qualified lawyer is a person with whom he should be ultra-careful and suspicious in any dealings. It has . . . been felt . . . that an accused person is likely to be prejudiced rather than assisted by a legal 'friend' at a court martial: party because of this suspicion of all legal forms,

processes and persons, partly because an outsider can know nothing of the ways of the seas or the Service. Thus a revolution would almost be necessary to bring about the establishment of a Naval Legal Branch, or the mentality necessary to receive it.[7]

The need for major reform in an area of notorious complexity was not left entirely for the Navy to ponder. The interest of Australian politicians in the disciplinary codes of all three Services, was partly prompted by concerns as to the operation and jurisdiction of Australian and Imperial laws over Australian servicemen.[8] This interest was met with cooperation from the Army, which wanted an Australian disciplinary code; conditional cooperation from the RAAF, which wanted the new code to mirror the British code as much as possible, but with staunch resistance from the Navy.

Both newspaper editorials and parliamentary debates on *Voyager* in 1964 revealed some obvious disquiet about naval discipline. As that disquiet took the form of a lack of faith in the integrity of those charged with the maintenance of discipline and the just and impartial treatment of accused persons, it was to be expected that the press and the parliament would seek an external investigation of the circumstances relating to the disaster. Of course, those within the Navy, especially those with an involvement in the day-to-day task of maintaining discipline, saw little wrong with the system. Naval law and the practice of discipline may not have always rested on ensuring justice; but it did serve to promote what was best for the Service. Legal technicalities were of little consequence. It may have been rough justice but it was seen as eminently practical.

The overwhelming rejection of the Navy's procedures following the loss of *Voyager* led to a complete change of attitude to naval discipline. Something needed to be done to restore confidence in naval law and Service discipline both inside and outside the Navy. Preston contends that a change of personalities in the Naval Board was also responsible for a change in the Navy's attitude towards a uniform Australian disciplinary code.[9]

In spite of being the most intransigent of the three services towards a new discipline code throughout the 1950s and early 1960s, the Navy attempted to reinvigorate interest in the undertaking from 1965. Although there is no document specifically linking *Voyager* with this change of attitude, there is little doubt that the Navy's confidence in the system as it existed throughout 1964 was shaken.[10]

In reconsidering its disciplinary procedures, the Navy was also bound to review the competency of the people who administered these procedures. The RAN did not believe until about the mid-1960s, that there was any call for full-time legal officers. Any advice it required for matters relating to naval policy came from either the Attorney-General's Department or the Crown Solicitor's office, as requested and when required. The Service relied upon its own officers of the Supply and Secretariat Branch, who were given some very elementary training in the law as sub-lieutenants at the Royal Naval College at Greenwich, and later a broad introduction at the same college as part of the prerequisites for promotion to lieutenant commander.

In 1963, the CNJA, Commander Larry Winch, a qualified barrister, put the view that the Navy could no longer afford to rely on legal advice from officers who had a general overview of the law in England and knowledge which had been acquired at varying points in their careers. He was prompted by criticism from the Courts Martial Appeal Tribunal, which was formed in 1955, of a court martial conducted in 1962. The Mannion Appeal, as it was known, saw the Navy severely criticised for the handling of the trial, particularly the naval judge advocate. Later in 1963, a panel of lawyers was established from various elements within the Citizen Naval Forces with the aim of using them as a source of legal advice.[11]

The Navy did not give consideration to having full-time legal officers until late in 1964 when three officers were permitted to undertake the New South Wales Barristers' Admission Board Examinations, and for them to read full-time in a barrister's chambers for six months after completing the course. These were the first and faltering steps, prompted by external pressures more than anything else.

However, by early 1964 the new legal organisation was still not fully in place. It was not until 8 April 1964 that Chaney publicly stated that the Navy was considering the appointment of a Judge Advocate General (JAG). The RAAF had had a JAG for many years. What prompted the Navy announcement was presumably the loss of *Voyager*. On 8 May 1964, Chaney announced that His Honour Judge Trevor Rapke of the Victorian County Court had been appointed. He was the first and only incumbent as the title was later to change. Rapke served in that capacity for thirteen years. He was the principal legal adviser to CNS and sought to maintain his independence by refusing to take rank. Around the same time, thought was given to making the CNJA the Director of Naval Legal Services to highlight the establishment of a distinct professional group within the Navy. But all of this happened after *Voyager* had been lost. Although it is easy to be critical, it is always difficult to prepare for the unexpected.

The Naval Board believed its procedures were adequate because they were largely those inherited from Britain where they had stood the test of time. However, the Admiralty never had to deal with an accident of the magnitude of *Voyager*. Other than the disastrous loss of HMS *Camperdown* and HMS *Victoria* after a peacetime collision in 1893, there does not appear to have been a collision involving two British warships investigated by a non-Royal Navy tribunal. There have been civilian Board of Trade inquiries into collisions involving Royal Navy ships and merchant ships. Much to its credit, the Royal Navy has not had a tragedy like *Voyager* since World War II and none of its carriers had been involved in major navigational incidents.

With this background, it might be assumed that had an accident like *Voyager* occurred within the Royal Navy at that time, the Admiralty would have been left to investigate the causes by its usual means. But this is only speculation. The lack of a precedent in the Australian situation did not prevent the *Voyager* Royal Commission. It would take the occurrence of a similar collision in Britain to demonstrate the extent of public and Government confidence in the Admiralty's procedures.

Of greatest relevance to this study is an American case remarkably similar in navigational aspects to the loss of *Voyager*. On 26 April 1952 the 1,700 ton destroyer USS *Hobson* collided with aircraft carrier USS *Wasp* in 15,000 feet of water, 725 miles north west of the Azores (Figure 28). *Hobson* sank in four minutes while *Wasp* limped back to New York with 75 feet of her bow torn away. The dead numbered 176, including the captain, and only 61 were rescued from the sinking destroyer.[12] As its regulations required, a Naval Court of Inquiry consisting of three rear-admirals was convened.

The collision was the product of a series of mistakes. *Wasp* was preparing to make a wide U-turn into the wind to enable her aircraft to practise deck landings. *Wasp* was not burning navigation lights. To take her station as planeguard, *Hobson* was ordered to turn to starboard. At the direction of her captain, Lieutenant Commander W. J. Tierney, *Hobson* altered to port and cut across *Wasp's* bows at 37 knots. The Court in its findings offered the following explanation for Tierney's actions.[13]

> He became completely confused and, having lost the tactical picture, mistakenly continued to believe that he could turn left into position and so ordered 'left rudder'.
>
> He decided against his planned final left turn after he started the evolution but told no one of his decision and inadvertently ordered 'left rudder' when he meant 'right rudder' which in fact would have placed him near his intended position.
>
> He made an error in judging his position relative to the *Wasp*, which, as noted was darkened except for the red aircraft warning lights, and, thinking he was on the *Wasp*'s starboard bow, when he was in fact on the port bow, turned left to avoid crossing ahead.[14]

The OOW in *Hobson*, Lieutenant W. Hoefer, tried to dissuade Tierney from altering to port but Tierney was convinced about the correctness of the manoeuvre. Tierney went down with his ship. The captain of *Wasp* was commended for the way he handled his ship both before and after the collision.

Sole blame for the collision was placed on Tierney. All other officers were cleared of any responsibility for the tragedy, at least publicly. The statement issued to Congress and the press varied from the actual findings of the Board of Inquiry which presented a majority and minority report to the convening officer, the Commander-in-Chief U.S. Atlantic Fleet (CINCLANT).

When considered together, the two reports submitted by the Court managed to allege negligence on the part of the captain and the OOW of *Wasp*. Captain B. McCaffree, USN, was criticised for the turning signal he gave *Hobson* because its execution involved a risk of collision; for the conditions under which the exercise was conducted noting speeds and ships' lighting; for making assumptions about *Hobson*'s movements which should have been challenged much earlier; for not seeking a fuller appreciation of *Hobson*'s position and relative movement; for signalling a flying course adjustment while a turn was in progress; for not keeping his ship on an advised course; and for not realising earlier that a collision situation was developing. He was not criticised for failing to sound any signal to warn *Hobson* although this fact was duly noted in the reports. The reports criticised *Wasps*'s OOW, Lieutenant Herbst, for failing to keep a proper lookout.

> Although [he] was watching the lights of *Hobson*, no ranges were requested, or deemed necessary for their complete tactical understanding. Lookouts, concentrating their attention on planes in the air, failed to observe and report significant changes of surface ship positions. Other sources of information available to the bridge were not used.[15]

If Robertson and Bate were treated harshly, one can only have extreme sympathy for McCaffree and Herbst. The attitude of the convening authority to these allegations of negligence, similar as they are to those brought against the *Melbourne* officers, could be considered a possible guide as to the way a RAN convening authority may have chosen to deal with a similar report from a RAN board of inquiry into the loss of *Voyager*.

To ascertain whether a charge of negligence was warranted against McCaffree, CINCLANT, Admiral L. D. McCormick, applied two criteria.

> Was there any action or lack of action on the part of the *Wasp* which, varying from the ordinary and approved practices of U.S. naval vessels, contributed either directly or indirectly to the making of the collision situation? If the alleged negligent act had not been committed, would the course of events have been altered in any way?[16]

It was clear that notwithstanding anything *Wasp* did or might have done with additional information, a collision would have occurred. As for the OOW, the Admiral accepted that his watchkeeping had not been perfect, 'but it is certain that any more complete information he might have obtained could not have altered the circumstances'. He added that the alleged negligent acts or derelictions of duty had not been shown to have either contributed to the collision or had a causal relationship with it. On this basis, 'neither officer should be held responsible in any degree for the collision'.[17]

So while the U.S. Navy had presented its eventual findings to the public, it withheld the essence of its deliberations. Both the majority and minority reports were much more critical than Spicer had been, and these were criticisms offered by naval experts. If there is any consistency in the views of naval experts and if the RAN's professional standards were as high as those of the U.S. Navy, an Australian Naval board of inquiry into the loss of *Voyager* should have made similar criticisms of *Melbourne*'s officers. In fact, every criticism made of McCaffree's performance, whether fair or not, could have been brought against Robertson. This would have put the Naval Board in a difficult position. Would it have dealt with Robertson, Kelly and Bate as the U.S. Navy had dealt with allegations against McCaffree and Herbst? And if it did, what would have been the reaction of the Parliament and the press, should it ever have learned of the Board's deliberations?

If the case of the loss of *Hobson* is any guide, the Naval Board may have been pleased to see an external inquiry. Although it may not have been the best solution, an external inquiry obviated the possible charge that the Naval Board had arranged an inquiry which protected the guilty and produced findings which best suited its interests. There is no doubt that if a Naval board of inquiry into *Voyager* produced an outcome similar to that for the loss of *Hobson*, the Naval Board would have been confronted with an insurmountable dilemma and an even bigger controversy than that which followed the first Royal Commission.

There was much to be said for the Marine Court of Inquiry method as provided by the various State and Commonwealth *Navigation Acts*. Indeed, the suggestion was made during the parliamentary debate in 1967 that the Navy ought to have regulations allowing for such an inquiry which placed a judge over two or more nautical assessors. However, naval ships are excluded from the Act. There was no doubt that such regulations were needed if only for the purpose of expanding the Government's range of options. As it was, once Menzies decided that the Naval board of inquiry was inadequate, he had no other alternative but to hold a Royal Commission. It was either a Naval board of inquiry or a Royal Commission although it appears he did not realise the limited number of alternatives to the normal naval procedure.

Having suffered an ordeal by Royal Commission, the Naval Board sought to prevent this ever being repeated. The Board believed the best way to avoid a Royal Commission and limit outside involvement in naval affairs was to establish a Naval Court of Inquiry along the lines proposed by Menzies in 1950. Chipp argued that the absence of such a court was a 'gap in justice' as the Departments of Civil Aviation and Transport, and the RAAF, had regulations providing for such a court.[18] Whether or not the time was right to propose new regulations for the Navy, Chipp suggested the matter should be presented to Cabinet.

Three arguments were put in its favour.

First, it would be a step towards a uniform policy for Courts of Inquiry; second, it would 'have saved a Royal Commission on *Voyager*[19]; and third, it could be made to cover naval aviation as well. There were, however, some concerns expressed by the Naval Board. Would such a court replace the Naval board of inquiry? Would the Navy lose the 'right of court martial'? While opinions were sought from the Attorney-General's Department on this matter, a draft Cabinet submission was prepared late in 1967 proposing a regulation providing for such a court to be established under the *Naval Defence Act*.[20] However, the matter was passed to the Defence Department for comment.

Discussions between the Navy and the Attorney General's Department had proceeded since Menzies's announcement of the first *Voyager* Commission. However, they had been kept low key during the Commission and after it as well, when the Cabban allegations were gradually surfacing. The new regulation would provide for a Naval Court consisting of a Federal or State judge and two naval assessors, a registrar, deputy registrar and other officials as required to assist in the court's proceedings. This was meant to provide for a full and public independent judicial investigation. It would have the power to subpoena witnesses and to take evidence on oath. The Board argued that it was preferable to a Royal Commission in that there could be professional naval experts appointed as assessors.

The Board went as far as saying that had the 1950 regulations been in place in February 1964, the 'full public investigation conducted by a judge' announced by Menzies, would have been achieved by convening a Naval court of inquiry. Whatever traditional feelings of preference for the purely Naval board of inquiry might have persisted, an incident the magnitude of the loss of *Voyager* showed that there could be situations when the existing provisions were inadequate and that change was necessary to give the Navy procedures and a jurisdiction like those which existed within the RAAF, civil aviation and the merchant marine.

In spite of the submission being prepared during the second Commission, the Minister believed action had to commence on a new regulation.

> The problem of timing still exists. Indeed it could be said to have been accentuated, in view of the appointment of the present Royal Commission into the Cabban allegations ...
>
> Nevertheless, I am becoming increasingly concerned at this gap in Navy procedures, which means that no provision exists for public and judicial inquiry into accidents other than by Royal Commission.[22]

It was because of the timing that the submission and the draft regulation were shelved and not brought before Cabinet.[22] Fortunately for the RAN, the regulations were not needed in the period that it took for them to be finalised.

Twenty years after Menzies convened the first *Voyager* Royal Commission, legislation was finally passed providing for a General Court of Inquiry which could be appointed by the Minister for Defence under Part II of the Defence (Inquiry) Regulations to inquire into any matter affecting the Defence Force. The Court would be presided over by a judge or 'an experienced legal practitioner' with the power to summon witnesses to give evidence or produce documents, to hear evidence on oath or affirmation, to hear evidence in public or in camera, or to prohibit disclosure of information.[23] In essence, this Court has all the powers and privileges of a Royal Commission including the disqualification of evidence or the final report of the court in any other legal action. It was better late than never.

How, then, should the loss of *Voyager* have been investigated? It should have been investigated by the Naval court of inquiry that would have been created in 1950 had it not been for the attitude of the Naval Board. As this form of inquiry did not exist, Menzies made the only decision possible in holding a Royal Commission.

The Navy benefited in the long run from a Royal Commission being held. There is doubt that the RAN and its means of inquiry could have stood up to sustained and detailed public scrutiny. There is also room for doubting whether the Naval Board was either prepared or administratively empowered to handle all the possible outcomes of a naval inquiry and the problems they might have produced. Given the state of the naval law in 1964 and the reputation of its practice, there were justified reservations about the RAN's ability to conduct a searching inquiry fair to all the parties involved.

Had the Naval Board insisted on investigating the collision itself and arrived through a board of inquiry at a finding, however reasoned and justifiable, that did not sit easily with public expectations, it would have had an even greater effect on the Board's already battered reputation. This was something the RAN could have done without.

# 20

# Why Did the Ships Collide?

A FTER, AND IN SPITE OF, all the evidence that was presented to the two Royal Commissions, is it possible to arrive at a convincing explanation as to why the ships collided? This remains the most pressing and vital question of all.

There are two ways to approach the problem of ascertaining the causes of the collision. The first method is to propose a theory which uses but does not conflict with the evidence. Although not all of the available evidence need be used in support of the theory, the theory should not be in contradiction with evidence not cited. This theory eventually becomes the explanation for the collision.

The other method begins with a number of possible theories. This is a preferable approach because it admits all the possibilities. In the case of *Voyager*, there are four main theories with a number of variations. Each of the theories is reduced until an unacceptable probability or a conflict with the known facts is identified. It can then be discarded. Given that there can only be one correct set of primary and contributory causes for the collision, the one theory that remains becomes the most convincing explanation for the collision, if not the actual description of why it happened.

The method adopted throughout both Royal Commissions was the first one. The reasons for this are unambiguous. Counsel appearing at the inquiries were bound to present the theory that showed their clients in the best possible light. Their purpose was not necessarily to find the causes of the collision. The 'adversary' approach to the inquiries gave that responsibility to counsel assisting. In the first Commission, Smyth was distracted from this objective by other concerns. In the second, Burt offered very few views on the causes of the collision. In fact, he was not prepared to admit that one theory was any better than another.

It might also be said that both Commissions required a standard of proof higher than any of the theories could provide. Thus, one theory may have emerged as being most likely, if indeed not probable, but would not be adopted by the Commissioners because of insufficient incontrovertible evidence. A historian is not confronted with the same problem. It is not that the standard of proof demanded in history is anything less than that required in a Royal Commission, but that history, when written with a commitment to achieve the greatest objectivity, is (or should be) indifferent to the feelings of those whose actions are analysed, and to its audience. Royal Commissions are buffeted by a vast array of concerns which reflect the pressures of prevailing mood, whereas history enjoys much greater freedom.

With this understanding of history and employing the second of the two approaches outlined above, it is possible to provide an explanation for the collision. While it must be conceded that the available body of evidence is limited, the evidence of those from *Melbourne*'s bridge and references to the movements and orders issued by *Voyager*'s officers is sufficient, when examined in conjunction with evidence from other sources, to enable the causes of the collision to be established with a fair measure of confidence.

From the first few days after the collision, it appeared as though the reason for the collision could lie in one or all of five areas. First, that signals sent between the ships did not reflect the intentions of the originator. Second, that *Voyager* had mistaken her position relative to *Melbourne*. Third, that *Voyager* correctly assessed her position relative to the carrier but miscalculated the area in which she had to manoeuvre. Fourth, that the state of training and readiness in either or both ships was poor, and fifth, that there was an equipment failure in either or both ships that went undetected. The latter three were either rejected during the two inquiries or earlier in this book.

The two primary theories that remain were proposed by Robertson — that *Voyager*'s bridge staff became confused and believed they were on the port side of *Melbourne* rather than the starboard; and by Street — that a mistaken signal was involved. If the first is reduced even further, it becomes a matter of whether *Voyager* correctly assessed her position relative to *Melbourne* when ordered to turn to the flying course of 020 degrees. If she did, her final movements were intentional and need to be probed as the reason for them is likely to be the initiating cause of the collision. If *Voyager* did mistake her position, the reasons for this error are likely to yield the answer.

It should be stressed that the present objective is to find the elusive initiating cause. There is no doubt that the collision occurred because *Voyager* failed to keep a proper lookout. Had the carrier been kept under closer observation any error in either perception or signals would have been noticed earlier and a collision averted. There can be no disputing that her captain and officer of the watch were responsible. But none of this serves to provide an explanation as to why the collision occurred.

The first step in assessing both theories is to eliminate *Melbourne* from any causative or contributory role. This can be done by looking at the final manoeuvre from the point of view of *Melbourne*'s officers. It is clear that *Melbourne* intended to alter her course from 060 to 020 degrees to conduct flying operations on a new course. She made two signals to effect this action. The first ordered an alteration of course to 020 degrees.[1] The second ordered flying stations on the same course.[2] *Melbourne*'s bridge staff believed that this later signal required the destroyer to take up planeguard station on execution. The signals were relayed correctly because they were actually heard by three of *Melbourne*'s senior bridge staff.[3]

There is no doubt that *Melbourne* carried out the turn using 20 degrees of rudder as previously declared and that approximately 60 seconds after ordering the course change she steadied on the new course of 020 degrees.[4] The manoeuvre was straightforward and *Melbourne* did not anticipate *Voyager* would have any difficulty in understanding or executing either of the signals. The officers on the carrier's bridge had no reason to believe the signals sent to the destroyer were incorrectly transmitted or that there was any reason why they might be misunderstood by *Voyager*'s bridge staff. As *Melbourne* carried out her signalled intentions, one can conclude that the initiating cause was conceived entirely on *Voyager*'s bridge.

What, then, are the defects and weaknesses of the theory posed by Robertson? The main obstacle in the way of accepting the 'mistaken bow' theory is that *Melbourne*'s green starboard sidelight was visible to *Voyager* throughout her turn to port from 060 to 020 degrees and should have left *Voyager* in no doubt that she was on *Melbourne*'s starboard bow (Figure 29). It is an obstacle that Robertson does not even acknowledge let alone attempt to counter. Instead, he deliberately draws attention away from this factor by suggesting that the difficulty inherent in assessing the apparent inclination of *Melbourne*'s silhouette was the cause of *Voyager*'s actions. While his emphasis on inclination was correct for exercises undertaken without navigation lights, such as was the case in the *Wasp-Hobson* collision, in an exercise where navigation lights were burning brightly, there was not the same problem of assessing inclination or relative position. *Voyager*'s officers did not need to study the appearance of *Melbourne*'s silhouette to know that they were on the starboard side of the carrier and that an alteration to port would have brought them towards *Melbourne*, had she been on a steady course. There is no reason to believe that the plainly visible starboard sidelight, located towards the bow of the carrier, would not have been seen by every individual of *Voyager*'s bridge. The only basis on which Robertson asserts that *Voyager* thought she was on the port bow was that her movements seemed to be consistent with such an error, and that Stevens would not pass ahead of the carrier's bows without permission. This was a superficial argument.

Robertson is correct when he says that Stevens would not cross *Melbourne*'s bow without permission. But to say that Stevens either thought he was on *Melbourne*'s port bow or 'lost the tactical picture' is to strain the credibility of his argument. The suggestion that Stevens might have been confused by the experimental red flight-deck floodlighting showing on the starboard side has little substance. Robertson knew that this was checked and found not to be the case twenty-four hours before the collision.[5] To avoid any possible confusion Robertson himself directed that *Voyager* be informed that *Melbourne* was conducting trials with these lights. There can be little doubt that the destroyer knew of these lights and how they were arranged. As a result, even greater vigilance on *Voyager*'s bridge would have been exercised to guard against any possible confusion. It needs to be stressed that *Voyager* reported no difficulty with the lights prior to the collision. If *Voyager* was able to see some red light on the starboard side from the upper experimental floodlight (the lower being obscured by the carriers bridge 'island'), the location of the light — very near to the masthead obstruction lights high on *Melbourne*'s superstructure — would have precluded the possibility of any confusion with a sidelight.

Robertson's theory was also dependent upon all of the other members of *Voyager*'s bridge staff similarly 'losing the tactical picture' and believing *Voyager* was on the port bow of *Melbourne*. This is so improbable as to render it most unlikely. For MacGregor, Cook, Price, Cullen and even the 2nd OOW, Sub-Lieutenant Davies, to have arrived at the same erroneous impression of the tactical situation, one which involved two ships executing straightforward manoeuvres, is beyond reasonable belief. There is no evidence to suggest they were confused or deceived by what they could have or did observe of the relative positions of the two ships. It is also extremely difficult to accept that if any of these officers had become aware of their confusion, they would not have informed Stevens or Price of the true situation and advised caution. It would be a severe indictment of the RAN if an officer were so afraid of his captain that he watched his ship come into collision without attempting to alert anyone.

Robertson was right when he noted the importance of Sumpter's evidence that Price was looking through his binoculars one minute before the collision. He would not look at *Melbourne* through binoculars if the carrier were obviously not where he expected it to be. The most reasonable explanation for him doing so was to confirm that *Melbourne* was doing what he expected her to do. Having observed *Melbourne* through binoculars, there would have been no avoiding the presence of the starboard sidelight.

The other aspect of Robertson's theory that requires comment relates to the performance of *Voyager*'s bridge staff. Because Samuels explained so capably what was required of both ships during the manoeuvres, he effectively made the action required by *Voyager* seem so simple that the errors he later ascribes to the destroyer's bridge staff are virtually unimaginable. By the end of the second inquiry, Robertson was prepared to ascribe an appalling lack of confidence and capability to *Voyager*'s captain and officers. Their training, experience, and competency demands that they be given far more credit than Robertson accords them. Although not an outstanding bridge team, they were much more able than Robertson needed them to be to have his theory accepted.

In fairness to Robertson, it was shown in an earlier discussion that he was less concerned to have the Commissioners accept his proposition that *Voyager* 'lost the tactical picture' than he was to establish a nexus between *Voyager* being on a continuous turn prior to the collision and his responsibility. Thus, Robertson was less interested in establishing the causes of the collision and more concerned with having his conduct freed of any censure. In effect, Samuels was particularly cunning in ensuring that his submissions that *Voyager* was on a continuous turn did not rely on the need to accept that the bridge staff became confused.

The circumstances of this particular night-flying exercise would also suggest that the attitude on *Voyager*'s bridge would have precluded any general inattentiveness. The early part of a work-up requires great concentration from all the bridge staff. In addition to the possibility that equipment could be faulty or maladjusted after a refit cycle, there is the inevitable 'rustiness' which would take a few days to overcome, and a settling period when officers and sailors learn to understand the ship's idiosyncrasies and handling. As ships usually take two to three months to achieve an acceptable level of operational readiness and efficiency, the start of a work-up is when a warship is most vulnerable to accidents or misadventure.

Although the theory proposed by Robertson is not inconsistent with the evidence, it lacks any positive corroboration and depends upon the existence of circumstances which are far too improbable for his theory to be accepted.

The other remaining possibility that needs to be considered is that the signals from *Melbourne* were either incorrectly relayed or misinterpreted on *Voyager*'s bridge. Variations on this theory were proposed by Street, Meares and Peek, while Spicer seemed to favour such a conclusion. There were several ways in which this could have occurred. They all revolve around the involvement of Tactical Operator Gary Evans.

Following the impact of the collision, Evans was thrown into the water. He told the 1964 Commission that he was unconscious for a period and sustained serious injuries. In a statement made on 4 March 1964, Evans recalled that the final signal received by *Voyager* before the collision was corpen foxtrot rather than foxtrot corpen. Reversing the first two words in the transmission would require a vastly different reaction from *Voyager*.

To reiterate the discussion of tactical signals in Chapter 3, the signal Robertson had sent to *Voyager*, foxtrot corpen — 'Estimated course for flying operations' — was an information signal advising *Voyager* that flying operations would be conducted on the ordered course. On receiving the signal, *Voyager* was to take planeguard station on *Melbourne*'s port quarter. If, however, the two words were reversed to become corpen foxtrot — 'Turn to the flying course' — *Voyager* would understand this to be an executive signal requiring her to turn to the ordered course.

The reversal of the two words in Evans's statement of 4 March 1964 was examined by Street during an *in camera* session of the first inquiry.

> Street: Your recollection was that the signal was as set out in the last two lines of the statement I have read to you?
>
> Evans: Yes, that is my recollection, apart from the fact that I think it is now 'foxtrot corpen'.
>
> Street: When did you change your mind about this 'foxtrot corpen'?
>
> Evans: After some thought, after quite a bit of thought.
>
> Street: You changed your mind before you came into the witness box yesterday, had you?
>
> Evans: Yes.
>
> Street: Until then your belief had been 'corpen foxtrot'?
>
> Evans: Yes.[6]

He was then probed by Meares on the same issue.

> Meares: Now I do not suppose that your mind has changed for this reason: that you have suddenly appreciated or at some time appreciated that if the course was 020 on the signal before [the turning signal] and 020 on the final signal and order, that if you were right about that then you could not have received a corpen foxtrot?
>
> Evans: Yes.
>
> Meares: So may I suggest to you that first thinking it was corpen foxtrot, then you have said to yourself: but wait a minute, I received 020 twice, therefore it must have been a foxtrot corpen. That is how you have done your best to work this thing out?
>
> Evans: Yes.
>
> Meares: And the reason you think now that the final signal was a foxtrot corpen is because you now appreciate that if you had understood the course as being 020 twice, then the second signal could not have been a foxtrot corpen?
>
> Evans: Yes.
>
> Meares: And that is why you have changed your mind, is it not?
>
> Evans: Yes.[7]

Alternatively, and this is something Meares did not cover, Evans may have heard the flying course as something other than 020. This view deserves to be favoured. Thus, Evans received the flying course signal from *Melbourne* but jumbled the digits. Having realised that the signal foxtrot corpen and the turning course signal should have been to the same course, Evans consciously decided that he must have heard corpen foxtrot. This would have made sense of his unconscious error.

However, Evans said he felt sure it was 'foxtrot corpen' because he had to look it up in the signal book. But this begs a vital question: why would he have looked up this signal at that time when he had earlier received the same signal? It is much more likely that he looked up corpen foxtrot just before the collision because this signal had not been transmitted previously that evening.

Spicer was inclined to believe that it was the turning course signal rather than the flying course signal that was mistaken. But this is inconsistent with the evidence and *Voyager*'s final movements, although consistent with his conclusions that were subsequently overturned. *Voyager*'s movement at 2052 to port does not exclude the possibility of the turning course having been mistaken as a westerly course. The fact that *Voyager* was observed to steady on a course of 020 degrees begins to erode its likelihood. However, for the flying course to have been given as 020 degrees, and for it to have induced the immediate starboard turn cancels out the mistaken signal theory and makes it no explanation at all. If any signal is to be mistaken, and for this mistake to have led ultimately to the collision, it needs to be the final signal. And for it to have induced a turn, rather than a stationkeeping manoeuvre, the two words 'foxtrot corpen' would need to be reversed.

Evans had obviously thought a great deal about the collision as his evidence contained elements of reconstruction rather than recollection. By way of example, the call signs of the two ships on the night of the collision were 07 for *Melbourne* and 44 for *Voyager*. Evans recalled the call signs in use that night were 21 and 59. These were the same call signs Leading Seaman Everett mentioned in his evidence. Evans gave his evidence after Everett. He was also no doubt aware of the reconstructions offered to the Commission by Robertson.

Evans, during examination by Smyth, stated: 'My impression of the cause of the accident is that *Melbourne* gave the final order to turn to port and failed to turn herself'.[8] Could this mean that the voice in the water was that of Evans? In notes for counsel, Robertson says of Patterson's evidence:

> If what Patterson says has any basis of truth in it, then it would seem that his statement that he heard somebody yelling out '*Melbourne* told us to turn to 270 and she didn't' was probably a misrepresentation of something said by Evans.[9]

Patterson was in no doubt that the voice was that of Evans. He told me that after realising that the voice he had heard was that of Evans, he mentioned the matter on three subsequent occasions to Evans.

Patterson said that on all three occasions Evans was aware of what he was referring to but would not comment.

The argument put by Street that Evans may have received the flying course and relayed it incorrectly is a compelling one. Evans was not an officer but a very junior communications sailor, inexperienced and under pressure to perform. It was an unusual exercise undertaken by a new bridge team after a long refit. Evans has recalled feeling that at the first inquiry there was a determination to blame him for what had happened.[10] He felt under attack and was naturally defensive. Of course, he was not to blame and could never have been held responsible for the collision. If any error had been made, it was the responsibility of the captain and the OOW to detect it and to initiate the correct action. This should have been stressed to Evans and to any other survivor who felt culpable before the inquiry began.

Having identified a possible initiating cause, it can be applied to the known facts of the collision (Figure 30). If the signal was relayed as corpen foxtrot and a course to the west, why did *Voyager* initially turn to starboard? The most likely explanation is that Price believed the signal was ordering *Voyager* to take planeguard station on *Melbourne*, which would be turning to the west. The order was countermanded by Stevens who believed (correctly) that the signal required *Voyager* to turn together with *Melbourne* to the new westerly course. As corpen foxtrot was a turning signal, *Voyager* would maintain true bearing and range (030 degrees at 1,000–1,500 yards) from *Melbourne*. On achieving the westerly course, *Voyager* would be ordered into planeguard station.

After countermanding Price's wheel order, Stevens stepped down into the chart table well and examined what was most likely to have been the tactical signalling manual.[11] Had Evans relayed the signal as corpen foxtrot, there would have been several reasons for thinking the signal was, or could have been, incomplete. Stevens could, for instance, have sought clarification from the signal book to show Cook, the navigator, or Cullen, the Communications Yeoman, that the correct interpretation of the signal did not involve the assumption of planeguard. Had Evans relayed the signal incorrectly, the existence of '22' at the end of the signal ('22' being the advised speed at which *Melbourne* would conduct flying operations) would have caused concern because turning course signals are not sent with an ordered speed. Evans volunteered the opinion that had he relayed the signal incorrectly, the '22' may have been taken as a time for the execution of the signal. If the signal had been relayed incorrectly there would have been reason for Stevens, Cook and Price to have consulted the signal book. The evidence of Evans suggests that this is what they did.[12]

If there was confusion or uncertainty about any of the signals transmitted from *Melbourne*, Stevens should have asked *Melbourne* for verification. The reason why this was not done relates to the character of Captain Stevens. It has been shown that Stevens was not an over-confident officer and relied on his subordinates more than most. Whereas Robertson was a trained specialist in communications, Stevens had not specialised in any area of operations. As the signals sent prior to the collision were straightforward, and *Voyager*'s concern was not prompted by the quality of signal reception but of tactical interpretation, Stevens may have been reluctant to question Robertson's signals. Thus, he may have been prepared to comply with a signal on the basis that Robertson was unlikely to have made such a simple mistake. Although there is no evidence that this was his attitude, it remains a possible reason for his decision not to verify a signal that had led him to refer to the signal book.

Having decided to turn to a westerly course, *Voyager* would need to make up for the range and bearing lost through Price's short starboard turn. The use of 10 degrees of wheel is more consistent with a turn than a stationkeeping manoeuvre. Indeed, Price's use of 15 degrees of wheel and its countermanding to 10 degrees by Stevens, strengthens the argument that Price initially misinterpreted the signal (believing that it required *Voyager* to move to planeguard station) and that Stevens corrected his action by executing a turn together to the mistaken westerly course. This was partly conceded by Robertson as Spicer noted: 'Captain Robertson thought that Port 10 in these circumstances would be an odd sort of wheel order to carry out the manoeuvre', if *Voyager* was assuming planeguard.[13]

The incorrectly relayed signal would have led *Voyager*'s bridge to believe their correct station would still have been 030 degrees at 1,000–1,500 yards from *Melbourne*. With a port turn in progress from around 2052 and 30 seconds, Price would have noticed that *Voyager* was gaining bearing while maintaining a correct range from *Melbourne*. This is what he expected to happen. He was also able to observe *Melbourne*'s starboard sidelight which would confirm the correctness of the bearings he could have taken. One minute prior to the collision, *Voyager*'s bearing and range from *Melbourne* was 056 degrees at 1,020 yards. This was what the bridge of *Voyager* would have hoped to observe. The ship was at an acceptable distance from *Melbourne* and gaining bearing, while her officers still may not have appreciated that *Melbourne* had not turned.

Over the next twenty seconds, when a collision became imminent, the bridge of *Voyager* realised that *Melbourne* had not turned. The first hint of this was MacGregor's inquiry to Patterson about *Melbourne*'s range. That possibly alerted the other bridge staff that something was wrong. Yet, it took another twenty seconds for Stevens and Price to react. *Voyager* continued to gain bearing from 056 degrees at one minute prior to the collision to 049 degrees at thirty seconds prior. As the carrier's range and inclination were difficult to assess, and given that the bridge radar in *Voyager* may not have been working properly, it is probable that Stevens and Price may not have been aware of *Melbourne*'s actual distance from *Voyager* until the two ships were *in extremis*. The final wheel and engine orders were a desperate attempt to avoid the collision but were far too late.

The turning action of the destroyer obscured the fact that *Melbourne* had not turned. Thus, at almost the same moment that Robertson realised a dangerous situation had developed, *Voyager*'s bridge came to the same view. In terms of the criticism to be levelled at either ship, if Robertson's defence about expecting the unexpected is accepted, the same standard ought to be applied to *Voyager*, notwithstanding the destroyer's duty to remain clear of the carrier. If Robertson was not aware that a collision was imminent until forty seconds before it occurred, it would be difficult to be more critical of the reaction on *Voyager*'s bridge.

If the foxtrot corpen signal had been relayed as corpen foxtrot with a course other than 020 degrees, it would have produced a situation where *Voyager*'s bridge staff thought they were in a different position with respect to *Melbourne* than was actually the case. Without committing the theory to unnecessary specifics, this explanation contends that *Voyager*'s bridge believed, for whatever reason, that the flying course was to be westerly rather than northerly, and that on execution, the ships would turn to that course with *Voyager* remaining in her former station — on a bearing of 030 degrees at a distance of 1,000–1,500 yards from the carrier.

This theory is not without its objections. Robertson believed that after altering to a course of 020 degrees, then to 060 degrees and back to 020 degrees, *Voyager*'s bridge would have been expecting the flying course to have been 020 degrees. But this is hindsight at work. While it was more than likely that flying would have been conducted on 020 degrees, *Voyager* had no reason not to expect another turn. Nearly ten minutes had elapsed between the alteration to 060 degrees then back again. With light variable winds it was just as likely that the wind was either insufficient or had shifted from 020 degrees and that *Melbourne* might need to turn back towards the south.

It could be argued that had Price believed the mistaken signal required *Voyager* to assume planeguard, he would not have turned to starboard as such a manoeuvre would have put *Voyager* astern of her station when completed. But this objection is ascribing too much competence in shiphandling to Price. When the two ships altered from the south to the north at 2042, *Voyager* executed the turn with too much wheel and consequently was left some distance from her correct station. This prompted a discussion between Stevens and Price about station-keeping and the dissimilar turning diameters of the two ships. Price was not confident and would have ensured any manoeuvre he ordered would not leave *Voyager* too close to the carrier. He may have thought that a turn to port left him with insufficient sea room, or that it would take longer to manoeuvre into station than a turn to starboard.

As for the Naval Board's reaction to the possibility of a mistaken signal, it was very unlikely that it could ever have publicly supported such an explanation because it involved a criticism of the signalling system and communications procedures. The Board may have privately conceded that this was a weakness, and the proposed changes and amendments to the Allied Naval Signal Book suggested this may have been the case. Indeed, it accepted the need for modifications to the tactical signalling manual as a consequence of the collision and sought the concurrence of its Allied partners, the Royal Navy and the U.S. Navy, for the changes it had proposed.

This theory also needs to overcome the hurdle that the 'voice in the water' stated that *Melbourne* signalled a course of 270 degrees and this is not a corruption consisting of the flying signal which consisted of zeros and twos. It is possible, and it was raised by Spicer, that *Melbourne*'s radio call sign that night — 07 — may have become a part of the signal transmission, resulting in the 270 degrees course. However, Patterson concedes that the numbers he heard could have been different and has confirmed this with me. Other than the evidence of Patterson, the direction of the mistaken course is left wide open.[14]

There are several possible ways in which the signal numerals could have been incorrectly transposed. For instance, the numbers could simply have become jumbled in Evans's haste to relay them after being reprimanded by Cullen a short time earlier. Alternatively, when a turning signal is passed from the tactical operator to the OOW, such as *Voyager*'s final turning signal, the words used are 'ships turning together to port to 020'. There is always the possibility that the word 'to' may be heard as 'two'. In this case, the tactical operator or the OOW could either hear or say the 'to' as part of the course, so that 020 becomes 202, or 200. Rather than there being three numerals to confuse there are actually four.

There is also the need to show why the mistaken signal was not detected in *Voyager*. It is likely that Evans was the only person on *Voyager*'s bridge to have heard the final two signals. Although fitted with two loudspeakers to amplify signals over the tactical communications net, Evans stated that the bridge speakers fitted were never very clear. They were of robust and sturdy construction built more to withstand the elements that to give clear reception. Mention has already been made of Burdett's evidence that one of the speakers was not working on the night of the collision while the other was not in a position to emit clear sound to the bridge. Lieutenant Conder, one of *Voyager*'s bridge watchkeeping officers, also said that it was very difficult to hear signals over this speaker at any time because of ambient bridge noise. There was obviously something in this as the Navy Board directed after the first inquiry that they be relocated in all other escort ships.

The presence of MacGregor, the First Lieutenant, on the bridge was virtually ignored throughout the two Royal Commissions. There is evidence that he was there two minutes before the collision when *Voyager* had reversed her wheel to port and that he was aware of the manoeuvre taking place.

> Leading Seaman Patterson, who was on duty in the Operations Room immediately prior to the collision, says that about two minutes before the impact Lt Cdr MacGregor called down in an anxious voice and asked whether Patterson had *Melbourne* or *Tabard* (a submarine) on radar? Patterson said he had a quick look at the radar, he could not see them and he reported this to the bridge.[15]

It is unclear why MacGregor would ask for this information and why he should do so in an anxious voice. It is also strange that he should ask about *Tabard* which was then twenty miles to the north.

What is likely, and consistent with this theory, is that MacGregor had doubts about the developing situation some time prior to the collision. The time cited by Spicer is not definite: Patterson stated in one place in his evidence that it could have been three minutes and in another, one minute. One suspects MacGregor may have become concerned that *Melbourne* might not have turned. If Patterson's estimate of the time when this happened is slightly inaccurate, in other words, if it was closer to one minute before the collision rather than two, MacGregor may have been the first to realise that *Melbourne* had not turned.

The wheel orders used in the final manoeuvre suggest there was some difference of opinion between Stevens and Price (and possibly Cook and Cullen as well) about *Voyager*'s new station. The first order, involving 15 degrees of wheel, was probably initiated by Price, as has been mentioned. The evidence of Degenhardt in the wheelhouse was that Price certainly relayed the order. Price responded promptly to the signal conveyed by Evans and used more wheel than Stevens was known to use in station-keeping.

The evidence suggests it took as much as forty seconds for Stevens and Price to determine that their ship was standing into danger.[16] Thus, it is reasonable to conclude that they were neither confused nor overly concerned by their perceptions of the relative movement of the two ships. Had they felt uncertain of *Voyager*'s relative position, the weight of their training would have been to take immediate avoiding action. As *Melbourne*'s navigation lights were consistent with what they expected to see, other than an awareness of closing range, there was little to prompt any corrective action.

As *Voyager* was still turning to port and had a heading of around 250 degrees at twenty seconds before the collision, and given that the intention of the bridge was to continue with this turn, she might have been turning to a course of at least 20 to 30 degrees further to the south, i.e., 210 or 220 degrees. Turning at the rate of 30 degrees every twenty-two seconds under 10 degrees of wheel at 21 knots, it is likely that at the very moment that *Voyager* expected to put the wheel amidships, the ships were *in extremis*. But it was not for as much as another twenty seconds that the destroyer's bridge realised that a collision was imminent. The lack of activity for such a long period suggests a lack of alarm rather than conscious confusion.

It should also be recalled that *Voyager* had executed turns together of this magnitude earlier in the evening. In fact, the turn together *Voyager* thought she was undertaking closely resembled those of 180 degrees at 1950 and 190 degrees at 2042. During these turns, *Voyager* showed no hesitation or difficulty in executing the required manoeuvres. And as the most likely mistaken courses were between 200 and 220, not far from the 190 course they had steered for over an hour earlier in the night, a flying course in that direction would not have been entirely unexpected.

The mistaken signal theory emerges far more strongly from this process of elimination. It has positive support from the evidence and none of the improbability faced by the 'lost tactical picture' theory. In the wake of the second inquiry which clearly established that *Voyager* was on a continuous turn prior to the collision, the arguments of Street and Meares have added strength and persuasiveness. Given that Evans's evidence taken in closed session clearly suggests that he did confuse one of the final signals; that Evans is now prepared to admit that the voice in the water could have been his; that other survivors told me they were called to the first inquiry to testify to what they had heard Evans say after the collision; that Patterson is certain the voice he heard in the water was that of Evans; and that a number of other survivors have told me that either Evans or Patterson referred to the voice in the water well before the first inquiry, the most compelling conclusion to be drawn is that there was an incorrectly relayed signal and that it did initiate the series of events which ultimately led to the collision.

The exact nature of the mistake or how a mistake was made, cannot be reliably determined. It is most likely to have been an error in the numerals of the turning course signal or the first two words of the flying course signal. Either way, there is no difficulty in placing such an interpretation over Robertson's reconstructions. At any rate, the origins of the mistaken signal are of secondary importance. That *Voyager*'s bridge believed they had been ordered onto a westerly course is sufficient to identify the primary and initiating cause which led to a series of concomitant contributory causes.

# 21

# The Survivors

THERE WAS NOTHING particularly remarkable about the ship's company of HMAS *Voyager* when she sailed for the East Australia Naval Exercise Area on the morning of 10 February 1964. By the end of that day, they were a group of men whose lives had been irrevocably changed.

Those who survived the impact of the collision had then to survive a prolonged period in the water before they were rescued. One of the survivors, John Milliner, told me:

> The rescue operation initiated by *Melbourne* from a survivor's viewpoint could not be faulted. Contrary to some survivors' evidence that they witnessed drownings, I find this hard to believe. *Melbourne*'s boats were on the scene very quickly and the helicopters were spotting for the boats. I had complete confidence in being picked up and when we were taken on board *Melbourne* the organisation was superb. Each survivor was allocated an escort who led us to the showers. After showering, we were led to a mountain of clothes (all donated by *Melbourne* crew), dressed and led to the wardroom and other designated areas where there was tea, coffee, biscuits and blankets. At about midnight, we were called out to see the aft section of *Voyager* eventually sink.[1]

The first group of survivors to arrive ashore were those embarked in a Search and Rescue (SAR) craft. There were 34 men on board; they were wearing either wet underpants or pyjama trousers, or were wrapped in blankets provided by the rescue craft. Those able to eat were fed and all were provided with clothing, towels, soap and other personal items. A second SAR craft arrived at 0130 with a further 36 survivors. At daybreak, the men were issued with fresh underwear, socks, handkerchiefs and footwear. At 0815, the survivors departed Jervis Bay and were transported to HMAS *Penguin* by Navy bus. The objective was to send the survivors on leave as quickly as possible. Two officers and eight men voluntarily remained at HMAS *Creswell* to identify two bodies which were due to arrive at 1300.[2]

The media were, as expected, very keen to talk with the survivors. By mid-morning the day after the collision, the survivors were in a number of locations. Some had been flown to Balmoral Naval Hospital (HMAS *Penguin*), others were at the Naval Hospital at NAS Nowra, or at the RAN College at Jervis Bay (HMAS *Creswell*). The Navy handled the media's requests for assistance very well. After advising that survivors who felt up to speaking with the media could do so but only outside naval establishments, the Navy realised the bad press this decision could have received and dropped the proviso . In any case, most of the survivors were not fit enough to leave the establishments to which they had been taken.

Of those who survived, cuts, bruises, lacerations and broken limbs were the main types of injury. Those sailors with the worst injuries were transferred from *Melbourne* to Balmoral, suffering from multiple abrasions and lacerations, renal injuries, amputated fingers, and inhalation and ingestion of fuel oil with pneumonitis.

The Navy's response to the ordeal of the sinking for the survivors and the sorrow of those who had lost loved ones was generous, despite the criticisms directed at the Navy.

The survivors were immediately given seven days' leave and duty travel warrants to allow them to travel to next-of-kin at Commonwealth expense by 'the quickest and most comfortable method of transport'.[3] This decision was made despite the lack of a laid-down regulation on survivors' leave. It was also anomalous in that the Board did not grant survivors' leave to aircrew involved in accidents.

Arrangements were made for each survivor to be met by someone from the Navy when they arrived in their home localities. They were given replacement uniforms, pay in advance, and instructions for claiming compensation for personal items lost in the collision.

Action was also taken to assist families of those lost in *Voyager* and to assure them that the Navy would be monitoring their situations and would render any assistance. Naval social workers visited all *Voyager* widows living in naval married quarters and informed them that they could continue to occupy their homes for three months. If any widow found it difficult to find alternative accommodation within that time, favourable consideration would be given for a further three months' occupancy. It was a big undertaking and there were, not unexpectedly, some deficiencies and shortcomings in the organisation of the effort and in arrangements made.

A story appeared in several newspapers in the week following the collision alleging that personnel at HMAS *Penguin* had offered to pay the difference between rail and air fares for those survivors whose normal means of transport was by rail, the Naval Board having advised that it was unable to fund the difference between the fares. A thorough investigation did not produce any evidence,[4] but the story had soured the Navy's efforts to provide for those who had suffered. The *Sun* newspaper did its best to sensationalise the incident by referring, among other things, to sixteen survivors who 'had been given second-class sit-up train accommodation ... Why didn't the Navy charter an aircraft?' These men deserved that kind of special treatment'.

The process of chartering an aircraft would have delayed the departure of the survivors and this was ruled out by the Navy which favoured sending them home promptly. The Naval Board was unable to authorise higher standards of travel than those normally allowed for duty travel in the absence of any regulations permitting the Navy to send the survivors home on leave with Government funded transport. Not to have given the survivors leave or leave travel would have been most uncaring. By going beyond the regulations, the Navy deserved some credit and not the unfair criticism it received. The Navy later conceded that travel arrangements could have been handled better.

> Some criticisms were made of travel arrangements and these arrangements would be altered in similar circumstances to provide the quickest and most comfortable travel for all survivors on any future similar occasion.[5]

When criticism of transport arrangements emerged in newspapers, Treasury officials stated that rules relating to travel could be relaxed in special circumstances if a request was made by the concerned department. On 13 February, the Federal Treasurer, Harold Holt, said in Parliament that 'If we had received such a request, it would have been examined promptly and sympathetically'. The Naval Board claimed in reply that bookings for second-class rail tickets for some survivors were the result of a misunderstanding among those actually making the bookings who were not aware of the Board's instructions. Whatever the real reasons, at its meeting on 14 February, the Board formally decided that 'survivors of HMAS *Voyager* returning to duty from leave should be provided with the class of rail accommodation provided by Interim Pay Instructions'.[6]

The Naval Board's reputation took a battering over its handling of the disaster. But there was a bright side to Spicer's report and one from which the Navy and the nation could at least draw great solace. The men of *both ships* had displayed remarkable courage and bravery during the collision. On 12 March 1964, the Navy Minister had announced that a number of personnel from *Voyager* and *Melbourne* had been awarded bravery medals, some posthumously.

In a press statement the minister said

> the awards were made in recognition of specific acts of heroism. Award recommendations were put forward only after every survivor from the *Voyager* had been interviewed. The fortitude of all concerned was a feature of the tragedy, and there were undoubtedly many cases of courage and devotion to duty that would never be known.[7]

The highest peacetime award, the George Cross, was posthumously conferred on *Voyager*'s coxswain, Chief Petty Officer Jonathan Rogers. The two other posthumously awarded were Albert Medals for Midshipman Kerry Marien and Electrical Mechanic First Class William

Condon. Six other medals were awarded — one George Medal and five British Empire Medals, while another three sailors were given the Queen's Commendation for Brave Conduct. Midshipman Marien was the only officer to receive an award.

Although the newspapers had included snippets of information about gallant conduct, it was not until those rescued from *Voyager* were able to explain some miraculous escapes that the full extent of the courage displayed became known. Undoubtedly the actions of Rogers and Marien had the greatest effect on the Commission, the Navy and the nation. Rogers was the most senior sailor on board; Marien the most junior officer. They were singled out by Spicer in his report. Mechanical Engineer Davis stated at the Commission that

> ... someone came swimming up to me and said 'Do you need any help?' and I noticed it was Midshipman Marien. I said no, that I did not need any help, and he said, 'I think there is someone up forward in the water. I will go up there and see if they need a hand'.

Marien was not seen again.

Radar Plotter Low had been trapped in the forward cafeteria after the collision. With Low and a group of others, Rogers was attempting to open the escape hatch in the cafeteria.

> ...he was telling everyone not to panic and we would all get out if they came through one at a time. He seemed very calm. I think he was more intent on getting the younger chaps out first before going out himself. I think perhaps he might have known that he would never have got out.

Able Seaman Matthews told the Commission

> I could hear the coxswain CPO Rogers, in the forward cafe, organising the escape of all the young fellows on the ship. I could hear him telling them not to panic, and he led them in a prayer and a hymn. Later on I heard him say to Leading Seaman Rich, 'I can't get out. You get all the young fellows out of the hatch'.

They were not the only heroes but inasmuch as one represented the Navy's heritage and the other the Navy's future, there was some solace for the Service.

There was great sympathy for the survivors and the next-of-kin of those who lost their lives in the collision. At its meeting on 18 February 1964, the Cabinet noted that all 'payments in respect of the disaster were being settled expeditiously'.[8]

The basic compensation entitlements for next-of-kin were prescribed in the *Commonwealth Employees' Compensation Act 1930–1962*. On 21 February in answer to a question from Senator J. A. Cooke, Forbes stated that

> I can assure you that all claims will be handled speedily and sympathetically. As all personnel on the *Voyager* were on duty for the purposes of the Act at the time of the collision, fully dependent next-of-kin will be virtually automatically entitled to the maximum payout under the Act of £3,000 plus £100 for each

dependent child under 16. In the circumstances, there should be no necessity for persons to be represented at the Royal Commission inquiry for the purpose of establishing claims under the Act.[9]

The living were not as expeditiously looked after as the interests of the dead.

During the period when Spicer was preparing his report, the Navy was confronted by concerns about the mental and physical state of the *Voyager* survivors. On 18 May Admiral Harrington wrote to inform all administrative authorities about the survivors.

> The following is the situation with regard to the *Voyager* survivors: 163 already returned to sea, 4 on draft to sea, 57 ashore.
>
> Some of these men could possibly suffer certain psychological upset consequent upon the loss of their ship. These effects may be difficult to detect or determine. Moreover, it is not possible to say when these effects may be expected to disappear.
>
> I have discussed this with the Second Naval Member and the Minister and we have decided that occasions could occur when it might be unwise to deal with these men by the conventional application of the regulations. Administrative authorities are therefore enjoined to be particularly careful in handling the affairs of these men and should there be any doubt as to the course of action which should be followed, immediate reference is to be made to the Naval Board indicating that the man is a *Voyager* survivor.
>
> This is not intended in any way to mean that these men are not always subject to all the ordinary rules and regulations appertaining to the conduct of naval affairs. Nevertheless it could occur that in a few cases there will be a mental trauma consequent upon the loss of HMAS *Voyager* and especially careful action will therefore be appropriate.[10]

By this time, two survivors had been treated for neurosis and psychosis and one was awaiting medical survey. A further two survivors were to be discharged as unfit for Naval service while nine were still not medical category A. Of the 232 survivors, 163 had been posted to seagoing units with four about to join a ship.[11]

Of all the commands to which this letter had been sent, only the commanding officer of HMAS *Sydney* sent a signal to the Fleet Commander and the Naval Board about the matter on 18 May 1964.

> In view of the number of psychiatric cases ex-*Voyager*, request psychological assessment of ex-*Voyager* ratings borne in *Sydney* may be undertaken prior to sailing.[12]

Harrington was not moved by the signal. He wrote three things on his copy: '(i) Why *Sydney*'s only? (ii) Induce psychotic symptoms?, (iii) Deal with as they arise'.[13] His attitude was generally representative of the Naval Board, consisting of admirals, some of whom had been in ships during the war while all had served with officers and men who had been in ships that had been lost. The Second Naval Member, Rear-Admiral Smith, had been 'sunk' twice during the war.

Harrington himself drafted a reply to *Sydney*'s signal although it was despatched under the Secretary's name. It illuminates the Naval Board's view of the average sailor in the Fleet.

> The Naval Board believe that the majority of sailors are sufficiently stable and temperamentally robust to be mentally unaffected by their experiences in HMAS *Voyager*, and therefore they may not wish to be subjected to psychological assessment.
>
> To treat all the survivors as potential psychiatric cases might well implant ideas of such disabilities in minds hitherto free of them and it is therefore not intended to carry out psychological assessment of survivors who are serving in HMAS *Sydney*, or elsewhere.[14]

The Naval Board's attitude toward the *Voyager* survivors was reminiscent of the advice given to those who fall off a horse — get back on again. Where possible, the Board directed that as many of the survivors as possible be sent to seagoing ships. A number remained ashore, most were sent to one of the remaining two *Daring* Class destroyers, or a little later, *Voyager*'s replacement, HMAS *Duchess*. On 28 June, the Minister visited *Sydney* to 'particularly discuss reaction of ex-*Voyager* ratings. [He was] told of one shipwright who is under psychiatric investigation and two junior rates who have shown some signs of anxiety. [He] seemed primarily interested in whether cases were genuine or merely a means of avoiding service'.[15]

Compensation for survivors and dependents of those lost in the collision was discussed by Cabinet on 21 October 1964. The matter of compensating the relatives of accident victims had been under review for a number of years, resurrected every time some misadventure occurred within the Forces. There was no legislation governing the liability of servicemen for tortious acts committed against other servicemen. The Naval Board stated at the time: 'The practice is not to disallow any claims for this reason and this practice will continue'.[16]

At that moment, the Attorney-General's Department and the Service Departments were working on new legislation to cover the Commonwealth's liability in cases of injury to servicemen.[17] In the case of *Voyager*, all claims were treated as being in an exceptional category although, until the new legislation was passed, the Commonwealth would not admit liability and would deny liability when it believed that 'the facts do not establish negligence'.[18] The matter was considered again by Cabinet the following day. It accepted the Attorney-General's recommendations that

(a) the Commonwealth does not deny the liability of the Commonwealth in respect of acts of servicemen in any action now current or which may arise out of the collision between *Melbourne* and *Voyager*;

(b) it endeavour to settle all *Voyager* actions on terms satisfactory to it; and

(c) where such settlement cannot be effected it facilitates the assessment of damages by the Court but opposes any action for the grant of a jury in such cases.[19]

Howson recorded in his diary, 'Cabinet meeting ... (b) Problems of compensation for *Voyager* victims. We agreed not to press this in court; and to apply similarly to the "Red Sales" dependents.[20] But to draft new legislation to cover cases in the future'.[21]

The only case that had been heard by the courts by the end of 1964 was that brought by the widow of the single civilian killed in the collision. Mrs Evelyn Parker successfully sued the Commonwealth for negligence on 30 March 1965. She received £11,300 and her daughter £600. The Commonwealth admitted liability, but Justice Windeyer made the point that although he accepted the right of a civilian to claim damages,

> the law does not enable a serving member of any of Her Majesty's forces to recover damages from a fellow member because acts done by him in the course of his duty were negligently done. And if the negligent person is not himself liable, the Commonwealth in my opinion cannot be liable.

He added:

> The courts of England have for nearly 200 years said ... that to allow a member of the forces to bring an action against another member for an act done in the course of duty would be destructive of morale, discipline and efficiency of the Service, and that for that reason the common law does not give a remedy even if the conduct complained of were malicious ... The immunity of a member of the forces from action by a fellow member ... arises from their common relationship to the Crown and from the special nature of their service. It is not that members have no duty to be careful. They have, for they are liable to punishment by court-martial for neglect of duty ... But that a man may be punished for carelessness does not mean that he had a common law duty of care, neglect of which could give rise to a civil action for damages.

The *Australian*'s Special Defence Correspondent, Captain John Robertson, in an article on 10 May 1965 entitled 'Relatives need a better deal', argued for the rights of dependents of those lost in *Voyager*.

> It is necessary for these dependents, left with little or no support, to undertake expensive litigation in an endeavour to obtain the suitable compensation which should be available to them as a matter of normal administrative procedure: and it is surely an indictment of the administration that such procedures have not been established for use in peace even though the defect does not exist in time of war.

Cabinet considered the matter of payments to survivors exactly twelve months after it first dealt with the matter. The only progress that had been made was that 'the Attorney-General and the Defence and Service Departments were in the process of developing proposals for new legislation dealing with the Crown's liability in cases of injury to servicemen'.[22] Few people would have expected that the matter of compensation for the survivors, a matter not even considered in 1965, would have been occupying Australian courts more than twenty-five years after the disaster.

Those whose lives were shattered and could not recover from the trauma of the collision felt entitled to some compensation. Yet most were overwhelmed by the force of High Court's ruling and did not press for their claims. However, the Court's previous judgement was largely overturned by a ruling in 1982. With the way opened for legal action to proceed, a determined fight for compensation by the survivors began in Australian courts during 1984.

The following year (1985) the Commonwealth Government accepted that the collision had been caused by negligence and agreed to waive the six-year Statute of Limitations. However, after the Victorian Supreme Court awarded damages to two survivors of around $250,000 each, the Commonwealth decided to enforce the Statute and avoid dealing with the other nearly ninety claims that had been made. The trial judge, Justice O'Bryan, accepted the view put at the next case that the collision had occurred during 'combat action' under which damages could not be claimed.

This was challenged by Bernard Verwayen, formerly a leading electrical mechanic in *Voyager*, and upheld by a majority of the full bench of the Victorian Supreme Court which said the Commonwealth had to abide by its earlier promise not to rely on the Statute of Limitations. In a 2-1 ruling, Justices Kaye and Marks said the Commonwealth was obliged to honour its original promise and, in effect, pay any damages assessed by a court. In their ruling, the judges said

> There can be little doubt ... that the promise by the respondent [the Commonwealth] to admit the claim and not plead the Statute was made deliberately and with the knowledge and intention that [Verwayen] pursue his claim and have his damages assessed.

The ruling also noted that *Voyager* had not been engaged in military operations at the time of the collision; rather, the collision had resulted from 'sheer carelessness in the control and navigation of the two vessels or in one of them'.

The Commonwealth appealed to the High Court arguing that the court erred in its finding that *Voyager* had not been engaged in 'activities of a purely military character, or in operations which could be described as training for battle'. It also claimed the full court should have found that Verwayen was required to show that he had suffered material disadvantage as a result of the accident.

In February 1990, the High Court ruled on the Commonwealth's appeal. In a 4–3 ruling, the court decided that the Commonwealth could not defend its claim on both grounds. Justices Deane, Dawson, Toohey and Gaudron dismissed the appeal; Chief Justice Mason and Justices Brennan and McHugh took a contrary stance. In his judgement, Justice Deane stated that the Commonwealth's original stance had had the undoubted advantage that it avoided the public impression 'of a mean-spirited and technical approach to those injured in the performance of their duties as members of their country's defence forces'. Justice Dawson said the Commonwealth's abrupt change of mind from its previous 'humane' approach, had represented a breach of the firm assurance it had deliberately given on a number of occasions. The absence of any attempt on its part to justify its actions, other than to say it was legally entitled to do so, led to the inevitable conclusion that in conscience it was unable to justify them. The Commonwealth was also ordered to pay Verwayen's legal costs.[23]

As Verwayen was a Queenslander, the Brisbane *Courier Mail* followed the case and commented on the High Court ruling in an editorial on 7 September 1990 headed 'Justice at Last'.

> The view that the Commonwealth has behaved with deplorable bureaucratic self-interest in the *Voyager* case would result in very little argument in the general community. . . . The ruling means that the Commonwealth as the employer of people paid to defend the country cannot claim exemptions from civil compensation if they come to harm in the course of normal duties. This is an important precedent. It is also elementary justice.

The remaining *Voyager* survivors held what they regarded was a belated funeral for their shipmates on 10 February 1991. The Navy provided HMAS *Swan* to convey a party of survivors and family members, including the widow and son of Captain Stevens, to the place of the collision. It was ironic that one of the ships acquired by the Navy to replace *Voyager* should be given the task. Wreaths were cast on the waters. I gave the commemorative address. Later in the day, a memorial service was held in *Voyager* Memorial Park at Huskisson on the shore of Jervis Bay. After a short march along the main street of the small town, a memorial plaque was erected to those lost in the collision. It was an emotional event and one which seemed to bring finality to the tragedy. Perhaps for the first time, the survivors felt they had paid a fitting tribute to those who did not survive.

The collision changed the lives of 232 men. It also changed the Navy.

# 22

# The Price of Vigilance

B Y THE MIDDLE of 1968, the Naval Board for a second time tried to put *Voyager* into the past. There were plenty of things to distract public and Service attention by the time the parliamentary debate on the Burbury Report was concluded in early April. New ships, submarines and aircraft were entering service. RAN destroyers, helicopters and mine clearance divers were engaged in operations in and around South Vietnam. *Sydney* was constantly employed ferrying troops and supplies to the war zone. For most of 1968 *Melbourne* was undergoing an extensive refit and modernisation at Garden Island Dockyard. On 14 February 1969 she was recommissioned and began a work-up off Jervis Bay before departing for South-East Asia on 5 May 1969. If anything, captains of RAN ships engaged in fleet operations were over-cautious. There was to be no repeat of the *Voyager* collision or anything like it. This was even made clear to the foreign navies with which the RAN was exercising in the South-East Asian region.

On the night of 2–3 June, *Melbourne* was exercising in the South China Sea with a combined naval force. The SEATO exercise, called 'Sea Spirit', consisted of *Melbourne* operating her aircraft with five escorts; three U.S. ships — *Keys*, *Larson* and *Frank E. Evans*; the RNZN cruiser *Blackpool* and the Royal Navy destroyer *Cleopatra*. Shortly after 0300, *Melbourne*'s commanding officer, Captain J. Philip Stevenson, ordered the *Evans* which was ahead of the carrier to take up planeguard station astern. Having witnessed all that had happened to Robertson five years earlier, Stevenson and the Fleet Commander at that time, Rear-Admiral Crabb, had given strong warnings to all of *Melbourne*'s consorts not to turn towards the carrier when taking station. Using voice radio, *Evans* was informed that *Melbourne*'s course was 260 degrees. The carrier's navigation lights were then turned to full brilliance. Unlike *Voyager*, *Evans* was not working-up and had performed the manoeuvre four times already that night.

For 30 seconds after receiving the signal, *Evans* altered neither course nor speed and was some 3,600 yards ahead of the carrier on her port bow. The destroyer's first alteration of course was to starboard —

towards the carrier. When she continued in this direction, Stevenson took immediate action to warn the destroyer over the voice radio that she was standing into danger: 'Watch it, you are on a collision course'. At the same time, he directed *Melbourne*'s operations room to 'watch *Evans*. She appears to be on a steady bearing'. Stevenson had done everything that Robertson was criticised for not doing with respect to *Voyager*'s final movements.

In the *Evans*, her captain, Commander Albert McLemore, was asleep in his bunk. Two very inexperienced OOWs, Lieutenants Ronald Ramsey and James Hopson, were on the bridge. Ramsey, who was 24, was not a qualified OOW, while Hopson who was 28, was at sea for the first time as an officer. With *Evans* now on a steady course towards the carrier producing a relative closing speed of over 40 knots, *Melbourne* expected the American destroyer to take action on the warning signal which *Evans* had acknowledged.

With *Evans* maintaining her course, a collision seemed inevitable and Stevenson took action to best protect his ship. Realising, again from the *Voyager* collision, that putting *Melbourne*'s engines astern would not achieve anything, Stevenson altered the carrier's course to port. Remembering Spicer's criticism of Robertson, Stevenson, with two blasts on *Melbourne*'s siren, signalled that her rudder was hard to port. It appeared as though the carrier's turn would allow *Evans* to pass narrowly ahead of her. But maintaining her stationing speed of 22 knots, the destroyer then reversed her wheel to starboard and under the carrier's bows. For the second time in five years, the hapless *Melbourne* cut another planeguard destroyer in half (Figure 31).

The bow section of *Evans* sank very quickly with the astern remaining afloat for some days, having been secured to the carrier after the collision. Of a ship's company of 273, seventy-four American sailors were lost, almost all of them in the forward section.

The Australian press featured headlines with the 'Here we go again' theme. *Melbourne* was tagged the 'jinx' ship and reporters alleged a hoodoo surrounded her every move. Comment was sought from Robertson but he resolutely refused. Mrs Robertson wrote to the *Sydney Morning Herald* on 5 June 1969. After mentioning that the collision brought back memories of *Voyager*, she commented

> May the lessons of two Royal Commissions have been learnt well. May the RAN, this time, stand behind its own officers concerned and may the tragedy of such a disaster not be lost sight of in a mire of verbal wrangle.

Admiral Hickling was not nearly so reticent. When asked the day after the collision whether a Royal Commission should be held, Hickling remarked

> That [first] commission made a hell of a mess of it. This time there should be a board of inquiry to establish the facts, and then a court-martial if necessary.

The Americans won't stand any bloody nonsense like a royal commission. They are far too practical for that.[1]

A USN-RAN Joint Board of Inquiry was established with representatives of the two navies. The president was Rear-Admiral Jerome King, USN. The five other members were Rear-Admiral David Stevenson, RAN, Captain Ken Shands, RAN, Captain John Davidson, RAN, and two USN captains.

The inquiry was certainly not what the Naval Board expected. In what was one of the most shameful incidents in the naval and national relations between Australia and the United States, every attempt was made to reduce the culpability of the American destroyer captain.

Rear-Admiral Anthony Horton, *Melbourne*'s navigator at the time of the collision, stated in a letter to me:

> Admiral King exercised undue licence as the senior officer of the court by dint of the manner in which the court procedures were construed, and his undoubted ability to question aggressively the Australian witnesses. That was his forte: he was intelligent and given a line of questioning ... he was certainly able to pursue the questioning to his own ends. In view of his responsibilities for the Squadron of which *Evans* was a part this was perhaps to be expected ... My only other comment at this time would be that Captain Stevenson felt let down by his superiors who appeared to acquiesce to what, I presume, were pressures from the U.S. Navy as regard court procedures and the subsequent manner and timing of further legal proceedings.[2]

Lieutenant Anthony Vincent, RANR, who was sent to the inquiry to assist the RAN's legal adviser Commander Harold Glass, QC, RANR, later said of Admiral King's performance:

> I hope that if any Australian officer conducted a Board on Inquiry in this fashion his conduct would be described as disgraceful.[3]

There was little doubt that privately the Americans accepted full responsibility. Publicly, their attitude was very different. In July 1969, before the findings of the Joint Board of Inquiry were made public, a British *Polaris* submarine captain wrote in a letter to an Australian submariner friend with some relevant information about the inquiry;

> I have been away for the past month on a liaison visit to the U.S. Pacific Fleet. It might interest you to know that when I called on Admiral Hyland (CINCPACFLT) a fortnight ago [10 July] in Pearl Harbor, he said to me 'Although I haven't read the report yet — you British need have no worries over the *Melbourne* accident — it was entirely our fault.[4]

This information was not forwarded to Captain Stevenson.

When Stevenson returned to Australia, the Naval Board was considering the report of the Joint Board of Investigation 'and decided the report should be forwarded to FOCAF for necessary action'.[5] FOCAF was the relevant administrative authority and any subsequent action had to be undertaken by him.[6] Admiral Crabb informed Stevenson that as the Board's report contained some criticisms of his conduct, he had to decide what course of action to take. Having provided Stevenson with a copy of the Board's report excluding its opinion as to responsibility for the collision, Crabb informed Stevenson that charges would be framed with a view to his court martial. This was the reappearance of the traditional role of the court martial as a 'name clearing' exercise and in its denial the chief cause of Robertson's unhappiness. Although the evidence could not really sustain the charge framed, namely that he failed to transmit to *Evans* a 'positive direction to correct course after he had determined that the destroyer was on a collision course', it was considered a means whereby the RAN could positively distance itself from the Subic Bay inquiry. The Naval Board believed that a court martial

> was the only really satisfactory method of providing Stevenson with the opportunity of having the imputations against him judged professionally. He had already stated that he intended to rebut any criticism of his conduct if such were made in the report.[7]

However, as Vincent points out,

> I do not know whether Rear-Admiral Crabb had hoped that I would tell him that Stevenson wanted a court martial in order to clear his name, as used to be the fashion in the Navy. Certainly Stevenson wanted no such thing and never gave any indication that he wanted to be court martialled.[8]

There was some political opposition to the decision among those who did not understand the use of the court martial for this purpose. Liberal backbencher Tom Hughes QC, later Commonwealth Attorney-General, attempted to prevent a court martial because he believed it would be 'contrary to justice' in the absence of an RAN inquiry that provided the basis for any charge to be laid.

In her book *No Case to Answer*,[9] Mrs Joanne Stevenson drew constant parallels between her husband's case and the treatment that Robertson suffered at the hands of the Naval Board.[10] She had written better than she knew. It was for the very reason that Robertson had been denied a court martial as a means of clearing his name that the Naval Board believed that Stevenson would be of a like mind. It felt that those who called for Robertson to be court martialled would have understood, and even appreciated, this decision.

Most of the newspapers saw the court martial as a travesty although the *Australian* on 6 January 1970 was a little more charitable in its editorial:

> After the *Voyager* tragedy, Captain Robertson did not have the opportunity to clear his name in immediate court-martial proceedings . . . In Captain Stevenson's case the lesson appeared to have been learned when the Navy initiated early court action.

At his court martial, Stevenson pleaded not guilty and submitted that he had no case to answer. This was accepted and the trial, which ran from 20 to 25 August 1969, acquitted him of both charges. However, Stevenson gained no pleasure from his acquittal. He believed he had been made a scapegoat and felt hurt that the court martial had been convened. From this point, the matter quickly developed into another controversy over personalities as Stevenson was appointed to a position he also felt was effectively a demotion. While possibly appearing to be similar to Robertson's situation, the facts of his posting suggest that the Naval Board had indeed learned a great deal from its handling of Robertson.

Stevenson had been told informally as early as 21 April 1969 that he would more than likely be posted as Chief of Staff to FOCAF at the end of that year. Although normally a senior post-captain's appointment, the incumbent at that time, Captain Ian Burnside, was a junior captain temporarily filling a vacancy when several senior captains had unexpectedly resigned from the Navy towards the end of 1968.[11] This probably gave Stevenson the wrong impression about the status of that appointment. On 5 May 1969, a month before the collision, Stevenson was formally advised that his next posting would be to the Sydney area to take effect at the end of 1969. Three weeks after the collision, Stevenson was advised that his replacement in command of *Melbourne* would be Captain Geoffrey Gladstone and that the intention to have him serve in the Sydney area remained. On 25 July the Naval Board considered the Subic Bay Report and decided that it be forwarded to the Fleet Commander for appropriate action. Four days later, Vice-Admiral Victor Smith, who was then CNS, wrote to Stevenson informing him that his next posting would be as Chief of Staff to FOICEA in January 1970. On 21 October 1969, Stevenson told Smith's Secretary that he could not accept the appointment on principle and intended to retire. This was the first formal indication the Naval Board had received regarding Stevenson's intentions. The positions of Chief of Staff to FOCAF and FOICEA were formally raised to commodore status on 24 November 1969 although there is nothing on record to show that this change was planned from early 1969 as Admiral Smith claimed. However, both positions have retained that status ever since.

On the same day (24 November 1969), Stevenson expressed the reasons for his dissatisfaction. Just over one week later, Stevenson's request to retire was received in Navy Office. Smith then wrote to Stevenson offering him a number of postings and a personal interview should he want to represent his views directly. There was no reply to this invitation. On 24 December the Naval Board refused his request to retire as the Navy could not satisfy the DFRB Board that his retirement was 'to meet the needs of the Service' in accordance with the DFRB Act Section 39 2b. Having decided to leave the Navy notwithstanding the Board's decision of 24 December, Stevenson submitted his resignation on 30 December 1969 and requested that it take effect on 3 April 1970. Two days later, the Board approved his application for leave and furlough and recommended to the Governor General that his resignation be accepted.

It was obvious that the Board had learned a great deal from the loss of *Voyager* and the resignation of Robertson. There was never any suggestion following the collision, the Joint Inquiry or his court martial, that Stevenson would be removed from command. He was given an opportunity to clear his name through a court martial and enjoyed the full confidence of the Naval Board. Whereas Robertson was kept at arm's length, Stevenson was offered a number of alternative appointments from command of the Naval Air Station to command of the destroyer tender HMAS *Stalwart*. Smith offered him the latter appointment to highlight the confidence he had in Stevenson's ability as a seagoing captain. But what Stevenson really wanted — a posting to the Imperial Defence College in London — Smith was not prepared to grant.

To arouse public and political sympathy, Stevenson and his supporters, including the redoubtable Jess, tried to draw a close parallel between the treatment of Robertson and Stevenson. The *Canberra Times* took the bait in two of its editorials dated 26 August and 17 September 1969. The first remarked:

> The case of Captain Stevenson contains certain parallels with the earlier episode. Captain Robertson was humiliated as a scapegoat for, in part, faulty naval procedures which had contributed to the tragedy. Captain Stevenson has been humiliated, albeit to a lesser degree.

The second:

> The second *Melbourne* disaster, like the first, and its aftermath, will go down in Australia's naval history as a sorry mess. Captain Stevenson's colleagues will not soon forget the example of what can happen to a blameless man who takes initiatives, accepts responsibility, and gets trapped by circumstances.

The tabloid *Sun* on 5 January 1970 followed suit.

> Captain Robertson and now Captain Stevenson! HMAS *Melbourne* is proving almost as dangerous to command as it is to confront ... The Government will be inviting trouble if it treats Captain Stevenson as shabbily as it treated the equally luckless Captain Robertson.

They were inaccurate comparisons that held little water. While the Naval Board could have been criticised indirectly for the conduct of proceedings at Subic Bay, it took every step imaginable to avoid any resemblance between the handling of Robertson and its handling of Stevenson. However, despite its best intentions, the Board still managed to create a controversy. Had the Board advised its representatives on the Joint Board to submit a minority report if they felt it was justified, and if Stevenson had been consulted over the matter of a court martial to clear his name, the whole event would have been handled with far less sensation.

The clearest thing to emerge from the disaster was that Stevenson's situation demonstrated problems in the Naval pension scheme, a situation that had existed since Robertson's resignation. Refusing to allow officers to retire and draw a pension after many years service was criticised by 'A Special Correspondent' — actually Tom Millar — in a *Canberra Times* article published before Stevenson had actually left the Service.

> What amounts to deliberate economic blackmail is exercised on Service Officers to compel them to continue however unwillingly or inefficiently in the career they chose perhaps thirty or more years earlier.[12]

Millar argued that 'no officer should be bound for service longer than 20 years'. It was with this in mind that Jess headed a parliamentary committee to review the existing pension, superannuation and death entitlements for servicemen and recommended that minimum pensionable service be reduced to 20 years and the removal of the odious requirement for officers to be retired 'in the interests of the Service'.

There was little in the Stevenson case for Jess to use and it was all over by 8 January 1970 when Stevenson relinquished command of the carrier and began three months' leave before formally retiring. The Naval Board in deciding to let Stevenson go had saved a great deal of turmoil and embarrassment for the Service. Despite Jess calling for an investigation of the matter on 3 January, and the appointment of an inspector-general to examine conditions and terms of service or a review of the RAN by a British naval officer,[13] there was little real enthusiasm for yet another naval inquiry. However, the controversy was helped along by the virulent attack on Jess by the new Minister for the Navy, Jim Killen, who said that Jess had made a 'childish outburst' and that he saw himself as a 'knight in shining armour ... without the horse'.[14] While Killen criticised Jess for making general allegations instead of laying specific charges, public sympathy lay with Jess and his right to ask questions about naval administration. Jess had also made his hand clear by stating that as long as Stevenson received his full pension entitlements 'then the thing is finished'.[15]

The loss of *Evans* did not trigger renewed calls for another review of naval training and operations. It became abundantly clear that the loss of *Evans* was caused by the appalling incompetence of the American destroyer's officers. Even the often merciless Australian press appeared to understand that all of the blame rested with the Americans. Compared to *Voyager*, the loss of *Evans* was almost a source of vindication for the RAN. The Naval Board had again been the subject of criticism but on this occasion there was some genuine sympathy for the Board from within the Government. Captain Stevenson entered civilian employment and took no further action with respect to the collision and his treatment.

Two major points emerged from the loss of *Evans*. The first was that aircraft carrier operations were especially dangerous and required additional vigilance for collisions to be averted. The second was that professional men should not always assume that their peers will be more understanding of their conduct than laymen.

# 23

# *The Legacy of* Voyager

WITHIN TWELVE MONTHS of the second *Voyager* Royal Commission, Admiral Hickling published *Postscript to Voyager*. This sequel was conceived with the same intentions as the first: to restate the case for Robertson, to assert that he and his supporters had been vindicated, and to record that justice had been served. As with the first book, the second was written quickly while the inquiry was still topical. Consequently, it suffers from the same defects although they are far more pronounced as Hickling moved towards his eightieth birthday.

The second book was shorter than the first and contains little discussion or analysis. Half of the text was either quotations or long extracts from the Reports of the two Royal Commissions, Commission transcripts, newspaper reports or Hansard. It neglects vital areas of the second Commission and its findings where they relate to matters other than those affecting Robertson. Not unexpectedly, it virtually avoided all of Cabban's allegations and skirted the difficult subject of Stevens's behaviour during 1963. It would have seemed to most readers that the Commission was about John Robertson and not the state of the RAN — something Hickling does not appear to acknowledge. Thus, he passes no comment on the effect of the whole tragedy on the RAN or the wider issues that became apparent during the six-month inquiry. As most of Hickling's opinions and judgements had been heard before, and the *Voyager* case was clearly closed, this second book was something of an anti-climax.

For the next five years, there was no public mention of *Voyager*. It was not until 4 February 1974, the tenth anniversary of the collision, that the matter was taken up again.[1] On this occasion, investigative journalist Evan Whitton prepared an article for publication in the *National Times*.[2] Whitton said he had first thought of the subject when reading a speech given by Whitlam in the parliamentary debate over the report of the 1967 Commission. Although both the managing editor and the editor of the paper were not convinced that he could uncover anything new, Whitton claimed that by arranging all the material in a certain way, it would 'disclose a new pattern'. The article took three months to research and write. It was described by Frank Devine, the editor of the Australian *Reader's Digest*, as the tightest piece of its kind he had seen in Australian journalism. It won Whitton a Walkley award for the Best Magazine Feature Story in 1974. But on closer inspection, it was inaccurate and misleading. There was certainly nothing 'new' in the article that the editors had initially sought.

Whitton headed his article 'Operation Cover-up' to reflect his thesis that *Voyager* was the 'most closely documented cover-up in Australian public life'.[3] The covering up was sustained, Whitton claimed, by the Parliament, particularly the Liberal Party, 'down through various echelons of the Navy', all of which were responsible for Stevens being on the bridge of *Voyager* at the time of the collision.[4] The central allegation in Whitton's article was that Stevens was a chronic alcoholic and that this was known by a great many people who conspired to cover up this fact. The central player in the cover-up was Sir Jack Stevens who, Whitton contends, was the 'ultimate establishment figure' with influence extending to the 'power centres of politics, business, the military and the Public Service'.[5] He also implied that Sir Jack was a close friend of Menzies. However, more than six years before Whitton wrote his article, Sir Jack privately sought to refute this suggestion.

(a) I cannot claim friendship with Sir Robert.

(b) I have never been alone with him in my life.

(c) Apart from my attendance at official meetings in the Cabinet room when I was a senior public servant, I have not met him more than 7 or 8 times. The first meeting was at Ivanhoe Grammar School about 1936; the next two at Puckapunyal in 1940; the fourth in Palestine in 1941 and the remainder at official or private dinners at which Sir Robert and I were among the guests.[6]

The Whitton article was rambling and highly impressionistic. It cited sections of the Cabban Statement and recalled the events leading to the collision, relying on Hickling's imaginative reconstructions and theories. It added little to what had already been said although two remarks by Robertson, which were based solely on rumour, attracted attention. Robertson asserted that Stevens's confidential report of January 1964 suggested that McNicoll was considering having Stevens replaced. There was no truth in this. Robertson also said he had heard that Sir Jack Stevens had attempted to contact Menzies during the night of the collision. This was also false, as has been shown. Yet it served to cast Sir Jack Stevens as a shadowy, conspiratorial figure and to heighten the element of controversy.

Whitton also made much of the 1967 Commission's decision not to hear medical evidence from McCallum and Rankin. The inference that this was part of an 'establishment' cover-up, which also involved the Royal Commissioners, revealed that Whitton had not properly read the

Commission's transcripts. It also showed his research was not as exhaustive as it could have been in that he failed to identify the connection between Morrow and Asprey. As for its accuracy, there were errors in the names of individuals as well as ships. Dates were also wrong. However, the article served to generate considerable public disquiet about the collision and the way it was investigated.

Five days later, Vice-Admiral McNicoll, recently returned Australian Ambassador to Turkey, attempted in an oblique way to answer the points raised by Whitton in an article that was published simultaneously in the *Age* and the *Sydney Morning Herald*. McNicoll described his article as a story 'never told before, a story of the inner councils of the Navy during these stressful years'.[7]

The article was an apologia for the Naval Board and an indictment of Smyth and flaws in the Royal Commission method of inquiry. The main thrust of the article was McNicoll's insistence that there was no connection between the Cabban Statement and the injustice felt by Robertson. Thus, he was harshly critical of Holt for agreeing to another Commission.

McNicoll's criticism extended to the Commission's report which he described as

> a muddly document of more than 250 closely printed pages. There was not even a complete summary of the findings, and its sentences were of such difficult construction that some of them yielded their meaning only after patient study and re-reading, and some of them not even then.

McNicoll's conclusion put the case against the 1967 Commission succinctly.

> The commissioners stepped right outside their terms of reference and did something they were not asked to do. They reviewed the navigational evidence and came to a different conclusion . . . The new conclusion about Robertson had no connection with the Cabban report, which need never have been published at all. But almost no one perceived this fact, or if they did, they made nothing of it. It was made to seem as if the new verdict on Robertson arose out of the Cabban report and that, therefore, anyone who had not been in favour of the Second Commission was denying him justice.

McNicoll says he was prevented from impressing this upon Gorton by the Prime Minister's secretary, Ainslie Gotto. This meant that it was left to Nigel Bowen to make this point but 'it was too late to be of any significance'.

Not unexpectedly, St John did not allow McNicoll's article to go unchallenged. Seizing on McNicoll's remark that the Cabban Statement was 'disgusting' and full of 'lies', St John said 'I spurn and repudiate these McNicoll allegations. The Cabban Statement was the work of a man of courage, high principle and complete integrity, whom I am proud to call friend'.[8] There was nothing new in what St John said in reply. What was most noteworthy was his failure to respond to

McNicoll's contention about the absence of a tangible connection between the Cabban Statement, the causes of the collision and the position of Robertson. St John urged Cabban to take defamation action against McNicoll but Cabban held to advice given by his counsel at the conclusion of the Commission to make no public comment.[9] After this brief exchange, *Voyager* returned to obscurity once more but not before the *Sydney Morning Herald* on 6 April 1989 described *Voyager* as

> the longest and sorriest story in our naval — perhaps our parliamentary — history. It is a sad record of evasion, dishonesty and incompetence. Ministers have prevaricated, Royal Commissions have blundered, naval officers have concealed the truth. Evidence has been destroyed and 'mislaid'.

The greatest tragedy for the RAN was that some of what was written in the *Sydney Morning Herald* was true.

I have tried in this book to achieve four aims. The first contained two parts: to describe the loss of *Voyager* and events immediately before and after the collision; and to account for the four-year aftermath.

At the beginning of 1964, the RAN did not enjoy the level of public confidence that navies are accorded in most countries. A series of incidents and accidents involving RAN ships between 1958 and 1963 created doubt about the RAN's professional standards and the quality of its administration and leadership. Whereas the Australian Parliament, press and people had been largely indifferent to the Navy, which occupied a position at the fringe of public life, the frequency and increasing gravity of these mishaps brought the Navy to public prominence. They came at a time when the RAN was emerging from a long period of decline after World War II and was seeking to achieve greater independence from the Royal Navy under Australian leadership. It was also preparing for an enhanced role in regional security affairs. The accidents were interpreted by the Labor Party Opposition in Parliament and the press as reflecting a gradual decline in naval standards, prompted by Government neglect and exacerbated by shortcomings in the Australians who had assumed control from Royal Navy officers in the early 1950s.

It was true that the RAN had been steadily declining in size and capability and that some of the Australian admirals were only of average ability as administrators. However, the charge that these accidents were a product of a wider milieu would have been more accurate if it had been applied to the period between 1954 and 1959 than to the five years that followed. The other point to be made is that all the accidents involved a different set of circumstances with causes specific to each.

The drowning of five junior officers from HMAS *Sydney* in late 1963 had added to the long list of mishaps but it was significant for another reason. The inquiry into the tragedy and subsequent court martial of three officers was badly handled. When two officers were admonished by a court martial and a conviction against a third was quashed by the Naval Board, the integrity of the RAN was called into question. This created the perception that the Naval Board was collectively arrogant and considered itself, and the Navy, above public reproach and parliamentary censure. With public trust in the Naval Board and the Navy's inquiry and disciplinary procedures severely eroded, the RAN could not afford to suffer any further accidents.

It was in this context that the news of the loss of *Voyager* was received. The magnitude of the disaster overwhelmed any claim the Navy could have made about its professionalism or its ability to conduct a fair inquiry. The reaction of the Parliament, the press and the public to the disaster contained two distinct elements. The first was a demand for a comprehensive review of naval operations and administration based on the belief that naval policies and procedures must have been fundamentally flawed to allow so many accidents. The Labor Opposition went further and asserted that professional standards had invariably fallen because the Government had neglected the needs of the Navy for so long.

The second reaction was an insistence that an independent tribunal be established to inquire into the loss of *Voyager*. This was based on widespread distrust and even outright contempt for Naval procedures and practices, and was seen as a means of highlighting the accountability of the Naval Board to the Parliament and ultimately the public.

Both reactions, and the beliefs on which they were founded, created an expectation that the inquiry into the collision would no doubt reveal the Navy's need for a complete overhaul and result in the rigorous implementation of remedial action to correct the deficiencies and weaknesses. The inquiry led to neither outcome. The particular circumstances and likely causes of the collision did not reveal any major institutional shortcoming in the manner in which the RAN was operated. The matériel state of *Voyager* and the conduct of the rescue operation was another matter. Many serious problems were identified. Although a number of changes in policy and procedure resulted from some of the inquiry's findings, both the Spicer Report and the Naval Board's response to it showed that the RAN was adequately operated and that, despite some innate institutional conservatism, a willingness existed to make changes when the need for them was demonstrated.

The wide-ranging review that the Labor Opposition and some elements of the press had demanded following the collision might have been justified and borne some fruit in 1958–59 when the Navy was stagnating and a large part of the Fleet was obsolete. But after five years under Gorton's leadership and the planned acquisition of many new ships, the Naval Board, as well as officers and sailors serving in ships and shore establishments, had come to accept the reality of rapid change and the need to improve naval operating procedures and administration to make the most of the new ships and latest technology.

It was not the matters being examined by Spicer that caused the Navy the greatest angst and which resulted in the greatest change, it was the method of inquiry. Menzies was aware of the political pressure he was under to set aside the normal naval investigation procedures. His alternative, a Royal Commission, was only a marginally better means, practically and politically, for inquiring into such a disaster. Most of the deficiencies in the Royal Commission method were manifest in the first inquiry and were perpetrated.

Smyth's combative approach and what appeared to be his determination to embarrass the Naval Board and to have blame attributed to Robertson, seems to have influenced the entire course of the inquiry and curtailed its capacity to make findings of fact. Whereas both the Naval Board and Robertson could have greatly assisted the Commission in ascertaining the causes of the collision, the vigorous and sustained attacks on both by Smyth forced them into defensive positions and the adoption of submissions which were aimed primarily at rebutting the allegations that he had made. The inquiry was distracted by Smyth's performance which alienated the Commissioner from much valuable evidence that he might have heard if Smyth had conducted himself in a different manner.

The outcome was an unconvincing report and a disappointed Parliament and press. Spicer offered no explanation for the collision, failed to identify a single contributory cause and made no prescriptions for the future safe operation of the RAN. While the Naval Board initiated a series of reforms and did learn a great deal from the tragedy, sections of the Parliament, the press, and the vast majority of people who wrote letters to their newspaper editors remained dissatisfied with the Spicer Report and unconvinced that the Navy had acted to either prevent a recurrence or to raise its professional standards.

The method of inquiry sowed the seeds of discontent for Robertson. In the absence of specific charges and in the face of Smyth's unrelenting attack on his probity as a witness and conduct as a naval captain, Robertson's position at the inquiry was always a precarious one. With counsel for the Navy effectively appearing for the Naval Board, there was an early divergence in interests and Robertson was left in a position of having to defend himself without necessarily having the support of the officers whose interests he could not realistically oppose. The Board sought to defend Robertson in its submission to Cabinet against what it considered were unfair criticisms by Spicer, but the tension between political imperatives, provisions in the *Royal Commissions Act* and the normal practice of naval justice produced an outcome that was contrary to Robertson's expectations as a naval officer subject to a parallel system of law, and one he was not prepared to accept. There was no means or right of appeal, either within the *Royal Commissions Act* or the *Naval Discipline Act*, against the damage that Robertson believed had been done to his interests. Given the subject of the inquiry, the circumstances in which it was conceived, and the inherent disadvantages in the Royal Commission method, the result of the inquiry was always likely to be controversial.

Conversely, if a Naval inquiry and court martial established a case against Robertson and convicted him on a charge of negligence, this being a possibility, there would still have been a controversy. Robertson would probably have resigned and still used Cabban to force another inquiry. There was also the possibility that at some time in the future, notwithstanding the position of Robertson, Cabban's allegations may have surfaced and caused a controversy.

As there were dangers and disadvantages with both the Naval board of inquiry and Royal Commission methods, the need existed for a form of inquiry which involved both the Judiciary and the Navy. The creation of a Naval Court of Inquiry would meet that need. The involvement of judges or lawyers would satisfy the requirement for independent and impartial consideration of matters referred to the court while naval officers sitting as assessors would provide expert opinion and ensure the Navy was involved in the inquiry process. Thus, the court would have the appearance of being a partially 'in-house' inquiry and avoid the suggestion that it was an external, and therefore unwanted, intrusion into naval affairs. Had this method of inquiry existed in 1964, it would have been by far the best means of investigating the collision and would have offered the greatest prospect of avoiding destructive controversy. The method of inquiry played too great a role in affecting the outcome of events in both 1964 and 1967.

The most significant outcome of the Spicer Report was the resignation of Robertson and the wave of sympathy which enveloped him. The resignation of Robertson was seized upon by some members of Parliament and certain elements of the press as a means to voice their disappointment with the findings of the Spicer Report but, more importantly, their disappointment that the Government had resisted pressure to institute a comprehensive review of naval policies and procedures. The controversy surrounding Robertson's resignation was, in effect, a useful means of gaining sympathy for an attack on the Naval Board. Thus, Robertson was conceived as a scapegoat for corporate failings at a higher level. Robertson was a willing participant in this campaign once he had decided to resign. He used public anger with the Naval Board as a means of gaining sympathy for his own cause.

Despite the enormous public interest in *Voyager* from February to

October 1964, by the end of the year *Voyager* had virtually passed into history, taking sympathy for Robertson with her. Over the next two years, Robertson's supporters sought to exploit general dissatisfaction with the Spicer Report, ill-will towards the Naval Board and continuing interest in the causes of the collision by holding out the attractive prospect of new and relevant evidence from Cabban. But this alone was not enough. It was only when Jess and Cabban were forced to act against their own personal interests — Jess by either taking the matter into Parliament against his party's wishes or by resigning his seat, and Cabban by allowing his Statement to be used to reopen an inquiry from which he stood to gain nothing — that sufficient political pressure could be exerted to force the Government into holding another inquiry.

The Naval Board considered it had every reason to oppose reopening the inquiry. The Board realised in 1965 when, among other indicators, recruiting applications continued to decline, that it had to re-establish goodwill and public confidence by a sustained, professional performance in operations or major exercises. With the delivery of new American-built destroyers and ships fitted with the latest technology, the RAN had what it needed to prove its worth. The Indonesian 'Confrontation' and the Vietnam Conflict were prime opportunities for the RAN to silence its critics and rebuild the pride of naval people in their Service. The last thing the Naval Board wanted to face in 1965–66 was another Royal Commission. The Board believed that the lessons of *Voyager* had been learned and that nothing useful could be gained from looking at it again in any respect.

The Naval Board resisted another inquiry into *Voyager* based specifically on the Cabban Statement for four reasons. First, at least two members of the Naval Board (McNicoll and Smith) believed it to be demonstrably inaccurate and untruthful. Second, they could see no causative connection between the Cabban allegations and the collision. This was their strongest argument. Third, the Board felt a continuing obligation to defend the reputation of Captain Stevens and, by implication, their actions in placing him in command. Finally, the Naval Board considered the very convening of a Royal Commission to be a criticism of itself. The efforts of certain officers, particularly McNicoll, in opposing another inquiry in 1965–66 were less than one would have expected from men in these positions of high responsibility.

There was almost nothing the Naval Board could do once Jess and St John had brought the issue to centre stage in the national political arena. The Board could express its views through its Minister, but that was all. However, in the period immediately before Holt decided to hold another inquiry, the Naval Board unnecessarily and unwisely identified the RAN with Captain Stevens and the interests of his family. This was chiefly the design of McNicoll. A common cause was established and the Naval Board's attitude was clear.

There was, as the newspaper editorials pointed out, no middle ground. People were either for Captain Stevens or against him in the same way that they were asked to be either against Cabban, or for him. Stevens was portrayed by the opposing sides as either a loyal, dedicated and professional naval officer, or he was a moody, incompetent and tyrannical drunk. The same was done with Cabban. He was courageous, principled and forthright, or he was a scheming, disloyal and compulsive liar. Those who sided with Stevens at the same time sided against Cabban. This was the attitude the Naval Board took from the outset so that it sought to vindicate Stevens and denigrate Cabban. Thus, even before the Commission was convened, naval personnel who knew something of Stevens's time in command could be in no doubt as to what the Board believed and what opinion it had formed as to the Cabban Statement. There was an expectation that officers and sailors would be of a like mind.

The Naval Board relied on expressions of loyalty to save it from much embarrassment. There was loyalty to Stevens personally and professionally; there were feelings of sympathy with the Stevens family; there was corporate loyalty to the Navy and its best interests; and there was also the loyalty usually felt to the sacred memory of the dead. There was also hostility to Cabban.

Cabban had broken one of the Navy's primary rules: he was disloyal. He had spoken against Stevens and, by implication, the system that had produced and preferred him to others. Cabban was an easy target. He was not a private school boy; he did not have independent means or influential parents and had no social standing. He had opposed the collective ethos of the Navy *as it was in 1963*, and found himself opposed by those who drew their self-esteem and social position from that ethos. These were the people the Navy had moulded from the age of thirteen.

While the Board opposed another inquiry on several grounds, those who were arguing for it saw it fulfilling a number of purposes. Jess saw a second inquiry as a means of correcting the injustice he believed Robertson had suffered in 1964. St John saw the inquiry as part of a righteous campaign against a faceless 'Establishment', of which some admirals and politicians were a part, which apparently believed it was beyond the reach of parliamentary accountability. The press assumed that it was about finding the causes of the collision.

When the second Commission began, there was no need for the Naval Board or any senior officer to attempt a cover-up. In addition to being morally wrong, it would have been foolish. As Burt remarked, the Navy had not been obstructionist but neither had it been enthusiastic about finding the truth. Intimidation was not needed. The culture of the Navy with its emphasis on things being done 'for the good of the Service', the ability of the Naval Board to make and break the careers of officers and sailors, and the imputation that anyone who corroborated the Cabban Statement had poor or faulty judgement, ensured that much that was known would never be told by officers and sailors who did not want to see the RAN's image tarnished by outsiders.

If properly understood, the importance of acting 'for the good of the Service' was primarily to serve the purposes of the Navy's senior officers who seemed to believe that what was good for them was good for the Service. Thus, it became apparent that counsel for the Navy at both Royal Commissions was concerned to lead the views and protect the interests of the Naval Board which was providing all the instructions. When the interests of Robertson, Kelly, Bate or even Cabban, McNeill, Tiller or Willis were divergent from those of the Naval Board, the interests of the Service were those of its leadership and not its constituency. It may well have been the case that they sought and, in fact, achieved what was in the best interests of the Service.

But despite these factors which worked in its favour, it was the zeal of the Naval Board's efforts to destroy Cabban before and during the second Commission that provided the best indication that there was some substance in his allegations. In arguing with more conviction than was needed, it became obvious that the Naval Board lacked faith in Stevens's reputation and his behaviour while in command of *Voyager*. If he was fit to command *Voyager* and the Cabban Statement was so obviously untruthful, the Naval Board should have been far less concerned about an investigation of his allegations. But it took the attitude it did for two reasons.

First, the Board either felt, or feared others would feel, that it was in some way specifically culpable for having posted Stevens to *Voyager* when he was unfit and indeed unsuitable for command. Whether or not the Board considered itself culpable cannot be established. Second, the Board was concerned by the general impression that would be formed of the RAN if it were established that an incompetent alcoholic could rise to its senior ranks. This amounted to a lack of faith in the Navy's performance reporting and promotion system. In the end, the Commission showed that there were some flaws in the way Navy Office managed officers' careers.

The second inquiry did lead to changes and reforms in naval administration. Yet it was an exercise for which too great a price was paid for too little gain. The connection between the Cabban Statement and the causes of the collision was never adequately demonstrated. Having failed to establish a causal link, the Commissioners made what could only be described as a guess that it must have had a bearing on the collision. However, there was not one piece of evidence — other than Stevens having allegedly consumed a triple brandy on the night of the collision — to this effect. What the 1967 Commission did was to rearrange some of the navigational evidence and argument so as to arrive at new conclusions.

Although there was a fresh set of findings on the circumstances of the collision, the Commissioners agreed with Spicer that the cause remained inexplicable.[10] The second inquiry was no closer to ascertaining the causes. Its role was to overturn demonstrably incorrect findings. It certainly had not, as St John supposes, 'ascertained the probable or the possible cause — the concealed unfitness, from whatever cause or combination of causes, of the captain'.[11] It cannot be stressed too strongly that none of the evidence showed that any unfitness on the part of Stevens contributed to the collision.

The general 'shake-up' that Jess and others may have felt the Navy needed had occurred after the first inquiry. The circumstances in which the collision was conceived had been the basis of change and particular deficiencies had been subject to review. The Board had acted, to the extent that it was able, to prevent a recurrence. This was what the Parliament sought and the public expected from the outset.

The other branch of the first objective of this book has been to explain why the controversy over the loss of *Voyager* persisted for so long. It was the result of numerous factors which again emanated from the form and mode of inquiry. For several reasons, including the reluctance of naval witnesses to give evidence which was critical of either their shipmates or superiors, not all that was relevant to the collision was made public at either inquiry. The conduct and report of the 1964 inquiry were inadequate in numerous respects and left space for persistent speculation. To exacerbate this situation, the vested interests of all the parties represented in the 1964 Commission, or even later, prevented them from vigorously seeking the true causes of the collision. The fact that the causes were not known allowed speculation to proliferate to the extent that uncertainty existed. As Spicer offered few firm findings, the possibility that Stevens's drinking may have been a factor was given much more credence than it would have otherwise gained.

A survey of collisions throughout history involving either warships or merchantmen reveals that collisions at sea, when taken to the law courts, are traditionally difficult to explain and resolve to the satisfaction of all concerned. When coupled with the vagaries, the tendency for imprecision and the various external pressures and expectations usually felt by a Royal Commission, the likelihood of a universally accepted outcome was most unlikely. Public discussion of *Voyager*, by any measure a professional embarrassment for the RAN, damaged the Navy's public standing and led the Naval Board to take some erratic action to limit the escalating controversy. This expanded the grounds for controversy and put the matter beyond the control of the Naval Board. The fact that *Voyager* became a controversy that was never properly resolved meant that the public's interest in the case would persist. This also explains why it remains controversial and the subject of continuing speculation.

My second objective was to offer the most convincing explanation, through navigational reconstruction, as to why the collision occurred and why two Royal Commissions concluded that the causes were inexplicable.

Evidence of what occurred on *Voyager*'s bridge in the four minutes prior to the collision is limited. But a sufficiently factual base does exist on which likely explanations can be tested. I have argued that only one explanation adequately fits the facts as they are known. It has been shown that the most probable, if not the actual, initiating cause of the collision was the corruption of a tactical signal on the bridge of *Voyager*. The signal ordering *Voyager* to take planeguard station on *Melbourne* was incorrectly relayed as a turning signal. The error implicit in this manoeuvre was not perceived on the bridge of *Voyager*, or in *Melbourne*, until a collision was unavoidable.

This explanation takes as its point of departure the evidence that five officers were on *Voyager*'s bridge at the time of the collision and none expressed any concern about the manoeuvre their ship was performing until a collision was imminent. Given that *Voyager*'s position relative to *Melbourne* was made plain by the carrier's starboard sidelight which was in clear view of *Voyager*'s bridge for a period of three minutes before the collision, the cause for the collision was most probably a mistaken signal. This explanation is proposed as the most probable cause. It cannot be established as the definite cause because the officers who were responsible for the navigation of *Voyager* were lost. Evidence of their thinking would be required before the initiating cause could be established with absolute certainty.

There were several reasons why this explanation, which was shown to be superior to those offered to date, was neither presented nor accepted at either inquiry as containing the most likely causes of the collision. At this point a distinction needs to be drawn between the two Commissions. The 1964 Commission was asked to find the circumstances and causes of the collision. The terms of reference of the 1967 Commission made the causes of the collision a peripheral concern. Indeed, counsel assisting the inquiry stressed that it was not entitled to hear any fresh navigational evidence. When the Commissioners finally agreed to hear argument (as apart from evidence) on the navigational aspects of the collision, they heard argument for and against the submissions which were put on Robertson's behalf. Thus, the case put by the Naval Board on navigational aspects was concerned with countering the submissions of Robertson rather than ascertaining the causes of the collision. Given that Robertson's submissions were aimed at overturning Spicer's criticisms of his conduct, examining possible causes for the collision would only be coincidental to the submissions presented.

It would be incorrect to imply that the causes of the collision were considered by two separate tribunals. Therefore, in answering the question of why the explanation offered in this book was neither presented nor accepted at the inquiries, the answer is only relevant to the first inquiry.

The predominant reason is that this explanation could not be argued to the satisfaction of the Commissioners in either inquiry, such was the limited evidence available. The influence of vested personal interests, the other major reason, has been mentioned as well. In 1964, counsel for those involved were engaged to put their clients' involvement in the most favourable light.

The best opportunity to ascertain the causes of the collision was in 1964. But with Smyth distracted by his efforts to attach blame to Robertson, and some of the Naval witnesses feeling either intimidated or even guilty of some complicity, vital information was withheld from the inquiry. By the time of the second inquiry, more than three years had passed and the memories of the majority of witnesses had faded.

In terms of elucidating the causes of the collision, the 1967 Commission was irrelevant. The unwillingness of Cabban's counsel in his final submission to project the force and effect of his client's allegations beyond the time Cabban left the ship to the collision, further demonstrated the absence of a connection.

The other difficulty, something already alluded to, in explaining the collision was the involvement of naval witnesses, many of whom were asked to give evidence that could have been in conflict with the views of the Naval Board.

The third objective of this book was to assess the effect — in terms of specific reforms and its influence on Service culture and professional ethos — that both the disaster and the inquiries that followed had on the RAN in the immediate and longer term.

There were six types of reforms resulting from the collision and the commissions. First, those specifically prompted by the collision and the rescue operation, such as the provision of helicopter wet-winch training and changes to the recording of personnel next-of-kin details. These changes were initiated on the basis of official reports and implemented immediately. Most had to do with damage control and emergency equipment.

Second, those specifically prompted by evidence presented at the first inquiry. They included the redesign of safety hatches and the location of life jacket stowages; changes in methods of signalling the progress of flying operations between ships; and timekeeping. The majority in this category related either to specific operating procedures or technical aspects of warship construction. In nearly every instance, the Board noted the need for improving or modifying equipment, or revising procedures. Many reforms were initiated before Spicer had submitted his report.

Third, changes prompted by evidence presented at the first Commission which were unrelated to the causes of the collision. The best example here is the reissuing of instructions to the Fleet on the consumption of alcohol at sea. Although there was no suggestion that alcohol was a relevant factor, the Board discovered that in some areas practice had deviated from policy to an unacceptable degree and ordered a return to regulations. It is difficult to make generalisations about the reforms initiated on this basis although the Board seems to have treated the Commission as an exercise in validating naval policies and procedures.

Fourth, changes prompted by the Spicer Report. There were very few reforms in this category. They included the need to stagger the relief of officers in command positions, and efforts to clarify the status and authority of the Officer in Tactical Command (OTC). As the Naval Board sought to prevent political and press criticism and to avoid further external involvement in naval affairs, the need for some of the changes implicit in the Spicer Report was anticipated by the Board and the necessary action taken. These changes were carried out to satisfy external pressure. As they did not eventuate until after the release of the Spicer Report, it is fair to assume the Board did not believe they warranted any priority.

Fifth, reforms prompted by evidence presented at the second Commission and by the Burbury Report. These included the redrafting of regulations dealing with command at sea, changes to the medical examination of officers and a review of procedures for recording punishments awarded to sailors. In general, these changes related to command and personnel administration. In addition to the need for reform, the Board seemed to have accepted, as it did in 1964, the need for a more stringent adherence to existing rules and guidelines. Many of the changes prompted by the second inquiry were initiated before the inquiry ended for much the same reasons that applied in 1964. Although both the evidence presented at the inquiry and the Burbury Report did not link the need for these changes with the causes of the collision, the Board seemed nonetheless prepared to take the need for them seriously and in doing so the Board belied its insistence that Cabban was lying.

Finally, there were those reforms prompted by the form of inquiry and the Naval Board's determination to avoid a repetition. Undertaking a review of board of inquiry and court martial procedures, showing an interest in establishing a Naval Court of Inquiry and creating a Naval

Legal Service were examples of this type of change.

Although a great deal of change and reforms in naval policies, procedures and practices initiated by the Naval Board between 1964 and 1968 resulted directly from the loss of *Voyager*, a component of this change and reform would possibly have resulted from other factors. The conduct of flying operations, the administration of ships' refits and the creation of a diverse naval public relations organisation are examples of changes and reforms which would probably have taken place in due course. In this instance, the collision and the commissions were *catalysts* for change. Rather than occurring at some time over the following five to ten years, these changes and reforms were instituted immediately.

In other areas, such as the provision and use of life-saving equipment and rules relating to the consumption of alcohol at sea, the action taken by the Naval Board was solely in response to the collision. In this respect, the collision and the inquiries were *stimuli* for change in that only a disaster could have highlighted the need for change while providing the necessary motivation to see necessary corrective action implemented. Had the collision not occurred, shortcomings in tactical signalling, for instance, would only have been addressed when the need was demonstrated elsewhere, possibly in an accident in another navy, or when the contingencies of operations prompted a general review of procedures as often happened with NATO publications.

While these conclusions have sought to particularise the bases and motivation for institutional reform in the naval context, making judgements on the rate of change is difficult. In many respects, the amount of change prompted by the loss of *Voyager* meant that it had to be implemented rapidly. Whereas the RAN had previously been consciously conservative in accepting the need for reform, the extent of change and the pace of implementation led to positive and constructive attitudes which were necessary if the RAN was to broaden its relationship with the U.S. Navy. Although it is unwise to speculate about what might have happened if *Voyager* had not been lost, the existence of substantial bureaucratic inertia in most navies justifies the contention that the RAN would not have reformed itself to anywhere near the extent that it did between 1964 and 1968, and may not have performed with as much confidence as it did thereafter.

The other major effect of the collision was to break down the walls of isolation that the Naval Board, and naval people generally, had erected around the RAN. There were, in fact, two worlds. The world of the Navy, and that which was outside. By 1967, the division between the 'two worlds' was crumbling. This is not to imply that *esprit de corps* was any weaker. The greatest change was the encroachment of the civilian world, with its divergent attitudes and values, on the naval environment. The RAN was no longer the 'closed shop' that it used to be. The second *Voyager* commission forced the Navy to liaise with external organisations from which it could draw expertise and assistance. Once the Naval Board looked beyond naval organisation, the benefits were immediately apparent. The Naval Board was more ready to seek and accept advice from outside specialists in both the public and private sectors. Discussion with other government departments was considered essential as the Navy began to see itself as a part of the executive branch of government rather than an enclave.

The first inquiry prompted the Board to establish a Naval Legal Service. The controversy produced by the second inquiry led the Board to devise a comprehensive public relations and recruiting strategy and programme. Civilian consultants were engaged to advise on management and personnel administration. The Board realised that its influence and prestige would increase by and through its contact with other areas of government and private enterprise, rather than being diminished by it. Isolation from the body politic was no longer a virtue. This change in attitude was one of the most lasting effects of the collision and the Commissions.

While this assimilation into the broad confines of Government and the wider fabric of society had its merits, the convening of a Royal Commission into the disaster and the subsequent treatment of Robertson was interpreted by most naval officers as a shameful display of political acquiescence and opportunism by the Naval Board. This severely diminished the standing of the Naval Board in the eyes of most officers and drove a wedge between the Navy's senior leadership and those being led. Near total ignorance of the political environment in which the Navy was administered and in which the disaster occurred, exacerbated the sentiments of distrust and disrespect that proliferated following Robertson's resignation. Political involvement in the events following the collision was neither excessive nor destructive. However, after 1964 there was a reluctance to rely on the expression of 'downwards' loyalty through the naval chain of command. There was also a feeling, given the perception of reluctance by the Naval Board to associate itself with Robertson's action, that officers and sailors were much more personally accountable for their actions than before the collision. Distrust and suspicion appeared and became an attitudinal attribute that persisted long after the Naval Board members of the mid-1960s had retired. The high ideal of maintaining the RAN as an 'extended family', especially among the officer group, could not be sustained after the loss of *Voyager*.

My final objective has been to look at why the loss of *Voyager* became a political and media *cause célèbre*. The loss of a warship and many lives will inevitably create a public controversy. The accidental death of a large number of people will always require a thorough investigation of the circumstances and causes associated with the incident, and the attribution of responsibility. There is also the inevitable public clamour for a guilty party to blame.

*Voyager* became a *cause célèbre* because the causes of the collision were not adequately explained by either of the Royal Commissions and this allowed speculation and suspicion to flourish. Indeed, both concluded that the cause of the collision was inexplicable. An inability to ascribe a clear intention to *Voyager*'s final movements and the loss of all the responsible officers on the bridge, precluded the possibility of making a finding of fact. This is not to say that either Spicer or the Commissioners in 1967 did not have their own views on the probable cause of the collision. However, there was insufficient evidence to reach the firm conclusions that were necessary to satisfy an interested public. With a great deal of uncertainty remaining and a residual interest in ascertaining the causes of the collision, ample scope existed for a plethora of theories and allegations to be made on the grounds that they might have offered the elusive initiating cause for the collision. And in the absence of an initiating cause, there was a search, prompted by Smyth and the press, for a range of contributing causes however tenuous their relevance to the circumstances of the collision might have been.

*Voyager* also possessed every attribute of a dramatic story and this continued to attract public interest. There was the drama of the collision and the rescue; the allegations and revelations of the first inquiry; the confrontation between Robertson and the Naval Board; the disquiet created by Spicer's finding that the collision was inexplicable. As expected, public interest gradually faded although curiosity about the causes of the collision remained. It was this situation that Jess and Hickling were able to exploit in seeking to free Robertson from Spicer's criticisms. By publicly portraying Cabban as the key to unlocking the causes of the collision, Jess made the most of an eagerness within the media to seize anything which offered an explanation. This was seasoned with allegations that the Naval Board was staging a cover-up. The number of issues involved had also expanded to include the actions of the Naval Board and naval personnel before and after the collision. The ingredients of a renewed controversy were in abundance. But the perception that *Voyager* had prompted a backbench revolt meant that it was no longer a controversy involving one of the Services. It was a political dispute that had divided the Government. The controversy could only proliferate in such circumstances.

The second inquiry did little to resolve the uncertainty. Robertson had achieved a result satisfactory to him but allegations, some of them well founded, that the Naval Board had tried to conceal evidence and influence witnesses prolonged the controversy until the Burbury Report was debated in Parliament. The two days of debate in both Houses of Parliament on the Burbury Report were inconclusive. The only issue that had been resolved was Spicer's criticism of Robertson although he had received his 'act of grace' payment before the debate began. There remained the problem of what to make of Stevens, Cabban and the attitude and actions of the Naval Board toward the Cabban Statement after Hickling's first book was published. For all the effort and anguish that was involved, the Parliament was no nearer a satisfactory explanation for the collision. The *Sydney Morning Herald* summed up the prevailing mood in its editorial of 6 April 1968. It was headed, '*Voyager*: Still Too Many Doubts'. *Voyager* should never have become, as veteran Australian journalist John Farquharson suggested twenty-five years after the collision, 'one of the three biggest political controversies in Canberra along with Petrov and the sacking of the Whitlam government'.[12] While doubt existed about the causes of the collision, and it must be said that some doubt will always exist, the loss of *Voyager* will remain a controversy.

In an unsolicited letter of sympathy sent shortly after the *Voyager* tragedy, the Second Sea Lord at the Admiralty, Admiral Sir Royston Wright, wrote:

> Collisions at sea can seldom be completely explained; with all the care and attention that we give to the training of our officers, they usually seem to be 'impossible'. Yet with relentless regularity they crop up in the best trained Fleets. The fact is that ours is a dangerous calling and every now and again Fate extracts a penalty'.[13]

It would appear that *Voyager*'s motto was well chosen. She had gone 'Where Fate Calls'.

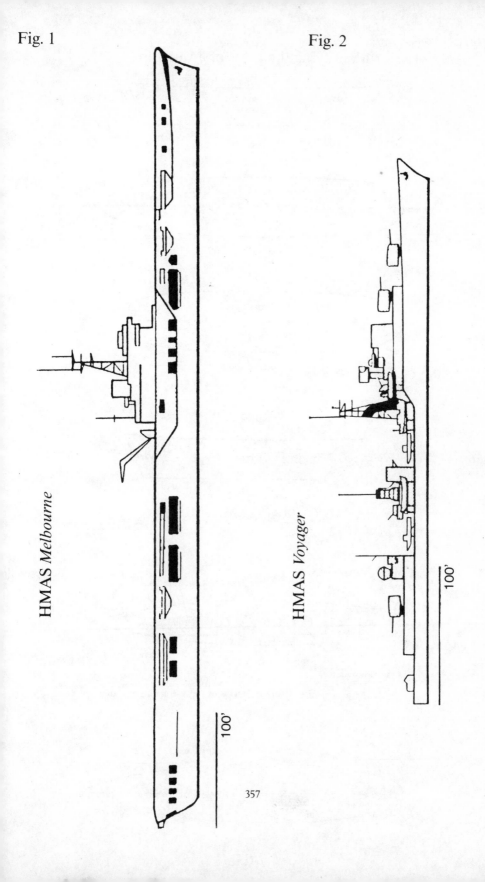

Fig. 1

Fig. 2

HMAS *Melbourne*

HMAS *Voyager*

100'

100'

357

## Fig. 3

# Identifying the parts of a warship

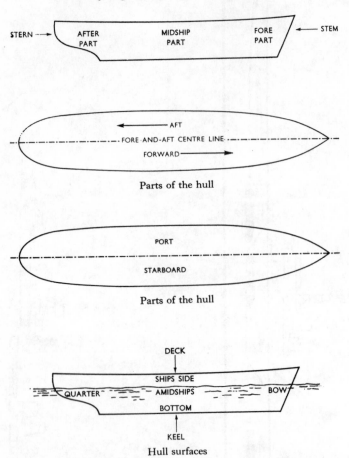

Parts of the hull

Parts of the hull

Hull surfaces

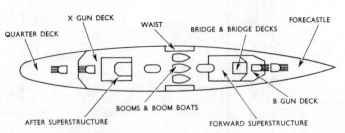

Arrangement of weather decks and superstructure of a ship

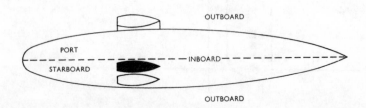

# Fig. 4

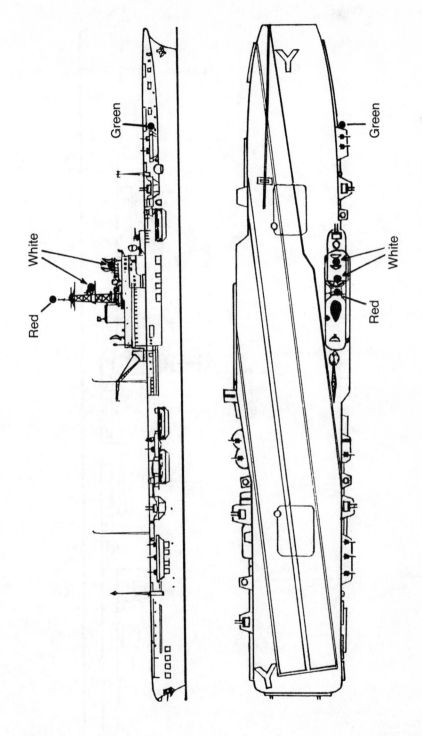

HMAS *Melbourne* – Operational and navigational lighting

Fig. 5

HMAS *Voyager* – Operational and navigational lighting

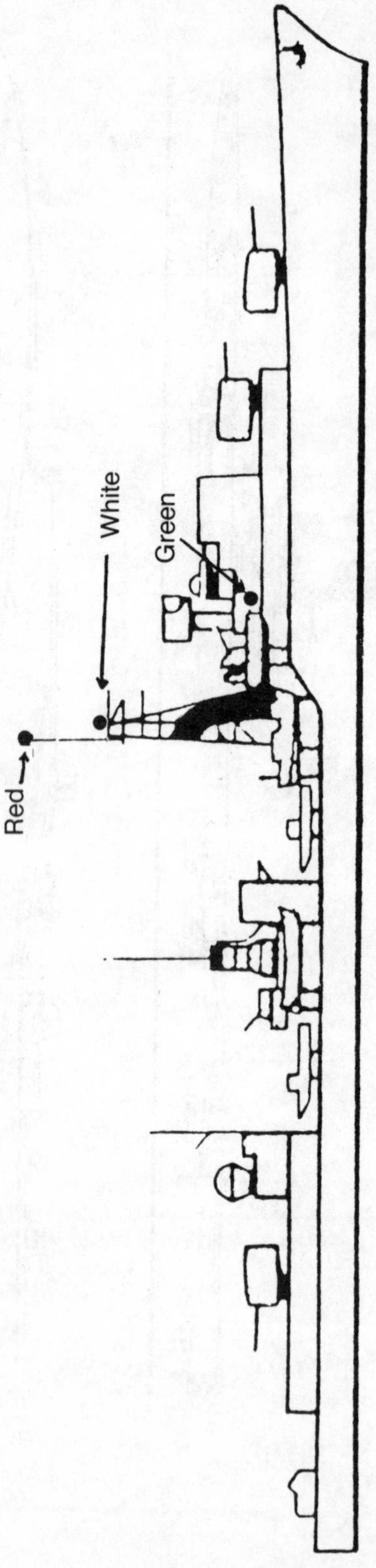

Red →

White

Green

Fig. 6

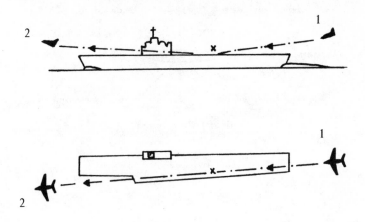

'Touch and go' procedure

Fig. 7

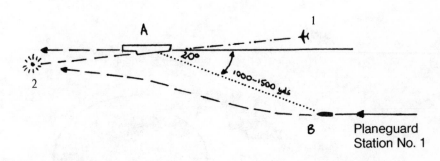

'Planeguard Station No. 1' and aircraft recovery procedure

Fig. 8

# True and relative bearings

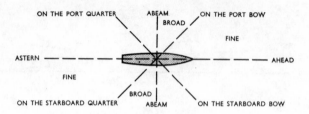

General relative bearings

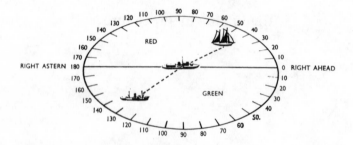

Red and green relative bearings

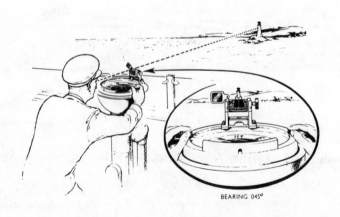

BEARING 045°

Taking a bearing

Fig. 9

Voyager's correct and actual position at 2047

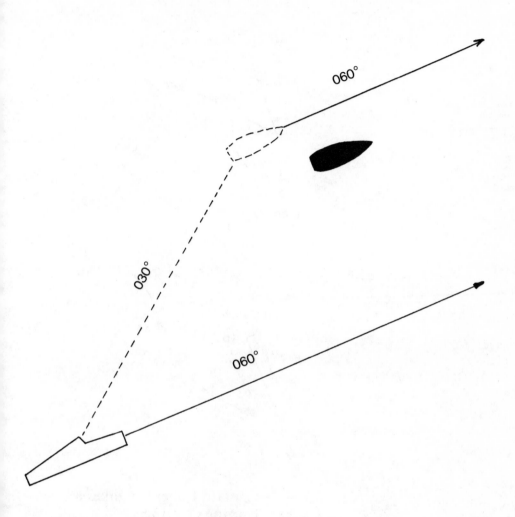

 Voyager's correct station at 2047

Voyager's actual position at 2047

# Fig. 10

## *Melbourne* and *Voyager* at 2054

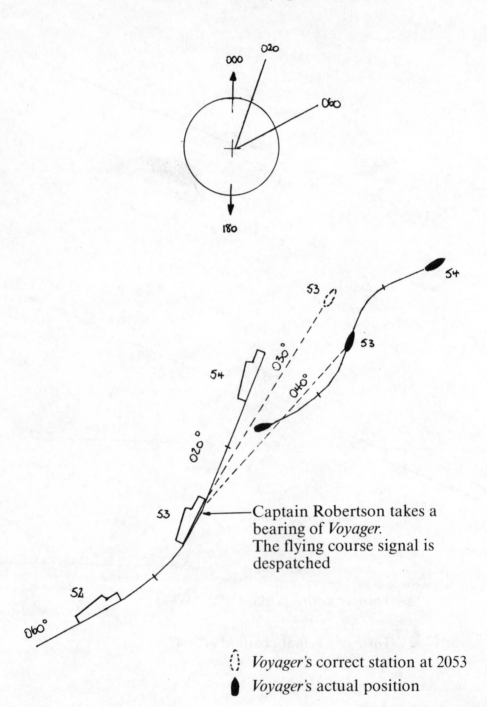

Captain Robertson takes a
bearing of *Voyager*.
The flying course signal is
despatched

*Voyager*'s correct station at 2053

*Voyager*'s actual position

Fig. 11

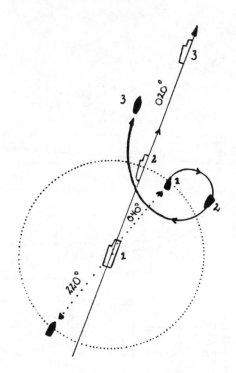

The 'usual' method of taking planeguard from forward of a carrier's bow

Fig. 12

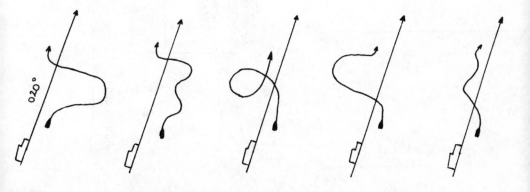

Alternative manoeuvres for taking planeguard station from forward of a carrier's bow

Fig. 13

Elevation of *Voyager*'s bridge superstructure

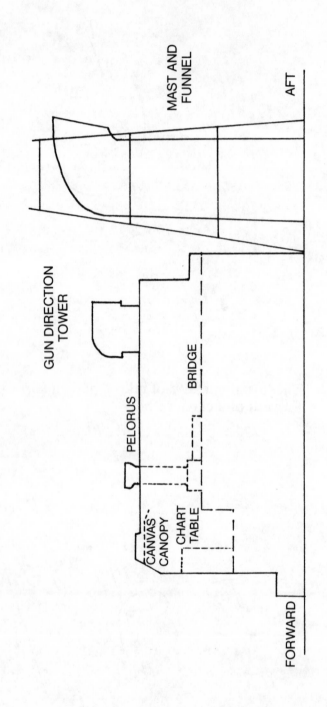

Fig. 14

Plan of *Melbourne*'s bridge

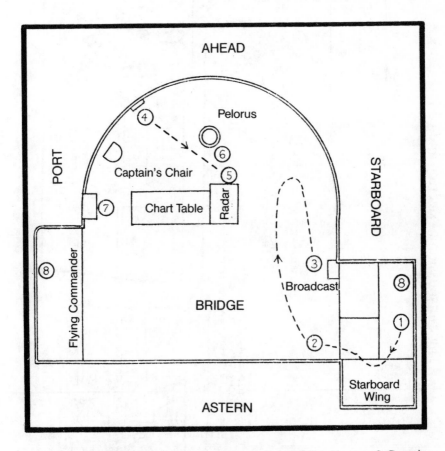

*Melbourne's* **bridge.** Key: 1 Captain Robertson watching *Voyager.* 2 Captain Robertson orders "Full speed astern". 3 Captain Robertson at broadcast. 4 Commander Kelly at anemometer, "looking for wind". 5 Commander Kelly orders "Stop both, half speed astern." 6 Officer of the watch. 7 Chief yeoman. 8 Lookouts.

Fig. 15

The transmission of steering and conning orders

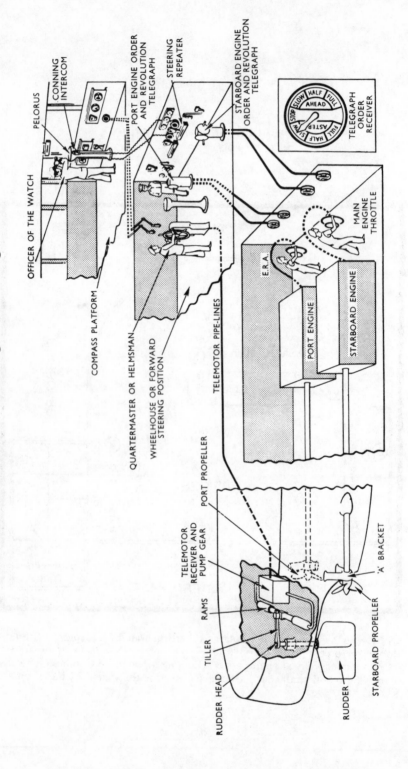

Fig. 16

Plan of *Voyager*'s bridge showing visual 'blind' arcs caused by gun director, mast, funnel and other fittings

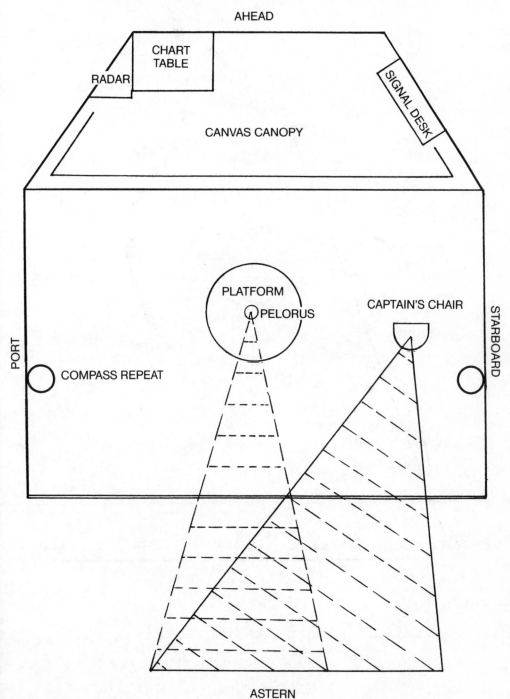

# Fig. 17

## Possible avoiding action at 2055

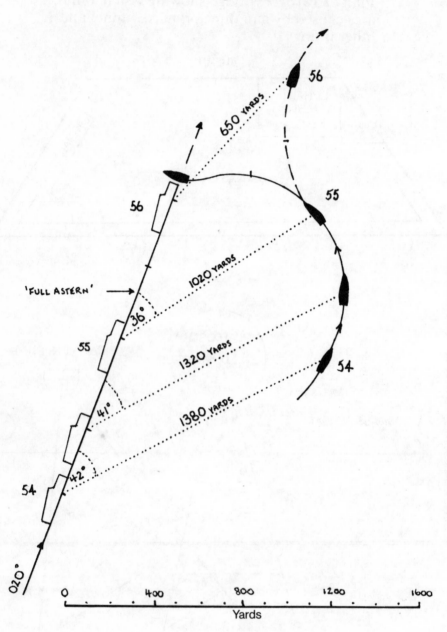

# Fig. 18

## Full astern effects

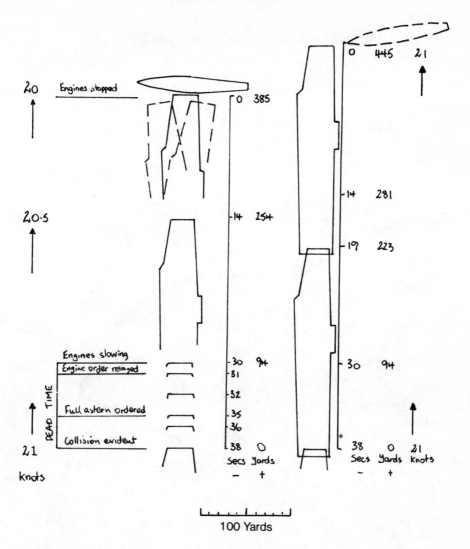

The effect of Robertson's action in ordering *Melbourne*'s engines astern is represented on the left.

Had the engine revolutions been unaltered, *Voyager* would have struck the starboard bow of *Melbourne* as shown on the right.

Had Robertson ordered the helm hard to port or starboard *Melbourne*'s heading at the point of collision would have been as indicated.

Fig. 19

*Melbourne – Voyager* tactical plot, 2055 – 2056

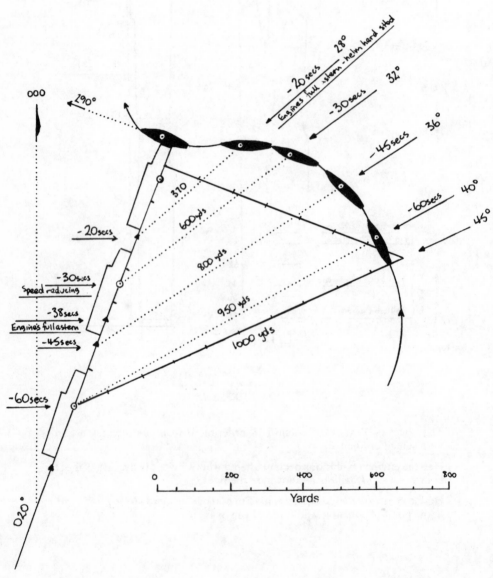

Fig. 20

## Tactical plot, 1929 – 2056

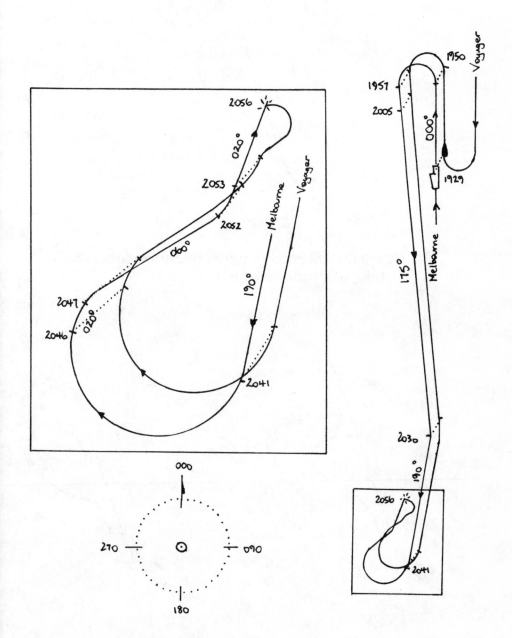

Fig. 21

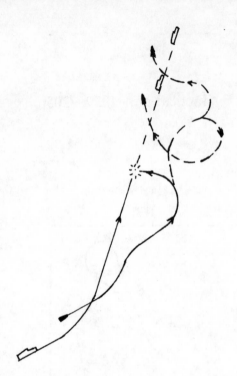

Captain Robertson's initial interpretation
of *Voyager*'s movements

Fig. 22

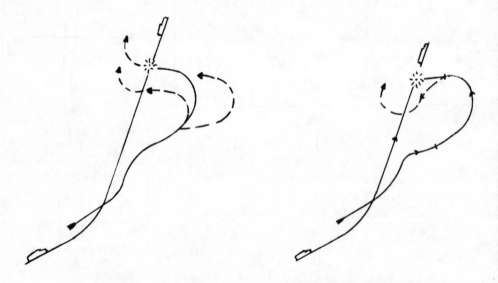

'Alternative methods for assuming planeguard station
where the initial turn to starboard was insufficient
and left *Voyager* with little room to manoeuvre.

Fig. 23

# Captain Robertson's reconstruction of 5 March 1964

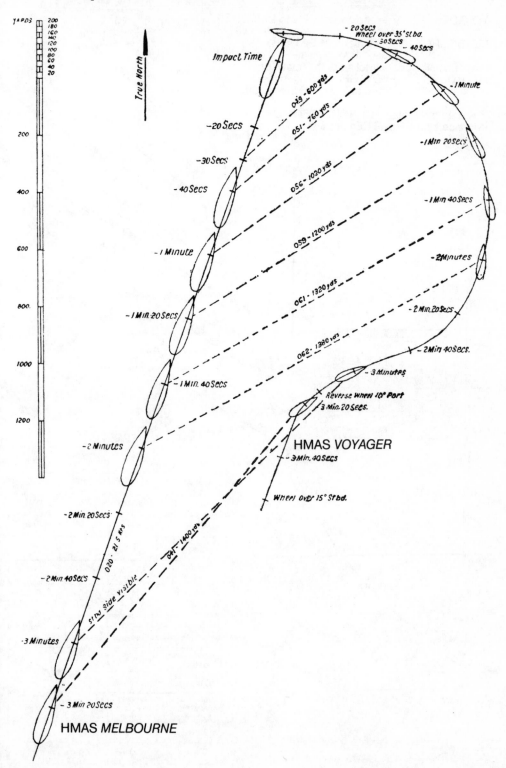

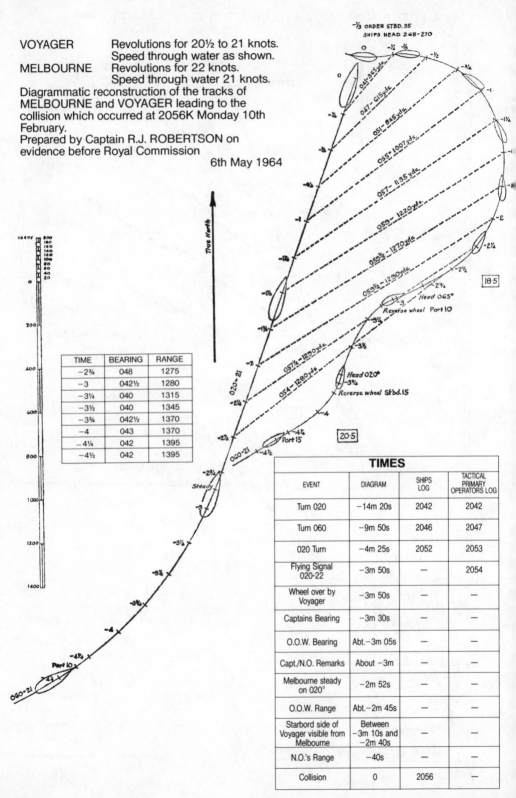

Fig. 24    Captain Robertson's reconstruction of 6 May 1964

VOYAGER    Revolutions for 20½ to 21 knots.
           Speed through water as shown.
MELBOURNE  Revolutions for 22 knots.
           Speed through water 21 knots.
Diagrammatic reconstruction of the tracks of
MELBOURNE and VOYAGER leading to the
collision which occurred at 2056K Monday 10th
February.
Prepared by Captain R.J. ROBERTSON on
evidence before Royal Commission
                          6th May 1964

| TIME | BEARING | RANGE |
|------|---------|-------|
| −2¾  | 048     | 1275  |
| −3   | 042½    | 1280  |
| −3¼  | 040     | 1315  |
| −3½  | 040     | 1345  |
| −3¾  | 042½    | 1370  |
| −4   | 043     | 1370  |
| −4¼  | 042     | 1395  |
| −4½  | 042     | 1395  |

| TIMES | | | |
|-------|---|---|---|
| EVENT | DIAGRAM | SHIPS LOG | TACTICAL PRIMARY OPERATORS LOG |
| Turn 020 | −14m 20s | 2042 | 2042 |
| Turn 060 | −9m 50s | 2046 | 2047 |
| 020 Turn | −4m 25s | 2052 | 2053 |
| Flying Signal 020-22 | −3m 50s | — | 2054 |
| Wheel over by Voyager | −3m 50s | — | — |
| Captains Bearing | −3m 30s | — | — |
| O.O.W. Bearing | Abt.−3m 05s | — | — |
| Capt./N.O. Remarks | About −3m | — | — |
| Melbourne steady on 020° | −2m 52s | — | — |
| O.O.W. Range | Abt.−2m 45s | — | — |
| Starbord side of Voyager visible from Melbourne | Between −3m 10s and −2m 40s | — | — |
| N.O.'s Range | −40s | — | — |
| Collision | 0 | 2056 | — |

Fig. 25

Mistaken signal theories proposed by Captain R.I. Peek

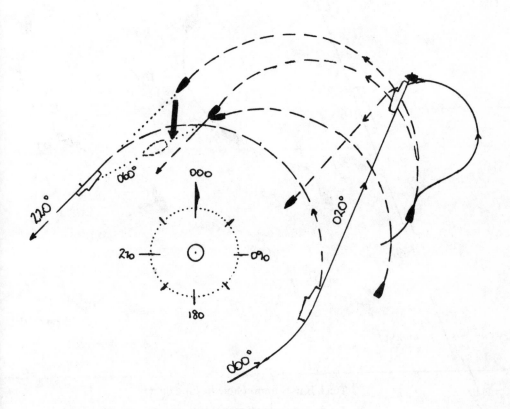

# Fig. 26

## Reconstruction of the collision based on the Spicer Report

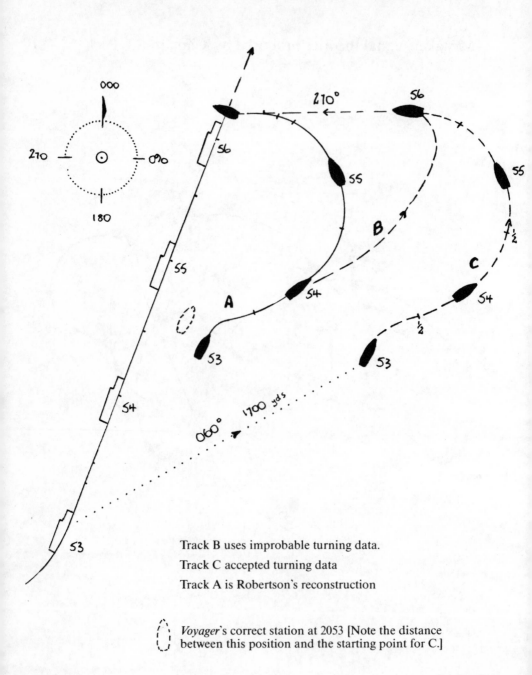

Track B uses improbable turning data.

Track C accepted turning data

Track A is Robertson's reconstruction

*Voyager's* correct station at 2053 [Note the distance between this position and the starting point for C.]

Fig. 27

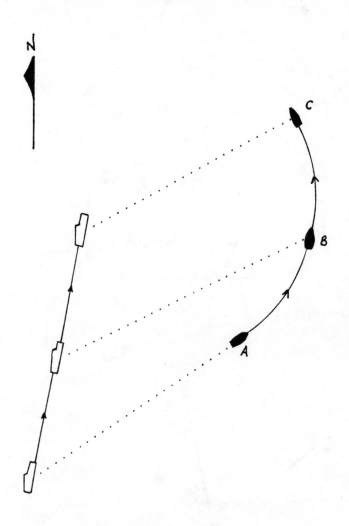

Representation of Spicer's findings
on Robertson's reconstruction

A.   Counsel considers action required.
     Commissioner considers doubt by Captain should have arisen.
     Captain believed change from 'fishtail' to zig-zag (double 'fishtail' in progress.
B.   Counsel alleges negligent failure.
     Commissioner considers inquiry by Captain required.
     Captain believed zig-zag in progress.
C.   Captain entertained doubt.
     Considered 'V' coming too far to port on zig-zag.

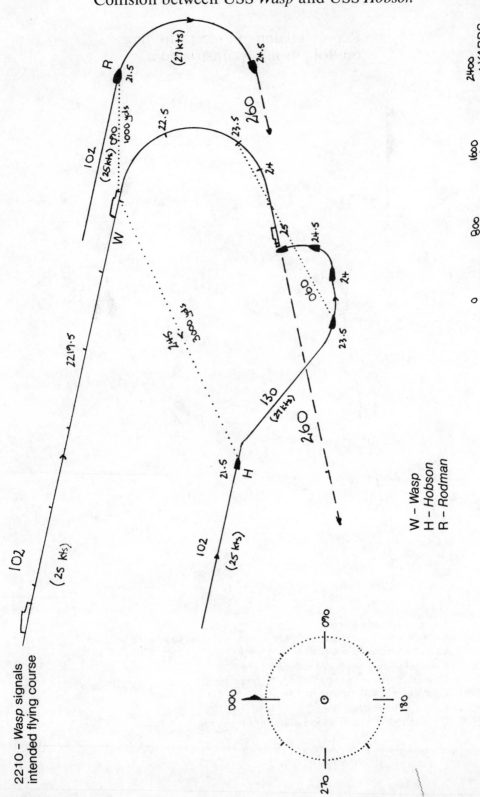

Fig. 28

Collision between USS *Wasp* and USS *Hobson*

2210 – *Wasp* signals intended flying course

W – Wasp
H – Hobson
R – Rodman

Fig. 29

# Arcs of navigation light visibility

Visibility Limit

*Melbourne*'s
starboard sidelight

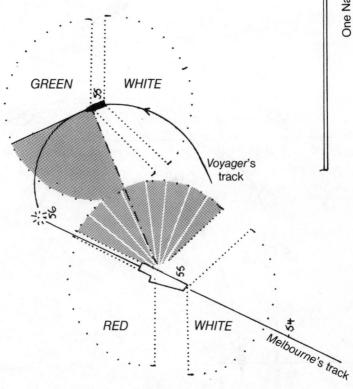

GREEN    WHITE

55

*Voyager*'s
track

56

55

RED    WHITE

44

*Melbourne*'s track

One Nautical Mile

N

Visibility Limit

*Voyager*'s
port sidelight

Fig. 30

Mistaken signal theory – possible explanation
for Lieut. Price's wheel orders
(based on a mistaken course of 270°)

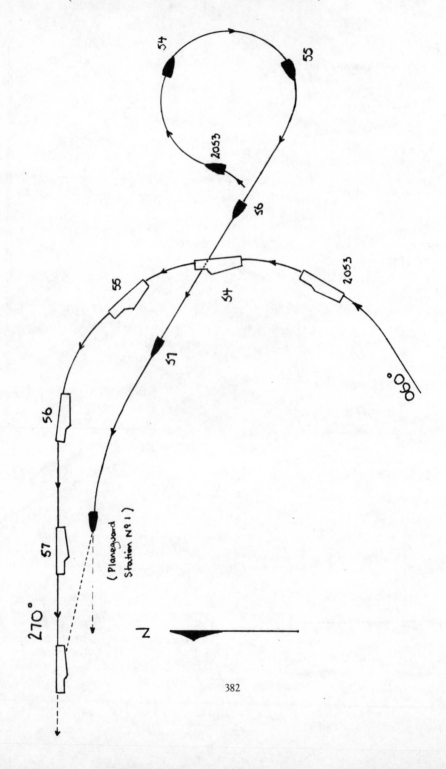

Fig. 31

Mistaken signal theory – possible explanation
of Captain Stevens's wheel orders
(based on a mistaken course of 270°)

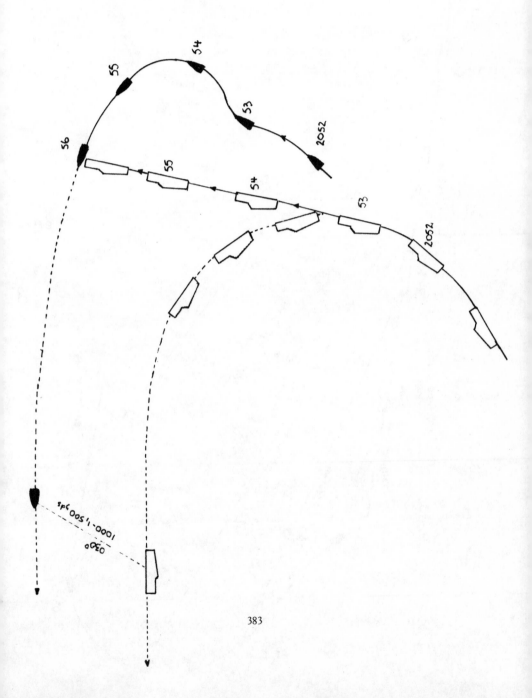

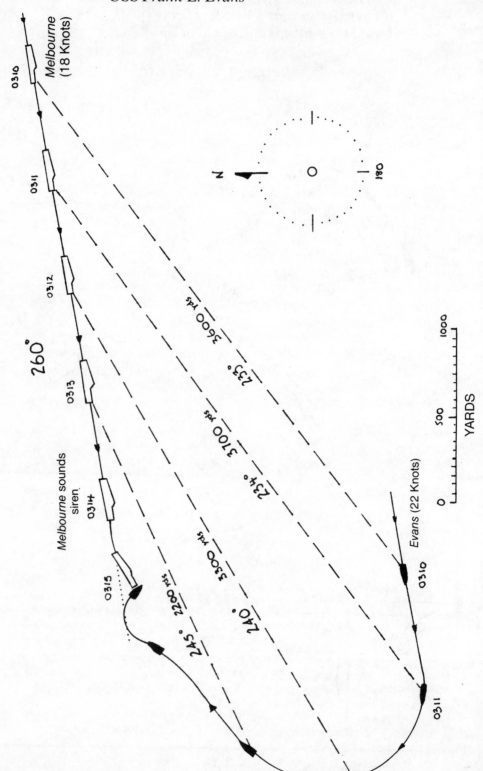

Fig. 32     Collision between HMAS *Melbourne* and USS *Frank E. Evans*

# Appendix 1
# The Cabban Statement

M Y NAME IS CABBAN. I joined *Voyager* in September 1962 as Executive Officer three days after Commander A. A. Willis took command and soon after we commenced the work-up. There were several new officers including the Navigating Officer, the Gunner Officer, the Captain and myself and the Engineer Officer. At the end of the work-up we were a reasonably well-knit team although Captain Stevens described the wardroom subsequently as the most depressed group of officers he had ever seen. And the reason is important.

When I joined *Voyager*, the day I joined, my predecessor carried on drinking with the officers until three in the afternoon. I had just left *Sydney* where I served as Executive Officer from the time of standing by till the conversion to troop carrier and I had insisted in *Sydney* that there would be no drinking at sea. Subsequently, with Commander Willis's complete support, I insisted that there would be no drinking at sea in *Voyager* and I also revised the bar hours in harbour and insisted on 100 per cent adherence to these hours except with the Captain's or my direct permission and in our presence.

These were not popular orders and they required firm discipline to maintain. However, shortly after Captain Stevens joining, two protests were lodged by the Engineer Officer, who was an Acting Commander, and the Supply Officer, a lieutenant commander, and I represented these protests to the captain on their behalf and he supported them to the extent of saying that he saw no objection to officers who had no watch and who had no direct contact with the ship's company having 'a beer' in the evening.

I should mention here that it was customary for the ship's company to be allowed to purchase a 26 ounce can of beer on most nights when no exercise took place. This didn't in any way affect my attitude towards officers drinking. I made it quite clear in the wardroom that this was the Captain's ruling and officers were free to abide by it as far as they wished but I still disapproved of any seaman officer drinking under any circumstances.

Subsequently none of the seaman officers drank at any time at sea with the exception of a gunner who joined the other two and although they were quite open with me that they disagreed, the remainder were very loyal officers and supported me to the end. They were also kind enough when I left the ship to say that although they had disagreed with me at the beginning they thought I had been right.

During the work-up Commander Willis had expressed the opinion quite strongly that the Navigating Officer was a poor ship handler. This is important because Captain Stevens on the first occasion that he took *Voyager* alongside collided with *Vampire* and subsequently rarely, if ever, handled the ship personally again, in my time on board, entering or leaving harbour, leaving it to Lt. Griffiths on almost every occasion. On two occasions I handled it, leaving harbour and entering harbour in the Far East and on the last occasion that I left harbour in a ship, which was from Sydney to Melbourne, I was given command. At that time I thought of it as a very generous gesture although the Captain was visibly affected by alcohol, on this occasion the time being 0800.

In his other shiphandling Captain Stevens was inconsistent. His station-keeping ability was extremely good and most officers would have been proud of it. But his handling was inclined to be affected by his temperament. On one notable occasion *Voyager* was taking *Ark Royal* in tow and almost collided by passing under the flight deck of *Ark Royal*, just clearing our main mast, and then in a fit of pique when the tow took too long to take up he rang on revolutions for 10 knots, with disastrous effects — parting the tow at the risk of all on the quarter deck. This was a rather ugly piece of seamanship in the face of the Fleet.

On another occasion when taking station on *Rothesay* for a transfer we overshot and roared in between her and the ship behind, which was at standard distance, missing them by the narrowest of margins with no credit.

He was subject to violent outbursts at the officer of the watch if he was either slow to react or if he made a mistake. Towards the end of the cruise the officers of the watch were able to cope with this but they were a little disconcerted earlier on. This extended even to abuse of the officers of the watch over the armament broadcast from the operations room.

In defence of Captain Stevens, he didn't consider that this should be taken seriously by the officers; after the event he expected them to learn and then to forget the tone in which he spoke. This took quite a bit of learning.

His temperament could range from buoyant good humour to depression when sober. He shared flashes of very fine leadership ability and I had the impression most of the time that the ship's company thought he was a very good captain. I may have been naive in this, for subsequently after the loss of the ship there was none of this respect reflected in the survivors to whom I spoke — to my great surprise.

I will now deal with the factors concerning Captain Stevens's drinking habits during the time that I served with him.

The first real flash I had of understanding Captain Stevens's drinking ability or habits was in our farewell party in Sydney where it was necessary for his wife to tell him publicly that it was time to leave.

When the ship proceeded to sea the Captain told me that he was ill, not having been to sea for some time, so I had command of the ship for the first twenty-four hours; *Vampire*, who was the senior ship present, being informed by signal at the Captain's instructions.

During the period in the Far East the situation became more than trying, it was quite desperate, as he drank for very long periods in harbour until he became violently ill and then would spend days in bed being treated by the doctor and his steward until he was fit to again start drinking.

Captain Stevens drank brandy almost exclusively but he was at times known to drink beer or whisky.

I became very anxious about the way things were developing and uncertain where to turn for advice. The Captain of the flagship was Captain R. I. Peek who had been my captain when I was Executive Officer of HMAS *Sydney*. Captain Peek received me when I called on him with my Captain's permission in Hong Kong and, most strange for him, he required me to remain standing. He was pleasant, formal, he asked me very briefly how the ship was and then I left. I had lost any opportunity I might have had to seek his advice simply because I felt instinctively that he knew and didn't want me to put myself into an impossible position.

It was an extremely trying period and this stage was climaxed by the Captain's birthday on which he was invited to a mess dinner as the guest of the mess. This was the first time on which he was invited in this manner and he arrived, although I had been warned ten minutes before that he had been drinking, completely under the influence but able to walk. It was obviously necessary for us to proceed with the dinner as quickly as possible if he was to last but unfortunately before anything else could be done he got on his hands and knees and crawled across the mess to the table. Before the soup had been finished I had to stand, make a very brief speech and take him from the mess, with the present that the mess had brought him, to his cabin. The officers and the stewards were outstandingly loyal on this occasion and a word of this incident never reached the Fleet, to my knowledge.

This pattern continued but it reached a climax during the visit to Tokyo. In Tokyo the Captain became worse to a degree that we hadn't seen before and on two occasions I took him (on one accompanied by the Engineer Officer) to steam baths to get him fit to deal with his social engagements at lunch time. One, a lunch with the Japanese Admiral.

But to little avail; he was carried from Captain Dollard's home after he had disgraced himself there. I've learned subsequently from Captain Robertson that he had in fact been sick all over the place on this occasion in Captain Dollard's home. And on the Sunday, which was the fourth day in Tokyo, he sent for me at 0630 to inform me that he would be unable to attend the church service that morning and I was to inform Captain [G. J.] Willis to this effect. The Captain when I saw him had his head on a pillow with a towel over it. The towel was soaked in vomit. I asked if I should get the doctor because he looked wretchedly sick and he said no. I saw the doctor and the doctor said that he wouldn't treat him — that he had warned the Captain that this would happen — and that it was his opinion that should the Captain rupture his ulcer at sea the Captain would die.

I went on board *Vampire* and informed Captain Willis of the Captain's condition and his message and of the doctor's opinion and explained my worry on the Captain's behalf. Captain Willis asked me to send the doctor to him, which I did, and he then went on board *Voyager* and went to the Captain's cabin where he spoke to him. Nobody else was present when Captain Willis spoke to Captain Stevens but during the next two months Captain Stevens did not have a single drink and that covered the period between Tokyo and Sydney which was quite a remarkable feat.

There is one other incident that I should mention in this period of which Mr Smyth was informed. It was a Captains' lunch in Hong Kong to which Captain Stevens was invited attended by the Captains of all RN ships present at the time. On this occasion a signal arrived in *Voyager* during the lunch hour to say 'YOUR CAPTAIN HAS PASSED OUT AND WILL BE RETURNED TO YOU WHEN HE IS FIT'. I replied asking was a doctor required and the reply came back 'NO'. The Captain did subsequently come back, said nothing and went straight to his cabin. I learned from Commander T. P. Irwin RN, the Engineer Officer of the *Rothesay*, that the Captain had passed out on the wardroom desk of *Rothesay* and the Captains present wanted to send him back to his ship in the condition he was, immediately. They were absolutely disgusted and considered that he was unfit to be there. Commander Irwin prevailed on them to allow him to place Captain Stevens in his cabin until he was fit to go back and they reluctantly allowed him to do this but offered no assistance. This indicated the feeling of the Fleet at the time.

Following the return to Sydney Captain Stevens arrived on board every morning that I was there at approximately 0800 very heavily under the influence of alcohol, told me that I had command and went to his cabin and retired for the day. He was wakened by his steward at 1600, he commenced drinking again and carried on ashore as soon as he had sufficient to get going. I submitted my resignation at this time and he was genuinely distressed at this and surprised. My decision was not a direct result of his conduct nor do I think it was greatly influenced by it although any last temptation I may have had to remain in the service at this stage was dispelled by this performance. Captain Stevens did not come on to the bridge after the ship left Sydney Harbour on the way to Melbourne to refit until it was ready to enter Port Phillip Bay. I had command of the ship for that stretch as well as while he lay in his bunk.

I'm sorry, I completely omitted the fact that immediately following our departure from Tokyo Captain Stevens told me that I had command of the ship for the next five days. That he wouldn't be coming from his cabin and my command was complete and I was to inform all the officers but not to send any signals indicating my command. He directed me that he was not to be disturbed on any account by anybody and this is exactly what happened. We were with the British Far East Fleet and running before a typhoon carrying out exercises.

During this period the ship was engaged in an intensive exercise programme which included no fewer than five refuellings or transfers and was under the close eye of the RN Flagship *Lion*. The ship's company, and the officers for that matter, were informed by me that the Captain was ill and were given no inkling of any other reason for the Captain's absence. The ship performed well and I was exceptionally proud of the conduct of the officers during this period. As I have said earlier, they were sympathetic to the Captain, considering him a sick man, and incredibly loyal.

Following the ship's arrival in Williamstown the Captain spent very little time on board with me, our leaves being taken at different times. However, he returned to the ship after the court martial of Captain W. J. Dovers of HMAS *Sydney* on which he had been a court member together with Captain Robertson, and he travelled by train from Sydney to Melbourne with Commander B. H. Loxton RAN, Captain of HMAS *Parramatta* at that time (correction, he was Captain of *Yarra* I believe — which was on the opposite side of the dock from us). Commander Loxton informed me that Captain Stevens had drunk a bottle of brandy on the train on the way down.

This statement didn't surprise me in the least. When I saw the Captain in his cabin, having missed him on the gangway, he expressed regret that I hadn't met him and was obviously well advanced on a bottle of brandy. At 1600 his steward came into the mess and asked for another bottle of brandy for the Captain. I knew that the first bottle had been full and asked if he had finished that and the steward said yes. At 1900 I called into the Captain's cabin to see if he was all right and he had half consumed this, which would have been his third bottle of brandy since leaving Sydney on the previous night. The next morning the steward came for me from the Captain to say that the Captain was sick and I found the Captain in the usual condition with a very vomit-soaked towel under his head, looking dreadful. He said that he was sick and to send the leading sick berth attendant to him as it would be about a week before he was on deck again.

This was a fairly accurate assessment as he was in fact inside his cabin for the next seven days although he was able to start drinking brandy again on about the fourth day taking it very gently. At this stage we had a new ship's company of recruits and it was important that they shouldn't have this knowledge of their captain. Unfortunately the stewards were new and I didn't know if I could rely entirely on their discretion and loyalty. However, at the time I had no indication that this didn't prevail.

Mr Smyth asked me in his chambers in Phillip Street in the office near where the enquiry was held at what time Captain Stevens started drinking and I replied that if he was having one of his periods of drinking he would have brandy in his coffee at breakfast time and go steadily on from then. This is not an exaggeration but is applied, as I say, to the periods when he was drinking. On these occasions when he drank he was inclined to become under the influence very quickly and he drank very large glasses of alcohol. His standard brandy on these occasions would be almost half a tumbler full of brandy topped up with water.

I was called to Mr Smyth's rooms after I had been interviewed by Commonwealth Police as I was the senior officer who had served in *Voyager* in the previous twelve months surrounding and in Australian waters. I was asked almost exclusively questions concerning the drinking habits of Captain Stevens and I replied to the questions that I was asked giving most of the story eventually that I have just outlined, perhaps even adding more instances which don't help at this stage. I was very anxious at this stage because I knew Captain Stevens didn't drink at sea, only in harbour, while I served with him, and I repeatedly stressed this to Mr Smyth who assured me that all was well and he understood this. I didn't want any slur on Captain Stevens's name; I was quite convinced that under no circumstances would he ever drink at sea.

I had taken the precaution even of informing my successor, Lt. Commander MacGregor, of the Captain's drinking habit and also stressing to him most strongly the necessity for the officers in the wardroom not to drink at sea because of the Captain's habit. He replied that he was capable of making his own decision in this matter and didn't agree with me. I spent approximately half an hour discussing this point with MacGregor but I learned subsequently that he reversed my decision and I have good reason to believe that all the officers in fact drank at sea following my succession. Perhaps this was a perfectly healthy reaction to my autocratic rule. However I would stress that of the officers in the wardroom when I left only one seaman officer,

Lt Dowling, who was killed, and the Electrical Officer, Commander Tapp, who was killed, had served in the ship in the Far East under Captain Stevens.

The work-up was planned under my co-ordination by the Staff Officers who left the ship so that Captain Stevens while approving the work-up had not planned it and he had not carried out a work-up with these officers or in the ship at all.

To come back to Mr Smyth. When Mr Smyth was questioning me I asked him straight out if he was trying to infer that Captain Stevens was drunk at the time of the collision. He asked why I questioned this; I said I have heard rumours to this effect, which I had from unexpected sources, and I said I wanted to make it quite clear that Captain Stevens would not drink at sea. Mr Smyth said that was clearly understood. When I was leaving Mr Smyth's office, which was after an interview lasting almost an hour, he said 'We'll be seeing a lot of you at the enquiry'.

Now subsequent to this I thought that it was important if Mr Smyth was going to call me and wanted this kind of evidence and believing that Captain Stevens wouldn't drink at sea that it was in the interest of his relatives that my statement should be known equally to them as well as Mr Smyth, so through my own solicitor I arranged to meet Mr Osborne who was the solicitor briefing Captain Stevens's relatives' counsel. Mr Osborne heard me and discussed it with me and came to the conclusion in fact that I did like Captain Stevens, which I don't dispute for a moment; he was a very likeable person but I had no respect for him, only pity.

Very soon after this I received a telephone call from the solicitor briefing the council representing the RAN, Mr Jenkyn QC. He sounded rather panicky and said that he understood that I had some information that I had offered to Mr Osborne and that were I to be called by Mr Smyth would I please see them, that is Mr Jenkyn's solicitors, and also allow them the knowledge that I had passed on. Some time after the Commission had started, and I had been careful not to leave the Sydney area in case I was called, I started to wonder if I were going to be called and went to see Mr Smyth and asked him. He said 'no'. He decided to reduce the other witnesses and I would no longer be required. Very shortly after this it became patently clear that I had been misled by Mr Smyth and others when the evidence was given that Captain Stevens had had a triple brandy on the bridge of *Voyager*.

It is very important at this stage that I mention that although Mr Smyth didn't deny that Captain Stevens had drunk anything, in fact, Mr Osborne did in saying that all Captain Stevens had had before the collision was a glass of brandy at lunchtime on the day before the collision. This I think is most important to understand because they at that time knew the truth. All the signs were then quite apparent that

Captain Robertson was being taken, as the Americans would say, for a ride and was going to be saddled with the entire responsibility. In some alarm of this injustice I rang Captain Robertson and offered to give evidence on his behalf although this was the last thing, I can assure you, that I wished to do in my own interest. I considered it a duty in the interest of justice to him. At this stage of my now civilian career the last thing I wanted was to be associated with anything smacking of a smear but the injustice in this case was so glaring that it couldn't be avoided.

I received a letter from the mother of the RN gunner who died on board the *Voyager*, following a letter that I wrote to her expressing sympathy. This officer had been court martialled on the previous year as officer of the watch of *Battleaxe* during her collision, and she said that she had received a letter shortly before my own from her son, written before he died but received subsequently, in which he said 'mother, I think this is going to be another *Battleaxe*'. This is interesting, particularly as during the previous year *Voyager* had been in at least five near collisions to my knowledge and in none of these do I think that *Voyager* was in any way to blame.

This illustrates a factor that isn't appreciated by the general public that near collisions in an active fleet are very common things. They were really very near. On three occasions I was on watch, twice while the Captain had command in the operations room and corrective action was taken by me as officer of the watch. But on two of the occasions the officer who was *Voyager*'s navigator at the time of the ultimate collision had been the navigator of the ship with which *Voyager* was in trouble, that is HMS *Caesar*, so that his influence in the ultimate collision may have been more significant than evidence can prove. I'll give more detail of one of these instances if you are in any way interested.

*Caesar* ordered *Voyager* to cross the screen from the starboard wing to the port wing at night having detached a SAU [Surface Action Unit]. The relative track was straight through *Caesar* so I asked the Captain to inform *Caesar* that we would pass astern of her. As we approached *Caesar* and were just about to pass astern, *Caesar* turned 180 degrees to starboard, that is towards us, and was suddenly on a collision course. It would have been impossible to turn to starboard to avoid it so that I was obliged to go hard a-port and full astern both engines, stopping dead in the water in front of the advancing convoy very close to it and no further than fifty feet from *Caesar*. Both ships stopped dead in the water. I switched all my lights on, needless to say, at this time, having been blacked out at the beginning of the manoeuvre. There was never any explanation asked for or offered for this incident. My memory is hazy on the details of the other incidents so I shan't attempt to remember it.

Another personality incident which may be of interest is that the officer of the watch of *Voyager* at the time of the collision had just completed a long period, I think probably twelve months, at HMAS *Watson* as instructor in the tactical floor so that his ship handling knowledge, although he may not have served in destroyers should have been as good as any officer on board.

Finally, I'd just like to say that I can envisage very clearly the situation on the bridge of *Voyager* at this time and if the officer of the watch had put the wheel in a direction which the Captain thought was wrong it wouldn't have been unlikely for the Captain to have shouted at the officer of the watch to put the wheel the other way and for the officer of the watch to become rattled, because the violence in the Captain's voice could have rattled him, put the wheel the other way and waited for the Captain who, in his opinion, had command, to give him another order and that would be the last thing that happened until the collision was inevitable with the officer of the watch dithering, not knowing whether he should do anything or not.

The size and complication of the bridge is such that a number of officers there was excessive and I discussed this with other officers who have served in *Voyager* with me and they all said the same thing — how often they have known a situation on those bridges where the officer of the watch didn't know what was happening simply because there were too many experts around. This, too, could have been a factor in the situation. The navigator, the 1st Lt, the officer of the watch, about two midshipmen, and the Captain, the yeoman and two signalmen crowd into the wretched bridge with so many levels it is not surprising that people weren't paying attention to what they should have been.

I think that concludes what I have to say. If any remarks are required on the personalities of some of the very good officers and men who lived and died I would be very happy to supply them.

The main facts outlined above were substantiated by Lt Commander Griffiths RAN, Navigating Officer of *Voyager* during the period in which I served in her, when interviewed by Mr Smyth QC.

# Appendix 2

## Signals Sent from HMAS Melbourne to HMAS Voyager on the Night of the Collision and their Interpretation

1929    Foxtrot Corpen 180 Tack 20. Station X-Ray 14 Tack 1. Mike Corpen 000 Tack 10.
*Execute to follow. Estimated course for impending aircraft operation is 180 (speed 20 knots). Take planeguard station No. 1. My course is 000 (my speed is 10 knots).*

1930    Stand by — Execute.

1950    Turn Foxtrot. Sierra Speed 25.
*Execute to follow — Turn to port into the wind for flight operations. I am at the same time as altering proceeding at 25 knots, the speed required for flying operations.*

1950    Stand by — Execute.

1956    Charlie Bravo 1
*Am ready to operate fixed-wing aircraft when wind conditions are suitable.*

1957    Mike Corpen 175
*My course is 175.*

2005    Mike Speed 22
*My speed is 22 knots.*

2006    Charlie Bravo 3
*Am operating fixed-wing aircraft.*

2030    Mike Corpen 190
*My course is 190.*

2040    Charlie Bravo 5
*My flight operations have been delayed temporarily (about 10 minutes).*

2041    Turn 020
*Execute to follow — Turn together to 020, ships turning to starboard.*

2042    Stand by — Execute.

2047   Turn 060

*Immediate execute — Turn together to 060, ships turning to starboard. I say again turn together to 060, ships turning to starboard — Stand by — Execute.*

2053   020 Turn

*Immediate execute — Turn together to 020, ships turning to port. I say again turn together to 020, ships turning to port — Stand by — Execute.*

2054   Foxtrot Corpen 020 Tack 22

*Estimated course for impending aircraft operation is 020 (speed 22 knots). Time 2054.*

# Appendix 3

# HMAS Voyager *Gallantry Awards and Citations*

*George Cross* (posthumous)
Chief Petty Officer Jonathan Rogers, DSM

*Albert Medal* (posthumous)
Midshipman Kerry Francis Marien
Electrical Mechanic First Class William Joseph Condon

*George Medal*
Petty Officer Douglas Moore, BEM

*British Empire Medal*
Petty Officer Geoffrey Percival Worth
Leading Seaman Raymond Ernest Rich
Leading Electrical Mechanic Brian Victor Longbotham
Leading Sick-Berth Attendant John Rennie Wilson
Able Seaman Eric Noel Robson

*Queen's Commendations*
Petty Officer Engineering Mechanic Edgar James McDermott
Engineering Mechanic Hugh Francis Gilvarry
Electrical Artificer Second Class Anthony Page

*Source:* Navy Public Relations Information Release No. 227/124, 12 March 1965.

# Appendix 4

## Officers and Men Lost at Sea in HMAS Voyager

Captain D. H. Stevens*
Commander E. W. Tapp
Lieutenant Commander I. A. G. MacGregor*
Lieutenant Commander B. L. Carrington
Lieutenant E. A. Brooks, RN
Lieutenant H. D. Cook*
Lieutenant J. L. Dowling
Lieutenant D. H. M. Price, RN*
Sub-Lieutenant E. S. Beavis
Acting Sub-Lieutenant J. S. Davies*
Midshipman B. C. L. Lindsey
Midshipman K. F. Marien, AM
Midshipman R. W. Maunder
Midshipman F. J. Morgan

Chief Petty Officer Jonathan Rogers, GC, DSM
Chief Petty Officer Cook L. D. Vincent

Petty Officer J. B. Guy
Petty Officer E. K. Harcla
Communications Yeoman K. B. Cullen*
Petty Officer Engineering Mechanic D. R. Macartney
Engine Room Artificer L. J. Leeson
Ordnance Artificer G. L. Nuss
Ordnance Artificer D. W. Reid

Leading Seaman J. E. Sparrowhawk
Leading Seaman K. C. Tait
Leading Engineering Mechanic N. J. Ashwell
Leading Electrical Mechanic C. G. Legg
Leading Radio Operator D. E. MacFarlane
Leading Airman B. M. Schmidt
Leading Cook W. J. Smye

Leading Steward K. J. Davis

Acting Leading Seaman F. B. Sharkey
Acting Leading Tactical Operator A. W. Teape
Acting Leading Electrical Mechanic J. McG. Fenwick
Acting Leading Steward N. E. Kingston

Able Seaman N. B. Brown
Able Seaman P. R. Carr
Able Seaman N. C. Glennie
Able Seaman S. Hale
Able Seaman U. J. Lambert
Able Seaman G. E. McLean
Able Seaman R. W. Parker
Able Seaman A. J. Solomon
Able Seaman P. G. Stocker
Able Seaman F. T. Taylor
Able Seaman J. Williams
Tactical Operator P. L. Harris
Engineering Mechanic J. N. Curgenven
Engineering Mechanic N. G. Diepenbroek
Engineering Mechanic L. J. Garrett
Engineering Mechanic K. S. Keddie
Engineering Mechanic R. E. McDonald
Engineering Mechanic G. E. Perrett
Engineering Mechanic R. A. Taylor
Electrical Mechanic P. L. Clarke
Electrical Mechanic W. J. Condon, AM
Electrical Mechanic J. C. G. Deans
Radio Electrical Mechanic G. S. Walker
Radio Operator R. A. Denham
Stores Assistant G. F. Cobban
Steward A. W. Thompson

Ordinary Seaman P. W. Bermingham
Ordinary Seaman M. A. Brokate
Ordinary Seaman W. G. Butts
Ordinary Seaman B. E. Castle
Ordinary Seaman J. D. Clayton
Ordinary Seaman G. D. Fitzallen
Ordinary Seaman L. B. Fleming
Ordinary Seaman G. J. Kelly
Ordinary Seaman L. C. Lehman
Ordinary Seaman E. L. O'Leary
Ordinary Seaman B. A. Scott

Ordinary Seaman A. V. W. Syaranamual
Ordinary Seaman R. A. West
Ordinary Seaman R. E. W. Woodward
Ordinary Tactical Operator R. W. Hendy
Ordinary Tactical Operator K. L. Muller
Ordinary Radio Operator E. R. Owen
Ordinary Radio Operator J. B. Trautman
Assistant Cook P. D. Milbourne
Assistant Steward J. N. Earl

Mr H. S. Parker
(Civil Technical Officer, HMA Naval Dockyard Williamstown).

* Denotes known to have been on the bridge at the time of the collision.

# Appendix 5

## Officers and Men Who Survived the Loss of HMAS Voyager

Lieutenant Commander P. W. Coombs
Lieutenant J. K. Conder, RN
Lieutenant J. R. Face
Lieutenant C. J. Nisbet
Lieutenant J. K. Perrett
Lieutenant C. B. Tuke, RN
Midshipman K. J. Perry

Chief Petty Officer R. W. Gough
Chief Petty Officer W. J. Lloyd
Chief Engineering Mechanic J. H. Hankin
Chief Engineering Mechanic T. V. Sharkey
Chief Naval Shipwright J. L. Webb
Chief Naval Shipwright A. G. Maine
Chief Electrician B. Cameron
Chief Engineroom Artificer A. J. Cameron
Chief Ordnance Artificer V. M. McDade
Chief Radio Supervisor D. F. Tindall

Petty Officer J. Curtis
Petty Officer N. J. Donnelly
Petty Officer W. N. Jackson
Petty Officer D. Moore, BEM
Petty Officer C. F. O'Flynn
Petty Officer R. Palmer
Petty Officer W. S. Strachan
Petty Officer N. W. Swinnerton
Petty Officer G. Worth, BEM

Petty Officer Writer G. J. Darcy
Stores Petty Officer M. Field
Stores Petty Officer K. A. Rees

Ordnance Artificer R. K. Chippendale
Ordnance Artificer J. H. Cullen
Ordnance Artificer D. H. Falconer
Ordnance Artificer G. A. Le Pavoux
Ordnance Artificer J. N. R. McDonald

Petty Officer Engineering Mechanic H. S. Baker
Petty Officer Engineering Mechanic E. J. Dillon
Petty Officer Engineering Mechanic E. J. McDermott
Petty Officer Engineering Mechanic B. J. Parkes
Petty Officer Engineering Mechanic L. L. Tippett
Petty Officer Engineering Mechanic A. G. Walsh
Petty Officer Electrical Mechanic B. Cumming
Petty Officer Radio Engineer G. J. Lincoln

Naval Shipwright J. L. Webb
Naval Shipwright T. James

Engineroom Artificer C. Bullworthy
Engineroom Artificer Corrigan
Engineroom Artificer K. G. Edge
Engineroom Artificer K. J. Fanker
Engineroom Artificer M. W. J. Hallen
Engineroom Artificer J. T. Hatton
Engineroom Artificer J. L. McGrath
Engineroom Artificer A. Page
Engineroom Artificer J. G. Steeden
Engineroom Artificer W. J. Schofield
Engineroom Artificer J. A. Stallard
Engineroom Artificer G. H. Weir
Engineroom Artificer L. T. White
Engineroom Artificer T. V. Williams
Acting Engineroom Artificer W. Beetham

Leading Seaman D. R. Alice
Leading Seaman F. J. Brennan
Leading Seaman L. C. Butcher
Leading Seaman K. S. Casas
Leading Seaman D. R. Elliss
Leading Seaman L. J. Graham
Leading Seaman W. E. Pallot
Leading Seaman M. J. Patterson
Leading Seaman R. E. Rich, BEM
Leading Seaman M. A. Webster

Leading Stores Assistant G. S. Richardson
Leading Stores Assistant C. W. Bell

Leading Engineering Mechanic A. G. Addison
Leading Engineering Mechanic W. N. Baker
Leading Engineering Mechanic A. T. Clarke
Leading Engineering Mechanic A. J. Ekert
Leading Engineering Mechanic R. C. Layfield
Leading Engineering Mechanic S. K. Page
Leading Engineering Mechanic T. Scarsi
Leading Engineering Mechanic W. F. Wood
Acting Leading Engineering Mechanic B. D. Cox

Leading Electrical Mechanic P. J. Brian
Leading Electrical Mechanic P. F. Gracie
Leading Electrical Mechanic J. P. Larkin
Leading Electrical Mechanic B. V. Longbottom, BEM
Leading Electrical Mechanic L. J. Moorfoot
Leading Electrical Mechanic S. C. Porter
Leading Electrical Mechanic P. J. Ryan
Leading Electrical Mechanic B. L. Verwayen
Leading Writer W. L. Harris
Leading Seaman Sick-Berth Attendant J. R. Wilson, BEM
Leading Radio Operator G. R. Smith
Leading Radio Electrical Mechanic A. J. Milliner
Leading Cook D. W. Love
Leading Airman C. W. Bell
Leading Airman A. E. Newcombe
Leading Airman R. J. Reynolds

Able Seaman J. W. Bannister
Able Seaman R. Bizzard
Able Seaman B. J. Britton
Able Seaman M. A. Brownless
Able Seaman G. A. Clarke
Able Seaman R. N. Clarke
Able Seaman P. W. Dusting
Able Seaman B. F. Fitzgerald
Able Seaman A. J. Fleay
Able Seaman G. J. Franklin
Able Seaman B. J. Gow
Able Seaman T. J. Harper
Able Seaman T. J. Hartler
Able Seaman P. Howis
Able Seaman K. J. Hamilton

Able Seaman C. A. Halliwell
Able Seaman D. R. Jones
Able Seaman A. R. Kahn
Able Seaman J. Kroeger
Able Seaman P. R. Low
Able Seaman C. G. Mackie
Able Seaman A. B. Matthews
Able Seaman L. D. Mead
Able Seaman E. N. Robson, BEM
Able Seaman K. J. Ryan
Able Seaman C. E. Tidball
Able Seaman R. I. Vizard

Writer R. A. Bird
Writer W. T. Grundy

Tactical Operator R. J. Burdett
Tactical Operator G. W. Evans

Radio Operator J. C. Beedham
Radio Operator P. F. Cox
Radio Operator A. D. Hellier
Radio Operator G. J. Luttrell
Radio Operator R. F. Pola

Engineering Mechanic B. G. Allen
Engineering Mechanic D. Andrew
Engineering Mechanic D. F. Barker
Engineering Mechanic M. M. Collins
Engineering Mechanic D. A. Cox
Engineering Mechanic J. H. Cracknell
Engineering Mechanic G. L. Davis
Engineering Mechanic F. Dorn
Engineering Mechanic G. Doust
Engineering Mechanic J. R. Fleming
Engineering Mechanic G. R. Gerhart
Engineering Mechanic H. F. Gilvarry
Engineering Mechanic J. K. Hannay
Engineering Mechanic B. F. Hopkins
Engineering Mechanic L. E. Henny
Engineering Mechanic M. R. Itchins
Engineering Mechanic R. J. Johnson
Engineering Mechanic I. C. Jones
Engineering Mechanic N. J. Kendall
Engineering Mechanic B. C. Manning

Engineering Mechanic M. M. Mullins
Engineering Mechanic N. A. McCaskill
Engineering Mechanic A. V. O'Brien
Engineering Mechanic D. M. Powell
Engineering Mechanic P. M. Quinn
Engineering Mechanic M. G. Skidmore
Engineering Mechanic R. Totterdell
Engineering Mechanic B. G. Walker
Engineering Mechanic J. D. Walker

Electrical Mechanic R. M. Bobko
Electrical Mechanic B. J. Coughlan
Electrical Mechanic O. R. Geary
Electrical Mechanic D. T. Hallam
Electrical Mechanic P. R. Martin
Electrical Mechanic B. J. McNamara
Electrical Mechanic E. W. Willcocks

Radio Electrical Mechanic K. I. Livingstone
Radio Electrical Mechanic R. J. Terry

Stores Assistant R. S. Dunbar
Stores Assistant J. W. Duncan
Cook B. P. Dunn
Cook J. L. Parkinson
Cook B. J. Rowe
Cook G. B. Roberts
Cook A. J. Vadasz

Steward R. Eddy
Steward J. K. Hannah
Steward R. Ogsy
Steward F. W. Oudyn
Steward B. V. Partridge

Ordinary Seaman M. Benyk
Ordinary Seaman T. V. Boseley
Ordinary Seaman C. L. Brown
Ordinary Seaman D. J. Corrigan
Ordinary Seaman B. W. Davis
Ordinary Seaman W. A. Degenhardt
Ordinary Seaman H. A. Dobell
Ordinary Seaman R. J. Dobell
Ordinary Seaman G. A. Ducker
Ordinary Seaman B. T. Eastwood

Ordinary Seaman P. J. Edge
Ordinary Seaman W. Fenwick
Ordinary Seaman D. Fletcher
Ordinary Seaman D. Flynn
Ordinary Seaman T. J. Freer
Ordinary Seaman E. M. Geaky
Ordinary Seaman A. W. Hall
Ordinary Seaman P. R. Hall
Ordinary Seaman I. B. Haigh
Ordinary Seaman R. C. Halloran
Ordinary Seaman R. P. Hemsley
Ordinary Seaman A. T. Hume
Ordinary Seaman B. J. Hyland
Ordinary Seaman P. Jeffrey
Ordinary Seaman J. F. Jersovs
Ordinary Seaman S. Kaz
Ordinary Seaman L. H. Kuster
Ordinary Seaman T. L. McCormick
Ordinary Seaman R. H. McFerran
Ordinary Seaman I. R. McKay
Ordinary Seaman G. W. McKewen
Ordinary Seaman T. D. McNair
Ordinary Seaman J. L. Monaghan
Ordinary Seaman G. N. Perrin
Ordinary Seaman C. Rowland
Ordinary Seaman L. R. Richmond
Ordinary Seaman P. D. Roberts
Ordinary Seaman W. R. Sale
Ordinary Seaman H. G. Stephenson
Ordinary Seaman I. L. Smith
Ordinary Seaman D. R. Sharp
Ordinary Seaman S. J. Singleton
Ordinary Seaman E. J. Stanley
Ordinary Seaman A. Stevenson
Ordinary Seaman R. N. Storer
Ordinary Seaman E. D. Sturt
Ordinary Seaman B. W. Sumpter
Ordinary Seaman R. J. Thomas
Ordinary Seaman F. J. Verco
Ordinary Seaman R. J. Vonarx
Ordinary Seaman D. J. Walker
Ordinary Seaman R. G. Walsh
Ordinary Seaman F. M. Wilson
Mechanic D. E. Rochow
Ordinary Radio Operator J. D. Withers

Ordinary Tactical Operator R. N. Jocumsen
Ordinary Tactical Operator N. S. Sampson
Ordinary Tactical Operator O. D. E. Sparks
Ordinary Stores Assistant H. Sluiter

Mr E. E. Bird
(Civilian Technical Officer, HMA Naval Dockyard Williamstown)

# Notes and References

## Chapter 1

1. Quoted in the *Times*, 23 December 1918.
2. The history of the College is described by Frank Eldridge, *A History of the Royal Australian Naval College* (Georgian House, Melbourne, 1949) and Ian Cunningham, *Work Hard, Play Hard* (AGPS, Canberra, 1988).
3. R. Hyslop, *Australian Naval Administration, 1900–1939* (Hawthorn Press, Melbourne, 1973) p. 181.
4. The Naval Board was part of the Department of Defence until 1915 when a separate Department of the Navy, with its own minister, was formed. As a consequence of post-World War I defence reductions, the Navy Department was merged back into the Defence Department although this did not affect the functioning of the Naval Board. In 1939, the Navy again became a separate department. The existence of three service departments continued until 1973 when they were again merged back into the Defence Department. The Naval Board continued to exist until 1976 with very few formal changes to its place in the administrative machinery of government.
5. Much was made of any praise the RAN received from the Royal Navy. The Deputy Chief of Naval Staff's Newsletter of October 1957 included a letter from Admiral Sir Alan Scott-Moncrieff, the departing British Commander-in-Chief, Far East Station, to the Australian Chief of Naval Staff, Vice-Admiral Sir Roy Dowling: 'It was very pleasant for me to be able to say, in my opinion, the Royal Australian Navy is second to none and that I capped that by saying I was in a good position to judge as I had served in and alongside so many other navies. Your men are splendid, fine upstanding types, steady on parade, and able and willing to talk.'
6. Seamus, 'Class, Ethics and Image: A theory of naval decline', *Naval Review*, Vol. 74, No. 2, April 1986, p. 118.
7. The two Battle Class destroyers *Anzac* and *Tobruk* were built as part of an extended wartime programme. They were World War II design ships built to keep the expanded wartime staffs in employment at the two naval shipyards, Williamstown and Cockatoo Island.
8. Robert Hyslop, *Aye Aye, Minister: Australian Naval Administration 1939–1959* (AGPS, Canberra, 1990).
9. N. A. M. Rodger, 'The Intellectual Formation of the Officer', *Naval Review*, Vol. 74, October 1986, pp. 392–3.
10. R. Hyslop (1990), op. cit., p. 32.
11. Alan Trengrove, *John Grey Gorton — An Informal Biography* (Cassell, Sydney, 1969) p. 139.
12. Gorton told me that Menzies paid scant attention to the Services other than when they caused him political problems. If anything, Gorton believed Menzies may have been better disposed towards the Navy. Certainly the Prime Minister always looked forward to taking passage in an RAN ship. Interview with the Rt Hon. Sir John Gorton, 2 August 1990.

## Chapter 2

1. Biographical entry on R. J. Robertson in F. B. Eldridge, *A History of the Royal Australian Naval College* (Georgian House, Melbourne, 1949) pp. 410–11.
2. Details of Robertson's decorations, awards and citations are listed by J. J. Atkinson, *By Skill and Valour* (Spink & Son, Sydney, 1986) pp. 103, 187.
3. Lieutenant Commander Ean McDonald to author, 5 June 1991.

4. Report of Inspection (Form AS 425) by Rear-Admiral Alan McNicoll dated 29 July 1963 — Navy file 18/206/33.
5. Navy file 1624/211/14 covered Naval Gunfire Support (NGS) firings and 1624/211/15 surface firings. Problems with the operation of *Voyager*'s equipment were examined in Navy files 704/52/74 and 725/52/185.
6. Interview with Rear-Admiral Peter Sinclair, 21 May 1991.
7. ACNB Minute 60/1963. Also Navy file 1211/251/115.
8. Contained on Navy file 18/6/198. Curiously, this report dated in December 1963 was not received in Navy Office until 11 March 1964.
9. The constraints imposed by the size of *Voyager*'s refit allocation were outlined in Navy file 203/4/65 'HMAS *Voyager* — Repair and Refit Allocation 1963/64' and 1215/251/226 which deals with *Voyager*'s two-year refit cycle.
10. Charles Thomason to author, 4 April 1991.
11. Navy file 1215/55/295 covers *Voyager*'s 1963 refit in Williamstown. Defects requiring attention after the refit were recorded in Navy file 1215/55/318. As they were reported and appear on the file, none seemed to have been sufficiently serious to have prevented the ship from sailing in February 1964.
12. ACNB Minute 40/63 and Navy file 203/4/66 refers.
13. Interview with Rear-Admiral Sinclair, 21 May 1991.
14. Interview with Rear-Admiral Sinclair, 21 May 1991.
15. Letter from Commander Tony Grazebrook, RANR, to author, 13 April 1991.
16. The text of the following extracts from Form S450 were contained in Signal DTG 111445Z Feb 64 from ANRUK to ACNB. Note: the only consistent reference in naval signals from this period was the Date–Time–Group (DTG). The first two numerals denote the day of the month; the next four numerals denote Greenwich Mean Time (GMT) or Z Time (International Time Zone 'Zulu') by the twenty-four hour clock and refer to the time the signal was electronically transmitted. The local time, in this case the Eastern Standard Time (EST), is obtained by adding ten hours to the Z Time. Thus, Signal DTG 111313Z Feb 64 was transmitted at 2313 local time on 11 February 1964.
17. Interview with Captain James Kelly, 9 May 1991.
18. Interview with Commodore Toz Dadswell, 21 April 1991.

# Chapter 3

1. In fact, the distances were even smaller. *Melbourne*'s position was taken from her bridge and did not include the 100 yards forward of that point to her bow. Similarly, *Voyager* had around 40 yards forward of her bridge.
2. The orders 'Full ahead' and 'Full astern' are reserved for emergencies. Although the engine telegraphs are normally set at 'Half ahead' or 'Half astern' for normal manoeuvring, this does not mean that a ship is steaming at half her top speed — whatever that might be. The speed is controlled by engine revolutions which are relayed from the bridge to the wheelhouse and rung down to the engine-room which physically alters engine revolutions. When 'Full ahead' is ordered, the engine-room is required to operate the engines at all available power. Survivors from *Voyager* later said the pipe they heard was 'hands to collision stations'. It is noteworthy that no such pipe existed in naval instructions. The correct pipe was 'Emergency, Emergency, Emergency — Hands to Emergency Stations — Close all red openings'. 'Red openings' were those watertight doors and hatches which were partly painted red to indicate that they were crucial to preserving the watertight integrity of the ship should it be damaged by collision or enemy action.
3. John Milliner to author, 17 July 1991.
4. Signal DTG 101100Z Feb 64 from *Melbourne* to FOICEA.
5. Interview with Commander George Halley, 21 December 1989.
6. Signal DTG 101114Z Feb 64 from *Melbourne* to FOICEA info ACNB, FOCAF, NOICJB, NAS Nowra.
7. Signal DTG 101140Z Feb 64 from *Melbourne* to addressees of previous signal.
8. HMA Ships *Hawk* (Lt Cdr B. G. Dunn), *Curlew* (Lt Cdr M. deV. Salmon), *Ibis* (Lt A. R. Cummins), *Teal* (Lt K. Murray), *Snipe* (Lt B. I. Hamill); *Ton* Class Minesweepers acquired from the Royal Navy in 1962. Signal DTG 101158Z Feb 64 From FOICEA to *Melbourne* info ACNB, NOICJB, NAS Nowra, 16 M[inesweeping] S[quadron].

9. Signal DTG 101214Z Feb 64 from FOICEA to *Kimbla*.
10. The absence of a damage report from *Melbourne* prompted FOICEA to ask in signal DTG 101236Z Feb 64, 'What is condition *Melbourne?*'
11. Signal DTG 101216Z Feb 64 from *Melbourne* to ACNB, info FOICEA.
12. Admiral Becher's movements detailed in signal DTG 101300Z Feb 64 from FOCAF to *Melbourne*.
13. Halley interview, 21 December 1989.
14. Signal DTG 101355Z Feb 64 from *Melbourne* to ACNB, info FOICEA.
15. Signal DTG 101418Z from *Melbourne* to ACNB, info FOCAF and FOICEA.
16. Interview with John Farquharson, 1 February 1989.
17. Record of conversation between Robert Hyslop and Tony Eggleton, 1988, p. 12. Copy held by Hyslop.
18. Ibid.
19. The text of this press statement was provided to all Naval Area Commanders by signal DTG 101515Z Feb 64 from ACNB.
20. Record of conversation, Hyslop-Eggleton, p. 13.
21. *Scotsman*, 11 February 1964.
22. Interview with Tony Eggleton, 31 January 1989.
23. Signal DTG 101356Z Feb 64 from *Melbourne* to ACNB, FOICEA and FOCAF.
24. *Melbourne*'s intentions were conveyed by signal DTG 101900Z Feb 64 to FOICEA, info ACNB, NAS Nowra and NOICJB.
25. Signal DTG 110110Z Feb 64 from FOCAF to ACNB.
26. R.Adm. Becher to CNS dated 'Tuesday morning [11 February 1964] at sea'. Original contained in unnumbered Navy file 'Loss of HMAS *Voyager*'.
27. Signal DTG 102050Z Feb 64 from *Stuart* to FOICEA, info ACNB, NAS Nowra, FOCAF and *Melbourne*.
28. Signal DTG 102350 from *Stuart* to addressees as per previous signal.
29. Signal from *Stuart* to FOICEA and ACNB dated 11 February 1964.
30. Signal DTG 110635Z Feb 64 from FOICEA to *Stuart*, NAS Nowra and NOICJB, info ACNB, FOCAF and *Melbourne*.
31. Signal DTG 110832Z Feb 64 from *Stuart* to FOICEA.
32. Signal DTG 111228Z Feb 64 from FOICEA to *Stuart*.
33. Signal DTG 1202212 Feb 64 from ACNB to FOICEA, confirmed in Signal DTG 130425Z Feb 64 from FOICEA to ACNB and FOCAF.
34. Signal DTG 121055Z Feb 64 from ACNB to FOICEA, info FOCAF, 16MS, NAS Nowra.
35. Signal DTG 160734Z Mar 64 from ACNB to FOICEA refers.
36. Signals DTG 200607Z Feb 64 from ACNB to FOICEA and DTG 250731Z Feb 64 from ACNB to all ships and shore establishments, refer.
37. Signal DTG 110133Z Feb 64 from ACNB to all ships and shore establishments.
38. Signal DTG 110419Z Feb 64 from ACNB to FOCAF and NAS Nowra, info FOICEA and *Melbourne*.
39. *Melbourne* letter No. 01/13, 11 February 1964.
40. Official letter from Commanding Officer, HMAS *Melbourne* to FOCAF, 11 February 1964. (Original copy in Robertson papers.)
41. Both the Report of Proceedings and the supplementary letter were placed on Navy file 1288/201/13.
42. FOCAF letter AF 38/28, 12 February 1964 to SecNav. Navy file 1288/501/12.
43. Signal from Navy Office to all ships and shore establishments, 12 February 1964 refers. Also Navy file 123/1/22 '*Voyager* Dependents' Relief Fund'.
44. *Age*, 14 February 1964.
45. Signal DTG 102046Z Feb 64 from Admiralty to ACNB, info ANRUK.
46. Telegram contained in signal DTG 120615Z Feb 64.
47. SecNav minute, 14 February 1964 to Naval Board members and signal DTG 140452Z Feb 64 from ACNB to FOCAF, FOICEA, Naval Area Commanders and the Admiralty.
48. Details of the funeral for Captain Stevens were conveyed to CNS by R. Adm. Smith in a handwritten note, 13 February 1964 which was placed on unnumbered Navy file 'Loss of HMAS *Voyager*'.
49. The body of Able Seaman R. W. Parker was buried at sea from HMAS *Vampire* on 14 February. Details of the arrangement were conveyed in a signal from FOCAF to FOICEA and *Vampire*, 13 February.

50. Details of the funeral protocol were contained in a signal from FOICEA to the Fleet, 13 February.
51. Letter from R. W. Cook to FOCAF, 28 February 1964. Copy contained in unnumbered Navy file 'Loss of HMAS *Voyager*'.
52. The text of the sermon preached by Bishop Muldoon was issued as a press statement by the Catholic Church in Sydney. The copy cited was contained in the private papers of the Ven. John Were RAN, Senior Anglican Naval Chaplain, held by the Museum of HMAS *Cerberus*.
53. Buckingham Palace Court Circular published in the *Times*, 3 March 1964.


# Chapter 4

1. The scope and extent of the particular risks faced by naval ships was detailed in a Deputy Chief of Naval Staff (DCNS) (T. K. Morrison) minute dated 20 February 1964 to Secretary of the Department of the Navy (SecNav) (Landau). It concluded, 'Accidents will happen, but there is no trend in those that have occurred in the RAN which should have led to any special instructions being issued by the Naval Board'.
2. D. Brown, *Warship Losses of World War II* (Arms and Armour Press, London, 1990) p. 228.
3. Admiralty Fleet Order 1439/60. Admiralty Book of Reference (BR) 134 — Reports of Collisions and Groundings — is also relevant.
4. Ibid.
5. P. Padfield, *An Agony of Collisions* (Hodder & Stoughton, London, 1966) p. 193.
6. *Bulletin*, 26 September 1964, pp. 17–19.
7. The Acting Minister for the Navy, Fred Osborne, outlined the details of the accident to Parliament on 6 August 1958: 'The essential particulars of it are that, after the accident to *Vendetta* occurred, a board of inquiry was set up at once. The board found that the cause of the accident was that, although the correct orders had been given from the bridge when *Vendetta* was moving from her berth with the intention of going to sea for trials, a mistake was made by the rating responsible for transmitting the orders from the wheelhouse to the engine-room through the engine-room telegraph, with the result that the starboard engine, instead of going half astern, went half ahead. The correct order to stop the engines was given. An order was again given to put the starboard engine astern with the same result as before. The engines were again stopped and, because the ship was moving forward to a dangerous position, the order was given then for the starboard engine to go astern. Again, the same mistake was made and the ship moved forward. By that time it was not possible for the officer in charge to do anything but stop both engines and drop an anchor. That was done. It is quite apparent from the report of the board of inquiry that the mistake, though regrettable and costly, was a simple, human error'. *Commonwealth Parliamentary Debates* (Reps) (hereafter cited as *CPD* (Reps)), 6 August 1958, p. 78.
8. Rear-Admiral Victor Smith to Robertson, 6 January 1964 (Robertson papers).
9. BR 11, p. 22, 'Duties and responsibilities of commanding officers'.
10. Ibid.
11. Captain Ian Easton RN (Commanding Officer, HMAS *Watson*) to FOICEA (Rear-Admiral Gatacre), 26 January 1964 (Robertson papers).
12. Ibid.
13. This was certainly Robertson's view: 'To my mind, this background, and the general public unease about naval affairs, explains why the Prime Minister felt that the normal course of naval justice would not suit the case of the *Voyager* collision.' (Notes on *One Minute of Time*, Robertson papers.)


# Chapter 5

1. SecNav to RNZN Liaison Officer C05191, 26 November 1965. Navy file 1215/255/65, p. 2.
2. Interview with the Hon. Sir Frederick Chaney, 27 July 1990.
3. Interview with the Hon. Dr Jim Forbes, 26 April 1989, and interview with Stuart Philpott, 3 May 1991.
4. Chaney interview. I have confirmed this sequence of events with Dame Pattie Menzies; Heather Henderson, Menzies's daughter (letter to author, 24 June 1991); Hazel Craig (Menzies's private secretary); Sir John Bunting (interview 8 August 1990); and Sir Garfield Barwick. Sir John Carrick, then president of the NSW Liberal Party, saw Menzies early the morning after the collision and remarked that although Menzies was deeply saddened by the disaster, he made no mention of not having been told. At any rate, Carrick believed that whether or not Menzies had

been informed immediately would not have affected his decision on the investigation of the collision. (Interview with the Hon. Sir John Carrick, 27 May 1989.)

5. Interview with Lady Harrington, 23 August 1990.

6. *Daily Mirror*, 26 August 1964.

7. Killen, op. cit., p. 82.

8. By Captain Robertson in an article by Evan Whitton published in the *National Times*, 4 February 1973. However, there was subsequent contact between the two. Mrs Heather Henderson recalled her father (Menzies) 'saying he had been in touch with Stevens, the father of the captain, and what a good man he was. He felt very sympathetic for the Stevens family'. (Letter to author, 24 June 1991.) However, this contact occurred after that alleged by Robertson.

9. Memoirs of Sir Jack Stevens and letter from Mrs B. L. Legoe (formerly Stevens) to author, 11 September 1990.

10. *Melbourne* informed the Naval Board by signal DTG 101638Z Feb 64 that 'Body of Captain Stevens is in *Hawk*. Body of one other man who may be AB Baker but has not been positively identified are in the boat which is being towed to Jervis Bay by *Ibis*'.

11. Interview with the Rt Hon. Sir Garfield Barwick, 21 September 1989.

12. Barwick interview, 21 September 1989.

13. Minute of ACNB meeting 10/1964, 11 February 1964. Navy Office file 1288/201/12 refers.

14. Chaney said that he spoke with Vice-Admiral Sir John Collins after the inquiry and told him the Board accepted the need for a Royal Commission. Chaney said that Collins, who was privately opposed to a Royal Commission and assumed the Naval Board would collectively have felt the same way, appeared to change his view once he realised many factors were involved and the Board had 'agreed' to a Royal Commission being held. (Chaney interview, 21 July 1990.)

15. Interview with Sir John Gorton, 2 August 1990.

16. Assistant Parliamentary Draftsman to SecNav 50/455, 15 February 1950. Filed on Navy file 584/201/881.

17. This detail is recorded in the CNS branch file 'HMAS *Tarakan*' in a file note prepared by Naval Registrar, Ira Menear, 14 February 1964. The point should be made that Menear worked in the Naval buildings at Victoria Barracks in Melbourne where the Naval registry was located. He could only have known this detail if it had been relayed to him by a senior official at Navy Office. Interview with Robert Hyslop (former Assistant Secretary, Department of the Navy), 12 September 1991. Also conversation with Charles Hill, head of 'N' Branch in Navy Office during 1964, 16 September 1991.

18. Navy Office file 584/201/881.

19. Comment on discussion paper 'Regulations to provide for a naval court of inquiry' by 2NM dated 17 February 1950, p. 1.

20. Ibid.

21. SecNav letter No. 9685, 15 March 1950 (Navy Office file 584/201/881) which refers to Parliamentary Draftsman Memo. No. 50/155, 1 March 1950.

22. This is confirmed by Menear in his file note cited above.

23. Prime Ministerial Press Statement 10/1964, 11 February 1964.

24. Navy Press Statement No. 132, 11 February 1964.

25. Comments by Captain Robertson on draft chapter 6 of *One Minute of Time*, 23 May 1965 (Robertson papers).

26. Neil Preston worked with the Navy Department from 1940 until its demise in 1973, in the legislative area of naval administration.

27. Prime Ministerial Press Statement No. 12/1964, 'Naval Disaster', 13 February 1964.

28. Prime Ministerial Press Statement No. 13/1964, 'Royal Commission on Naval Disaster', 13 February 1964.

29. *CPD* (Reps), 25 February 1964, p. 30.

30. Gorton interview, 2 August 1990.

31. *Australian*, 22 September 1964.

32. Comments by Captain Robertson on draft Chapter 6 of *One Minute of Time*, undated but probably written in May 1965 (Robertson papers).

33. SecNav to RNZN Liaison Officer C05191, 26 November 1964. Navy file 1215/255/65.

34. *Daily Mirror*, 12 February 1964.

35. Comments by Captain Robertson on draft Chapter 6 of *One Minute of Time*, 23 May 1965 (Robertson papers).

36. Unpublished memoirs of Sir Jack Stevens, Vol. 2 unnumbered pages in bound volume. Written over 1963–1965. (Original held by D. E. Stevens.)
37. Captain Ian Cartwright, the Australian Naval Attache in Washington at the time the Royal Commission had ended, told me that American naval officers were 'amused' by the decision to hold a Royal Commission. (Interview with Captain Ian Cartwright, 30 August 1990.) The U.S. Navy had recently witnessed the end of a congressional inquiry into the loss of the nuclear submarine *Thresher* in 1963.
38. Deputy Crown Solicitor (DCS) to FOCAF (undated).
39. SecNav to DCS (undated), Navy file 1288/201/13.
40. Captain R. I. Peek to Robertson, 12 February 1964 (Robertson papers).
41. Navy Office Acquaint No. 11/64, 25 February 1964 refers.
42. Signal DTG 060133Z Feb 64 from ACNB to FOCAF. As Fleet Communications Officer he was also Fleet Intelligence Officer.
43. Interview with Commodore John Snow, 17 July 1989.
44. Although Menzies had discussed the appointment of counsel assisting the commission with Barwick, he made no mention of who the commissioner would be. (Barwick interview.)
45. Interviews with Commander Osborne on 18 July 1989 and 29 August 1990. Also *Who's Who In Australia*, 1988.
46. Gregory told the author that the Price family were of some means and would still have engaged junior counsel if the Commonwealth had refused to pay their legal costs. (Interview with W. H. Gregory QC, 18 July 1989.)
47. Gregory interview, 18 July 1989.
48. Royal Commission (hereafter RC) transcript, Day 1, p.4.
49. Interview with the Hon. Sir Laurence Street, 2 July 1990.
50. Interview with Commander Alex Bate, 23 November 1989.
51. Signal DTG 170136Z Feb 64 to ACNB.
52. Sec PM & C (Bunting), to SecNav, 64/6115 dated 12 March 1964.
53. SecNav to AsstSec, Naval East Australia Area (Neilson), 5 March 1964. The contents were transmitted to Jenkyn QC.

# Chapter 6

1. That it did not expect Smyth to take this line has been confirmed by Humfry Henchman in an interview with me on 16 July 1989. Gregory believed that Smyth was distracted from assisting by a determination to push his own view. He also thought that Smyth's intention was to show the Navy that it was accountable. (Interview with W. H. Gregory QC, 18 July 1989.)
2. Smyth's opening address covered 32 pages of transcript. RC transcript, Day 2, pp. 10–42.
3. This was also the understanding of Gordon Samuels QC and Ray Reynolds QC who were involved in later proceedings.
4. Robertson later remarked, 'From what I have been told by [Peek and Stevenson], Smyth went strictly his own way . . . Perhaps I might mention in passing that many of us who have talked about this affair are of the opinion that the very fact that Smyth had a naval captain who was continually trying to put him on the right track made it even more certain that he, Smyth, would go his own way. This conclusion rests, partly at least, on the characters of Smyth and Peek.' Notes on *One Minute of Time* (Robertson papers).
5. RC transcript, Day 2, pp. 77–8.
6. RC transcript, Day 2, p. 47.
7. RC transcript, Day 3, p. 110.
8. Ibid.
9. Ibid.
10. Robertson was later critical of the wisdom of hindsight that characterised the view of some naval officers. Several months later Robertson received a letter from a retired officer who had served with Becher: 'You may not know of this incident. It is a good example of the "vanity of Experience" that you talk about. I was Commander (Air) of *Melbourne* at the time the redoubtable Otto [Becher's first name] was the captain. We were about to leave Hong Kong harbour from alongside and the conditions in the harbour were a little dicey, the tide sweeping in through the pass, and a strong wind blowing in the same direction. Ignoring Red Merson's [the navigator] advice, Otto cast off and creamed down harbour, put his wheel hard to starboard and, halfway

round, found that he didn't have the horsepower to make it. He nearly collected four U.S. 'cans' that were moored in the middle and had to order full astern to just miss a French dredger that was at work near the end of the extension to Kai Tak runway'. (R. H. Hain to Robertson, 6 October 1964 (Robertson papers)). This was one of several stories relayed to Robertson about Becher's shiphandling after the admiral had given his evidence.

11. An incident described for Hickling by Robertson in private notes (Robertson papers).
12. RC transcript, Day 4, p. 269.
13. This part of Barker's evidence is covered in RC transcript, Day 6, pp. 305–7.
14. RC transcript, Day 6, p. 307.
15. RC transcript, Day 6, p. 310.
16. RC transcript, Day 6, pp. 321–6.
17. RC transcript, Day 6, p. 333.
18. RC transcript, Day 6, p. 311.
19. RC transcript, Day 24, p. 1779.
20. RC transcript, Day 6, p. 368.
21. RC transcript, Day 7, p. 384.
22. RC transcript, Day 7, p. 406.
23. RC transcript, Day 7, p. 397.
24. RC transcript, Day 7, pp. 398A–400.
25. RC transcript, Day 7, p. 441.
26. Ibid.
27. RC transcript, Day 7, p. 457.
28. Henchman states that Jenkyn only realised his brief was too large when Smyth made his opening address. He says that it was he who persuaded Robertson to engage separate representation although Jenkyn initially resisted this view. At any rate, Henchman believed that Spicer should have exerted greater control over Smyth. (Interview with Henchman.) For his part, Gregory thought the Navy counsel had not received good instructions from the Crown Solicitor and seemed not to know the line to take on several matters. (Interview with Gregory, 18 July 1989.) Meares blamed the Crown Solicitor's office for not having prevailed upon Robertson to engage counsel. (Interview with the Hon. Leycester Meares, 18 July 1989.)
29. RC transcript, Day 8, p. 459.
30. Telex, 1300, 25 March 1964. The telegram stated: 'Acting on legal advice from Counsel for the Navy I have decided to obtain legal representation for the remainder of the Royal Commission. Royal Commission has been adjourned for one week to enable me to do this. I respectfully request that the cost of this legal representation may be borne by the Government' (Robertson papers).
31. Snedden to Robertson, 26 March 1964 (Robertson papers).
32. Farncomb, on behalf of Alfred Rofe and Sons, Solicitors, to Attorney-General (Snedden), 29 March 1964 (Robertson papers).
33. Attorney-General (Snedden) to Farncomb, 13 April 1964 (Robertson papers).
34. Ibid.
35. Letter from Farncomb to Attorney-General (Snedden), 15 April 1964 (Robertson papers).
36. Robertson to Commanding Officer, HMAS *Kuttabul*, 16 April 1964 (Robertson papers).
37. Ibid.
38. Rear-Admiral Alan McNicoll to Robertson, 8 May 1964 (Robertson papers).
39. *CPD* (Reps), 6 May 1964, p. 1559.
40. Attorney-General (Snedden) to Harold Farncomb, 5 May 1964 (Robertson papers).
41. 'Notes for 18 March 1968 meeting between Sir Jack Stevens, Fred Osborne and Sam Benson'. (Stevens papers).
42. Minute, 28 February 1964 from DCNS to CNS and the SecNav. Filed on 'Loss of HMAS *Voyager*'.
43. Chaney to Hasluck, 3 March 1964. Copy contained on Navy file 1288/501/13.
44. Hasluck to Chaney, 3 March 1964. Copy contained on unnumbered CNS branch file 'HMAS *Voyager* Royal Commission'.
45. Henchman told me that he overheard Harrington telling Robertson in Sydney that he would have to 'stand him down for the duration of the Royal Commission', which the Naval Board evidently thought would continue for some time. This would have created the expectation in Robertson's mind that he would definitely be returning to his command. Robertson's personal papers suggest this meeting took place after an unscheduled Naval Board meeting on Saturday 21 March 1964.

However, Admiral Sir Victor Smith told the author that the Board had no intention of sending Robertson back to *Melbourne* although this was never communicated to him.

46. Unnumbered Navy Press Statement, 26 March 1964. Penscript notes 'For release 10.00am EST 26 March — FOCAF to inform *Melbourne* complement at about 9–9.30am'.

47. Hicks was not known as a strong advocate but he established an instant rapport with Robertson and the two communicated very well. Raine was a sergeant in the 2nd AIF but joined the RAN in the hope of seeing wartime action as an ordinary seaman.

48. RC transcript, Day 9, pp. 468–72 (Smyth's cross-examination of Bate).

49. RC transcript, Day 9, p. 468.

50. RC transcript, Day 9, p. 497.

51. Interview with Captain James Kelly, 9 May 1991.

52. RC transcript, Day 9, pp. 514–17.

53. RC transcript, Day 9, pp. 533–4.

54. RC transcript, Day 10, p. 557f.

55. RC transcript, Day 11, p. 643–4.

56. RC transcript, Day 10, p. 574.

57. RC transcript, Day 11, p. 631–3.

58. RC transcript, Day 12, p. 713.

59. Naval architect R. J. Herd told me that during a conversation he had with Hicks at the inquiry about Robertson's diagrams reconstructing the collision, Peek joined the 'discussion and assured Mr Hicks that he would not find that Captain Robertson's reconstructions were supported by all navigating officers in the Navy' (Herd to author, 8 May 1989). Herd produced a report for Smyth on 24 March 1964. Concerning Robertson's reconstruction he stated: 'why Robertson's diagrams were drawn without reference to speed and revolution loss during turns is not at all clear' (Letter to author). The Director of Navigation in the Commonwealth Department of Transport and Shipping, Norman Bolton, objected to Hicks's cross-examination of Herd, who had pointed out the shortcomings in Robertson's diagrams. Bolton said that the Naval Board had not provided expert opinion and suggested that Hicks ought to have criticised the Board rather than Herd. This was a valid point and highlighted the deficiencies in the assistance the Board could have given the Commission, and Robertson. (Interview with Bob Herd, 25 March 1989.)

60. Robertson made detailed notes on his selection of words for his counsel. He said that Rear-Admiral George Oldham had advised him to use words in common usage. He said that the term 'unseamanlike' would need to be explained to a layman and confusion could arise. At any rate, Robertson stressed in notes to his counsel that unseamanlike did not mean dangerous. As an example, he said that *Voyager* could have stopped both engines and dropped astern of *Melbourne* before putting her engines ahead again and taking station. Although this was unseamanlike, it could hardly be described as dangerous. Robertson's definition of unseamanlike was actually a description of 'unprofessional' performance.

61. RC transcript, Day 12, pp. 718–19.

62. RC transcript, Day 13, pp. 785–8.

63. RC transcript, Day 13, p. 783.

64. *Regulations and Instructions to the RAN* (ABR 5016) were later rewritten to state: 'Whenever a grounding, a collision or narrow escape from collision occurs, care is to be taken to preserve the ship's log, all engine-room registers, the navigating officer's notebook, the plot in use, and the charts by which the ship was being navigated at the time. Entries are not to be erased but if correction is found to be necessary, the entry is to be crossed through so that the correction may be shown and the alteration initialled. Subsequent marking or amendment of the chart or plot is not to be made in any circumstances.'

65. RC transcript, Day 14, pp. 856–7, 864.

66. RC transcript, Day 14, pp. 857–8.

67. RC transcript, Day 14, pp. 856, 864.

68. 'Notes for future use by Captain Robertson on the evidence of Cdr Kelly' contained in a file headed 'Notes on trascript prepared by R. J. R. |Robertson| during Royal Commission' (undated), p. 12 (Robertson papers).

69. RC transcript, Day 14, pp. 876–7.

70. This was partly conceded by Sumpter. RC transcript, Day 14, p. 876.

71. 'Notes for future use', p. 15.

72. RC transcript, Day 14, p. 884.

73. RC transcript, Day 14, p. 884.

74. RC transcript, Day 14, p. 903.
75. RC transcript, Day 14, p. 905.
76. RC transcript, Day 14, p. 885.
77. RC transcript, Day 15, p. 964.
78. RC transcript, Day 15, p. 972.
79. RC transcript, Day 16, p. 983.
80. RC transcript, Day 16, p. 983.
81. RC transcript, Day 29, p. 2161.
82. The rules for surface plotting were set out in BR 1982 A Part 2. Paragraph 325 is particularly relevant. There are two basic rules. First, own ship's track is always kept up to date. Second, the initial positions of ships in company are plotted showing their stations but tracks are not kept up to date. Instead their positions are plotted on the radar screen and observed to ensure they do not move from their stations. The guide ship, in this case *Melbourne*, would be the highest priority with the operations room being ready if necessary to assist the OOW with relative velocity problems. This means that *Melbourne* would not necessarily plot *Voyager*'s track, but that *Voyager* should have kept *Melbourne*'s track up to date. In certain circumstances (when visibility is good or ships are in close formation and inside radar ground wave or sea clutter) these rules can be varied by the OOW or the Operations Room Officer with the OOW's concurrence. In this instance, with no operations room officer in attendance and the ships exercising for the first time after refitting, a plot of *Melbourne*'s track should have been maintained. Practically speaking, this was Patterson's specific duty in the operations room.
83. RC transcript, Day 21, p. 1465
84. RC transcript, Day 21, p. 1467.
85. RC transcript, Day 21, p. 1481. It was alleged that Patterson was trying to find excuses for his failure to have maintained *Melbourne*'s track. Robertson suggested to his counsel that 'the plot in *Voyager* at the time of the collision was about 5 to 8 minutes out of date and for this reason it left the impression in the mind of Patterson that it was a hook shape to the left'. (Notes prepared by Robertson for his counsel, undated (Robertson papers)).
86. RC transcript, Day 26, p. 1978.
87. RC transcript, Day 28, p. 1991.
88. This evidence was taken in camera, RC transcript, Day 24, p. 1697.
89. RC transcript, Day 24, p. 1698.
90. In a letter to me (19 August 1991), Patterson stated: 'The voice I heard in the water was that of T/O Gary Evans. I cannot, at this late stage, accurately recall as to how long after the collision I heard the voice. However, given that I was in the water for about five minutes before the forward section sank, it is my belief that it was between five and ten minutes after entering the water, that I heard the voice . . . From my conversations with him, I am certain that he does recall calling out in the water as I allege.'
91. RC transcript, Day 24, p. 1701.
92. Interview with Robert Jocumsen, 30 June 1991.
93. RC transcript, Day 28, p. 2037.
94. RC transcript, Day 28, p. 2082.
95. RC transcript, Day 30, p. 2070.
96. RC transcript, Day 28, p. 2049f.
97. Interview with Michael Patterson, 19 May 1991.
98. RC transcript, Day 30, p. 2205.
99. RC transcript, Day 31, p. 2335.
100. Notes by Robertson on draft Chapter 12 of *One Minute of Time*, dated 3 July 1965, p. 1 (Robertson papers).
101. RC transcript, Day 30, p. 2081.
102. John Milliner to author, 23 August 1991.
103. RC transcript, Day 29, p. 2112.
104. RC transcript, Day 32, p. 2375.
105. RC transcript. Day 17, p. 1153.
106. RC transcript, Day 17, pp. 1153–6.
107. Robertson offered this description of Degenhardt in notes made during the Commission for his counsel (Robertson papers).
108. Contained in an enclosure to a letter from Robertson to Hickling dated 25 February 1965 (Robertson papers).

109. RC transcript, Day 38, p. 2856.
110. Beer was sold to liberty men from canteens in RN ships when in ports where beer could not be purchased ashore. The rum issue was discontinued in the RN in 1967 and several years later in the RNZN.
111. RC transcript, Day 38, p. 2868.
112. RC transcript, Day 38, p. 2868.
113. Ibid.
114. Letter from FOICEA to SecNav dated 1 April 1964. Copy contained in unnumbered CNS branch file 'HMAS *Voyager* Royal Commission'.
115. Rear-Admiral G. G. O. Gatacre to SecNav, 1 April 1964.
116. Galfrey Gatacre, *Reports of Proceedings* (Nautical Press, Manly, 1982) p. 368.
117. Gatacre, op. cit., pp. 371–2.
118. Gatacre was a close friend of Captain Stevens and had some dealings with Sir Jack Stevens. On 24 June 1962, Gatacre wrote to Captain Stevens telling him he would be on the 30 June 1962 promotion signal thanks to Gatacre's efforts at the promotion board. It was highly irregular for Gatacre to have given Stevens this information. However, it reflects the closeness of their friendship and suggests a desire in Gatacre to have Stevens feel indebted to him for his promotion. (G. G. O. Gatacre to D. H. Stevens, 24 June 1962) (Stevens papers).
119. CNS to FOCAF, 18 May 1964. Copy contained on unnumbered Navy file 'HMAS *Voyager* Royal Commission'.
120. Gatacre letter of 1 April, op. cit., p. 5.
121. Gatacre's contention was thoroughly examined by the Naval Staff and detailed references from tactical publications cited to show his error. The Director of Communications (Cdr R. E. Lesh) briefed Jenkyn QC on this matter on 6 April 1964. A record of the briefing is contained in unnumbered CNS branch file 'HMAS *Voyager* Royal Commission'.
122. Signal DTG 181138Z Aug 64 from FOCAF to ACNB stated, 'Captains employed on this duty understood the correct interpretation. There was no need for confirmation as they already knew what was correct'. Becher followed this signal with a personal letter dated 20 August 1964 in which he said he had not issued a memorandum on this matter as it seemed 'that the less official discussion of a matter which was being reviewed by the Royal Commission the better'. Original contain in unnumbered Navy file 'HMAS *Voyager* Royal Commission'.
123. Notes on *One Minute of Time* (Robertson papers).
124. RC transcript, Day 32, p. 2395.
125. RC transcript, Day 33, p. 2439.
126. Notes prepared for Hickling by Robertson, 25 November 1964 (Robertson papers).
127. RC transcript, Day 33, p. 2439.
128. RC transcript, Day 33, p. 2440.
129. RC transcript, Day 33, p. 2443.
130. Ibid.
131. RC transcript, Day 33, p. 2445.
132. RC transcript, Day 33, pp. 2446–9.
133. RC transcript, Day 34, pp. 2530.
134. RC transcript, Day 34, pp. 2531–2.
135. This statement is contained in notes prepared by Robertson during the Commission for his counsel (Robertson papers).
136. Ibid.
137. Notes prepared by Robertson for his counsel, page 65 (undated although prepared before final addresses were given) (Robertson papers).
138. RC transcript, Day 39, p. 2996–7
139. Signal DTG 180451 May 64 from FOICEA to ACNB, info FOCAF, NAS Nowra and *Melbourne*.
140. It appears that Robertson told Hickling about the conversation Barwick had with Hicks, and that reference to it was made in the first draft of *One Minute of Time*. In his comments on this draft, Hicks wrote, 'I want to make it clear that no reference, oblique or otherwise, can be made to a private discussion with the Attorney-General. In any event, the head of the Judiciary does not and cannot tell the Government what it should do' (undated page of comments by D. S. Hicks on chapters 12–16 of *One Minute of Time*) (Robertson papers). In his comments on the same chapters, Robertson says 'Hicks wants me to emphasise that the conversation he quotes from Barwick is particularly confidential. He does not want it to go any further than amongst those of us who have read it' (document titled "Further notes by Captain Robertson dated 27 June

1965") (Robertson papers). Moreover, Barwick told me that he believed suggesting Smyth had been a mistake. (Interview with the Rt Hon. Sir Garfield Barwick, 21 September 1989.) Chaney said that Barwick also told him he regretted the decision to appoint Smyth. (Interview with the Hon. Sir Frederick Chaney, 27 July 1990.)

141. Ibid.
142. RC transcript, Day 44, p. 3433.
143. Ibid.
144. RC transcript, Day 44, pp. 3434–8.
145. RC transcript, Day 44, p. 3450.

# Chapter 7

1. Smyth's final address is covered in RC transcript, Days 45–7, pp. 3469–697.
2. Jenkyn's final address is covered in RC transcript, Days 48–50, pp. 3699–968.
3. Minute from SecNav to all Board members, 11 June 1964. Landau had received information and Jenkyn's request from Neilson.
4. RC transcript, Day 48, p. 3699.
5. Ibid.
6. RC transcript, Day 48, p. 3752.
7. RC transcript, Day 50, p. 3916.
8. RC transcript, Day 50, p. 3917.
9. RC transcript, Day 48, p. 3758.
10. RC transcript, Day 49, p. 3779.
11. RC transcript, Day 50, p. 3919.
12. RC transcript, Day 49, p. 3823.
13. RC transcript, Day 49, p. 3824.
14. RC transcript, Day 49, p. 3847.
15. Ibid.
16. *Halsbury's Laws of England*, 3rd edn, ref. 35, p. 651.
17. RC transcript, Day 50, p. 3929.
18. Street's final address is covered in RC transcript, Day 51, pp. 3969–4048.
19. RC transcript, Day 51, pp. 3974–5, 4042.
20. RC transcript, Day 51, p. 3974.
21. Hon. Sir Laurence Street to author, 23 August 1989.
22. A point not lost on Spicer. RC transcript, Day 51, p. 4042.
23. RC transcript, Day 51, p. 3973.
24. Street seemed to be conscious of this despite arguing to the contrary. RC transcript, Day 51, pp. 4006–7.
25. Note prepared by J. E. S. Stevens titled 'My Own Cross-Examination' — submitted to W. P. Ash QC in 1967 but not dated.
26. Meares's final address is covered in RC transcript, Days 51–2, pp. 4048–105.
27. Gregory interview, 18 July 1989.
28. Hicks's final address is covered in RC transcript, Days 52–4, pp. 4105–246.
29. RC transcript, Day 52, p. 4112.
30. RC transcript, Day 52, p. 4120.
31. RC transcript, Day 52, p. 4123.
32. Ibid.
33. Ibid.
34. Undated notes prepared by Robertson for D. S. Hicks QC.
35. Smyth's closing address in reply is covered in RC transcript, Days 54–5, pp. 4292–377.
36. RC transcript, Day 55, p. 4372.
37. Signal DTG 1502162 Feb. 64, from Flag Officer Aircraft Carriers (RN) to *Eagle, Ark Royal, Victorious* and *Centaur*.
38. Letter to the author, 5 June 1991.
39. Interview with the author, 24 May 1991.
40. Interview with Admiral Sir Victor Smith, 22 June 1990.
41. Letter to the author, 21 May 1991.

# Chapter 8

1. *Report of Royal Commission on the 'Loss of HMAS* Voyager' — (Comonwealth Government Printer, Melbourne, 1964); hereafter called the Spicer Report.
2. *Daily Mirror*, 26 August 1964.
3. *Daily Mirror*, 27 August 1964.
4. *Age*, 1 September 1964.
5. *Daily Mirror*, 27 August 1964.
6. *Age*, 27 August 1964.
7. Spicer Report, p. 6.
8. Spicer Report, p. 10.
9. In an interview with me (17 April 1991), Commodore Thomas Dasdwell altered the diagram under his name in the Spicer Report to show *Voyager's* final steady course as a mean course rather than an actual course.
10. 'I take 2042 hours as a fair starting point', Spicer Report, p. 8.
11. There was some variation between the turning and stopping data given by Robertson and Herd. They both generally agree on *Melbourne's* track with a turning diameter of around 2,800 yards under 10 degrees of rudder. But whereas Robertson's reconstructions of *Voyager's* final movements were based on a speed of 21 knots until 2052, 20.5 knots until 2053 and 30 seconds, and 18.5 knots until the collision, with a turning diameter of 800 yards under 15 degrees of rudder and 1,100 yards under 10 degrees, Herd gives her the same 'theoretical' speeds but has her turning diameter as 850 yards under 15 degrees of rudder and 1,000 yards under 10 degrees. Both were of the opinion that the drag produced by the rudder moving from port 10 to starboard 35 would have negated the effect of the engines being brought to full ahead. In a letter to me (20 May 1989), Herd states, 'The manoeuvring data for the two ships which was available in 1964 did not include data specific to *Melbourne*. A collection of data from different sources was in use for *Melbourne*, whereas detailed trials data for *Voyager* was available. For this reason I made my *Melbourne* estimates conservative'.
12. Spicer Report, p. 18.
13. Ibid.
14. Spicer Report, p. 21.
15. Ibid.
16. Spicer Report, p. 22.
17. The concept of fault in relation to maritime collisions is discussed in S. Mankabady, *Collisions at Sea: A guide to their legal consequences* (North-Holland, New York, 1978) pp. 9–18.
18. Lord Maugham in *The Llanover* (1945), *Lloyds Law Reports*, No. 78, p. 461.
19. Spicer Report, p. 31.
20. Spicer Report, p. 38.
21. Minute from 2NM to CNS, 29 July 1964. Original contained on unnumbered CNS Branch file 'Matters Arising from Royal Commission'.
22. Memorandum 'Royal Commission — Loss of HMAS *Voyager*', prepared by Cdr Larry Winch for ACNB consideration, p. 1.
23. ACNB minute 80/1964 dated 24 July 1964 and Navy Office file 1288/201/14 refer. Winch was permitted to consult with the Attorney-General's Department and the newly appointed Naval Judge Advocate-General (Judge Trevor Rapke) as required. It is interesting that the Naval Board mentioned the 'whaler tragedy' in this context. It appears from this instance that the Naval Board actively sought to prevent making public documents relating to that incident and seems to have been alarmed by the prospect. The preponderance of interest in preventing the disclosure of information relating to this accident, but not of others, does not inspire confidence in the propriety of the handling of that matter.
24. Opinion provided to the Naval Board by Cdr Larry Winch, CNJA, 31 July 1964.
25. Ibid, p. 3.
26. Ibid. p. 4.
27. Ibid, p. 13.
28. Ibid.
29. ACNB minute 90/1964, 7 August 1964. ACNB minute 80/1964 is also relevant.
30. Cabinet Decision Nos 418 and 422, 25 and 26 August 1964 give direction to the Naval Board. At its meeting on 27 August, the Board endorsed the Navy's submission to Cabinet on the Royal Commission report. ACNB minute 97/1964, 27 August 1964 refers.

31. 'Report of Royal Commission on Loss of HMAS *Voyager* — Report by Naval Board' dated 1 September 1964, p. 2. Contained on unnumbered Navy file 'Matters Arising from *Voyager* Royal Commission'. The matter of timekeeping was standardised. See Navy file 519/252/35, 'Clocks in HMA Ships'. Commonwealth Naval Orders Nos 428 and 430 of 1964 also dealt with this subject to ensure uniformity of practice throughout the Fleet.
32. Ibid.
33. Ibid. pp. 3–4.
34. Ibid., pp. 4–9.
35. Ibid, p. 3.
36. 'Summary of Main Points in the Report and Naval Board Comments', Contained on unnumbered Navy file 'Matters Arising From *Voyager* Royal Commission', p. 1.
37. Ibid, p. 4.
38. Ibid, p. 3.
39. DCNS Newsletter, May 1965, Section B, para. B33.
40. Ibid.
41. Note for file 161/201/71, 'Navigational Lighting in HMA Ships', prepared by CNS dated 24 November 1964.
42. This remark was written by Harrington on a sheet of personalised notepaper and placed inside the advance copy (Copy No. 3) which he received of the report from Sir John Spicer.
43. Spicer Report, p. 9.
44. 'Summary of Main Points', p. 4.
45. Naval Board report on Spicer Report, 1 September 1964, pp. 10–12.
46. Cabinet submission, pp. 10–12
47. Minute from CNS to Chaney, 26 August 1964. An enclosure listed the command experience of seven RN officers who were then commanding British aircraft carriers. Each had had only one carrier command and only one previous seagoing command. To cite one example, the captain of the commando carrier HMS *Bulwark* had been ashore for eight and a half years before assuming command.
48. Ibid.
49. Naval Board submission to Cabinet on Spicer Report, 1 September 1964, p. 3.
50. Ibid.
51. Naval Board report on Spicer Report, 1 September 1964, pp. 27–35.
52. Navy file 16/201/72 'Communications — points arising from the *Voyager* inquiry' and 465/201/349 'Possible amendments to ATP 1A'.
53. In July 1964 with the release of the Spicer Report imminent, the Naval Board proposed a list of the most likely questions it would be asked as a consequence of the Royal Commission and the report, and suitable answers. There were 53 questions in all. Questions 41 and 42 dealt with fleetwork aspects. The proposed answers were redrafted throughout August 1964 and were distributed to Naval Board members under a minute from Landau. (Contained on unnumbered CNS branch file 'Matters arising from Royal Commission'.)
54. Ibid.
55. 'Answers to likely questions'. In reply to question 28: 'Is it a practice to allow officers and ratings to drink alcoholic liquor prior to ships engaging in exercises?'

# Chapter 9

1. A draft Cabinet decision from the 4 September meeting was provided to Landau by Bunting as a letter enclosure, dated 7 September 1964.
2. Draft Cabinet minute, 4 September 1964. No decision number appended.
3. Cabinet minute, 10 September 1964 (Decision No. 485).
4. *CPD* (Reps) 26 August 1964, p. 603.
5. Ibid. p. 2.
6. *CPD* (Reps) 15 September 1964, p. 1073.
7. *CPD* (Reps), p. 1074.
8. Ibid.
9. *CPD* (Reps), p. 1080.
10. *CPD* (Reps), 15 September 1964, p. 1088.
11. *CPD* (Reps), p. 1082.
12. *CPD* (Reps), p. 1083.

13. *CPD* (Reps), p. 1082.
14. *CPD* (Reps), p. 1086.
15. *Bulletin*, 26 September 1964, p. 21.
16. *Daily Mirror*, 22 September 1964.
17. Hon. Clyde Cameron to author, 15 May 1991.
18. *CPD* (Reps) 15 September 1964, p. 1090. In a letter to me, Cameron stated 'I treated the whole exercise as a cover-up of the Naval Board. My attitude was clearly indicated by my constant interjections'. (Cameron to author, 15 May 1990).
19. *CPD* (Reps), pp. 1097–100.
20. *CPD* (Reps), pp. 1101–04.
21. *Age*, 17 September 1964.
22. *Daily Mirror*, 16 September 1964.
23. *Herald*, 16 September 1964.
24. Chaney told me that the Navy portfolio was not a popular one and that most of his parliamentary colleagues said they were glad it was him and not they who had the *Voyager* controversy and the Navy with which to contend. (Interview with the Hon. Sir Frederick Chaney, 27 July 1990.)
25. The *Bulletin*, 26 September 1964, p. 21.
26. *SMH*, 26 September 1964.
27. *CPD* (Reps) 24 September 1964, p. 1473.
28. Ibid.
29. *CPD*, p. 1475.
30. *CPD* (Reps), p. 1480.
31. *CPD* (Reps), p. 1482.
32. *CPD* (Reps), p. 1485.
33. *CPD* (Reps), p. 1488.
34. *CPD* (Reps), p. 1490.
35. Ibid.
36. *CPD* (Reps), p. 1491.
37. *Australian*, 22 September 1964.
38. *Australian*, 25 September 1964.
39. *CPD* (Senate) 23 September 1964, p. 680.
40. Ibid.
41. Ibid.
42. *CPD* (Senate), p. 683.
43. *CPD* (Senate), p. 687.
44. Alan Trengrove, *John Grey Gorton — An Informal Biography* (Cassell, Sydney 1969) p. 144.
45. Don Whitington, *The Twelfth Man?* (Jacaranda, Brisbane, 1972) p. 137.
46. *The Twelfth Man?*, p. 136.
47. *CPD* (Senate) 23 September 1964, p. 688.
48. *CPD* (Senate), p. 690.
49. *CPD* (Senate), p. 692.
50. *CPD* (Senate), p. 694.
51. *CPD* (Senate), p. 695.
52. *CPD* (Senate), p. 697.
53. P. Howson and D. Aitken (ed.) *The Howson Diaries: The Life of Politics* (Viking Press, Melbourne, 1984), diary entry for 24 September 1964, p. 113.
54. *Australian*, 25 September 1964.
55. *Bulletin*, 26 September 1964, p. 19.
56. Reported in the *Australian*, 26 September 1964.
57. *Australian*, 30 October 1964.
58. Interview with Harrington's son, Captain Simon Harrington RAN, 17 July 1990.
59. Section B, para. B56.
60. See Navy file 165/1/70 'Public relations post-*Voyager* assessment and proposed measures to lessen the effect of adverse publicity'.
61. ACNB minute 108/64, 9 October 1964 and Navy file 8/2/35 refer.
62. ACNB minute 105/64, 25 September 1964.
63. ACNB minute 107/64, 6 October 1964.
64. Navy Press Release, 20 December 1964.
65. *CPD* (Reps), 1 April 1965.

66. Letter from Chipp to Holt dated 16 May 1967. Copy contained in Navy file 1288/201/44, folio 71.
67. Interview with Rear-Admiral Andrew Robertson, 4 July 1990.

# Chapter 10

1. N. A. Jenkyn QC to Robertson, 8 July 1964 (Robertson papers).
2. Naval Attache, Washington (Peel) to Captain Robertson, 27 August 1964 (Robertson papers).
3. Surgeon Commander Brian Treloar to Robertson, 11 July 1964 (Robertson papers).
4. Commodore James Ramsey to Robertson, 17 June 1964 (Robertson papers).
5. CNS to Robertson, 23 August 1964. (Original in Robertson papers.)
6. Interview with Admiral Sir Victor Smith, 22 June 1990.
7. Rear-Admiral Bill Graham said that Harrington's dislike of Robertson was evident to him when he (Graham) was serving as secretary to Vice-Admiral Sir Henry Burrell. Harrington's widow and his son, Captain Simon Harrington RAN, were under a similar general impression.
8. Interview with Commodore Ken Gray, 23 January 1991.
9. Philpott to Robertson, 7 May 1965 (Robertson papers).
10. Memorandum from SecNav to Minister, 26 August 1964. Copy No. 24, p. 4 cited.
11. *Sun*, 27 August 1964.
12. *Daily Mirror*, 27 August 1964.
13. Interview with Admiral Sir Victor Smith, 22 June 1990.
14. Harold Hickling, *One Minute of Time* (A. H. & A. W. Reed, Wellington, 1965) p. 228.
15. The full text of all correspondence relating to his resignation was provided to the press by Robertson at a conference he called on 29 September 1964. A copy of his prepared statement is included in the Robertson papers.
16. The opinion sought by the Naval Board and given by I. F. Sheppard and J. C. Braund, representing the DCS, 28 August 1964, was that charges could not be properly laid under the *Naval Discipline Act*. This advice evidently ignored a traditional use of the court martial to clear an officer's name.
17. Winch to Robertson, 12 October 1964 (Robertson papers).
18. R. J. Robertson, 'The Two Voices of the Naval Board', *Australian*, 5 October 1964.
19. *Australian*, 22 September 1964.
20. A single handwritten page included on the file 'Matters Arising from the Royal Commission into the Loss of HMAS *Voyager*'.
21. Minute from CNS to the Minister for the Navy, 15 September 1964.
22. Minute from 2NM to CNS and Secretary of the Navy Department, 16 September 1964. Both referred the matter to the Naval Board in their penscript at the head of the minute.
23. Ibid.
24. Interview with Sir Frederick Chaney 27 July 1990. Chaney felt that although Robertson understood what he was doing in resigning his commission, it surprised Chaney that Robertson immediately lobbied others to write to the Navy Minister to ask that he (Robertson) be granted a pension.
25. Cabinet minute, 22 September 1964 (Decision No. 489).
26. *Commonwealth Gazette*, 22 October 1964.
27. Minute from 2NM to SecNav, 22 September 1964.
28. Captain Anthony Synnot to Robertson, 30 September 1964 (Robertson papers).
29. James Ramsey to Robertson, 29 September 1964 (Robertson papers).
30. *Daily Mirror*, 30 September 1964.
31. A rough transcript of Robertson's remarks in response to questions from the press was made by the editor of *Navy News*, who was in attendance, and forwarded to Tony Eggleton, the CNPR.
32. Minute from 2NM to CNS and SecNav, 29 September 1964. Filed in 'Matters Arising'.
33. This matter was put strongly to Chaney by Landau in a minute headed 'Captain Robertson — Consultation with Naval Board', 13 October 1964. Filed in 'Matters Arising'.
34. Hickling, *One Minute of Time*, p. 56.
35. Contained in the private papers of the Ven. John Were (Museum of HMAS *Cerberus*).
36. Hugh Curnow (the *Bulletin*) to Robertson, 22 September 1964 (Robertson papers).
37. *Age*, 30 September 1964.
38. *Australian*, 22 September 1964.
39. *SMH*, 23 September 1964.

40. Winch, in a letter to Robertson (14 October 1964) remarked, 'Your newspaper articles were moderate in the extreme. The last article in particular, and the reference in the first about "loyalty down" really got to the heart of things' (Robertson papers).
41. *Australian*, 1 October 1964.
42. Notes prepared for counsel in 1967 (Robertson papers).

## Chapter 11

1. The Minister directed that the wreath-laying off Jervis Bay be concealed from the press until after the event. Filed on 'Loss of HMAS *Voyager*'.
2. The then Commodore Superintendent of Training at HMAS *Cerberus*, J. Philip Stevenson, remarks in a letter to the Secretary of the Navy Department that it had been 'decided that no special service should be held annually to distinguish *Voyager* from the loss of any other RAN ship'. *Cerberus* letter 61/3/2, 10 March 1965. Navy Office file 12/1/31.
3. Interview with Sir Frederick Chaney, 27 July 1990.
4. Hickling to Robertson, 18 November 1964 (Robertson papers).
5. Conversation with Mrs B. Robertson, 23 May 1991.
6. Hickling served for a brief period during World War I in the light cruiser HMAS *Melbourne*. At that time the ship was in European waters with a ship's company that was predominantly British.
7. In a letter to Robertson from Hickling's publishers (25 January 1965), Ray Richards mentioned the importance of signed documents and this may have been the reason for asking Cabban to sign his statement. Richards's advice was obscure. 'You will be consulting your barrister friends about obtaining signed statements giving additional evidence on the drink aspect, such evidence not to be used in the book now being written but being held in the event of threats or other pressure being applied to the book or to yourself. I realise how distasteful this aspect is to you but I would regard it important in a number of respects that it be obtained now in the event of urgent or future requirements' (Robertson papers). This letter would most likely have come into Robertson's possession the day before he met with Cabban.
8. Ray Richards to Robertson, 1 March 1965 (Robertson papers). Richards later in the same letter suggests that Robertson establish a dossier of information on Stevens's drinking habits to use in the event that Sir Jack Stevens might try to have the book withdrawn from sale.
9. Robertson from Mary Anstruther, 11 February 1965 (Robertson papers).
10. Richards to Robertson, 24 June 1965 (Robertson papers). Richards also sought evidence from Griffith but this request, based on Cabban's statement that his allegations could be corroborated by Griffith, was ignored by Robertson who was against any investigation of the Cabban Statement. Robertson informed Richards that Griffith could corroborate the statement although it is unclear whether Robertson actually spoke with Griffith or was merely reiterating the remark passed by Cabban at the end of his statement. However, Hickling did attempt to speak with Lieutenant Richard Carpendale who had returned to Britain after exchange with the RAN in *Voyager*.
11. Robertson to Hickling, 23 February 1965 (Robertson papers).
12. Hickling to Robertson, 13 May 1965 (Robertson papers).
13. Fowle to Hickling, 15 February 1965 (copy in Robertson papers).
14. Robertson to SecNav (Landau), 24 March 1965 (Robertson papers).
15. Director of Naval Intelligence to Robertson, 23 March 1965 (Robertson papers).
16. Landau to Robertson (1288/201/13), 8 April 1965 (Robertson papers).
17. Robertson to Landau, 14 April 1965 (Robertson papers).
18. Landau to Robertson (1288/201/13), 29 April 1965 (Robertson papers).
19. Robertson to Landau, 3 May 1965 (Robertson papers).
20. Landau to Robertson, 18 May 1965 (Robertson papers).
21. Handwritten note contained in a file of private papers held by Sir Frederick Chaney.
22. Chaney interview, 27 July 1990.
23. SecNav minute to Minister (Chaney), 23 August 1965. Navy file 1288/201/44, 'Allegations of former Lt Cdr Cabban'.
24. Ibid.
25. Ibid.
26. Interview with Sir John Gorton, 2 August 1990.
27. Ray Richards on behalf of A. H. & A. W. Reed (Publishers) to Robertson, 18 October 1965 (Robertson papers).

28. Hickling to Robertson, 13 May 1965 (Robertson papers).
29. Notes by Captain Robertson on *One Minute of Time*, dated 27 June 1965 (Robertson papers).
30. A copy of Hicks's comments (in type form) on Hickling's manuscript is contained in the Robertson papers.
31. Draft of *One Minute of Time*, p. 58.
32. Notes by Captain Robertson on draft of *One Minute of Time*, p. 5, 27 June 1965 (Robertson papers).
33. 'An Admiral Speaks His Mind', *Age*, December 1965.
34. *Naval Review*, Vol. 40, No. 2, April 1967, pp. 169–71 at p. 171.
35. '*Voyager*: A new look at tragedy', *Herald*, 4 December 1965.
36. 'Collision off Jervis Bay', *SMH*, 4 December 1965.
37. Quoted in the *Age*, 23 October 1965.
38. *One Minute of Time*, pp. 142–3.
39. T. B. Millar, 'Disaster Compounded', *Bulletin*, 20 November 1965, p. 56.
40. *CPD* (Reps), 9 December 1965, p. 3814.
41. Ibid.
42. Sam Benson to Sir Jack Stevens, 22 November 1965 (Stevens papers).
43. Quoted in the *Australian*, 24 November 1965, p. 5.
44. Extract of letter from Jess to Holt, quoted in a file memorandum by Sam Landau covering the Navy Minister's copy of the Cabban Statement. The memorandum states that the full text of the Cabban Statement was not seen by the Navy department until August 1966 when it enclosed with Jess's letter to Holt. AA 1288/201/44, folio 11.
45. Cabban to Jess, 10 August 1966. Copy passed to Minister for the Navy and placed on file AA 1288/201/44, folio 13.
46. Minute from First Assistant Crown Solicitor to the Attorney-General (Snedden), citing information from J. Braund of the Crown Solicitor's office, 23 August 1966. AA 1288/201/44, folio 20.
47. Jess to Holt , 11 August 1966. A copy was forwarded to the Department of the Navy and placed in file AA 1288/201/44, folio 14.
48. 'Notes on correspondence dated 11 August 1966 from Mr Jess MP to Prime Minister', probably prepared on 26 August 1966 by Sam Landau. 1288/201/44, folio 15.
49. Minute from McNicoll to Chaney, 23 August 1966. 1288/201/44, folio 16.
50. Ibid.
51. Chaney to Menzies, 24 August 1965, with enclosures. 1288/201/44.
52. Minute from Landau to Chipp (by hand of Philpott [Deputy Secretary of the Navy Department]), 22 December 1966. AA 1288/201/44, folio 21.
53. P. Howson, *The Howson Diaries* (Viking 1984), footnote to diary entry for 13 December 1966, p. 254.

# Chapter 12

1. St John's involvement is set out in detail in his book, *A Time To Speak* (Sun, Melbourne, 1969) pp. 80–115.
2. *CPD* (Reps), 7 March 1967.
3. Stevens to Benson, 13 March 1967 (Stevens papers).
4. Jess to Holt, 23 March 1967. Copy in Navy file 1288/201/44 folio 29.
5. W. Kent Hughes to Holt, 20 March 1967. Copy contained in Navy file 1288/201/44, folio 27.
6. 'Backbenchers', *Current Affairs Bulletin*, Vol. 37, No. 11, 18 April 1966, p. 165.
7. Howson, *The Howson Diaries* (Viking, 1984) diary entry for 10 April 1967, p. 285.
8. Jess explained the means by which he delivered this letter and the effort he had expended in doing so in a letter to Holt, 17 April 1967. Copy contained on Navy file 1288/201/44, folio 30.
9. Holt to Jess, 21 April 1967. Copy contained in Navy file 1288/201/44, folio 31.
10. McMahon to Holt, 12 April 1967. Copy contained on Navy file 1288/201/44, folio 33.
11. Interview with John Jess, 4 September 1989.
12. Interview with the Hon. Don Chipp, 5 September 1989.
13. Cabinet submission 'Royal Commission on loss of HMAS *Voyager*, 1964 and treatment of Captain R.J. Robertson', 27 April 1967, p. 2 (Executive Summary).
14. Ibid., p. 13.
15. Ibid., p. 9.

16. Ibid., pp. 13–14.
17. Cabinet minute, 2 May 1967 (Decision No. 296). Sir Nigel Bowen, who attended this meeting, told me that Cabinet held firm to its view that nothing would be gained from holding another inquiry as no satisfactory case had been made to show how the Cabban allegations might have had a bearing on the collision. Bowen said that it was more of a practical than a political decision. (Interview with Sir Nigel Bowen, 8 August 1991.)
18. D. L. Chipp & J. Larkin, *The Third Man* (Rigby, 1978), p. 74.
19. Memorandum, 28 April 1967, prepared for Chipp by McNicoll. Navy file 1288/201/44, folio 42.
20. McNicoll to Landau, 29 August 1964, and contained on unnumbered CNS branch file 'Matters Arising from Royal Commission'.
21. Stevens to Benson, 7 May 1967 (Stevens papers).
22. *Australian*, 8 May 1967.
23. Cabban told me that this was his rather than Jess's attitude in wanting another inquiry. (Conversation with Cabban, 5 June 1991.)
24. Mackay to Holt, 4 May 1967. Copy contained on Navy file 1288/201/44, folio 45.
25. Ibid.
26. Chipp & Larkin, *op. cit.*, p. 74.
27. Chipp & Larkin, op. cit., p. 74.
28. This meeting took place in St John's home on 7 May 1967 (St John, op. cit., p. 83).
29. Mackay to Holt, 8 May 1967. Copy contained in Navy file 1288/201/44, folio 47.
30. St John to Chipp, 15 May 1967. Original contained in Navy file 1288/201/44, folio 55.
31. Slip attached to letter, Bunting to Landau, 9 May 1967. After first being placed in file 60/40/12, it was held in 1288/201/44, folio 50 and 51.
32. Motion moved by Jess, seconded by Turner. Copy filed on Navy file 1288/201/44, folio 52.
33. Cabinet minute dated 10 May 1967 (Decision No. 331).
34. Mackay to Holt, 8 May 1967, Navy file 1288/201/44, folio 47.
35. 'Memorandum On Aspects of the *Voyager* Debate', prepared by McNicoll and forwarded to Chipp, p. 1 cited. Copy contained in Navy file 1288/201/44, folio 57.
36. Ibid., p. 2.
37. Chipp to Holt, 15 May 1967. McNicoll's memorandum and a minute from Surgeon Rear-Admiral Coplans were enclosed. Copy contained in Navy file 1288/201/44, folio 58.
38. Minute from Coplans through Landau to Chipp, 15 May 1967. Tabled in Parliament on 17 May 1967 and printed in *Loss of HMAS* Voyager, Parliamentary Paper No. 50, 1967.
39. Minute from Coplans through Landau to Chipp, 15 May 1967. (This was a different minute to that referred to in the previous footnote.) The minute never reached Chipp. The original is contained in Navy file 1288/201/44, folio 64.
40. *Loss of HMAS* Voyager, Parliamentary Paper No. 50, 17 May 1967.
41. Landau to G. J. Willis, 19 April 1967. Copy contained in Navy file 1288/201/44, folio 17.
42. Interview with Rear-Admiral A. A. Willis, 24 May 1991.
43. Signal DTG 240941Z Apr 67 from ANRUK to ACNB refers.
44. Landau to Smyth, 21 April 1967. Copy contained in Navy file 1288/201/44.
45. The details of the following narrative are taken from a 'Note for File' prepared and signed by Landau, 9 May 1967. Contained in Navy file 1288/201/44, folio 37.
46. Ibid.
47. Landau to Smyth, 11 May 1967. Copy contained on Navy file 1288/201/44, folio 40.
48. Chipp, op. cit., p. 75.
49. It was subsequently reconstructed by Tiller.
50. Interview with Dr Michael Tiller, 27 July 1990.
51. Smyth to Landau, 27 April 1967. Copy contained in Navy file 1288/201/44, folio 31.
52. Letter from Dr M.C. Tiller to the author, 25 June 1990.
53. Statement by M.C. Tiller taken at Perth by Burt and Neal in the presence of George Sadlier, solicitor, on Friday 11 August 1967, p. 10.
54. Tiller statement of 7 August 1967, p. 8.
55. *Loss of HMAS* Voyager, Parliamentary Paper No. 50, p. 12.
55a. Currently Chief Justice of the High Court of Australia.
56. 'Statement of Lieutenant Commander Griffith RAN, Navigating Officer of *Voyager* during the period July 1962 to January 1964', taken by the Solicitor General, 15 May 1967. Copy contained in Navy file 1288/201/44, folio 41.
57. Interview with Lieutenant Commander S.B. Griffith, 9 August 1990.

58. St John claims that Nigel Bowen was in possession of Griffith's statement of 15 May 1967 when the Parliamentary debate began. However, the statement was not tabled. Interview with Ted St John, 15 July 1989.
59. Cabinet minute, 16 May 1967 (Decision No. 332).
60. *CPD* (Reps), 16 May 1967, p. 2149.
61. *CPD* (Reps), p. 2161.
62. *CPD* (Reps), p. 2165-6.
63. Chipp & Larkin, op. cit., p. 76.
64. *CPD* (Reps), p. 2167.
65. *CPD* (Reps), p. 2169.
66. Ibid.
67. Ibid.
68. Interview with Sir Nigel Bowen, 8 August 1991.
69. *CPD* (Reps), p. 2171.
70. *CPD* (Reps), p. 2146.
71. *Adelaide News*, 18 May 1967.
72. Quoted by St John, op cit., p. 89.
73. *Australian*, 20 May 1967.
74. *CPD* (Reps), p. 2175.
75. *CPD* (Reps), p. 2178.
76. *CPD* (Reps), 17 May 1967, p. 2245.
77. *CPD* (Reps), p. 2246.
78. *CPD* (Reps), p. 2245.
79. Hon. C.R. Cameron to author, 15 May 1967.
80. *CPD* (Reps), p. 2253.
81. A citation from *CPD* (Reps), 15 September 1964, p. 1086.
82. *CPD* (Reps), 17 May 1967, p. 2255.
83. The Opposition's strategy during the debate represented a marked departure from the way it should have been handled. As Cameron explained: 'prior to Gough Whitlam becoming leader of the Federal Parliamentary Labor Party [FPLP] on 8 February 1967, the Opposition didn't have what is now called a "Shadow Cabinet" with each member of it being treated as a spokesman for a designated department. Instead, the frontbenchers were described as the FPLP Executive and its members would lead on any subject which the leader felt appropriate. That ended when Gough was elected to the leadership. He established a Shadow Cabinet which proved to be a vast improvement . . . In choosing me to lead for the Opposition on 17 May, Mr Whitlam was out of step with his subsequent rule for Shadow Cabinet responsibility. My first assignment in his Shadow Cabinet was housing'. (Cameron to author, 15 May 1991.)
84. *CPD* (Reps), p. 2259.
85. Select Committees, also known as *ad hoc* committees, are set up to examine and report upon particular matters. They need to be differentiated from Standing Committees, which have a continuing function and a mandate to consider and comment upon matters in a defined field. Both types generally include members from all major parties in both the Senate and the House of Representatives.
86. Cabinet minute, 17 May 1967 (Decision No. 348).
87. *CPD* (Reps), p. 2279.
88. Ibid.
89. *CPD* (Reps), 18 May 1967, p. 2309.
90. Ibid.
91. Interview with Sir Nigel Bowen, 8 August 1991.
92. In spite of a Royal Commission being established, Jess told me he would have preferred a Senate Inquiry but had accepted the best he could get (Jess interview, 5 September 1989).
93. *Salmon Report* (HMSO, 1966), para. 7.
94. *Israel Law Review*, No. 2, 1976, pp. 313-14.

## Chapter 13

1. E.H. St John, *A Time to Speak* (Sun, 1969) p. 90. Jess states that Bowen asked him if the terms of reference were acceptable. In reply, Jess complained that they were too narrow but Bowen would not agree to them being redrafted. (Jess interview.)

2.  Cabinet minute, 25 May 1967 (Decision No. 356).
3.  Ibid.
4.  Interview with Sir Nigel Bowen (8 August 1991).
5.  *Australian,* 22 May 1967.
6.  John Stubbs, 'This Week in Parliament', *Australian,* 20 May 1967.
7.  Alan Reid, *The Gorton Experiment* (Shakespeare Head, Sydney, 1971) p. 36.
8.  Interview with Sir John Gorton, 2 August 1990.
9.  *CPD* (Reps), 19 May 1967, p. 2439.
10. Press statement issued by Mrs B.L. Stevens, 18 May 1967. (Original in the Stevens papers.)
11. Press statement by Major General Sir Jack Stevens, 18 May 1967. (Original in the Stevens papers.)
12. S. B. Griffith to B. L. Stevens, 18 February 1964 (Stevens papers).
13. D. J. Martin to B. L. Stevens, 15 February 1964 (Stevens papers).
14. T. J. Redman to B. L. Stevens dated 15 February 1964 (Stevens papers).
15. T. K. Morrison to B. L. Stevens, 12 February 1964 (Stevens papers).
16. V. A. Smith to B. L. Stevens, 12 February 1964 (Stevens papers).
17. B. L. Stevens to R. B. McMurrick, 23 May 1967 (Stevens papers).
18. R. B. McMurrick to B. L. Stevens, 9 July 1967 (Stevens papers).
19. Notes for counsel, 2 June 1967 (Stevens papers).
20. Notes for counsel, 2 June 1967 (Stevens papers).
21. D. H. D. Smyth to B. L. Stevens, 23 June 1967 (Stevens papers).
22. D. H. D. Smyth to F. M. Osborne, 23 June 1967 (Stevens papers).
23. G. J. Willis to B. L. Stevens, 26 June 1967 (Stevens papers).
24. G. J. Willis to B. L. Stevens, 10 July 1967 (Stevens papers). When he was finally called to give evidence at the Commission, he was in Vancouver on the IDC's summer tour as part of his staff course. By then he had seen little news of the Commission and had minimal contact with Australian naval personnel in the few days he spent in Australia to appear before the inquiry. (Interview with Vice-Admiral Sir James Willis, 29 January 1991)
25. *CPD* (Reps), 4 October 1967, pp. 1647–48.
26. Interview with the Hon. Sir Stanley Burbury, 25 May 1991.
27. Interview with the Hon. K.W. Asprey, 29 August 1990.
28. Interview with the Hon. George Lucas, 25 May 1991.
29. Interview with Chester Porter QC, 22 May 1991.

# Chapter 14

1.  'Cabban' Royal Commission (hereafter RC II) transcript, Day 1, p. 6.
2.  RC II transcript, Day 2, p. 14.
3.  RC II transcript, Day 2 p. 53.
4.  RC II transcript, Day 2, p. 27.
5.  RC II transcript, Day 2, p. 43–4.
6.  RC II transcript, Day 2, p. 50.
7.  RC II transcript, Day 2, p. 16.
8.  RC II transcript, Day 3, pp. 68–77.
9.  Draft of 'Statement for Royal Commission', 20 June 1967, B. L. Stevens (Stevens papers).
10. Cabban was examined by Burt on the third and fourth day of hearings.
11. RC II transcript, Day 5, pp. 239–241.
12. RC II transcript, Day 5, p. 240.
13. Herman Wouk, *The Caine Mutiny* (Jonathan Cape, London, 1951).
14. RC II transcript, Day 5, p. 240.
15. RC II transcript, Day 5, p. 242.
16. RC II transcript, Day 5, p. 246.
17. RC II transcript, Day 6, p. 295. Mutiny was the unlawful removal of an officer from command, while insubordination was the wilful disobedience of a lawful order. If Stevens had attempted to bring any action against Cabban, it would have been for insubordination in that he sent a signal advising that Stevens was not in command when he was directed to make no signal. However, inasmuch as Stevens's order would have been unlawful, Cabban could not have been convicted of any offence under the *Naval Discipline Act.*
18. RC II transcript, Day 6, p. 340.
19. RC II transcript, Day 6, p. 360.

20. RC II transcript, Day 7 , p. 375.
21. RC II transcript, Day 7, pp. 388, 389.
22. RC II transcript, Day 7, p. 392.
23. Cabban Statement.
24. Cabban Statement.
25. Interview with Commander the Hon. Fred Osborne, 29 August 1990.
26. Interview with Justice Peter Murphy, 5 September 1989.
27. Quoted in RC II transcript, Day 8, p. 517.
28. Later in the inquiry, the U.S. Navy weather station at Guam produced a weather report for that area on the dates in question which confirmed the existence of the typhoon. This served to cast doubt on the accuracy or the truthfulness of yet another of the logs maintained by RAN ships and presented to the Commission.
29. RC II transcript, Day 9, pp. 548–9.
30. RC II transcript, Day 9, p. 563.
31. Ibid. pp. 564–5.
32. RC II transcript, Day 9, p. 589.
33. The equivalent of a 'Collins Street' specialist in Melbourne or a 'Harley Street' specialist in London.
34. However, Stevens was given a cigarette lighter as a birthday gift by the officers of *Voyager* in 1963.
35. RC II transcript, Day 14, p. 1000.
36. RC II transcript, Day 15, pp. 1020, 1022.
37. RC II transcript, Day 15, pp. 1022–3.
38. Interview with Surgeon Rear-Admiral Brian Treloar, 21 March 1991.
39. RC II transcript, Day 15, pp. 1063–4.
40. Surgeon Rear-Admiral Coplans told the Commission that the Navy's policy was 'to discourage personnel from seeking private consultations. The doctor they go to invariably has no idea that they are in the Service and he may discover something which is not recorded' (RC II transcript, Day 16, p. 1080). But if Morrow was a consultant to the Navy, and he knew that Stevens was a naval officer in command of a destroyer, in spite of Stevens seeing him in a private capacity he was under the same obligation as a naval medical officer to submit official reports as required by the Naval Board. Morrow should have warned Stevens before the consultation began that he was obliged to report to the Naval Board anything that was required by naval regulations. Indeed, Coplans suggested that Morrow's consultation with Stevens was inadequate and that had he seen Stevens he would have directed him to undergo more detailed examination (RC II transcript, Day 16, p. 1138).
41. Recorded on Form E. 190 dated 26/1/39.
42. HMAS *Vendetta* letter, 1 January 1942. (Copy in Stevens papers).
43. Statement of sea service, Captain D.H. Stevens, enclosure to NOL 351/20/235, 26 March 1964 (Stevens papers).
44. SecNav to Flag Officer Commanding Sydney, NOL 589/202/559 (1880), 18 January 1949.
45. FOCE, Sydney to Sec Nav, NSW letter 2860/682/2/11, 18 January 1950. The Commendation was subsequently endorsed by the Board.
46. NOL 443/202/488, 17 November 1950.
47. There was some thought at this stage that alcohol may have contributed to his condition. (Interview with Surgeon Rear-Admiral Brian Treloar, 21 March 1991.)
48. Penscript on Cabban Statement contained in Stevens papers.
49. C. H. Morgan, *The Gunroom* (Chatto & Windus, London, 1991).

# Chapter 15

1. Submission to the Law Reform Commission of Canada and quoted in L. A. Hallet, *Royal Commissions and Boards of Inquiry: Some Legal and Procedural Aspects* (Law Book Co., Melbourne, 1982) p. 215.
2. Ibid.
3. RC II transcript, Day 10, p. 671.
4. Ibid.
5. Ibid.
6. RC II transcript, Day 10, p. 675.

7. Notes for counsel, undated (Robertson papers).
8. RC II transcript, Day 11, p. 685.
9. RC II transcript, Day 12, p. 799.
10. Ibid.
11. RC II transcript, Day 12, p. 802.
12. RC II transcript, Day 13, pp. 842–3.
13. RC II transcript, Day 13, p. 843.
14. Ibid.
15. RC II transcript, Day 39, p. 2847.
16. Ibid.
17. RC II transcript, Day 39, p. 2859.
18. RC II transcript, Day 40, p. 2863.
19. RC II transcript, Day 50, pp. 3620–1.
20. Letter to the author from Hon. Justice I. F. Sheppard, 24 August 1990.
21. RC II transcript, Day 53, pp. 3775–6.
22. RC II transcript, Day 54, p. 3849.

# Chapter 16

1. Hon. Justice G. J. Samuels to author, 19 September 1990.
2. Burt's closing address is covered in RC II transcript, Days 67 and 68, pp. 4676–776.
3. RC II transcript, Day 67, p. 4716.
4. Hiatt's final submission is covered in RC II transcript, Days 69, 70, 71, pp. 4776–916.
5. Cabban's motives in making the Statement are covered in RC II transcript, Day 69, p. 4810.
6. A submission on the punishment returns is developed in RC II transcript, Day 70, p. 4881–8.
7. Ash's final submission is covered in RC II transcript, Days 71–4, pp. 4917–5207.
8. Murphy's final submission is covered in RC II transcript, Days 75–76, pp. 5220–96.
9. Interview with Hon. Justice Peter Murphy, 5 September 1989.
10. RC II transcript, Day 75, p. 5258.
11. RC II transcript, Day 75, p. 5263.
12. RC II transcript, Day 75, p. 5262.
13. Murphy interview, 5 September 1989.
14. RC II transcript, Day 75, p. 5287.
15. RC II transcript, Day 76, p. 5297.
16. RC II transcript, Day 76, p. 5311.
17. Samuels's final submission is covered in RC II transcript, Days 76–80, pp. 5297–614.
18. RC II transcript, Day 76, p. 5321.
19. RC II transcript, Day 76 p. 5343.
20. RC II transcript, Day 76, p. 5357.
21. Notebook contained in the Robertson papers.
22. Robertson papers.
23. Penscript by Robertson on notes for submission to counsel (probably Samuels) (Robertson papers).
24. RC II transcript, Day 77, p. 5430.
25. RC II transcript, Day 77, p. 5478.
26. RC II transcript, Day 80, p. 5614.
27. 'Notes for final submission, Counsel for Captain Stevens' (Stevens papers).
28. Ibid.
29. The five occasions were the birthday dinner in Singapore, the dinner in HMS *Rothesay* and on three occasions while in Tokyo. Ash said he accepted 'moral blame' for the birthday dinner and the Tokyo instances.
30. Ibid.
31. Notes prepared by Ash (Stevens papers).
32. Interview with Commander the Hon. F. M. Osborne, 29 August 1990.
33. Hon. Sir Lawrence Street to author, 23 August 1989.
34. RC II transcript, Day 85, p. 5932.
35. *Corbin On Contracts*, Vol. 6, 1962 edition, para. 1303.
36. Letter to the author, September 1990.

# Chapter 17

1. St John had wanted Professor Blackburn's evidence (RC II, transcript, Day 39, pp. 2865–9) to be made the subject of a specific term of reference, suggesting that it provided the link between Cabban's evidence and the collision. (E. H. St John, *A Time to Speak* (Sun, 1969)).
2. Dr Michael Tiller to author, 25 June 1990.
3. Dr Vern Plueckhahn, Report to Royal Commission, 7 November 1967 (RC II exhibit 60A).
4. Report submitted to the Royal Commission by Dr Vern Pleuckhahn, 7 November 1967.
5. St John, in his book, dwelt on the Commissioners' decision not to hear McCallum and Rankin. (St John, op. cit., p. 103). As the Commissioners' understanding was that both would offer similar views to Birrell, they saw no point in protracting the inquiry by hearing their opinions. The point ought also to be made that Birrell was neither a surgeon nor a scientist (nor was he a policeman) whereas Morrow was a specialist physician and Goulston a researching medical scientist.
6. Dr John Birrell to author, 29 May 1989.
7. This was Birrell's area of special interest in his work with the Victorian Police Force, having studied the effects of alcohol consumption on motor vehicle driving performance.
8. It is noteworthy that Birrell's opinions were not as conclusive nor offered with as much conviction as St John suggested. While Birrell may have told St John outside the Commission that he thought Stevens was an alcoholic, he was circumspect on this issue in his testimony (RC II transcript, Day 66, p. 4541).
9. Discussion with Dr Kerry Goulston, 3 September 1991.
10. Dr Kerry Goulston to author, 6 September 1991, citing Harrison's *Principles of Internal Medicine* (4th ed) and *Clinics in Gastroenterology*, vol. 13, no. 2, May 1984, eds J. I. Isenberg and C. Johansson.
11. Dr James Rankin (Head of Biomedical Research and Medicine at the Addiction Research Foundation of Canada) to author, 31 May 1989.
12. Hyland's evidence is covered in RC II transcript, Day 56, pp. 3880–98A.
13. 'There is a strong Naval tradition that those officers who are concerned with the navigation of the ship should not drink at sea.' Comments by McNicoll in 'Memorandum on aspects of the *Voyager* debate', 15 May 1967, Navy file 1288/201/44, p. 2.
14. Commodore Ken Gray recalls Stevens making this point while commanding *Quickmatch* and at the Royal Naval Staff College, Greenwich, when both were students in 1960 (interview with Commodore Ken Gray, 23 January 1991).
15. A pamphlet issued to prospective warship commanding officers by the Royal Navy in the 1950s, *Your ship: advice to officers assuming their first command,* revealed that a 'study of court martial returns and a catalogue of loggings over one year would show that the great majority of offences committed by officers are caused directly or indirectly by drink, by which is not meant drunkenness but a lapse of duty or conduct through drink. Many of those, which appear ordinary offences in neglect of duty, are brought about by weakening of willpower and sense of duty by drinking too much . . . That you yourself [as a commanding officer] may be able to drink without apparent effect is unfortunately not enough, for in all things your officers will try to copy you. Officers have been ruined for life by getting into a habit of drinking when young, often due to the bad example set by their senior officers'.
16. RC II transcript, Day 32, pp. 2294–5 and RC II transcript, Day 33, p. 2358.
17. Letter to his wife, 1963, tabled as Exhibit 171.
18. RC II transcript, Day 31, pp. 2233, 2240–1.
19. RC II transcript, Day 38, pp. 2742–3.
20. RC II transcript, Day 18, pp. 1256–7.
21. RC II transcript, Day 30 pp. 2172–4.
22. RC II transcript, Day 46, p. 3316.
23. RC II transcript, Day 18, p. 1291.
24. RC II transcript, Day 21, p. 1501.
25. RC II transcript, Day 27, p. 1972.
26. RC II transcript.
27. RC II transcript, Day 47, p. 3357.
28. RC II transcript, Day 25, p. 1794.
29. RC II transcript, Day 48, p. 3488.
30. RC II transcript, Day 17, pp. 1161–2.
31. RC II transcript, Day 18, p. 1224.
32. RC II transcript, Day 52, p. 3732.
33. Evidence of Commander Peter Irwin, RN, RC II transcript, Day49, pp. 3526–8.

34. RC II transcript, Day 19, pp. 1331, 1336.
35. RC II transcript, Day 56, pp. 4111–18.
36. RC II transcript, Day 17, pp. 1175, 1204.
37. RC II transcript, Day 17, p. 1209.
38. RC II transcript, Day 19, pp. 1303–7, 1312–19.
39. RC II transcript, Day 60, p. 4210.
40. RC II transcript, Day 58, p. 4113.
41. RC II transcript, Day 60, p. 4209.
42. RC II transcript, Day 65, p. 4429ff.
43. RC II transcript, Day 58, pp. 4113–14.
44. RC II transcript, Day 26, pp. 1892–3.
45. RC II transcript, Day 34, p. 2495.
46. RC II transcript, Day 43, pp. 3095–6.
47. RC II transcript, Day 52, pp. 3752–6.
48. RC II transcript, Day 37, pp. 2660, 2665.
49. RC II transcript, Day 44, p. 3197.
50. RC II transcript, Day 20, p. 1434 and Day 21, p. 1445.
51. RC II Exhibit 171 also RC II transcript, Day61, pp. 4272–3, Day 62, pp. 4309–11, and Day 70, p. 4880.
52. RC II transcript, Day 31, pp. 2217–20.
53. RC II transcript, Day 49, p. 3495.
54. RC II transcript, Day 17, pp. 1171, 1215.
55. RC II transcript, Day 18, pp. 1275–6, Day 34, pp. 2430–1 and Day 73, p. 5144.
56. RC II transcript, Day 25, pp. 1777–8.
57. RC II transcript, Day 18, pp. 1263–4.
58. RC II transcript, Day 20, pp. 1395–6, 1398.
59. RC II transcript, Day 17, pp. 1195–9.
60. RC II transcript, Day 23, pp. 1614–16.
61. RC II transcript, Day 31, p. 2254.
62. RC II transcript, Day 20, pp. 1383–5.
63. RC II transcript, Day 39, p. 2833.
64. RC II transcript, Day 62, pp. 4329–35.
65. RC II transcript, Day 28, p. 2031.
66. RC II transcript, Day 20, p. 1407.
67. RC II transcript, Day 21, p. 1488.
68. Clarke was Stevens's Naval College term-mate.
69. RC II transcript, Day 41, p. 3009.
70. Notes for final submission — counsel for Captain Stevens (Stevens papers).
71. 'Notes for discussion with Osborne and Benson – 11 March 1968', prepared by Sir Jack Stevens (Stevens papers).
72. D. L. Chipp & J. Larkin, *The Third Man* (Rigby, 1978), p. 82.
73. Peter Young 'Collision that caused an outcry and left a mystery', *Australian*, 10 February 1984, p. 7.
74. RC II transcript, Day 25, p. 1755.
75. RC II transcript, Day 44, p. 3168.
76. Ibid.
77. RC II transcript, Day 44, p. 3169.
78. RC II transcript, Day 44, p. 3170.
79. Statement by Dr Michael Tiller taken at Perth by Burt and Neil in the presence of George Sadlier, solicitor, on 11 August 1967, p. 9. Copy provided to author by Tiller.
80. Tiller made some handwritten notes of the conversation shortly afterwards. A copy of the notes was supplied to me by Dr Michael Tiller. The questions related mainly to matters he had covered in his statement to Burt of 11 August 1967. Tiller was informed at the end of the conversation that the matter would not be raised again with him.
81. B. S. J. O'Keefe to M. C. Tiller, 5 October 1967. Copy supplied to author by Dr Michael Tiller.
82. Interview with the Hon. Sir Francis Burt, 25 July 1990.
83. The words in quotation are Wilson's recollection of what Stevens had said to him. John Wilson to author, 2 June 1991.
84. J. R. Wilson to author, 2 June 1991.

85. Ibid.
86. Interviews with Asprey, 29 August 1989; Burbury, 24 May 1991; and Lucas, 24 May 1991.
87. Hon. Sir Stanley Burbury to author, 29 September 1990.
88. Interview with the Hon. Don Chipp, 5 September 1989. When the substance of Chipp's remarks were relayed to the now Hon. Justice Peter Murphy, he stated: 'Mr Don Chipp was the Minister for the Navy at the time. I have not read the book to which you refer . . . The several assertions that you make in your letter [the evidence of the unnamed doctor relating to amphetamines] can find no support from me, and I remember nothing which would suggest to me that they have any substance in them'. (Hon. Justice Peter Murphy to author, 14 August 1990).
89. Interview with John Jess, 4 September 1989.
90. Interview with Rear-Admiral Peter Sinclair, 21 May 1991.

# Chapter 18

1. *Report of Royal Commissioners on the Statement of Lieutenant Commander Cabban and Matters Incidental Thereto* (hereafter Burbury Report) (Commonwealth Government Printer, Canberra, 1968).
2. Report of Naval 'Committee on Public Relations following the *Voyager* Royal Commission', 13 December 1967, p. 6.
3. Ibid., diary entry for 22 February 1968, p. 397.
4. T. P. E. Hewat & D. Wilson, *Don Chipp* (Visa, Camberwell, 1978) p. 26.
5. Burbury Report, pp. 31, 40, 45, 223.
6. Burbury Report, p. 223.
7. Burbury Report, p. 107.
8. Burbury Report, p. 109.
9. Burbury Report, p. 118.
10. Burbury Report, pp. 122–3.
11. Interview with Lieutenant Commander S. B. Griffith, 9 August 1990.
12. Op. cit., p. 126.
13. Op. cit., p. 122.
14. Burbury Report, p. 145.
15. Interview with Sir Francis Burt, 25 July 1990.
16. Burbury Report, p. 158.
17. Burbury Report, p. 224.
18. Burbury Report, p. 175.
19. Burbury Report, p. 177.
20. Burbury Report, pp. 176–7.
21. Burbury Report, p. 179.
22. Interview with the Hon K. W. Asprey, 29 August 1989.
23. When I asked Justice Lucas why the Commissioners had not produced their own reconstruction, he stated 'that judges and lawyers ought not to give more opinion than they are asked for'. (Interview with the Hon. G.A.G. Lucas, 25 May 1991.)
24. Burbury Report, pp. 228–9.
25. Interview with Ted St John QC, 15 July 1989.
26. 'Notes for Discussion with Messrs Osborne and Benson' prepared by Sir Jack Stevens for a meeting on 11 March 1968. Stevens says in these notes that the purpose of this meeting was to help Benson with his speech in Parliament.
27. Ibid.
28. Interview with Commander the Hon. F. M. Osborne, 29 August 1990.
29. 'Notes for Discussion' prepared by Stevens.
30. Ibid.
31. Ibid.
32. *Australian*, February 1988. After the Spicer Report was released, Martin consulted Commander Peter Doyle and explained to him that he had certain misgivings about the contents of the Report and its principal findings. He was advised against taking any further action as the matter was considered over. (Interview with Rear-Admiral Peter Doyle, 15 March 1989.)
33. The first instance Sir David Martin refers to was during exchange service with the Royal Navy when posted to HMS *Battleaxe*. While in that ship it collided with HM Ships *Apollo* and *Wakeful* in Portsmouth Harbour.

34. Interview with Rear-Admiral Sir David Martin, 20 July 1990.
35. *West Australian*, 27 February 1968.
36. *Australian*, 1 March 1968.
37. *Sun-Herald*, 3 March 1968.
38. Interview with Sir John Gorton, 2 August 1990.
39. Cabinet minute, 28/29 February 1968 (Decision No. 58).
40. Cabinet minute, 12 March 1968 (Decision No. 62).
41. Ibid.
42. *CPD* (Reps) 13 March 1968, p. 32.
43. An amount, which, if it had attracted tax, would have become around $60,000.
44. Quoted in the *Sydney Morning Herald*, 19 March 1968.
45. Quoted in the *Age*, 3 April 1968.
46. *Age*, 20 March 1968.
47. *CPD* (Reps), 2 April 1968, p. 669.
48. *CPD* (Reps), p. 670
49. *CPD* (Reps), p. 674. This incident was added to two other notorious actions by Whitlam in Parliament: a reference to Sir Garfield Barwick and throwing a glass of water into the face of Paul Hasluck. However, Clyde Cameron states, 'I supported Whitlam's attack on [Landau] and the public service generally; and called for an amendment to the *Public Service Act* to permit the instant dismissal of a bureaucrat who gave false or misleading information to a minister'. (Cameron to author, 15 May 1991.)
50. *CPD* (Reps), pp. 682–3.
51. *CPD* (Reps), p. 683.
52. *CPD* (Reps), p. 685.
53. *CPD* (Reps), p. 696.
54. *CPD* (Reps), p. 697.
55. Ibid.
56. *CPD* (Reps), p. 699.
57. *CPD* (Reps), p. 702.
58. *CPD* (Reps), 3 April 1968, p. 718.
59. *CPD* (Reps), p. 721.
60. *CPD* (Reps), p. 723.
61. *CPD* (Reps), p. 724.
62. *CPD* (Reps), pp. 724, 725, 727.
63. *CPD* (Reps), p. 729.
64. *CPD* (Reps), p. 737.
65. *CPD* (Reps), p. 738.
66. *CPD* (Reps), p. 742.
67. *CPD* (Reps), pp. 742–3.
68. *CPD* (Reps), p. 743.
69. Ibid.
70. *CPD* (Reps), p. 744.
71. *CPD* (Reps), p. 745.
72. *CPD* (Reps), p. 747.
73. *CPD* (Reps), p. 747.
74. *CPD* (Reps), p. 757.
75. *CPD* (Reps), p. 758.
76. *CPD* (Reps), p. 762.
77. Ibid.
78. *CPD* (Reps), pp. 764–5.
79. *CPD* (Reps), p. 766.
80. *CPD* (Reps), p. 767.
81. Minute from Sec CNS to SecNav, 16 November 1967. This minute was referred to the Naval Board.
82. Minute from McNicoll to Minister for the Navy (through SecNav), 30 November 1967. Folio 1, File 2/204/81 — 'Formulation of Suitable Naval Public Relations Programme Consequent Upon Matters Arising — (A) *Voyager* Inquiry (B) W. D. Scott Report on Recruiting'. The Naval Board formally resolved to investigate engaging a public relations firm to assist in the formulation of a PR plan and strategy in its meeting of 8 December 1967. Naval Board minute No. 114 of 1967 refers.

83. The Committe on Public Relations met for the first time on 13 December 1967. The first draft of its first report was placed on file 2/204/81.
84. 'Report of Committee on Public Relations Following *Voyager* Inquiry', p. 10.
85. Signal DTG 050355Z68 from ACNB to COMFEF.
86. 'Report of Public Relations Committee Following *Voyager* Inquiry' (file 2/204/81), p. 4.

# Chapter 19

1. George Zdenkowski, 'Is that inquiry really necessary?', *Bulletin*, 28 May 1991, p.30.
2. L.A. Hallett, *Royal Commissions and Boards of Inquiry: Some Legal and Procedural Aspects* (Law Book Company, Melbourne, 1982) p.10.
3. D.J. Killen, *Inside Australian Politics* (Methuen Haynes, Sydney, 1985) p.82.
4. D.L. Chipp & J. Larkin, *The Third Man*, (Rigby, Melbourne, 1978) p. 66.
5. RAN personnel were brought to trial by court martial under the *Naval Discipline Act 1957* (UK) as modified and adopted by Naval Forces Regulation No. 8 (Statutory Rule 1958 No.88) to the Naval Forces of the Commonwealth. *Queen's Regulations and Admiralty Instructions* (QR & AI) applied to the RAN by virtue of section 36 of the *Naval Discipline Act*.
6. Interview with Sir John Carrick, 27 March 1989.
7. *Australian Law Journal*, Vol. 24, No.7, p. 274.
8. Beddie explains that the 'manner in which the British legislation was made to apply to the Australian services was simple. The relevant British Act was 'incorporated' in Australian legislation 'by reference'; that is, by naming, but not reproducing either the text or the content of, the British Act. If (and for long this was the practice) the name of the British Act was not followed by a date which served to specify its provisions at a precise time, future amendments to the Act made by the Parliament at Westminster would automatically apply to the Australian services. The principal British Acts incorporated into Australian legislation were the *Naval Discipline Act*, the *Army Act* and the *Air Force Act*.' (B.D. Beddie, 'The Australian Navy and Imperial Legislation', *War & Society*, Vol. 5 No.2, September 1987, p.73.)
9. Neil Preston, 'The Development of Defence Force Disciplinary Law 1901-1985: An Outline', ANU Work-in-Progress Seminar presented 29 November 1988, p.12.
10. In late 1964, extensive changes were made in Defence legislation. As Beddie outlines, 'The manner in which the *Naval Discipline Act* applied to the RAN was included in the changes. Sections 34 to 37 of the *Naval Defence Act* were deleted with the result that there ceased to be any situations in which the *Naval Discipline Act* operated without modification'. (Beddie, op. cit., p.85).
11. The only other lawyer in the Navy Department was a civil servant, Gordon Beatty, who worked in 'N' Branch until early retirement in 1965.
12. Narrative of action is reproduced in the *Army, Navy Air Force Journal*, 3 May 1952.
13. The facts and quotations cited with respect to this inquiry are drawn from a confidential report provided to the Naval Board at its request following the loss of *Voyager*. The copy has no pagination or file markings. It was filed on unnumbered CNS branch file, '*Voyager* Royal Commission'.
14. 'Pertinent extracts from the findings of a Naval court of inquiry into the circumstances surrounding the collision between USS *Wasp* and USS *Hobson* on 26 April 1952', under cover of a letter from U.S. Naval Attache, Canberra, to SecNav, 27 April 1964. Quoted in Ed Frede, 'A Sinking Stirs Up Memories', the *Virginian Pilot*, 12 February 1964.
15. 'Pertinent extracts', op.cit., p.5.
16. Report of CINCLANT FF1-Z/A17-4, 19 July 1952, p.3.
17. Report of CINCLANT, op. cit., p.4.
18. Penscript notes attached to Naval Board meeting agenda papers, 25 September 1967.
19. Ibid.
20. The handling of this submission was covered in SecNav minute to Naval Board members, 21 September 1967. Included in ACNB minutes and on Navy Office file 321/201/43.
21. Draft Cabinet submission, 'Naval Courts of Inquiry', prepared for signature of Minister for the Navy (Chipp), 21 September 1967. Navy Office file 321/201/43. Filed with Naval Board Minutes.
22. The final action on this matter seems to have been taken at the Naval Board meeting held on 25 September 1967. The Minister asked for a legal opinion on the relationship of the proposed regulations with the *Royal Commissions Act*. Naval Board Minute 88/67, 25 September 1967.
23. Defence Instruction (General) — Administration — 34–1 issued 22 August 1986. The Naval Courts of Inquiry legislation was passed with the *Defence Force Discipline Act* in 1982, coming into force on 3 July 1985.

## Chapter 20

1. Testimony of Robertson (RC transcript, p.2437), Everett (RC Transcript, p.266A, 273) and Bate (RC transcript, p.388).
2. Testimony of Robertson (RC transcript, pp. 2435, 2437, 2439-41, 2523, 2624, 2625-6), Bate (RC transcript, pp. 388, 394), Barker (RC transcript, pp. 377, 364), Everett (RC transcript, pp. 266A, 273), Kelly (RC transcript, p. 519) and Evans (RC transcript, pp.889–90, 897, 903).
3. Testimony of Robertson (RC transcript, pp. 2437-9), Barker (RC transcript, pp.301, 311–12) and Everett (RC transcript, p.276).
4. Testimony of Robertson (RC transcript, pp. 2426, 2430), Barker (RC transcript, p.301) and Everett (RC transcript, pp. 266A, 273).
5. He also stated in his main report on the collision, HMAS *Melbourne* letter 01/13, 5 March 1964, that at the time of the collision *Melbourne* was showing the prescribed lights, including 'Red floodlighting of the Flight Deck from the screened lights fixed to the Island structure (showing to port only)' (Robertson papers).
6. RC transcript, Day 15, pp. 918, 923ff.
7. RC transcript, Day 40, p.940.
8. RC transcript, Day 14, page 890.
9. Undated notes for counsel prepared by Robertson (Robertson papers).
10. Interview with Gary Evans, 12 August 1991.
11. Testimony of Evans (RC transcript, pp.890-1, 903) and Burdett (RC transcript, p.967).
12. Certainly, the different interpretations for these signals expressed at the first Commission made it clear that a number of different views were held. In the naval staff paper prepared on this matter following the release of Spicer's report, the RAN proposed 18 changes to ATP 1A to resolve the confusion and ambiguity of signals relating to carrier flying operations. Nearly all these proposals were adopted in the form advised by the RAN.
13. RC transcript, p. 2531.
14. Interview with Michael Patterson, 18 May 1991.
15. Spicer Report, p.12.
16. Even Robertson conceded that 'if reaction started on *Voyager's* bridge at the time that *Melbourne* bore Red 75 and this reaction was translated into an order to the wheelhouse to go hard astarboard and full ahead, then it took them from about minus 1 minute to minus 20 seconds [to the collision] to decide to take this action. In other words, about 40 seconds'. Undated manuscript prepared by Robertson titled 'Various Notes' in a file headed 'Notes on transcript prepared by RJR during Royal Commission' (Robertson papers).

## Chapter 21

1. Letter to author, 17 July 1991.
2. *Creswell* letter 01/4/95(2), 19 February 1964.
3. Signal DTG 130714Z Feb 64 from ACNB to FOICEA, *Melbourne* and *Watson* refers.
4. Signal DTG 240225Z Feb 64 from ACNB to *Penguin* and FOICEA: 'Allegations have been made that officers and men at *Penguin* offered to make ex-gratia payment either out of their own pockets or welfare fund to enable 16 *Voyager* survivors to fly to Melbourne or travel first class by rail on 11 February and offer was refused by, quote, someone in the Navy, unquote. Request urgent report'. No confirmation of the allegations was revealed after inquiries by staff at *Penguin* and in Naval Area Commands.
5. SecNav to RNZN Liaison Officer, op. cit., p. 9.
6. ACNB Minute 12/64, 14 February 1964. Also Navy file 1288/201/12.
7. Navy press release 227/124, 12 March 1964.
8. Cabinet minute, 18 February 1964, Decision No. 46.
9. Telegram from Forbes to Cooke, 21 February 1964.
10. CNS to All Administrative Authorities, 18 May 1964 contained in unnumbered Navy file 'Loss of HMAS *Voyager*'. Also Navy file 333/201/139 dealing with psychological surveying of survivors.
11. Minute from DCNP to CNS, 18 May 1964.
12. HMAS *Sydney* signal DTG 182316Z May 64 to Naval Board, Navy Office file 333/201/139.
13. Ibid.
14. NOL, 22 May 1964, Navy Office file 333/201/139.
15. Signal DTG 281239Z Feb 64 from *Sydney* to ACNB marked 'Exclusive secret'.
16. SecNav to RNZN Liaison Officer, op. cit., p. 10.

17. Cabinet minute, 21 October 1964 (Decision No. 1324).
18. Ibid.
19. Cabinet minute, 22 October 1964 (Decision No. 548). The Attorney-General was 'authorised to give a public indication that the High Court is the appropriate place in which actions against the Commonwealth should be brought'. See Navy file 125/1/133 on handling of claims by the Commonwealth.
20. The 'Red Sales' were the RAAF's aerobatic team, all of whom perished in an accident in August 1962.
21. Howson, *The Howson Diaries* (Viking 1984), diary entry for 22 October 1964, p. 118.
22. Cabinet minute, 21 October 1964 (Decision No. 1324).
23. At the time of writing (November 1991), legal action on claims lodged by another eighty *Voyager* survivors for damages was continuing.

# Chapter 22

1. The *Australian*, 4 June 1969, p. 11.
2. Rear-Admiral Antony Horton to author, 8 August 1988.
3. A. Vincent, 'Collision! The Subic Bay Inquiry', *Quadrant*, October 1975, pp. 12-21, p. 18 cited.
4. Lt Cdr G. Dalrymple to Capt. I. M. Burnside, RAN, 24 July 1969. Original held by Commodore Ian Burnside.
5. Naval Board minute 94/1969.
6. Vincent, op. cit., p. 20.
7. Memorandum for file 'Schedule of events concerning Captain J. P. Stevenson, RAN', prepared by Secretary to CNS. (Undated).
8. Vincent, op. cit., p. 20.
9. Joanne Stevenson, *No Case To Answer* (Alpha Books, Sydney, 1971).
10. Ibid. pp. 7–9, 40, 48, 92, 165, 199.
11. Memorandum 'Posting of Captain J.P. Stevenson' prepared by Captain Ian Burnside, RAN.
12. 'In the interests of the Service', T.B. Millar, *Canberra Times*, 8 January 1970.
13. *SMH*, 5 January 1970.
14. Quoted in the *Sun-Herald*, 11 January 1970. When Killen was given the Navy portfolio he received a telegram from Chaney which read: 'Congratulations on the Navy portfolio. Ha! Ha!'. (Interview with Sir Frederick Chaney, 27 July 1990.)
15. Quoted in the *Canberra Times*, 7 January 1970.

# Chapter 23

1. Evan Whitton, '*Voyager*: Operation Cover-up', *National Times*, 4 February 1974, pp. 18–24.
2. The background to this article is described in detail by John Hurst in *The Walkley Awards: Australia's Best Journalists in Action* (John Kerr Pty Ltd, Richmond, 1988) pp. 288–91.
3. Ibid. p. 18.
4. Ibid., p.18.
5. Ibid.
6. Ibid. Added to these remarks, Stevens wrote: 'I do not want this raised in the House unless any inference is made to Sir Robert's alleged friendship with me'.
7. A.W.R. McNicoll, 'The *Voyager* Story', *SMH*, 9 February 1974.
8. Letters to the Editor, *SMH*, 13 February 1974.
9. Interview with C.A. Porter, QC, 22 May 1991.
10. Burbury Report, p. 202.
11. St John, op. cit., p. 111.
12. J. Farquharson, *Canberra Times*, 4 February 1989.
13. Contained in 'HMAS *Voyager* sympathy notes' unbound and unnumbered collection of letters retained by CNS (Harrington).

# Bibliography

PRIMARY SOURCES

**Official reports**

Australian Commonwealth Law Reform Commission, *Civil Admiralty Jurisdiction*, Report No. 33 (AGPS, Canberra, 1986)

*Report of the Royal Commissioner into the Loss of HMAS Voyager* (Commonwealth Government Printer, Melbourne, 1964)

*Report of the Royal Commission on the Statement of Lieutenant Commander Cabban and Matters Incidental Thereto* (Commonwealth Government Printer, Canberra, 1968)

**Official printed papers**

*Commonwealth Parliamentary Debates (Representatives)*

*Commonwealth Parliamentary Debates (Senate)*

Commonwealth Parliamentary Papers 1964–66; Vol. XIII, pp. 289–341

Commonwealth Parliamentary Papers 1968; Vol. 1, pp. 967–1245.

**Official printed sources:** Navy Office, Canberra

Allied Tactical Publications (ATPs)

Australian Commonwealth Naval Board, Minutes of Meetings and agenda papers

DCNS Newsletters (1957–1968)

'Record of Service' cards (officers)

Signal logs (classified and unclassified)

Australian Fleet Orders

Commonwealth Naval Orders

*Queens Regulations and Admiralty Instructions*

*Regulations and Instructions for the RAN*

**Official published sources**

*Admiralty Manuals of Navigation* (Vols I, II, III)

*Admiralty Manual of Seamanship* (Vols I, II, III, IV)

437

*A Statistical Analysis of Selected Marine Collisions Occurring During Fiscal Years 1957, 1958, 1959* (U.S. Government Printer, Washington, 1960)

*Naval War Manual* (BR 1806, 1958)

*Notes on the Royal Navy* (BR 1868, 1958)

*RAN 1911–1961, Golden Jubilee* (Government Printer, 1961)


## ARCHIVAL HOLDINGS

### Australian Archives

A 1255: 1964 *Voyager* Royal Commission — Transcripts of evidence

A 1256: 1964 *Voyager* Royal Commission — Exhibits

A 1257: 1964 *Voyager* Royal Commission — Secretary's correspondence files

A 1258: 1964 *Voyager* Royal Commission — Secretary's notes on evidence

A 1529: 1964 *Voyager* Royal Commission — Documents presented as evidence

AA 1972/329: Papers dealing with the loss of HMAS *Voyager*, and the inquiry into the Statement of Lt Cdr Cabban

AA 2265: Papers relating to the Royal Commission into Cockatoo Island Dockyard (1921)

AA 2289: Papers relating to the Royal Commission into Naval and Defence Administration (1917–19)

AA 2446: Papers relating to the Royal Commission of inquiry into the circumstances associated with the retirement of Lieutenant Commander Alan Dermot Casey from the RAN (1934)

AA 2585: Australian Commonwealth Naval Board Minute Books (1905–1976)

AA 2586: Alphabetical index to Australian Commonwealth Naval Board Minute Books (1922–1976)

MP 1049/17: 1964 *Voyager* Royal Commission — Transcripts, statements and miscellaneous papers (27 boxes)

SP 551/1: HMAS *Voyager* Ship's Log (Bundle 782)

SP 917/1: Records and transcripts of the Royal Commission on the sinking of *Voyager* and the Royal Commission into the allegations of Lt Cdr Cabban

ST 2695/1: Copies of statements, reports, exhibits from 1967 Cabban Royal Commission

### Australian Broadcasting Commission (Film Archive)

'*Melbourne–Voyager* — 1964'

Catalog Nos NF 1546, NG 1098, NK 1245, RU 95

'This Fabulous Century' (1977)

Transcript of interview between Peter Luck and Captain John Robertson

### Australian War Memorial

AWM 178: 1964 *Voyager* Royal Commission (13 boxes)

AWM 179: 1967 *Voyager* Royal Commission (15 boxes)

**Public Record Office, London**

ADM 116/4351: Report of Board of Inquiry into the loss of HMS *Hood*

ADM 116/4352: Report of the Second Board of Inquiry into the loss of HMS *Hood*

ADM 205/76: Correspondence between the First Naval Member and the First Sea Lord — 1951

ADM 205/110: Correspondence betwen the First Naval Member and the First Sea Lord — 1956

**State Library of New South Wales**

ML MSS 2676: 1964 *Voyager* Royal Commission — Papers of L. W. Street QC


NON-ARCHIVAL OFFICIAL HOLDINGS

**Unnumbered Chief of Naval Staff branch files**

'Loss of HMAS *Voyager*'
'*Voyager* — Sympathy notes'
'HMAS *Voyager* Royal Commission'
'Answers to likely questions'
'Naval Board Cabinet submission — Spicer Report'
'Matters Arising from the Royal Commission into the Loss of HMAS *Voyager*'
'Royal Navy Replacement for HMAS *Voyager*'
'Long-term Replacement for HMAS *Voyager*'
'Royal Commission — Fleet Bulletins' (1967)

**Navy Office files**

2/204/24: Operational readiness and sea training

2/204/81: Naval Public Relations Programme consequent on (a) *Voyager* inquiry (b) W. D. Scott report on recruiting (1967)

12/1/31: '*Voyager* Lament' by Wilmot James

16/201/72: Communications — points arising from the *Voyager* inquiry

18/6/198: HMAS *Voyager* — request for reason for delay of proceedings for Nov. 1963

18/201/33: Collision complaint re: conducting of Royal Commission and treatment of Captain Robertson

18/206/33: Report of Inspection — HMAS *Voyager*

20/1/13: RAN Escort Vessels

38/201/20: Loss of HMAS *Voyager* — recommendations for awards for acts of gallantry (1964)

43/1/38: Regional Strategic Assessments

62/40/12: Parliamentary questions re — *Voyager* witnesses

125/1/109: Payment for loss of personal affects by survivors of HMAS *Voyager* collision

165/1/70: Public Relations — Post *Voyager* assessment and proposed measures to lessen the effect of unfavourable publicity (1964)

177/1/40: Parliamentary question re: escape scuttles

202/3/44: Navy Estimates — 1963/4

202/201/22: Estimates of expenditure — 1962/3

203/4/65: HMAS *Voyager* — Repair and refit allocation 1963/4

333/201/139: Psychological assessment of survivors of HMAS *Voyager* collision

343/201/5: HMAS *Voyager* — Loss of after collision with HMAS *Melbourne* (a) survivors, casualties, and notification of NOK (b) burial arrangements

518/251/56: Life jacket stowages in HMA Ships

519/252/35: Clocks in HMA Ships

1205/251/4: Construction, Modernisation and Conversion programme for the RAN

1211/4/3: *Ton* Class Minesweepers

1211/51/158: Review of escape scuttles, HMA Ships *Vampire* and *Vendetta*

1211/51/452: Lookout Placement in HMA Ships

1211/252/37: RAN Escort vessels — suitability of present layout of loudspeakers on bridges of vessels (1964)

1213/201/19: Role of HMAS *Sydney*

1215/251/226: HMAS *Voyager* — Two-year refit cycle

1215/259/52: HMAS *Voyager* — Extension of refit

1285/202/39: Composition of HMA Fleet for planning purposes

1288/1/21: Theories of interaction between ships on parallel course

1288/1/22: HMAS *Voyager* disaster — inquiry by S. J. Benson MP on the correctness of the order passed to *Voyager* to 'turn together' more than 90 degrees (1964)

1288/1/56: HMAS *Voyager* — Royal Commission 1967 — Expenditure involved

1288/1/63: HMAS *Voyager* — Royal Commission 1967 — Distribution of Report

1288/1/88: Messages of Condolence

1288/201/12: HMAS *Voyager* — Loss by sinking after collision with HMAS *Melbourne* off Jervis Bay (1964)

1288/201/13: Security problems involved in presentation of evidence

1288/201/14: Royal Commission into sinking of HMAS *Voyager* — Matters Arising From (1964)

1288/201/17: HMAS *Melbourne/Voyager* — Royal Commission Report and subsequent events arising from report (1964) (Parts 1 & 2)

1288/201/44: HMAS *Melbourne/Voyager* — Allegation by former Lt Cmdr Cabban

1288/201/45: *Voyager* Inquiry 1967 — Royal Commission

1288/201/46: Royal Commission into Allegations of HMAS *Melbourne*/HMAS *Voyager* collision by Lt Cmdr Cabban — List of deficiencies and/or weaknesses on the present Navy Procedures, Regulations, Instructions or Organisation — Policy

1624/211/14: HMAS *Voyager* — NGS firings

1624/211/15: HMAS *Voyager* — Surface firings

4301/104/17: *Tide Austral* — Commissioning into RAN


## PRIMARY PUBLISHED SOURCES

Chipp, D. L. & Larkin, J., *The Third Man* (Rigby, 1978)

Gatacre, G., *Reports of Proceedings* (Nautical Press, Manly, 1982)

Howson, P., *The Howson Diaries* (Viking, 1984)

Killen, J., *Inside Australian Politics* (Methuen, Sydney, 1985)

St John, E. H., *A Time to Speak* (Sun, 1969)


## PRIVATE COLLECTIONS

Chaney papers (in possession of the Hon. Sir Fred Chaney)

Harrington papers (in possession of Captain C. S. H. Harrington RAN)

Robertson papers (in possession of author)

Stevens papers (in possession of Mr D. E. Stevens)

Unpublished memoirs of Major General Sir Jack Stevens (in possession of Mr D. E. Stevens)

Were papers (Museum of HMAS *Cerberus*)


## INTERVIEWS

Asprey, Hon. K. W.
Barwick, Rt Hon. Sir Garfield
Bate, Commander J. A.
Bateman, Commodore W. S. G.
Berger, Commodore H. P.
Birrell, Dr J. H. W.
Bowen, Hon. Sir Nigel
Broben, Commodore I. W.
Bunting, Sir John
Burbury, Hon. Sir Stanley
Burnside, Commodore I. M.
Burt, Hon. Sir Francis
Cabban, Lieutenant Commander P. T.
Cairns, Hon. Dr J. F.
Cameron, Hon. C.
Carrick, Hon. Sir John
Cartwright, Captain I. H. S.
Chaney, Hon. Sir Frederick
Chipp, Hon. D. L.
Craig, Miss H.

Dadswell, Commodore T. A.
Doyle, Rear-Admiral P. H.
Evans, Petty Officer Signals Yeoman G. W.
Forbes, Hon. Dr A. J.
Gorton, Rt Hon. Sir John
Graham, Rear-Admiral W. H. D.
Gray, Commodore K. D.
Gregory, Mr W. H.
Griffith, Lieutenant Commander S. B.
Hagerty, Mr W. A. E.
Halley, Commander G.
Hannay, Mr J.
Harders, Sir Clarrie
Harrington, Lady [Janet]
Henchman, Mr H. J. H.
Herd, Mr R. J.
Hill, Mr C. J.
Hugonnet, Captain P.
Hyslop, Mr R.
Jess, Mr J. D.

Jocumsen, Warrant Officer Signals
    Yeoman R. N.
Kelly, Captain J. M.
Legoe (formerly Stevens), Mrs B. L.
Martin, Rear-Admiral Sir David
Meares, Hon. C. L. D.
Merson, Commodore J. L. W.
Murphy, Hon. Justice P.
Osborne, Commander the Hon. F. M.
Patterson, Leading Seaman Radar
    Plotter M. J.
Philpott, Mr T. S.
Porter, Mr C. A.
Preston, Mr A. N.
Reynolds, Hon. R. G.
Robertson, Rear-Admiral A. J.
Robertson, Captain B. D.
Robertson, Mrs B.
Robertson, Mr M.
Samuels, Hon. Justice G. J.

Sinclair, Rear-Admiral P. R.
Smyth, Commodore D. H. D.
Snow, Commodore J. B.
Sparks, Mr O. D. E.
Stevens, Mr D. E.
Stevens, Rear-Admiral J. D.
Street, Hon. Sir Laurence
St John, Mr E. H.
Tiller, Dr M. C.
Townsend, Captain A. A.
Treloar, Surgeon Rear-Admiral B. T.
Verwayen, Leading Electrical Mechanic
    B. L.
Walls, Rear-Admiral R. A. K.
Whitlam, Hon. E. G.
Willis, Rear-Admiral A. A.
Willis, Vice-Admiral Sir James
Wilson, Chief Petty Officer Medical
    J. R.
Wright, Commander W. G.

## CORRESPONDENCE

Allard, Dr D. C. (5 November 1990)
Asprey, Hon. K. W. (6 September 1990)
Barwick, Rt Hon. Sir Garfield (1 August 1989)
Birrell, Dr J. H. W. (26 June 1989)
Boutilier, Dr J. (12 October 1990)
Bowen, Hon. Sir Nigel (15 May 1991)
Burbury, Sir Stanley (25 September 1990, 8 April 1991)
Burnside, Commodore I. M. (2 June 1990)
Cairns, Dr J. F. (25 April 1991)
Cameron, Hon. C. R. (15 May 1991)
Chaney, Hon. Sir Fred (30 January 1990)
Douglas, Commander W. A. B. (7 September 1990)
Glover, Lieutenant W. (CF) (7 November 1990)
Goldrick, Lieutenant Commander J. V. P. (9 March 1991)
Gorton, Rt Hon. Sir John (28 June 1990)
Goulston, Dr K. J. (6 September 1991)
Hagan, Professor K. (12 February 1991)
Halley, Commander G. (21 December 1989, 30 April 1991)
Heath, D. J. (3 December 1991)
Henderson, Mrs H. (24 June 1991)
Henchman, H. J. H. (20 May 1989, 17 July 1989)
Herd, R. J. (8 May 1989)
Hudson, Admiral M. W. (4 May 1991)
Jess, J. D. (7 August 1989)
Legoe (Stevens), Mrs B. L. (4 August 1990, 23 June 1991)
Lucas, Hon. G. A. G. (24 March 1991)
Martin, Dr A. W. (31 July 1989)
McCausland, J. (25 January 1990)
McDonald, Lt Commander E. (5 June 1991, 4 July 1991)
McGibbon, I. (11 October 1990)

Meares, Hon. C. L. D. (27 May 1989)
Menzies, Dame Pattie (13 August 1990)
Merson, Commodore J. L. W. (9 April 1991)
Milliner, A. J. (17 July 1991, 23 August 1991)
Morrice, Captain J. O. (12 July 1990)
Murphy, Hon. Justice P. (14 August 1990)
O'Keefe QC, B. S. J. (7 September 1990)
Osborne, Commander the Hon. (29 July 1989)
Patterson, M. J. (10 April 1991, 19 August 1991)
Peek, Vice-Admiral Sir Richard (7 August 1989)
Robertson, Rear-Admiral A. J. (11 March 1990)
Samuels, Hon. Justice G. J. (19 September 1990)
Sheppard, Hon. Justice I. F. (26 June 1989, 24 August 1990)
Snow, Commodore J. B. (15 May 1989)
Stevens, Rear-Admiral J. D. (12 December 1990)
Street, Hon. Sir Laurence (17 July 1989, 23 August 1989)
St John, E. H. (2 June 1989, 21 July 1989, 18 May 1991)
Thomason, C. H. S. (14 April 1991, 3 July 1991)
Tiller, Dr M. C. (25 June 1990, 17 December 1990)
Verwayen, B. L. (13 March 1991)
White QC, M. W. D. (25 March 1991, 28 June 1991)
Whitton, E. (26 October 1990)
Willis, Rear-Admiral A. A. (23 April 1991)
Wilson, J. R. (2 June 1991)
Wright, Commander W. G. (31 March 1991)


JOURNALS AND PERIODICALS

*Australian Law Journal*
*Bulletin*
*Current Affairs Bulletin*
*Janes Fighting Ships*
*Lloyd's Law Reports*
*Naval Review*
*Navy News*
' *Shipping and Shipbuilding Record*
*The Navy*
*United States Naval Institute Proceedings*
*War and Society*
*Who's Who in Australia*


NEWSPAPERS

*Age*
*Australian*
*Canberra Times*
*Daily Mirror*
*Daily Telegraph*
*Herald*
*Sun*
*Sydney Morning Herald*
*Truth*

## PUBLISHED SECONDARY SOURCES

### Monographs

Atkinson, J. J., *By Skill and Valour* (Spink and Son, Sydney, 1986)

Bastock, J., *Australia's Ships of War* (Angus & Robertson, Sydney, 1975)

Bennett, J. M., *A History of the Supreme Court of NSW* (Law Book Co., Sydney, 1974)

Brown, D., *Warship Losses of World War II* (Arms and Armour Press, London, 1990)

Cahill, R. A., *Collisions and Their Causes* (Fairplay, London, 1983)

Callender, G., & Hinsley, F. H., *The British Side of Naval History* (Christophers, London, 1952)

Cockcroft, A. N., & Lameijer, J., *A Guide to the Collision Avoidance Rules*, 3rd edn (Stanford Maritime Press, London, 1982)

Cowen, Z., *Federal Jurisdiction in Australia* (Oxford Univ. Press, Melbourne, 1959)

Cunningham, I. J., *Work Hard, Play Hard* (AGPS, Canberra, 1988)

Eldridge, F. B., *History of the Royal Australian Naval College* (Georgian House, Melbourne, 1949)

Degenhardt, H. W., *Maritime Affairs — A World Handbook* (Longman, Essex, 1985)

Dockrill, M., *British Defence Since 1945* (Basil Blackwell, Oxford, 1988)

Downs, I., *The Last Mountain* (Univ. of Queensland Press, St. Lucia, 1986)

Elliott, P., *Allied Escort Ships of World War II* (Macdonald and Janes, London, 1977)

Frame, T. R., *The Garden Island* (Kangaroo Press, Kenthurst, 1990)

Frame, T. R., & Goldrick, J. V. P., *Reflections on the RAN* (Kangaroo Press, Kenthurst, 1991)

Frame, T. R., & Swinden, G. J., *First In, Last Out! The Navy at Gallipoli* (Kangaroo Press, Kenthurst, 1990)

German, A., *The Sea Is At Our Gates* (McClelland & Stewart, Toronto, 1990)

Gray, E., *Few Survived: A Comprehensive Survey of Submarine Accidents and Disasters* (Leo Cooper, London, 1986)

Grove, E. J., *Vanguard to Trident* (U.S. Naval Institue Press, Maryland, 1987)

Hall, T., *HMAS Melbourne* (Allen & Unwin, Sydney, 1982)

Hallet, L. A., *Royal Commissions, Select Committees and Boards of Inquiry* (Law Book Co., Melbourne, 1982)

Hampshire, A. C., *The Royal Navy Since 1945* (William Kimber, London, 1975)

Hewat, T. E. P., & Wilson, D., *Don Chipp* (Visa, Camberwell, 1978)

Hickling, H., *One Minute of Time* (Reed, Auckland, 1965)

Hickling, H., *Postscript to Voyager* (Reed, Auckland, 1969)

Hodges, P., *Battle Class Destroyers* (Almark, London, 1971)

Hurst, J., *The Walkley Awards* (John Kerr Pty Ltd, Richmond, 1988)

Hyslop, R., *Australian Naval Administration 1900–39* (Hawthorn Press, Melbourne, 1973)

Hyslop, R., *Aye Aye, Minister: Australian Naval Administration 1939–59* (AGPS, Canberra, 1990)

Jose, A. W., *Official History of Australia in the War of 1914–18*, Vol. IX, *Royal Australian Navy* (Angus and Robertson, Sydney, 1943)

Joske, P. E., *Australian Federal Government*, 3rd edn (Butterworths, Melbourne, 1976)

Lenton, H. T., *Warships of the British and Commonwealth Navies* (Ian Allan, London, 1969)

Love, R., *Changing Interpretations and New Sources in Naval History* (U.S. Naval Academy, Annapolis, 1980)

Lucy, R., *Pieces of Politics*, 2nd edn (MacMillan, Melbourne, 1979)

Macandie, G., *The Genesis of the RAN* (Commonwealth Government Printer, 1949)

McGuffie, K. C., *Marsden: The Law of Collisions at Sea*, 11th edn (Stevens & Sons, London, 1961)

MacPherson, K., & Burgess, J., *The Ships of Canada's Naval Forces 1910–1981* (Toronto, 1981)

Mankabady, S., *Collisions at Sea: A Guide to Their Legal Consequences* (North-Holland, London, 1978)

Marriott, J., *Disaster at Sea* (Arrow, London, 1987)

Marsden, R. G., *Documents Relating to the Law and Custom of the Sea* (Navy Records Society, Vols. 49 & 50)

Morgan, C. H., *The Gunroom* (Chatto & Windus, London, 1919)

Moscow, A., *Collision Course* (Pan, London, 1959)

O'Neill, R., *Australia in the Korean War 1950–53*, Vol. II, *Combat Operations* (AGPS, Canberra, 1985)

Overacker, L., *Australian Parties in a Changing Society, 1945–67* (Cheshire, Melbourne, 1968)

Padfield, P., *An Agony of Collisions* (Routledge & Kegan Paul, London, 1966)

Reid, A., *The Gorton Experiment* (Shakespeare, Sydney, 1971)

Reid, A., *The Power Struggle* (Shakespeare, Sydney, 1969)

Reynolds, C., *History and the Sea* (Univ. of South Carolina Press, South Carolina, 1989)

Silverstone, P., *U.S. Warships of World War II* (Ian Allan Ltd, London, 1965)

Smith, H. A., *The Law and Custom of the Sea* (Stevens & Sons, London, 1959)

Stevenson, J., *No Case to Answer* (Alpha Books, Sydney, 1971)

Thompson, R., *The Judges* (Allen & Unwin, Sydney, 1987)

Trengrove, A., *John Grey Gorton* (Cassell, Sydney, 1969)

Tunstall, B., *The Realities of Naval History* (Allen and Unwin, London, 1936)

Wouk, H., *The Caine Mutiny* (Jonathan Cape Ltd, London, 1951)

Young, J., *A Dictionary of Ships of the Royal Navy of the Second World War* (Patrick Stephens, Cambridge, 1975)

## Articles

'Backbenchers', *Current Affairs Bulletin*, Vol. 37, No. 11, 18 April 1966

Beattie, J. H., 'Marine Collision', *USNI Proceedings*, June 1962

Beddie, B. D., 'The Australian Navy and Imperial Legislation', *War and Society*, Vol. 8, No. 2, September 1987

'Continuing a Fine Tradition', *The Navy*, February 1959

DesRoches, J. A., 'Military Law in Contemporary Democratic Societies', U.S. Army Legal Services Conference, 27 September 1988

Frame, T., 'The *Voyager* Disaster: 25 Years On, a New Perspective', *Canberra Times*, 4 February 1989

Frede, E., 'A sinking stirs up memories', *Virginian Pilot*, 12 February 1964

Gibbs, B. G., 'The Naval Legal Services and the Role of the Naval Lawyer — Past, Present and Future', 6th RAN Legal Conference, HMAS *Penguin*, 20 January 1980

Gorton, J. G., 'The Navy — An Investment in Tomorrow', *The Navy*, September 1963

Hallet, L., 'Judges as Royal Commissioners', *Law Institute Journal* (Vic), Vol. 61, No. 8, August 1987

Higgins, T., 'Royal Commissions', in P. Grabosky (ed.), *Government Illegality*, Proceedings of a seminar held by the Australian Institute of Criminology (AIC, Canberra, 1987)

McGovern, T., 'Radar and the Rule of the Road', *Shipping and Shipbuilding Record*, 25 January 1960

McNicoll, A. W., 'The *Voyager* Story', *SMH*, 4 February 1974

Millar, T. B., 'Disaster Compounded', *Bulletin*, 20 November 1963

Millar, T. B., 'The Navy after years of decline', *Bulletin*, 13 November 1965

Nyman, T., 'Royal Commissions: A Time for Pause', *Law Society Journal*, February 1986

Ogilvie, A. G., 'Courts of Marine Inquiry in Australia', *Australian Law Journal*, No. 53, 1979

Preston, N., 'The Development of Defence Force Disciplinary Law, 1901–1985', Australian National University, Work-in-progress seminar, 29 November 1988

Rintoul, S., 'The *Voyager* Outcasts', *The Weekend Australian*, 4 February 1989

Robertson, R. J., 'The *Voyager* Disaster', *Australian*, 1 October 1964

Robertson, R. J., 'Collision Course', *Australian*, 2 October 1964

Robertson, R. J., 'Why I Resigned from the Navy', *Australian*, 3 October 1964

Robertson, R. J., 'The Two Voices of the Naval Board', *Australian*, 5 October 1964

Robertson, R. J., 'What's Wrong with the Navy?', *Australian*, 6 October 1964

Rodger, N. A. M., 'The Intellectual Formation of the Officer', *Naval Review*, Vol. 74, No. 4, October 1986

'Seamus', 'Class, Ethics and Image: A Theory of Naval Decline', *Naval Review*, Vol. 74, No. 2, April 1986

'Taffrail', 'Trinitas in Unitate', *The Navy*, February 1959

Thompson, A. L., 'A Forgotten Episode in Australia's Legal History', Naval Legal Seminar, HMAS *Encounter*, 26 July 1980

Vincent, A., 'Collision! The Subic Bay Inquiry', *Quadrant*, October 1975

Whitton, E., '*Voyager*: Operation Cover-up', *National Times*, 4 February 1974

Winterton, G., 'Judges as Royal Commissioners', *UNSW Law Journal*, Vol. 10, No. 1, 1987

Wylie, F. J., 'Rules of the Road', *Shipping and Shipbuilding Record*, 17 October 1963

Young, P. J., 'Collision that Caused an Outcry and Left a Mystery', *Australian*, 10 February 1984

**Thesis**

R. N. Wallace, 'The Australian Purchase of Three United States Guided Missile Destroyers: A Study of the Defence Aspect of Australian-American Relations', PhD dissertation, Tufts University, Massachusetts, 1980